Lecture Notes in Computer Science 8517

Commenced Publication in 1973
Founding and Former Series Editors:
Gerhard Goos, Juris Hartmanis, and Jan van Leeuwen

Aaron Marcus (Ed.)

Design, User Experience, and Usability

Theories, Methods, and Tools
for Designing the User Experience

Third International Conference, DUXU 2014
Held as Part of HCI International 2014
Heraklion, Crete, Greece, June 22-27, 2014
Proceedings, Part I

 Springer

Volume Editor

Aaron Marcus
Aaron Marcus and Associates, Inc.
1196 Euclid Avenue, Suite 1F, Berkeley, CA 94708-1640, USA
E-mail: aaron.marcus@AMandA.com

ISSN 0302-9743   e-ISSN 1611-3349
ISBN 978-3-319-07667-6   e-ISBN 978-3-319-07668-3
DOI 10.1007/978-3-319-07668-3
Springer Cham Heidelberg New York Dordrecht London

Library of Congress Control Number: 2014939619

LNCS Sublibrary: SL 3 – Information Systems and Application, incl. Internet/Web
and HCI

Typesetting: Camera-ready by author, data conversion by Scientific Publishing Services, Chennai, India

Printed on acid-free paper

Springer is part of Springer Science+Business Media (www.springer.com)

Foreword

The 16th International Conference on Human–Computer Interaction, HCI International 2014, was held in Heraklion, Crete, Greece, during June 22–27, 2014, incorporating 14 conferences/thematic areas:

Thematic areas:

- Human–Computer Interaction
- Human Interface and the Management of Information

Affiliated conferences:

- 11th International Conference on Engineering Psychology and Cognitive Ergonomics
- 8th International Conference on Universal Access in Human–Computer Interaction
- 6th International Conference on Virtual, Augmented and Mixed Reality
- 6th International Conference on Cross-Cultural Design
- 6th International Conference on Social Computing and Social Media
- 8th International Conference on Augmented Cognition
- 5th International Conference on Digital Human Modeling and Applications in Health, Safety, Ergonomics and Risk Management
- Third International Conference on Design, User Experience and Usability
- Second International Conference on Distributed, Ambient and Pervasive Interactions
- Second International Conference on Human Aspects of Information Security, Privacy and Trust
- First International Conference on HCI in Business
- First International Conference on Learning and Collaboration Technologies

A total of 4,766 individuals from academia, research institutes, industry, and governmental agencies from 78 countries submitted contributions, and 1,476 papers and 225 posters were included in the proceedings. These papers address the latest research and development efforts and highlight the human aspects of design and use of computing systems. The papers thoroughly cover the entire field of human–computer interaction, addressing major advances in knowledge and effective use of computers in a variety of application areas.

This volume, edited by Aaron Marcus, contains papers focusing on the thematic area of Design, User Experience and Usability, addressing the following major topics:

- Design theories, methods and tools
- User experience evaluation

- Heuristic evaluation
- Media and design
- Design and creativity

The remaining volumes of the HCI International 2014 proceedings are:

- Volume 1, LNCS 8510, Human–Computer Interaction: HCI Theories, Methods and Tools (Part I), edited by Masaaki Kurosu
- Volume 2, LNCS 8511, Human–Computer Interaction: Advanced Interaction Modalities and Techniques (Part II), edited by Masaaki Kurosu
- Volume 3, LNCS 8512, Human–Computer Interaction: Applications and Services (Part III), edited by Masaaki Kurosu
- Volume 4, LNCS 8513, Universal Access in Human–Computer Interaction: Design and Development Methods for Universal Access (Part I), edited by Constantine Stephanidis and Margherita Antona
- Volume 5, LNCS 8514, Universal Access in Human–Computer Interaction: Universal Access to Information and Knowledge (Part II), edited by Constantine Stephanidis and Margherita Antona
- Volume 6, LNCS 8515, Universal Access in Human–Computer Interaction: Aging and Assistive Environments (Part III), edited by Constantine Stephanidis and Margherita Antona
- Volume 7, LNCS 8516, Universal Access in Human–Computer Interaction: Design for All and Accessibility Practice (Part IV), edited by Constantine Stephanidis and Margherita Antona
- Volume 9, LNCS 8518, Design, User Experience, and Usability: User Experience Design for Diverse Interaction Platforms and Environments (Part II), edited by Aaron Marcus
- Volume 10, LNCS 8519, Design, User Experience, and Usability: User Experience Design for Everyday Life Applications and Services (Part III), edited by Aaron Marcus
- Volume 11, LNCS 8520, Design, User Experience, and Usability: User Experience Design Practice (Part IV), edited by Aaron Marcus
- Volume 12, LNCS 8521, Human Interface and the Management of Information: Information and Knowledge Design and Evaluation (Part I), edited by Sakae Yamamoto
- Volume 13, LNCS 8522, Human Interface and the Management of Information: Information and Knowledge in Applications and Services (Part II), edited by Sakae Yamamoto
- Volume 14, LNCS 8523, Learning and Collaboration Technologies: Designing and Developing Novel Learning Experiences (Part I), edited by Panayiotis Zaphiris and Andri Ioannou
- Volume 15, LNCS 8524, Learning and Collaboration Technologies: Technology-rich Environments for Learning and Collaboration (Part II), edited by Panayiotis Zaphiris and Andri Ioannou
- Volume 16, LNCS 8525, Virtual, Augmented and Mixed Reality: Designing and Developing Virtual and Augmented Environments (Part I), edited by Randall Shumaker and Stephanie Lackey

- Volume 17, LNCS 8526, Virtual, Augmented and Mixed Reality: Applications of Virtual and Augmented Reality (Part II), edited by Randall Shumaker and Stephanie Lackey
- Volume 18, LNCS 8527, HCI in Business, edited by Fiona Fui-Hoon Nah
- Volume 19, LNCS 8528, Cross-Cultural Design, edited by P.L. Patrick Rau
- Volume 20, LNCS 8529, Digital Human Modeling and Applications in Health, Safety, Ergonomics and Risk Management, edited by Vincent G. Duffy
- Volume 21, LNCS 8530, Distributed, Ambient, and Pervasive Interactions, edited by Norbert Streitz and Panos Markopoulos
- Volume 22, LNCS 8531, Social Computing and Social Media, edited by Gabriele Meiselwitz
- Volume 23, LNAI 8532, Engineering Psychology and Cognitive Ergonomics, edited by Don Harris
- Volume 24, LNCS 8533, Human Aspects of Information Security, Privacy and Trust, edited by Theo Tryfonas and Ioannis Askoxylakis
- Volume 25, LNAI 8534, Foundations of Augmented Cognition, edited by Dylan D. Schmorrow and Cali M. Fidopiastis
- Volume 26, CCIS 434, HCI International 2014 Posters Proceedings (Part I), edited by Constantine Stephanidis
- Volume 27, CCIS 435, HCI International 2014 Posters Proceedings (Part II), edited by Constantine Stephanidis

I would like to thank the Program Chairs and the members of the Program Boards of all affiliated conferences and thematic areas, listed below, for their contribution to the highest scientific quality and the overall success of the HCI International 2014 Conference.

This conference could not have been possible without the continuous support and advice of the founding chair and conference scientific advisor, Prof. Gavriel Salvendy, as well as the dedicated work and outstanding efforts of the communications chair and editor of *HCI International News*, Dr. Abbas Moallem.

I would also like to thank for their contribution towards the smooth organization of the HCI International 2014 Conference the members of the Human–Computer Interaction Laboratory of ICS-FORTH, and in particular George Paparoulis, Maria Pitsoulaki, Maria Bouhli, and George Kapnas.

April 2014   Constantine Stephanidis
                                          General Chair, HCI International 2014

Organization

Human–Computer Interaction

Program Chair: Masaaki Kurosu, Japan

Jose Abdelnour-Nocera, UK
Sebastiano Bagnara, Italy
Simone Barbosa, Brazil
Adriana Betiol, Brazil
Simone Borsci, UK
Henry Duh, Australia
Xiaowen Fang, USA
Vicki Hanson, UK
Wonil Hwang, Korea
Minna Isomursu, Finland
Yong Gu Ji, Korea
Anirudha Joshi, India
Esther Jun, USA
Kyungdoh Kim, Korea

Heidi Krömker, Germany
Chen Ling, USA
Chang S. Nam, USA
Naoko Okuizumi, Japan
Philippe Palanque, France
Ling Rothrock, USA
Naoki Sakakibara, Japan
Dominique Scapin, France
Guangfeng Song, USA
Sanjay Tripathi, India
Chui Yin Wong, Malaysia
Toshiki Yamaoka, Japan
Kazuhiko Yamazaki, Japan
Ryoji Yoshitake, Japan

Human Interface and the Management of Information

Program Chair: Sakae Yamamoto, Japan

Alan Chan, Hong Kong
Denis A. Coelho, Portugal
Linda Elliott, USA
Shin'ichi Fukuzumi, Japan
Michitaka Hirose, Japan
Makoto Itoh, Japan
Yen-Yu Kang, Taiwan
Koji Kimita, Japan
Daiji Kobayashi, Japan

Hiroyuki Miki, Japan
Shogo Nishida, Japan
Robert Proctor, USA
Youngho Rhee, Korea
Ryosuke Saga, Japan
Katsunori Shimohara, Japan
Kim-Phuong Vu, USA
Tomio Watanabe, Japan

Engineering Psychology and Cognitive Ergonomics

Program Chair: Don Harris, UK

Guy Andre Boy, USA
Shan Fu, P.R. China
Hung-Sying Jing, Taiwan
Wen-Chin Li, Taiwan
Mark Neerincx, The Netherlands
Jan Noyes, UK
Paul Salmon, Australia

Axel Schulte, Germany
Siraj Shaikh, UK
Sarah Sharples, UK
Anthony Smoker, UK
Neville Stanton, UK
Alex Stedmon, UK
Andrew Thatcher, South Africa

Universal Access in Human–Computer Interaction

Program Chairs: Constantine Stephanidis, Greece, and Margherita Antona, Greece

Julio Abascal, Spain
Gisela Susanne Bahr, USA
João Barroso, Portugal
Margrit Betke, USA
Anthony Brooks, Denmark
Christian Bühler, Germany
Stefan Carmien, Spain
Hua Dong, P.R. China
Carlos Duarte, Portugal
Pier Luigi Emiliani, Italy
Qin Gao, P.R. China
Andrina Granić, Croatia
Andreas Holzinger, Austria
Josette Jones, USA
Simeon Keates, UK

Georgios Kouroupetroglou, Greece
Patrick Langdon, UK
Barbara Leporini, Italy
Eugene Loos, The Netherlands
Ana Isabel Paraguay, Brazil
Helen Petrie, UK
Michael Pieper, Germany
Enrico Pontelli, USA
Jaime Sanchez, Chile
Alberto Sanna, Italy
Anthony Savidis, Greece
Christian Stary, Austria
Hirotada Ueda, Japan
Gerhard Weber, Germany
Harald Weber, Germany

Virtual, Augmented and Mixed Reality

Program Chairs: Randall Shumaker, USA, and Stephanie Lackey, USA

Roland Blach, Germany
Sheryl Brahnam, USA
Juan Cendan, USA
Jessie Chen, USA
Panagiotis D. Kaklis, UK

Hirokazu Kato, Japan
Denis Laurendeau, Canada
Fotis Liarokapis, UK
Michael Macedonia, USA
Gordon Mair, UK

Jose San Martin, Spain
Tabitha Peck, USA
Christian Sandor, Australia

Christopher Stapleton, USA
Gregory Welch, USA

Cross-Cultural Design

Program Chair: P.L. Patrick Rau, P.R. China

Yee-Yin Choong, USA
Paul Fu, USA
Zhiyong Fu, P.R. China
Pin-Chao Liao, P.R. China
Dyi-Yih Michael Lin, Taiwan
Rungtai Lin, Taiwan
Ta-Ping (Robert) Lu, Taiwan
Liang Ma, P.R. China
Alexander Mädche, Germany

Sheau-Farn Max Liang, Taiwan
Katsuhiko Ogawa, Japan
Tom Plocher, USA
Huatong Sun, USA
Emil Tso, P.R. China
Hsiu-Ping Yueh, Taiwan
Liang (Leon) Zeng, USA
Jia Zhou, P.R. China

Online Communities and Social Media

Program Chair: Gabriele Meiselwitz, USA

Leonelo Almeida, Brazil
Chee Siang Ang, UK
Aneesha Bakharia, Australia
Ania Bobrowicz, UK
James Braman, USA
Farzin Deravi, UK
Carsten Kleiner, Germany
Niki Lambropoulos, Greece
Soo Ling Lim, UK

Anthony Norcio, USA
Portia Pusey, USA
Panote Siriaraya, UK
Stefan Stieglitz, Germany
Giovanni Vincenti, USA
Yuanqiong (Kathy) Wang, USA
June Wei, USA
Brian Wentz, USA

Augmented Cognition

**Program Chairs: Dylan D. Schmorrow, USA,
and Cali M. Fidopiastis, USA**

Ahmed Abdelkhalek, USA
Robert Atkinson, USA
Monique Beaudoin, USA
John Blitch, USA
Alenka Brown, USA

Rosario Cannavò, Italy
Joseph Cohn, USA
Andrew J. Cowell, USA
Martha Crosby, USA
Wai-Tat Fu, USA

Rodolphe Gentili, USA
Frederick Gregory, USA
Michael W. Hail, USA
Monte Hancock, USA
Fei Hu, USA
Ion Juvina, USA
Joe Keebler, USA
Philip Mangos, USA
Rao Mannepalli, USA
David Martinez, USA
Yvonne R. Masakowski, USA
Santosh Mathan, USA
Ranjeev Mittu, USA

Keith Niall, USA
Tatana Olson, USA
Debra Patton, USA
June Pilcher, USA
Robinson Pino, USA
Tiffany Poeppelman, USA
Victoria Romero, USA
Amela Sadagic, USA
Anna Skinner, USA
Ann Speed, USA
Robert Sottilare, USA
Peter Walker, USA

Digital Human Modeling and Applications in Health, Safety, Ergonomics and Risk Management

Program Chair: Vincent G. Duffy, USA

Giuseppe Andreoni, Italy
Daniel Carruth, USA
Elsbeth De Korte, The Netherlands
Afzal A. Godil, USA
Ravindra Goonetilleke, Hong Kong
Noriaki Kuwahara, Japan
Kang Li, USA
Zhizhong Li, P.R. China

Tim Marler, USA
Jianwei Niu, P.R. China
Michelle Robertson, USA
Matthias Rötting, Germany
Mao-Jiun Wang, Taiwan
Xuguang Wang, France
James Yang, USA

Design, User Experience, and Usability

Program Chair: Aaron Marcus, USA

Sisira Adikari, Australia
Claire Ancient, USA
Arne Berger, Germany
Jamie Blustein, Canada
Ana Boa-Ventura, USA
Jan Brejcha, Czech Republic
Lorenzo Cantoni, Switzerland
Marc Fabri, UK
Luciane Maria Fadel, Brazil
Tricia Flanagan, Hong Kong
Jorge Frascara, Mexico

Federico Gobbo, Italy
Emilie Gould, USA
Rüdiger Heimgärtner, Germany
Brigitte Herrmann, Germany
Steffen Hess, Germany
Nouf Khashman, Canada
Fabiola Guillermina Noël, Mexico
Francisco Rebelo, Portugal
Kerem Rızvanoğlu, Turkey
Marcelo Soares, Brazil
Carla Spinillo, Brazil

Distributed, Ambient and Pervasive Interactions

**Program Chairs: Norbert Streitz, Germany,
and Panos Markopoulos, The Netherlands**

Juan Carlos Augusto, UK
Jose Bravo, Spain
Adrian Cheok, UK
Boris de Ruyter, The Netherlands
Anind Dey, USA
Dimitris Grammenos, Greece
Nuno Guimaraes, Portugal
Achilles Kameas, Greece
Javed Vassilis Khan, The Netherlands
Shin'ichi Konomi, Japan
Carsten Magerkurth, Switzerland

Ingrid Mulder, The Netherlands
Anton Nijholt, The Netherlands
Fabio Paternó, Italy
Carsten Röcker, Germany
Teresa Romao, Portugal
Albert Ali Salah, Turkey
Manfred Tscheligi, Austria
Reiner Wichert, Germany
Woontack Woo, Korea
Xenophon Zabulis, Greece

Human Aspects of Information Security, Privacy and Trust

**Program Chairs: Theo Tryfonas, UK,
and Ioannis Askoxylakis, Greece**

Claudio Agostino Ardagna, Italy
Zinaida Benenson, Germany
Daniele Catteddu, Italy
Raoul Chiesa, Italy
Bryan Cline, USA
Sadie Creese, UK
Jorge Cuellar, Germany
Marc Dacier, USA
Dieter Gollmann, Germany
Kirstie Hawkey, Canada
Jaap-Henk Hoepman, The Netherlands
Cagatay Karabat, Turkey
Angelos Keromytis, USA
Ayako Komatsu, Japan
Ronald Leenes, The Netherlands
Javier Lopez, Spain
Steve Marsh, Canada

Gregorio Martinez, Spain
Emilio Mordini, Italy
Yuko Murayama, Japan
Masakatsu Nishigaki, Japan
Aljosa Pasic, Spain
Milan Petković, The Netherlands
Joachim Posegga, Germany
Jean-Jacques Quisquater, Belgium
Damien Sauveron, France
George Spanoudakis, UK
Kerry-Lynn Thomson, South Africa
Julien Touzeau, France
Theo Tryfonas, UK
João Vilela, Portugal
Claire Vishik, UK
Melanie Volkamer, Germany

HCI in Business

Program Chair: Fiona Fui-Hoon Nah, USA

Andreas Auinger, Austria
Michel Avital, Denmark
Traci Carte, USA
Hock Chuan Chan, Singapore
Constantinos Coursaris, USA
Soussan Djamasbi, USA
Brenda Eschenbrenner, USA
Nobuyuki Fukawa, USA
Khaled Hassanein, Canada
Milena Head, Canada
Susanna (Shuk Ying) Ho, Australia
Jack Zhenhui Jiang, Singapore
Jinwoo Kim, Korea
Zoonky Lee, Korea
Honglei Li, UK
Nicholas Lockwood, USA
Eleanor T. Loiacono, USA
Mei Lu, USA

Scott McCoy, USA
Brian Mennecke, USA
Robin Poston, USA
Lingyun Qiu, P.R. China
Rene Riedl, Austria
Matti Rossi, Finland
April Savoy, USA
Shu Schiller, USA
Hong Sheng, USA
Choon Ling Sia, Hong Kong
Chee-Wee Tan, Denmark
Chuan Hoo Tan, Hong Kong
Noam Tractinsky, Israel
Horst Treiblmaier, Austria
Virpi Tuunainen, Finland
Dezhi Wu, USA
I-Chin Wu, Taiwan

Learning and Collaboration Technologies

Program Chairs: Panayiotis Zaphiris, Cyprus, and Andri Ioannou, Cyprus

Ruthi Aladjem, Israel
Abdulaziz Aldaej, UK
John M. Carroll, USA
Maka Eradze, Estonia
Mikhail Fominykh, Norway
Denis Gillet, Switzerland
Mustafa Murat Inceoglu, Turkey
Pernilla Josefsson, Sweden
Marie Joubert, UK
Sauli Kiviranta, Finland
Tomaž Klobučar, Slovenia
Elena Kyza, Cyprus
Maarten de Laat, The Netherlands
David Lamas, Estonia

Edmund Laugasson, Estonia
Ana Loureiro, Portugal
Katherine Maillet, France
Nadia Pantidi, UK
Antigoni Parmaxi, Cyprus
Borzoo Pourabdollahian, Italy
Janet C. Read, UK
Christophe Reffay, France
Nicos Souleles, Cyprus
Ana Luísa Torres, Portugal
Stefan Trausan-Matu, Romania
Aimilia Tzanavari, Cyprus
Johnny Yuen, Hong Kong
Carmen Zahn, Switzerland

External Reviewers

Ilia Adami, Greece
Iosif Klironomos, Greece
Maria Korozi, Greece
Vassilis Kouroumalis, Greece

Asterios Leonidis, Greece
George Margetis, Greece
Stavroula Ntoa, Greece
Nikolaos Partarakis, Greece

HCI International 2015

The 15th International Conference on Human–Computer Interaction, HCI International 2015, will be held jointly with the affiliated conferences in Los Angeles, CA, USA, in the Westin Bonaventure Hotel, August 2–7, 2015. It will cover a broad spectrum of themes related to HCI, including theoretical issues, methods, tools, processes, and case studies in HCI design, as well as novel interaction techniques, interfaces, and applications. The proceedings will be published by Springer. More information will be available on the conference website: http://www.hcii2015.org/

General Chair
Professor Constantine Stephanidis
University of Crete and ICS-FORTH
Heraklion, Crete, Greece
E-mail: cs@ics.forth.gr

Table of Contents – Part I

Design Theories, Methods and Tools

Experience Report: The Effectiveness of Paper Prototyping for
Interactive Visualizations 3
  Bastian Bansemir, Franziska Hannß, Berit Lochner,
  Jan Wojdziak, and Rainer Groh

A Review of Empirical Intercultural Usability Studies 14
  Victoria Böhm and Christian Wolff

Towards a Vocabulary of Prototypes in Interaction Design –
A Criticism of Current Practice 25
  Arne Berger, Michael Heidt, and Maximilian Eibl

Agile Usability Patterns for UCD Early Stages 33
  Ana Paula O. Bertholdo, Tiago Silva da Silva, Claudia de O. Melo,
  Fabio Kon, and Milene Selbach Silveira

Ideologies in HCI: A Semiotic Perspective 45
  Jan Brejcha

The Language Game 55
  Roman Danylak and Kyeong Kang

On the Idea of Design: Analyzing the Ideal Form of Cars 64
  Arash Faroughi and Semir Maslo

M4REMAIP: Method for Requirements Elicitation Based on Mobile
Applications under an Interaction Perspective 74
  Sarah Gomes Sakamoto and Leonardo Cunha de Miranda

A Mixed-Method Approach for In-Depth Contextual User Research 86
  Walkyria Goode, Caroline Little, Andrew Schall, Renae Geraci, and
  Vanessa Brown

Reframing Design under Technical Conditions 96
  Moritz Greiner-Petter and Claudia Mareis

Developing UX for Collaborative Mobile Prototyping 104
  Isabella Hastreiter, Sascha Krause, Tim Schneidermeier, and
  Christian Wolff

Deconstructivist Design within HCI 115
  Michael Heidt, Andreas Bischof, and Paul Rosenthal

Using Agile Methods in Intercultural HCI Design Projects   123
   Rüdiger Heimgärtner and Alkesh Solanki

Revisiting Graspable User Interfaces: A Design Process for Developing
User Interface Metaphors   130
   Mandy Keck, Esther Lapczyna, and Rainer Groh

Tracing Design Work through Contextual Activity Sampling   142
   *Tarja-Kaarina Laamanen, Pirita Seitamaa-Hakkarainen, and
   Kai Hakkarainen*

Techno-Theoretical Paradigm: Performance, Fashion and Wearables   153
   Valérie Lamontagne

A User Experience Design Toolkit   163
   *Ioanna Michailidou, Constantin von Saucken, Simon Kremer, and
   Udo Lindemann*

How Two become One – Creating Synergy Effects by Applying the
Joint Interview Method to Design Wearable Technology   173
   Ulrike Schmuntzsch and Lea H. Feldhaus

In-Depth Analysis of Non-deterministic Aspects of Human-Machine
Interaction and Update of Dedicated Functional Mock-Ups   185
   Stefano Filippi and Daniela Barattin

Grammatical Analysis of User Interface Events for Task
Identification   197
   Yonglei Tao

Model-Based User Interface Development for Adaptive Self-Service
Systems   206
   Enes Yigitbas, Holger Fischer, and Stefan Sauer

User Experience Evaluation

Usability Evaluation of Mobile Passenger Information Systems   217
   *Shirley Beul-Leusmann, Christian Samsel, Maximilian Wiederhold,
   Karl-Heinz Krempels, Eva-Maria Jakobs, and Martina Ziefle*

SCENE: A Structured Means for Creating and Evaluating Behavioral
Nudges in a Cyber Security Environment   229
   Lynne Coventry, Pam Briggs, Debora Jeske, and Aad van Moorsel

Attempts to Quantitative Analyze for the Change of Human Brain
Activity with Physical and Psychological Load   240
   *Hiroaki Inoue, Shunji Shimizu, Hiroyuki Nara, Takeshi Tsuruga,
   Fumikazu Miwakeichi, Nobuhide Hirai, Senichiro Kikuchi,
   Eiju Watanabe, and Satoshi Kato*

Measuring Confidence in Internet Use: The Development of an Internet
Self-efficacy Scale   250
  Mary Joyce and Jurek Kirakowski

Customer Journey Mapping of an Experience-Centric Service by Mobile
Self-reporting: Testing the Qualiwall Tool   261
  Inka Kojo, Mikko Heiskala, and Juho-Pekka Virtanen

Evaluation of Tablet PC Application Interfaces with Low Vision Users:
Focusing on Usability   273
  Cínthia Costa Kulpa and Fernando Gonçalves Amaral

Relationship between Elements of the Usability and Emotions Reported
after Use: A Mexican Case   285
  Irma Cecilia Landa Ávila and Lilia Roselia Prado León

Experimental Research in Applying Generative Design and 3D Printers
in User Participating Design   296
  Lin-Chien James Lee and Ming-Huang Lin

Building a Semantic Differential Scale as Tool for Assisting UX
Evaluation with Home Appliances   308
  Vanessa Macedo and Caio Marcio Silva

Evaluating Quality and Usability of the User Interface: A Practical
Study on Comparing Methods with and without Users   318
  *Caio Marcio Silva, Vanessa Macedo, Rafaela Lemos, and
  Maria Lúcia L.R. Okimoto*

Multicultural Text Entry: A Usability Study   329
  *Cristina Olaverri-Monreal, Maria Lúcia L.R. Okimoto, and
  Klaus Bengler*

Subjective and Objective Assessment of Mashup Tools   340
  Tihomir Orehovački and Toni Granollers

Usability Analysis of Smartphone Applications for Drivers   352
  Manuela Quaresma and Rafael Gonçalves

Eye Tracking Insights into Effective Navigation Design   363
  Andrew Schall

Changing Paradigm – Changing Experience?- Comparative Usability
Evaluation of *Windows 7* and *Windows 8*   371
  Tim Schneidermeier, Franziska Hertlein, and Christian Wolff

Applying the User Experience Questionnaire (UEQ) in Different
Evaluation Scenarios   383
  Martin Schrepp, Andreas Hinderks, and Jörg Thomaschewski

Online Psychometric Design (OnPsyD) Tool   393
  Shiny Verghese, Paul van Schaik, and Steve Green

Comparing Effectiveness, Efficiency, Ease of Use, Usability and User
Experience When Using Tablets and Laptops   402
  Werner Wetzlinger, Andreas Auinger, and Michael Dörflinger

Heuristic Evaluation

Heuristics for Evaluating the Usability of Mobile Launchers for Elderly
People   415
  Muna S. Al-Razgan, Hend S. Al-Khalifa, and Mona D. Al-Shahrani

Heuristic Inspection to Assess Persuasiveness: A Case Study of a
Mathematics E-learning Program   425
  Eric Brangier and Michel C. Desmarais

Design as a Tool for Managing Risks and Vulnerabilities Regarding
Artifacts of Public Safety   437
  Walter F.M. Correia, Sérgio Ximenes da Silva, Fábio F.C. Campos,
  Marina L.N. Barros, and Marcelo Márcio Soares

Enhancing Usability Engineering in Rural Areas Using Agile
Methods   445
  Rüdiger Heimgärtner, Alkesh Solanki, and Bernd Hollerit

Serious Games and Heuristic Evaluation – The Cross-Comparison of
Existing Heuristic Evaluation Methods for Games   453
  Natalia Jerzak and Francisco Rebelo

Towards the Development of Usability Heuristics for Native Smartphone
Mobile Applications   465
  Ger Joyce and Mariana Lilley

Common Industry Format (CIF) Report Customization for UX
Heuristic Evaluation   475
  Llúcia Masip, Marta Oliva, and Toni Granollers

Evaluating the Usability on Multimodal Interfaces: A Case Study on
Tablets Applications   484
  Edvar Vilar Neto and Fábio F.C. Campos

Developing Playability Heuristics for Computer Games from Online
Reviews   496
  Miaoqi Zhu and Xiaowen Fang

Media and Design

Designing Real-Time: On How Events Affect Audiovisual Narrative   509
Marcus Bastos

Post Media: Towards a User Interface Architecture   519
Jiří Bystřický and Jan Brejcha

Interactive Film: The Computer as Medium   527
Roman Danylak

Digital Self: Fiction and Non-fiction on the Internet   537
*Ana Carol Pontes de França, Luciano Rogério de Lemos Meira, and
Marcelo Márcio Soares*

The Bridge – A Transmedia Dialogue between TV, Film and Gaming . . .   548
Herlander Elias

Fishtank Everywhere: Improving Viewing Experience over 3D
Content   560
*Lucas S. Figueiredo, Edvar Vilar Neto, Ermano Arruda,
João Marcelo Teixeira, and Veronica Teichrieb*

The Database on Near-Future Technologies for User Interface Design
from SciFi Movies   572
Jun Iio, Shigeyoshi Iizuka, and Hideyuki Matsubara

User Interfaces That Appeared in SciFi Movies and Their Reality   580
Masaaki Kurosu

Bridging the Gap: Methods and Teaching of F-A-S-T - Framing-Art-
Science-Technology   589
*Deborah Schmidt, Grit Koalick, Sebastian Gassel, Christian Sery,
Rainer Groh, and Markus Wacker*

Film – System – Communication   601
Katrin Vodrazkova

Design and Creativity

User Experience Technique in Computer Digital Arts Production:
Paper Prototyping Used as Material to Define Intentionality   613
Marília Lyra Bergamo

Cultural Creativity in Experience Design Model   622
Shu Hsuan Chang, Chi-Hsien Hsu, and Rung Tai Lin

Keeping Creative Writing on Track: Co-designing a Framework to
Support Behavior Change   631
Paul Doney, Rebecca Evans, and Marc Fabri

Challenges in Designing New Interfaces for Musical Expression.......... 643
  *Rodrigo Medeiros, Filipe Calegario, Giordano Cabral, and
  Geber Ramalho*

Collaboration Space for Creative Knowledge Work – Analysis of
Industrial Pilots 653
  *Mika P. Nieminen, Mikael Runonen, Mari Tyllinen, and
  Marko Nieminen*

Ornamental Images and Their Digital Occurrences 663
  Michael Renner

Affording Creativity and New Media Possibilities 675
  Zoie So

basil.js - Bridging Mouse and Code Based Design Strategies 686
  Ludwig Zeller, Benedikt Groß, and Ted Davis

Author Index... 697

Table of Contents – Part II

Design for the Web

The Common Implementation Framework as Service – Towards Novel
Applications for Streamlined Presentation of 3D Content on the Web ...   3
    Andreas Aderhold, Katarzyna Wilkosinska, Massimiliano Corsini,
    Yvonne Jung, Holger Graf, and Arjan Kuijper

Website Design Based on Cultures: An Investigation of Saudis,
Filipinos, and Indians Government Websites' Attributes   15
    Hend S. Al-Khalifa and Regina A. Garcia

The Role of Avatars in e-Government Interfaces   28
    Badr Almutairi and Dimitrios Rigas

Towards Data Confidentiality and Portability in Cloud Storage   38
    Ebtesam Ahmad Alomari and Muhammad Mostafa Monowar

A Usability Study on Elder Adults Utilizing Social Networking Sites....   50
    Jessica Arfaa and Yuanqiong (Kathy) Wang

An Alternative Media Experience: LiveLeak   62
    Fatih Çömlekçi and Serhat Güney

E-government and the Digital Agenda for Europe: A Study of the User
Involvement in the Digitalisation of Citizen Services in Denmark   71
    Jane Billestrup and Jan Stage

The Paradigm of Meta-interface as a Facilitator of Websites Usability
and Accessibility   81
    Fábio F.C. Campos, Edvar Vilar Neto, Maria Neves, and
    Walter F.M. Correia

Experience-Centered Web Design Model   92
    Luciane Maria Fadel

Online Shopping Websites: An Evaluation of User Experience and
Interface Ergonomic Criteria from the Perspective of Older Users   104
    Fabiane Rodriguez Fernandes and Luis Carlos Paschoarelli

HCI Knowledge for UX Practices in the Web Development Process   116
    Idyawati Hussein, Murni Mahmud, and Abu Osman Md Tap

Cultural Divergence in Website Interaction Spanish vs. English   127
    Nicholas Iuliucci and Ania Rodriguez

A Study of Cultural Reflection in Egyptian Government Websites   139
    Nouf Khashman and Elaine Ménard

Towards a Friendly User Interface on the Cloud   148
    Heba A. Kurdi, Safwat Hamad, and Amal Khalifa

The Cultural Conceptual Model for Simplifying the Design of Localized
Websites   158
    Abdalghani Mushtaha and Olga De Troyer

Design for the Mobile Experience

Left vs. Right-Handed UX: A Comparative User Study on a Mobile
Application with Left and Right-Handed Users   173
    Sinan Aşçı and Kerem Rızvanoğlu

Scissors – A Precise Pointing Widget for Touch Screen Devices   184
    *Felipe Breyer, Luis A. Vasconcelos, Antônio Rivero, and
    Judith Kelner*

Ergonomics and Usability in Sound Dimension: Evaluation of a Haptic
and Acoustic Interface Application for Mobile Devices   193
    *Guilherme Orlandini, Gilson Ap. Castadelli, and
    Lígia Maria Presumido Braccialli*

Information Design – Qualitative Approach for Corporative App
in iPad   203
    *Jacqueline Aparecida G.F. de Castro, Marcelo V. Rino, and
    Julia Yuri Landim Goya*

An Analysis of Design Methodologies of Interactive System
for Mobiles   213
    *Adriana Chammas, Manuela Quaresma, and
    Cláudia Renata Mont'Alvão*

Smart-Islands: Enhancing User Experience for Mediterranean Islands
for Tourism Support   223
    Umberto Di Staso, Daniele Magliocchetti, and Raffaele De Amicis

Detection of Churned and Retained Users with Machine Learning
Methods for Mobile Applications   234
    Merve Gençer, Gökhan Bilgin, Özgür Zan, and Tansel Voyvodaoğlu

A Research Framework for the Smartphone-Based Contextual Study of
Mobile Knowledge Work   246
    *Mikko Heiskala, Eero Palomäki, Matti Vartiainen,
    Kai Hakkarainen, and Hanni Muukkonen*

The Happiness Machine: Mobile Behavior Change   258
  Aaron Marcus

Equivalence of Navigation Widgets for Mobile Platforms   269
  Amilcar Meneses Viveros, Erika Hernández Rubio, and
  Dario Emmanuel Vázquez Ceballos

Gestural Interfaces Touchscreen: Thinking Interactions beyond the
Button from Interaction Design for Gmail Android App   279
  Tobias Mulling, Cristiano Lopes, and Arthur Cabreira

Tracking Mobile Workers' Daily Activities with the Contextual Activity
Sampling System   289
  Hanni Muukkonen, Kai Hakkarainen, Shupin Li, and
  Matti Vartiainen

Methods to Study Everyday Activities in a Mobile Work
Context – A Literature Overview   301
  Eero Palomäki, Kai Hakkarainen, Matti Vartiainen, and
  Mikko Heiskala

Building a Quality Mobile Application: A User-Centered Study
Focusing on Design Thinking, User Experience and Usability   313
  Danielly F.O. de Paula, Bianca H.X.M. Menezes, and
  Cristiano C. Araújo

Territorial Brand Graphic Interface Management in Mobile Applications
Focused on User Experience   323
  Luiz Salomão Ribas Gomez and Valéria Casaroto Feijó

Device Agnostic CASS Client   334
  Kari Salo, Udeep Shakya, and Michael Damena

To What Extent System Usability Effects User Satisfaction: A Case
Study of Smart Phone Features Analysis for Learning of Novice   346
  Muhammad Shafiq, Muddesar Iqbal, Jin-Ghoo Choi, Zeeshan Rafi,
  Maqbool Ahmad, Wasif Ali, and Saqib Rasool

Cutting Edge Design or a Beginner's Mistake? – A Semiotic Inspection
of iOS7 Icon Design Changes   358
  Christian Stickel, Hans-Martin Pohl, and Jan-Thorsten Milde

Design of Visual Information

Developing a Verbal Assistance System for Line Graph
Comprehension   373
  Cengiz Acartürk, Özge Alaçam, and Christopher Habel

Multimedia Surveillance in Event Detection: Crowd Analytics
in Hajj 383
    Layla Al-Salhie, Mona Al-Zuhair, and Areej Al-Wabil

A Visual Programming Approach to Big Data Analytics 393
    Christian Bockermann

Management of Visual Clutter in Annotated 3D CAD Models:
A Comparative Study 405
    Jorge Camba, Manuel Contero, and Michael Johnson

Effect of Perception-Compatibility, Learning-Factor, and
Symbol-Carrier on Single LED Symbol System Recognizing 417
    Chun-Chieh Chang and T.K. Philip Hwang

Interfacing CBIR: Designing Interactive Widgets to Query Attribute
Data in Face Image Retrieval 425
    Ted Davis

Wearable Networks, Creating Hybrid Spaces with Soft Circuits 435
    T. Raune Frankjaer and Daniel Gilgen

Aluminum CT Image Defect Detection Based on Segmentation
and Feature Extraction 446
    Ning He, Lulu Zhang, and Ke Lu

Interface as a Medium: Creating Effective Visual Services through
a User-Experiences Perspective 455
    Tingyi S. Lin

Taking Decisions with Systems Oriented to the General
Public - Applying Visual Information Based on Viennese
Method 463
    André S. Monat, Marcel Befort, and Ricardo Cunha Lima

Interactive Visualizations in Learning Mathematics: Implications for
Information Design and User Experience 472
    Virginia Tiradentes Souto

Need Driven Prototype Design for a Policy Modeling Authoring
Interface 481
    Dimitris Spiliotopoulos, Athanasios Dalianis, and Dimitris Koryzis

Beyond Perspective – A Model-Based Approach for Camera-Based
3D-Interface Design 488
    Jan Wojdziak and Rainer Groh

Design for Novel Interaction Techniques and Realities

Use of Immersive Reality and Haptic Devices in Rehabilitation after
Cerebral Vascular Accident: Clinical Perspectives and Neuro-Image
Evidence.. 501
  *Helda Oliveira Barros, Marcelo Márcio Soares, and
  Epitácio Leite Rolim Filho*

Extending ActionSketch for New Interaction Styles: Gestural Interfaces
and Interactive Environments...................................... 509
  Gil Barros

Syntactic/Semantic Formalizations and Metrics of Residential
Applications Based on Gestural Interface........................... 521
  *Ana Carla de Carvalho Correia, Paulo Leonardo Souza Brizolara,
  Leonardo Cunha de Miranda, and Juvane Nunes Marciano*

Controlling Light Environments Using Segmented Light Sources
and Mobile Devices 533
  *Brian Eschrich, Dietrich Kammer, Karol Kozak, Jan Hesse, and
  Rainer Groh*

Can Virtual Reality Increase Emotional Responses (Arousal and
Valence)? A Pilot Study 541
  *Sergio Estupiñán, Francisco Rebelo, Paulo Noriega,
  Carlos Ferreira, and Emília Duarte*

In-Place Natural and Effortless Navigation for Large Industrial
Scenarios 550
  *Lucas S. Figueiredo, Mariana Pinheiro, Edvar Vilar Neto,
  Thiago Menezes, João Marcelo Teixeira, Veronica Teichrieb,
  Pedro Alessio, and Daniel Freitas*

Beyond Fingers and Thumbs – A Graceful Touch UI: Elegant
Multi-touch and Gesture UI with Context Dependent Prompting....... 562
  Sue Hessey, Szu Han Chen, and Catherine White

Embodied Tele-Presence System (ETS): Designing Tele-Presence for
Video Teleconferencing 574
  Muhammad Sikandar Lal Khan, Haibo Li, and Shafiq ur Réhman

Gestures: The Reformer of the User's Mental Model in Mobile HCI..... 586
  *Tian Lei, Luyao Xiong, Kun Chen, Xu Liu, Yin Cao, Qi Zhang,
  Dongyuan Liu, and Sisi Guo*

Sound Bending – Talking Bodies Quantum Sound Suits 598
  Kristin Neidlinger and Wendy Ju

Augmenting a Wearable Display with Skin Surface as an Expanded
Input Area   606
   Masa Ogata, Yuta Sugiura, Yasutoshi Makino,
   Masahiko Inami, and Michita Imai

Affordances and Gestural Interaction on Multi-touch Interface Systems:
Building New Mental Models   615
   Adriano Bernardo Renzi and Sydney Freitas

Augmented Reality in Design: Thinking about Hybrid Forms of Virtual
and Physical Space in Design   624
   Christine Schranz

Diving in? How Users Experience Virtual Environments Using the
Virtual Theatre   636
   Katharina Schuster, Max Hoffmann, Ursula Bach,
   Anja Richert, and Sabina Jeschke

Designing Information for Mediated Reality Systems   647
   Luis A. Vasconcelos, Felipe Breyer, Bernardo Reis, Aline Silveira,
   Daniela Falcone, Judith Kelner, and Ubiratan Carmo

Games and Gamification

Cutscenes in Computer Games as an Information System   661
   Daniel Říha

Challenge Design and Categorization in Video Game Design   669
   Michael Brandse and Kiyoshi Tomimatsu

A Study about Designing Reward for Gamified Crowdsourcing
System   678
   Joohee Choi, Heejin Choi, Woonsub So, Jaeki Lee, and JongJun You

Evolution of the Physical Interfaces in Videogames as a Support to the
Narrative and the Gaming Experience   688
   Alan Richard da Luz

Skyfarer: Design Case Study of a Mixed Reality Rehabilitation Video
Game   699
   Marientina Gotsis, Vangelis Lympouridis, Phil Requejo,
   Lisa L. Haubert, Irina C. Poulos, Fotos Frangoudes,
   David Turpin, and Maryalice Jordan-Marsh

Wanting the Unwanted – What Games Can Teach Us about the Future
of Software Development   711
   Daniel Hellweg

Empirical Analysis of Playability vs. Usability in a Computer Game   720
David Novick, Juan Vicario, Baltazar Santaella, and Iván Gris

The Study of the Relations between the *BrainHex* Player Profiles,
MBTI Psychological Types and Emotions as Means to Enhance User
Experience   732
*Rafael Eduardo Paulin, André Luiz Battaiola, and
Márcia Maria Alves*

A Review of Gamification for Health-Related Contexts................   742
Pedro Pereira, Emília Duarte, Francisco Rebelo, and Paulo Noriega

Game Design Techniques in User Research Methods – A New Way to
Reach the High Score in Development Teams   754
Eva Rügenhagen and Theo Held

A New Design Process for Viewer Participation in Interactive TV
Program: Focused on the Interactive TV Game Show Hae-un-dae   763
*Jeongbeom Shin, Hyun Jung Kim, Jea In Kim,
Bong Gwan Jun, and Chung-Kon Shi*

Immersive Interactive Narratives in Augmented Reality Games   773
Bruno Santos Viana and Ricardo Nakamura

Serious Economic Games: Designing a Simulation Game for an
Economic Experiment   782
Danilo Wanner

Interface Design for Somatosensory Interaction   794
Qiong Wu, Xun Rong Li, and Guan Shang Wu

Author Index   803

Table of Contents – Part III

Design for Health

User Experience in Training a Personalized Hearing System 3
    Gabriel Aldaz, Tyler Haydell, Dafna Szafer, Martin Steinert, and
    Larry Leifer

Developing mHealth Apps with Researchers: Multi-Stakeholder Design
Considerations 15
    Michael P. Craven, Alexandra R. Lang, and Jennifer L. Martin

Accessing Web Based Health Care and Resources for Mental Health:
Interface Design Considerations for People Experiencing Mental
Illness 25
    Alice Good and Arunasalam Sambhanthan

Reading Digital Medicine Leaflets in Mobile Devices an Interactive
Study Conducted in Brazil 34
    Christopher Hammerschmidt and Carla Galvão Spinillo

Visual Design in Healthcare for Low-Literate Users – A Case Study of
Healthcare Leaflets for New Immigrants in Taiwan 44
    Yah-Ling Hung and Catherine Stones

Enhanced Hospital Information System by Cloud Computing:
SHEFA'A 56
    Lamiaa Fattouh Ibrahim, Suzan Sadek, Shahd Hakeem,
    Lana Al-Sabban, Asmaa Ibrahim Mohammed Ahmed, and
    Alaa Hassan Al-Sayed

Exploring Possibilities of Designing Virtual Personal Health Coach in
Relation to Gender Differences 63
    Hakan Kuru and Armagan Kuru

Wayfinding in Hospital: A Case Study 72
    Laura Bezerra Martins and Hugo Fernando Vasconcelos de Melo

Health Care Professionals *vs* Other Professionals: Do They Have
Different Perceptions about Health Care Waste and Dangerous
Products Pictograms? Some Findings Using a Digital Device in Field
Survey 83
    Cláudia Renata Mont'Alvão

"How am I Doing?" - Personifying Health through Animated
Characters 91
    Andreas Schmeil and Suzanne Suggs

SPARK: Personalized Parkinson Disease Interventions through Synergy
between a Smartphone and a Smartwatch 103
    Vinod Sharma, Kunal Mankodiya, Fernando De La Torre,
    Ada Zhang, Neal Ryan, Thanh G.N. Ton, Rajeev Gandhi, and
    Samay Jain

How Do Patient Information Leaflets Aid Medicine Usage? A Proposal
for Assessing Usability of Medicine Inserts 115
    Carla Galvão Spinillo

Usability Improvement of a Clinical Decision Support System 125
    Frederick Thum, Min Soon Kim, Nicholas Genes, Laura Rivera,
    Rosemary Beato, Jared Soriano, Joseph Kannry, Kevin Baumlin,
    and Ula Hwang

Information about Medicines for Patients in Europe: To Impede or to
Empower? 132
    Karel van der Waarde

A Collaborative Change Experiment: Telecare as a Means for Delivery
of Home Care Services 141
    Suhas Govind Joshi and Anita Woll

Design for Reading and Learning

Innovative Educational Technology for Special Education and Usability
Issues 155
    Kursat Cagiltay, Filiz Cicek, Necdet Karasu, Hasan Cakir, and
    Goknur Kaplan Akilli

Examining the Interfaces to E-journal Articles: What Do Users
Expect? 164
    Mary C. Dyson and Elizabeth M. Jennings

The Impact of Media and Background Color on Handwriting 173
    Chao-Yang Yang, Wei-Lin Hsu, and Ting-Yi Chou Huang

The Relation between Online and Print Information Graphics for
Newspapers 184
    Ricardo Cunha Lima, Rafael de Castro Andrade,
    André S. Monat, and Carla Galvão Spinillo

Prototyping in a Learning Environment - Digital Publishing Projects
from the Escola Superior de Desenho Industrial 195
    Marcos André Franco Martins

Logograms: Memory Aids for Learning, and an Example with
Hearing-Impaired Students 207
    Ligia Medeiros, Marcos Brod Júnior, and Luiz Vidal Gomes

SMART Note: Student-Centered Multimedia Active Reading Tools for
Tablet Textbooks 217
  Jennifer George-Palilonis and Davide Bolchini

Design, User-Experience and Teaching-Learning...................... 230
  Cristina Portugal

Design for Mobility, Transport and Safety

Challenges in Implementation of TVM (Ticket Vending Machine) in
Developing Countries for Mass Transport System: A Study of Human
Behavior while Interacting with Ticket Vending Machine-TVM 245
  Mazhar Abbas

Simulation of Wireless Sensor Network for Flood Monitoring System ... 255
  Manal Abdullah

Enhance User Experience Moving in Campus through Understanding
Human Spatial Cognition 265
  *Szu-Miao Chen, Yi-Shin Deng, Sheng-Fen Chien, and
  Hsiao-Chen You*

Pilgrim Smart Identification Using RFID Technology (PSI)............ 273
  *Abeer Geabel, Khlood Jastaniah, Roaa Abu Hassan, Roaa Aljehani,
  Mona Babadr, and Maysoon Abulkhair*

Timeaxis Design of a Service System Growing Values of Mobility Using
the M-V Model 281
  *Kei Kamiya, Akira Kito, Jaime Alvarez, Koichiro Sato,
  Hidekazu Nishimura, Yoshiyuki Matsuoka, and Satoru Furugori*

Developing the HMI of Electric Vehicles: On the Necessity of a Broader
Understanding of Automotive User Interface Engineering.............. 293
  Christian Knoll, Roman Vilimek, and Inken Schulze

Examining the Functionality and Usability of Interactive Wayfinding
Design within Cities in China.................................... 305
  Fung Ha Sandy Lai

The Encourage Operators to Promote Manual Flight Operations- a
Pandemic in Modern Aviation 317
  *Edgard Thomas Martins, Isnard Thomas Martins, and
  Marcelo Márcio Soares*

Hardwired Critical Action Panels for Emergency Preparedness: Design
Principles and CAP Design for Offshore Petroleum Platforms 326
  Bojana Petkov and Alf Ove Braseth

Designing the User Experience for C4ISR Systems in the U.S. Army 338
Pamela Savage-Knepshield, Jeffrey Thomas, Christopher Paulillo,
James Davis, Diane Quarles, and Diane Mitchell

A Mobile Application for Controlling Domestic Gas Cylinders
Remotely 347
Wafaa M. Shalash, Salha Al-Behairi, Nada Al-Qahtani,
Mashael Al-Muzaini, Bayan Sharahili, and Aisha Alawi

Virtual Personas: A Case Study on Truck Cabin Design 357
Jos Thalen and Mascha van der Voort

A Pilot Study Using Virtual Reality to Investigate the Effects of
Emergency Egress Signs Competing with Environmental Variables on
Route Choices 369
Elisângela Vilar, Emília Duarte, Francisco Rebelo,
Paulo Noriega, and Ernesto Filgueiras Vilar

Impact of Multi-sensory On-Bicycle Rider Assistance Devices on Rider
Concentration and Safety 378
Chao-Yang Yang, Yu-Ting Wu, and Cheng-Tse Wu

Design for Rural, Low Literacy and Developing Communities

Barriers and Reforms for Promoting ICTs in Rural Areas of Pakistan ... 391
Aneela Abbas, Mubbashar Hussain, Muddesar Iqbal, Sidra Arshad,
Saqib Rasool, Muhammad Shafiq, Wasif Ali, and Nadeem Yaqub

Positive Technology and User Experience for Human Needs in
Developing Countries: Some Considerations 400
Nils Backhaus, Stefan Brandenburg, and Anna Trapp

Transforming Data into Information Experiences 411
María González de Cossío

Design for Rural Community Regarding Health 423
Shahzaib Iftikhar, Umar Muzaffer, Abbas Illyas, Tayyab Asif Butt,
Hassan Ejaz, and Muhammad Faraz Khokhar

Content Management and User Interface for Uneducated People 432
Zainab Mahmood, Syeda Sana Shahzadi, and Sahar Tariq

Rural Area Development through Multi-interface Technology and
Virtual Learning System 442
Faizan ul Mustafa, Adeel Mushtaq, Shakra Mehak, Salman Akbar,
Usman Ahmad, Sara Mobeen, Hassan Ejaz, Tayyab Asif Butt, and
Muhammad Faraz Khokhar

Traffic Management in Rural Networks 452
    *Rodrigo Emiliano, Fernando Silva, Luís Frazão, João Barroso, and
    António Pereira*

Usability Guidelines for Designing Knowledge Base in Rural Areas:
Towards Women Empowerment 462
    Javed Anjum Sheikh, Hafsa Shareef Dar, and Farzan Javed Sheikh

The Contemporary Rural Landscape in the South-Western Region of
Poland (Sudeten Region) – A Search for Spatial Order 470
    Elzbieta Trocka-Leszczynska

Mobile Money System Design for Illiterate Users in Rural Ethiopia 482
    *Mesfin F. Woldmariam, Gheorghita Ghinea, Solomon Atnafu, and
    Tor-Morten Grønli*

Design for Environment and Sustainability

Using Soft Systems Methodology (SSM) in Understanding
Current User-Support Scenario in the Climate Science Domain of
Cyber-Infrastructures 495
    Hashim Iqbal Chunpir, Thomas Ludwig, and Amgad Ali Badewi

Improving Sustainability through Usability 507
    Vincent G. Duffy

Energy Graph Feedback: Attention, Cognition and Behavior
Intentions 520
    June A. Flora and Banny Banerjee

User-Centred Design of an Audio Feedback System for Power Demand
Management 530
    *Rebecca Ford, Joe Penn, Yu-Chieh Liu, Ken Nixon,
    Willie Cronje, and Malcolm McCulloch*

Personalized Energy Priorities: A User-Centric Application for Energy
Advice 542
    Rebecca Ford, Ondrej Sumavsky, Auren Clarke, and Paul Thorsnes

Experiencing CSR in Asia: A Social Media Perspective from the
Outside In 554
    Constance Kampf

Pumping Up the Citizen Muscle Bootcamp: Improving User Experience
in Online Learning 562
    Beth Karlin, Birgit Penzenstadler, and Allison Cook

Enhancement of Usability for Farmers: User Interface for Rural
Community 574
  Muhammad Faraz Khokhar, Hassan Ejaz, Tayyab Asif Butt,
  Shahzaib Iftikhar, Umar Muzaffer, Abbas Illyas, Faizan ul Mustafa,
  Adeel Mushtaq, Usman Ahmad, and Usman Asghar

User-Experience for Personal Sustainability Software: Applying Design
Philosophy and Principles 583
  Aaron Marcus, Jennifer Dumpert, and Laurie Wigham

Energy Consumption Feedback: Engagement by Design 594
  Ruth Rettie, Kevin Burchell, and Tim Harries

The Design and Evaluation of Intelligent Energy Dashboard for
Sustainability in the Workplace 605
  Ray Yun, Azizan Aziz, Bertrand Lasternas, Chenlu Zhang,
  Vivian Loftness, Peter Scupelli, Yunjeong Mo, Jie Zhao, and
  Nana Wilberforce

Investigating Sustainability Stages in the Workplace 616
  Ray Yun, Peter Scupelli, Azizan Aziz, Bertrand Lasternas,
  Vivian Loftness, and Nana Wilberforce

Public Perception and Acceptance of Electric Vehicles: Exploring Users'
Perceived Benefits and Drawbacks 628
  Martina Ziefle, Shirley Beul-Leusmann, Kai Kasugai, and
  Maximilian Schwalm

Design for Human-Computer Symbiosis

FX e-Makeup for Muscle Based Interaction 643
  Katia Vega, Abel Arrieta, Felipe Esteves, and Hugo Fuks

The HARSim Application to the Task of Carrying School Supplies 653
  Ricardo Dagge and Ernesto Filgueiras Vilar

Human-Bed Interaction: A Methodology and Tool to Measure Postural
Behavior during Sleep of the Air Force Military 662
  Gustavo Desouzart, Ernesto Filgueiras Vilar, Filipe Melo, and
  Rui Matos

A Vibrant Evolution: From Wearable Devices to Objects as Mediators
of Experience 675
  Patricia J. Flanagan

Extended Senses in Responsive Environments: An Artistic Research
Project on Atmosphere 687
  Christiane Heibach, Andreas Simon, and Jan-Lewe Torpus

Ultralight Backpack System for Heavy Loaded Users   699
  Michal Pelczarski

Human Interactive Wearable Devices: Applications of Artificial
Electronic Skins and Smart Bandages.............................   710
  Kuniharu Takei

Aesthetically Enhanced RFID Inkjet Antenna Logos on
Skin (AERIALS)...   719
  James Tribe, Will Whittow, and John Batchelor

ReFlexLab: Designing Transitive Wearable Technologies towards Poetic
Aesthetics..   731
  Clemens Winkler and Soomi Park

Author Index   739

Table of Contents – Part IV

DUXU in the Enterprise

Methodological Framework for Control Centres Evaluation and
Optimization   3
   Ana Almeida, Francisco Rebelo, and Paulo Noriega

A UX Maturity Model: Effective Introduction of UX into
Organizations   12
   Lorraine Chapman and Scott Plewes

A Perception Oriented Approach for Usable and Secure Interface
Development   23
   Mehmet Göktürk and İbrahim Şişaneci

Activities to Improve System Integration and Service
Quality and Add Additional Values - Reducing the Cost in
Applying Human-Centered-Design Process -   32
   Rieko Hamachi, Ichiro Tsukida, and Hisashi Noda

ISO 9241-210 and Culture? – The Impact of Culture on the Standard
Usability Engineering Process   39
   Rüdiger Heimgärtner

Design, Deployment and Evaluation of a Social Tool for Developing
Effective Working Relationships in Large Organizations   49
   Athanasios Karapantelakis and Yonghui Guo

Humanizing the Enterprise: Delivering Best in Class User Experience
to Business Software Users   61
   Janaki Kumar

Designing Financial Literacy and Saving Tools for the Unbanked and
under-banked in Brazil   71
   Ananya Mukherjee, Catherine Winfield, Shan He,
   Federico Casalegno, and Wilson Ruggiero

Enabling Better User Experiences across Domains: Challenges and
Opportunities Facing a Human Factors Professional   81
   Emrah Onal, Susan McDonald, Corey Morgan, and Olga Onal

Brands Analysis Using Informational Ergonomics Concepts:
A Proposal   90
   João Carlos Riccó Plácido da Silva, Luis Carlos Paschoarelli, and
   José Carlos Plácido da Silva

Design for Diverse Target Users

The Design and Development of Empathetic Serious Games for
Dyslexia: BCI Arabic Phonological Processing Training Systems   105
    Arwa Al-Rubaian, Lama Alssum, Rawan Alharbi,
    Wafa Alrajhi, Haifa Aldayel, Nora Alangari, Hadeel Al-Negheimish,
    Aljohara Alfayez, Sara Alwaalan, Rania Aljindan, Ashwag Alshathri,
    Dania Alomar, Ghada Alhudhud, and Areej Al-Wabil

Considering People Living with Dementia When Designing Interfaces . . .   113
    Claire Ancient and Alice Good

Ergonomic Evaluation of Manual Force Levels of the Elderly in the
Handling of Products: An Analysis Using Virtual Reality   124
    Rafaela Q. Barros, Marcelo Márcio Soares, and
    Maria Goretti Fernandes

Accessibility of Mobile Platforms.   133
    Alireza Darvishy

TAC-ACCESS - Technologies to Support Communication from
Interfaces Accessible and Multimodal for People with Disabilities and
Diversity: Context-Centered Design of Usage   141
    Cristiani de Oliveira Dias, Liliana Maria Passerino,
    Carlos de Castro Lozano, and Enrique García Salcines

Designing with the User in Mind a Cognitive Category Based Design
Methodology   152
    Joseph Kramer and Sunil Noronha

The Impact of Human Likeness on the Older Adults' Perceptions and
Preferences of Humanoid Robot Appearance.   164
    Kerem Rızvanoğlu, Özgürol Öztürk, and Öner Adıyaman

Aging and New Technologies: Challenges and Perspectives   173
    Cláudia Stamato, Manuela Quaresma, and
    Cláudia Renata Mont'Alvão

A Challenging Design Case Study for Interactive Media Design
Education: Interactive Media for Individuals with Autism   185
    Asım Evren Yantaç, Simge Esin Orhun, and Ayça Ünlüer Çimen

Emotional and Persuasion Design

Further Investigation of the Effects of Font Styles on Perceived Visual
Aesthetics of Website Interface Design   199
    Ahamed Altaboli

You Can Interact with Your TV and You May Like It an Investigation
on Persuasive Aspects for an iDTV Application   208
    Samuel B. Buchdid, Roberto Pereira, and M. Cecília C. Baranauskas

Mood Boards as a Universal Tool for Investigating Emotional
Experience   220
    Huang-Ming Chang, Marta Díaz, Andreu Catalá, Wei Chen, and
    Matthias Rauterberg

Cool in Business: Developing a Data-Based Instrument Measuring
"Cool"   232
    Carol Farnsworth, Karen Holtzblatt, Theo Held, and Shantanu Pai

From Inexperienced Users to Co-creators: An Exploration of a
Generative Method   244
    Chrysoula Gatsou

From Wearables to Soft-Wear: Developing Soft User Interfaces
by Seamlessly Integrating Interactive Technology into Fashionable
Apparel   253
    Daniel Gilgen and T. Raune Frankjaer

Beyond Wearables: Experiences and Trends in Design of Portable
Medical Devices   261
    Rafael Gomez and Anna Harrison

On Feelings of Comfort, Motivation and Joy that GUI and TUI
Evoke   273
    Julián Esteban Gutiérrez Posada, Elaine C.S. Hayashi, and
    M. Cecília C. Baranauskas

The Wearable Self: Braiding a Feminist Critique within a Somaesthetics
Framework for Design   285
    Emily Ip, Wynnie (Wing Yi) Chung, Sunmin Lee, and
    Thecla Schiphorst

Throwing a Smile: Using Smile Icons to Design Social Interfaces   297
    Kyoko Ito, Shumpei Hanibuchi, and Shogo Nishida

User Experience Milestones: Structuring the Development of Experience
Products   308
    Simon Kremer, Ioanna Michailidou, Constantin von Saucken, and
    Udo Lindemann

Not So Fun? The Challenges of Applying Gamification to Smartphone
Measurement   319
    Michael W. Link, Jennie Lai, and Kelly Bristol

The Power of Negative Feedback from an Artificial Agent to Promote
Energy Saving Behavior 328
    Cees Midden and Jaap Ham

Emotion, Affectivity and Usability in Interface Design 339
    Renato Nascimento, Carlos Dias Limeira,
    André Luís Santos de Pinho, and
    José Guilherme Santa Rosa

New Methods for Measuring Emotional Engagement................. 347
    Andrew Schall

Does Social User Experience Improve Motivation for Runners? A Diary
Study Comparing Mobile Health Applications 358
    Frank Spillers and Stavros Asimakopoulos

Motive-Oriented Design: Helping Automobile Engineers to Take the
User's Perspective! 370
    Constantin von Saucken, Ioanna Michailidou, Simon Kremer, and
    Udo Lindemann

User Experience Case Studies

A Validation Study of a Visual Analytics Tool with End Users 381
    Heloisa Candello, Victor Fernandes Cavalcante, Alan Braz, and
    Rogério Abreu De Paula

User Support System in the Complex Environment 392
    Hashim Iqbal Chunpir, Amgad Ali Badewi, and Thomas Ludwig

Increasing Family Involvement in Elderly Care...................... 403
    Jasper Jeurens, Koen van Turnhout, and René Bakker

User Experience of Video-on-Demand Applications for Smart TVs:
A Case Study 412
    Linda Miesler, Bettina Gehring, Frank Hannich, and
    Adrian Wüthrich

Usability Methodological Procedures Applied on an Institutional Site ... 423
    Lúcia Satiko Nomiso and Luis Carlos Paschoarelli

Interactions around a Multi-touch Tabletop: A Rapid Ethnographic
Study in a Museum 434
    Evelyn Patsoule

Skill Specific Spoken Dialogues Based Personalized Atm Design to
Maximize Effective Interaction for Visually Impaired Persona   446
    Muhammad Shafiq, Jin-Ghoo Choi, Muddesar Iqbal,
    Muhammad Faheem, Maqbool Ahmad, Imran Ashraf, and
    Azeem Irshad

Consideration for Interpretation of Brain Activity Pattern during Car
Driving Based on Human Movements   458
    Shunji Shimizu, Hiroaki Inoue, Hiroyuki Nara,
    Fumikazu Miwakeichi, Nobuhide Hirai, Senichiro Kikuchi,
    Eiju Watanabe, and Satoshi Kato

Cross-Platform Product Usability and Large Screen User Experience:
A Teleconference System U&E Research   469
    Yinting Zhang, Chuncheng Zhao, Gang Liu, and Ting Han

Author Index   481

Design Theories, Methods and Tools

Experience Report: The Effectiveness of Paper Prototyping for Interactive Visualizations

Bastian Bansemir[1], Franziska Hannß[2], Berit Lochner[1],
Jan Wojdziak[2], and Rainer Groh[3]

[1] BMW Group, München, Germany
{bastian.bansemir,berit.lochner}@bmw.de
[2] Gesellschaft für Technische Visualistik mbH - GTV, Dresden Germany
{franziska.hannss,jan.wojdziak}@visuativ.com
[3] Chair of Media Design, Technische Universität Dresden, Germany
rainer.groh@tu-dresden.de

Abstract. This article describes the designing process of an interactive visualization at BMW. Paper prototyping is introduced as a part of the user-centered-design process and put into practice as a novel method for software development. During the development process paper prototypes have been used as a tool for communicating and testing within the interdisciplinary team of operational experts, visualization experts, designers and software developers. In conclusion the integration of paper prototyping benefits the design process positively. The interactive visualization meets the expectations of the user.

Keywords: paper prototyping, design research, interaction design, interface design, software development, interactive systems.

1   Introduction

Companies engage in speeding-up their software development cycles [1], due to harder competition, raising instability, increasing complexity or changing customer preferences [2, 3]. Indeed, notable successes have been achieved while moving away from traditional software development models, such as the waterfall model, to scrum-based or other agile models [4, 5].

This agile movement is impeded by the tendency to specialize employees, to intensify the workload for each employee, and to globally distribute employees [6]. Many issues evolve around agile models if employees do not work at the same or close location or even time zone or are not able to participate in daily meetings. However, realizing a high frequency in such situations, necessary for iterative software development, is often not handy or even impossible. Hence, agile models often fail to live-up to expectations companies often have [6].

At the intersection point between 'the dream of agility' and 'the daily reality' of a highly distributed workforce, paper prototyping is gaining momentum as one possible solution for solving this seeming contradiction. Paper prototyping may be understood

A. Marcus (Ed.): DUXU 2014, Part I, LNCS 8517, pp. 3–13, 2014.

as a cheap and quick tool to support the understanding between designers, developers, managers, engineers, customers and users of different design-stages during the development process [7].

Whilst extensive research has already studied various aspects of prototyping in the field of Human Computer Interaction in great detail [8-10] and has achieved compelling results, we focus in our case study on the use of paper prototyping. The major research question may be formulated as follows: How to use paper prototyping for user interface development of complex interactive systems? The study reports results from a case study conducted at and with BMW concerning the software development of a small-scale IT project. The main focus of software development concerned interface design of an interactive software project. Results indicate that paper prototyping may indeed close the gap between requirements of agile development and daily challenges of distributed workplaces.

The following sections shed light on first prototyping methods, second methodological proceeding applying paper prototyping and third outcomes of the paper prototyping process.

2   Prototyping in the Design Process

Within the process of interface design, prototyping is an essential tool for requirements elicitation, testing, communicating and decision-making. Prototypes represent a part or the complete user interface of the interactive system. They can be made with pen, paper and cardboard or by typing code. Prototypes may be segregated concerning their level of (i) completeness and (ii) fidelity.

First, prototyping methods are used to address special issues of the current state of the design and development process. In other words, it might either be necessary to give an impression of the whole system from the user's point of view or have an

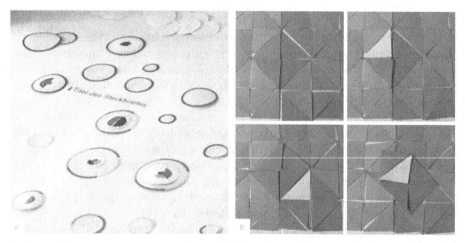

Fig. 1. Examples of Prototyping strategies: (a) horizontal prototype for a design decision process and (b) vertical prototyping as a stop motion video [11]

in-depth discussion on a specific element of the system under development. Hence, concerning the completeness of a prototype, two different types are distinguished: If a prototype presents a big range (or even the full set) of features of the interface, it is called a horizontal prototype [8]. Fig. 1a introduces an example of a horizontal paper prototype for a design decision process of the complex interactive system that was developed during the second cycle of the prototyping process (see chapter 3). Contrary, to estimate the usability or feasibility of a specific feature of a given system a vertical prototype is used. Gaining a first impression of a feature's functionality is the main objective of vertical prototypes. Fig. 1b shows a vertical prototype made out of paper. To achieve a better understanding of the functionality from a user's interaction perspective a stop-motion video is used to explicate the interaction aspect.

Second, due to their complexity prototypes may be characterized as low- or high-fidelity prototypes. Low-fidelity prototypes are characterized by low development costs, are mainly used for evaluation of competing design concepts and are most useful as a communication device within the developer team [12]. Furthermore they help to make design decisions at an early stage of the design process (see fig. 2b). Low-fidelity prototypes allow teams to experiment with a big number of design alternatives (especially when compared to high-fidelity prototypes) [13]. On the other hand, high-fidelity prototypes show the look and feel close to the final application. Therefore, they often represent the full set of functions and inhabit full interactivity. These prototypes are often used for exploring issue related to navigation and testing [12]. Fig 2a presents an interactive functional model of a product design process, i.e. a so-called work model.

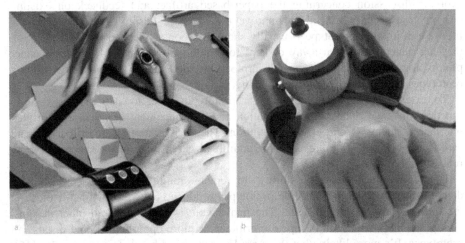

Fig. 2. Examples of prototyping methods regarding the level of fidelity: (a) low-fidelity prototypes for a decision making process concerning an interface structure and (b) high-fidelity prototyping as an interactive functional model of a product design process [11]

2.1   The Concept of Paper Prototyping

Paper prototyping (also called offline prototyping) may result in artifacts, such as paper sketches, illustrated storyboard, cardboard mock-ups or stop motion videos [14]. Paper prototyping is mostly used to get a fast and direct feedback from users in an early stage of the design process. Furthermore, they help to uncover relevant information about users and their work processes that should be supported [14].

Fast ways to create prototypes include the use of cardboards, paper, transparent paper, pens, and post-it notes. Literature on paper prototyping emphasizes, that creating a common understanding of an interface using a quickly drawn sketch positively influences the development process. In other words, users and developers often find it easier to understand a sketch, compared to discuss design options using a written document. Sketches or paper prototypes show first ideas and build the basis for discussions of further iteration stages. Additionally, they serve as a thinking tool, which support content-based analysis [7]. First low-fidelity prototypes, by means of sketches, are later transformed into more dynamic and flexible paper prototypes to encourage users to test, evaluate and change design ideas. This modular framework includes paper-based prototype-elements and placeholders. The elements can be fixed or dynamic to be placed individually during the design decision process. Placeholders are use to be drawn on and function as additional new elements of the interface. Moreover, alterable paper prototypes inspire a productive design discussion. With this modular framework [7] the developer-team gains valuable user feedback during the development process. This user feedback and the expression of user's ideas feed into subsequent stages of the interface design process. For the developer-team, the evolving discussion concerning the paper-based artifact and feedback on existing designs is especially fruitful to improve the interface design [15]. However, the lifecycle of a paper prototype is usually short. As soon as they served their purpose, they are generally thrown away or kept for emotional reasons [14]. In sum, paper prototyping is used for horizontal prototyping and mostly remain low-fidelity prototypes to show the overall functionality.

To extend the applicability of paper prototyping, i.e. to also discuss specific functions in great detail, the combination and rearrangement of previously printed interface elements is one efficient solution. The used materials are still paper and cardboard. Pen and glue are used for additional extensions during the prototyping process.

DOW introduces the possibility to create multiple prototypes [15]. He demonstrates that sharing multiple prototypes produce better results than dedicating the time to only one design idea. The final layout is inspired by all other designs. Group members will be more open to criticize, explore opportunities and discuss all prototypes. It's more likely, that there are less emotional bonds to any one idea [15]. "Collaborating on paper prototypes not only increases participation in the design process, but also improves communication among team members and increases the likelihood that the final design solution will be well accepted" [14]. However, it seems to be adequate to use multiple prototypes only in situations in which a creative mode of interaction among users and developers is really wanted.

2.2   Advantages and Disadvantages of Paper Prototyping

Paper prototyping is known as a fast way to mock up an interface and to get fast and direct feedback from the user [16]. Therefore it is used in the early development in the field of interface design. SNYDER quotes that due to paper prototyping the communication in a multidisciplinary team, the user as a part of the team, is easier. Furthermore it encourages creativity from the developer team and the user as well. With paper as material for prototypes it is possible to produce different design solutions and present a variety of interface mock ups. Therefore paper prototyping is used for an effective decision finding process [15]. By examining the alternative designs, it is possible to choose the most efficient one [14].

One of the disadvantages is that there will be no code produced. A paper prototype cannot refer to all problems of the interface. Especially the fast and easy way of an interaction is hard to recreate. Furthermore the user might get a wrong impression of the interface [16].

3   Paper Prototyping and Interactive Visualizations

To study the main research question an in-depth case study method is applied [17], analyzing an interface design project at BMW. BMW is the world leading car manufacturer in the premium segment. BMW has to challenge existing processes, methods and models to maintain this market position. To address this challenge, BMW always searches for new ways to do things even better. Paper prototyping is seen as an innovative approach to create better results faster.

More specifically, paper prototyping is embedded in an interface design process of an HTML5 web interface that enables a new business process. Numerous experts concerning the design of the business process, technological experts, and operation experts contributed to the success of the project. This process addresses stages such as requirements felicitation, prototyping, and refinement in iterative cycles. In other words, it follows the idea of design science [18], while putting a rapid form of prototyping, in this case paper prototyping [19], at the center of design efforts.

To consolidate the framework of design science the user centered design [20] is applied. In four iterative cycles an interactive visualization is developed by putting users into the center of the design process without confronting them with technical details. Hence, our interdisciplinary team used paper prototyping throughout all cycles. This method allowed us to get the same understanding of the visualization and build a common language through images. Interaction possibilities were also simulated using paper prototypes. In detail, the following cycles with the respective stages of task analysis, design, prototype and test [21] were part of the development process:

1st cycle: Developing rough sketches
2nd cycle: Elaborate the visualization concept
3rd cycle: Enhance the visualization with an interaction concept
4th cycle: Implementing a HTML5 interactive visualization

First cycle, we started by analyzing the task of the visualization. In the presented case we focused on developing a visualization for a new business process which shows complex information such as dependencies and a high number of dimensions. To prepare the paper prototyping the design phase aimed for a creative mood through inspiration (see fig. 3).

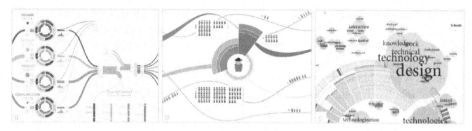

Fig. 3. Visualization-concepts as inspiration: (a) structure and efficiency of a School of Design [22], (b) Friendship-visualization [23], (c) „Total Interaction- " connections between the book's content [24]

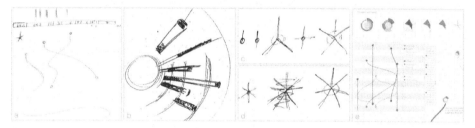

Fig. 4. Paper prototyping, first iteration: (a-d) rough sketches of ideas and (e) first iterations of the sketches on the PC

On this basis, first ideas were brainstormed and put into rough sketches (see fig. 4), which were reviewed by experts during the test phase.

Second cycle, with the most favored design idea the visualization concept was elaborated. To prepare the paper prototyping we identified the essential data and design elements and developed their first graphical representation (see circles in fig. 5). Putting all elements together as a paper prototype allowed the team and the users to discuss the visualization concept in detail and enhance it. Therefore we placed the single elements on a drawing area (see fig. 5), rearranged them and brought new design ideas into the scene. By drawing on existing elements, creating new sketches or printing new designs the graphical representations were designed and tested in an intuitive and rapid manner.

Third cycle, the paper prototype of the visualization allowed us to develop an interaction concept easily. In line with BEAUDOUIN-LAFON [14] we distinguished that the offline prototype made it comfortable for the team and the users to try different activities. The paper prototype facilitates to analyze, design, prototype and test diverse scenarios with varying interaction concepts and impact on the visualization. Simulating different tasks increased the comprehension of the user's needs.

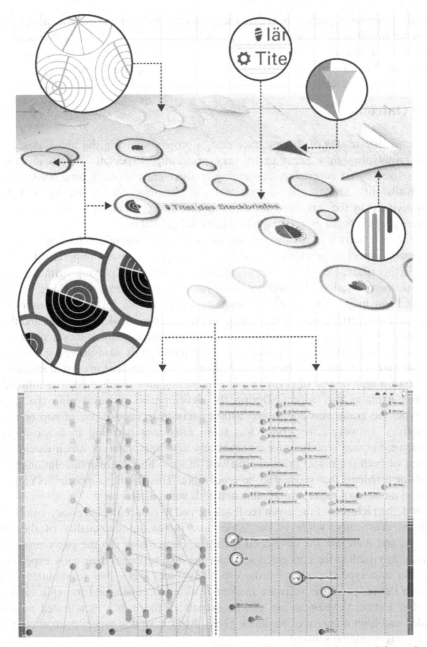

Fig. 5. Paper prototyping for interactive visualizations: Paper prototyping used for a design decision process (top) and results of the prototyping process implemented to the interface (bottom)

Fourth cycle, based on the developed concept we implemented an interactive visualization with HTML5 (see bottom part of fig. 5). The prior iterations helped to generate a common ground on requirements, so that the design, implementation and test in the fourth cycle were focused on technical details. Indeed, for further needs of clarification the paper prototype was used. That allowed the interdisciplinary team to discuss specifications in deep and overcome the issue of special terminology.

4   Outcome

Altogether, the results of the interface design project applying the above described paper prototyping flow seem to be very promising. Especially in circumstances characterized by (i) uncertainty concerning requirements, (ii) high time pressure and low availability among the experts able to formulate requirements, and (iii) innovativeness of the conceived software i.e. the most difficult situation to execute a software project, paper prototyping unfolds its full potential.

In our case study five advantages become apparent to the research team. First, the **enjoyment aspect** of working with a paper prototype is a very important facet we found in this study. Developers and users achieved a state of 'playing' with the paper material, the colored circles and lines, the net pieces, and texts. Watching children playing Lego may come closest to this state we observed. In this state, users and developers are working very concentrated on the prototype, make jokes here and there but always work as a whole group. In sum, enjoyment enables to set up a very concentrated atmosphere among a diverse set of participants, also under conditions of time pressure. This aspect of paper prototyping is widely ignored in current literature.

Second, a high degree of **creativity** among participants is achieved. The following situation explains this aspect. During the development process using the paper prototype, the group was confronted with a decision to choose one of two or more alternatives. However, the group was more often not deciding in favor of one alternative, but was searching for a completely new interpretation which would take the best of both (or more) prior alternatives. In sum, highly creative solutions were found for problems that seemed to be unsolvable. This finding supports SNYDER's list of advantages of paper prototyping, and adds some detail.

Third, the **richness** of the given feedback helped to reduce the necessary number of iterations drastically, while at the same time increasing the quality of the user interface and therefore the developed software. Participants use the paper prototype not only to visualize the conceived solution, but also reflected their daily experience upon the prototype. In other words, especially users were able to simulate or to envision the usage of the software in their work environment and to explicate their thoughts. Hence, developers are able to empathize the user's view based on very detailed and high quantity of feedback given. Especially this aspect contradicts with disadvantages often discussed.

Fourth, **acceptance** of the software in later stages increased drastically. This finding is especially remarkable as the development team was not able to include by far not all wishes or requirements. The acceptance of the software is mostly based on the feeling of all participants to be a part of the development team, which is in part true. So, introducing the new software is achieved more fluent.

Fifth, the **time** needed to occupy experts and to develop the software was reduced significantly. All the prior mentioned aspects result in drastic efficiency gains. Less meetings, instant solutions of wicked problems, good understanding of requirements and highly accepted solutions are the outcomes of the paper prototyping project in this study.

Besides these positive outcomes, we also found a backside of paper prototyping. First, getting participants into **creative mode** is a challenge. As long as participants do not touch the paper the positive effects may not unfold as described above. Instead, developers as well as users stick to a discussion and may get distracted. So getting participants into a mode in which they work pro-actively with the paper material is essential.

Second, developers who prepare the paper prototyping session may get **stuck to a particular design**. This finding seems to be natural as the developers spend a lot of time with preparing the materials and have the time to develop an own understanding of the software. This effect is tricky as the developers are often unaware about this process as the development of an own understanding happens unconsciously. To not fall into this trap as a developer the only way is to remain open minded and curious.

5   Conclusion

The major aim of this paper was to close the gap between advantages of agile software development methods and challenges raised by a distributed workforce, such as existing at BMW. For this study a single in-depth case study approach was applied, following a design science paradigm. In greater detail, the method of paper prototyping was applied in four cycles of interface design of an innovative business application to be implemented at BMW.

The results of the study show that paper prototyping is superior to other methods of software development, mainly by realizing five main advantages. Two disadvantages were also identified. On the one hand, advantages include (1) enjoyment of all participants along the design process, (2) a high level of creativity that is unleashed, (3) high richness of feedback given by users, (4) the acceptance of the developed design in later stages of development, and (5) drastic reduction in development time. On the other hand, disadvantages include (1) the challenge to get all participants in a creative mode, and (2) developers being stuck to their previously developed design propositions. Altogether advantages overweight the disadvantages by far, not only on quantifiable measures such as development time and coding quality etc. but also on more subjective measures such as enjoying the development process. In sum, we were able to show how paper prototyping may be applied in distributed development teams in a big organization and the positive and negative effects of paper prototyping.

Future work could shed more light on the four development stages we applied. Specifically, it should be tested if the stages we identified hold also in other contexts or may be distinct to the in-depth case study at BMW. Furthermore, we also found that not every participant (developer and user) was able to give input in every stage. E.g., developers were more involved in early stages of drawing sketches while users involved more in working with the elements of the later paper prototype. Hence, future work could address this issue by identifying roles the different stakeholders play and exploring how these different roles may be included most effectively.

Summarizing this study, we were able to show how paper prototyping in an interface design process may work within a big company, and how paper prototyping effects the development process altogether. Avenues for future research are also shown.

References

1. Blackburn, J.D., Scudder, G.D., Van Wassenhove, L.N.: Improving Speed and Productivity of Software Development: A Global Survey of Software Developers. IEEE Transactions on Software Engineering 22(12), 875–885 (1996)
2. Dag, J.N., Gervasi, V., Brinkkemper, S., Regnell, B.: Speeding up Requirements Management in a Product Software Company: Linking Customer Wishes to Product Requirements through Linguistic Engineering. In: 12th IEEE International Requirements Engineering Conference (RE 2004), pp. 283–294. IEEE Computer Society (2004)
3. Cohen, D., Lindvall, M., Costa, P.: Agile Software Development. DACS State-of-the-Art/Practice Report, Fraunhofer Center Maryland (2003)
4. Highsmith, J.: Extreme programming. White Paper, Arlington (2000)
5. Beck, K., Beedle, M., Bennekum, A., van Cockburn, A., Cunningham, W., Fowler, M., Grenning, J., Highsmith, J., Hunt, A., Jeffries, R., Kern, J., Marick, B., Martin, R.C., Mellor, S., Schwaber, K., Sutherland, J., Thomas, D.: Manifesto for Agile Software Development, http://agilemanifesto.org
6. Ramasubbu, N., Balan, R.K.: Globally Distributed Software Development Project Performance: An Empirical Analysis. In: 6th Joint Meeting of the European Software Engineering Conference and the ACM SIGSOFT Symposium on the Foundations of Software Engineering (ESEC-FSE 2007), pp. 125–134. ACM Press, New York (2007)
7. Knöfel, A., Koalick, G., Lapczyna, E., Groh, R.: Pimp your prototype. In: 5th International Scientific Conference "Printing Future Days 2013", pp. 131–136. VWB - Verlag für Wissenschaft und Bildung, Berlin (2013)
8. Nielsen, J.: Usability Engineering. Academic Press, London (1994)
9. Sears, A., Jacko, J.A.: The Human-Computer Interaction Handbook: Fundamentals, Evolving Technologies and Emerging Applications. Lawrence Erlbaum Associates, Taylor & Francis Group, New York, London (2012)
10. Moggridge, B.: Designing Interactions. The MIT Press, Cambridge (2007)
11. Chair of Media-Design: Werkstatt, http://werkstatt.inf.tu-dresden.de
12. Rudd, J., Stern, K., Isensee, S.: Low vs. High-Fidelity Prototyping Debate. Interactions 3(1), 76–85 (1996)
13. Rettig, M.: Prototyping for Tiny Fingers. Communications of the ACM 37(4), 21–27 (1994)
14. Beaudouin-Lafon, M., Mackay, W.E.: Prototyping Tools and Techniques. In: Sears, A., Jacko, J.A. (eds.) The Human-Computer Interaction Handbook: Fundamentals, Evolving Technologies and Emerging Applications, pp. 1017–1039. Lawrence Erlbaum Associates, Taylor & Francis Group, New York, London (2012)
15. Dow, S.: How prototyping practices affect design results. Interactions 18(3), 54–59 (2011)
16. Snyder, C.: Paper Prototyping: The Fast and Easy Way to Design and Refine User Interfaces. Morgan Kaufmann Publishers, San Francisco (2003)

17. Yin, R.K.: Case Study Research: Design and Methods. SAGE Publications, Los Angeles (2009)
18. Hevner, A., Chatterjee, S.: Design Research in Information Systems. Springer Science+Business Media, New York (2010)
19. Sefelin, R., Tscheligi, M., Giller, V.: Paper Prototyping - What is it good for? A Comparison of Paper- and Computer-based Low-fidelity Prototyping. In: Extended Abstracts on Human Factors in Computing Systems (CHI 2003), pp. 778–779. ACM Press, New York (2003)
20. Norman, D.: Design Principles for Human-Computer Interfaces. In: Conference on Human Factors in Computing Systems (CHI 1983), pp. 1–10. ACM, New York (1983)
21. Tory, M., Möller, T.: Human Factors in Visualization Research. IEEE Transactions on Visualization and Computer Graphics 10(1), 72–84 (2004)
22. De Donno, S.: Visualizing the School of Design, http://www.densitydesign.org/2013/04/visualizing-the-school-of-design/
23. Eschrich, B., Leitner, H.: Freundschaft, http://issuu.com/brino/docs/freundschaft
24. Rembold, M., Späth, J.: http://www.munterbund.de, http://www.munterbund.de

A Review of Empirical Intercultural Usability Studies

Victoria Böhm and Christian Wolff

University of Regensburg, Media Informatics Group, Universitätsstrasse 31,
93053 Regensburg, Germany
{victoria.boehm,christian.wolff}@ur.de

Abstract. In this paper, we discuss the applicability of usability engineering methods to software engineering projects in intercultural contexts. We have conducted a review of 55 empirical studies from the field of intercultural usability engineering. Categories from ISO TR 16982 were used as a classification framework.

1   Introduction

This paper presents first results of a literature review of usability engineering methods in intercultural interaction design and usability engineering projects. Our goal is to describe which different types of methods have already been researched regarding their applicability in intercultural contexts. A sample of 55 articles is analyzed and categorized according to the methodological framework given in the international standard ISO TR 16982 [1] (Ergonomics of human-system interaction – Usability methods supporting human-centered design) [1]. Besides a quantitative analysis we also discuss qualitative aspects of method usage and conclude with a brief description of future modifications in the review procedure and scope of analysis.

2   Motivation and Objectives

In intercultural software development projects people from different cultures are confronted and work together as, e. g., moderators, subjects, programmers or, more generally, as stakeholders. These people obviously differ in nationality and native language. But there are also subtle differences in patterns of non-verbal communication and values that guide their behavior. These distinctions have presumably impact on the procedure and also on the results of usability engineering methods. Therefore the applicability of methods should be investigated.

In studies which address this topic, three main reasons are given, why the application of specific usability engineering methods should be considered in research: One reason is the origin of methods: The majority of methods was developed in the western world

---

[1] The standard is going to be replaced by ISO 9241-230 [66]. We have used the scheme from ISO TR 16982, because in the current state of the new version the distinction of methods seems to be too fine-grained and the standard is not yet finished.

A. Marcus (Ed.): DUXU 2014, Part I, LNCS 8517, pp. 14–24, 2014.
© Springer International Publishing Switzerland 2014

and therefore the adequacy and applicability of these techniques outside their original cultural context is questionable ([2], [3], [4]).

The second and more relevant factor is the impact of culture on the results of usability testing methods which could be observed in some studies. [5] conducted an evaluation with both, subjective methods as well as objective evaluation methods. As objective measures task completion and errors were reported and questionnaires and interviews were used as qualitative methods. The results of both method types did not correlate. The users' performance with the system tested was poor but the results of the questionnaire and interview were positive. The different outcomes were attributed to the culture of the subjects from the far east, who probably were afraid of losing face.

Besides the effect of culture on the results of a method, specific problems with the practical application of the method itself were observed. Evers used three different techniques to evaluate a university website: Interview, thinking aloud and questionnaires. Participants with different cultural background were tested with the same procedures. Subjects were divided into four groups: UK, USA, NL, JP. Depending on the culture of the subjects specific problems could be observed with the methods: Japanese participants had difficulties to speak out loud during the thinking aloud while North American subjects seemed to answer the questionnaire in a quiz-like manner and tried to give the appropriate, "right" answer [6].

3   Review Methodology

In our ongoing literature review current research from the field of intercultural usability engineering is collected and classified into different categories of usability methodology. The goal of this analysis is twofold: First, we want to identify clusters of research, methods that have been widely investigated, but also gaps where research appears to be missing. Second, the classification serves as a framework for clustering best practices in the future.

3.1   Data Sources

Articles were taken from four different databases:

- Proceedings from the *International Workshop on Internationalization of Products and Systems* of the last two years (IWIPS 2010, 2011)
- A current handbook on intercultural design [7] (References from the chapter „methodology" were analyzed)
- *HCI Bibliography* (http://hcibib.org), an international bibliography for literature in the domain of human-computer interaction studies
- *Digital Library Mensch-Computer-Interaktion* (http://dl.mensch-und-computer.de), a digital library collecting HCI literature primarily from German language countries.

3.2   Selection of Articles

The following three criteria were defined to model the requirements for further analysis. Only articles which met all three criteria were investigated and classified:

1. Explicit focus on at least one usability engineering method
2. Empirical nature of research: usability engineering methods are applied in a empirical study
3. Intercultural context: A usability engineering method is investigated with regard to a specific culture, or several cultures in comparison.

3.3   Classification Framework

As a classification framework we have employed the classification of usability engineering methods from the Standard DIN EN ISO TR 16982 „Ergonomics of human-system interaction – Usability methods supporting human-centered design". We have selected this standard as a reference framework because it appears to be a reliable and distinct source of different categories and a good starting point for getting an overview over the field of investigated methods. The standard describes twelve classes of usability engineering methods. We conflated Expert evaluation and Document based methods (Table 1).

Table 1. Classification of usability engineering methods from DIN EN ISO TR 16982

Direct involvement of users	Indirect involvement of users
1. Observation of users 2. Performance measurement 3. Critical incidents analysis 4. Questionnaires 5. Interviews 6. Thinking aloud 7. Collaborative design and evaluation 8. Creativity methods	9. Document based methods/Expert evaluation 10. Model based approaches 11. Automated evaluation

Process was added as a category to that model in order to capture research that investigates the process of usability engineering. For some methods from the standard a short description is provided in the appendix, if the according techniques to a term were vague (see Table 2).

4   Results

So far, we have classified 55 empirical studies with respect to the framework which were published between 1996 und 2013. The following diagram shows the distribution of publication dates:

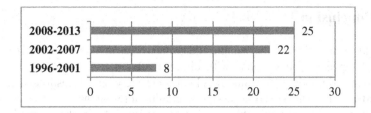

Fig. 1. Publication dates

A quantitative analysis of classes shows that the majority of studies employed *interview techniques*, 21 studies out of 55 conducted interviews. The second most frequent methods are *questionnaires* and *thinking aloud*. They were used 19 respectively twelve times. Half as much studies used *performance measurement methods* or *collaborative design and evaluation techniques*, for each category ten studies out of 55. In eight articles users were *observed*.

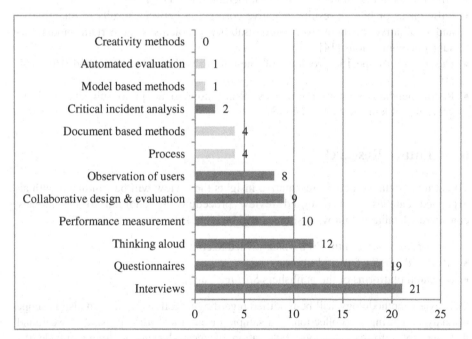

Fig. 2. Classification into categories from DIN ISO 16982

Four times the process of usability engineering in intercultural contexts was regarded and document based methods like style guides were used to evaluate or design an application.

The remaining usability engineering methods were investigated less often in our sample, with frequencies ranging from zero to four times. Details on the classification are given in the appendix (see Table 3).

5   Conclusion

Due to the small size of the sample, quantitative results must be interpreted with caution. It appears that methods with direct involvement of users are investigated more often. Methods like thinking aloud, interview and questionnaires can be identified as dominant areas (clusters) of intercultural research.

Different reasons are plausible for this observation: First, direct involvement of users leads to more potential bias in usability engineering methods and therefore these methods are more questioned. Second, there are more relevant sources for adoptions from other disciplines available, like guidelines for the application or translation of surveys ([8], [9], [10], [11]).

Beyond the quantitative disproportion of research conducted among the different methods, there are some interesting qualitative findings. In the empirical intercultural usability studies four categories of qualitative information can be found:

* Differences in the implementation of a method ([12], [13])
* Differences or bias in results: negative correlation between results of quantitative and qualitative methods [6], more usability problems with certain moderator-subject combinations [14]
* Description of specific problems of one culture with a specific method ([6], [15], [16])
* Recommendations or best practices: Rules how to adopt to subjects needs to prevent problems or bias ([17], [18]).

6   Future Research

To get more detailed and representative insights the review will be continued with an expanded database and modified review procedure. In addition to the already considered databases following sources will be included:

* *Web of Knowledge* (http://www.isiknowledge.com/)
* *ACM* und *IEEE CS* digital libraries
* Research platforms of the publishers *Springer* and *Elsevier*

The review methodology will be modified regarding selection criteria and also in scope of analysis. During the collection of a sample of empirical usability studies we found that relevant information about localization of methods can be found outside the discipline boundaries of HCI research. A good example is the guideline from Schaffer and Riordan, who describe in detail how to accommodate research in a intercultural context [19]. Their work includes several adoptions and recommendations which can also be applied in usability engineering. Thus, the selection criteria will be accommodated and also non-usability studies will be collected, just as non-empirical work, which can potentially bundle best practices ([20], [21], [22]).

Beyond these selection requirements, the scope of investigation shifts from quantitative analysis to a more qualitative approach. Not only usability methods will be regarded, but also the three typical observations mentioned above: Best practices, specific problems and observed bias. All these modifications provide the basis to build a framework of prevalent problems and their solutions.

References

1. International Standards Organization: ISO TR 16982 - Ergonomics of human-system interaction – Usability methods supporting human-centered design. In: DIN Deutsches Institut für Normung (ed.) Software Ergonomie- Empfehlungen für die Programmierung und Auswahl von Software. Beuth, Berlin (2004)
2. Sakala, L.: Participatory Design in a Cross-Cultural Design Context (2009)
3. Lee, J.-J., Lee, K.-P.: Cultural Differences and Design Methods for User Experience Research: Dutch and Korean Participants Compared. In: Proceedings of the 2007 Conference on Designing Pleasurable Products and Interfaces, pp. 21–34. ACM, New York (2007)
4. Jagne, J., Smith, S.G., Duncker, E., Curzon, P., Campus, T.P.: Cross-cultural interface design strategy. Univers. Access Inf. Soc., 1–8 (2006)
5. Herman, L.: Towards effective usability evaluation in Asia: cross-cultural differences. In: Sixth Australian Conference on Computer-Human Interaction, pp. 135–136 (1996)
6. Evers, V.: Cross-cultural Applicability of User Evaluation Methods: A Case Study Amongst Japanese, North-American, English and Dutch Users. In: CHI 2002 Extended Abstracts on Human Factors in Computing Systems, pp. 740–741. ACM, New York (2002)
7. Rau, P.-L.P., Plocher, T., Choong, Y.: Cross Cultural Design for IT Products and Services. CRC Press, Boca Raton (2013)
8. Survey Research Center: Guidelines for Best Practice in Cross-Cultural Surveys (2011)
9. Hoffmeyer-Zlotnik, J.H., Harkness, J.A.: Methodological Aspects in Cross-National Research. Gesis Verlag, Mannheim (2005)
10. Harkness, J.A., Braun, M., Edwards, B., Johnson, T.P., Lyberg, L.E., Mohler, P.P., Pennell, B.-E., Smith, T.W. (eds.): Survey methods in multinational, multiregional, and multicultural contexts. Wiley, Hoboken (2010)
11. Orlando, B., Kenneth, L.: Translating Questionnaires and Other Research Instruments: Problems and Solutions. Sage, London (2000)
12. Clemmensen, T.: Templates for Cross-Cultural and Culturally Specific Usability Testing: Results From Field Studies and Ethnographic Interviewing in Three Countries. Int. J. Hum. Comput. Interact. 27, 634–669 (2011)
13. Shi, Q.: A Field Study of the Relationship and Communication Between Chinese Evaluators and Users in Thinking Aloud Usability Tests. In: Proceedings of the 5th Nordic Conference on Human-computer Interaction: Building Bridges, pp. 344–352. ACM, New York (2008)
14. Vatrapu, R., Perez-Quinones, M.: Culture and Usability Evaluation: The Effects of Culture in Structured Interviews. J. Usability Stud. 1, 156–170 (2006)
15. Oyugi, C., Dunckley, L., Smith, A.: Evaluation methods and cultural differences: studies across three continents. In: NordiCHI 2008: Using Bridges, pp. 318–325. ACM (2008)
16. Yeo, A., Barbour, R.H., Apperley, M.: Usability Testing: A Malaysian Study. Department of Computer Science. University of Waikato (1997)

17. Day, D., Evers, V.: Questionnaire Development for Multicultural Data Collection (1999)
18. Vermeeren, A., Attema, J., Akar, E., de Ridder, H., von Doorn, A., Erbuğ, C., Berkman, A., Maguire, M.: Usability Problem Reports for Comparative Studies: Consistency and Inspectability. Human-Computer Interact 23, 329–380 (2008)
19. Schaffer, B.S., Riordan, C.M.: A Review of Cross-Cultural Methodologies for Organizational Research: A Best- Practices Approach. Organ. Res. Methods 6, 169–215 (2003)
20. Nielsen, L.: Personas - User Focused Design. Springer, London (2012)
21. Biesterfeldt, J., Capra, M.: Leading International UX Research Projects. In: Marcus, A. (ed.) HCII 2011 and DUXU 2011, Part I. LNCS, vol. 6769, pp. 368–377. Springer, Heidelberg (2011)
22. Gorlenko, L., Krause, S.: Managing International Usability Projects: Cooperative Strategy. In: CHI 2006 Extended Abstracts on Human Factors in Computing Systems, pp. 159–164. ACM, New York (2006)
23. Sun, X., Shi, Q.: Language Issues in Cross Cultural Usability Testing: A Pilot Study in China. In: Aykin, N. (ed.) Usability and Internationalization, Part II, HCII 2007. LNCS, vol. 4560, pp. 274–284. Springer, Heidelberg (2007)
24. Puri, S.K., Byrne, E., Nhampossa, J.L., Quraishi, Z.B.: Contextuality of Participation in IS Design: A Developing Country Perspective. In: Proceedings of the Eighth Conference on Participatory Design: Artful Integration: Interweaving Media, Materials and Practices, vol. 1, pp. 42–52. ACM, New York (2004)
25. Oreglia, E., Liu, Y., Zhao, W.: Designing for Emerging Rural Users: Experiences from China. In: Proceedings of the SIGCHI Conference on Human Factors in Computing Systems, pp. 1433–1436. ACM, New York (2011)
26. Honold, P.: Culture and Context: An Empirical Study for the Development of a Framework for the Elicitation of Cultural Influence in Product Usage. Int. J. Hum. Comput. Interact. 12, 327–345 (2000)
27. Bourges-Waldegg, P., Scrivener, S.A.R.: Meaning, the central issue in cross-cultural HCI design. Interact. Comput. 9, 287–309 (1998)
28. Asano, K., Yamazaki, K.: Observation Analysis Method for Culture Centered Design – Proposal of KH Method –. In: Marcus, A. (ed.) DUXU/HCII 2013, Part II. LNCS, vol. 8013, pp. 11–19. Springer, Heidelberg (2013)
29. You, M., Xu, Y.-J.: A Usability Testing of Chinese Character Writing System for Foreign Learners. In: Marcus, A. (ed.) DUXU/HCII 2013, Part II. LNCS, vol. 8013, pp. 149–157. Springer, Heidelberg (2013)
30. Vatrapu, R., Suthers, D.: Intra- and Inter-Cultural Usability in Computer-Supported Collaboration. J. Usability Stud. 5, 172–197 (2010)
31. Ford, G.: The Effects of Culture on Performance Achieved through the use of Human Computer Interaction. Human-Computer Interact., 218–230 (2003)
32. Bilal, D.: Measuring the usability of an international user interface: Culture and design representations. In: Human-Computer Interaction Symposium, Austin, TX (2006)
33. Yan, Q., Gu, G.: A remote study on east-west cultural differences in mobile user experience. In: Aykin, N. (ed.) Usability and Internationalization, Part II, HCII 2007. LNCS, vol. 4560, pp. 537–545. Springer, Heidelberg (2007)
34. Lee, Y.S., Ryu, Y.S., Smith-Jackson, T.L., Shin, D.J., Nussbaum, M.A., Tomioka, K.: Usability testing with cultural groups in developing a cell phone navigation system. In: Proceedings of HCI International (2005)

35. Sturm, C., Strube, G., Gouda, S.: Localization beyond National Characteristics: The Impact of Language on Users' Performance with Different Menu Structures. In: Marcus, A. (ed.) DUXU/HCII 2013, Part II. LNCS, vol. 8013, pp. 105–114. Springer, Heidelberg (2013)
36. Rau, P.-L.P., Liang, S.-F.: Internationalization and localization: evaluating and testing a Website for Asian users. Ergonomics 46, 255–270 (2003)
37. Hartson, H.R., Castillo, J.C., Kelso, J., Neale, W.C.: Remote Evaluation: The Network As an Extension of the Usability Laboratory. In: Proceedings of the SIGCHI Conference on Human Factors in Computing Systems, pp. 228–235. ACM, New York (1996)
38. Liu, J., Liu, Y., Rau, P.-L.P., Li, H., Wang, X., Li, D.: How Socio-economic Structure Influences Rural Users' Acceptance of Mobile Entertainment. In: Proceedings of the SIGCHI Conference on Human Factors in Computing Systems, pp. 2203–2212. ACM, New York (2010)
39. Wang, L., Rau, P.P., Salvendy, G.: A Cross-Culture Study on Older Adults Information Technology Acceptance. Int. J. Mob. Commun. 9, 421–440 (2011)
40. Tractinsky, N.: Aesthetics and Apparent Usability: Empirically Assessing Cultural and Methodological Issues. In: Proceedings of the ACM SIGCHI Conference on Human Factors in Computing Systems, pp. 115–122. ACM, New York (1997)
41. Clemmensen, T., Goyal, S.: Cross cultural usability testing. The relationship between evaluator and test user (2005)
42. Ménard, E., Khashman, N., Dorey, J.: Two Solitudes Revisited: A Cross-Cultural Exploration of Online Image Searcher's Behaviors. In: Marcus, A. (ed.) DUXU/HCII 2013, Part II. LNCS, vol. 8013, pp. 79–88. Springer, Heidelberg (2013)
43. Wang, M.-Y., Tang, D.-L., Kao, C.-T., Sun, V.C.: Banner Evaluation Predicted by Eye Tracking Performance and the Median Thinking Style. In: Marcus, A. (ed.) DUXU/HCII 2013, Part II. LNCS, vol. 8013, pp. 129–138. Springer, Heidelberg (2013)
44. Walsh, T., Nurkka, P., Koponen, T., Varsaluoma, J., Kujala, S., Belt, S.: Collecting Cross-cultural User Data with Internationalized Storyboard Survey. In: Proceedings of the 23rd Australian Computer-Human Interaction Conference, pp. 301–310. ACM, New York (2011)
45. Graffigna, G., Bosio, A.C., Olson, K.: Face-to-Face versus Online Focus Groups in Two Different Countries: Do Qualitative Data Collection Strategies Work the Same Way in Different Cultural Contexts? Doing Cross-Cultural Research. In: Ethical and Methodological Perspectives, pp. 265–286 (2008)
46. Diehl, J.C., Christiaans, H.H.C.: Globalization and cross- cultural product design. In: Marjanovic, D. (ed.) Proceedings of the 9th International Design Conference, pp. 503–510
47. Hunter, M.G., Beck, J.E.: Using Repertory Grids to Conduct Cross-Cultural Information Systems Research. Info. Sys. Res. 11, 93–101 (2000)
48. Vatrapu, R., Perez-Quinones, M.A.: Culture and International Usability Testing: The Effects of Culture in Structured Interviews. J. Usability Stud. 1, 156–170 (2004)
49. Tomico, O., Karapanos, E., Levy, P., Mizutani, N., Yamanaka, T.: The Repertory Grid Technique as a Method for the Study of Cultural Differences. Int. J. Des. Vol 3(3) (2009)
50. Sun, H.: Building a Culturally-competent Corporate Web Site: An Exploratory Study of Cultural Markers in Multilingual Web Design. In: Proceedings of the 19th Annual International Conference on Computer Documentation, pp. 95–102. ACM, New York (2001)
51. Yammiyavar, P.G., Torkil Clemmensen, J.K.: Influence of Cultural Background on Non-verbal Communication in a Usability Testing Situation. Int. J. Des. 2(3)

52. Plocher, T., Zhao, C.: Photo interview approach to understanding independent living needs of elderly Chinese: A case study. In: Dai, G. (ed.) Proceedings of 5th Asia-Pacific Conference on Computer-Human Interaction. Science Press (2002)

53. Law, E.L.-C., Hvannberg, E.T.: Analysis of Combinatorial User Effect in International Usability Tests. In: Proceedings of the SIGCHI Conference on Human Factors in Computing Systems, pp. 9–16. ACM, New York (2004)

54. Brush, A.J.B., Ames, M., Davis, J.: A Comparison of Synchronous Remote and Local Usability Studies for an Expert Interface. In: CHI 2004 Extended Abstracts on Human Factors in Computing Systems, pp. 1179–1182. ACM, New York (2004)

55. Yasuoka, M., Sakurai, R.: Out of Scandinavia to Asia: Adaptability of Participatory Design in Culturally Distant Society. In: Proceedings of the 12th Participatory Design Conference: Exploratory Papers, Workshop Descriptions, Industry Cases, vol. 2, pp. 21–24. ACM, New York (2012)

56. Clarke, R., Wright, P.: Evocative of Experience: Crafting Cross-cultural Digital Narratives Through Stories and Portraits. In: Proceedings of the 7th Nordic Conference on Human-Computer Interaction: Making Sense Through Design, pp. 318–321. ACM, New York (2012)

57. Lee, J.-J., Lee, K.-P.: Cultural Differences and Design Methods for User Experience Research: Dutch and Korean Participants Compared. In: Proceedings of the 2007 Conference on Designing Pleasurable Products and Interfaces, pp. 21–34. ACM, New York (2007)

58. Chavan, A.L.: Another culture another method. In: HCII 2005 Conference Proceedings, pp. 344–352 (2005)

59. Bidwell, N.J., Reitmaier, T., Marsden, G., Hansen, S.: Designing with Mobile Digital Storytelling in Rural Africa. In: Proceedings of the SIGCHI Conference on Human Factors in Computing Systems, pp. 1593–1602. ACM, New York (2010)

60. Abdelnour-Nocera, J., Austin, A., Michaelides, M., Modi, S.: A Cross-Cultural Evaluation of HCI Student Performance – Reflections for the Curriculum. In: Marcus, A. (ed.) DUXU/HCII 2013, Part II. LNCS, vol. 8013, pp. 161–170. Springer, Heidelberg (2013)

61. Díaz, J., Rusu, C., Pow-Sang, J.A., Roncagliolo, S.: A Cultural-oriented Usability Heuristics Proposal. In: Proceedings of the 2013 Chilean Conference on Human - Computer Interaction, pp. 82–87. ACM, New York (2013)

62. Katre, D.S.: Position Paper On Cross-cultural Usability Issues of Bilingual (Hindi & English) Mobile Phones. In: Clemmensen, T., Yammiyavar, P. (eds.) Proceedings of Indo-Danish HCI Research Symposium. Indian Institute of Technology, Guwahati (2006)

63. Smith, A., Dunckley, L., French, T., Minocha, S., Chang, Y.: Reprint of a Process Model for Developing Usable Cross-cultural Websites. Interact. Comput. 24, 174–187 (2012)

64. Elbaz, P., Galal, P., Galal-Edeen, H., Gheith, M.: The Influence of Culture on Systems Usability. Int. J. Softw. Eng. 4, 93–114 (2011)

65. Röse, K.: Usability-Engineering in the Context of Product Development. In: Proceedings of the 17th World Congress The International Federation of Automatic Control, pp. 8124–8128

66. ISO 9241-210:2010(en) (Ergonomics of human-system interaction — Part 210: Human-centred design for interactive systems),
https://www.iso.org/obp/ui/#iso:std:iso:9241:-210:ed-1:v1:en

Appendix

Table 2. Brief description of method categories in DIN EN ISO TR 16982

Observation of users	Collection of information about the user's behavior and the performance in the context of a specific task during user activity.
Performance related measures	Collection of quantifiable measurements (time to complete a task, number of errors, number of commands).
Critical incidents analysis	Systematic collection of specific events (positive or negative). Incidents are described in the form of short reports which provide information about the context.
Collaborative design and evaluation	Methods which allow different types of participants to collaborate in the evaluation and design of a system. Users play an important role in design and evaluation. (*card sorting[1], prototyping, cultural probes*)
Creativity methods	Methods which involve the elicitation of new system features usually extracted from group interaction (*Creativity techniques like SCAMPER, six thinking hats.*)
Document based methods/ Expert evaluation	Usability expert uses existing checklists or documents /his own judgment to carry out design or evaluation. (evaluation based on style guides, handbooks, standards, evaluation grids)
Model based methods	a) Formal methods that are based on models to predict users performance (KLM, GOMS) b) User interface specification and design methods are applied to create models of users behavior (flow chart diagrams interaction diagrams, state diagrams or task descriptions; *use cases, stories, scenarios, personas*)
Automated evaluation	a) Algorithms are used which focuse on usability criteria and are able to diagnose the deficiencies of a product (perceptive screen complexity, presentation quality) *b) automated collection of user data (web-logs).*

---

[1] Methods formatted in italics were added by the authors to clarify the categories.

Table 3. Explicit Classification of the sample

Method	References	#
Observation of users	[23][6][24][25][26][27][28][29]	8
Performance measurement	[5][18][30][31][32][33][34][35][29][36]	10
Critical incident analysis	[37][18]	2
Questionnaires	[5][17][6][34][16][30][38][39] [40][37][27][33][15][41][42][35] [43][29][44]	19
Interviews	[14][5][45][46][24][47][48][3][16][25][38][49] [26][27][50][51][52][41][28][42][35]	21
Thinking aloud	[12][13][51][15][6][16][53][27][54][34] [41][29]	12
Collaborative design	[2][55][56][57][58][52][59] [46][28]	9
Document based methods	[36][60][61][62]	4
Automated evaluation	[16]	1
Model based approaches	[36]	1
Process	[4][63][64][65]	4

Towards a Vocabulary of Prototypes in Interaction Design – A Criticism of Current Practice

Arne Berger, Michael Heidt, and Maximilian Eibl

Chemnitz University of Technology,
Strasse der Nationen 62,
09107 Chemnitz, Germany
{arne.berger,michael.heidt,
maximilian.eibl}@informatik.tu-chemnitz.de

Abstract. A methodological framework and a constructivist meta theory for formulating a vocabulary of prototype characteristics in interaction design are presented. Motivation for this research approach is drawn from cognitive psychology which hypothesizes that the aesthetic cognition of artifacts lies outside the scope of verbal appreciation. First, the shortcomings of the related design research literature are discussed in an attempt to frame a suitable methodology for overcoming these issues. It is also shown how the analysis of existing literature, protocols and observations will fit into this research scheme. Second, an accompanying meta theory building on Latours [15, 16] account of artifact–subject relations within the actor network theory, is described.

Keywords: aesthetic cognition, ANT, design theory, prototypes, methodology.

1   Motivation

The German »Entwurf« is farther-reaching than the two english terms »draft«, as in preliminary version, and »design«, as in final artifact. Every final design is the draft of a new design. This circle is fundamentally endless and as much based on the professional agency of designing as it is based on conscious and subconscious processes of aesthetic cognition. This dualistic peculiarity of the »Entwurf« may be one of the reasons, why German writing design researchers find it arcane to partake in English publications. Solely embracing professional agency, the very idea of »Entwurf« would be fundamentally incomplete. This dualism is, however, more than linguistic quibbling. The alternation of aesthetic cognition of existing artifacts, subsequent designing of future artifacts and subsequent aesthetic cognition is their very focus.

 Design activities of professional individuals and groups have been studied quite extensively since Donald Schöns seminal book »The Reflective Practitioner« [27]. Schöns initial insights into reflective practice are still the main anchor points [2] for contemporary design research. What Schön coined as »reflective practice« is nowadays mainly investigated with the help of interviews, protocol- and observation

A. Marcus (Ed.): DUXU 2014, Part I, LNCS 8517, pp. 25–32, 2014.
© Springer International Publishing Switzerland 2014

studies. See e.g. [7, 22]. Schöns depiction of design work as a »conversation with the material« is particularly well studied by e.g. Goldschmidt [10, 11] or Gero [9].

However, within the scope of design research, the role of aesthetic cognition in the before mentioned circle of »Entwurf« following »Entwurf« without hard boundaries between draft and design is barely researched. Among the few noteworthy are Petruschats [24, 25] remarks on the cognitive similarities between the decisions of designers while designing artifacts and those of users when choosing and using said artifacts. This resonates well with Whitfields [29] account of aesthetics as pre-linguistic knowledge. Hence aesthetics are not conceived as an »artistic« aspect of design, »but rather as a fundamental process for acquiring and creating knowledge« [29] which depends on the aesthetic perception of every involved individual and not the designer alone. While both Petruschat, a cultural scientist, and Whitfield, a psychologist, refer back to Damasios [5] somatic marker hypothesis, they both alike close the circle between draft and design, thus moving the artifact and its aesthetic cognition into the centre of attention.

If both and Domasio are right, design research needs to take a step aside from investigating how designers work to researching the very characteristics of design artifacts, inducing said aesthetic processes, once again acknowledging Daley [4]. This presumption moves the focus from investigating design processes to the research of the aesthetic cognition of design artifacts. This may be approached from two main directions that inevitably inform each other. With cognitive psychology being the first, design research can contribute to the understanding of the very characteristics of design artifacts. Both disciplines need to inform each other, albeit are quite different to be embraced in a single scientific endeavor. Hence, the paper at hand concentrates on the description of an evolving methodology for characterizing design artifacts, especially those in interaction design, which in particular receive little interest.

2   Related Work

Design artifact centered research ranges from the discipline independent investigation of, e.g. pivotal qualities of sketches [10, 11] to the very particularities of design arti-facts in product and engineering design, where e.g. Pei [23] counts 37 different kinds of design representations. This growing and ongoing interest to describe what design artifacts are and what they do slowly expands to the specifics of prototypes in interaction design. Most remarkably and simultaneously singular is Lim et al. [19] recent approach to an anatomy of prototypes. Thus moving forward from an exhaustive body of literature, e.g. [8, 13, 28] that exclusively describes the utilization of prototypes in software engineering and interface design but not their inherent specifics.

Accordingly, we share Lims view that current research into the dimensions of prototypes in interaction design is not sufficient because it deals only with »what to do with prototypes without understanding what they actually are« [19] However, Lims approach to »establish a fundamental definition of prototypes« [19] is limited for a couple of reasons.

First, their approach »is not meant to be complete; it is, however, meant to be useful« [19] Thus, the anatomy of prototypes is a somewhat simplified version of what prototypes in interaction design are, limiting it to a tool for designers only [19]. Second, their approach is based »on the fact that prototypes are not the same as the final design« [19]. Because of this assumption, this constrained collection of preliminary prototype attributes may not be extended to those of interaction design artifacts in general. Consequently, those limitations severely restrict the usage of this collection of attributes. Neither it is suited for facilitating communication between stakeholders, nor is it sufficient for a complete description of prototypes from the direction of other stakeholders, nor from the direction of the artifact itself. On these grounds the proposed list of attributes is ultimately not useful as a framework for investigating aesthetic cognition of said artifacts.

Lastly, and furthermore problematic, the methods Lim et al. applied, have not been clearly described, making it hard to replicate results in more exhaustive settings. We aim to address those issues with a substantial meta theory and a clearly defined methodology in the prospective building of a vocabulary for prototypes in interaction design. The focus of this short paper is the proposition of a meta theory and an operation breakdown of the applied methodology.

3   Methodology and Applied Methods

The approach to form an exhaustive definition of dimensions of prototypes is building on four stages of analysis. The first stage is a meta theory that will be described in depth in the next chapter. The meta theory is based on Latour [15, 16] who developed a symmetric view of how artifacts and subjects are interrelated forming a framework for further analysis. In the second stage, this framework is used to categorize existing dimensions of prototypes from three bodies of literature. The first corpus of categories emerges from efforts of Floyd [8] and Houde et al. [13] among others who aim to describe entry-points into the perception of design prototypes for different stakeholders. The second corpus of categories has been gathered from various sources discussing »fidelity«. Quite remarkably, the overwhelming body of literature about prototypes in interaction design is still in the middle of a debate about this very fidelity [1, 3, 17, 21]. This discussion aims at finding a definite model for categorizing the varieties between low fidelity sketches vs. high fidelity models and between non-functioning vs. working prototypes. However, this body of literature is a rich resource for categorizing concepts that researchers used to describe attributes of prototypes. In that way the fidelity debate can, after all, indirectly inform our research about what prototypes are. A third corpus of emerging categories is provided by researches who are trying to establish vocabulary lists to precisely describe specific aspects of prototypes. Most noteworthy among them are the interaction attributes proposed by Diefenbach [6] and Lim [18]. In a third stage, the thereby evolved preliminary categories are validated and advanced with the analysis of protocols of discussions between interaction designers and software engineers about the evolution of different mobile interaction applications. The fourth and final step is set to validate the completeness of the emerged categories. In design research this is usually accomplished via the analysis of expert interviews or observation studies. This feedback may instead very well derive from an analysis in cognitive psychology of appropriate design actions.

Following the tracks of socio and cultural research and protocol studies in design research, e.g. [10, 22], Mayrings [20] qualitative content analysis method is being applied. The method is particularly qualified to establish a corpus of categories where none existed. It is also well suited to analyze both text, as in interviews and protocols, and image, as in sketches or prototypes.

4   Fundamental Specification of Subject-Artifact-Relations

A robust meta theory is prerequisite for a legit vocabulary of interaction design prototypes. Therefore our research is based on a meta theory of fundamental artifact-subject relationships. We adopted Latours [15, 16] proposition for the approachability of its symmetric view of artifact–subject relationships. However, Latours proposal is empirical sound in its very nature and thus fundamentally grounded in practice. A possible future meta theory may as well be based on the data provided by cognitive psychology.According to Latour the state of artifacts within the agency of human subjects is usually seen as fundamentally binary. The artifact may as well change the subject as the subject may change the artifact [15]. This oversimplification suggests ontological contradictions, thus four distinctions of this amalgamation are more likely. They are proposed by Latour as translation, composition, blackboxing and delegation.

4.1   Translation

Neither the subject nor the artifact act on their own. Instead a subject-artifact or an artifact-subject is being composed as a hybrid »actant« that follows a third objective that is different from the aim of the artifact (its inscription) or the subject alone [16].

4.2   Composition

Agency is usually a combination of interleaved artifact-subject-relations that are taking effect together. Effective user agency can only be achieved by using those connected actants. Those actants include already inscribed means of agency that enable future activity. Thus activity is a combination of actants [16].

4.3   Blackboxing

Consequently time and space are folded as they interweave multiple subject artifact agencies. In turn they concurrently unfold those underlying cascades. Artifacts are as well single elements as they are compositions of multiplexed artifact-subject-configurations [16]. An artifact is as well a singular component as it is the sum of folded artifact subject configurations. The interweaved nature of those complex and nested subroutines stays implicit as long as an artifact is properly operating or as long as the subject refuses detailed appreciation. However, the moment an artifact breaks, its enclosed cascading blackboxes are unfolding.

4.4   Delegation

These accumulations continue to delegate actions of absent subjects [16]. An artifact contains coagulated work of other actants that in turn transform the artifact into an actant on its own. Latour exemplifies the concept of delegation with a »sleeping policeman« a speed bump designed to slow down motorists in urban areas [16]. The moral goal to safeguard pedestrians is translated to the car drivers selfish goal to safeguard his vehicle. This translation is not apparent, as the ultimate goal remains unchanged. In turn the goal may have been accomplished by other means, as e.g. traffic signs. In both cases the manifestation in concrete material changed while the intended goal remains unchanged [16]. Additionally the changed material may result in driver reactions that are unforeseen by the designers of the speed bump or the traffic sign alike. The initial intention may permanently remain unknown.

Latours propositions are relevant, as they explain that those bonded aspects need to be taken into account when discussing the role of artifacts in human agency. Artifacts are not only relational objects with a locked-in meaning, that is activated whenever triggered. Instead artifacts can very well delate an inscribed meaning of now absent subjects. However, this connection of delation and absent is the base for a broad interpretation by currently present subjects. In relation to artifacts in interaction design, as the topic at hand, a shift between the designers intention and the users interpretation occurs. This once again seconds the very concept of aesthetic cognition.

There are other concurrent research approaches for a proposed application of these theoretical findings in a practice-oriented context. Schäffer [26] e.g. generalizes Latours propositions to an in-between of artifact and subject, that very well may help the understanding of facilitated human agency. However, focusing on the in-between considers this connection as a mere »contagion« of subjects by artifacts, thus disguising the discussion of concrete dimensions between artifact and user. An antithesis is proposed by Janlert [14]. Their radical description merely sees artifacts as »things in themselves« [14 p.3]. The lack of practical relevance of this account is apparent, as the author himself is an interpreting subject that is observing other interpreting subjects. Hence the »thing in itself« may very well exist but can never be experienced without human interference.

We have chosen a middle ground different from these accounts by Schäffer and Janlert. We do not exclude human agency of intention and interpretation. In addition, we do not intertwine artifacts and subjects to an inseparable amalgamation. Hence the confrontation of artifact (sketch, prototype, product) and subject (designer, user, stakeholder) is three parted.

1. The artifact by itself is solidified intention in specific material. Some of the characteristics of intention and material are interchanging. Speaking with Latour, the

speed bump made of concrete becomes a police man and the intention of the police is materialized in concrete [16]. Different processes of exchange are possible. The same intention may be manifested in different material. Interpretations of the same material may profoundly differ.

2. The designer of an artifact is following a specific intention that leads her to inscribe specific semantic aspects into the artifact. Those very aspects may be manifested in various materials. The intentions behind a speed bump or a traffic sign are fundamentally equal. Yet their specific semantic and material manifestations are fundamentally different.

3. Users interpretation of an artifact evolves from the perception of its material. Maybe the car driver will never realize the designers intention to safeguard pedestrians. He will interpret the speed bumps materialization in concrete as a thread to his car. He as well may interpret the traffic sign as beautifully colored or yet another patronization. Still, at least in theory, both artifacts may lead to safer roads.

These three aspects differentiate between artifacts intentions and interpretations, thus shaping a nuanced approach for the analysis of their aspects. The concept of artifacts as black boxes explains different interpretations of an artifacts intention. To a lesser extend it also explains its semantic body between intention and its material. Different stakeholders are interconnected through the artifact as a) their interpretations are based on the artifact, b) their intentions and their knowledge are inscribed into the artifact and c) their interpretations are once again based on the artifact (sic).

5   Interpreter, Intention, Content, Material

Following these theoretical accounts four base categories may be deducted to structure the interconnection between subjects and artifacts in interaction design. The distinction between professional designer and utilizing user falls short considering our meta theory and considering aesthetic cognition. The artifact for reducing speed has multiple dimensions. The first dimension being its specific material. The materialization of the artifact is foremost following technological considerations. To a certain extend decisions about the material are subordinate to the semantic body of the artifact. The speed bump may very well be a steel construction, as the traffic sign may be an image on a display instead of a drawing on a steel plate. The artifact always bonds the material and the designers intention. We specifically imply that the material may not have been consciously chosen but found or recombined as long as it complies with the designers intention. The designers intention may temporarily or permanently remain unknown. Maybe the car shall be damaged after all. Once again, the material is only an afterthought. The car may be damaged with steel or concrete as pedestrians may be safeguarded with symbols on signs.

There is another layer of differentiation between material and intention, especially considering professional design activity. We propose the concept of »semantic body« as a working hypothesis. Body describes how the artifact is build to achieve the designers intention. This is different from a manifestation in concrete material, as outlined below.

Body describes which actions, data, functions and interactions the artifact embodies. We reach the limits of the scope of the speed bumps as an example: made of concrete or steel, the speed bumps function is very simple. It may as well be an interactive device that automatically reacts to the volume of traffic. Its functionality as well as its interactivity would fundamentally differ; still it may be manifested in unchanged material. This can as well be expanded to the traffic sign at the roadside. It may be a screen, fixed to display a permanent speed limit, it may manually be set to different speed limits, automatically by a timer switch or interactive by a traffic surveillance system. All four possibilities leave the materialization unchanged but incorporate more information to achieve certain levels of interactivity.

The dimension of the artifacts body characterize the aspects of function, interaction, semantic and appearance. They enable the artifact to take effect and lie in-between the intention and the material. The dimensions of the body are implemented in specific material, while the intention lies behind both body and material, qualifying the designers objective.

6   Future Work

Within the scope of this work, an exhaustive application of the described methodology is pending. It is currently being applied on relatively small samples to show its usefulness and the resulting »completeness« of the vocabulary. Sample size being an issue, consequently this methodology may be adapted for a larger scale for some of the experiments. Outside the scope of this work, an application of the vocabulary within cognitive psychology is pending, subsequently responding in a follow-up application in a design research setting.

References

1. Buxton, B.: Sketching User Experiences. Morgan Kaufmann (2007)
2. Chai, K.-H., Xiao, X.: Understanding design research: A bibliometric analysis of Design Studies (1996-2010). Design Studies 33(1), 24–43 (2012)
3. Coyette, A., Kieffer, S., Vanderdonckt, J.: Multi-fidelity Prototyping of User Interfaces. In: Baranauskas, C., Abascal, J., Barbosa, S.D.J., et al. (eds.) INTERACT 2007, Part I. LNCS, vol. 4662, pp. 150–164. Springer, Heidelberg (2007)
4. Daley, J.: Design creativity and the understanding of objects. Design Studies (1982)
5. Damásio, A.R.: Descartes' error: emotion, reason, and the human brain (1994)
6. Diefenbach, S., et al.: Ein Interaktionsvokabular: Dimensionen zur Beschreibung der Ästhetik von Interaktion. Usability Professionals, 27–32 (2010)
7. Dorst, K.: Design problems and design paradoxes. Design Issues 22(3), 4–17 (2006)
8. Floyd, C.: A systematic look at prototyping. Approaches to Prototyping 1, 1–18 (1984)
9. Gero, J.S.: Design prototypes: a knowledge representation schema for design. AI Magazine 11(4), 26 (1990)
10. Goldschmidt, G.: Serial Sketching: Visual Problem Solving in Designing. Cybernetics and Systems 23(2), 191–219 (1992)

11. Goldschmidt, G.: The Dialectics of Sketching. Creativity Research Journal 4, 123–143 (1991)
12. Berger, A.: Design Thinking for Search User Interface Design. In: Wilson, M. (ed.) Proceedings of the 1st European Workshop on Human-Computer Interaction and Information Retrieval. Workshop in: 2011 British Computer Society Conference on Human-Computer Interaction (BCS-HCI 2011). ACM, New York (2011)
13. Houde, S., Hill, C.: What do prototypes prototype. In: Handbook of Human-computer Interaction, vol. 2, pp. 367–380 (1997)
14. Janlert, L.E., Stolterman, E.: Complex Interaction. ACM Transactions on Computer-Human Interaction 17, 1–32 (2010)
15. Latour, B.: Die Hoffnung der Pandora. suhrkamp taschenbuch wissenschaft (2002)
16. Latour, B.: Pandora&s hope (1999)
17. Lim, Y., et al.: Comparative analysis of high-and low-fidelity prototypes for more valid usability evaluations of mobile devices. In: Proceedings of the 4th Nordic Conference on Human-computer Interaction: Changing Roles, pp. 291–300 (2006)
18. Lim, Y., et al.: Interactivity attributes: a new way of thinking and describing interactivity. In: Proceedings of the 27th International Conference on Human Factors in Computing Systems, pp. 105–108 (2009)
19. Lim, Y.-K., et al.: The anatomy of prototypes. ACM Transactions on Computer-Human Interaction 15(2), 1–27 (2008)
20. Mayring, P.: Qualitative Inhaltsanalyse: Grundlagen und Techniken. Beltz (2010)
21. McCurdy, M., et al.: Breaking the fidelity barrier: an examination of our current charcterization of prototypes and an example of a mixed-fidelity success, New York, NY, USA, pp. 1233–1242 (2006)
22. Paton, B., Dorst, K.: Briefing and reframing: A situated practice. Design Studies 32(6), 573–587 (2011)
23. Pei, E.: Building a Common Language of Design Representations, pp. 1–689 (October 2009)
24. Petruschat, J.: Das Leben ist bunt. Technical Report #21. form+zweck (2005)
25. Petruschat, J.: Wicked Problems. practice based research (2011)
26. Schäffer, B.: Kontagion" mit dem Technischen. Zur dokumentarischen Interpretation der generationenspezifischen Einbindung in die Welt medientechnischer Dinge. In: Bohnsack, R., et al. (eds.) Die Dokumentarische Methode und ihre Forschungspraxis, pp. 45–67. VS Verlag für Sozialwissenschaften (2007)
27. Schön, D.A.: The reflective practitioner: how professionals think in action. Basic Books (1983)
28. Virzi, R.A.: What can you Learn from a Low-Fidelity Prototype? Proceedings of the Human Factors and Ergonomics Society Annual Meeting. In: Proceedings of the Human Factors and Ergonomics Society Annual Meeting, pp. 224–228 (October 1989)
29. Whitfield, T.W.A.: Aesthetics as Pre-linguistic Knowledge: A Psychological Perspective. Design Issues 21, 3–17 (2005)

Agile Usability Patterns for UCD Early Stages

Ana Paula O. Bertholdo[1], Tiago Silva da Silva[2], Claudia de O. Melo[1,3],
Fabio Kon[1], and Milene Selbach Silveira[4]

[1] IME/USP - Universidade de São Paulo
{ana,fabio.kon}@ime.usp.br
[2] ICT/UNIFESP - Universidade Federal de São Paulo
silvadasilva@unifesp.br
[3] Thoughtworks
cmelo@thoughtworks.com
[4] FACIN/PUCRS - Pontifícia Universidade Católica do Rio Grande do Sul
milene.silveira@pucrs.br

Abstract. The integration between agile methods and UCD has been addressed by several authors in recent years. However, a gap remains regarding how the practices have been described, lacking a standard that both designers and agile practitioners can understand and apply.

This study aims to propose agile usability patterns based on the literature, with a focus on the User-Centered Design early stages. The goal of the proposed patterns is to facilitate the use of the best agile usability practices by identifying more clearly in which context the pattern can be applied, and what is the problem that each pattern solves, presenting examples.

Keywords: agile usability, agile UCD, agile UX, best practices, patterns.

1 Introduction

The adoption of agile development methods has grown steadily in the software industry, since their creation [1, 2]. According to Larman [3], agile methods apply time boxed iterative and evolutionary development, adaptive planning, promote evolutionary delivery, and include other values and practices that encourage agility – rapid and flexible response to change.

Agile development values are in accordance to the underlying principles of User-Centered Design (UCD) [4], e.g., focusing on individuals and interactions and collaborating with customer. By integrating UCD and agile methods, we can ensure the software produced adds value to the business and to the end user. As observed by Ratcliffe and McNeill [2], there is no motivation in using software if it does not add value.

With regard to usable practices or methods, agile methods are considered lightweight, *i.e.*, the team should only do what is necessary to bring value to the customer. On the other hand, UCD shows the importance of real users in system development. If used together, UCD and agile methods will benefit, since

A. Marcus (Ed.): DUXU 2014, Part I, LNCS 8517, pp. 33–44, 2014.

software is developed by and for people. This integration between agile methods and UCD has been addressed by several authors in recent years. For instance, Sy [5], Fox *et al.* [6] and Silva *et al.* [7] arrived at very similar proposals.

However, it is still necessary a breakdown of each stage of these proposals. Moreover, a gap remains regarding how the practices have been described, lacking a standard that both designers and agile practitioners can understand and apply. Patterns can help in understanding how to integrate the practices of the two communities involved and allow us to visualize the commonalities shared.

This study aims to propose agile usability patterns based on the literature [8], with a focus on the User-Centered Design early stages: Identify need for human centered design; Specify context of use; and Specify requirements [4]. The research question for this study is: what are the best usability practices used in the agile methods community related to UCD early stages?

The remainder of this paper is structured as follows: Section 2 presents key concepts for the research and a brief summary of recent related work; Section 3 presents how the synthesis and collection of data was performed to rate usability practices in patterns; Section 4 presents the Agile Usability Patterns related to UCD early stages; and Section 5 brings up conclusions as well as future directions for the research.

2   Background

Agile methods entail adaptive planning and iterative processes. Having an iterative process means a project is divided into subsets of features, unlike the waterfall that divides a project based on requirements analysis, design, coding, and tests. In the iterative style, the development cycle is composed of a series of small incremental releases. Each release is set at regular intervals, typically from two to four weeks, which are called sprints in Scrum [9] or iterations in eXtreme Programming (XP) [10], in which the team carries out a complete development cycle of a subset of the requirements.

There is an international standard that is the basis for many UCD methodologies. This standard (ISO 13407: Human-Centred Design Process) defines a general process for including human-centered activities through a development life-cycle, but does not specify exact methods. In this model, once the need to use a human centered design process has been identified, four activities form the main cycle of work: (*i*) Specify Context of Use; (*ii*) Specify Requirements; (*iii*) Produce Design Solutions; (*iv*) Evaluate Designs.

While usability methods have focused primarily on the typical users of the system that actually use it, agile methods are concerned with the fulfillment of customer needs, more related to the system business values. The concern for the users therefore is present in both, however they differ with respect to the type of user considered. Thus, the integration of these areas benefited the users, whatever the type or profile they belong.

The systematic literature review on UCD and agile methods conducted by Silva *et al.* [7] presented 58 studies addressing this topic. Some of them depict an overall picture for the integration of UCD and agile methods, such as Fox *et al.* [6], and Sy [5]. 31 studies of the systematic review addressed the early stages of the UCD. However, classifying the studies according to the UCD stages is a hard task. Due to the agile projects iterative nature some UCD stages overlap.

The literature suggests that for a smooth integration between UCD and Agile, UCD should take advantage of the iterative nature of Agile. For instance, Sy [5] suggests that breaking designs down into cycle-sized chunks gives them the freedom to mix and match different types of usability investigations into the same session, which enables them to juggle more than one design, and more than one type of usability investigation at the same time. In order to do so, UCD should be performed aiming at applying all activities of the UCD cycle for each subset of features. This is the aim of Agile UCD, breaking UCD stages down into the agile cycles size.

3   Method

The goal of data collection was to find the usability practices most used by the agile community. The search criteria was defined as follows:

- (("usability" OR "usability methods" OR "User Centered Design" OR "User eXperience" OR "Human-Computer Interaction" OR "Computer-Human Interaction") AND ("agile methods" OR "agile development" OR "eXtreme Programming" OR "Scrum" OR "agile")).

The filtering process consisted of: (*i*) Reading the title, (*ii*) Reading the summary, and (*iii*) Reading the complete study. For each phase, the studies that were not in accordance to the inclusion criteria were excluded.

The synthesis of the collected data was performed by checking the items that define a pattern – name, context, problem, solution and examples – in each practice. Practices that did not have the data for each of these items were excluded from the pattern. A pattern would need to have at least three similar practices for the same problem. Furthermore, for a practice to be defined as a pattern example, it should belong to different projects among the pattern examples considered.

4   Agile Usability Patterns for UCD Early Stages

In this study, a pattern is defined according to Alexander *et al.* [11], *i.e.*, a pattern is a structured method of describing good design practices within a field of expertise. Still following Alexander's definition [11], we describe the patterns by presenting (*i*) Name; (*ii*) Context; (*iii*) Problem; (*iv*) Solution; and (*v*) Example.

The patterns are presented according to the UCD stages [4], which facilitates the understanding of the goal of each pattern described. This paper focuses only on the usability practices which comprises the following steps of the UCD: (1) Identify Needs for Human-Centered Design; (2) Specify Context of Use; and (3) Specify Requirements.

Tullis and Albert reported the difference between the terms usability and User Experience (UX): "Usability is generally considered the user's ability in using something to accomplish a task successfully, while user experience has a broader view, looking at the full interaction of the individual, as well as their thoughts, feelings and perceptions that result from this interaction" [12].

In the agile community, it is extremely common to use the term User Experience to any activity related to user research, UCD, usability, or interface design. Therefore, in the patterns described below, we use the same term. However, the term not necessarily indicates that all UX activities were really performed.

Based on the method defined in Section 3, we propose the following set of Agile Usability Patterns related to UCD early stages.

4.1 Identify Needs for Human-Centered Design

Pattern: *Sprint Zero*

Context: Sprint Zero is a practice that aims at better defining a broader view of the project. It is a stage before starting the project implementation, to define product view and general goals, to roughly plan future sprints, to define design principles and to clarify roles of the team members and communication methods.

It is also a critical sprint to do any work of UX or usability before the start of code production. In the agile community, it is usually performed by a UX or usability team, composed of usability specialists, designers, and UX managers who study the user and draw some screens to communicate the raised ideas. Some teams involve other members, such as developers.

Problem: Missing the "big picture" of the system in the beginning of the development with agile methods. In addition, priorities might be unclear and team members might work with wrong things because they did not understand which the real priorities were. Therefore, they report unnecessary work. Also, there is little time for upfront design. The main forces involved are:

- **Force 1**: The UX team needs to clarify the "big picture" of the system.
- **Force 2**: Short time to understand the "big picture" of the system during the Sprints, where there are parallel UX and development activities.

Solution: A short Sprint before the code implementation to define a broader view of the product, general goals, to roughly plan the next sprints and to define design principles.

Example: Chamberlain *et al.* suggest Sprint Zero should be done before the Planning Game, an agile planning meeting, so that usability aspects can be discussed during the Planning Game [13]. Belchev and Baker report contextual inquiry being used as one-to-one interviews conducted in the users workplace, which aim at observing ongoing work [14].

Pattern: *One Sprint Ahead*

Context: The iteration time is considered too short to perform all the UX activities and implement their results. Therefore, UX professionals need to work one sprint ahead of the development team. Thus, the UX team is able to conduct user research and produce design solutions to the upcoming development iteration. At the same time, the UX team evaluate the already coded functionalities from the previous iteration. In this context, there are two work tracks within the project: UX and development.

Problem: Making the development and the UX team syncrhonized, then both can collaborate and provide input to the development workflow. Main forces involved:

- **Force 1**: Developers need design definitions and system requirements to analyze and implement functionalities.
- **Force 2**: The UX team needs to evaluate designs implemented by developers according to user needs.
- **Force 3**: The UX team needs to interact with users and customers to define design requirements and solutions.
- **Force 4**: Iteration usually offers short time to perform the activities described in the three first forces.

Solution: The UX team works at least one iteration ahead of development team.

Example: The systematic review conducted on UCD and agile methods [7] described several articles [13, 15, 16] that address the One Sprint Ahead issue. They reported the use of one sprint ahead concept, that in summary consists of UX or usability specialists performing tasks related to user research, design and user interface evaluations while the development team implements the code of stories designed in the previous sprint and fix problems found by the UX team.

Pattern: *UX Specialists as Product Owners*

Context: Customers usually provide business requirements that the system need to attend. When hybrid versions – composed by Scrum and XP – are followed, Product Backlog items are described as User Stories. The adoption of UX specialists as Product Owners means that real users interests will be taken into account as well as customers interests. The Product Owner shares user needs with the team and the team defines what functionalities they will be able to finish until the next Sprint. Software development with agile methods is iterative or divided into iterations or sprints.

Problem: Integrating business requirements into usability requirements. Main forces involved:

- **Force 1**: Adding real users needs to a development environment without leaving business requirements behind.
- **Force 2**: Combining customers and real users needs.

Solution: UX specialists composing a Product Owners team.

Example: Gothelf describes his experience as Product Owner in an agile team using Scrum [17]. He thinks that UX designers work is the link between business and customer. By addressing this information under the view of the Product Owner, it is possible to come up with ideas for design early and accordingly with business requirements.

Pattern: *Users Time is Valuable*

Context: In agile methods, all the activities are related to a subset of functionalities at each iteration or sprint. Therefore, when carrying out user research, it is necessary to save some time for gathering requirements for the upcoming iterations and evaluations of the former ones. From a single visit, it is possible to use time for several activities with users. In general, the activities related to users are performed in a face-to-face format and only by members of the UX team.

Problem: Short time to conduct usability tests and user research. Main forces involved:

- **Force 1**: UX activities are performed during sprints or iterations.
- **Force 2**: Sprints or iterations are too short to be divided into a specific type of activity (evaluation, design or research) at each meeting with the user.

Solution: Each meeting with typical users is used for several activities, such as usability tests of the design developed in the previous iteration and user research to define requirements dor the upcoming iteration.

Example: Patton states that the practice called "Leverage user time for multiple activities" is one of the best practices when integrating UX into an Agile environment, since in this kind of environment, time is short to go deeper into the user research and evaluation [18].

Pattern: *Parallel Tracks*

Context: In agile environments concerned about UX or usability research, it is common to have a team in charge of UX-related activities, a team in charge of development activities and team leaders. In this context, one team provides the others with input through delivering results from user research, prototyping of new screens and interface evaluation, whereas the development team will share the code integrated to the interface delivered by the UX team. In this situation, there are parallel tracks involving the UX and development teams. Each team is responsible for its own activities, but communicating to each other during the cycle.

Problem: Fixing design flow in agile cycles, clarify doubts regarding design releases, get the design job done in one iteration, and validate designs. Main forces involved:

- **Force 1**: Performing UX activities synchronized with the features under development.
- **Force 2**: Implementation of the features already defined by UX research and design activities, and fix features based on UX evaluations.

Solution: UX or usability team working in a parallel track with the development team in order to synchronize their activities.

Example: The pattern follows the agile UCD cycle proposed by Sy [5]. Parallel tracks aims at synchronizing the UX activities with the development sprints [19].

Pattern: *UX Specialists as Full-Time Member of the Agile Team*

Context: Traditionally, UX or usability teams work on several projects at the same time, i.e. they are not fully dedicated to a unique project. This traditional UX styles of working does not fit into Agile development. In this case, UX specialists would start losing important updated data during the iterations. Moreover, UX professionals had not much time to dedicate themselves to each project and perform design activities. For these reasons, UX specialists started to be dedicated to one project at a time, reinforcing that all members are fully committed to the systems quality.

Problem: The UX team feels left out of the cycle or loses crucial information, with short time for design activities. Main forces involved:

- **Force 1**: In agile methods, all the participants must be committed and not just involved to the project. Daily communication and co-location are important.
- **Force 2**: UX teams might work with several projects at the same time. Thus, the communication between the UX team and the development team becomes even more difficult.

Solution: Participants working full-time in a single agile team. UX specialists should not work at multiple projects concurrently. Moreover, the pair designing practice – as in pair programming – is strongly recommended.

Example: Nielsen describes the practice named "Decline of the centralized UX department" as a result of his experiences. He says that all his case studies indicate that UX personnel should be co-located with developers and other members of the project. Thus, the UX team would be considered part of the project team [20].

4.2 Specify Context of Use

Pattern: *Little Design Up Front*

Context: The design upfront as proposed in traditional UX research does not fit into the agile values. Regarding agile values, requirements changes are considered inherent to the development process and it is not necessary to spend much time with planning and designing of requirements upfront. Due to these values, agile development advocates little design upfront the development, then just the necessary work is done, reducing waste. In this context, UX specialists focus only on the job related to those features for a specific iteration. Then, they share their results with the development team, according to the Parallel Tracks pattern definition.

Problem: Traditionally, user research is carried out before development starts. This is incompatible with agile values. Main forces involved:

- **Force 1**: In agile methods, only the features that will fit into the next iteration need to be detailed.
- **Force 2**: User research and the analysis of collected data that result in requirements definition are usually performed ahead of the start of the development.

Solution: Carrying out research with less granularity of details, focusing only on a set of essential features for the next iteration, i.e., chunking design work into small pieces.

Example: Cho [16] states that less time should be spent with high-fidelity design. The focus should be on defining problems and finding solutions collaboratively. Before starting the sprint cycle, the UX specialists team gets ready for the next sprint through holding sessions to define problems and develop solutions and this happens during the last week of the previous sprint.

Pattern: *Contact Plan of Users*

Context: Conducting research with real users depends on knowing who the typical users of a system are and then finding users willing to participate in research, design and testing stages. Additionally, in order to have these activities done before the next iteration, it is not possible to think about which users should be called. Having a contact plan of users is helpful in such a situation. Contact Plan of Users consists of a list of users who meet the systems profile, their contact data, and possibilities of participation are kept up-to-date.

Problem: Being unable to reach the right users in time, not getting feedback in time for the project, depending on beta-users, and delivering a design without any evaluation. Main forces involved:

- **Force 1**: The need for typical users to participate in activities such as requirements gathering, design and evaluation.
- **Force 2**: Check if the users are available to participate in UX activities is in accordance to project schedule.

Solution: Create an early channel for communication with final users in order to guarantee stable feedback.

Example: In [21] report constant planning of future feedback from users during development. According to the authors, the UX practitioner may does not know exactly what will be asked in two weeks, it could be a feedback for a prototype or several questions and answers involving typical users. However, it is necessary to schedule meetings with users on a regular basis to obtain feedback quickly.

4.3   Specify Requirements

Pattern: *User Stories*

Context: In XP, user stories are written by customers such requirements the system needs to meet for them. They are similar to case scenarios but they do not have only the working description of a user interface. User stories are the basis for creating acceptance tests. The aim is to check if the user story was implemented correctly. The aim of writing user stories in agile teams is to meet user needs, not to specify user interfaces. However, when UX activities are integrated into agile methods, besides adding the real users point of view of the system and not only the customers – focused more on business requirements –, it is also common to include interface drafts into user stories. These drafts aim at improve the understanding of ideas previously discussed and creation of prototypes. Also, personas are used to better describe the user profile present in each story and usability issues can be inserted into the story acceptance criteria.

Problem: Traditionally, usability requirements are defined and described in detailed documents which contain task analysis, personas, an overview and case scenarios. However, extensive documentation does not fit into agile methods scenarios. Main forces involved:

- **Force 1**: In agile methods, extensive documentation is considered as a time consuming activity that can be easily outdated due to requirements changes.
- **Force 2**: Requirements definition with UX methods or usability usually describe in details user needs according to the results of user profiles.

Solution: Inclusion of usability requirements into user stories, defining acceptance criteria for each story.

Example: Hussain *et al.* state that user research can be used to develop user stories [22]. Sohaib and Kahn report that user stories must be integrated into design based on scenarios [23].

Pattern: *More Collaboration, Less Documents*

Context: More collaboration, less documentation refers to values that have been already shared in agile environments, but expanded to UX activities or usability. In this context, sharing research findings happens orally and though low-fidelity prototypes, such as paper drawings made with pencils in a way that the ideas are easily and quickly shared and validated. Also, in these cases, low and medium-fidelity prototypes are used as specification along with user stories, which share the same value – just the enough for understanding.

Problem: Non-understandable designs, designs left behind during implementation, agile team does not understand UX activities. Main forces involved:

- **Force 1**: Research findings and evaluations need to be shared among the team as soon as possible in the development process.
- **Force 2**: More detailed descriptions of the UX research findings or usability last longer because of the process of documentation.

Solution: Design and design processes being frequently updated; continuous communication during implementation and testing. Also, some teams use UX professionals as design facilitators who collect information from the people involved, such as users, customers and developers, sharing them among all project members.

Example: Six [24] informs that UX practitioners need to adapt their deliveries because when someone are working with the rest of the team, one can answer their questions directly rather than writing a style guide. Instead of writting a 90-page report, problems from a usability test can be immediately adress.Less time authoring unnecessary documentation means more time for you to help make a great product. The author also highlights the fact that since UX practitioners are much more involved with tasks outside their immediate specialty, such as development and testing, they find new ways of using their UX knowledge.

Pattern: *Prototypes as Specification*

Context: As part of the idea previously described in the pattern "More collaboration, less documents", several teams use prototypes as specification rather than extensive documents aiming at gathering users and customers requirements for discussion as soon as possible. In this context, prototypes are used to quickly communicate and validate ideas related to user interface requirements. Usually, they are built by UX specialists and along with user stories they are the main sources for specifying system requirements.

Problem: Sharing interface requirements that meet user needs faster than documents of requirements specifications. Mains forces involved:

- **Force 1**: To spread knowledge related to user needs, which need to be met by the system in a faster way and early in the development process.
- **Force 2**: Need for registering requirements defined and shared with the team.

Solution: Use prototypes to specify user interface requirements.

Example: In [25], user interface prototypes are used to make customer requirements be known as soon as possible during discussions and make them work as a template for development.

5   Conclusion

The problem of combining User-Centered Design and agile methods is an example of a context-dependent issue. We believe that presenting usability practices as patterns – providing context, problem, solution, and example – will increase their applicability and improve their reliability. However, this is an ongoing work and it still needs further study in order to validate the proposed patterns.

Usability should be part of the development process, not only with the aim of creating usable products, but also usable practices, involving all team members related to the context in which the systems will be used. Thus, an agile and usability-based team will have all members focused on meeting the customers and typical users needs, since all of them are required to understand the importance of doing so.

All members participating in the development of a system are users of methods or practices in software development. When it comes to choosing the best method in software development, it is necessary to consider who the users are, what they need, how and in which context they perform their tasks in order to focus on the human beings involved in the project. In other words, apply to the user of development methods the same tasks used to understand the end users of a system.

It is not necessary to use methods with great formality, regarding their application or documentation. However, it is necessary to have a collaborative environment, where all the people involved with the project share both the knowledge acquired from close contact with real users and the knowledge required to develop the product, starting from the data collection and specification of the context of use to the development and testing.

In this context, each project member benefits from the previous knowledge of the others, allowing a greater comprehension of the software development project as a whole. Also, it is possible to improve the usability of the product and the development process.

Patterns can help in understanding how to integrate the practices of the two communities involved and allow us to visualize the commonalities shared. The goal of the proposed patterns is to facilitate the use of the best agile usability practices by identifying more clearly in which context the pattern can be applied, and what is the problem that each pattern solves, presenting examples.

References

[1] Dingsøyr, T., Dybå, T., Moe, N.B.: Agile Software Development - Current Research and Future Directions, 1st edn. Springer (2010)

[2] Ratcliffe, L., McNeill, M.: Agile Experience Design: A Digital Designer's Guide to Agile, Lean, and Continuous. New Riders (2012)

[3] Larman, C.: Agile and Iterative Development: A Manager's Guide. Pearson Education (2003)

[4] Association, U.E.P.: What is user-centered design? (January 2014)

[5] Sy, D.: Adapting usability investigations for agile user-centered design. Journal of Usability Studies 2(3), 112–132 (2007)

[6] Fox, D., Sillito, J., Maurer, F.: Agile methods and user-centered design: How these two methodologies are being successfully integrated in industry. In: Agile 2008 Conference, pp. 63–72 (2008)

[7] Silva da Silva, T., Martin, A., Maurer, F., Silveira, M.: User-centered design and agile methods: A systematic review. In: Society, I.C. (ed.) Agile Conference, Agile 2011, pp. 77–86 (2011)

[8] Santos, A.P.O.: Application of agile usability practices in free and open source software. 131 p. thesis (master in computer science) (2012); Institute of Mathematics and Statistics, University of Sao Paulo, Sao Paulo,
http://www.teses.usp.br/teses/disponiveis/45/45134/tde-22082012-154721

[9] Schwaber, K., Beedle, M.: Agile Software Development with Scrum, 1st edn. Prentice Hall PTR, Upper Saddle River (2001)

[10] Beck, K., Andres, C.: Extreme Programming Explained: Embrace Change, 2nd edn. Addison-Wesley Professional (2004)

[11] Alexander, C., Ishikawa, S., Silverstein, M., Jacobson, M., King, I.F., Angel, S.: A Pattern Language: Towns, Buildings, Construction. Center for Environmental Structure Series. Oxford University Press (1977)

[12] Tullis, T., Albert, B.: Measuring the User Experience: Collecting, Analysing, and Presenting Usability Metrics. Morgan Kaufmann (March 2008)

[13] Chamberlain, S., Sharp, H., Maiden, N.: Towards a framework for integrating agile development and user-centred design. In: Abrahamsson, P., Marchesi, M., Succi, G. (eds.) XP 2006. LNCS, vol. 4044, pp. 143–153. Springer, Heidelberg (2006)

[14] Belchev, B., Baker, P.: Improving obama campaign software: Learning from users. In: Agile 2009 Conference, pp. 395–399 (2009)

[15] Sy, D., Miller, L.: Optimizing agile user-centred design. In: CHI 2008 Extended Abstracts on Human Factors in Computing Systems, pp. 3897–3900. ACM, New York (2008)

[16] Cho, L.: Adopting an agile culture. In: Proceedings of the 2009 Agile Conference, AGILE 2009, pp. 400–403. IEEE Computer Society, Washington, DC (2009)

[17] Gothelf, J.: Ux designer as product owner (February 2011), http://www.jeffgothelf.com/blog/ux-designer-as-product-owner/

[18] Patton, J.: Emerging best agile ux practice (2008), http://agileproductdesign.com/blog/emerging_best_agile_ux_practice.html

[19] Lu, C., Rauch, T., Miller, L.: Agile teams: Best practices for agile development 9(1), 6–10 (2010)

[20] Nielsen, J.: Agile user experience projects (2009), http://www.useit.com/alertbox/agile-user-experience.html

[21] Enterprise, E.: Incorporating user-centered design into an agile development process (December 2011), http://experoinc.com/incorporating-user-centered-design-into-an-agile-development-process/ (acessed on: December 2011)

[22] Hussain, Z., Milchrahm, H., Shahzad, S., Slany, W., Tscheligi, M., Wolkerstorfer, P.: Integration of extreme programming and user-centered design: Lessons learned. Agile Processes in Software Engineering and Extreme Programming 31, 174–179 (2009)

[23] Sohaib, O., Khan, K.: Integrating usability engineering and agile software development: A literature review. In: 2010 International Conference on Computer Design and Applications ICCDA, vol. 2 (2010)

[24] Six, J.M.: Integrating ux into agile development (April 2011), http://www.uxmatters.com/mt/archives/2011/04/integrating-ux-into-agile-development.php (accessed on: December 2011)

[25] Broschinsky, D., Baker, L.: Using persona with xp at landesk software, an avocent company. In: Proceedings of the Agile 2008, pp. 543–548. IEEE Computer Society, Washington, DC (2008)

Ideologies in HCI: A Semiotic Perspective

Jan Brejcha

Information Science and Librarianship, Charles University, Prague, Czech Republic
jan@brejcha.name

Abstract. The user-interface (UI) of interactive systems is the meeting point of people with interactive communication technology (ICT). As a human product, it forms a part of culture that determines us, often without our full awareness. The values and goals of the designers are implicitly encoded in the interface and the documentation but can be in conflict with the values of the user. This is when both the intentional and unintentional manipulation with the user starts because he or she is presented with inappropriate choices or even inappropriate goals. The aim of this article is to show how this manipulation works, in which regards it is unavoidable and how can we deal with it. Ideologies are a special means of manipulation and we can counter them by suitable education and analysis.

Keywords: User-interface, ideology, values, ethics, manipulation, persuasion, rhetorics, culture.

1   Introduction

The user-interface (UI) of interactive systems is the meeting point of people with interactive communication technology (ICT). As a human product, it forms a part of culture that determines us, often without our full awareness. The UI is constructed according to a set of values of the designer and other stakeholders in the production process. Their values and goals are implicitly encoded in the UI and the documentation, and can be in conflict with the values of the user. This means the UI directs the user interaction often according to the intent of the designer. This is when both the intentional and unintentional manipulation of the user starts because he or she is presented with choices, or even goals, that are incompatible for his or her intent. For the purpose of unmasking and decoding the inner workings of the UI, we have chosen a semiotics approach, with the emphasis on pragmatics, as defined by Charles Morris [23]. Semiotics is a study of semiosis, or sense-making, which has a syntactic (syntax), semantic (meaning) and pragmatic (purpose) dimension.

Pragmatics, "deals with the biotic aspects of semiosis, that is, with all the psychological, biological, and sociological phenomena which occur in the functioning of signs." [23][page 30]. This most complex dimension focuses on how we use or interpret vehicle/object relation, *i.e.*, what is the signs' purpose? The pragmatic

A. Marcus (Ed.): DUXU 2014, Part I, LNCS 8517, pp. 45–54, 2014.

dimension governs how signs are used or understood in their conventional and symbolic form.

Each and every UI is a result of diverse influences during the design process. Stakeholders in the process have their own goals and expectations that try to put into the final product. For example, the sales and marketing department could have strategic aims of short time-to-market, easy adoption of the product from the users and gimmicks to strengthen the brand and the product family. The programmers, on the other hand, might want to incorporate an advanced and clever technology, while the designers might want to create a simple and good-looking UI. All of these often conflicting values can have an input into the final product at the cost of the final user who expects the product to satisfy his or her needs and help achieve his or her goals. Often, such expectation falls short and the user is forced to become a "detective" trying to guess the motive of the designer in order to understand how to use the product in a sensible way. [8] In this light, the user should be aware as much as possible of the techniques used during the development process as well as the prevailing ideologies driving the UI production.

From our standpoint, the UI is an example of a complex language. Consequently, we can apply different UI language components such as: discrete elements, interaction sentences, narration, rhetorical tropes, and patterns. [3] Discrete elements are the smallest elements to have a meaning. The interaction sentence is a meaningful unit describing a task in the user's interaction. The narrative in UI is made both by the designers' meta-communication and the temporal and/or sequential aspects of perceiving UI elements. Rhetorical tropes are devices of persuasion and emphasis, such as metaphors. Patterns are typical configurations of UI language components in different settings.

By analyzing the individual statements exposed through the interaction with the software, we can follow an entire argumentation constructed with the help of the different UI elements. A simple way of doing this is transcribing the "interaction sentences" [3] that the user encounters while performing a certain task. The interaction sentences can be analyzed further in terms of what goals the designers have and what assumptions they have about his or her users. By exploring different parts of the system through the UI, we can extract the inherent values. We argue that when the UI follows the structure of natural language, it both behaves user-friendlier and conveys the designer's intent more effectively.

2   Ideology and HCI

For the purposes of this article, we understand ideology as:

"[A] logically coherent system of symbols which, within a more or less sophisticated conception of history, links the cognitive and evaluative perception of one's social condition – especially its prospects for the future – to a program of collective action for the maintenance, alteration or transformation of society." [24][page 510]

What criteria should we then use to recognize ideologies and analyze them further? Again, according to Mullins, these components are: cognitive power, evaluative power, action-orientation and logical coherence. (*Ibid.*). By (2.1) cognitive power, he means the "cognition and retention of information" (*Ibid.*), when we identify and symbolize our recurrent experience. After having done this cognitive process we can simplify, order and abstract it for making choices between information, *e.g.* on different causal forces. The (2.2) evaluative power is then based on this understanding of information. Political ideology, "incorporates evaluations of what is conceived" and can anticipate "possible events and conditions." (*Ibid.*) The (2.3) action-orientation is based on the power of the ideology to "communicate conditions, evaluations, ideals, and purposes among members of groups (...) and thereby facilitates the mobilization and direction of energies and resources for common political undertakings." (*Ibid.*) Finally, the (2.4) logical coherence or consistency between various ideology components means, "the ideology must 'make sense' and not result in logical absurdities." (*Ibid.*)

As the word suggests, ideology is related to ideas. On this level, it is needed to focus on the relation between UI and image. As Mitchell put it,

"The concept of ideology is grounded, as the word suggests, in the notion of mental entities or 'ideas' that provide the materials for thought. Insofar as these ideas are understood as images - as pictorial, graphic signs imprinted or projected on the medium of consciousness - then ideology, the science of ideas, is really an iconology, a theory of imagery." [22][page 164]

Currently, in the context of ICT, ideology comes to us from a rather unexpected direction. As Galloway [16] points out, citing Althusser, ideology that was, "traditionally defined as an 'imaginary relationship to real conditions' (Althusser)" [16][page 953] has been superseded by simulation. He understands simulation as an "'imaginary relationship to ideological conditions." In short, "ideology gets modeled in software." (*Ibid.*) Therefore, software serves as a prime example of current ideologies acting on us according to all the four criteria.

2.1   Cognitive Power

Software models ideology and is made visible through the way software works. This reflects the cognitive power of ideology. It does so by relating to the underlying hardware in a specific way:

"In a formal sense computers are understood as comprising software and hardware are ideology machines. They fulfill almost every formal definition of ideology we have (...). Software, or perhaps more precisely operating systems, offer us an imaginary relationship to our hardware: they do not represent transistors but rather desktops and recycling bins." [6][page 43]

Most importantly, as Chun continues, "software produces 'users'." [6][page 43] Software creates both a relation with hardware as well as with users. Hardware is what the user encounters first, although the focus is then shifted to the software and the UI as a whole.

UI is regarded as an entrance into a simulated world, but UI is also forms a media layer between the "real" world and the user. "The doorway/window/threshold definition is so prevalent today that interfaces are often taken to be synonymous with media themselves." [16][page 936] An even more poignant definition relates the UI more tightly to the effect it has on the interacting users:

"The interface is this state of 'being on the boundary.' It is that moment where one significant material is understood as distinct from another significant material. In other words, an interface is not a thing; an interface is always an effect. It is always a process or a translation." [16][page 939]

The UI works thus not only on a semiotic level by differentiating symbols, but also on a psychological level when it creates relations and effects. For the UI to be effective and enjoyable, it is important to work "as a 'mirror' depicting the user's self-image, not only a 'window' looking into a world of content(...)." [21][page 53]

The differentiation work of the UI done between the user and users' self-image leads us to think about the UI in the terms of an active self-organizing entity. This notion is close to what Derrida [9] called "différence". Following Derrida's argumentation, the UI presents a different idea from the original one (or content) just by the way it is mediated. Thus, different media can go only as far as their structure permits. The medium of text can express other things than speech (*e.g.* Derrida's example of difference vs. différence, both of which are read the same); the medium of image can express other things than text, *etc.* The medium of the UI thus expresses its content differently.

The primacy of text for Derrida is something we can also observe very well in software. Software can go past the interacting subject, which is in contrast with the UI, which is bound in the subject/object relation [9] simply because it requires a user. And because the action is done through the UI, the UI privileges the content it presents. In this way, the UI not only tells us how to read a certain idea but can also pre-select for us which ideas we can possibly read. As Winograd and Flores state that: "Computers have an especially large scope, for they are machines that work with language. By using them, we join a discourse set up in the limits made by programmers." [27][page 178]

Each UI presupposes a certain paradigm of use which is not always visualized. When built correctly, the UI lets us see only what has to be seen. The UI itself stands on a certain ideology. It defines relations which are to be made. The relations made by ideology are political in as much as they are social.

While the prevalent UI definition is connected with a gateway as a passage into another world, beyond the entrance this world is structured by another narrative. By analyzing the narrative, we can gain a better insight into the UI structure and the underlying ideology:

"In temporal terms, narrative is about what already happened while simulation is about what could happen. Because of its static essence, narrative has been used by our culture to make statements. (...) The potential of simulation is not as a conveyor of values, but as a way to explore the mechanics of dynamic systems." [14][page 86]

2.2   Evaluative Power

The user is presented with information "designed to program the spectators of techno-images to behave in a specific way and this in turn serves as a feedback to the programs calculating these techno-images." [11] Here, techno-images are computer-generated images in Flusser's theory.

Therefore, for building new UIs, we ought to deconstruct the present ones and uncover their design/intent. Winograd and Flores also suggest this by stating that: "design is the interaction between understanding a creation... [We therefore] need to set up a theoretical framework not to watch how the devices operate, but what they cause. " [27][page 53] This is frequently the only way to understand new UIs in a situation when we do not have a suitable interpretation key - we do not know their code. It is, in a way, something like "reverse engineering" known from computer science.

2.3   Action Orientation

In order to use the UI, different *languages* are present in the form of action paradigms. "Action paradigms define a set of instructions that are available at any given moment. The paradigms offered by the system should match those the user needs so that she's not forced to perform an action she didn't intend." [1][page 91] For example, take the interaction game for putting the computer to sleep in Microsoft® Windows® XP. Here the user has to first click on Start, then Shut Down, only then is he or she presented with the intended Sleep button. Thus, for putting the computer to sleep, we have to choose from UI language components that are in conflict with our intent. Even when something does not work as expected, we can gather interesting data out of it. When we interpret a connection between an UI sign and a proposed function, this mental connection is what forms our image of the system. "Systems work because they don't work. Non-functionality remains essential for functionality." [16][page 931] Similar oppositions build the interaction space as "...the 'choices' operating systems offer limit the visible and the invisible, the imaginable and the unimaginable." [6][page 43]

The action-orientation of ideology also works when the medialization (*i.e.* how the content is presented to the user) is not trustworthy. In such a case, however, the medialization works the other way round: it influences our intent according to what can be medialized. However, for a UI to be effective, it should be both trustworthy and familiar: "Designing for familiarity is crucial when trying to persuade people to behave in unfamiliar ways." [26][page 99]

The user actuates the computer (or *apparatus*) to use it together with their technical imagination to create something but, paradoxically, one of the computer function is the user's intent. [12] This is so because the apparatus is predisposed only for some type of code and program cycles. As Bogost says: "Software establishes rules of execution, tasks and actions that can and cannot be performed." [5][page 4] Therefore, for the designer's intention to be fulfilled, he or she can intend only what is doable.

Only using a specific apparatus for the chosen job can the designers' intent be fulfilled:

"The freedom of decision of pressing a button with one's fingertips turns out to be a programmed freedom. A choice of prescribed possibilities. I choose according to the regulations..." [13][page 93] Such freedom leads to the illusion of nearly unconfined freedom, however, our interactions are latently directed to a certain goal. This freedom leads us to take over the thinking of the designer.

The above-mentioned "programmed freedom" is closely connected with procedures as sequences of action. Again, with Bogost, "[p]rocedures are sometimes related to ideology; they can cloud our ability to see other ways of thinking (...)." [5][page 3] We can take the action-orientation element of ideology as a form of rhetoric.

Since Aristotle, rhetoric was used in different media to state arguments of the designer in order to make the audience believe in the presented reality. Persuasion as a technique has made its way into ICTs and has even been transformed into a tool. Fogg defines a persuasive technology tool as "an interactive product designed to change attitudes or behaviors or both by making a desired outcome easier to achieve." [15][page 32]

In the ICT environment, the persuasive tools are supported by the inner workings of software, as we have stated above. These workings, based on procedures, help to get predefined arguments to the users. Bogost calls it "procedural rhetoric". "Procedural rhetoric is a technique for making arguments with computational systems and for unpacking computational arguments others have created." [5][pages 2-3]

A specific characteristic of procedural rhetoric is that it does not build arguments using techno-images, but "through the authorship of rules of behavior, the construction of dynamic models." [5][page 29] Therefore, proce-dural rhetoric works in the space of medialization between design/intent and design/form. In such a manner, it is close to a "UI grammar" [3], where language plays the part of a rule system. In the system, the UI designer establishes grammar rules (syntax) for the combination of its elements. The manner in which UIs are built is governed by a set of rules given by the designer, *e.g.*, every UI produced can follow a different intrinsic UI grammar. The choice of elements is then subject to the pragmatics of the entire UI.

2.4   Logical Coherence

Mullins suggests that ideology should be coherent, *i.e.* syntagmatic rather than paradigmatic, since it needs to help create a seamless experience. From the perspective of internal connectedness, design fulfills the same function as art, technics and machines for they manipulate and try to master the original state of things, nature. [13] As Flusser [13][page 19] continues: "This is the design that is the basis of all culture: to deceive nature by means of technology, to replace what is natural with what is artificial and build a machine out of which there comes a god who is ourselves." What is important here is that the ideology perpetuates itself beyond the human reach.

Furthermore, "Programmers are not the important elements for the functioning of techno-images, but the structures of apparatuses they produce. Techno-images are imperativistic not because they are used by some ideologists to manipulate the society, but because they are a projection of such a pixel universe that pretends to present the world pixel by pixel." [11]

In the above quote, what is imperativistic is the constructed artificial world that forces us to take it for reality. What is imperialistic is the tendency of the producers (or even the producing automata of techno-images themselves) to colonize the semiotic space with signs (techno-images) referring to other techno-images and leaving out all the rest. Such tendency is supported by a number of ideologies embedded in the UI.

What are then the emerging ideologies present in the UI? Since its inception, the modernistic tradition of ideology orbits around five main concepts: emancipation (on a personal as well as social level), individuality (liberal ideology), time/space (fear of the stranger), work (with its emphasis on productivity) and community (nationalism, unity). We shift from "heavy" and "solid", hardware-focused modernity to a "light" and "liquid", software-based modernity. [2] In order to tackle this problem, a shift of analysis towards this liquid phase is needed. We argue that software - both on the personal (user) and social (society) level - should be regarded as a driving force, a catalyst, for a certain type of behavior. What happens when images are computer-generated, when they are "techno-images", as Flusser [12] coined them?

In the field of UI design, different instances of ideology are present. So far, one of the most prominent is the ideology of hypertext [4] - As Nielsen states, "[hypertext] makes individual users the masters of the content and lets them access and manipulate it in any way they please." [25] This user-empowering approach is contrasted by choice-obfuscation (*e.g.* when navigation links are not readily visible) or even user oppression (when user choice is limited or eliminated, *e.g.* in splash screens or ads). (*Ibid.*). Currently, the semantic space of UI ideology is somewhat centered around the terms "simple, fast, intuitive, social, minimal, choice, useful, fun", as a series of interviews with web designers suggest. [7]

Another important ideology is the ideology of ease. Dilger [10] presents the ideology of ease, which dissects users into the "computer illiterate" and "techies" and suggests that this "will ensure that the historical boundaries of gender, race and class are reproduced in computing practices for years to come." By ideologies, he means the "frameworks of thinking and calculation about the world - the 'ideas' that people use to figure out how the social world works, what their place is in it, and what they ought to do." (According to Dilger's reading of Hall, 1986). This is pretty much with Mullins' view, since the way the world works refers to cognitive and evaluative power, people's place in it and what they ought to do then refers to the action-orientation. Dilger states, that ease is gendered, which is to be seen in the connotation of an "easy" to use computer system as feminine. Ease has a different meaning in connection to work and leisure, during the former it has to be supported by the system, during the latter a certain difficulty could be desirable, *e.g.* in chess. At work, moreover, a task may not seem worthwhile if it does not seem easy. Pictures may furthermore seem easier to understand than text, which is supported by various media, such as television or comics. The notion of speed is also connected to anything which would be labeled as easy including learning. Finally, the gain of ease is matched by a loss in choice, security, privacy, or health. (*Ibid.*)

Some of the HCI ideologies may even have a more pronounced impact on the user's behavior through the use of social cues and persuasion techniques. In the mobile context this has been carried out by Aaron Marcus and Associates, Inc., in a series of mobile applications. The applications may lead the users to act in a reduce their ecological footprint [20], reduce weight and improve dietary behavior [19], manage wealth after retirement [17], or share memories and family wisdom [18], among others.

3   Summary

In this paper, we have presented semiotics as an analytic method especially in its most complex dimension – pragmatics. Pragmatics stands in the design process at the beginning because it forms the strategy and purpose of the developed UI. In the sign, context pragmatics leads the meaning interpretation – what semantics will be assigned to which syntax elements. Not only is this a process of interpretation, but also the UI development strategy is subject to ideology in a large extent. Such ideology adapts its specific form in the UI. For the purposes of developing new UIs, but also for interacting with the UIs already in place, it is important to know the ways in which pragmatics, as an interpreting principle, is coded and mediated. We can then counter the ideologies by proper education and analysis.

A solution of how to address such a situation is therefore, on one hand, maximizing one's competence in terms of coding forms and medialization that has a big impact on the creation of UI. On the other hand, developing methods to analyze the influence of such UI on the society, the creation and modification of meaning and human relations that would be able to uncover the design behind every design. This article shows a possible approach based on UI language components analysis. This is in line also with Fogg's suggestion:

"One useful approach is to conduct a stakeholder analysis, to identify all those affected by a persuasive technology, and what each stakeholder in the technology stands to gain or lose. By conducting such an analysis, it is possible to identify ethical concerns in a systematic way." [15][page 233]

References

1. Andersen, P.B.: A theory of computer semiotics. Cambridge: Cambridge University Press (1997) ISBN 0521448689
2. Bauman, Z.: Liquid Modernity. Polity (2000) ISBN 9780745624105
3. Brejcha, J., Marcus, A.: Semiotics of interaction: Towards a UI Alphabet. In: Kurosu, M. (ed.) HCII/HCI 2013, Part I. LNCS, vol. 8004, pp. 13–21. Springer, Heidelberg (2013)

4. Bush, V.: As We May Think. In: The Atlantic Online (July 1945), http://www.theatlantic.com/doc/194507/bush (accessed August 10, 2009), ISSN 1072-7825
5. Bogost, I.: Persuasive Games: The expressive power of videogames. The MIT Press, Cambridge (2007) ISBN 9780262514880
6. Chun, W.H.K.: On Software, or the Persistence of Visual Knowledge. Grey Room, 26-51 (2005) ISSN 1526-3819
7. Chang, E.: Design 2.0: Minimalism, Transparency, and You, http://www.emilychang.com/go/weblog/comments/design-20-minimalism-transparency-and-you/ (accessed January 5, 2009)
8. De Souza, C.S.: The semiotic engineering of human-computer interaction. MIT Press, Cambridge (2005) ISBN 0262042207
9. Derrida, J.: Writing and difference. University of Chicago Press (1978) ISBN 9780226143293
10. Dilger, B.: The Ideology of Ease. Journal of Electronic Publishing 6 (September 2000), http://quod.lib.umich.edu/cgi/t/text/text-idx?c=jep;view=text;rgn=main;idno=3336451.0006.104 (accessed March 4, 2009), ISSN 1080-2711
11. Flusser, V.: Lob der Oberflächlichkeit. Bollmann Verlag, Mannheim (1995)
12. Flusser, V.: Into the Universe of Technical Images, University of Minnesota Press (2011) ISBN 978-0-8166-7020-8
13. Flusser, V.: The Shape of Things: A Philosophy of Design. Reaktion Books (1999) ISBN 1861890559
14. Frasca, G.: Videogames of the oppressed: Critical thinking, education, tolerance, and other trivial issues. In: Wardrip-Fruin, N. (ed.) First Person: New Media as Story, Performance, and Game, pp. 85–94. MIT (2004) ISBN 0262731754
15. Fogg, B.J.: Persuasive Technology: Using computers to change what we think and do. Morgan Kaufman Publishers, San Francisco (2003) ISBN 9781558606432
16. Galloway, A.R.: The Unworkable Interface. New Literary History 39, 931–955 (2009) ISSN 0028-6087
17. Marcus, A.: The Money Machine: Helping Baby Boomers Retire. User Experience 11(2), 24–27 (2012a)
18. Marcus, A.: The Story Machine: a Mobile App to Change Family Story-Sharing Behavior. In: Procedings of CHI 2012, pp. 1–4 (2012b)
19. Marcus, A.: Health machine. Information Design Journal 19(1), 69–89 (2011)
20. Marcus, A., Jean, J.: Going green at home: the green machine. Information Design Journal 17(3), 235–245 (2009)
21. Marcus, A.: Metaphor design in user interfaces. SIGDOC Asterisk Journal of Computer Documentation 22(2) (1998) ISSN 0731-1001
22. Mitchell, W.J.T.: Iconology: Image, Text, Ideology. University of Chicago Press (July 1987) ISBN 0226532291
23. Morris, C.W.: Foundations of the Theory of Signs. University of Chicago Press, Chicago (1970) ISBN 0226532321
24. Mullins, W.A.: On the Concept of Ideology in Political Science. The American Political Science Review 66, 498–510 (1972) ISSN 0003-0554

25. Nielsen, J.: Mastery, Mystery, and Misery: The Ideologies of Web Design. UseIt.com (2004), http://www.useit.com/alertbox/20040830.html (accessed March 4, 2009), ISSN 1548-5552
26. Wai, C., Mortensen, P.: Persuasive technologies should be boring. In: de Kort, Y.A.W., IJsselsteijn, W.A., Midden, C., Eggen, B., Fogg, B.J. (eds.) PERSUASIVE 2007. LNCS, vol. 4744, pp. 96–99. Springer, Heidelberg (2007)
27. Winograd, T., Flores, F.: Understanding computers and cognition: A new foundation for design. Addison-Wesley, Boston (1987) ISBN 0201112973

The Language Game

Roman Danylak and Kyeong Kang

Faculty of Engineering and Information Technology,
University of Technology, Sydney
roman@emotionalcomputing.com, kyeong.kang@uts.edu.au

Abstract. With rise of the computer since the 1950's there has been a constant evolution for ways to further enable calculating capacities. It is ironic, that a machine derived with such thoughtful and sophisticated process mathematically, has found a key and increasingly dominant expression in games, which has a reputation for a lack of seriousness. Games continue to rise as a very popular form of interaction. The paper examines the notion of language as a game to partly explain the phenomenon. The paper reflects upon the philosophical writings of Wittgenstein who proposed that language is a game. In addition semiotic analysis, a linguistic meta-tool, will be applied to a game with the aim of shedding light on the usefulness of semiotics in user interaction design.

Keywords: Semiotics: Sign/symbol/icon design and DUXU, Games, Philosophy.

1   Language: A Definition

Just about everybody uses language. When we enter a foreign country and we are deprived of our language we become acutely aware of how important it is. For the purposes of this commentary, the comments made by Saussure [1], a key founder of semiotics, is useful in understanding what language is.

Language is a well-defined object in the heterogeneous mass of speech facts. It can be localized in the limited segment of the speaking-circuit where an auditory image becomes associated with a concept. It is the social side of speech, outside the individual who can never create nor modify it by himself; it exists only by virtue of a sort of contract signed by the members of a community. Moreover, the individual must always serve an apprenticeship in order to learn the functioning of language; a child assimilates it only gradually. It is such a distant thing that a man deprived of the use of speaking retains it provided that he understands the vocal signs that he hears. [1] (Saussure, [1916] 1966, p.14)

There are three facts that Saussure establishes here: firstly language is heterogeneous, meaning that it is complex because of its variety. Secondly he establishes the nature of the personal contract that all language users engage in. Thirdly, he establishes it as a trans-temporal phenomenon, that is, it endures over time, and that it is learnt and stands in this way outside of the individual biological human.

A. Marcus (Ed.): DUXU 2014, Part I, LNCS 8517, pp. 55–63, 2014.

Saussure establishes first that language 'is'; which answers an ontological question of 'how do we know that we are seeing / experiencing anything at all?' The manifestation of the phenomenon of language is established as 'auditory image', referring to the conceptual attachment that occurs with the verbal utterance, an interior activity. What is seen, and what is heard is referenced in social contract which language secures, for without it there could be no meaning and no comprehension of the text written on this page. Therefore language is an enduring and shared phenomenon. The auditory image is what can be termed the linking of the sign to the signifier. For example the symbols d –o –g are symbols representing the sound that we understand are a rather common four legged fury animals that is often domesticated - and we may see the image of the animal in the minds' eye when we say the word. Thus, there is a fundamental connection between what we hear and what we see. This fact forms the foundations of semiotics.

The notion that semiotics could be useful in human computer interaction occurs because semiotics is the science of signs, symbols and their interpretation, the application to computational devices could be directly made considering that the computer is a symbol processing machine or as Winnograd states [2], 'a language machine'.

2   Language as a Game: Wittgenstein

The word 'game' has its origins in an Old English word 'gamen', meaning 'fun, amusement' [3]. The literature on general game theory is substantial, and the concept has been significantly developed in mathematics, for example, in the writings of Von Neumann [4]. Games here will be characterised by the merging of linear narrative with interactive processes [5].   As Schell [6] states, interactive games show a duality of story - that is narrative - and gameplay. Hence, a game has both linear and probability aspects to it.

The writings of Wittgenstein (1889-1951) are particularly pertinent to the notion of language as a game. Twenty four published works of his remain [7] the most famous being *Tractatus Logico-Philosophicus* [8] published in 1913 for which he received a doctorate from Cambridge University. Originally a mechanical engineer, Wittgenstein studied under Bertrand Russell. However, his posthumously published *Philosophical Investigations* [9] was unique in its construction, consisting of aphorisms exercising the reader's mind through the problems of language. Wittgenstein posited that language was like a game where rules were followed.

In the practice of the use of language … one party calls out the words, the other acts on them. In instruction in the language the following process will occur: the learner names the objects; that is, he utters the word when the teacher points to the stone. – And there will be this still simpler exercise: the pupil repeats the words after the teacher - both of these being processes resembling language.

We can also think of the whole process of using words … as one of those games by means of which children learn their native language. I will call these games 'language-games' and will sometimes speak of a primitive language as a language-game.

And the processes of naming the stones and of repeating words after someone might also be called language-games like ring-a-ring-a-roses.

I shall also call the whole, consisting of language and the actions into which it is woven, the 'language-game.' [9](Wittgenstein, [1958] 1988 p. 5e).

From this we can see, which might not be readily apparent, that factors such as probability and agreement of meaning are part of language as a game.

3   Examples of Games and Electronic Games

3.1   Art as Game: Jean Arp

Jean Arp was a member of Cabaret Voltaire, the avante-garde group of artists who created prodigious and influential work at the beginning of the 20th Century on which Modernism was founded, used chance, that is the randomness of events, as an element in the composition of an artwork [10]. He tore sheets of scrap paper and allowed them to fall at random on a sheet of paper, accepting the compositional pattern as it was. This indicated that the actions by which artworks were made were as important as the artwork itself. It changed the focus from the object to the action of making, and was a precursor of human-computer gestural interaction where the process of the action may be continuously engaged. In this way, probability was considered to be a compositional element and the visual order typical of preceding art was now being displaced by the chaos of random probability (see Figure 1).

Fig. 1. Jean Arp Collage with Squares Arranged

According to the Laws of Chance, 1916-17 <http://arthistory.about.com/od/dada/ig/Dadaat MoMAZurich/dada_zurich_02.htm>

3.2 Virtusphere: Immersive Games

Virtusphere is an immersive Virtual Reality system with simulation platform allows lifelike movements in cyberspace. It was designed for Police or Military training scenarios. VirtuSphere is a commercial product offering six degrees of freedom – to move in any direction: to walk; to crawl; or to run over unlimited distances [11]. Virtusphere is compatible with all computer-based simulations. The tasks are controlled by software, but to change the terrain, new software is required. It uses an new omni-directional locomotion interface and a smart-turntable system to give users the ability to move freely in any direction within virtual environments without loosing sight of the displayed images despite their projection on a limited large screen that do not provide surrounding or 360 degrees of visual feedback. A head mounted display is also utilised; however, there are no wires attached. The user can make many full body rotations without losing sight of the environment (see Figure 2).

Fig. 2. Virtusphere <http://www.virtusphere.net/>

3.3 Console Games

Grand Theft Auto V, a console game, the latest version launched in September 2013, in three-and-a-half months to 32.5 million copies were sold. It uses Playstation 3 and X Box and grossed $1 billion in three days claiming the sales record in that timeframe for *any* form of entertainment, video game or otherwise. The next biggest seller, revenue-wise, is *Call of Duty: Black Ops 2*, which took over two weeks to achieve the same figure, (12) (see Figure 3).

Fig. 3. Grand Theft Auto 2013 [12]

3.4   Interactive Art Game to Be or Not to Be

There is a growing field where aesthetic human computer interactions known as Interactive art. The interactive artwork game *To be or not to be* was designed and developed at The Creativity and Cognition Studios (CCS), University of Technology, Sydney by Danylak and Weakley [13] and evaluated in Sydney's Powerhouse Museum for audience interaction at the CCS interactive art space beta_space. The game format was a key aspect designed in conjunction with the film narrative. The aim of the game was to interact with 23 gesture puzzles and in doing so to assemble the film narrative. The gesture rhythms were based on the syntactic patterns of the dialogue. Interactors were invited to solve a walking gesture/word puzzle using an on-screen interactive map. When solved, by being in the right place at the right time, triggering in sequence a 36 square floor pad system, sections of a film narrative based on Shakespeare's play Hamlet would appear. Usability studies showed high levels of gestural interaction and an above average predicted emotional response to the film content. An online video description is available (see Figures 4 (a) (b)).

Fig. 4a. To be or not to be mode 1   **Fig. 4b.** To be or not to be mode 2
http://www.youtube.com/watch?v=jKNvSpXG0Z0/
http://www.betaspace.net.au/content/view/36/.

The system comprised of a 36 square pressure sensitive floor pad grid, approximately 3 m x 3 m in total, connected to an Apple Mac and a video projector, illuminating a semi- transparent perspex projection screen approximately 3 m x 4 m using back projection. The pads are commonly used in commercial house alarm systems. The system was programmed using Max/MSP, a multimedia programme with a high degree of design freedom and data recording capacity.

Figures shows the interactor engaging in the floorpad using walking gestures to solve the game puzzle using the interactive position map in the left hand corner of the screen; (b) shows the interactor observing one film segment being played back after successfully achieving the word / gesture puzzle, the interactor being in the right place at the right time. There are twenty-three such film sequences which playback as one film - the final game goal.

4   Applying Semiotics: *Monopoly*

The sheer variety of games is presents a difficult analysis and can baffle the most capable designer. Applying semiotic analysis to games, in particular Jakobson's notion of metaphor and metonymy [14], reduces the complexity significantly allowing for the experience of the language aspect in the game to emerge. In linguistics this is known as aphasia, a linguistic disorder. If we say 'dog' this is a metaphor; if we say 'claw' which belongs to the dog, this a metonymy. In this way metaphors are higher order representations, whilst metonymy is the explication, or the exhaustion of the metaphor. This is also know as the two axes of association, the paradigmatic and the syntagmatic plains [15].

A further distinction which bears agreeable comparison is that 'a metaphor is a way in which one entity is viewed as another' whilst a metaphor is 'one entity standing for another' [16]. Metaphor, then, is the association made with the mental image, the higher order association that forms in the paradigmatic plain to which sound is attached through signification; whilst, metonymy is the sequence – the syntagmatic plain - or the chain-like process that is characterised by the linear structure of words which explicates the metaphor.

Even more simply put we can say that metaphors as figures of speech where ' this is that' or this represents that are usually unique and stand alone as representations; whilst metonymies refers to the association that is closer to understanding of the real world. For example if I was to denigrate someone by calling them ' a dog' and I have used the word pejoratively, that is negatively, this connotative use tends more to a metaphoric use because I refer to the specially attached meaning. On the hand, if I say ' the ' dog is over there drinking water' then tends more to the metonymic, because, the language I use is denotative, that is, what I say, is what you get; the equation in denotation is more straightforward.

Hence, in a simple board game, say in the ever popular *Monopoly,* invented by the Parker Brothers in 1903 (17) and is now owned by Hasbro Toys. The game overall is a metaphor of the process of commercial property trading (see Figures 5 (a) (b) (c).)

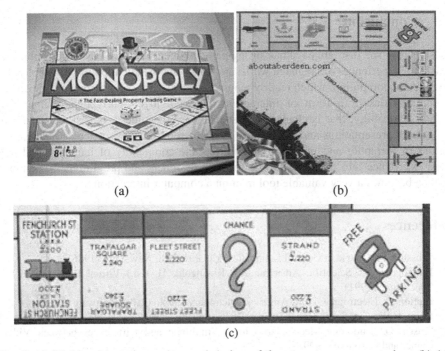

Fig. 5. (a) (b) (c)   (a) section and expanded view of the property square metaphors (b) (c). Monopoly: Parker Brothers (1903) source: Google images

The game consists of a square board with segmented smaller squares placed along the perimeter of the board. Players are individuals who are give a counter representing themselves, throwing a dice and moving along the squares according to chance. Each player then randomly may land on a perimeter square. The perimeter square mainly represent different properties and rang in low to high cost. Each player is given money and has the opportunity to buy properties, utilities, gets special chances offered or can be penalised by going to gaol for a short time. If a player lands on another persons property - square, then they must pay rent. The object of the game is to monopolise the market and to gain a s much rent from the other players as possible. In short, the game is a metaphor of real estate capitalism.

An objection may be made that we can see two levels of metaphors; there is the overall game as a metaphor of property trading yet there are the individual metaphor squares of properties – Pall Mall, The Strand and so on. This is correct, the semiotic analysis can present many levels of metaphor in operation so a hierarchy must be established. At the level of player experience it is the passage around the board landing on different property – metaphors that resembles a life experience. Again, each of these metaphors are unique. The metonymic element here the regulation of the movement around the board: players can only move between one and twelve spaces, based on the throw of the dice. Whilst the game is clearly made interesting by the random probabilities generated by the dice throw.

5   Conclusion

Thus, we can see that language has strong game elements and are easily verifiable by own daily experiences of language whilst also enjoying the attention of philosophy. In the realm of computing, which readily manipulates the symbols of language, the game aspect pervades as a form of interaction and is enjoyed unrivalled commercial success. Probabilty, that is chance – a usual feature of games - is easily adapted to computer representations and interactions. Whilst, semiotics, in particular Jakobson's notions of metaphor and metonymy, simplifies the complexity of language and the game experience into workable format for both designers and programmers. Semiotics then becomes a very valuable tool in human computer interaction.

References

1. Saussure, F.: Course in General Linguistics. McGraw-Hill, New York (1986)
2. Winnograd, T.: Scientific American. In: Rheingold, H. (ed.) Virtual Reality, p. 215. Touchstone (1991)
3. Dictionary, Electronic Oxford American Dictionary Version 1.0.2. Software (2005)
4. Kuhn, H.W.: Classics in Game Theory. Princeton University Press (1997)
5. Frasca, G.: Ludology Meets Narratology: Similitude and Differences between Video Games and Narrative (1999),
   http://www.Futurelab.org.uk/resources/publications-reports-articles/web-articles/Web-Article528 (viewed October 10, 2007)
6. Schell, J.: Understanding Entertainment: Story and Gameplay Are One. In: Jacko, J.A., Sears, A. (eds.) The Human-Computer Interaction Handbook, p. 836. Lawrence Erlbaum & Associates, New Jersey (2003)
7. Kaal, H., McKinnon, A.: The Published Works of Ludwig Wittgenstein. InteLex Corporation, University of Chicago Library (2007),
   http://www.lib.uchicago.edu/efts/WITT/WITT.bib.html
   (viewed January 12, 2007)
8. Wittgenstein, L.: Tractatus Logico-Philosophicus. Routledge, London (1922, 1974)
9. Wittgenstein, L.: Philosophical Investigations. Basil Blackwell, Oxford (1958, 1988)
10. Hughes, R.: The Shock of the New. British Broadcasting Corporation, London (1980)
11. Bouguila, L., Ishii, M., Sato, M.: Realizing a New Step-in-Place Locomotion Interface for Virtual Environment with Large Display System. In: Proceedings of the Workshop on Virtual Environments (2002)
12. Grand Theft Auto in, http://techland.time.com/2014/02/04/rockstar-grandtheftauto-v-was-2013s-best-selling-video-game/ (viewed February 1, 2014)
13. Danylak, R., Weakley, A.: To Be or Not To Be. Sydney: Exhibition, Powerhouse Museum (2007), http://www.youtube.com/watch?v=jKNvSpXG0Z0/,
    http://www.betaspace.net.au/content/view/36/
14. Jakobson, R.: Two Aspects of Language and Two Types of Aphasic Disturbances. In: Pomorska, K., Rudy, S. (eds.) Language and Literature. Harvard University Press, Cambridge (1956)

15. Barthes, R.: Elements of Semiology, vol. 58, pp. 13–15. Hill and Wang, New York (1964)
16. Fass, D.: International Conference on Computational Linguistics, Proceedings of the 12th Conference on Computational Linguistics, vol. 1, pp. 177–181 (1988)
17. Orbanes, P.E.: Monopoly: The World's Most Famous Game & How Got that Way, p. 22. Da Capo Press (2006)

On the Idea of Design: Analyzing the Ideal Form of Cars

Arash Faroughi and Semir Maslo

Cologne University of Applied Sciences, Germany
University of Burgos, Spain
{arash.faroughi,semir.maslo}@fh-koeln.de

Abstract. This paper calls the Renaissance the 'Golden Age of Design' due to the high meaning of the original design theory. It seeks to answer the question what was the *'Idea'* behind *'Disegno'*. To achieve this, we analyze different books of the Classical Antiquity and the Renaissance that were mainly important for its invention. Then, the paper will introduce an investigation concept, which takes the peculiarities of the original design into account. Finally, parts of the proposed concept will be tested by analyzing the ideal form of cars.

Keywords: Disegno, Design theory, Renaissance, Design philosophy, Platonic Idea, car, automobile.

1 Introduction

By recognizing the marvelous artworks of the Renaissance – such as the works of Brunelleschi, Da Vinci or Michelangelo – it is interesting to know that the concept of design (*'Disegno'*) was mainly responsible for a higher status of the visual arts. During medieval times, the departments of knowledge were divided into two categories: arts of the mind *'Artes Liberales'* ('Liberal Arts') and arts of the hand *'Artes Mechanicae'* ('Mechanical Arts'). While the Liberal Arts were taught in the medieval universities, the Mechanical Arts were placed below them in the hierarchy of knowledge and thus their subjects were excluded from universities. Architecture, painting and sculpture were placed amongst the mechanical arts and therefore they had a low position in the hierarchy of knowledge. For this reason, scientists and artists of the Italian Renaissance battled to elevate their status. Interestingly, in contrast to most scholars, Giorgio Vasari tried to find an agreement and harmony between the visual arts and found it in the concept of design. He declared architecture, painting and sculpture as its arts - (*'arti del disegno'*). With this concept, the visual arts were no longer rivals, but *'sisters, born of one father'* – design. They were no longer *'arts of the hand'* but, through design, theoretical constructs. Consequently, the door was opened for the first art academy in Europe. Under the major influence of Vasari, the Florentine *'Accademia delle Arti del Disegno'* ('Academy of the Arts of Design') was founded in 1563.

A. Marcus (Ed.): DUXU 2014, Part I, LNCS 8517, pp. 64–73, 2014.
© Springer International Publishing Switzerland 2014

Design was one of the central concepts of the Renaissance period. It was the foundation and theory of all fine arts, the creative power needed to develop 'never-before-seen' things and thus the light of all inventions. Due to its high meaning, we call the Renaissance the *'Golden Age of Design'*. The paper aims to answer the question what was the *'Idea'* behind *'Disegno'*. Therefore, we select important sources of the Classical Antiquity and Renaissance in order to understand the movements for the invention of the original design. Next, the paper presents a concept that focuses on the investigation of *'Idea'* of things. Finally, we test parts of the concept by analyzing the ideal form of cars.

2   On the Analysis

To gain a better understanding of why the original design concept was developed we performed two different analyses. Both of them are proposed in recently related works [13][14] and thus this paper will describe them shortly. The first one, called *'Litterarum Lumen'*, analyses the movement, which originated from Petrarch, the father of the intellectual and literary movement *'Humanism'*. As Burckhardt points out, literature preceded the visual arts and gave them their main impulse [8]. Hence, the analysis includes the work of six important Renaissance humanists and of six authors of the Classical antiquity, which mainly influenced the humanistic movement. It focuses on the following classical subjects: poetry, rhetoric and philosophy. Figure 1 represents the selected authors for the analysis.

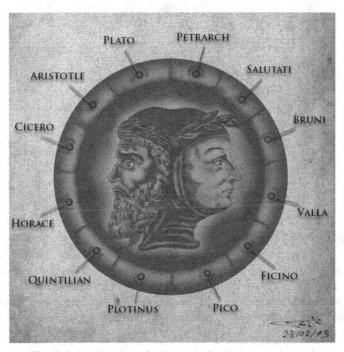

Fig. 1. Selected authors for the analysis *'Litterarum Lumen'*

The second analysis is called *'Arti del Disegno'* and focuses on the visual arts *'Architecture'*, *'Painting'* and *'Sculpture'*. The selected books for the analysis did not only deal with the mentioned arts, but have also significantly influenced the original meaning of design. The aim of the analysis is to characterize why design was of such great importance during the Renaissance period. Moreover, it builds also the connection to the first analysis *'Litterarum Lumen'* with the aim to characterize, how the *'light of literature'* shined over the visual arts. As depicted in Figure 2, six important authors are included – beginning with Marcus Vitruvius Pollio, who is known as the father of architectural theory and ending with Giorgio Vasari, the father or art history and design.

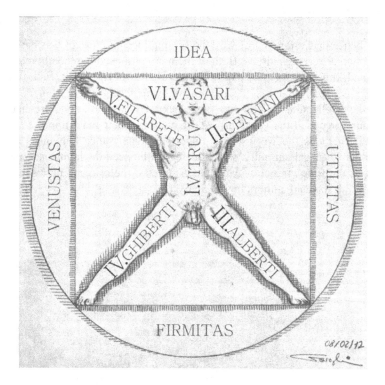

Fig. 2. Selected authors for the analysis *'Arti del Disegno'*[1]

3   The Idea of Disegno

Based on the analyses, the characteristics and *'Idea'* of the original design theory (*'Disegno'*) can be summarized as follows: *'Disegno'* was regarded as the *'knowledge of forms'* and the *'foundation'* of all created things. According to Filarete, it was useful for the creation of *'correct'* and *'worthy'* things [6]. Inspired by Aristotle and

---

[1] For details cs. [14]

Pliny the Elder, it was not only a useful science, but also a noble and *'liberal'* one [5] [18]. For example, Aristotle wrote the following words in his book on *'Politics'*: *"to be always seeking what is useful, is unworthy of a liberal, and inconsistent with an elevated, character"* [5, p. 299]. For this reason, *'Disegno'* was a noble science, because it had the power for discovering *'countless beauties'* [6]. Furthermore, the ancient philosophy of *'form'* and *'matter'* was of great importance for the theory of *'Disegno'*. Plato, Aristotle and Plotinus defined form as the principle of matter. For Aristotle, all things could only be created, if the form pre-exists in the mind of the creator [3]. This philosophy was especially used in the Renaissance theory of architecture. According to Alberti, the art of building was composed into two parts: *'Disegno'*[2] and *'construction'* [2]. While *'Disegno'* was related to form, the act of *'construction'* was associated to matter. Hence, *'Disegno'* was separated from the act of construction. Moreover, it was defined as an intellectual activity and thus it was the work of the *'mind'* and not of *'hand'*. Based on the Renaissance theory, the main work of an architect is therefore to plan and form the building and not to construct it. The superiority of form over matter can be shown with the analogy between God and nature. For Ficino, God is *"the creator of all forms"* and nature *"the craftsman of the world"* [16, p. 19]. For this reason, Vasari and Zuccari characterized God as a designer who formed the things of nature after an *'Idea'*. Interestingly, Zuccari argued that *'Disegno'* has the following etymological meaning: *'Segno di Dio'* ('Sign of God in Man') [23]. Only through *'Disegno'*, man is able to create *'a new or second World'*. Finally, this can be defined as the *'Idea'* of *'Disegno'*: to create a *'Golden World'* or a *'Paradise on Earth'*.

4   Investigating the Idea of a Thing

One of the peculiarities of *'Disegno'* was to form a thing according to the *'Idea'*. Hence, a designer should be able to understand the *'principles'* and *'hidden secrets'* of nature and thus be able to invent something new. Moreover, by seeing the ideal forms, he is able to complete something to perfection. The Renaissance scholars were mainly inspired by Cicero who wrote in his book *'De Oratore'* ('On the Orator') that every study should focus on the *'Platonic Idea'* and should thus create a clear image of the ideal form of the analyzed subject [11]. Therefore, during the Renaissance period, this goal was not limited in *'Disegno'* and visual arts, but also used in literature. For example, they built an image of an *'ideal orator'*, *'ideal courtier'*, *'ideal city'* or *'ideal palace'*. Hence, we analyzed how the Renaissance scholars investigate the *'Idea'* of a thing. Based on this, we developed a concept that considers the peculiarities of that time. Our proposed concept is depicted in Figure 3.

---

[2] Alberti did not use the Italian term *'Disegno'* in his treatise *'De re aedificatoria'* ('On the Art of Building'), because it was written in Latin. But Cosimo Bartoli translated his treatise into Italian in 1550 and replaced the term *'lineamento'* with *'disegno'*.

Fig. 3. The battle between philosophy and poetry

In general, the concept unifies philosophical with poetical concepts. This unification is used due to the following reason: the theory of *'Disegno'* was strongly influenced by philosophical and poetical concepts. The function of philosophy was according to Ficino to analyze the *'principles of all things'* and to find the *'Ideas'* they are based upon [15]. He concludes that philosophy could lead to a *'Golden Age'*. Like philosophy, poetry had the power to create an *'ideal world'*. It was praised as a divine art and through poetic frenzy or inspiration, an artist could create divine things. Moreover, according to Salutati, poetry can turn all things into *'something else'* [10]. He does not only see poetry in words, but in actions and objects as well. As shown in the Figure above, the philosophical and poetical concepts are presented in a dichotomous structure and are composed of four parts of investigation. The reason for this structure is the following: During the Renaissance, *'creative competitions'* or *'scientific battles'* lead to positive changes and thus to a progression towards perfection. Therefore, we build a *'scientific arena'* where philosophical and poetical concepts battle each other according to the parts of investigation. The parts will be described shortly by the following list:

1. **Term:** According to Epicurean philosophy, all scientific works should begin with a *'terminological'* analysis. Words should correspond to the used concepts. Based on Plato and Neoplatonic sources, *'dialectic'* is the art of speech and the ability to speak clearly about all concepts [19]. It seeks to define *'what'* a thing is. [19] [17]. On the other hand, the poetic *'licence'* has the power to free the researcher from clear concepts and terms by using poetic techniques such as metaphors or

periphrases. It aims to encourage creativity and imagination of the researcher for forming *'something new'*.

2. **Comparison:** *'Comparison'* is a powerful concept for both philosophy and poetry. While philosophy uses this concept mostly for defining the *'different'* qualities of things, poetry focuses on *'similarities'*. According to Salutati, poetry is a science that searches especially for similitudes between things [20].

3. **Types:** A main step to understand the nature of a thing is to analyze their types. Investigating the *'original'* types and principles of a thing is mainly a subject of philosophy. Poetry, however, focuses on potentiality and thus dreams on a potential *'future'* [4].

4. **Essence:** Finally, the last part of investigation focuses on the essence of a thing. According to Neoplatonic philosophy, the essential form of a thing can be *'simple'* or *'composite'*. While the simple form is, according to Plotinus, always uncompounded, the composite one is a composition of different *'Ideas'*. The aim of the philosophical concept is to *'simplify'* the form of a thing according to its essential nature. In contrast to this, the poetical concept seeks to *'compound'* additional characteristics to the essential form and thus to build something new. This can be achieved by using poetical techniques such as *'ephitets'*.

5   Designing the Ideal Form of Cars

The year 1885 is often considered as the birth of the automobile. In this year, the German engineer Karl Benz invented the first *'horseless carriage'* – the modern automobile. But interestingly, the 'Idea' of a self-propelled car was formulated for the first time in the 13th century by the English philosopher Roger Bacon. In his letter *'De mirabile potestate artis et natura'* ('On the Marvelous Power of Art and Nature'), he wrote the following: *"It is possible that a car shall be made which will move with inestimable speed, and the motion will be without the help of any living creature"* [7, p. 26]. Moreover, the Renaissance scholars Giovanni Fontana and Leonardo da Vinci were the first to design this idea. About 1420, Fontana drew a self-propelled vehicle in his technological treatise *'Bellicorum instrumentorum liber'* ('Book on the instruments of war'). Leonardo da Vinci's self-propelled car was drawn around the year 1478 and can be found in his *'Codice Atlantico'* ('Atlantic Codex'). During the Renaissance period, as Filarete pointed out, design (*'Disegno'*) gave birth to an *'Idea'* and thus it is not necessary to build own inventions. For this reason, most of the inventions of that time remained, unfortunately, on paper. However, according to this thinking, it can be said that the self-propelled car is the invention of the Renaissance.

To test our concept, we searched for a subject that is both relevant today and that was also in the focus during the Renaissance period. Hence, we selected the design subject *'the ideal form of cars'*. To design an ideal form of an object, the Renaissance scholars used a fascinating methodology: they draw an analogy of the analyzed object with *'the most perfect being'* - the humans. For them, man is, due to his likeness and image of God, perfectly designed. Surely, they were inspired by the ancient authors

Cicero and Vitruvius. Cicero wrote in his treatise *'De Natura Deorum'* ('On the Nature of the Gods') that man is perfect, not only because of his intellect, but also for his body: *"What composition of limbs, what conformation of lineaments, what form, what aspect, can be more beautiful than the human? Each member is formed, not only for convenience but also for beauty"* [12, p. 12]. For Vitruvius, the form of a building should have *"an exact system of correspondence to the likeness of a well-formed human being"* [22, p. 47]. Mainly in architecture, the Renaissance scholars Filarete and Vasari described the ideal form of a city or palace by comparing it with the human being [6][21]. Hence, in our study, we built the same analogy. The paper presents some of the result of our analysis that dealt with the human body in particular. Moreover, the form of our study is *'Renaissance'* based and is mainly inspired by the studies and drawings of Leonardo da Vinci and Francesco di Giorgio Martini. The following subsections describe the results of the investigation parts *'term'* and *'comparison'*.

5.1   The Results of the Investigation Part *'Term'*

Etymologically, the term *'car'* is derived from the Latin word *'currus'* or *'carrum'* and means a *'wheeled vehicle'*. In the ancient time, *'currus'* was a chariot, mainly used in racing or for battles and its main purpose was speed traveling. Generally, for describing the concept of *'currus'*, we need two other terms: *'animals'* and *'driver'*: the *'currus'* was designed to be pulled by *'animals'*, especially by horses, and the *'driver'* was responsible for the controlling of it movement. Francis Bacon also used the Latin term *'currus'*, but changed, as written above, the *'Idea'* of it. The term that correspondence with his *'Idea'* is *'automobile'*. The word *'automobile'* is etymologically a hybrid word, a combination of the Ancient Greek term 'αὐτός' ('autós', 'self') and the Latin *'mobilis'* ('movable'), and means literally *'moved of itself'*. Therefore, a *'car'* is a *'wheeled vehicle'* that *'moves of itself'*, that means *'without the help of any living creature'* and is controlled by a *'driver'*.

For the poetic concept *'licence'*, we used the following metaphor: the driver 'is the Soul of a Car'. This metaphor is mainly inspired by Aristotle's book *'De Anima'* ('On the Soul'). In his book, Aristotle argued that the soul is on the one hand the *'mover of the body'* and on the other, due to its location in body, *'moved by the body'*. For this reason, we draw an analogy between *'soul'* and *'driver'*. Like the philosophers debates on the *'seat'* of the soul, we analyzed therefore the seat of the *'driver'*. Mostly, as also visualized in Figure 4, the ancient philosophers believed that the seat of the soul is either in the *'heart'* or in the *'head'*[3]. Very roughly, we can say that the actual seat of the driver in a car is comparable with the position of the heart in human body. But to see the seat of the driver in the *'head'*, helps to create new *'Ideas'* for a car. According to Plato, the head is *'the most divine part'* of the human body. For Pacioli, the head is set to the top of the human body to be their *'guardian'*. As depicted in Figure 4, the head of the woman moves independently from her body. Hence, like a *'guardian'*, she is able to oversee the street without changing the position of her body.

---

[3] More concretely, the brain is recognized to be the seat of the soul.

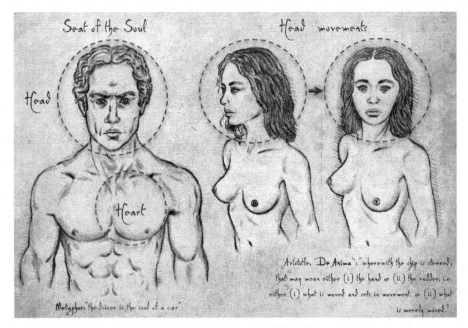

Fig. 4. Study on head movement

Subsequently, we analyze the connection between *'soul'* and *'movement'*. Interestingly, like the *'Idea'* of automobile, the soul is characterized in Platonic and Neoplatonic sources as *'self-moving'*. Based on Ficino's book *'Theologia platonica'* ('Platonic Theology'), the soul moves perfectly that means in *'circular motion'* [16]. Hence, the *'circular motion'* was considered as the ideal form of movement. According to the results of this investigation part, the *'Idea'* is to add a *'moveable head'* to the form of cars that can move in *'circular motion'* and hence to differentiate between *'head'* and *'body movements'*. With this *'Idea'*, backward-driving with poor visibility could become a *'problem of the past'*.

5.2   The Results of the Investigation Part *'Comparison'*

Consequently, while the investigation part *'term'* analyzed the head movements, the part *'Comparison'* focuses on the movements of the body. It compares the movement system of the human body with that of a car. The Renaissance scholar who wrote about body movements was Leon Battista Alberti. In his treatise on Painting, he argued that the painter should study particularly the body movements that are *"generated only [...] when the position changes"* [1]. Inspired by the ancient orator Quintilian, he described the different directions of movement that change the position of the body. Basically, as shown in Figure 5, the following direction can be differentiated from each other: (A) vertical {up, down}; (B) horizontal or lateral {left, right}; (C) circular and (D) diagonal {up/left, up/right, down/right, down/left}. If we compare the movements of human and car, we recognize that the human can move in all basic directions (A, B, C, D). The car, however, moves only in the directions of A and C.

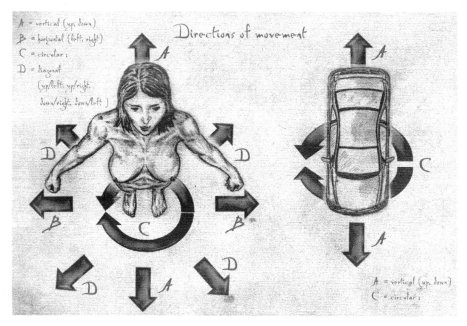

Fig. 5. Directions of movement

Hence, the *'differences'* between the movement system of human and car lie in the *'diagonal'* and *'lateral movements'*. An *'ideal'* vehicle motion system should be able to move in all directions. For this reason, the *'Idea'* of this investigation part is to add the *'diagonal'* and *'lateral movement'* to the motion system of a car. With the *'Idea'* of diagonal movement, a car could change the lane without rotating its body. The *'lateral movements'* can change especially the behavior of parallel or sideway parking. With this *'Idea'*, the driver is able to park easily even in the narrowest gaps.

6   Conclusion

In summary, the aim of the paper was to find out what were the peculiarities of the original design theory *'Disegno'* and what was the *'Idea'* behind it. Therefore, we first analyzed significant works from the Classical Antiquity and Renaissance. Then, based on our analysis, we proposed an investigation concept that focuses on analyzing the *'Idea'* of thing. Finally, we tested the investigation parts *'term'* and *'comparison'* of our proposed concept by analyzing the *'ideal form of cars'*.

References

1. Alberti, L.B.: De Pictura, 1435, translated by Spencer, J. R., On Painting. Yale University Press, New Haven (1967)
2. Alberti, L.B.: De re aedificatoria, 1452, translated by Rykwert, J., On the Art of Building in Ten Books. MIT Press, Cambridge (1988)

3. Aristotle. The Metaphysics of Aristotle, 350 BC, Translated by M'Mahon, J.H., Bohn, H.G., York Street, Covent Garden, London (1857)
4. Aristotle, Poetics, 335 BC, Translated by Bywater, I. Dodo Press, Boston (2006)
5. Aristotle. Politics, 350 BC, Translated by Gillies, J., Aristotle's Ethics and Politics, comprising his practical philosophy. T. Cadell and W. Davies, London (1813)
6. Averlino, A. (Filarete), Trattato d'architettura, 1464, Translated by Spencer, J.R., Treatise on Architecture. Yale University Press, New Haven (1965)
7. Bacon, R.: De mirabile potestate artis et natura, 1214–1294, Translated by Davis, T. L. Chemical Publishing Company, Easton (1923)
8. Burckhardt, J.: Die Kultur der Renaissance in Italien. Phaidon Verlag, Wien (1930)
9. Castiglione, B.: The Book of the Courtier from the Italian of Count Baldassare Castiglione, 1528, Translated by Sir Hobby, D. Nutt (1900)
10. Cennini, C.: Il libro dell'arte, 1400, translated by Thompson, D.V., The Craftsman's Handbook. Dover Publications, New York (1965)
11. Cicero, M. T., de Oratore, 55 BC, Translated or Edited by J.S. Watson, On Oratory and Orators. Southern Illinois University Press, Carbondale (1970)
12. Cicero, M. T., De Natura Deorum, 45 BC, Transalted by Walsh, P.G., The Nature of the Gods, Digireads.com Publishing, Stilwell (2007)
13. Faroughi, A., Faroughi, R.: On the Poetry of Design. In: Marcus, A. (ed.) DUXU/HCII 2013, Part I. LNCS, vol. 8012, pp. 38–47. Springer, Heidelberg (2013)
14. Faroughi, A., Faroughi, R.: Über die Synthese der MCI basierend auf dem Ursprung des Designs. In: Reiterer, H., Deussen, O. (eds.) Mensch & Computer 2012: interaktiv informiert – allgegenwärtig und allumfassend!?, pp. 213–222. Oldenbourg Verlag, München (2012)
15. Ficino, M.: Commentaries on Plato's Republic, Laws and Epinomis, 1496, Translated by Farndell, A., When Philosophers Rule.Shepheard-Walwyn, London (2009)
16. Ficino, M.: Theoloia Platonica, 1482, Transtalted by Allen, J.B., Platonic Theology, Cambridge. I Tatti Renaissance Library, vol. 2 (2002)
17. Mirandola, G.P.: (1486). De hominis dignitae, Translated by Von der Gönna, G. Rede über die Würde des Menschen, Reclam (1997)
18. Pliny the Elder, Naturalis historia, 77-79, Translated by Bostock, J., Riley, H.T. The Natural History of Pliny. Henry G. Bohn, London (1857)
19. Plotinus, E.: 270, Translated by MacKenna, S., Page, B.S., The Six Enneads of Plotinus, Philip Lee Warner, London (1917)
20. Salutati, C.: De laboribus Herculis, 1406, vol. 1. Translated by Ullman, B.L. (eds.) In aedibus Thesauri mundi (1951)
21. Vasari, G.: Le vite dei più eccellenti architetti, pittori et scultori italiani, 1568, Translated by Brown, B.B. et al, Vasari on Technique. Dover Publications, New York (1960)
22. Vitruvius, P.: De Architectura libri decem, 22 BC, Vitruvius: The Ten Books On Architecture. Echo Lib., UK (2008)
23. Zuccari, F.: L'Idea de Pittori Scultori Ed Architetti, 1607, In: Heikamp, D. (edt), Scritti d'arte di Frederico. Zuccaro, Florence (1961)

M4REMAIP: Method for Requirements Elicitation Based on Mobile Applications under an Interaction Perspective

Sarah Gomes Sakamoto and Leonardo Cunha de Miranda

Department of Informatics and Applied Mathematics,
Federal University of Rio Grande do Norte (UFRN), Natal, Brazil
sarahsakamoto@ppgsc.ufrn.br, leonardo@dimap.ufrn.br

Abstract. In recent years mobile usage has increased remarkably, attracting new adopters. Mobile applications, or mobile apps, have become essential tools for daily tasks, enhancing productivity, communication and entertainment. Nowadays, there is a great demand for updated software in order to meet customer expectations. Interaction aspects and aesthetic characteristics stand out as an important differential, which must guide the product development process. Therefore, it is necessary to elicit functional requirements based on existing products, which are available in repositories, i.e. mobile app stores. We present M4REMAIP, a method for requirements elicitation based on mobile applications under an interaction perspective, as well as results of this method's application in order to demonstrate its practical usefulness for requirements elicitation in the context of home control applications.

Keywords: apps, requirements engineering, mobile interface, home control, home automation, smart home.

1   Introduction

Requirements elicitation requires an understanding of the problem domain in order to analyze and identify product characteristics which reflect user needs [1]. It is a complex process with intense information capture and is crucial for development of high quality products. Nowadays, there is a great demand for updated software in order to meet – ever more selective – customer expectations. Interaction aspects and aesthetic characteristics stand out as an important differential [2,3], which deserve careful attention and must guide the product development process. Constant software updates and user interface modifications mark out a paradigm shift. A possibility of facilitating interaction is to integrate new solutions into the existing "ecosystem" of already available products, aiming at improving user interaction.

Mobile devices are integrated into our everyday life activities. In recent years the use of mobile devices has increased remarkably, attracting new users. Mobile applications, or mobile apps, have become essential tools for daily tasks, enhancing productivity, communication and entertainment. Users of these platforms are no longer restricted to applications supplied by device manufactures. Mobile platforms

A. Marcus (Ed.): DUXU 2014, Part I, LNCS 8517, pp. 74–85, 2014.

provide several third-party apps through their repositories, i.e. mobile app stores, enabling users to search and install apps in a quick, easy and central manner, and sometimes, free of charge.

Due to this ever increasing adoption of mobile technology, it is fundamental to observe these apps under the Human-Computer Interaction (HCI) perspective, attempting to interface and interaction aspects of these solutions. Nowadays, several apps are available from various segments. Just like the mobile phone context, mobile apps for home control are closely related with people daily tasks. These apps provide control of home elements, whether single appliances such as a lamp, or several appliances connected to a home automation system. Home control via mobile devices [4,5,6] is a thriving sector, attracting interest of academy and industry. People used fixed control panels inside the house to control home systems, but with the advantages of mobile devices, people can control home in an effective and convenient way.

In this paper, we propose a method for requirements elicitation based on apps under the interaction perspective. Moreover, we present the results of method's application for requirements identification of Android apps for home control. This work is inserted into a research project related to smart homes based on open-source infrastructures [7] and interaction with multiple interfaces, such as mobile [11] and gesture-based interfaces [8,9,10].

The paper is organized as follows: Section 2 describes the method; Section 3 presents a case study based on the application of the method in order to identify requirements of Android apps for home control; Section 4 discuss the results and research issues; Section 5 concludes the paper.

2   M4REMAIP

The M4REMAIP (Method for Requirements Elicitation based on Mobile Applications under an Interaction Perspective) aims at eliciting requirements based on apps' usage. Based on description analysis gathered from such use, it is possible to identify important characteristics of apps, aiming at improving user interaction. This method – Fig. 1 shows an overview of the method – can be applied in different domains and at different stages in the design lifecycle, e.g. when starting a new project or updating an existing one. It was inspired by previous work from our research group [12].

The method consists of five steps, performed in two distinct phases: phase I comprises three steps and occurs before the apps' usage, phase II comprises two steps and focuses on the use of apps and requirements capture. Thus, the five steps of the method are as follows: (I.1) definition, (I.2) search, (I.3) setup, (II.4) evaluation, and (II.5) extraction.

The definition step (I.1) consists of the target definition. In this step, the elicitation objective is defined, as well as the target platform – e.g. tablet or smartphone –, the operating system and, based on this information, the specific device to be used during the process. The search step (I.2) consists of the search specification and the subsequent search execution. In the search specification, search parameters are specified: search strategy – i.e. automatic and/or manual –, keywords, selection criteria – i.e. inclusion and exclusion –, and database. Depending on information gathered from the definition step, the database will be a specific app store, such as Google Play®, App Store®, Samsung Apps®, BlackBerry World®, and Windows Phone Store®. During search execution, the search is conducted according to specification. The setup step (I.3) consists of download and installation of apps derived from the search step.

The evaluation step (II.4) is based on exploratory use and textual description of mobile apps. An average time is defined for the exploratory use of each app – e.g. 30 minutes –, and during the usage, an analysis of features, design and interaction characteristics is performed. This analysis is performed manually, in order to provide an observation focusing on HCI aspects, with details from a user perspective. Subsequently, during the description activity, each app is described textually, with information regarding main functionality and interface characteristics, as well as positive and negative aspects. During description activity, each app may be used again in order to provide a brief verification of app interface details.

The extraction step (II.5) consists of the description analysis and the requirements definition. The description analysis involves reading these textual descriptions, identifying common or deemed important features, and analyzing whether these functionalities are relevant requirements for the respective context.

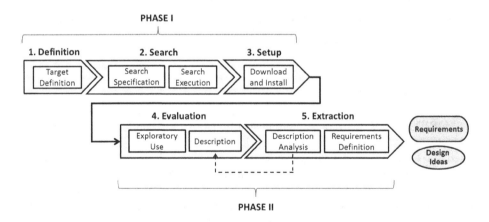

Fig. 1. Overview of the M4REMAIP

At the end of the method, requirements are obtained. In addition to functional requirements elicitation, this method might also be applied to identify possible design solutions for the domain (vide Fig. 1). These possible design solutions may be obtained from descriptions reading focusing on a specific feature, observing the differences regarding how it is provided by apps.

In Fig. 1, it is possible to observe a dashed line from description analysis (extraction; II.5) to description (evaluation; II.4). This is due to the fact that during the description analysis some characteristics may be deemed more relevant, requiring a deeper and detailed description. Another aspect is that each step tends to act as a filter, reducing the volume of input – total amount of apps – from one step to another. For example, in search step, input may be all apps in a repository, but after search execution, only a substrate is output. Subsequently, not all apps of this resulting set can be downloaded or installed successfully, therefore after setup step, other substrate is generated. Moreover, depending on amount of apps to be installed, a single, sequential performance of all method steps might not be possible, since some mobile devices may present limitations regarding memory and storage. In this case, steps 3 and 4 should be executed with subsets of the total amount of apps, with each subset uninstall before executing the procedure again.

3   Application of M4REMAIP

This section presents the application of M4REMAIP in the context of eliciting functional requirements of Android apps for home control. First, we present Phase I of the method, then Phase II, and subsequently the results obtained with applying the method in this specific domain.

3.1   Phase I

In the definition step (step 1) the smartphone was defined as target platform, since it is a more restrictive device in comparison with the tablet, e.g., regarding screen size. Android was chosen as operating system, and the specifications of device used in this study are: a smartphone Motorola Razr i XT890, with Android 4.1.2 (Jelly Bean), configured with Portuguese language, Intel Atom Z2460 2GHz GPU, 1GB RAM, screen size 4.3" (540x960).

In the search step (step 2), the search strategy was automatic and manual search in Google Play®. For automatic search, the following keywords were established (in alphabetical order): "arduino", "automação", "automatizada", "casa", "control", "domotica", "home", "residencial", and "smart". The app was included if it, according to the app's description, proposed controlling home element or home automation system. The manual search consisted of selection among related apps indicated by Google Play®, according the following inclusion criteria: the app must present home, building or lamp as icons, or the app must have "control/controle" or "automation/automação" terms in its tittle. In both search strategies, the exclusion criteria were: be paid or be shown after 10th position (due to time viability reasons of application of method).

The setup step (step 3) had 35 apps as input from the previous step. All apps were downloaded and installed successfully, and continued to next step. Steps 3 and 4 were performed sequentially, with no need of division into apps subsets and uninstall.

3.2   Phase II

In the evaluation step (step 4), 1 app from the total amount of 35 apps could not be started: Domotic Center (by Showroom), version 1.5 demo. Therefore, only 34 apps were analyzed. We defined 30 minutes for the exploratory use of each app, and subsequently wrote the description. During the description activity, some apps were used again, with the average duration of 10 to 15 minutes, enabling verification of details regarding interface and some characteristics.

In order to demonstrate the execution of this step, summarized descriptions of apps are presented follows. We indicate the app developer next to each app name, so as to facilitate possible searches at Google Play®. In the extraction step (step 5), we point out relevant aspects identified based on use of apps, which indicate requirements. These aspects are highlighted in cyan.

Several apps required user authentication, not enabling a continued exploratory use. Such was the case of QW Home Automation (by Qingjun Wei), Rogers Smart Home Monitoring (by Rogers Communications Inc.), HCA Home Control Assistant (by Advanced Quonset Technology, Inc.) and BeHome 247 (by BeHome247.com). InControl Home Automation Free (by Moonlit Software) is another example: when started, it shows a sequence of instructions for installing and configuring the server, which leads to the system's authentication screen. Another case is INSTEON for SmartLinc (by INSTEON), which provides two options: one for new users and another for already existing users. For new users, it shows prerequisites for system operation, and then, requires authentication.

Smart Automation Experience (by Possible World Wide) starts in authentication screen, requesting a code, and exhibiting a help button and a link for registration. We performed the registration procedure, however, did not receive the authentication code requested to visualize the demo. InSideControl HD (by Schneider Electric Industries SAS) starts exhibiting a screen on landscape mode, and when we clicked on information option, the app – v.1.1.0 – crashed. Arduino Lamp (by Benhur Quintino de Souza) provides lamp control. This app can only run five times, and does not enable visualization of options regarding its features, only a tutorial and simple settings.

Since we performed the use of apps without a home infrastructure, several apps exhibited an empty home screen, with a black background along with an overflow button, which reveals an options menu. Such was the case of wdISY (by 222Designs) and Casa Domotica com Arduino Mega (by Excontrol Automatización y Domotica). AzHomeTouch (by Azcom Technology S.r.l) also shows this kind of interface after the authentication process. Its authentication screen exhibits an auto-login option; after login, there are settings options which include preferences, import configuration file, logoff and exit. DroidSeer TRIAL Version (by SPVSOFT) also exhibits an empty screen at startup, however, it allows to add, modify and remove appliances or events, with names to be specified by users.

AtMyHomeLE (by DevQ S.r.l.) exhibits options in a grid. Among them, there are lighting, automation, cameras, scenarios, installations and favorites. It is possible to navigate between options but when an option is selected, any information is provided. MyHomeManagerLite (by Pascal Duray) is a limited version, providing only a subset of features. When the app starts, it exhibits a message with information about the available features on this version, in order to notify users.

When SoulissApp (by Alessandro Del Pex) is started for the first time, it exhibits a user license. The app has three main options at the main screen and a brief description is provided for each one. For appliances control, it is possible to activate commands based on time, users' geographical position or sensor data. This app also provides an icon set, with 53 different options, and connection test feature. Just like SoulissApp, domRemote for Domintell system (by KZ Software) also starts exhibiting a message with terms and conditions. MobiLinc Lite (by Mobile Integrated Solutions) provides a link to information regarding terms and conditions, to be shown on a web page.

Domodroid beta 1.1 (by Pierre Lainé) starts exhibiting a welcome message. The initial screen shows two options: House and Map. Although we could not access these features without a home infrastructure, Map encompasses the idea of visualizing a home map, but it was not possible to verify it. FIBARO (by Fibaro) starts showing a sequence of screens with a step-by-step guide, and subsequently the app main screen. The main screen is composed of views with grayed out options, indicating blocked or inactive functionality. A carousel menu at the bottom of the screen also shows options through swipe interaction.

Home Buddy (by rakstar somar) starts exhibiting configuration options, which include: setting auto-refresh interval and enable/disable vibration. The main screen has two swipe views in order to show devices and scenes. There is also an action bar with action items, indicating voice interaction and refresh, and an overflow button with more options. AutHomationHD (by Garrett Power) has an interface composed of tabs and two sidebars, accessed by swipe. These sidebars show several options, such as: search; refresh; voice; about; sort by name, type, alphabetical order or inverse; and settings. In this last one, options are shown in different settings categories. The app sends an audio feedback if a voice command is not found. HAL-Home Automation @ Language (by Richard T. Schaefer) provides voice interaction and also enables users to assign touch gestures to commands. When the app is started it emits audio instructions regarding user settings and its interface is composed of swipe views.

Several apps provide a home control simulation in a demo mode. SRGio (by Alexus Art) offers a demo through authentication with user/password as guest/guest and its interface is composed of tabs. An important characteristic regarding appliances control is a single button to turn on/off, which also indicates the current state. Vera Mobile (by Alexus Art) is identical to the previous app as well as MiControl (by Alexus Art), but the last one is a Spanish version. I-WISH Smart Home (by Innova Egypt) provides demo with authentication with user/password filled in automatically. The app enables selecting or adding a server, and to assign a name, address and port to it. Other characteristic is the language selection, with two available idioms, i.e. English and Arabic.

Lifedomus (by Lifedomus) also provides a demo mode. Its interface is based on tabs, with several options, such as visualization by rooms and activities history (log). Regarding log feature, it is possible to show a complete log or filtering by alarms or events (requested actions). ayControl KNX and more (by easyMOBIZ.com) starts in demo mode, exhibiting rooms grouped by home floor. It is possible to import profiles, visualize and enable/disable log, and customize the interface with themes. SmartHome One by SMARTIF (by SMARTIF) starts showing options regarding authentication and demo offline, and displays household appliances by rooms or by type. Like other apps, Cisco SC Residence (by Cisco Systems, Inc.) provides a simulation mode and has a graphical interface with appliances arranged in a circle. Depending on selected appliance, different control elements are displayed, and for each device, an icon indicates the current status.

HSTouch Home Automation (by HomeSeer Technologies) and CMClient (by ComfortClick) provide simulation through a demo server. HSTouch Home Automation allows controlling home appliances, checking room climate and sending commands based on events. For appliances control, the app displays a dedicated screen for each appliance with its control options. In settings, it is possible to change server data, and separately, authentication data. CMClient presents a user interface similar to a desktop or launcher, with several options and a menu at the bottom of the screen accessed by swipe. Among options, there are calendar, mode selection, energy consumption, language selection and messages, which include e-mail, alerts and events.

ImperiHome (by Evertygo) offers interaction via tap, hold, swipe and voice. The main screen is composed of swipe views organized by main rooms. The app provides scenes, which allow execution of commands set. Regarding home appliances – home objects – it is possible to modify its name and icon, and add each one as favorite, hide or exhibit it. Also, images set represent the different status of the home objects. Moreover, users may add a scene shortcut in device home screen.

Table 1 summarizes 34 apps addressed in Phase II of the method. This table presents the column names: "Ver." indicates app version; "Infra." indicates the app availability for use without infrastructure; "Conn." indicates whether connection data, e.g. IP address, URL, is presented – and how – at user interface; and "Auth." indicates whether authentication data, e.g. user/password, is presented – and how – at user interface. At column "Infra." we used the following classification: (N)one when app does not provide navigation; (P)artial functionality, when app provides some functionality, however does not allow to simulate appliances control; and (F)ull functionality, when app provides all functionality and allows simulating appliances control. At columns "Conn." and "Auth.", we used the following caption: "N" for does not require, "S" for require on screen, and "C" for requires in configuration settings.

Table 1. Android apps identified and analyzed applying M4REMAIP

Icon	Name	Ver.	Infra.	Conn.	Auth.	Language
	QW Home Automation	1.1.11	N	S	S	English
	Rogers Smart Home Monitoring	5.0.5	N	N	S	English
	HCA Home Control Assistant	11.2.11	N	C	N	English
	BeHome 247	1.1.1	N	N	S	English
	InControl Home Automation Free	2.0.9	N	N	S	English
	INSTEON for SmartLinc	1.2.3	N	N	S	English

Table 1. (*continued*)

	Smart Automation Experience	7.1.1	N	N	N	English
	InSideControl HD	1.1.0	N	C	N	English
	Arduino Lamp	1.0	N	N	N	English
	wdISY	-	N	C	C	English
	Casa Domotica con Arduino Mega	4.0	N	S	N	English
	AzHomeTouch	0.6.5	N	C	S	English
	DroidSeer Trial Version	-	P	S	S	English
	atMyHomeLE	1.0.56	P	N	N	Portuguese
	MyHomeManagerLite	1.0.1.0	P	C	N	English
	SoulissApp	1.2.31	P	N	N	Portuguese
	domRemote for Domintell system	1.1.22	P	C	N	English
	MobiLinc Lite	1.2.4	P	N	S	English
	Domodroid beta 1.1	1.1	P	C	N	English
	FIBARO	1.1	P	S	S	English
	Home Buddy	0.37	P	C	N	English
	AutHomationHD	3.1.3.5	P	C	C	English
	HAL-Home Automation @ Language	1.006	P	S	S	English
	SRGio	1.9.107	F	N	S	English
	Vera Mobile	1.9.107	F	N	S	English
	Micontrol	1.9.409	F	N	S	Spanish
	I-WISH Smart Home	1.1	F	C	S	English/ Arabic
	Lifedomus	1.4.1	F	S	N	Portuguese
	ayControl KNX and more	3.0.9	F	N	N	English
	SmartHome One by SMARTIF	1.8.9.2	F	S	S	Portuguese
	Cisco SC Residence	2.5.2.210567	F	N	S	English
	HSTouch Home Automation	1.35	F	C	C	English
	CMClient	2.0.2	F	C	C	English/ Others
	ImperiHome	1.9.2	F	C	C	English

3.3   Requirements and Design Ideas

After executing Phases I and II of the method, we identified 45 functional requirements, organized in eight categories: (a) general, (b) first startup, (c) configuration, (d) connection, (e) authentication, (f) feedback, (g) home objects, and (h) control.

(a) GENERAL – **R1. About:** Provide information about the app; **R2. Available features:** Provide information regarding available features, especially when the app is a limited version; **R3. Brief description:** Provide a brief description of each feature; **R4. Demo:** Provide a simulation of home infrastructure in order to enable appliances control. Thus, users may interact and test app features. This simulation may be provided by demo mode, demo server, or authentication with user/password filled out automatically.

(b) FIRST STARTUP – **R5. User license:** Exhibit user license, with options to accept or refuse terms and conditions; **R6. Welcome message:** Exhibit a welcome message; **R7. Tutorial/instructions/step-by-step:** Provide instructions and presentation of apps features, in a sequence of screens with a step-by-step guide; **R8. Prerequisites for system operation:** Display information about required hardware/software artifacts and necessary conditions for system operation; **R9. Help:** Provide an option with help information.

(c) CONFIGURATION – **R10. Settings categories:** Exhibit options grouped into categories, according similar configuration purposes; **R11. Configuration file:** Provide an option to send a configuration file, containing settings data; **R12. Connection and authentication separately:** Exhibit server connection information separately from authentication; **R13. Language:** Provide options to language selection, in order to change the idiom of displayed information.

(d) CONNECTION – **R14. Server data:** Provide options for data input related to server such as name, address and port; **R15. Connection test:** Provide connection test in order to user test connection with home system; **R16. Refresh:** Provide option to refresh, implying in a new query and update of displayed information manually; **R17. Auto-refresh:** Provide automatic updates based on new queries to the system; **R18. Refresh interval:** Provide option which enables users set the time interval to automatic updates; **R19. Logout option:** Provide an option which enables users to close the connection with the home system.

(e) AUTHENTICATION – **R20. User/password:** Provide authentication with user and password; **R21. Auto-login:** Provide an option which enables users to choose to login to the system automatically during the app startup.

(f) FEEDBACK – **R22. Audio feedback:** Provide audio feedback, in order to warn users of actions performed in the system; **R23. Haptic feedback:** Provide haptic feedback, in order to notify users of actions performed in the system; **R24. Enable/disable audio/haptic feedback:** Provide option to enable/disable the audio or haptic feedback; **R25. User interface with grayed out options:** Display interface grayed out elements if features provided through interaction with these elements are blocked or inactive; **R26. Full log:** Provide a full history of actions occurred in the system; **R27. Log with filter by alarms and events:** Provide filtering options regarding log information, enabling filtering by alarms or events (requested actions); **R28. Enable/disable log:** Provide option to enable/disable log functionality; **R29.**

Alert messages: Display messages with urgent information (alerts); **R30. Event messages:** Display messages with information regarding actions performed by the system.

(g) HOME OBJECTS – **R31. Objects displayed by rooms:** Display home objects by rooms; **R32. Objects displayed by type:** Display home objects by type of appliance; **R33. Modify name:** Provide an option which enables users to modify object names identifying each appliance; **R34. Modify icon:** Provide an option which enables users to modify object icon identifying each appliance; **R35. Icon set:** Provide an icon set, enabling user to assign an icon to each object; **R36. Images indicating status:** Provide images which represent home objects and their current status. An image set must represent different status of each home object; **R37. Favorites:** Provide an option which enables users to select objects and mark them as favorites.

(h) CONTROL – **R38. Commands based on time:** Activate commands based on a predefined time; **R39. Commands based on position:** Activate commands based on users' geographical positions; **R40. Commands based on sensor:** Activate commands based on sensor data; **R41. Commands based on events:** Activate commands based on events occurred in the home system; **R42. Single button to turn on/off:** Provide a single button to turn on and turn off actions; **R43. Dedicated screen for each appliance:** Display a dedicated screen for control options of each appliance; **R44. Scenes:** Provide an option which enables executing a command set related to a particular usage scenario; **R45. Scenes shortcuts:** Provide shortcuts to scenes activation.

We also identified some possible solutions with regard to interaction: graphical interface with tap, hold and swipe gestures; voice commands. Moreover, we identified some possible solutions for the "Settings" functionality, which include possible icons to represent the functionality and possible locations inside mobile app interface. Some possible locations include: pop-menu in an overflow button at action bar; carousel menu at the bottom of the screen; navigation drawer (sidebar); button at home screen. With regard to icon aspects, we identified some suggestions, as shown in Fig. 2.

Fig. 2. Some possible design solutions – icons – to functionality "Settings"

4   Discussion

The results presented in previous section represent a non-exhaustive set of functional requirements for Android apps for home control. Some considerations show relevant aspects and are outlined below. Firstly, a difficulty in applying this method for this specific domain is that many apps require a real home infrastructure in order to evaluate all functionalities. Despite we could not proceed with exploratory use with several apps, this method demonstrated to be useful and enabled identifying requirements for this domain. Moreover, implementing requirements addressed in this paper also requires home system and the infrastructure integrated to the app.

With regard to user interface, it may be observed that most apps do not follow Android design patterns. Several apps do not provide the ActionBar, and some solutions provide both logout and exit buttons, contrary to the guidelines [13]. Another important observation is that most app interfaces use dark tones, with gray and black colors. This is contrary to the design principles of current automated and smart homes, which adopt glass and transparent materials and use white and light colors. Regarding user interaction, it is worth mentioning that some apps provide voice interaction, using Android resources for voice recognition. However, apps still lack the use of other interaction modes. During exploratory use, we did not identify the use of accelerometers for a direct interaction related to control, such as command activation or feature selection. Regarding language, although some apps provide major information in a local language, some messages or interface elements are not translated. This fact emphasizes the importance of language support, as well as other localization and internationalization aspects of app design.

There are some interesting remarks regarding the method which deserve further comments. The two activities related to evaluation step – exploratory use and description – are mutually complementary. Exploratory use provides an overview of interface aspects and app features, while the description activity enables attempting to interaction details. Subsequently, the extraction step provides the deeper analysis and identification of functional requirements.

Several requirements impact interaction aspects of an app, e.g. log, and might be discovered by applying the method proposed in this paper. The proposed categories for functional requirements aim to aid understanding of the context and implementation of such requirements, however, other classifications could be proposed for this purpose. Moreover, based on descriptions and the design solutions, it is also possible to identify design patterns [13] used in apps, as clearly noted in location suggestions to functionality "Settings". Regarding possible solutions, we focused on interactions and the "Settings" functionality in order to demonstrate some examples, but other design solutions could be found.

It is noteworthy that requirements elicitation methods from the point of view of Software Engineering are often directed by the perspective of user interaction via a graphical interface and involve document investigation or contact with people associated with product/system usage. This method might be useful for different audiences, from academia, such as researches trying to identify characteristics on apps for this research domain, to industry, such as autonomous developers, startups or companies with small development teams.

5   Conclusion

This paper presented the definition of a method – M4REMAIP – and results of its application in requirements elicitation of Android apps for home control. In order to achieve this, we analyzed apps in this specific domain under an HCI perspective, considering design and interaction issues. Based on this analysis, we identified important features and characteristics for Android apps for home control. Results obtained with the execution of this method demonstrate its usefulness for functional requirements elicitation focusing on interaction aspects.

For future work, we envision the design and implementation of an Android app based on functional requirements identified in this paper, and also, application of the method defined in this work to other domains.

Acknowledgements. This work was partially supported by the Brazilian Federal Agency for Support and Evaluation of Graduate Education (CAPES), and by the Physical Artifacts of Interaction Research Group (PAIRG) at Federal University of Rio Grande do Norte (UFRN), Brazil.

References

1. Kotonya, G., Sommerville, I.: Requirements Engineering: Processes and Techniques. Wiley (1998)
2. Charland, A., Leroux, B.: Mobile Application Development: Web vs. Native. Commun. ACM. 54, 49–53 (2011)
3. De Angeli, A., Sutcliffe, A., Hartmann, J.: Interaction, Usability and Aesthetics: What Influences Users' Preferences? In: 6th Conference on Designing Interactive Systems, pp. 271–280. ACM (2006)
4. Tarrini, L., Bianchi Bandinelli, R., Miori, V., Bertini, G.: Remote Control of Home Automation Systems with Mobile Devices. In: Paternó, F. (ed.) Mobile HCI 2002. LNCS, vol. 2411, pp. 364–368. Springer, Heidelberg (2002)
5. Marusic, L., Skocir, P., Petric, A., Jezic, G.: Home-in-Palm - A Mobile Service for Remote Control of Household Energy Consumption. In: 11th International Conference on Telecommunications, pp. 109–116. IEEE (2011)
6. Potts, J., Sukittanon, S.: Exploiting Bluetooth on Android Mobile Devices for Home Security Application. In: IEEE Southeastcon, pp. 1–4. IEEE (2012)
7. Oliveira, D.H.D., Mendes, G.A.V., Miranda, L.C., Miranda, E.E.C., Silva, L.F.: Domotic based on Arduino Platform: State of the Art and New Hardware Trends. In: XXXIX Latin America Conference on Informatics, pp. 1–11 (2013) (in Portuguese)
8. Sakamoto, S.G., Miranda, L.C., Hornung, H.H.: Home Control via Mobile Devices: State of the Art and HCI Challenges under the Perspective of Diversity. In: 16th International Conference on Human-Computer Interaction. Springer (in press, 2014)
9. de Carvalho Correia, A.C., de Miranda, L.C., Hornung, H.: Gesture-based Interaction in Domotic Environments: State of the Art and HCI Framework Inspired by the Diversity. In: Kotzé, P., Marsden, G., Lindgaard, G., Wesson, J., Winckler, M. (eds.) INTERACT 2013, Part II. LNCS, vol. 8118, pp. 300–317. Springer, Heidelberg (2013)
10. Correia, A.C.C., Miranda, L.C., Hornung, H.H., Marciano, J.N.: Recommendations for Gesture-based Residential Interactive Systems Inspired by Diversity. In: 16th International Conference on Human-Computer Interaction. Springer (in press, 2014)
11. Correia, A.C.C., Miranda, L.C., Marciano, J.N.: Syntactic/Semantic Formalizations and Metrics of Residential Applications based on Gestural Interface. In: 16th International Conference on Human-Computer Interaction. Springer (in press, 2014)
12. Marciano, J.N., Miranda, L.C., Miranda, E.E.C., Pereira, R.: Android MALL Apps for Japanese Language: Identifying and Eliciting Interface/Interaction Requirements through the Semiotic Framework. In: XXXIX Latin America Conference on Informatics, pp. 1–11 (2013)
13. Nudelman, G.: Android Design Patterns: Interaction Design Solutions for Developers. Wiley (2013)

A Mixed-Method Approach for In-Depth Contextual User Research

Walkyria Goode[1], Caroline Little[1], Andrew Schall[1], Renae Geraci[2],
and Vanessa Brown[2]

[1] SPARK Experience, Bethesda, MD, USA
[2] Bose Corporation, Framingham, MA, USA
{walky,caroline,andrew}@sparkexperience.com,
{Renae_Geraci,Vanessa_Brown}@bose.com

Abstract. Successful design requires an in-depth understanding of user behavior. The paper will describe how we applied a mixed-method research approach, which combines a traditional contextual inquiry with a modified diary study, in three different studies. The proposed methodology permits the inclusion of more participants in a larger geographical area, maximizing research resources, and the collection of longitudinal data. A summary of lessons learned from the new hybrid method will be presented.

Keywords: contextual inquiry, diary study, design research, HCI.

1 Introduction

Successful interface design relies upon a multifaceted understanding of users – their behaviors, thoughts, interests, feelings and emotions. The HCI field has proposed several techniques to gather this kind of complex information about users, including contextual inquiry and diary studies. The design of a product intended for a major market can require in-depth research studies with numerous participants and unique use cases across multiple locations and with repeated tasks and interactions. In order to accomplish such studies, we are proposing a mixed approach, which combines a traditional contextual inquiry with a modified diary study.

1.1 Contextual Inquiry

Contextual inquiry is a research methodology that involves researchers observing and interviewing participants in their natural environment. While derived from traditional ethnography, in contextual inquiry the researcher does not seek to integrate seamlessly into the participant culture but instead adopt a collaborative relationship with research participants as Master (participant) and Apprentice (researcher) [1]. Creating this relationship is important for a few reasons: it provides researchers a framework for behavior rather than asking them to follow particular rules for

A. Marcus (Ed.): DUXU 2014, Part I, LNCS 8517, pp. 86–95, 2014.

communication with participants, and it creates a model that naturally draws out relevant information from the participant while enabling learning for the researcher [2]. While a master may not be a natural teacher, by teaching in the context of his or her work, describing actions as they occur, the apprentice learns. The apprentice-master model thus allows participants to talk about their work as it happens, explaining it, rather than the researcher trying to draw out that information from user as in a traditional interview scenario.

As defined by Beyer and Holtzblatt [2], contextual inquiry is based on four principles: context, partnership, interpretation, and focus. Context is critical to the method as it allows the researcher to understand and collect information on the ongoing experience, that is, what is happening now versus what the user may remember or think is important to recount. In a traditional interview, the participant may summarize the experience for the researcher, leaving out critical details and lumping like scenarios together into one abstraction. Contextual inquiry methodology focuses on collecting concrete data, the specific and not general experience. Partnership refers to both to the apprentice-master model and how that relationship between researcher and participant fosters the ability to share and analyze design possibilities in the moment. This interpretation is a key benefit of using contextual inquiry, as it allows the researcher to test assumptions in the exact moment the user is completing a task. The user should then be able to modify the idea as he or she can compare it directly to the current state. Finally, the principle of focus, while important for all research activities, is critical for contextual inquiry because of the undefined nature of user's environment. The interviewer needs to know and be cognizant of the goals of the session and be able to guide the conversation in a productive direction. As such, the interviewer should prepare a moderator guide with a list of questions that can prompt the participant and structure the interview [14].

Contextual inquiry is best used for understanding how specific environmental factors influence or impact user behavior [6]. While a qualitative method, contextual inquiry mitigates some of the problems inherent in user interviews because it gives researchers a fuller picture of the user experience and grounds insights in reality – what users actually do and not simply what they say they do. One downside of the methodology is that it only accounts for one slice in time of the user experience. Researchers may miss critical activities, challenges, or behaviors if they are not present during a specific time. Additionally, contextual inquiry may be seen as lacking rigor as it takes place in an uncontrolled environment and relies heavily on the subjective interpretation of the researcher of anecdotal data [15].

1.2 Diary Study

Diary study is a research method in which participants self-log their activities over a discrete period of time [20, 9]. Participants are asked to describe their activities, user needs, context information and thoughts on a daily basis, either at the end of the day or as soon as the activity of interest has occurred. Since the diary entries portray relatively recent events, participants usually provide a rich summary of their thoughts, feelings and reflections on the logged activities [7, 18]. Diary studies that monitor data collection allow researchers to both encourage participants to complete their required log as well as expand or clarify on their entries. The diary method is particularly useful because it requires minimal research resources while at the same time capturing contextual and user-submitted data. This method is commonly used for understanding behavior, predicting behavior or guiding product design [4, 3, 15].

A key advantage of a diary study is that participants' entries are recorded directly after an activity is performed, minimizing demands on memory usually present in regular interviews or surveys [19]. Having participants record information immediately reduces common effects of recall such as saliency and recency. Diary methods also help diminish aggregation errors. Aggregation errors are observed in survey and interview responses, when participants are asked to estimate the frequency in which they perform a particular activity. The logging of such activities over a period of time allows for a direct frequency count rather than asking for a frequency estimate. This decrease in response bias increases the ecological validity of the study [18].

The main drawback of diary studies is that they rely on participant cooperation, which can diminish over time as logging data can be tedious or time-consuming [7]. The importance of engaging participants throughout the process makes a proper study design even more critical. Diary designs can vary from simple entries with free format and a date stamp to involved questionnaires with branching logic [19]. A good balance is needed between collecting a lot of data and not overwhelming participants in order to reduce attrition rates.

1.3   Mixed Method Approach

Traditionally, a contextual inquiry and diary study are considered two separate methodologies. The authors propose and have tested a technique wherein the two methods are combined into one comprehensive study. The benefits of such an approach are obvious: the limitations of each method are complemented by the strength in the other. For example, contextual inquiry lacks a longitudinal focus that can be compensated for by a diary study. A diary study also helps sharpens the qualitative data collected in a contextual inquiry by providing information directly submitted by users, without being filtered through the lens of a researcher. On the other hand, contextual inquiry balances out the raw, unfiltered view of user-submitted data and allows researchers to begin to understand a user's actual world instead of a simple description of it.

Other researchers have utilized a mixed-method approach to understanding the holistic user experience with a type of product or life event. Müller, Gove, and Webb used a combination of written and video diaries, in-home interviews, and contextual inquiry to understand the primary and secondary activities users perform on tablet devices, as well as common locations and times of day tablets are used [11]. The range of data collected- both longitudinal, user-generated, and researcher-observed- gave the team a fuller view on the role tablets play in users lives and allowed them to provide guidance on key areas of focus for website and app developers when designing for the tablet experience.

Leedy and Downes-Le Guin [10] used a similar approach when studying one very specific experience: how men select engagement rings and think about the betrothal process. The research team asked participants to complete pre- and post-visit surveys and conducted a contextual inquiry. In this case the surveys acted as a type of diary study, without the longitudinal component, as they provided user-submitted data and allowed users to document their own reflections on the experience.

2   Study

2.1   Method

Following is a description of the mixed method approach employed in three studies on telework technologies, audio listening behavior and HR resources and tools. The telework technologies study investigated how workers use telepresence technology – what works and what doesn't – as well as formulating a strategy based on user needs for new solutions for the future. The listening behavior study examined different population segments and their behaviors around collecting, listening to and sharing audio content. The HR resources and tools study researched the environment in which HR personnel perform their jobs and what tools and resources they use and need. The approach did not vary and will be summarized once. The description is followed by the methodological results from all studies and will detail result characteristics that can be obtained when applying this mixed method approach.

2.2   Participants

Each study had unique requirements for participation based on the goals of the study. In general, participants needed to be willing and able to let researchers observe them in a variety of scenarios and environments. This can be an issue in contextual inquiry especially when potential participants deal with sensitive information in their work or have concern about allowing a research team to visit them in their office environment. Participants also needed to be tech-savvy enough to use the remote diary study tools, including online surveys and a mobile app, and take digital photos. In the case where participants did not have a smartphone, an online option was always provided as an alternative.

The first study – telework technologies study – involved (24) professionals from four major US cities who either conducted work remotely (in their homes or other locations) or who communicated with remote coworkers (or a combination thereof). In order to observe and document a range of experiences, participants were selected who used technologies including but not limited to phone calls, including conference call systems, videoconference tools like Skype or GoToMeeting, screen-sharing applications like JoinMe, and in-office based telepresence systems.

For the audio listening behavior study (40) participants from three major US cities were recruited based on specific criteria related to the needs to the study, including frequency of audio listening and devices and technology used. In order to screen participants more thoroughly, the client created a battery of questions included as part of recruitment that segmented the participants per pre-defined market research categories.

The HR resources and tools study involved (24) participants, all of whom work for a central organization at unique sites, in four geographic locations around the US. Each participant had the same role in their organization, managing benefits and HR tasks, but had slightly different duties depending on the needs of their specific organization.

2.3   Procedure

Contextual Inquiry. The contextual inquiry complements the longitudinal diary study component of the study by providing an in-depth snapshot into the daily activities of a participant. The goal of the in-person method is to understand specific user behavior as it relates to his or her environment.

Researchers visited participants on-site (at a location that made sense for particular study objectives). Sample locations included: a participant's home, a coffee shop, and an office. While just one participant was recruited for the in-person interview, in some instances related individuals were interviewed "on the spot" in context to the study subject (e.g. a colleague or roommate).

The research sessions, as defined by the contextual inquiry methodology, included elements of observation of user behavior and directly interviewing participants, either prompting them to teach or "show and tell" a particular environment or task or through pre-defined questions brought into shape the interview.

During observation, researchers focused on documenting the following types of activities:

- User tasks performed - specifically noticing any "workarounds" or challenges
- Tools used and materials, artifacts, or other individuals referenced or consulted
- Interactions, both impromptu and scheduled, between participants and other individuals
- Environment, including physical model and space set-up and technology/devices

A team of two researchers attended each session; one led the session and guided the interview, while the second researcher took notes, ran the video camera, and took relevant photos.

Diary Study. The diary study is a longitudinal journal that helps capture a day in the life of participants, track their routine tasks and situations and identify resources used, both on a regular or less frequent basis.

The diary study began with a remote briefing session using web video technology to ensure participants fully understand the type of information desired and when to input an entry, as well as a walkthrough of the different technologies that will be used for the study. This instructional briefing was given 1-to-3 days before data collection began. In addition, participants were emailed a detailed manual with instructions related to the study and the technologies they would be using.

The actual data collection was both signal contingent, meaning a signaling device was used to prompt the participants to make an entry in their journal, and event contingent, where participants were asked to record a journal entry each time a specific event occurred. The signal contingent tools included calendar reminders, text messages, and emails to prompt participants to record data. Event contingent tools included note-sharing applications with image capability [12], web-based surveys [16, 17], and a mobile app documentation tool [8].

The data entry portion used a semi-structured design, which included both closed- and open-ended questions. Closed-ended questions were included to ensure consistency in response and increase validity and reliability. Open-ended questions were included to elicit personal thoughts and experiences. Entries were designed to be as simple and concise as possible to encourage voluntary logging. Participants reported on their day-to-day activities including:

- Resources that they use as part of the monitored activity
- Image captures of their workspace, documents, screen shots of websites or application, tools (hardware, artifacts) used
- Thoughts, feelings, emotions and issues encountered

All participants were constantly monitored. Ad hoc surveys were sent to ask specific questions about participant's entries and any issues they raised regarding user behavior, problems, and needs. Participants responded with more detail. At the end of the longitudinal portion, the researcher interviewed a group of participants individually for an in-depth debrief.

Mixed Method. The data collection concluded with a final remote video-based debriefing session with participants from both the contextual inquiries and diary studies. This "focus group style" session encouraged participants to interact with one another and allowed researchers to direct the conversation toward global themes and solutions. Examples of items discussed are:

- Typical and atypical situations that occurred for participants
- Resources and tools that participants use and how they use them
- Group brainstorm of ideas for solving challenges common to the group

2.4   Methodological Results

Many of the types of results expected to be found from contextual inquiry also occur in the mixed-methods approach, including work models, physical models, and artifact models. These models are a way to explain the user behavior in one, visual representation. A work model depicts the structure of the participant's activity. The physical model illustrates the physical environment related to the activity. The artifact model shows both physical and electronic objects that are used or created by the user [5]. For all three studies, different models were created to express different pieces of the environment or system that impact user behavior.

The additional longitudinal data gathered in the diary study methodology also allows researchers to create in-depth personas describing user characteristics as well as supporting storyboards that reflect how a particular persona behaves over the course of a set period of time. A persona is a description of a typical user based on the composite of several users with similar behaviors, interests and user needs. Each persona, given a fictional name and demographic information, describes the needs and tasks this user has in relation to the research area and to their physical, social and technological environment [13].

The combination of overall system/environmental understanding, created by the models, combined with the in-depth insight into specific user behavior as defined by the personas provides a holistic view of challenges and gaps. This knowledge can lead to concepts addressing both existing problems as well as the development of new products or services.

3   Discussion

In general, the studies to which the mixed methodological approach was applied had successful outcomes, as the research objectives were achieved. As with any study that involves a large number of participants in multiple locations, as well as both in-person and remote activities, coordination and management is challenging. However, the benefits of combining the diary study component with the contextual inquiry outweigh the additional time and resources needed. Understanding the user perspective through their direct entries not only provides more information about participants, but also allows for another touch point between the research team and user, making it easier for researchers to ask follow-up questions or receive clarity about an experience. Additionally, having more information about participant behavior over time accounted for behaviors that were not seen during the contextual inquiry session. For example, how a specific piece of technology malfunctioning impacted a participant workflow or how the experience of going to a concert with a friend affected future music listening choices. The debrief sessions at the end of the study were critical for linking the in-person research experience with the diary study entries, giving researchers the opportunity to co-design with not just a single participant, but with a group. This group dynamic was important for allowing participants to build off one another's idea and compare and share experiences.

The authors hope that this approach can be improved upon and refined in future studies. Opportunities exist to add in more efficiency to the study protocols and for ensuring more consistency between types of participant responses to allow for more direct comparison.

3.1   Lessons Learned

Experience with using this mixed-method approach in three different studies taught us several lessons.

Contextual Inquiry. First, proper recruitment of participants is vital for the contextual inquiry portion. The carrying out of the contextual inquiry process involves many man-hours (scheduling, traveling, meeting). Due to this investment, it is of critical importance to ensure participants fit the correct behavioral and demographic profile for the study. Our second study – the audio listening behavior study – required a very specific segmentation of the target population. On a couple of occasions we had to eliminate participants because they did not fit the intended segment.

Second, semi-structured interviews should be the norm with some allowance of new ideas to be brought up. A moderator guide with standard questions will ensure that at least some common questions are addressed to the group of participants as a whole. Permitting the flow of new ideas allowed the researchers to learn of new perspectives that were not initially considered. These new ideas were integrated in later interviews and the diary study to confirm their relevance.

Third, visual recordings of the participant's environment are extremely helpful. Even if participants are requested to take photos as part of the diary exercise, taking additional photos and creating sketches of the environment during the contextual inquiry can be very useful. In many instances, the participants took more detailed focused photographs of the artifacts, while the researcher took more comprehensive photographs of the user's environment.

Diary Study. First, make several types of logging artifacts available. Our first study – the telework technologies study – required the use of a specific note-sharing application. The target population for this study was extremely tech-savvy and didn't have problems learning to use the application. In fact, some already were already expert users. This wasn't the case for the other two studies. The audio listening behavior study had a target population that was mobile and required a logging artifact that allowed data entry on the go. For this study we initially decided to use a smart phone app that would capture images and text. We soon discovered that not all participants had access to a smart phone. Thus, we provided an online option that could be accessed via a 'non-smart' phone or computer. The third study – the HR resources and tools study – had a target population with varying degrees of technological sophistication. In this case, we utilized an online survey that was both user-friendly and accessible from any device.

Second, an initial briefing is paramount before data collection starts. This purpose for this briefing is twofold. First, it helps participants understand the areas of interest that they should log. Entry examples are provided to illustrate this point. Second, it helps participant become comfortable with the logging technology to use. A walkthrough is performed and simple instructional manual is given.

A third lesson is the importance of personal interactions. Researchers would send out friendly reminders for participants to log their entries. In addition, diary entries were closely monitored. If the participant hadn't entered data by the end of the day, the researcher would nudge him/her to do so. The close monitoring also prompted researchers to dive deeper or ask clarification about a particular point or entry. The researcher then reached out the participant via email or a short ad hoc survey.

A fourth lesson is to start participants in waves. Different start days allow enough time to schedule initial briefings and to monitor data. Not all participants should start on the same day. It takes a participant at least a day to get comfortable with entering data and clarification requests are most common at the beginning.

A fifth lesson is flexibility. The researcher must be willing and able to interact with participants at their convenience.

A final lesson refers to data interpretation and coding. This is a resource intensive process. Every entry needs to be read and analyzed. In the case of multiple researchers, an agreement should be reached beforehand on how to approach this analysis to maintain a high inter-rater reliability.

Mixed Method. First, select a representative sample of participants for the focus-group debrief. Including – and specifically scheduling – all participants will be impossible. Since the debrief will be using remote technologies a smaller size than a regular focus group is recommended, approximately 6 to 8 participants.

Second, use a structured interview that will guide discussion to pinpoint areas of interest. Participants in remote sessions tend to lose interest more quickly than in-person sessions. If a participant starts dominating the discussion or taking it in a different direction, others will get easily distracted and not participate. Incorporating activities as part of the debrief, such as asking participants to note in a viewable shared document all the tools they use for their job, is helpful in soliciting and maintaining participant attention.

3.2   Limitations

As with any qualitative study, this mixed- method approach is subjective in nature and cannot be used to derive certainties. Additionally, the combination of contextual inquiry with a diary study is more time and resource intensive and requires additional collaboration between research team members to ensure data is being collected and interpreted in a standardized fashion.

References

1. Beyer, H.R., Holtzblatt, K.: Apprenticing with the customer. Communications of the ACM 38(5), 45–52 (1995)
2. Beyer, H.R., Holtzblatt, K.: Contextual Design: Defining Customer-Centered Systems. Morgan Kaufmann Publishers, San Francisco (1998)
3. Czerwinski, M., Horvitz, E., Wilhite, S.: A diary study of task switching and interruptions. In: Monk, A.F., Olsen, D. (eds.) CHI 2004, pp. 175–182. ACM Press, Vienna (2004)
4. Higgins, C.A., McClean, R.J., Conrath, D.W.: The accuracy and biases of diary communication data. Social Networks 7, 173–187 (1985)
5. Holtzblatt, K., Burns Wendell, J., Wood, S.: Rapid Contextual Design: A How-To Guide to Key Techniques for User-Centered Design. Morgan Kaufmann Publishers, San Francisco (2005)

6. Hom, J.: The Usability Methods Toolbox Handbook (1998),
   http://www.idemployee.id.tue.nl/g.w.m.rauterberg/
   lecturenotes/UsabilityMethodsToolboxHandbook.pdf (retrieved)
7. Hyldegard, J.: Using diaries in group based information behavior research- a methodological study. In: Information Interaction in Context, IIiX, Copenhagen, Denmark, pp. 153–161 (2006)
8. iSurvey, http://www.isurveysoft.com (last visited February 3, 2014)
9. Liu, N., Liu, Y., Wang, X.: Data logging plus e-diary: Towards an online evaluation approach of mobile service field trial. In: MobileCHI 2010, Lisbon, Portugal, pp. 287–290 (2010)
10. Leedey, E., Downes-Le Guin, T.: A sum greater than the parts: Combining contextual inquiry with other methods to maximize research insights into social transitions. In: EPIC 2006, pp. 41–48 (2006)
11. Muller, H., Gove, J.L., Webb, J.S.: Understanding tablet use: A multi-method exploration. In: MobileHCI 2012, pp. 1–10 (2012)
12. Pachikov, S.: Evernote (Version 5.4.4), Application (2014), http://evernote.com/
13. Persona (n.d.) In How to & Tools of What & Why Usability from Usability.gov., http://www.usability.gov/how-to-and-tools/methods/personas.html (retrieved)
14. Potts, L., Bartocci, G.: <Methods> Experience design </Methods>. In: SIGDOC 2009, Bloomington, Indiana, pp. 17–21 (2009)
15. Rieman, J.: The diary study: A workplace-oriented research tool to guide laboratory efforts. In: INTERCHI 1993, pp. 321–326 (1993)
16. SurveyGizmo, http://www.surveygizmo.com (last visited February 3, 2014)
17. SurveyMonkey, http://www.surveymonkey.com (last visited February 3, 2014)
18. Vannier, S.A., O'Sullivan, L.F.: The feasibility and acceptability of handheld computers in a prospective diary study of adolescent sexual behavior. The Canadian Journal of Human Sexuality 17(4), 183–192 (2008)
19. Wild, P.J., McMahon, C., Liu, S.: A diary study of information need and document usage in the engineering domain. Design Studies 31, 46–73 (2010)
20. Zimmerman, D.H., Wider, L.D.: Diary-interview method. Urban Life 5(4), 479–498 (1977)

Reframing Design under Technical Conditions

Moritz Greiner-Petter and Claudia Mareis

Institute of Research in Art and Design, Basel, Switzerland
{moritz.greinerpetter,claudia.mareis}@fhnw.ch

Abstract. In recent years concepts and approaches of scientific epistemology and sociology of science have been applied to the field of design and thereby considerably exposed the epistemological qualities and socio-material configurations in the practice of designing. However, technical paradigms and characteristics of design practice as a specific form of technical activity have been slightly neglected. In considering positions from the philosophy and sociology of technology as well as media theory, we attempt to resume promising approaches that move in this direction and indicate what the implications of such approaches might be for creative practices. By elaborating these aspects, we aim to reframe contemporary design cultures and practices within technical conditions.

Keywords: Design Theory, Design Philosophy, Epistemology, Technical Cultures in Design, Science and Technology Studies (STS), Tools, Software.

1 Introduction

In this paper, we want to gain a deeper understanding of technically driven design cultures and practices. This we aim to do by elaborating and differentiating the role of technical objects within design processes. In a more general view, we are interested in an up-dated notion of *the technical* respectively *techné* within contemporary design cultures and practices, especially in the realm of digital media practices and interaction design.

Over the past few years, design has been increasingly discussed within the framework of scientific epistemology as well as from the perspective of Science and Technology Studies (STS). Thus, the epistemological qualities of design cultures and practices, their potential in the production of new knowledge have been widely researched and discussed in-depth. Scholars from both STS, and design, artistic, and architectural research fields have been investigating architectural practices [1,2] design cultures and techniques [3,4], as well as the epistemic role of models [5], sketches, or drawings [6,7]. Special attention has been given here to the visual and material dimensions of designing, especially to the notion of "objects" and "things" [8,9]. Slightly less attention however has been given to the aspects of tools and instruments, as well as to technical paradigms of designing.

A. Marcus (Ed.): DUXU 2014, Part I, LNCS 8517, pp. 96–103, 2014.
© Springer International Publishing Switzerland 2014

Design always has been and is increasingly becoming a discipline bound to technological domains. It is vital in designing to exploit the potentialities of production techniques in creative ways and to expand its means of creation through technological research. That way, it also reshapes its very scope of application by exploring new design spaces along technological advancement in general. In that sense, complex tools like computers and especially software constitute a significant background for contemporary design practices to unfold. We consider it important to foster a critique of digital media regarding its stake in structuring creative practices, shaping aesthetics of production and establishing conceptual and discourse paradigms in design.

2   Technical Objects

The growing theoretical interest in design as a knowledge-intensive discipline draws from previous work in social studies of science and technology and those studies' research into the epistemological status of material relations, artifacts and representations within creative practices. The conceptualization of "epistemic objects" and "technical objects" by historian of science Hans-Jörg Rheinberger [10] has been an especially fruitful resource for analysis of knowledge production embedded in material environments beyond scientific domains. Ewenstein and Whyte [11] have recently differentiated these kinds of objects and how they come into use in architectural practice. Drawing on Rheinberger, they distinguish between "technical objects," "epistemic objects," and "boundary objects". While technical objects are described as "taken-for-granted" [11, p.9], "fixed and stable tools" that are "ready-to-hand, complete and unproblematic instruments," epistemic objects are characterized in a more dynamic, somewhat fuzzy way by their "lack and incompleteness," "partially expressed in multiple instantiations," "continuously evolving" [11, p.10]. On the contrary, the concept of "boundary objects," first described by Star [12] and Star/Griesemer [13], is described as being less material, more discursive and interactive: as an "object that is differently interpreted and provides a holding ground for ideas for communication, translation and standardization of meaning" [11, p.10].

While the concepts of both epistemic and boundary objects have been discussed thoroughly, the description of technical objects appears to lack more detailed elaboration. This observation seems to be accompanied by or is even based on a rather indifferent, out-dated notion of *the technical* and *techné* within the analysis of contemporary design. Looking at design cultures and practices through the lens of epistemology has certainly led to a better understanding of design. However, due to the subsuming and subordination of technical aspects under the auspices of epistemic (mostly scientific) concepts, a somewhat shortened, indifferent understanding of design now seems to dominate the discourse – in terms of knowledge production and innovation processes.

3   Problematizing Technical Objects

The understanding of technical objects as stable and unproblematic tools, merely as taken-for-granted instruments, might become questionable in the context of the technical transformation of creative settings. When conceptualizing the technical equipment in which practices are embedded simply as a means to an end, the productivity of their specific mediality is underestimated. The materiality and structure of technical media always create a deficit as well as a surplus of meaning and expressive qualities that are beyond the explicit control of the user [14].

In a similar notion, Don Ihde turns the attention in his philosophical analysis of technology not only to common aspects of amplification and enhancement but also to their potential in reducing spaces of perception [15]. As he puts it, "for every revealing transformation there is a simultaneously concealing transformation of the world, which is given through a technological mediation. Technologies transform experience, however subtly, and that is one root of their non-neutrality" [15, p.49]. Referring to optical technologies like the microscope and telescope, Ihde highlights the transformation of perceptions through technological instrumentation: As a such instruments reveal previously unknown phenomena with magnification, bringing them closer and focally into the center of vision, the instruments simultaneously reduce an observer's sense of depth and the size and location of the objects in their context [15, p.50]. The technological mediation is transforming the very sense of bodily and world space as it were, diminishing the foreground in magnifying what lies in the background of perception.

Comparable to Ihde, Albert Borgmann argues in his philosophy of technology against supposedly dominating promises of liberation and enrichment concerning modern technologies [16]. Beyond perceptual transformations, Borgmann focuses on the displacement of practices and social dimensions connected to technological progress. Referring to Martin Heidegger, he develops the distinction between "things" and "devices" in his analysis. According to him, "things" are traditional technological configurations that constitute complex practices around themselves. They are highly contextual, unfold focusing and centering qualities, thus serve as orienting experiences that demand manifold bodily and social engagement [16, p.41]. As they incorporate means and ends inseparably, they convey a sense of depth and integrity [17, p.210]. Modern technologies seek to subvert these focal practices and reconstitute "things" as "devices." This way, they reduce the complex qualities of the original "thing" that they have achieved in replacing with a mere commodity, narrowed to a limited purpose. Transformed in an instantaneous, available, safe, and easy technology [16, p.41], they are detached from a definite context, exhibiting a distinction of means and ends [16, p.43]. Their commodious character renders "devices" as being less demanding, less engaging, shallow experiences [17, p.206]. Borgmann exemplifies this "device paradigm" with the central heating plant, which technologically has transformed the fireplace into a device to merely provide warmth as a commodity, and as such the social and cultural dimensions of the practices of work, skill, knowledge, and sociality surrounding the traditional stove are diminished [16, p.42].

Although debatable in their implications, the two techno-critical standpoints outlined above serve to broaden the perspective on technical objects and question a notion of them as unproblematic tools. Drawing from Ihde and Borgmann in the context of creative practices, the question can be raised: How does the technical transformation of tools involved in designing also alter the space for expression and the very condition for creativity? Similar to the argument for optical technologies, it can be argued that the use of information technology and communication media influences the relationship between sense and skill and conceptions of time and space. As Ihde also points out, technical instrumentation has transformed and is transforming the contexts within which disciplines produce knowledge or artifacts and are understood, be it science or artistic and designerly practices [15, p.187], as they settle new spaces of experience or objectifications of sense. By enabling distinct modes of creation and framing specific production aesthetics in design, the technical ensembles might become problematic regarding their productive agency. Put differently, the qualities and intricate structure of knowledge-intensive creative practices might reflect the modalities of the tools and equipment that assist in composing design work. These questions gain relevance especially in contemporary design culture, where a majority of activity in practice is mediated by digital technologies – from research, inspiration, and visualization to creation, generation, and production. The intensity and dynamic of these interactions makes up the ambiguity of technical objects that, we argue, needs to be refined to further comprehend creative practices.

4   An Updated Notion of "The Technical"

Thinking about technical conditions in contemporary design practices more specifically beyond the realms of philosophy of technology could address not only but at least two levels of consideration. On the one hand, the instrumental notion of the tool needs to be expanded in order to grasp the processual dimension of technical activity embedded in a complex and distributed configuration. On the other hand, in a movement connected to that but facing the opposite direction, particular modalities and structures within specific technical elements and the effects arising from them need to be considered.

Technology has long been conceptualized in an exteriority or an organic extension of its user in a relationship described in categories of purposefulness, utility, and instrumentality [18,19]. In terms of the history of ideas, it was mainly conceived in a manner of distinction or opposition, be it from nature, culture, or society [19]. The development of the technological condition of today, namely an expansive media-technological pervasion, has provoked a theoretical sensibility for the trans-instrumental, non-intentional, distributed, and processual characters of human-machine-relations. Already the ancient notion of *the technical* or *techné* comprised an ensemble of things, actors, and activities in which technical actions are embedded and constituted [20]. It could articulate technical activity in a processual manner, implicating a form of social activity [19, p.42]. That notion has been updated and elaborated in the last decades not only but most prominently at the hands of the Actor

Network Theory, which posits an ontological symmetry of human and non-human actors [19, p.40]. That way, technical activity in contemporary technological conditions became graspable in terms of situated hybrids of human-machine interactions and agency – the capacity for action – as temporally emergent phenomena, distributed across a social and material field of actants. Tools in that sense expand far beyond a particular material instrument that can be conceptualized as a single object outside of and opposite to its user. The boundaries of the conception of a tool become rather ambiguous, incorporating a mesh of practices that exhibit operative behavior. Technical activity then is the effect of a movement along the human-machine-boundary, between objectification and subjectification, where technologies can become actors in the same way as human practices can become methods or commodities [21]. Along these lines, while the inseparable and mutually constituting human-machine relationships must be recognized, particular accountabilites [21] or degrees of distribution [19] of agency can be located nevertheless. This understanding of a Heideggerian "equipmental whole" [20] in the context of design practices is more interested in the processual and emergent dimension and relationships of dependence of the technical embeddedness than its instrumental character. It is apt to make graspable, how the economy of associations, aesthetic negotiations, and creative agency is distributed throughout production environments and could be mapped out and rendered visible. *The technical* then encompasses the interplay of embodied as well as externalized, mediated, communicative, and social qualities that constitute the activity of designing.

At the same time, complex apparatuses like computational tools can themselves be viewed as assemblages of different concepts, functions, and structures. This way, approaching the transformation of creative settings on the level of specific technological manifestations and unfolding their particular characteristics can be a strategy to gain understanding of design under technical conditions. Both Matthew Fuller with his "software criticism" [22] and Lev Manovich in his attempt to establish a "software studies" [23] argue for an "unfolding of particularities" [22] in the workings of digital media tools in order to understand their involvement in transforming aesthetic cultures or shaping conceptual models of creative practices. In analyzing common media content production software in terms of interface metaphors, the working of commands, and surrounding workflows, Manovich tries to reveal how they invoke critical displacements on all kinds of levels [24,23]. Instancing digital video compositing software, he points out how certain software paradigms enabled the emergence of new visual languages and logics of form. Foremost, the integration of traditionally separated media forms in digital software lead to new media hybrids that exhibit deep remixability. Pre-digital media operations that are now rendered with computer software change in their inner logic and functioning as they get digitally augmented and parameterized. Conceptual metaphors provided by these tools like layers, transparency, and compositing tend to change the designer's or artist's understanding of what a moving image is, how to think about it and how to design it. He underlines that in mentioning how the idea of animated form enters architectural thinking via concepts established in video compositing software, which finally results in computational and generative aesthetics in architecture that differ from traditional designing based on spatial typologies, for instance. Due to the widespread availability of and the unification of media forms by software, Manovich argues furthermore that professional boundaries between different fields of design have become less important. In considering software tools from the bottom up, looking at particular interface elements and functions, an approach like Manovich's tries to expose the traces of technicality to be found in mental models of designers, everyday workflow structures up to media cultures and aesthetic languages within a field of practice.

Both levels of consideration outlined above are complementary or transitional and lie on a spectrum of possible entry points into an understanding of the technicality of a practice like that of design. Specific materialities, constraints and possibilities of particular (digital) tools afford skillful or instrumental, non-intentional, automatized or routinized, messy or improvisational engagements which entangle intricate ways of socio-material relations and activities, mobilize and coordinate forms of knowledge, communications or imaginations, which also applies the other way around for each of these.

5   Design as a Technical Activity

Some of the implications of transferring the outlined positions from philosophy, sociology, and the aesthetics of technology to design practices were already implied and need to be elaborated in the future. In conclusion, we want to put forth possible interpretations concerning the aspect of creativity in computationally transformed creative settings.

The cultivation of creativity is a central concern of design practices, which seek to facilitate contextual innovation in a more or less systematic or methodological manner. Facilitating creativity has long been connected to efforts of systematization and cognitive techniques [3]. In contemporary technology-saturated work contexts, creativity, artistic expressiveness, and virtuosity are for great parts realized within software environments. With Ihde and Borgmann the techno-logical effects of amplification and reduction came into view. The technologization of processes and their specific mediality opens up spaces for expression and innovation, while diminishing others at the same time. An ambivalence regarding technicality in designing arises from the efforts to technologically implement and translate qualities like creative intention, skills, and practical knowing that might be all at once hard to systematize and to articulate. From the perspective of Manovich, the design of the computational tools involved becomes problematic as it can effect crucial aspects of practice and workflow – from the conceptual models of media and content that are established to the amount of structure imposed on the work or process, the kinds and qualities of representations, the levels of abstraction necessary, the kinds of manipulations implemented to the openness, and extensibility of the tool [25]. In a wider context of distributed agency, it can be asked then: How is the accountability for creativity, aesthetic judgments and design decisions socio-materially negotiated and coordinated and spread across the *equipmental whole*. The advances in generative and parameterized design, for instance, could be seen as forms of co-creation and -authoring with algorithms that enable and demand the designer to react to the logic of forms and aesthetics rendered by the computational tools in changing degrees.

Furthermore, the specific materialities of computing have also become a place for design exploration itself. Fields like interaction design and new media design explicitly investigate the idiosyncratic expressive potentials of computational media and the interface between humans and computers. Systemic properties like interactivity, generativity, computational complexity, networked behavior, and emergence become categories for designing and get part of the palette of expressive materials to work with. These computational possibilities also seem to open up the design space for practitioners for whom coding and programming techniques are ever more often becoming part of their technical and conceptual repertoire.

6   Conclusions

While several fields of designerly as well as artistic practice have been analyzed quite intensively in the context of epistemology and new knowledge production introduced in recent years, in this paper we wanted to shift the focus to their technical condition of possibility. We put forth some promising reflections in order to look at contemporary practices in design from the perspective of their technicality. According to our view, the technical instruments themselves still remain somewhat marginalized in the analysis of creative practices, especially considering digital media tools.

With the notions presented here, we wanted to propose some of the possible coordinates for a refinement in the analysis of contemporary design practices with an emphasis on its technical conditions. Further research is needed to better understand the ways in which tools are structuring and mediating creative practices. This could lead to insights not only into the nature of contemporary design activities but also enhancements in knowledge for designing digital tools that support creative work. Furthermore, considering a pervasiveness of practices of programming in fields like digital media design and interaction design, the adoption of coding practices and the interference with technical paradigms from realms outside design need further exploration. As technologies tend to withdraw, to be perceived as *ready-to-hand* tools and embedded in other qualities of practices, specific modes of researching their interactions and transformations require elaboration as well. To make creative practices like designing more comprehensible, the complex interplay of actors within technical ensembles as well as material and knowledge practices needs to be uncovered further. This aims at strengthening a position of research that approaches design practices as an intricate interplay of knowledge, technologies, and actions.

References

1. Yaneva, A.: The making of a building: a pragmatist approach to architecture. Peter Lang, Oxford (2009)
2. Ammon, S., Froschauer, E.M. (eds.): Wissenschaft entwerfen: vom forschenden Entwerfen zur Entwurfsforschung der Architektur. Fink, München (2013)

3. Mareis, C.: Design als Wissenskultur: Interferenzen zwischen Design- und Wissensdiskursen seit 1960. Transcript, Bielefeld (2011)
4. Gethmann, D., Hauser, S. (eds.): Kulturtechnik Entwerfen: Praktiken, Konzepte und Medien in Architektur und Design Science. Transcript, Bielefeld (2009)
5. Wendler, R.: Das Modell zwischen Kunst und Wissenschaft. Fink, München (2013)
6. Latour, B.: Drawing Things Together. In: Lynch, M., Woolgar, S. (eds.) Representation in Scientific Practice, pp. 19–68. MIT Press, Cambridge (1990)
7. Wittmann, B.: Papierprojekte. Die Zeichnung als Instrument des Entwurfs. Z. Für Medien. Kult. 2012, pp. 123–138 (2012).
8. Latour, B.: A Cautious Prometheus? A Few Steps Toward a Philosophy of Design (With Special Attention to Peter Sloterdijk). In: Hackne, F., Glynne, J., Minton, V. (eds.) Proceedings of the 2008 Annual International Conference of the Design History Society, pp. 2–10. Universal Publishers, Falmouth (2009)
9. Ehn, P.: Participation in design things. In: Proceedings of the Tenth Anniversary Conference on Participatory Design, pp. 92–101. Indiana University, Indianapolis (2008)
10. Rheinberger, H.-J.: Toward a history of epistemic things: synthesizing proteins in the test tube. Stanford University Press, Stanford (1997)
11. Ewenstein, B., Whyte, J.: Knowledge Practices in Design: The Role of Visual Representations as 'Epistemic Objects'. Organ. Stud. 30, 7–30 (2009)
12. Star, S.L.: The structure of ill-structured solutions: boundary objects and heterogeneous distributed problem solving. In: Gasser, L.G., Huhns, M.N. (eds.) Distributed Artificial Intelligence, vol. 2. Pitman, London (1989)
13. Star, S.L., Griesemer, J.R.: Institutional Ecology, 'Translations' and Boundary Objects: Amateurs and Professionals in Berkeley's Museum of Vertebrate Zoology, 1907-39. Soc. Stud. Sci. 19, 387–420 (1989)
14. Krämer, S.: Das Medium als Spur und als Apparat. In: Krämer, S. (ed.) Medien, Computer, Realität. Wirklichkeitsvorstellungen und Neue Medien, pp. 73–94. Suhrkamp, Frankfurt am Main (1998)
15. Ihde, D.: Technology and the lifeworld: from garden to earth. Indiana University Press, Bloomington (1990)
16. Borgmann, A.: Technology and the character of contemporary life: a philosophical inquiry. University of Chicago Press, Chicago (1987)
17. Borgmann, A.: Focal Things and Practices. In: Dreyfus, H.L., Wrathall, M.A. (eds.) Heidegger Reexamined, pp. 194–210. Routledge, New York (2002)
18. Hörl, E. (ed.): Die technologische Bedingung: Beiträge zur Beschreibung der technischen Welt. Suhrkamp, Berlin (2011)
19. Rammert, W.: Technik – Handeln – Wissen: zu einer pragmatistischen Technik- und Sozialtheorie. VS Verlag für Sozialwissenschaften, Wiesbaden (2007)
20. Uhlig, F.: Robinsons Pflug. Werkzeuge zwischen Nachbau und Erfindung. In: Schmitz, T.H., Grohninger, H. (eds.) Werkzeug-Denkzeug: manuelle Intelligenz und Transmedialität kreativer Prozesse, pp. 165–190. Transcript, Bielefeld (2012)
21. Suchman, L.A.: Human-machine reconfigurations: plans and situated actions. Cambridge University Press, Cambridge (2007)
22. Fuller, M.: Behind the blip: Software as culture. Nettime Mail. List. 7 (2002)
23. Manovich, L.: Software takes command: extending the language of new media. Bloomsbury, New York (2013)
24. Manovich, L.: Inside Photoshop. Comput. Cult. 1 (2011)
25. National Research Council (U.S.): Beyond productivity: information technology, innovation, and creativity. National Academies Press, Washington, DC (2003)

Developing UX for Collaborative Mobile Prototyping

Isabella Hastreiter, Sascha Krause, Tim Schneidermeier, and Christian Wolff

Media Informatics Group, University of Regensburg
{Tim.Schneidermeier,Christian.Wolff}@ur.de,
{Sascha.Krause,Isabella.Hastreiter}@stud.uni-regensburg.de

Abstract. Prototyping is an essential part of the user-centered design process (UCD). Since the emergence of touch-based mobile devices in recent years, a broad range of efforts has been taken to adapt professional prototyping tools to the mobile context. However, none of the existing mobile prototyping solutions adapts sufficiently to the needs of multidisciplinary teams or considers the experience of the users' working environments explicitly. Our goal was to develop a mobile prototyping tool that supports the users in their tasks with special attention to the context of use. We especially considered the holistic experience relating all tasks of the human-centered design process. Our approach of requirements engineering focused on UX methods to get a deep insight not only on pragmatic features but also emotional demands (i.e. hedonic qualities). Therefore we tried to strengthen the hedonic qualities to support action mode usage for leveraging creative potentials. We'd like to reveal whether and to what extent a detailed look on UX can ensure the working progress efficiency and motivation of a multidisciplinary software engineering team practicing agile methods. We will illustrate this by presenting the development process of our mobile prototyping tool *Prime*, especially concerning new perspectives of a design process that focuses on hedonic parameters.

Keywords: user experience, user centered design, prototyping tools, mobile applications, hedonic quality, joy of use, holistic experience.

1 Introduction

The focus of software design has increasingly shifted towards human factors in the last decades [15]. Usability covers a great deal of human needs in a working environment such as efficiency of the system, effectiveness in the work process and satisfaction of the user [18]. Nevertheless, there is software which is perfectly designed for these requirements and still isn't attractive for a broader audience. This might be due to the fact that user experience aspects are not sufficiently assessed during design. This is why we tried to focus on UX while developing a mobile prototyping application for the human centered design process.

The organization of the rest of this paper is as follows: In Ch. 2 we introduce the human-centered design process and discuss the role of prototyping within that process. Ch. 3 focusses on the UX methods that can be used during the design process

A. Marcus (Ed.): DUXU 2014, Part I, LNCS 8517, pp. 104–114, 2014.

for mobile applications. Finally, in Ch. 4 we present Prime, a tablet-based prototyping tool for mobile applications. A short outlook concludes the paper.

2   The Human Centered Design Process and User Experience (UX)

The Human Centered Design Process, as defined in ISO 9241 210 [13], based on the key principles of "the active involvement of the prospective user and clear understanding of user and task requirements", "an appropriate allocation of function between user and system", "iteration of design solutions" and "multi-disciplinary design teams" [19] has become a valuable approach for putting the user in the focus of the software development process and focusing on his real needs.

The requirements engineering process not only consists of the identification of features providing benefits to the user and her task in context, but in the explicit interface providing the functionality. Ensuring the usability of the product during the development is key to utility of the product and ultimately its market success. In order to develop an adequate design solution for a given problem there are different approaches to software evaluation. Besides Usability, which is already a very common part of the process, UX is the approach to understand which values are important for the users. Consequently the main task of studies in User Experience (UX) should focus on answering this question. "A system or device is not just task orientated; it is a signifier of the user's identity, interest, lifestyle and values." is the defined target by Holt and Lock. [11]

2.1   Prototyping

Prototyping is widely accepted as a useful tool in application development since it can be used in various ways and be adapted to multiple issues. From the different approaches to prototyping, from low fidelity sketches describing only functions, screen elements and proportions to high fidelity mockups providing interactivity and basic backend business logic, especially low fidelity techniques like paper prototyping proved to be most helpful for requirements engineering in human centered design development flows [23]. Focusing on early development stages, collecting functional requirements from prospective users is not sufficient to develop adequate design solutions. A detailed understanding of the user's task, context, aims and workflow in which the product will be embedded is essential to adapt the design to his needs. According to human centered design principles of end user involvement it is essential to gather that information from real users from the very beginning of the development process. In this process, the verbalization of design requirements is a very tedious task for the participant, separating the function from its realization. Prototyping proved to be able to facilitate the communication process between the users participating in the requirements engineering process and the development team, building a general language developers and users can relate to [23]. By applying participatory design in combination with a low-fidelity prototyping approach like paper prototyping the user can be empowered to communicate requirements.

In the following, the generated prototypes can serve as a data source regarding mental user models and the context in which the collected features have to be seen. Furthermore the development team can rely on them as a reference of requirements to be met when developing the user interface. As low fidelity prototyping is a very fast and cost-efficient method [22] for generating a wide range of different solutions, it represents a great approach to further developing first sketches from the user's requirements, quickly discusses the results and iterate on them in order to produce adequate design solutions. The variety of ideas can be enhanced by collaboration of not only user interface designers but all members of the development team. This is crucial in the early phases of development because there is never just a single perfect solution for a given problem. It seems that not only the diversity but the quality of the solutions can be positively influenced by collaboration in prototyping [6] which gives evidence that supporting cooperation on prototyping is a necessity.

Getting feedback on the developed solutions from the end users, low fidelity prototypes often fall short of communicating the purpose of the elements depicted. Since the results from rapidly prototyping on a low fidelity are very rough and sketchy in general, it is hard for peer users to identify the depicted elements intuitively [24]. In most cases the participant is not familiar with this technique and user interface design in general, leading to misinterpretations of the given sketches and making it hard to identify interactive elements since the discrepancy between the elements is often not distinct enough to identify their purpose, making a guided walkthrough evaluation techniques necessary. To enable the user to evaluate the developed screens in a more exploratory manner, the visual fidelity of early prototypes could be enhanced to support the recognition and interpretation of UI elements.

2.2   The Mobile Context

Rapidly prototyping mobile applications adds further layers of complexity and problems to the process [24] regarding hardware constraints like display metrics and the paradigm of touch interaction. Smartphone screen sizes make it essential to consider the dimensions of screen elements even in first draft sketches to develop solutions to hide complexity and make it accessible regarding touch target sizes. Paper sketching is by its nature is not capable of providing reasonable constraints needed in order to support adequate solutions. Furthermore the anticipated context of use is far more important regarding mobile applications than the traditional desktop environment because of the ubiquitous nature of mobile devices. Being such an influential factor, recent concepts suggest to shift the prototyping process out of the lab into context of use [25], adapting mobile devices providing a realistic feeling for the prototype as a medium overcoming the restrictions of paper prototypes.

In order to provide a functional solution for mobile prototyping, we had to define our target audience to be able to gather the right requirements. Since the complex process of application development requires a multitude of skills and knowledge, most development teams consist of members with different focuses fulfilling different roles, like usability engineers, programmers and project managers. We decided to take these circumstances into account and focus our project to meet the needs of small development teams practicing agile methods of software development.

2.3   Pleasure as a Factor in UX

Regardless of the mobile context there are generic concepts of UX we integrate in our work. Hassenzahl und Tractinsky [9] argue that there is a lack of empirical studies in the field of UX and therefore create a system combining Usability and UX. They define pragmatic and hedonic aspects and create the AttrakDiff metric, a valid tool to measure those qualities. Beyond the purely cognitive and task oriented view they want to give feedback on the dimensions of the stimulation, identification and attractiveness of UX. Similar classifications can be found in different approaches. Jordan [14] established a basic classification of four different pleasures: The socio-, physio-, psycho- and ideo-sphere describe the impact of social factors, sensory perception, cognitive challenges and ideological values. Lock & Holt [11] are polishing those spheres in drawing more specific conclusions for designing a system. In a hierarchical analysis they define the details of pleasure as "(...) a positive emotional state experienced when needs or desires are fulfilled, either from external or internal stimuli" [11]. The assessment criteria they provide are more specific than the top level illustration of Jordan.

Based on this model we try to identify special needs for a mobile prototyping tool by considering them in our methodological structure. Through Laddering [28] it should be possible to understand which of those components is most important to our tool and how we can gain functions for our tool.

3   UX Methods during the Mobile App Developing Process

We want to show in which areas of use mobile prototyping can be supported by a tablet-based tool. Due to the related work we assume that in situ might be a valuable support. During our developing process we concentrated especially on how to optimize the UX. Therefore we combined different methods and discuss the output of our experiences.

Since the emergence of tablet devices, great effort has been taken to leverage their potential not only for entertainment purposes but for professional use as well. In the context of user interface development several companies have tried to adapt sketching and prototyping tools for mobile application platforms, mostly iOS and Android. In the context of our project we decided to evaluate those existing solutions by a competitive analysis. We identified the features those products implemented to provide a mobile prototyping solution for professional use to get additional insight about the requirements.

We found a broad range concerning the fidelity of the prototypes produced by the existing tools, from low-fidelity, sketchy style to fully functional click trough products. Regarding the functionality, the main focus of the existing solutions seems to provide a rich palette of UI elements and stencils which can be manipulated by the user in their size, visual appearance and content. Because of the sheer number of available objects, most of the tools struggled with the interface and information architecture to provide access to them.

In addition we performed an expert evaluation of the usability of the products, using Nielsen's "Ten usability heuristics for user interface design" [20], which is a solid framework providing guidelines to evaluate user interfaces independent from the platform of the application to evaluate. The evaluation was performed based on simple tasks in a mobile situation to simulate a real working scenario as closely as possible. We discovered that most remarkably the tools implementing a high fidelity approach became very complex to use when the prototype was supposed to make use of the available interactive elements. This observation corresponded with the fear of the participants of the focus group regarding the generation of high fidelity prototypes in a mobile scenario.

We have applied a range of UX methods, starting with SHIRA [10], a qualitative analysis in which the peer user is included to get a deeper understanding of his needs by associating adjectives and justifying his or her choice. 'Structured Hierarchical Interview for Requirement Analysis' (SHIRA) is an interviewing technique that seeks to explore the meaning of abstract product qualities such as 'controllable', 'simple', 'impressive' or 'innovative' for a specific software product in a specific context of use [10]. The test persons were asked to choose three out of a list of pragmatic and hedonic issues. After a brief description of how our tool works we asked four people with usability engineering background to choose three adjectives with the highest importance to them. After selecting one of the attributes they were asked to explain explicitly what features could support this adjective in the prototyping tool. All four users chose the value clearly structured, which according to them could be achieved when using breadcrumbs, designing infoboxes, using view buttons and showing the most important information. Each of the following adjectives was chosen twice. As simple functions a wizard for unused functions and an intuitive connection between the different layers were mentioned. Creative could be achieved through a broader color selection and a broader variety of forms available. As practical the test persons described functions like easy export and a rapid assembling of a prototype. The words the participants selected were mainly out of the pragmatic field, except for the adjective creative. But even the detailed description of this attribute only leads to pragmatic and functional conclusions. In relation to our goal, to get impact on the UX, this is not very satisfying. We have therefore decided to undertake further UX considerations regarding our own tool.

In the next step we applied the AttrakDiff. This is a semantic differential developed by Marc Hassenzahl et al. [8]. The tool has been available free of charge since 2002 on www.attrakdiff.de. Up to 2007 it has been used by 302 groups in research and economic projects [7]. It can be applied to the user centered design cycle when functional software or prototypes are already available to be tested. Based on the competitive analysis we decided to evaluate the AppCooker (http://www.appcooker.com/), our competing reference product with good results in usability tests and a great variety of features, with the AttrakDiff to gain a better understanding of the user's expectation on a mobile prototyping tool. AttrakDiff is based on the understanding of pragmatic and hedonic qualities [1]. We asked 15 participants to undergo our usability setting where they were asked to fulfill a task based usability test and follow up completing the AttrakDiff. None of the participants was familiar with the tool and therefore they were not biased.

In the evaluation of confidence the product is on a scale between neutral and self oriented and therefore has neutral to positive values in the pragmatic as well as in the hedonic field and potential to optimize. Since our special interest was to find out which attributes makes the tool more eventful the question remains which steps to perform to do so. Nevertheless this assessment initially showed us how the basic functions of those tools can be classified.

A special concern lies in understanding how a multidisciplinary group of software engineers work together on a user centered design process in their daily routine and in which way our tool can support their realities. Subsequently, we combined the methods of a focus group with SHIRA and explicitly drew the attention to hedonic values. We invited small worlds, which is a consulting team in questions on usability engineering. They are already working with prototyping in their engineering cycle and therefore where an ideal group for our interest. The focus group consists of four members: A programmer, a project manager and two usability engineers. Since we are missing out on hedonic qualities in our former data collection, we decided to let every participant choose one adjective which we analyzed carefully and combined the method with a usual focus group, in which the participants are discussing a variety of issues the moderators stimulate them to [17]. The outcome of this combination of methods was convincing: In the first phase the participants introduced themselves and the specific tasks they fulfill in the engineering team. They also gave insight on the others they are working with and their collaboration. The second part treated the mobile context. The participants started to explain when and in which context they need to prototype. During the third part every participant took one attribute from the SHIRA pool. The positive effect in this respect was that every subscriber was presenting his choice in front of the group and therefore many different ideas were generated. Due to the process they had to justify their choice towards the others and because of that the descriptions were very specific.

Table 1. Valuable features identified by the focus group

Function	Description
Inserting camera pictures	Very empowering during the creative process of generating ideas.
non proprietary Export	To support interactive prototyping the export must be better.
Preview	Create a Preview version which can be annotated by the other team members.
Push Notification	To ensure a smooth operation the team must be informed by the system, when changes were made.
Sharing	To support collaborative Working there need to be sharing possibilities inside the tools
Frames	To make the prototypes more realistic a variation of frames should be included
Heuristic Feedback	Automatized evaluation tool which is oriented on the Golden Rules of usability experts. Instant feedback.

Finally we matched the results with the layers of Jordan [11] and focused our further design on the socio layer to create a collaborative mobile prototyping tool. Our requirements engineering process provided detailed insights in the demands of a multidisciplinary development team, practicing agile methods. As mentioned the existing solutions don't meet the requirements specified by our peer users yet. In particular features targeting the socio layer of the prototyping process and its inherent collaborative nature were not implemented. As our participants noted supporting team collaboration independent from the actual location of the individual team member could greatly enhance the productivity and the social experience of a mobile prototyping solution. This becomes even more important since the everyday working situation of an individual team member is not necessarily related to a fixed work station. The complexity of a mobile prototyping solution should be stripped down as much as possible. That incorporates not only the reduction of available ready to use user interface stencils to a minimum but also the reduction of the fidelity of the prototypes, which the tool should be capable of. As emphasized by the participants, the creation of complex interactive high fidelity prototypes in a mobile work setting is not practical. The number of steps required for their generation and the functions needed is too complex to handle when distracted by environmental factors. The purpose of a mobile prototyping solution is perceived as a digital sketching tool for rapid generation of concepts and quick iterating upon them. The participants experienced in the application of prototyping methods to the development process emphasized particularly the potential of a mobile prototyping tool for a collaborative approach and a simplified in-team communication, independent from the actual physical location of the participating individuals. This is especially important, because successful cooperation is generally based on geographical proximity. Existing mobile solutions are not supporting collaboration, which was emphasized as an essential part of the development process. This could be an explanation for the lacking adoption of these tools in a professional context.

A mobile prototyping tool could enable the development team to generate ideas and iterate on results independently from another but still stay in touch with the rest of the team and their results. All team members should be automatically informed when new results are generated by a participant. The resulting workflow can speed up the development process significantly and provide an adequate solution for the prototyping of mobile applications. We therefore identified the socio sphere as the most potential target for further optimization of our base product, and to evaluate whether supporting the social perception of our product could enhance overall product experience. Furthermore a mobile device based prototyping tool is seen as a sensible approach to take mobile context specific considerations into account at early development stage. Making use of a mobile device as an all-in-one solution for prototyping makes it very comfortable to prototype in the future context of use and adapt the application in development to the circumstances.

4   Prime, a Simple Prototyping Tool for Android Tablets

Our product, a simple prototyping tool for android 10" tablets resulting from another project already incorporates the basic functionality for mobile prototyping enabling the user to sketch mobile applications with a set of basic, customizable objects. The interface consists of a drawing area the size of the Nexus 4, the android reference phone from google, and an objects palette from where the user can simply drag and drop objects onto the canvas where they can be directly manipulated to fit the users' needs. The tool realizes a mixed fidelity approach using basic android user interface elements like buttons, lists, grids, input elements etc. and the hardware camera to incorporate sketches and drawings into the prototype. The hedonic dimension of prototyping has not yet been targeted in the existing concept thus making it an ideal candidate for further optimization.

According to the results of our focus group, the number of objects available doesn't have to be extensive, meaning that every UI element should be available, but provide flexible elements, which can be adapted to model a wide range of interfaces by combination and creative use. As a result, a simple objects palette will help to strip down complexity and meet the requirement of an easy to use minimalistic interface, leveraging creativity and enabling novice users in the context of requirements engineering process to participate.

Regarding the visual fidelity of the interface elements, the participants indicated that realistic appearance can positively influence the hedonic perception of the prototype and support the recognition of elements and associated functions by novice users which also conforms to other findings [24].

Since the results of the SHIRA and focus group suggest that a high fidelity approach is not feasible in a mobile environment, we decided to focus our work on providing low fidelity realization of the prototyping functionality. In other words our tool will not be capable of building interactive click-through prototypes, since the participants mentioned that a mobile sketching tool would simplify their rapid prototyping process in the means of collaborative idea generation to a greater extent and the task of creating real interactive prototypes in a mobile setting would be hard to handle.

Based on the prioritization of the requirements, we identified the socio sphere as most potential to incorporate hedonic values in our base product. The participants stated that a feature supporting the active participation in the prototyping process would not only enhance the utility but also the hedonic perception of the product. In order to enable our product to support a collaborative approach on prototyping we implemented an online backend based on parse.com, a cloud platform providing easy to set up user accounts with different privileges and a database to store arbitrary objects. The cloud platform enables the product to create projects, invite team members and automatically sync user data to other team members as soon as a data connection is available to the device. According to our requirements, team members are not restricted to specific roles and rights, enabling them to engage as equitable partners in the process. To support dynamic formation of teams, or subteams working on a specific feature, each user can participate in an unlimited number of projects and create new projects as required. To keep the sketching process structured each project can contain any number of screens as a concept modelling application screens in the tool to develop. At screen level the actual sketches are presented to the user by separating them in user and team sketches implemented as two vertical scrolling lists on the same app-screen to enable the user to compare them and get inspired by the different solutions presented. To further develop promising ideas, the user can clone existing sketches and perform his amendments to avoid confusion, which would arise when a user edits a sketch made by one of the other team members. To inform members of the availability of a new sketch the product makes use of parse.com to send a push notification to the projects related participants. To support a more efficient discussion and enable the team members to make reference to specific sketches, all screens are labeled with consecutive numbers and can be commented on.

Fig. 1. Snapshot of our prototyping tool PRIME

5   Conclusion

SHIRA and the AttrakDiff alone don't allow any specific customization. This leads to vague orientation and most of the results concentrate on pragmatic factors. In our case only the combination of SHIRA and the focus group in which we were working with laddering brought concrete tasks to develop our tool. Based on the four pleasures of Jordan as a theoretical concept we could draw conclusions with a concept for the implementation. Maybe a broad consulting of methods might already be considered a useful approach for our goal. But during our human centered design process we came to the conclusion that it would be very valuable to have a standalone method set for the hedonic sphere that does not include pragmatic enquiries. Current tools don't fully concentrate on the hedonic aspect. They mostly combine a holistic approach of

Usability and UX. So how can we support a deeper understanding of the user's hedonic values? We think that a stronger focus on the hedonic sphere during the methodological approach is already a good start, but there still is a lack of methods concentrating on UX. Nevertheless the future task of research has to design a method set to emphasizing requirements and to evaluate ideas during the engineering process.

The comments during the usability testing point out that a tool with an innovative and fresh character is given a greater hedonic weight. Prerequisite is the general compliance of proven usability principles and a system oriented on the mental model of the user. In the context of our project we focused on the collaborative experience of the engineering team. The statements during the system requirement analyses suggest that there still is potential for optimization in the ideo and psycho pleasure.

References

1. AttrakDiff, http://attrakdiff.de/index-en.html (retrieved)
2. IHM-HCI 2001: Treizièmes journées sur L'ingénierie de l'Interaction Homme-Machine de l'AFIHM: 13th Annual Conference of "Association Francophone d'Interaction Homme-Machine" (AFIHM): 15th Annual Conference of the Human-Computer Interaction Group of the British Computer Society: Quinzième conference annuelle du group "Human-Computer Interaction" de la "British Computer Society". Cepadues-Editions, Toulouse (2001)
3. CHI 2006 extended abstracts on Human factors in computing systems. ACM, New York (2006)
4. Proceedings of the 11th International Conference on Human-Computer Interaction with Mobile Devices and Services. ACM, New York (2009)
5. Czerwinski, M. (ed.): Proceedings of the Twenty-sixth Annual SIGCHI Conference on Human Factors in Computing Systems. ACM Press, New York (2008)
6. Dow, S., Glassco, A., Kass, J., Schwarz, M., Schwartz, D., Klemmer, S.: Parallel prototyping leads to better design results, more divergence, and increased selfefficacy. ACM 17(4) (2010)
7. Hassenzahl, M., Burmester, M., Koller, F.: Der User Experience (UX) auf der Spur: Zum Einsatz von, http://www.attrakdiff.de, http://attrakdiff.de/files/up08_ux_auf_der_spur.pdf (retrieved)
8. Hassenzahl, M., Burmester, M., Koller, F.: AttrakDiff: Ein Fragebogen zur Messung wahrgenommener hedonischer und pragmatischer Qualität. In: Szwillus, G. (ed.) Interaktion in Bewegung, 1st edn., vol. 2003, pp. 187–196. Teubner, Stuttgart (2003)
9. Hassenzahl, M., Tractinsky, N.: User esperience - a research agenda. Behaviour & Information Technology 25(2), 91–97 (2005), https://ccrma.stanford.edu/sleitman/ UserExperienceAResearchAgenda.pdf (retrived)
10. Hassenzahl, M., Wessler, R., Hamborg, K.-C.: Exploring and understanding product qualitites that users desire. In: IHM-HCI 2001. Treizièmes journées sur L'ingénierie de l'Interaction Homme-Machine de l'AFIHM: 13th Annual Conference of "Association Francophone d'Interaction Homme-Machine" (AFIHM): 15th Annual Conference of the Human-Computer Interaction Group of the British Computer Society: Quinzième Conference annuelle du group "Human-Computer Interaction" de la "British Computer Society". Cepadues-Editions, Toulouse (2001)

11. Holt, J., Lock, S.: Understanding and Deconstructing Pleasure: A Hierarchical Approach. In: Czerwinski, M. (ed.) Proceedings of the Twenty-sixth Annual SIGCHI Conference on Human Factors in Computing Systems, ACM Press, New York (2008), http://www.chi2008.org/altchisystem/submissions/submission_jane66_0.pdf (retrieved)

12. Proceedings: August 19-20, Redondo Beach, California [u.a.]. IEEE Computer Society, Los Alamitos (2004)

13. DIN 9241 210

14. Jordan, P.W.: Designing pleasurable products: An introduction to the new human factors. Taylor & Francis e-Library, London (2003)

15. Karwowski, W.: The Discipline of Human Factors and Ergonomics. In: Salvendy, G. (ed.) Handbook of Human Factors and Ergonomics, 4th edn., pp. 3–33. Wiley, Hoboken (2012)

16. Kinoe, Y., Horikawa, Y.: Eliciting requirements for a new product's user interface design: The customer prototype express. Technical Report TR58-0963 (1991)

17. Kontio, J., Lehtola, L., Bragge, J.: Using the Focus Group Method in Software Engineering: Obtaining Practitioner and User Experiences. In: Proceedings, Redondo Beach, California, August 19-20, pp. 271–280. IEEE Computer Society, Los Alamitos (2004)

18. Lewis, J.R.: Usability Testing. In: Salvendy, G. (ed.) Handbook of Human Factors and Ergonomics, 4th edn., pp. 1267–1305. Wiley, Hoboken (2012)

19. Maguire, M.: Methods to support human-centred design. ACM 55(4), 587–634 (2001)

20. Nielsen, J.: Heuristic evaluation. In: Nielsen, J., Mack, R.L. (eds.) Usability Inspection Methods, Wiley, New York (1994)

21. Nielsen, J., Mack, R.L. (eds.): Usability inspection methods. Wiley, New York (1994)

22. Rettig, M.: Prototyping for tiny fingers. ACM 37(4), 21–27 (1994)

23. Rudd, J., Stern, K., Isensee, S.: Low vs. high-fidelity prototyping debate. ACM 3(1), 76–85 (1996)

24. de Sá, M., Carriço, L.: Low-fi prototyping for mobile devices. In: CHI 2006 Extended Abstracts on Human Factors in Computing Systems, pp. 694–699. ACM, New York (2006), http://dl.acm.org/citation.cfm?doid=1125451.1125592 (retrieved)

25. de Sà, M., Carriço, L.: A mobile tool for in-situ prototyping. In: Proceedings of the 11th International Conference on Human-Computer Interaction with Mobile Devices and Services. ACM, New York (2009), http://doi.acm.org/10.1145/1613858.1613884 (retrieved)

26. Salvendy, G. (ed.): Handbook of human factors and ergonomics, 4th edn. Wiley, Hoboken (2012)

27. Szwillus, G. (ed.): Interaktion in Bewegung (1. Aufl). Teubner, Stuttgart (2003)

28. Vanden Abeele, V., Zaman, B.: Laddering the User Experience!, https://lirias.kuleuven.be/bitstream/123456789/267307/4/laddering (retrieved)

Deconstructivist Design within HCI

Michael Heidt[1], Andreas Bischof[1], and Paul Rosenthal[2]

[1] Chemnitz University of Technology, Research Training Group crossWorlds,
Thüringer Weg 5, Chemnitz 09126, Germany
[2] Chemnitz University of Technology, Visual Computing Group, Straße der Nationen
62, Chemnitz 09111, Germany
{michael.heidt,paul.rosenthal}@informatik.tu-chemnitz.de,
andreas.bischof@phil.tu-chemnitz.de

Abstract. Every HCI artefact reproduces a specific stance towards its
users. Influential within the academic sphere is the notion of a *User-
Centered-Design* process. However, observing actual design practice renders the assumption of the centrality of users problematic. To this end,
the text conducts an exploration of the relationship between discourse
within the fields of HCI and architecture. A special focus are the formal
expressions of *deconstructivism* within architecture and their potential
counterparts within HCI design.

Keywords: deconstruction, interdisciplinarity, cultural informatics,
critical technical practice.

1 Introduction

Centrality of users is one of the most prevalent topoi within HCI design and
theory. It has been stipulated in the form of a standardised user-centered-design
(UCD) process [7] and continues to be an omnipresent point of reference. However, it does not always become clear whose interests get reflected within UCD
processes.

At the same time, HCI is in a process of questioning fundamental assumptions
embodied within its guiding methodological and theoretical artefacts [12]. By doing this, it responds to a perceived rise in significance attributed to its products.
Interactive artefacts continue to permeate social reality. Consequently, the field
of HCI has to produce new conceptualisations and theories trying to account
for its new responsibilities. At the same time, theorists outside the discipline
of HCI call for development of new intellectual agendas and stances towards
what is perceived as new qualities of this technological permeation of social processes. In this situation, rethinking strategies embodied within HCI practices
and intellectual positions is equipped with a new level of urgency.

We seek to contribute to the discussion process outlined by exploring potential
links between architecture and HCI. Specifically, we will discuss possible implications of applying ideas adopted from *deconstructivism* within architecture.

A. Marcus (Ed.): DUXU 2014, Part I, LNCS 8517, pp. 115–122, 2014.

2   HCI Self-images

The discussion will commence by questioning the position of users and humans within the fields of HCI and architecture. This is is done in order to provide conceptual distinctions able to designate possible differences and translations between the two fields.

2.1   Humanness

Following its self-descriptions, The Human stands at the center of HCI. After all it gave the discipline its name. Since its inception, the discipline has dealt with questions of the relationships between technological systems and its social other. Initially conceptualised as a cognitive subsystem of sign-manipulating organisational structures, the roles of humans within HCI have diversified over time. Apart from resources, as socio-organic means of production, they have come to be more frequently seen as consumers or as discriminating vendors of their own skills and resources. HCI techniques have since adopted stances of user-friendlyness. Not only the effiency of an organisational system is to be optimised, but products are to be produced that need to stand the test of consumer-scrutiny. HCI now lives in a world, where potential users could say no. At the same time, the organisations conducting HCI have changed in a less radical manner. While it is no longer a single organisation, trying to integrate human operators as processors, users still can be understood as being part of a system. Even if they are consumers, structures creating consumer needs and those that satisfy these can be construed as crucial, sidestepping the figure of autonomous users.

If one accepts that a paradigm change has taken place within HCI, one has to ask how the relationship of humans and computers had to be conceptualised in the past. HCI did evolve in settings of administration and office work, not at sites one would be tempted to identify with 'humanness' as such. Only now has technology become ubiquitous enough that it is perceived as an integral part of virtually every aspect of life. Mobile devices seem to be our most loyal companions, we touch them more often than our lovers or life-partners.

2.2   Centrality

As pointed out, HCI discourse organises itself according to a principle of *centrality*. Interestingly, the problem of periphery seldom is put under conceptual scrutiny within the HCI community. The topos of user-centrality is employed in order to distance oneself from positions articulated within the period of classical HCI [12]. Within classical HCI, what appeared to be central were matters of information processing. It thus marked an instance of 'technical talk'.

The encountered gesture is ubiquitous within HCI: Technical problems are not central *anymore*. Does this really designate the main problem, a focus on technology? Or does the perceived ubiquity of technical talk mask yet another underlying dynamic, resisting designation within HCI communities? If deconstruction had anything to contribute might it be not merely questioning centrality of users but also that of technology?

3 Architecture

3.1 History

The history of computer-science already covers discussions of deconstructive architecture. In their famous debate [4] architects Christopher Alexander and Peter Eisenman discuss the position of deconstruction and formality. Alexander has been extremely influential for design in computer-science both in respect to his early work on mathematically principled form finding [1] as well as with respect to his later writings on patterns [2]. The latter have inspired the design pattern movement within software engineering.

In the aforementioned debate, Eisenman puts forward the view of a building as a formal text. Notions of formality continued and continue to pervade his work, generating interest from researchers within the formal sciences. Our discussion will adopt the conceptual lens of *complexity* in order to provide a perspective allowing for translations into the language of informatics.

3.2 Complexity

Ostwald and Vaughan [10] employ the concept of *complexity* in order to inquire into the nature of Eisenman's early buildings. His series of Houses I-VI can be

Fig. 1. Eisenman's House VI. *Photographic work by Pedro Xing. Image in Public Domain, licensed CC0 1.0.*

read as effort to produce what he called "pure form" (House VI is shown in figure 1). Eisenman strived to create *non-representational* architecture, structures that cannot be read as function of functionality or context. This is in contrast with systems perspectives, which emphasise the interplay of entities (diagrammatically expressed in figure 2). According to the authors, Eisenman's proclaimed intention of invariant complexity indeed is met. Materialised within the building is no dialogue between system and environment but an instance of what Eisenman calls 'pure form'. They can be read as purely formal entities.

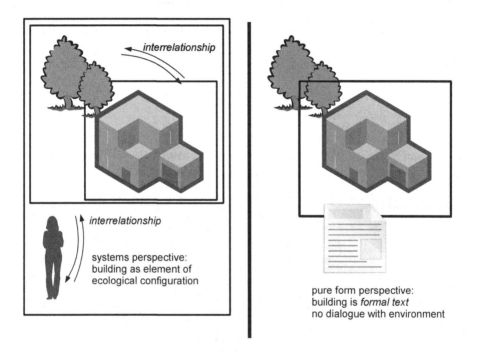

Fig. 2. Building as system-component and as formal text

3.3   Alienation

This is in line with a conception of pure technicality: Technical discussions, as Andrew Feenberg points out [5], have a tendency to suppress the context of technological artefacts. Consequently, decontextualisation has been read into the essence of technology. Theory in this respect points towards technology as an alienating aspect of modern life.

Alienation is usually seen as a problem, a worrying feature of modern lifestyles and technological objects occuring in them. Eisenman on the other hand seems to embrace alienation. Formality and decontextualisation are celebrated. His deconstructivist architecture can thus be viewed as continuation of tendencies within modernist architecture. These however emphasised the importance of *function*.

Deconstructivist making no longer creates forms that bring about certain functions. Form is seen as independent structure, worth making and reading for its own sake. The design aspect of making thus seems to have been relegated to a secondary position. The made product no longer serves innocent purposes, it tries to resist its usefulness. Eisenman thus anticipates characteristics of electronic products: In an environment where the product does not meet positive needs, it can situate itself as an autonomous entity.

3.4   Inhumanness

Indeed, the topic of inhuman practice is not altogether alien to HCI literature. Dunne provides an account of (In)Human Factors [3]. He thereby criticises notions of design aimed at production of market-oriented forms. His discussion is aimed at thinking an alternative to conceptions of optimalisations of form.

4   Deconstructivist HCI

During our discussion of the architecture-deconstructivism problemset, two subjects have kept resurfacing, *centrality* and *alienation*. This section will interpret these subjects as challenges and discuss how they might be addressed designerly, in a strategic manner.

4.1   Decentralisation

Would not decentralisation be a suitable architectural reply to the challenge of user-centeredness? How could it be translated into the language of HCI?

Within the field of IT architecture, distributed systems are a well established field of study. Distributed Systems researchers analyse and build architectures that are dispersed in space and heterogeneous in their construction. This heterogeneity is exhibited both on a technical as well as on an institutional level. In fact, some authors argue that it is indeed administrative complexity that dominates contemporary distributed architectures and thus constitutes the most pressing research challenges. Following these developments, there is a growing body of literature, discussing human-factors in distributed systems [11].

User-experience however is an entity which cannot be directly controlled by means of system design. Distributed architecture does not create a more distributed or decentred experience for users. Indeed on a physiological level, the user as physio-biological entity is a highly distributed system herself. Information processing, immuno-endocrine processes all happen concurrently, while the nervous system exhibits a massive degree of parallelisation.

While the distributed nature of technical internet architecture might not immediately prove to be consequential, social implications prove to be more variegated. Not only does society consist of a heterogeneous array of sites, individuals, institutions, practices. Processes of interaction exhibit a distributed dynamic. If one accepts *attribution* as a constitutive feature of interaction-dynamics, there are no non-distributed processes. Every entity always is decentered, what it is depends on what others attribute to it.

Keeping this in mind, we have to state, that HCI entities *always already are distributed*.

We revisit the question whether the distributed nature of media creates an awareness of distribution or decenteredness. Is not the opposite true, does not the distributed, ubiquitous nature of contemporary device ecologies contribute to an individualisation of users? They might send messages to technical systems dispersed around the globe. Their communications however appear to be centered more reflexively onto their own person than ever before.

How can these insights be employed in order to create elements on the level of experience relating to distribution? Necessarily such a practice would produce an element of disorientation. This however in itself is insufficient to evoke a sense of distribution or decenteredness.

4.2   Deconstructivist HCI Strategies

Has the shift from signal processing to user-centredness to be rethought? Has the 'cultural turn' inside HCI been masking what goes on below the surface logic of postmodern consumer practice?

It would do tremendous injustice to the devices of deconstruction to conclude with a definite answer. It might be tempting to do so, thereby supplying an element of irony. This however, might still prove to be an empty gesture, a mere formal joke, a reflexive manouever limited to the text itself without reference or effect.

We will try to provide a more conventional explanation of Deconstructive HCI (DHCI). Following engineering practices, the text will employ the pedagogical device of bullet-points:

- DHCI could enrich users' experience by alienating them.
- DHCI might allow them to experience alienation collectively.
- Theorists that posit alienation as a defining feature of contempoary society might be tempted to construe this process as an emancipatory one.
- Hereby a transition to positions of enlightenment philosophies becomes possible.

Within this conceptual frame, creation of alienation would not be seen as a problem. It is detrimental to the user-experience in so far, as users would feel 'worse'. If this feeling becomes shared, it could break an isolation felt before.

Deconstructivist HCI is distinct from bad design. While the latter is ubiquitous, both in theory as well as in practice, it does not produce any interesting effects.

It thus adopts a perspective similar to that covered with respect to deconstructivist architecture. The interactive artefact is substituted for the building constructed (as diagrammatically explained by virtue of figure 3).

DHCI allows a user to become a reader of the formal text otherwise hidden beneath the blackbox.

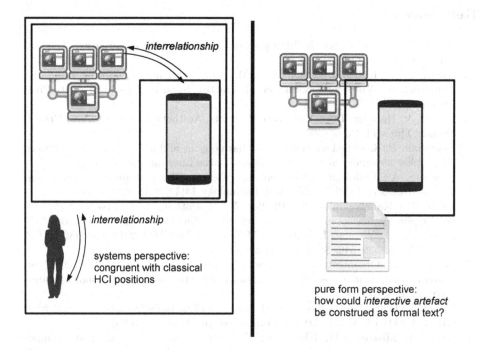

Fig. 3. interactive artefact: can it be construed in analogy to a building?

It does so not only in the technical sense of baring the formal 'guts' of materialised formal systems. If it wants to align itself with deconstructivism in its
critical sense, it has to expose the hidden formal texts that give rise to user positions. These equally are formal. They can be texts on the level of administration
or economics, politics or culture.

Deconstruction does not want to optimise a correspondence between form and
its cultural environment, it does not want to recontextualise technology. Maybe
if one wants to bring deconstructivist strategies to bear they would have to be
embedded into a wider array of practices. The concept of design and interface
ecologies [8,9,6] might reasonably be amended with that of theory ecologies.

5   Conclusion

As pointed out, creating effects of alienation could be a powerful ingredient of
a strategy of this kind. If we really live in a world were experiences of alienation and individualisation are as ubiquitous as the mobile technologies we use,
deconstructivist strategies might still prove useful. By allowing feelings of in-
significance and alienation to be experienced jointly they might even contribute
to new forms of social awareness.

References

1. Alexander, C.: Notes on the Synthesis of Form (Harvard Paperbacks). Harvard University Press (October 1964)
2. Alexander, C., Ishikawa, S., Silverstein, M.: A Pattern Language: Towns, Buildings, Construction (Center for Environmental Structure Series). Oxford University Press (August 1978)
3. Dunne, A.: Hertzian Tales: Electronic Products, Aesthetic Experience, and Critical Design. The MIT Press (2006)
4. Eisenman, P.: Contrasting concepts of harmony in architecture: Debate between christopher alexander and peter eisenman. Lotus International 40, 67 (1983)
5. Feenberg, A.: Philosophy Documentation Center: Ten paradoxes of technology. Techné: Research in Philosophy and Technology 14(1), 3–15 (2010)
6. Heidt, M., Kanellopoulos, K., Pfeiffer, L., Rosenthal, P.: Diverse ecologies interdisciplinary development for cultural education. In: Kotzé, P., Marsden, G., Lindgaard, G., Wesson, J., Winckler, M. (eds.) INTERACT 2013, Part IV. LNCS, vol. 8120, pp. 539–546. Springer, Heidelberg (2013)
7. International Organization for Standardization (ISO), S.: 9241-210: 2010. ergonomics of human system interaction-part 210: Human-centred design for interactive systems (2009)
8. Kerne, A.: Doing interface ecology: the practice of metadisciplinary. In: ACM SIGGRAPH 2005 Electronic Art and Animation, pp. 181–185 (2005)
9. Kerne, A., Mistrot, J.M., Khandelwal, M., Sundaram, V., Koh, E.: Using composition to re-present personal collections of hypersigns. Interfaces (September 2004)
10. Ostwald, M.J., Vaughan, J.: A data-cluster analysis of facade complexity in the early house designs of peter eisenman. NOVA. The University of Newcastle's Digital Repository (2009)
11. Ranganathan, A., Campbell, R.H.: What is the complexity of a distributed computing system? Complexity 12(6), 37–45 (2007)
12. Rogers, Y.: HCI theory: Classical, modern, and contemporary. Synthesis Lectures on Human-Centered Informatics 5(2), 1–129 (2012)

Using Agile Methods in Intercultural HCI Design Projects

Rüdiger Heimgärtner[1] and Alkesh Solanki[2]

[1] Intercultural User Interface Consulting (IUIC),
Lindenstraße 9, 93152 Undorf, Germany
ruediger.heimgaertner@iuic.de
[2] Continental Engineering Services GmbH,
Osterhofenerstraße 17, Regensburg, Germany
alkesh.solanki@conti-engineering.com

Abstract. In this paper, examples from intercultural HCI design projects are presented and analyzed with regard to applying agile methods to expedite the HCI design process while reducing resources. First, the products and the processes are considered with regard to culture. Then, the reasons of paradigm-shift from Waterfall/V-model to the application of agile methods are put forward. At same time, the benefits of using agile methods (SCRUM) in the user-centered design process are identified.

Keywords: Agile, SCRUM, User-Centered Design, ISO 9241-210, Culture, HCI, Approach, Process, Structure, V model, Waterfall model, Product, Cultural Dimension, HCI Dimension, HCI Style, Intercultural, Intercultural User Interface Design, Standard, Usability Engineering, Intercultural Usability Engineering.

1 Introduction

With competition in mind in the search for flexibility and overall effort reduction in standard (static and rigid) HCI design projects, there have been endeavors in the past exhausting all customization possibilities up to the customer's written approval (cf. [1]). But the standard V-Model process based on a waterfall model does not fit well when 1) the product requirements are not clear in the beginning (which is even more certain in the case of pre-development projects), and 2) the requirements get developed during the development phases and therefore the requirements change more often than not (which is always the case for Human Computer Interface Design/Development even up to the last phase of development) (cf. [2]). The customer project in question has both the characteristics of a HCI concept development project as well as those of a high-fidelity prototype (demonstrator) pre-development project (cf. Figure 1).

A. Marcus (Ed.): DUXU 2014, Part I, LNCS 8517, pp. 123–129, 2014.
© Springer International Publishing Switzerland 2014

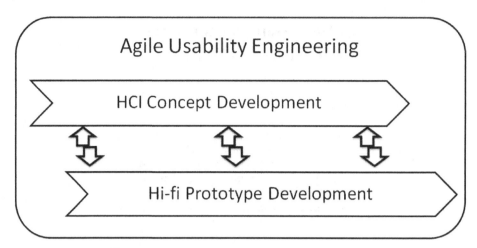

Fig. 1. Integrated Agile Usability Engineering Process

2   Products and Processes

The intercultural HCI design projects mentioned above are normally executed by multicultural teams (cf. [3]) (in our case members from Pakistan, India, the Czech Republic, Germany, Romania, England, Mexico, Nepal and China). The typical products are automotive driver information and infotainment systems such as instrument clusters, secondary displays, head-up displays, multimedia systems and rear-seat entertainment systems (cf. [4]).

All phases in the development process are affected (analysis, design, implementation and evaluation phases). For instance, on the one hand, the colleagues coming from a certain type of culture demanded a great amount system engineer's time until they grasped it, but that only concerned the part of, the task they could do. At this point then they worked through it like a robot (without thinking about the overall task). Moreover, they worked on the current tasks rather narrow mindedly and therefore missed the overall view of the task and the system. In fact, short before delivery of the system to customer, integration tests revealed a show stopper requiring necessary system design changes: certain aspects of the system were completely overlooked because of the inability to think of the system at the abstract level and they were therefore unable to inform the team in time, possibly because of high power distance (cf. [5], cf. Figure 2).

Furthermore, some tasks were even unexplainable to these colleague because of different world views. Nevertheless, after several attempts, they accepted the task without knowing why and executed the task correctly because of their hierarchical thinking (cf. [5]). On the other hand, this was not the case with other colleagues because they only do things if they know why in order to be sure of the benefit of their efforts. This is because of their individualistic behavior (cf. [5]). These are just some examples of process hurdles that can arise in multicultural teams of intercultural HCI design projects without having to generalize it.

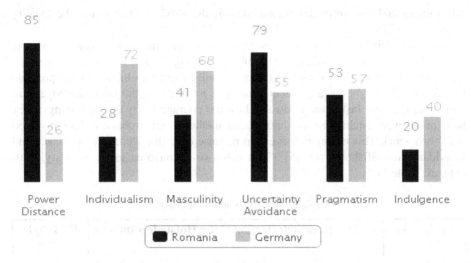

Fig. 2. Hofstede's Indices for Romania and Germany

3   From Waterfall/V-Model to Agile Methods

While trying to avoid such problems arising from strict hierarchies and inflexible process models in our intercultural innovation/platform projects, we had positive experience of with practically using and deploying some of the agile principles and methods (cf. [6]) focused on getting (iteratively and incrementally) 'right things' done (to increase product quality) rather than getting things done right (to increase process quality).

Having lost a precious 20% of resource capacity and time in the "analysis paralysis" of the product requirements, which were neither complete nor final, it was decided to introduce agile development methods in order not to fail to deliver the values matching the customer's high expectations and to avoid losing the customer for ever. Customers do not trust you as supplier anymore. The supplier loses face (cf. [7]). Different interpretations of the agile manifesto are represented by various methodologies such as SCRUM, XP, Lean Driven, Kanban, and others (cf. [8]).

All of them have risk management, test and customer validation and acceptance as a major value. Furthermore, they all have artifacts – customer requirements, tests, working software as well as engineering processes that are repeatable and similar companywide: for instance rules the methodology and the customization done in the company (cf. [9]). Since the agile methods require a culture and mindset change, initially there was great resistance from the team/stakeholders.

To overcome the barriers for increased flexibility and adaptation to change was yet another hurdle. As the expectations of transparency and accountability were being raised there was a great amount of insecurity and the increased sense of being continuously monitored (cf. [10]). Most of the team members were not used to continuous and high volume communication. This changed significantly after on the job training and tips from the Scrum Master, the Product Owner and the Quality Assurance Engineer.

Most interestingly, Romanians refused to adopt agile methods in general. This is indebted to their culture: hierarchical thinking; waiting for and following commands; only after consulting the boss were employees willing to hear others. It is not possible to talk directly to employees to steer them, you must go via the boss. Employees do only what they are instructed to do and lack the courage to try out new things; they hold on to well established and introduced methods and processes ("not invented here"-behavior). This means risk aversion because of high uncertainty avoidance and individualistic selfishness (cf. [5]). This behavior is mirrored in the HCI style (cf. [11], cf. Table 1).

Table 1. HCI Styles around the World

HCI Style	Cultural characterization using Hofstede's Indices	HCI Style Score
Asian	PDI high, IDV low, MAS middle, UAI low, LTO high	90
Indian	PDI high, IDV middle, MAS middle, UAI middle, LTO middle	70
African	PDI high, IDV low, MAS middle, UAI middle, LTO low	60
Scandinavian	PDI low, IDV high, MAS low, UAI middle, LTO low	40
Slavic	PDI high, IDV middle, MAS middle, UAI high, LTO low	30
Angle-Saxon	PDI low, IDV high, MAS middle, UAI low, LTO low	20
German	PDI low, IDV middle, MAS high, UAI middle, LTO low	10

3.1   Phases of the HCI Design Process According to ISO 9241-210

Agile usability (cf. [12]) is a reasonable approach to optimize the process of HCI design. In the following, we describe our experiences in the main phases of the HCI design process according to ISO 9241-210.

Analysis. Use agile methods in HCI projects from the very beginning where the uncertainty is very high regarding contractual requirements and thereby commit to a mid-to-long term contract. In agile risk and contract management, bravery and self confidence comes from manageable refactoring cycles. This ensures robust system architecture by allowing change requests by end users and stakeholders. Due to unclear contractual requirements from the customer it is also difficult for the supplier to calculate a realistic and competitive offers. Therefore the supplier is compelled to add a risk premium which makes the offer costly for the customer. Using agile methods generally reduces the risks for both because of iterative and incremental risk management and contracting. Further from the process point of view, as mentioned above, the requirements development has become more effortless with customer's involvement and early feedback.

Design / Implementation. Since from the beginning the focus has been on doing right thing, the first tasks/user stories that were taken up were of SW/HCI system architecture (System User Stories) (cf. [13]). In the first six weeks of development refactoring has already been done twice. Implementation (extreme) reviews are also being practically implemented with the focus on improving the design for future flexibility and also for testability/maintainability (cf. [8]). As shown in Figure 1 above, the analysis sprints, the design sprints and the evaluation sprints of the HCI concept development process are running in parallel to the implementation sprints of the Hi-fi prototype development process with certain predefined synchronization stages between these two processes.

Evaluation. Tests have been planned for each iteration at the unit test level as well as at the system test level (cf. [9]). There is still much scope for improving and automating tests. The focus changed from extensive documentation to working software, from processes to people and interpersonal skills and from following a plan to being able to respond to changes. Customer satisfaction increased through continuous delivery. The whole development was accelerated through continuous customer involvement and early feedback. This also helped in finalizing the requirements faster and earlier. Since the development got broken down into smaller incremental iterations, there were no inhibitions in documenting and analyzing the requirements under discussions. And those few requirements were also immediately implemented and were delivered to the customer for final acceptance.

3.2   HCI Concept Process Management

Supplier processes regarding product release and product acceptance are executed by the product owner. Engineering processes such as requirements analysis, software design and software construction as well as software/system integration and testing are at the core of the agile methodology done by the cross-functional core team and managed by the product owner at the system level. Resource management, training and project infrastructure is an intrinsic demand on agile methods managed by the product owner, the scrum master and the stakeholders. Process improvement is continuously in focus in agile development prescribing the continuous monitoring of the learning curve and efficiency. Product evaluation and change management (including problem resolution management) is enhanced by reviewing and re-prioritizing requirements and errors within the sprint planning. Process related documentation and configuration management must be done only to the extent that it satisfies the fulfillment of a desired maturity/capability level.

If we map ASPICE (cf. [14]) to SCRUM in intercultural HCI design projects in the automotive context, some of the generic practices of the Process Attributes 3.1 and 3.2 can be mostly ("largely") or fully ("fully") achieved. However, to fulfill all process attributes up to ASPICE level 3 in all process areas, extensive additional documentation as well as intelligent extension of existing SCRUM templates would be necessary (e.g. to achieve bidirectional traceability at level 1).

4   Implications and Discussion

The team is slowly getting adapted to the new culture and mindset necessary for using agile methods within an intercultural HCI design project. The team's creativity has increased. Helping each other is taking the first place. It can be felt that everyone is becoming more and more pro-active. The team's speed is also slowly improving. New ideas are getting generated almost every day. Everyday something new gets tried out. There is no fear of failure. Failures are seen as learning opportunities. It appears that the team has started enjoying a certain freedom for creativity, experimentation, exploration, and learning new things with and from each other. There are signs that team members are starting to take up the collective responsibilities and slowly self-organization is creeping in.

However, the retrospective review revealed that the version and change management system used was not directly compatible (due to its complexity and inflexibility) with the SCRUM methodology being deployed. Nevertheless, that the SCRUM methodology does work in a distributed development setup has been proved once again in this project.

Furthermore, if the agile development processes are supported by some auxiliary processes, it is possible to achieve up to capability level 3 for most of the process areas according to an ASPICE HIS scope[1], which is very important for intercultural HCI design projects in the automotive context.

The principles of the agile manifesto: individuals and interactions over processes and tools; working software over comprehensive documentation; customer collaboration over contract negotiation are applied at the same time and thereby staying compatible with the process capability model of ASPICE.

From this point of view, it is reasonable to determine to what extent the implemented agile development process in this project covers ASPICE process capability levels and that it is deployable in projects with high demand for certified quality.

---

[1] Reduced ASPICE scope agreed by certain car manufacturers (cf. URL=http://portal.automotive-his.de/index.php?lang=english, last access 02|24|2014).

5   Conclusion

Using agile methods in intercultural HCI design projects works from our point of view and will definitely be pursued in our future intercultural HCI design projects.

References

1. Balzert, H.: Lehrbuch der Software-Technik. [2], Softwaremanagement. Spektrum, Akad. Verl., Heidelberg (2008)
2. Ressin, M., Abdelnour-Nocera, J., Smith, A.: Lost in agility? approaching software localization in agile software development. In: International Conference on Agile Processes in Software, Engineering, Extreme Programming, X.P (2011)
3. Schoper, Y., Heimgärtner, R.: Lessons from Intercultural Project Management for the Intercultural HCI Design Process. In: Marcus, A. (ed.) DUXU/HCII 2013, Part II. LNCS, vol. 8013, pp. 95–104. Springer, Heidelberg (2013)
4. Heimgärtner, R.: Towards Cultural Adaptability in Driver Information and -Assistance Systems. In: Aykin, N. (ed.) Usability and Internationalization, Part II, HCII 2007. LNCS, vol. 4560, pp. 372–381. Springer, Heidelberg (2007)
5. Hofstede, G., Hofstede, G.J.: Cultures and organizations: software of the mind. McGraw-Hill, New York (2010)
6. Cockburn, A., Highsmith, J.: Agile Software Development: The People Factor. Computer 34(11), 131–133 (2001)
7. Victor, D.A.: International business communication, 7th edn., p. 280. Harper Collins, New York (1998)
8. Highsmith, J., Cockburn, A.: Agile Software Development: The Business of Innovation. Computer 34(9), 120–122 (2001)
9. Rätzmann, M.: Software-Testing & Internationalisierung. 2. Aufl. Galileo Press, Bonn (2004)
10. Blankl, M., Biersack, P., Heimgärtner, R.: Lessons Learned from Projects in Japan and Korea Relevant for Intercultural HCI Development. In: Marcus, A. (ed.) DUXU/HCII 2013, Part II. LNCS, vol. 8013, pp. 20–27. Springer, Heidelberg (2013)
11. Heimgärtner, R.: Reflections on a Model of Culturally Influenced Human Computer Interaction to Cover Cultural Contexts in HCI Design. International Journal of Human-Computer Interaction (2013)
12. Gundelsweiler, F., Memmel, T., Reiterer, H.: Agile Usability Engineering. In: Keil-Slawik, R., Selke, H., Szwillus, G. (eds.) Mensch & Computer 2004: Allgegenwärtige Interaktion, pp. 33–42. Oldenbourg Verlag, München (2004)
13. Walsh, T., et al.: Collecting cross-cultural user data with internationalized storyboard survey. In: Proceedings of the 23rd Australian Computer-Human Interaction Conference, pp. 301–310. ACM, Canberra, Australia (2011)
14. van Loon, H.: Process Assessment and ISO/IEC 15504: A Reference Book. Springer (2007)

Revisiting Graspable User Interfaces

A Design Process for Developing User Interface Metaphors

Mandy Keck, Esther Lapczyna, and Rainer Groh

Chair of Media Design, Technische Universität Dresden, 01062 Dresden, Germany
{mandy.keck,esther.lapczyna,rainer.groh}@tu-dresden.de

Abstract. The use of metaphors can support the understanding of novel interfaces approaches and increase the ease of use. But the design of novel holistic and adaptable metaphors is still challenging for interface designers. While most literature provides no systematic instruction for metaphor design or recommend to use a repertoire of known metaphors, we present a method that focuses on the generation of new metaphors based on the analysis and abstraction of everyday objects and the separate analysis of the given problem domain. Several methods of the field of human-computer interaction and traditional design support these analyzes. The methods presented in this paper are suitable especially for graspable user interfaces and illustrated by examples from several workshops.

Keywords: Metaphor design, Interface design method, Rapid prototyping, Operation metaphor, Graspable User Interfaces.

1   Introduction

Dealing with complex, abstract data and novel devices constantly poses new challenges to interface designers. On the one hand, suitable representations for abstract formless data are required. On the other hand, new interaction techniques have to be developed, which meet the requirements of technological innovations and the user's needs. These problems can be addressed by using metaphors. They can wrap abstract data, which initially has no inherent perceptual form, visual representation or shape. Hence, the use of metaphors within the design process can support the user in understanding novel interface approaches. Furthermore, a complex formless data structure can be made graspable by exploiting a known form repertoire and its associated interaction patterns.

However, it is challenging to create and to integrate a suitable metaphor, which fits well to the specific interaction paradigms of new technological innovations and also transfers the given data into a graspable interface for the user. To address these problems, we will present a method to develop holistic metaphors. This method was developed with a strong focus on didactic aspects and was tested in a series of experimental student workshops. We suggest that our approach is especially suitable for developing graspable interfaces, which require manipulation of finite data using hands, body or gestures.

A. Marcus (Ed.): DUXU 2014, Part I, LNCS 8517, pp. 130–141, 2014.

Therefore, we have a strong focus on experimenting with everyday objects to deduce materiality, form and affordances from everyday objects. Furthermore, this approach encourages the intuitive, transparent and playful interaction with given data objects to bring joy and excitement to the user interface as demanded by [1].

In this paper, we start with a short introduction to traditional approaches of interface metaphors. Next, we explain our method which focuses on the development of Operation Metaphors for graspable interfaces.

2   Metaphors in Interface Design

Lakoff & Johnson establish the terms of source domain and target domain: "The essence of metaphor is understanding and experiencing one kind of thing in terms of another" [2]. Hence, a whole concept and its structural connections will be assigned from a familiar situation (*source domain*) to an unknown problem (*target-domain*).

Although the concept of metaphor originates from the field of linguistics, it became a common approach in user interface design. When applied correctly, user interface metaphors offer numerous advantages [3]. By grounding user interface actions, tasks, and goals in a familiar framework of concepts that are already understood, the metaphor becomes a powerful tool, which can facilitate learning and understanding of complex content, increase ease of memorization and use, and stimulate user's interest [3], [4], [5]. Designed inappropriately, there is the risk that metaphors can promote misunderstanding, are not recognized by the user or invite assumptions about the target domain that are not valid [3], [5], [6]. To avoid these problems, it is essential to understand and improve strategies for developing user interface metaphors [5].

It is almost impossible to "find the right metaphor" that covers every aspect of functionality of the target domain [6]. The tension between metaphorical representation based on real-world systems and the need to extend computer functionality beyond real-world source domains entails unavoidable mismatches between the source and target domains [5]. Smith addressed this problem and established the terms "literal" and "magic" features. Literal features are defined to be those that are consistent with the metaphor, whereas magic features are defined to be those capabilities that violate the metaphor in order to provide enhanced functionality [7]. Although adding magical features and functions is unavoidable and appropriate as long as expectations set by the metaphor do not mislead the user, similarities (matches) and dissimilarities (mismatches) between the source and target domain play a prominent role in how metaphors work [5].

2.1   Types of User Interfaces Metaphors

There are several different types of metaphors, which can be transferred to the field of interface design. Lakoff & Johnson provide a taxonomy with a strong philosophical and linguistic view [2]. Barr et al. extend this taxonomy especially for user interface metaphors [8]. They distinguish between Orientational, Ontological and Structural Metaphors, which are divided into Process and Element Metaphors.

Table 1. Types of User Interface Metaphors according to Barr et al. [8], Morville & Rosenfeld [9] and Groh et al. [10]

Barr et al.	Morville & Rosenfeld	Groh et al.
Orientational Metaphor		Orientational Metaphor
Structural Metaphor	Organizational Metaphor	
Process Metaphor	Functional Metaphor	Operation Metaphor
Element Metaphor	Visual Metaphor	
Ontological Metaphor		

A similar classification was established by Morville & Rosenfeld [9]. Their classification of metaphors for web sites distinguishes between Organizational, Functional and Visual Metaphors (see Table 1).

Orientational Metaphors can be characterized as metaphors, which provide a concept with a spatial orientation [2]. Such metaphors are strongly based in the users physical and cultural experiences of the world [8]. Structural and Organizational Metaphors are used in a similar way and transfer a familiar organizational structure to a new system's organization. There are similarities in Process Metaphors and Functional Metaphors as well, which create a link between familiar tasks in the traditional environment and tasks in the new environment [9]. Element Metaphors as well as Visual Metaphors can use familiar graphic elements (in case of Element Metaphors also sounds, text, touch and anything else that the user can perceive through the senses) to create a connection to new interface elements, whereas Ontological Metaphors explain concepts in terms of the very basic categories of our existence [2]. Element Metaphors or Visual Metaphors and Ontological Metaphors are not considered in this paper, because we comprehend the user interface metaphor as a complex holistic system of signs and their relations, which can contain single (or atomic) elements like these.

In the context of developing design methods for a metaphoric interface, we distinguish between two different types of metaphors, depending on the aim of the interaction: the Orientational Metaphor and the Operation Metaphor [10].

The Orientational Metaphor supports orientation in immersive, memorable environments. It enriches the dynamic spatial image with spatial and structural patterns. The Operation Metaphor is used for operational forms of interaction. The relation between the user and the digital artifacts is static in nature and thus be called "emersive" in contrast to the immersive experience in dynamic environments. Whereas the Orientational Metaphor is dominated by the visual perception, the Operation Metaphor should provide affordances, which invite manual interaction with the given limited data set in order to make them graspable.

2.2   Design Process for Interfaces Metaphors

Novel devices that exploit new technologies always change the form and meaning of everyday computing. Digital artifacts in interactive systems are flexible, dynamic and intelligent, in contrast to artifacts in a traditional understanding [11]. This shift in thinking requires an integrated view on interactive systems as a whole, which influences the drafting process. The aesthetic or experiential qualities of these artifacts cannot be fully investigated by current user-centered design approaches, because they do not address analytic approaches and functional qualities of interaction [12]. Recent trends in (HCI) design research take this into account and explore the role of aesthetics and materiality. Lim et al. [11] emphasizes that the aesthetics of an interactive artifact cannot be limited to visual appearance. Rather, it is a matter of the holistic experience of usage.

For this purpose, Jung & Stolterman [12] demand a new theoretical and methodological foundation. Their proposal for a form-driven perspective on interaction design introduces a new interaction design research model through the lens of form and materiality. This Material Turn [13] makes hybrid forms possible. Tangible User Interfaces bridge the mental gap between physical and digital material interaction.

The metaphorical mapping is an important foundation for the creation process of interactive artifacts, because novel technologies influence their interaction patterns and visualization. Marcus provides a systematic approach for metaphor design consisting of five stages: (1) Identify items among data and functions that should be targets, (2) Identify source of metaphorical reference (3), Generate many possible metaphors, (4) Identify and evaluate matches and mismatches, (5) Revise metaphors to strengthen effective matches and reduce harmful mismatches [3]. Neale & Carroll offer a similar approach and point out some guidelines for each stage [5]. However, particularly the stage of generating possible metaphors is described insufficiently or bases on the re-use of known metaphors. In contrast, our method presented in section 3 can be used for developing novel interface metaphors, especially Operation Metaphors. The method has a didactical structure and provides a methodological toolbox, which can be used for analysis and abstraction of source and target domain to generate a holistic, subtle metaphor – according to Marcus, who demanded that a metaphor should be subtle, unconscious, or invisible [3]. In the following section, we will introduce our method and describe the different stages to develop an Operation Metaphor.

3   Developing Operation Metaphors

According to Neale & Carroll [5] the generation of possible metaphors is a heuristic and highly creative process, which is difficult to structure. Our approach enables to discover and prepare suitable metaphors. The underlying hypothesis of our process is: Every morphologically limited metaphor is suitable to every limited gestalt (in terms of an unit object with known states).

Fig. 2 illustrates the metaphor design process. The first part is divided into two columns: the left column characterizes the source domain and the right column describes the target domain. Both columns include methods to analyze and abstract the chosen repertoire as well as the given problem and involve methods of different disciplines to provide systematic instructions. The goal of each column is to generate an abstract model, which is ready for a fusion of the form (left column) to the meaning (right column). The Operation metaphor is the result of the metaphorically mapping from shapes (source domain) to states of the finite data (target domain). The resulting holistic approach empowers the user to understand the meaning beyond the original content. Unlike an iconic association, which links reality and image by similarity, the metaphor is characterized by the assignment of informal, shapeless information and a gestalt, which shows various states of the data. Our method creates a generative, synthetic and programmable shape – a technical image [14].

The source domain represents the repertoire of structures with defined shapes. The exploration of this repertoire provides enormous possibilities. However, not all shapes are suitable to be used. A decisive condition is that both source domain and target domain must be prepared in a comparable form – the same level of abstraction.

3.1   Gestalt Analysis

The gestalt analysis (see Fig. 2, left side) explores the richness and the variability of the selected shape. This sensual contention requires training and an analytical perception. University courses for design and architecture students such as the german "Bauhaus Vorkurse" train these skills in a didactical manner. The origin of their visual contention should be formed by the cognition of formal principles [15], [16], [17] at an elementary level. The traditional design theory provides specific methods for the reduction and decomposition of an object or subject. All of these methods teach the competence of visual thinking und use drawing and sketching as tools to narrow the own perception. They offer an experimental access to become familiar with complex problems [18], [19], [20]. Their didactically motivated methods use the analysis as stimulus within the design process. Possible suggestions to explore the geometrical relationship are to reveal regular states, transitions and relations. Furthermore, different views of the object to deduce a grid or an internal order can be studied.

Depending on the complexity of the chosen object, it can be attributed to one or more gestalt categories. They are distinguished by their dimensionality and require specific methods of formal analysis. To explore the variability of the shape, we used a series of experiments as a methodical tool. They reduce dimensions and analyze inherent interaction patterns and affordances. In a first step, we analyzed the structure and the behavior of malleable substances and their potential for manually tangible interaction. In this context, we developed the experimental setup explore Table [21]. This analysis tool allows the exploration of tangible interaction patterns on a planar surface. Two video cameras, which are attached above and underneath a table with an acryl glass plane, capture the user interaction process (see Fig. 1 – liquids and eggs).

Based on these insights, we elicit spatial affordances, by studying the behavior of substances in a spatial context. The initial outcome of this analysis was the DepthTouch system – an interactive tabletop with an elastic display [22] (see Fig. 1, top right and Fig. 4, right). The aim of these experiments is to create environments that address natural human (anthropomorphic) qualities.

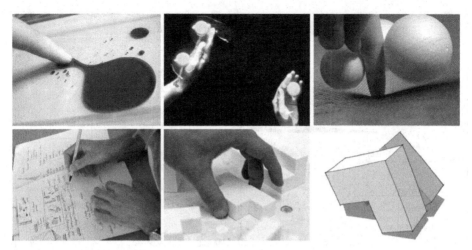

Fig. 1. Examples for gestalt analysis (top): liquids, eggs, fabrics; analysis process (bottom): drafts (left), experimenting with prototypes made of foamcore (middle), exploring different functions in a virtual 3D model (right)

Interaction design for novel interfaces becomes tangible and plastic. To focus this kind of design research, Eschrich et al. introduce a shape-oriented approach to deduce capable, useful interaction mappings from the gestalt analysis [23] (see Fig. 1, below).

It is important to constitute that these experimental studies form the beginning of the method. They sensitize the designer for the broad spectrum of possibilities in order to generate an extensive repertoire. Not all gestalts are equally to be used in an interactive metaphor. Therefore, we established the following criteria to limit the available repertoire by behavior, reversibility, plasticity, granularity, transformability or stability.

Visual Grammar. The gestalt analysis provides a rich repertoire of gestalt characteristics. This unordered result set of the top-down analysis process has to be translated into gestalt patterns and interactive features. A first step to organize the repertoire is a systematical structuring in geometric relations or transitions (evoked by interaction patterns) and material qualities. This categorization can help to fill blank spots in the analysis. This ordered set of graphical elements and their properties – structures and rules of its use – constitute a visual grammar [24].

3.2   Problem Analysis

The target domain is concerned with the problem definition of the design process. The time-dependent multivariate data structures are characterized by different levels of complexity. Naive connections between source and target domain do not support the understanding of the problem domain. The task of the designer is to develop a synthetical image for a problem, which is neither physically nor concrete.

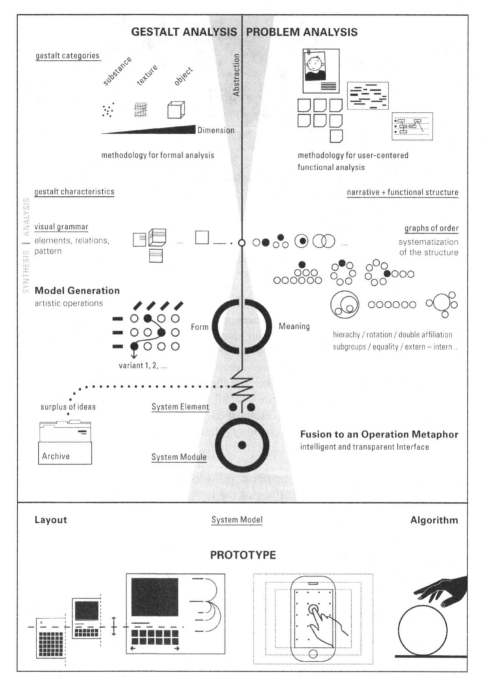

Fig. 2. Method for developing Operation Metaphors

For a successful mapping of the metaphor, the conceptions of source and target domain must be prepared and associated in a similar form. Similar to the gestalt analysis, the source material of the problem has to be analyzed to discover narrative and functional structures. There are different analytical methods that are well known from user-centered design and information architecture [25] such as personas, scenarios and use cases. These methods are not elaborated further in the context of this paper.

Graphs of Order. To transfer this clarification in a comparable degree of abstraction, the results require a visual notation, which creates an order like a pattern language. Graphs of order are such a sign system. The narrative structure of the problem is searched systematically to the following criteria: conditions, proportions, arrangements, figures, directions or typical relations (triangle, symmetry, etc.) Croy [26] and Frutiger [27] make suggestions to record all identified characteristics in a consistent form.

3.3   Model Generation and Fusion

Both data structure and gestalt repertoire were analyzed and abstracted progressively with the visual grammar (source domain) and the graphs of order (target do-main). Based on these elements and their relations or their qualitative and quantitative features of the visual language, the designer synthesizes a conceptual model. The fusion links the model to the graphs of order and creates an Operation Metaphor. This mapping fosters an intelligent and transparent interface that empowers the user to derive an own mental model of the interactive system. The synthesis generates a visual system, which is primarily the result of an elementary variation of the repertoire [28]. The design of interactive artifacts requires a generative design approach, whose elements and design rules are transparent. This holistic thinking is not a new phenomenon. Already progressive thinkers like the protagonists of swiss design in the 60's operated with systematic methods and tools, to derive a systemic relation between elements and the whole [29], [30]. An example for the variety of artificial operations is the morphological box [31] – a heuristic but systematic method, which Gerstner used for his algorithmic problem solutions of design issues [29]. Fig. 3 demonstrates a potential combination of the visual elements and their interactive aspects, but a new combination of several views and states of the gestalt are also possible.

The scheme of the metaphor generation (see Fig. 2) strictly divides between source and target domain. Both sides pose their independent challenges and require different analysis methods. Until both sides are ready to be fused, this separation should be maintained, to avoid rash solutions and ensure the development of universally expandable metaphors. Furthermore, this approach supports a profound and unprejudiced analysis, which generates a large variance. The fusion maps a shape to a set of properties of the data structures. By applying a systemic approach, both system elements become a system module. The whole of these system modules constitutes a system model once the essential graphs of order are linked. Both sides have a dialectic relationship and may have to be varied further.

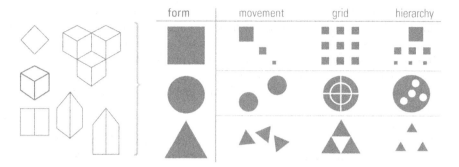

Fig. 3. Model variations (left) and an example for a morphological box (right)

To this end, further suitable experiments with the experimental setup of the gestalt analysis can be helpful. If the fusion between form and meaning is not satisfactory, an iteration loop is possible.

3.4   Prototyping

In the prototyping phase, the generated system model of compatible variants of the gestalt repertoire is developed further into a consistent draft. The goal of this phase is to test and algorithmise different variants and iteratively arrive a final solution by using mockups and prototypes. Until this phase, no technical restrictions are considered to avoid disturbing the creative process. Depending on the chosen technology, various prototyping techniques are suitable. To evaluate different variants, *offline prototypes* such as paper prototypes and mockups made of cardboard or foamcore can be created in a very short period of time. With these low-fidelity prototypes, designers can get a quick idea of a wide variety of different layout and interaction alternatives [32], [33]. In the case of multitouch interaction, we used paper prototypes to map different states of our model to a planar layout. The discovered forms and structures of the previous phases can be arranged into a grid, which structures and encapsulates the states of the interactive system [20]. To ensure that the layout is suitable for direct manipulation, we used different sizes of paper prototypes (in the size of mobile devices, tablets and multitouch monitors) and defined a minimum size for interaction objects of 1 x 1cm (see Fig. 4, left).

With video prototyping, we illustrated how users can interact with the system and get an immediate impression of how various gestures are suited to different devices [34]. Stop motion animations make it relatively easy to create a variety of low-cost special effects e.g. speeding up or reversing time, or give inanimate objects magical properties (e.g. changing the shape of an interaction object when touched) [35].

In contrast, *online prototypes* can be used to give an impression of the final interface in selected scenarios [33]. These high-fidelity prototypes are used to find algorithms for regular forms in the system model and to simulate the behavior of the interaction objects. Moreover, they allow the exploration of haptic and tangible, interactive or multi-sensory qualities [36].

Fig. 4. Paper prototyping for multitouch interfaces (left), online prototypes made of Arduino (middle) and fabrics as flexible projection surface (right)

Fig. 4 shows two online prototypes made of a simple plastic model, sensors and Arduino (middle) or fabrics as flexible projection surface (right) that allow a quick impression of various interaction techniques.

4 Conclusion

The presented method offers a methodological toolbox for developing novel interfaces metaphors. In comparison to the systematic approach of metaphor design provided by Marcus [3] or Neale and Carroll [5], it focuses on the stage of generating new metaphors and merge several interdisciplinary methods of the field of human-computer interaction and traditional design. The method separates the metaphor generation process into two subproblems: the analysis and abstraction of the source domain and the target domain. Both sides can be processed by two different designers. When used for teaching, we suggest to start with the analysis of the source domain to avoid restrictions and rash solutions conveyed by the given problem.

While the methods to identify problems and requirements on the side of the target domain are well described in the literature, we focus on the analysis and abstraction of the source domain and provide several instructions as well as experimental setups. We emphasize that it is important to arrive at the same level of abstraction on both sides in order to create an adaptable, subtle metaphor. The provided method is well-suited for Operation Metaphors because the experimental setup supports the finding of affordances that invite manual interaction with the data set. An extension of the methodological toolbox for the orientation metaphor is part of future work and requires different methods for the analysis of the source domain and additional experiments.

Acknowledgements. On behalf of Mandy Keck this work has been supported by the European Union and the Free State Saxony through the European Regional Development Fund. We thank all students, colleagues and advisors who participated in realizing the design cases presented in this paper.

References

1. Norman, D.A.: Introduction to This Special Section on Beauty, Goodness, and Usability. Human-Computer Interaction 19(4), 311–318 (2004)
2. Lakoff, G., Johnson, M.: Metaphors We Live By. The University of Chicago Press (1980)
3. Marcus, A.: Metaphor design in user interfaces. Journal of Computer Documentation 22, 43–57 (1998)
4. Carroll, J.M., Thomas, J.C.: Metaphor and the cognitive representations of computing systems. IEEE Transactions on Systems, Man, and Cybernetics 12(2), 107–116 (1982)
5. Neale, D.C., Carroll, J.M.: The Role of Metaphors in User Interface Design. In: Helander, M., Landauer, T.K., Prabhu, P. (eds.) Handbook of Human-Computer Interaction, 2nd revised edn. Elsevier Science, B.V., The Hague (1997)
6. Cooper, A.: The myth of metaphor. published in Visual Basis Programmer's Journal 5(6) (1995)
7. Smith, R.B.: Experiences with the alternate Reality Kit – An example of the tension between Realism and Magic. In: Proceedings of Human Factors in Computing Systems and Graphical Interfaces, Toronto (1987)
8. Barr, P., Biddle, R., Noble, J.: A taxonomy of user-interface metaphors. In: Proceedings of the SIGCHI-NZ Symposium on Computer-Human Interaction (CHINZ 2002), pp. 25–30. ACM, New York (2002)
9. Morville, P., Rosenfeld, L.: Information Architecture for the World Wide Web: Designing Large-Scale Web Sites, 3rd edn. O'Reilly Media (2006)
10. Groh, R., Gründer, T., Keck, M.: Production of Metaphors for Graspable User Interfaces (Metaphernproduktion für Begreifbare Benutzerschnittstellen). i-com: Zeitschrift für interaktive und kooperative Medien 11(2) (2012)
11. Lim, Y., Stolterman, E., Jung, H., Donaldson, J.: Interaction Gestalt and the Design of Aesthetic Interactions. In: Proceedings of the 2007 Conference on Designing Pleasurable Products and Interfaces, pp. S. 239–S. 254. ACM, New York (2007)
12. Jung, H., Stolterman, E.: Digital Form and Materiality: Propositions for a New Approach to Interaction Design Research. In: Proceedings of the 7th Nordic Conference on Human-Computer Interaction: Making Sense Through Design, pp. S. 645–S. 654. ACM, New York (2012)
13. Wiberg, M., Ishii, H., Dourish, P., Vallgårda, A., Kerridge, T., Sundström, P., Rosner, D., Rolston, M.: Materiality matters—experience materials. Interactions 20(2), 54–57 (2013)
14. Flusser, V.: Into the universe of technical images. University of Minnesota Press, Minneapolis (2011)
15. Arnheim, R.: Art and visual perception: a psychology of the creative eye. University of California Press, Berkeley (2004)
16. Metzger, W.: Laws of seeing. MIT Press, Cambridge (2006)
17. Dondis, D.A.: A primer of visual literacy. MIT Press, Cambridge (1973)
18. Lupton, E., Miller, J.A.: The ABCs of triangle, square and circle - the Bauhaus and design theory. Princeton Architectural Press, Princeton (1993)
19. Jenny, P.: Drawing techniques. Princeton Architectural Press, New York (2012)
20. Lupton, E.: Graphic design thinking: beyond brainstorming. Princeton Architectural Press, New York (2011)
21. Brade, M., Kammer, D., Keck, M., Groh, R.: Immersive Data Grasping Using the eXplore Table. In: Proceedings of the Fifth International Conference on Tangible, Embedded, Embodied Interaction, Funchal, Portugal (2011)

22. Peschke, J., Göbel, F., Gründer, T., Keck, M., Kammer, D., Groh, R.: DepthTouch: An Elastic Surface for Tangible Computing. In: Proceedings of the International Working Conference on Advanced Visual Interfaces, New York, NY, USA, pp. S. 770–S. 771 (2012)

23. Eschrich, B., Knöfel, A., Gründer, T., Keck, M., Groh, R.: A Shape-Oriented Approach for Creating Novel Tangible Interfaces. In: Mensch & Computer 2013: Interaktive Vielfalt. Oldenbourg Verlag, Bremen (2013)

24. Leborg, C.: Visual grammar, 1st English edn. Princeton Architectural Press, New York (2006)

25. Ebenreuter, N., Geerts, M.: Design Strategy: Towards an Understanding of Different Methods and Perspectives. In: Proceedings of the 2011 Conference on Designing Pleasurable Products and Interfaces, pp. 51:1–51:8. ACM, New York (2011)

26. Croy, P.: Signs and their message. Musterschmidt, Göttingen (1972)

27. Frutiger, A.: Signs and symbols: their design and meaning. Van Nostrand Reinhold, New York (1989)

28. Hofmann, A.: Graphic Design Manual. Principles and Practice. Niggli, Niederteufen (1988)

29. Gerstner, K.: Designing programmes. Müller, Baden (2007)

30. Ruder, E.: Typography. Niggli, Sulgen (1996)

31. Zwicky, F.: Discovery, Invention, Research Through the Morphological Approach, 1st american edn. MacMillan (1969)

32. Sears, A., Jacko, J.A.: Human-Computer Interaction: Development Process. RC Press, Boca Raton (2009)

33. Wiethoff, A., Schneider, H., Rohs, M., Butz, A., Greenberg, S.: Sketch-a-TUI: Low Cost Prototyping of Tangible Interactions Using Cardboard and Conductive Ink. In: Proceedings of the 6th International ACM Conference on Tangible, Embedded and Embodied Interaction, TEI 2012, Kingston, Canada, February 19-22 (2012)

34. Kammer, D., Schmidt, D., Keck, M., Groh, R.: Developing Mobile Interface Metaphors and Gestures. In: Proceedings of the 15th International Conference on Human-computer Interaction with Mobile Devices and Services Companion, MobileHCI 2013. ACM, New York (2013)

35. Bonanni, L., Ishii, H.: Stop-motion prototyping for tangible interfaces. In: 3rd International Conference on Tangible and Embedded Interaction, pp. 315–316 (2009)

36. Knöfel, A., Koalick, G., Lapczyna, E., Groh, R.: Pimp your prototype. In: Proc. 5th International Scientific Conference on Print; Media Technology, pp. 131–136. VWB - Verlag für Wissenschaft und Bildung, Chemnitz (2013)

Tracing Design Work through Contextual Activity Sampling

Tarja-Kaarina Laamanen[1], Pirita Seitamaa-Hakkarainen[1], and Kai Hakkarainen[2]

[1] University of Helsinki, Department of Teacher Education, Helsinki, Finland
[2] University of Turku, Department of Education, Turku, Finland
{tarja-kaarina.laamanen,
pirita.seitamaa-hakkarainen}@helsinki.fi,
kai.hakkarainen@utu.fi

Abstract. The present study investigated professional designers' practices in context, the role of their design tools and materials, the organization of their daily work and social connections related to their ongoing design projects. We examined the feasibility of using contextual event sampling as a method of studying professional design practices; this method involves repeated sampling of design events and actions in their social and cultural context. The data were collected electronically with Contextual Activity Sampling System (CASS), the rationale and usage of which are described in detail. The data analysis provided a view of the basic features of designers' work; their activity, social interaction, and changes in location as well as the emotional dimensions of their experiences. Results indicated that designers' work was multilayered, but they were not disturbed by the fluid and varying nature of the work and found satisfaction in it. We found the CASS- technology suitable for design research as it captures multimodal data and is applicable to variety of design interests and fields. Methodological implications regarding the contextual study of design practices and ideas of the tool development are discussed.

Keywords: design, event sampling, design practice.

1   Introduction

Design practice involves multifaceted activities related to working with various design tools and materials within limited time and resources, as well as communicating with clients. In current design research, there is increasing interest in developing frameworks that assist in investigating design practice in context, that is, as a multi-level phenomenon that, beyond individuals, takes place in a particular social and material context. It is important to understand how designers over the long term, and in context, develop new artifacts, and ways of working. It is also important to learn how the designers experience the design work—that is routine and challenging design aspects. Designing is a complicated long-term creative process, where designers work with open-ended, ill-defined problems, and apply domain-specific knowledge in order to find the solution to a design problem [1],[3]. Design processes and design thinking have been areas of intensive investigation. However, there has been also increasing interest in

A. Marcus (Ed.): DUXU 2014, Part I, LNCS 8517, pp. 142–152, 2014.

investigating design as a holistic activity that involves designer, design process, design object and design context [2]. One can analyze design work from four perspectives: what is done and why (assignments, tasks, objects; with whom; how (work and communicative actions and practices); and where and when (space and time) [see also 12]. The distribution of work, in one form or another, is an overarching characteristic of all aspects of knowledge work. Designers are working in project-based design teams that are mustered for solving one particular design task; consequently, they must have skills of creating and maintaining personal social networks and quickly adapting in multi-professional environments [see also 4].

The present paper examined how repeated sampling of design events taking place in the context of everyday activity can be used to investigate and document various aspects of design. Event sampling refers to the research strategy for studying ongoing daily experiences as they occur in the ebb and flow of everyday life, instead of retrospective generalization of experiences [10]. This method relies on various research instruments designed to provide detailed descriptions of specific moments in a person's life. The methods of event sampling provide information, for instance, on participants' on-going experiences, emotions, and social activities in their natural context of occurrence. By collecting real-time data of participants' actions, it is possible to examine how various factors, such as perceived challenge and situational competence interact, or how their mutual relation develops across time [5]. These methods have been identified either with the experience sampling method (ESM) [5] or the ecological momentary assessment (EMA) method [11]. Towards that end, we used Contextual Activity Sampling System [8]. It is a research instrument under development; it is a procedure that uses 3G mobile phones for sampling various aspects of learning and design in their actual context of occurrence. We wanted also to examine how the CASS method and instrument could be developed better to account for the contextual aspects of design. The method provides information, for instance, on participants' on-going experiences, emotions, and social activities in their actual context of occurrence. The challenge is to develop research methods to account for various aspects of actual design activities instead of mere beliefs or conceptions of the participants, after the fact.

2   Method

2.1   Participants

We were interested in individual designers' practices, the role of the tools and materials, organization of their daily work, and their social connections related to their ongoing projects. We asked designers who had worked as professionals for at least two years, to participate. All of them were "entrepreneur-designers," defined as freelance designers or designers who have their own small design enterprise. The participants are mainly working alone; they have their own permanent partnerships or networks working with, for example, manufacturers, customers and fabric bulk salesmen. Table 1 contains the background information of the participants and their design cases during the data collection. All the participants worked in the area of Helsinki, Finland.

Table 1. Designers background information and their design case

Participants	Age	Experience (years)	Design case
Fashion Designer A	32	10	Ideation phase of children's collection + women's collection manufacturing phase
Fashion Designer B	31	8	Designing prints to sportswear collection prototypes
Interior Designer C	46	10	Familiarizing herself with new design cases and new customers, checking and continuing with the previous designs with customers
Interior Designer D	34	11	Ideation phase + designs team meeting
Textile Designer E	26	2	Working old pattern-ideas into new ones to be shown and sold to manufacturers in Sweden + arranging meetings with manufacturers
Wooden wall Designer F	49	25	Translating the trade-related brochures and processing texts in order to make a portfolio to the international exhibition in Köln

2.2   Event-Sampling Method as a Part of CASS System

In the present study, event-contingent sampling was used. We chose to use the term 'event sampling' as a theoretically neutral term to refer to repeated sampling of participants' activities, whether they are psychological experiences or external actions, in the contexts of everyday activity. We defined design practice as a process consisting of a sequence of interrelated specific design events. These events represent various aspects of designing, such as an episode of conceptual designing, construction of a prototype or dealing with business-related matters. These design events generally capture temporal aspects of participants' daily activities and domain content. Participants were requested to identify the main design events of their design practices and to respond to a pre-determined query (set of questions) whenever a new design event emerged.

2.3   CASS-Query for Tracing Design Practices and Data Collection

Contextual Activity Sampling System (CASS) was investigated to determine the feasibility of using mobile phones in full-scale processes of event sampling. The CASS allowed us to generate various sets of questions related to the designing events. It provided a possibility to take into account the participants' (individual) time schedules and allowed different kinds of response formats. In other words, the designers activated the questionnaire in mobile telephones each time the designing events occurred. Then, the designers (individually) responded to the activated questions by writing a text message, taking photos or making audio notes. CASS sent the data directly to the database, recording date and time of sampling. Further, the designers were also asked to make audio notes (i.e., audio diary) concerning their day at the end of each working day.

The query was designed following the feedback from the previously executed survey about knowledge work activity and practices [13].   In the present, pilot study, designers answered a CASS query (set of questions) concerning their ongoing design projects, emotions, and personal social networks. We categorized the query items according to four different spaces of design practices: 1) physical space, 2) tool and material space, 3) social space, and 4) mental space [9], [12]. The *physical space* as well as *tool and material space* relate to the context, the instruments and materials with which the designer was involved during the event. The *social space* relates to personal social networks and partnerships the designers were dealing with. *Mental space and work orientation* refers to the designers' emotions and experienced competence related to their work.

The query consisted of 20 questions: a) what, where, how and why questions, b) Likert type structured questions, which called for ratings according to a five-step scale as well as c) instructions for taking photos. The questions 1, 6 and 8 related to the query of the context of physical space. The participants were requested to respond to questions concerning the place they were working. They were asked to take a photo of their working place in that moment, to answer why they were there, and to evaluate how well the place supported their work. Questions 2, 9, 10, 11 and 12 related to physical tools and instruments as well as material the designers were working with (i.e. tool and material space). They were asked to photograph the tools and equipment they used and requested to describe how well the tools and material supported their work. Questions 3, 4, 5 enquired about the collaboration designers had, with whom they were interacting and how it supported their work about (i.e., social space). For the mental space questions (16-20), we utilized part of 'Flow state scale' [6]. We were interested in various kinds of mental states designers may have had during their work; for example, how creative they felt at the moment or how well they were able to concentrate at that point. Finally, four questions (7, 13, 14, 15) were related to the designers' work orientation. These questions concerned attaining the task, overlapping and routine tasks and related challenges of the task. The entire query was designed to be completed in 5-10 minutes.

Participants were asked to answer the questionnaire several times a day and record a separate end-of-day spoken diary in the phone, once a day, during the five working days i.e., one week. Designers were instructed to activate the questionnaire in mobile telephones each time the work related event changed to another event or task. CASS sent the data directly to the database, recording date and time. All the audio notes were recorded in the phone, transmitted to the database, and transcribed word for word.

2.4   Method of Data Analysis

We first organized the data collected with CASS queries in separate, respective, individual designer's documents consisting of all CASS entries of each day. Transcribed audio diaries were included to the analysis. The organized data were analyzed in accordance with the spaces presented above, which provided the main structure for preliminary categories. A more detailed classification scheme, however, emerged from the data itself. Figure 1 represents the main categories according to which we analyzed the participants' responses.

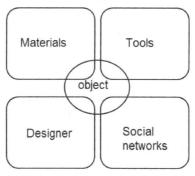

Fig. 1. The main categories of the study

Table 2 below presents the content of the analyzed categories: 1) the object of activity i.e. what they were doing, 2) designers experiences and emotions, 3) design tools they were using 4) materials they were using and their social   networks.

Table 2. Content of the analyzed categories

Object of activity	e.g. finishing the products, designing a new product and testing it, mapping the business papers
Designer	Reported experiences, emotions (e.g. concentration, enjoyment)
Design tools	a) sketching tools, b) fabrication tools, c), Information management tools, d) communication tools and e) assistant tools (e.g. dummy)
Materials	a) idea materials, b) materials for sketching and designing, c) materials for prototyping, d) materials for process organizing and product design (product tables, timetable) and e) materials related to the customer (e.g., interiors concepts book)
Social Networks	a) personal networks (peer designers, friends, family), and b) professional networks (manufacturers, sales representatives and fabric bulk salesmen, customers)

3   Results

3.1   Overview of the CASS Query

Of six participants, three completed the query for five days and three designers missed one day. Four entries were incomplete due to the technical problems related to server and that data were excluded from the analysis. Designer A and B were the most active in providing the CASS data whereas designer C provided CASS query only once a day. Five of the designers provided end-of-the-day audio recording for each day's practices. In the present study, the designers' work areas and design cases differed within each other, and we are not able to compare designers' professional activities in a detailed way. However, the CASS query elicited data indicating some general features of the designers' working practices.

The following section describes how the designers experienced their work emotionally and how they met their challenges related to work at hand. In the second section we report the design tools and materials related their work practices. The third section highlights the multilayered design work, i.e., how and where designers worked during the CASS query.

3.2   Work Orientation and Emotional Commitment

The designers were asked to identify the main design events of their design practices and to respond to the CASS query whenever a new design event emerged. As a part of query, the participants were asked to assess in the context of each design event 1) how challenging they experienced the situation to be, 2) how well they were able to concentrate on the task, 3) how creative they feel, and 4) how they enjoy the work. Following, data will be reported regarding frequency distribution of such assessments, summarized across events reported by all of the participants. The designers estimated that their ability match on the challenge of the task quite well or very well 27%, (f=18), moderately 40% (f=27) and only little or not at all 27% (f=18). This indicates that, overall, designers experienced their current tasks as demanding, but usually had resources sufficient to meet the challenges. In general they felt that they were able to concentrate well or very well on their work approximately 73% (f= 49), moderately or only little 18% (f=12) during their CASS query. The designers estimated that they enjoyed their work a good deal or very much 51% (f=34) of the cases; moderately or little 40% (f=27) of the query entries. The designers were rather motivated, engaged and goal oriented during their working days. The reported enjoyment of the events indicates that they were not disturbed by the changeable nature of design work and could find satisfaction of it. Figure 2 depicts Designer's B reported events (date and time) related to her experience of challenge of work, enjoyment and creativity.

The query revealed that Designer B appeared to work with a quite challenging task from Tuesday (1.7) to Thursday (3.7) and she was enjoying her work a good deal (scale values 4 to 5), most of the time. During this CASS query week she was mainly at her home because the Internet connection was not functioning at her own studio. She reported in her audio diary, that she was slightly disturbed working at home. Further, according the query entries (see Figure 2) she felt herself moderately or quite creative at the beginning of the week (Tuesday and Wednesday) while she was working with her print and embroidery designs for the coming season. In the middle of the week, she took care of the business-related matters in addition to print designing. Also, during Tuesday and Wednesday she was in touch with her partners

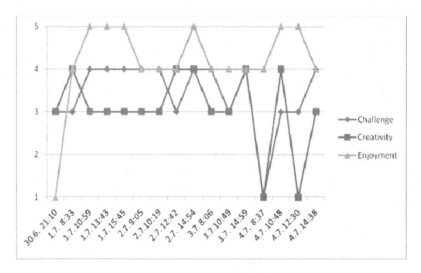

Fig. 2. Designer B's reported CASS query events related to her experience of challenge of work, enjoyment and creativity

by Skype-conference and by e-mail, and she got the prints ready in Thursday. On Friday (4.7) she was mapping her papers and moving her archives, and the line chart shows that she did not feel creative. However, the line chart reveals that she still enjoyed very much of her working day.   In the following excerpt of audio diary, she complemented the Thursday CASS-query entries in her own words.

> "Today has been one of those days, I've been putting the finishing touches on the fleece   jackets and the last of the weight patterns which earlier didn't seem to work but now,   they're all done, so the winter 2010 collection   printing and embroidery is all done. This puts me in a good mood as the client is just leaving for a vacation, and this week...or the person I've been working with, hopefully after this week we'll have everything up to speed. On the other hand, it's very difficult to work from home, because there is so much here that I would rather be doing than work, hopefully they will fix the Internet at the office soon. What else...I feel very tired recently, but it's good in a way, with all the changes coming and how I've made progress with some people who are hard to deal with. On the other hand, because I'm only in the initial phase of this business, I've been able to work on some business things." (DB; Audio diary 3.7.2008)

In general, the results revealed that designers considered some of their professional practices as routine tasks, such as paper work and reading e-mails. They often reported that routine tasks had clear goals and that they completed the task in one event. As expected, they considered designing events more creative and challenging, and they felt that the final goals of their design tasks were more open-ended in nature.

3.3   Design Tools and Materials Used

As a part of query, the participants were asked to assess in the context of each design event the support for their process provided, respectively, by 1) the design tools, 2) the materials and 3) the place. Further data will be reported regarding frequency distribution of such assessments summarized across events, reported by all of the participants.

The designers reported a diversity of design tools that they used during their working. They considered that the design tools supported their working very well 61% (f=41) or quite well 19% (f=13). As expected, most of the designers used sketching tools (i.e., design software, paper and pen). All of them used information managing tools and communication tools. Computer-aided drafting was reported in the data, but it was merely used for editing and altering sketches.

Further, the designers considered that material that they were using supported their working moderately 33% (f=22), quite well 21% (f=14) and very well 30% (f=20). Depending on the design phase, the designers used different materials. Designer F mainly worked with trade-related brochures and processed her own text in order to make a portfolio to the international exhibition. Designer A and E were in the preliminary designing phase, and they needed to collect idea materials to inspire their designing. Designer E used pictures from nature books for inspiration, and designer A used internet materials as an inspiration source and as an aid in framing the current idea space for children's collection. Designers A and B used materials for sketching and designing as well as for experimenting, for example, when producing preliminary plans, sketches, and prints. Designer A described in her audio diary how she started to design the children's collection:

> "I began working on the children's clothing collection color coordination and brainstorming (idea space), mainly I collected model and color samples and was pondering which colors would be good and then I searched the internet for suitable picture and idea patterns." (DA; Audio diary 10.6.08)

Figure 3 presents photos taken by the designer B during CASS query. As stated earlier, Designer B worked with the prototypes of her sportswear collection, so she used paper prints and visualizations of embroidery as materials for executing prototype.

Fig. 3. Designer B's photos from CASS query events

3.4   Multi-layered Design Work

The CASS query revealed the multi-layered nature of the design work, which was related to the physical and social spaces of working. The designers reported a variety of physical places (i.e., home, studios) and virtual and social spaces (Skype, Net meeting, meeting customer or colleagues in face-to-face) where they worked. The designers' work and communicative actions took place in "hybrid workspaces" that can be seen as combination of physical, virtual and social settings [13]. These settings were blended together and varied when designer shifted from one event to another, i.e., by working sometime physically alone and then with others, virtually or face-to-face contacts.. As expected, the designers mainly worked at their own studios; some of them had studios at their home, whereas others had a separate working studio. In addition working at home or in studio, designers also reported other places related to design work, which were used only temporarily (post office, fabric bulk, salesman office, art supply store, coffee shop).

4   Discussion

The purpose of our research was to overcome some of the methodological challenges of studying design practice. At one level, we highlighted the situational aspects to contextualize design practices. At the other level, the aim was to explore the feasibility of collecting research data using mobile technology (i.e., CASS query) and apply an event sampling method in the context of actual design work.

In the present study, the data indicated these basic features of designers' work; designers activity, social interaction, and changes in location as well as emotional dimensions of experiences. According the query entries, we may conclude that designers were quite motivated and engaged during their working days. Designers' working days were multilayered; the participants had multiple and different kinds of tasks. They were not disturbed by the changeable nature of design work, and they enjoyed the work in general. As expected, various domain-specific tools and materials were used to support design work.

The results presented in this article, it should be stated, are quite general, and we depicted the designers' everyday working practices and workflow at the particular level we chose. Due to the heterogeneity of the design fields and small sample size, we were not able compare designers or to conduct a statistical analysis of the data. There might be individual differences and variance between participants related, for example, to the complexity, enjoyment or concentration of the work.   In the following, we will critically discuss advantages and disadvantages of the event-sampling method and CASS query as a research instrument, in particular.

The heterogeneous participant sample can be considered as one limitation of the study, as it caused disintegration (i.e. diversity and variegation in the data) and made it difficult to describe specific viewpoints of designers work. The study needs to be replicated with homogenous samples in terms of design field.   By nature, event-sampling research depends on participants' ability and willingness to comply with instructions; their responses are likely affected by factors such as social desirability and demand characteristics.   Sampling bias may be systematic (not reporting in more demanding situations) and affect the results of investigations. Some participants of the present investigations failed to actively report their design activities. The nature of the multi-tasking design work could have made it hard to identify a design event. These gaps became apparent, since two research "instruments" i.e. CASS query and the end-of-day diary complemented each other in a way that we were able to compare the relevance and authenticity of CASS query towards descriptions of the daily workflow from the end-of-day diaries and vice versa.

In any case, since we have now gathered some basic structure of design events, it is more straightforward to develop instructions for designers to keep records of their practices. If researchers wish to address, for example, a particular aspect of design, such as certain conditions governing the use of specific tool, activity or particular type of interaction, they may instruct a designer to supply information when the condition is satisfied. In this way, one can specify the particular events and reduce the designer's burden of answering the query.

CASS system implemented on 3G mobile devices provides multiple ways of capturing multimodal data: short video clips, audio notes, photos and text notes. The CASS system in a mobile device can be also used as a critical incident method, where designers will be given a specific theme (for example, ideation process / inspiration searching) on which to take photos during a period of time, audio tape (or text) a short notes related to incidents. CASS query can also be applied to the participatory design (or self-documentation in user studies), where a design project is intended to understand people's feelings, pleasure and values related to future products to be designed i.e. design probes [7]. To conclude, we can see various ways of conducting event-sampling method using CASS query in design research. We believe that the CASS method is applicable to a variety of research interests and the exploitation of CASS will be possible since the CASS system will be available in open source terms for interested parties. The CASS query tool could provide the methodological transparency what design research requires.

References

1. Akin, Ö.: Psychology of architectural design. Pion Limited, London (1986)
2. Dorst, K.: Design research, a revolution - waiting - to happen. Design Studies 29(1), 4–11 (2008)
3. Goel, V.: Sketches of Thought. MIT Press, Cambridge (1995)
4. Hakkarainen, K., Palonen, T., Paavola, S., Lehtinen, E.: Communities of networked expertise. Elsevier, Amsterdam (2004)
5. Hektner, J., Schmidt, J., Csikszentmihalyi, M.: Experience sampling method: Measuring the quality of everyday life. Sage, Thousand Oaks (2007)
6. Jackson, S.A., Marsh, H.W.: Development and validation of scale to measure optimal experience: flow state scale. Journal of Sport and Exercise Psychology 18(1), 17–35 (1996)
7. Mattelmäki, T.: Design Probes. University of Art and Design UIAH, Helsinki (2006)

8. Muukkonen, H., Inkinen, M., Kosonen, K., Hakkarainen, K., Karlgren, K., Lachmann, H., Vesikivi, P.: Research on knowledge practices with the Contextual Activity Sampling System. In: Proceedings of the 9th International Conference of Computer Supported Collaborative Learning, Rhodes, Greece, vol. 1, pp. 385–394. International Society of the Learning Sciences (2009)

9. Nonaka, I., Konno, N., Toyama, R.: The concept of "BA": A conceptual framework for the continuous and self-transcending process of knowledge creation. In: Nonaka, I., Nishiguchi, T. (eds.) Knowledge Emergence, pp. 13–29. Oxford University Press, Oxford (2001)

10. Reis, H.T., Gable, S.L.: Event sampling and Other Methods for Studying Everyday Experience. In: Reis, H.T., Judd, C.M. (eds.) Handbook of Research Methods In Social and Personality Psychology, pp. 190–222. Cambridge University Press, USA (2000)

11. Shiffman, S.: Real-time self-report of momentary states in the natural environment: Computerized ecological momentary assessment. In: Stone, A., Turkkan, J., Jobe, J., et al. (eds.) The Science of Self-report: Implications for Research and Practice, pp. 277–296. Lawrence Erlbaum Associates, Inc., Mahwah (2000)

12. Vartiainen, M., Hakonen, K., Koivisto, S., Mannonen, P., Nieminen, M.P., Ruohomäki, V., Vartola, A.: Distributed and mobile work: Places, people, & technology. Gaudeamus, Espoo (2007)

13. Vartiainen, M., Ruohomäki, V., Hakkarainen, K., Jalonen, S., Kosonen, K.: Studying hindrances and enablers in knowledge work with CASS-method. In: A paper presented at Activity 2008 (Activity Analyses for Developing Work) Conference, May 12-14. Finnish Institute of Occupational Health, Helsinki (2008)

Techno-Theoretical Paradigm:
Performance, Fashion and Wearables

Valérie Lamontagne

Concordia University, Design & Computation Arts, 1515 St. Catherine St. West,
Montréal, Québec, Canada H3G 2W1
valerie@3lectromode.com

Abstract. This paper seeks to formulate a theoretical ground from which to analyze wearables as performative. My aim is to argue that wearables are theoretically (and practically) situated somewhere between the performance art costume and that of the fashion garment.

Keywords: Wearables, performance, laboratory culture, design, embodiment, interface culture, textiles, prototyping.

1 Introduction

First I examine a critical analysis of the body-garment dynamic present within performance studies and fashion theory. The aim is to first establish the link between the garment and the body as being inherently performative. This performance angle will then be built upon by looking at the relationships between technology, performance and the body. The first section of this paper investigates the legacy of the "Performative Turn" in expanding the notion of performance beyond the stage, associating it with the important role of body politics, props, costumes and contexts in shaping meaning. The second section examines fashion theory's construction of meaning through the visual orchestration of the body and garments within performance and event-based contexts related to fashion, including the runway and the street. The performative analysis of garments and bodies within both fields (performance art and fashion) serve as a foundation through which we will later investigate the links between garments, bodies and the technologies present within wearables. Lastly I will probe how media culture in relation to the body amplifies and extends its range and types of expressions.

2 Performance Theory and the Performance of the Body

We begin with an overview of performance theories relating to the body. Particularly, we look to performance examples from outside the tradition of theatrical stage scholarship—in which costume traditionally plays a supporting role—to focus on contexts in which costumes are at centre stage in the construction of characters, narrative, and meaning. These contexts encompass the use of non-actor elements such

A. Marcus (Ed.): DUXU 2014, Part I, LNCS 8517, pp. 153–162, 2014.

as props, make-up and more particularly, costumes to create meaning within both artistic and every day contexts.

The first performance context is the artistic genre known as "performance art." Emerging at the turn of the century, performance art gained prominent acceptance from the art world in the 1960s. The foundations for performance art, as distinguished from those of theatre, were developed outside the parameters of the black box/stage, with "real world" contexts, objects, and settings fueling the construction of events. In short, performance art is about acting in real world settings and with a high degree of context awareness in which the objects, people and settings at hand are key players within the performance. This is not to argue that performance art is more "real"—it contains a high degree of imagination and abstraction—however, it does aim to create theatricality built on an actual situation in the real world, as opposed to creating imaginary realms divorced from the immediate setting as in theatre. As a craft, performance art often highlights the actual actors and their unique bodies (i.e. gender, race, sexual orientation), and costumes are used as highly codified and important elements to the construction and interpretation of the performance and the performer. In addition, the disarming charm and appeal of performance art is tied to its convergence with the "real." Performance art and performance studies theoreticians such as Carlson, Schechner and Goldberg have observed how the use of costumes, props, and settings are enlisted in creating performance within the everyday and by means of visual as opposed to dramaturgical codification [1; 2; 3; 4; 5].

The idea that performance can be built upon the everyday, and that the everyday is a type of performance came to the fore in the 1960s through a movement known as the "Performative Turn." The "Performative Turn" explores methodologies and analysis of the everyday rooted in bodily actions—rituals, play, games, sports, individual and social practices of society—wherein an emphasis is placed on performance as the key to understanding these actions. These modes of research— engaging with, observing and analyzing the uses of performance in rituals [5]; and constative utterances such as the phrase pronounced at weddings, "I do take this woman to be my lawful wedded wife," [6] shape the thinking around external and contextual elements playing an important role in performance in the everyday. What is more, the negotiation and flux of public identity through "social" performances [7] as well as the understanding of rituals and play in sports and society via props, costumes, and situations take on greater meaning when viewed from this angle [8; 9; 10; 11]. The "Performative Turn" spawned modes of knowledge production anchored in action, fieldwork, and everyday social dramas in which the combined action of bodies and costume/props/settings gained important signification. As McNamara and Schechner note in their introduction to Turner's From Ritual to Theatre: "Performance is no longer easy to define or locate: the concept and structure has spread all over the place. It is ethnic and intercultural, historical and ahistorical, aesthetic and ritual, sociological and political." [11]. This lateral adoption of the theories of performance in the "Performative Turn" have had an important effect in defining performance as a way of understanding the construction of human events in tandem with the environment.

The role of the body becomes increasingly important within theories of performance, from art to sociology/anthropology. Marcel Mauss' notion of the "techniques of the body" explores how the ways in which the body in movement and display is symbolically crafted [12]. Furthermore, the body itself becomes a highly contested zone of artistic and political agency—keenly tied to socially engaged performance art practices in the 80s and 90s—which sought to re-map the meaning(s) of people in the arts, performance arts stages, and the general public sphere by way of performative actions [13; 14]. The expanding importance of performance, on both a symbolic and a practiced scale, is important when considering wearables as artistic artifacts occurring at the interstice of the body and fashion/technology, for it points to how the body, in consort with costumes, creates performance.

3   Fashion Theory and the Performance of the Adorned Body

Performance theories previously discussed were principally focused on the creation of meaning through performance contexts highlighting the body and costumes/props. However, fashion discourse is specifically focused on the garment's contribution to the construction of meaning when worn on the body. Fashion has built its own set of theories and means of interpretation attached to various practices of adornment and its relationship to the body, the individual, and society. These theories differ from those stemming from performance studies, as their primary departure point for expression is clothing, as opposed to the body. In fashion theory, emphasis is mainly placed on understanding social codes and influences as expressed through sartorial choices and public displays of style, both of which are keenly mapped onto social and economic hierarchic structures. A number of theoretical avenues explored in fashion theory can guide us towards a richer understanding of "performativity" in wearables, specifically from the perspective of the garment's contribution to expression. Of particular interest is the relationship between the body and the garment and how, when combined, new forms of performances of self can occur. As much as performance studies theory can guide us in a better understanding of the body's actions, fashion theory has a more intimate handle on the specific contribution of the garment in shaping meaning at the intersection of the body and clothing.

Theories around dress and fashion start with the garment itself. The main modes of analysis focus on two dominant narratives: emulation (based on social and economic stratification) and communication (based on individual and collective expressiveness) [15]. Early sociological texts focus on emulation in fashion, postulating that styles began at the top of the social hierarchy, with the elite forging a distinctive style of dress, which are then emulated by the lower classes, hence the "trickle-down effect" [16]. Theories of emulation are heavily reliant on a unidirectional social flow from rich to poor, leaving little opening for individual "expressiveness" in fashion or for stylistic "reverse engineering." However, emulation also proposes tensions in expressions of individualism versus collectivism, a creative push and pull still at play today between the classes [16]. Other emulation theories reliant on a psychoanalytical model see fashion as a "social regulating system," entwined in personal psychology and collective desires and other mores often found at the brink of disruption, deviation and change [17]. Philosophical and historical overviews probe the nature of emulation in fashion, revealing the increasingly democratic power of clothes where fashion is not bounded by class but rather affords a fluid political and social trajectory since the modern era [18].

Communication theory, for its part, revolves around the individual's choices in fashion and clothing to express both personal identity as well as group adherence [19; 20; 21]. From this viewpoint, clothing becomes a conduit for "the expressive culture of a community" [15]. Within a communication system, however, where clothing acquires the ability to be "read," there is a danger of also reducing clothing to sign (or semiotic interplay), divorced of bodies, action and performative "events." For example, some texts focus on a strict system of semiotic meaning to explain fashion, such as through print, such as in the case of fashion magazines [22].

Recent fashion theory has begun to incorporate performance as part of fashion's expression. As fashion's influence is increasingly mediated through performance and communication technologies such as photography, film, video, runway shows and the Internet, the importance of fashion "performance" is also coming to the fore. With the rapid stylistic flux associated with fashion, change is intrinsic to its survival (in terms of both economics and relevance), and has propelled more diverse and dynamic developments conflating strict "emulation" or "communication" systems. Fashion is "of the moment" and in this way, it can be appreciated as part of a Zeitgeist linked to performance, event making, and the constructions of mediatized time-based arts [20]. Moreover, fashion as art embodies the "phrasing of human life" which encompasses historical, mediated and performance-based modes of cultural presence [23; 24].

4   Technology as an Extension of the Self

Some analysis of our relationship with technology has to be elaborated in order to discuss the impact of wearable technologies on the body when embedded into fashion/garments. The Canadian philosopher Marshall McLuhan viewed technology as an extension of our bodies, wherein our senses were solicited to interpret and experience media [25]. McLuhan noted that "...the electric age ushers us into a world in which we live and breathe and listen with the entire epidermis" [25]. This epidermis, by which McLuhan means the outer layer of the human skin that protects the flesh, can be used as a metaphor for the second skin that is wearable technologies. As techno-fashion researcher Sabine Seymour notes, digital displays from mobile and networked environments are merging with the organic epidermis of our bodies through wearable technologies [26]. Hence, our bodies increasingly become interfaces, mediated through technologies from interactive art, for handheld or embedded devices. This techno-organic epidermis constructs new relationships with technology, which use wearable technologies to blur the traditional limits between object, garments, information and entertainment. As the concept of the mediatized "epidermis" evolves to represent the meeting of body and technology, new kinds of technological experiences emerge. As technology becomes as extension of the garments and networks in which we participate on a daily basis (Facebook, email, blogs, news feeds, etc.) it also become closer to our body, more immediate in access and more available to interact with other interfaces. Technologies that use somatic inputs are an important element to consider in the "performance" of wearable technologies. Further examples of user interfaces that depend on the body—along with media arts expression via the body—will be investigated to reveal the changing and increasingly intimate relationship we are developing with media interfaces [27; 28; 25; 29: 30].1.4

5   Performative Wearables and Laboratory Cultures

We now look at the atelier/laboratory culture currently involved in wearables research and production. As these sites cultivate the materials, technologies and modes from which techno-fashion is developed, they also stage the ways in which these objects become technologically and somatically performative. In order to follow and engage with this techno-cultural scientific design field, I look at the ways in which Science Technology and Society (STS) theories of laboratory research and knowledge production have used performance as a platform from which to analyze labs [31; 32; 33; 34; 35; 36]. In particular, I look at the branch of STS literature in which performance concepts are used to examine scientific research occurring in laboratories. STS describes events taking place in the laboratory—such as material testing, prototype development, fabrication of new materials, note taking and technology testing—as "performative." Within this theoretical frame, individuals working with technology, materials and various test equipment are considered to be "performative" factors within the development of this research. This "performative" focus is used to analyze laboratories in which individuals and materials play equally "performative" roles in the process of shaping research outcomes. It owes much to mid-twentieth century sociological and anthropological theories of performance, previously described. However, STS theories of performativity expand into the unheralded territory of scientific and material research in order to question the otherwise deductive reasoning of laboratory operations and findings. Performativity from an STS viewpoint, as applied to wearables sites of production offers a unique way to highlight the actions of all involved, from technologies and materials to individuals.

Wearables are complex designs bringing together expertise from the disparate fields of garment making, textiles, engineering, computation and somatic knowledge. One way of examining the intertwined collaborations contributing to the design and technological innovations of wearables is through the optics of performance-focused research as proposed by STS literature. The advantage of using STS performance theories has two principal purposes: a) these theories provide an opportunity to look at a rich and varied spectrum of contributing factors, including the various individuals, material sciences, technologies, and social organizations that shape each unique wearable, and b) they encompass the ateliers/laboratories within the narrative of performative events that traces its history and seeds the modalities of use on and with the body. In this way, an analysis of the studies pertaining to ateliers/laboratories that produce wearables gives us the opportunity to reveal the nuances of the individuals (scientists, designers, engineers) and materials (tools, matter, technologies) that have an impact on design and use outcomes. The perception of the laboratory as a place of genesis for performative wearables informs the story of how they come into being materially and expressively.

As Andrew Pickering notes, technoscientific practices in the field of STS are engendering a shift from a representational model to a performative one, wherein the mechanics of knowledge production, the specific uses of equipment, and the functioning of human/nonhuman "actants" are shaping scientific paradigms. Researchers such as Pickering and Karen Barad propagate this performative perspective. It refutes the premise that scientific knowledge is encoded in only inscriptive forms such as documents, theoretical frameworks, papers, texts and other techniques of traditional knowledge capture and creation [31; 32; 33; 35; 36]. Such a framework maps a shift in science research away from representational modes of knowledge production and toward performative, enacted modes that bridge the gap between knowledge and material through performativity and action [31]. This performative reading of science "shifts the focus from questions of correspondence between descriptions and reality (e.g., do they mirror nature or culture) to matters of practices/doings/actions" [31]. Building on—and departing from—the sociology of scientific knowledge (SSK) theories from the 1970s, discussions of the performativity of both materials and machines becomes important to the understanding of a scientific enquiry that does not want to minimize the contribution of "actions" to knowledge production [35]. In fact, this knowledge is built on the accommodations of human and nonhuman agencies in the process of scientific experimentation [37; 35]. Furthermore, this focus on materiality, from a feminist and scientific realm, is part of a larger, emergent trend occurring in philosophical studies: that of materialities gaining critical ground [38; 39].

Laboratories and their operational structures, the sites where science, technoscience, and techno-artistic research are produced, have emerged arguably as one of paradigmatic loci of analysis for STS. To better understand the processes of knowledge production, the performative contributions of human (scientists and researchers or, in the case of wearables, fashion designers and engineers) and nonhuman agencies (materials, machines) or, as Bruno Latour has called them, actants, are considered as equals in analysis [40; 41; 42; 43; 44; 45; 35; 36]. This permits science to be reevaluated beyond previous Modern schemas of knowledge production that were divorced from the "mangle" of disruptive forces supplied by nonhuman agencies such as machines, materials and tools [35; 37]. By focusing on the tools, matter, and modalities under which scientific objects (and ideas) are measured, shaped, described and harnessed, human contributions are valued on par to nonhuman artifacts, with both influencing and shaping an experiment's goals and results [46; 42]. This ethnography of science practice has been arrived at primarily through sociologists embedding themselves at the sites of material research (labs) to witness the "intimate processes of scientific work." This close analysis of scientific process, viewed from a sociological angle, aims to bridge gaps between "human affairs" and "scientific production" as seen in the production of wearable technologies [42].

6   DIY and the Changing Face of the Laboratory

The changing face of the laboratory—especially in regards to craft, technology and physical computing for artists and designers—also needs to be addressed when discussing wearables. There is a growing body of literature describing the shift in production paradigms taking place as a result of the agglomeration and access to new technologies, machines, and shared expertise. Examples of this increased access range from the proliferation of physical spaces for creating technologies and rapid-prototyping objects (such as FabLabs and Hacker Spaces) to the increased networked possibilities of "print on demand" services for 3D printing, textile printing, and circuit printing. Increasingly, the arts and design "laboratory" has much in common with the cottage industries from before the industrial revolution, with the artist/artisan playing critical roles in fabrication processes and choices and retaining control over the end product or design—an element that Modern production chains had all but erased [47]. Hence, for a field such as wearables design - having direct access to expert machines and technicians can make all the difference. Much like fashion designers who begin their careers with a collection of accessible equipment such as home sewing machines and sergers housed in a basement or studio, the wearables designer and techno-crafter now has access to an increasingly expanding palette of technologies and tools from LilyPad Arduinos, conductive threads, laser cutters and more.

In setting up a context for my own comparative analysis of four studio-labs involved in the design and production of wearables, I make reference to a number of key STS case studies of scientific, natural, social and/or technology-based research in order to develop my own research into the performative elements at play in wearables ateliers/laboratories. Examples such as Bruno Latour's analysis of the failure of the Parisian transportation systems as described in his book Aramis [44], Michel Callon's analysis of the domestication of scallops on the Northern coast of France and anthropologist Georgina Born's embedded narrative of the development of avant-garde music from within France's most famous sound research studio IRCAM [48] all are useful in analyzing the coupling of machines, technologies and tools together with human use, expectations and bodies that underlie the research at hand. By understanding the couplings of individuals and machines residing in studio-lab/ateliers we can better identify the ways in which wearables become materially and socially performative.

7   Wearables: How Do They Perform?

The characteristics valued in wearables can be explored and defined through three different lenses: a) the relationship of the body to fashion and technology; b) the types of material explorations developed to implement technology into the garment; and c) the symbolic expression(s) created by the implementation of technology into fashion and its use on the body.

The first quality relates to the intimate relationship that is forged between the wearable and the body. In particular, it looks at how the body, when combined with technology, is transformed. By this I refer to how the unique mechanical-somatic exchange, created by implementing techno-fashion on the body, proposes new ways of thinking about, moving, and living in the body. The relationship of the body to fashion and technology is particularly expressed in wearables because it does not seek to solve a design/medical/health/safety/social problem, but rather explores how we experience the body in connection with technology and fashion. In this way, wearables are speculative fashion designs that seek to create new experiences for the wearer that are not deterministic, or even tangibly practical.

A second quality that can help us outline wearables for the purposes of this thesis is the type of materials and technologies used in the garments. These include electrical and mechanical technologies that enact some kind of state or material change. These material and technological explorations are found at the juncture of futuristic fashion material innovations such as 3D printing and knitting, digital printing and weaving combined with mechanical and electrical engineering and computational systems. The combination of these innovative fashion and engineering technologies produces design-focused state changes adapted to garments, such as dynamic transformations in shape, colour and illumination.

The third quality investigates the exteriorization of wearables: i.e. what they display, express and project onto the public. Where the first quality of wearables is concerned with the interiorization of the experience of the wearer, this section focuses on what techno-garments express outwards. The range of effects is linked to the materials and techniques used to produce them in the ateliers/laboratories where they are designed and developed. Both stylistically and technically, the range of effects available to wearables varies depending on the milieu in which they are produced (i.e. fashion vs. academia). Each milieu's distinguishing tools, materials, technologies, and design cultures end up shaping the expressions, narratives, and meanings attached to a particular wearable. In all cases, the uniqueness of wearables is expressed outwards, much like how fashion makes a statement about the individual wearing the garment. However, it has the added dimension of technology to generate new meanings and expressions. I situate wearables as tied to performance art through the use of time-based transformation and display on the body. In fashion, as in performance, a story, statement or expression is conjured for a public. It is within this culture of display and expression that I situate wearables gain meaning.

8   Conclusions

In this paper, I seek to situate body-based practices from three distinct yet related fields: (1) the use of the body as object within art historical notions of performance art and performance theory, (2) fashion's understanding of the garments and body in terms of public displays and social significance, and (3) the understanding of media and technology as influencing the somatic. On the one hand, performance art and performance theory constructs and comments on the uses of the body as a symbolic and expressive tool within performance as linked to the everyday, and in connection with objects. On the other hand, fashion theory maps out and categorizes the role of the garment as social construction and personal expression in performance contexts such as the catwalk, film, photography, and street culture. Where one field (performance studies/art) probes the everyday context of the body to create performance, the other (fashion) brings garments into the fold of performance through display, show and media promotion. Finally, in the case of the encroaching importance of technology as a "second skin," wearables and the added layer of media devices seen in society become critical to the understanding of the relationship of technology to the body. In all cases, a theory of bodies and objects is elaborated in which performance is the glue that secures its meaning.

References

1. Carlson, M.: Performance: A Critical Introduction. Routledge, London (1996)
2. Goldberg, R.: Performance Art: From Futurism to the Present. Harry N. Abrams, New York (1979)
3. Schneider, R.: The Explicit Body in Performance. Routledge, London (1997)
4. Schechner, R.: Performance Studies: An Introduction. Routledge, London (2002)
5. Schechner, R.: Performance Theory. Routledge, London (2008)
6. Austin, J.L.: How to Do Things with Words. Harvard University Press (1975)
7. Goffman, E.: The Presentation of Self in Everyday Life. Anchor Books, New York (1959)
8. Conquergood, D.: Poetics, Play, Process and Power: The Performative Turn in Anthropology. Text and Performance Quarterly 9(1), 82–95 (1989)
9. Turner, V.: The Ritual Process: Structure and Anti-Structure. Aldine (1995)
10. Turner, V.: Dramas, Fields and Metaphors: Symbolic Action in Human Society. Cornell University Press (1975)
11. Turner, V.: From Ritual to Theatre: The Human Seriousness of Play. PAJ Publications (1982)
12. Mauss, M.: Techniques of the body. Economy and Society 2(1), 70–88 (1973)
13. Jones, A.: Body Art, Performing The Subject. University of Minnesota Press, Minneapolis (1998)
14. Phelan, P.: Unmarked: The Politics of Performance. Routledge, London (1993)
15. Entwistle, J.: The Fashioned Body: Fashion, Dress and Modern Social Theory. Polity, Cambridge (2000)
16. Simmel, G.: On Individuality and Social Forms. University of Chicago Press, London (1904/1971)
17. König, R.: À la mode: On the Social Psychology of Fashion, trans. F. Bradley. Seabury Press (1974)
18. Lipovetsky, G.: The Empire of Fashion: Dressing Modern Democracy, trans. Catherine Porter. Princeton University Press, Princeton (1994)
19. Barnard, M.: Fashion as Communication. Routledge, London (2002)
20. Davis, F.: Fashion, Culture and Identity. University of Chicago Press, London (1994)
21. Wilson, E.: Adorned in Dreams: Fashion and Modernity. Virago, London (1985)
22. Barthes, R.: Système de la Mode. Éditions du Seuil, Paris (1967)
23. Brand, J., Teunissen, J. (eds.): Fashion and Imagination: About Clothes and Art. ArtEZ Press (2010)
24. Hollander, A.: Feeding the Eye. Douglas & McIntyre / Fsg Adult (1999)

25. McLuhan, M.: Understanding Media: The Extensions of Man. The MIT Press, Cambridge (1964/1994)
26. Seymour, S.: Fashionable Technology: The Intersection of Design, Fashion, Science, and Technology. Springer, Heidelberg (2008)
27. Hansen, M.B.: New Philosophy for New Media. The MIT Press, Cambridge (2006)
28. Hayles, N.K.: How We Became Posthuman: Virtual Bodies in Cybernetics, Literature, and Informatics. The University of Chicago Press, London (1999)
29. Turkle, S.: Life on the Screen. Simon & Schuster, New York (1995)
30. Turkle, S.: The Second Self. The MIT Press, Cambridge (2005)
31. Barad, K.: Posthumanist Performativity: Toward an Understanding of How Matter Comes to Matter. Signs: Journal of Women in Culture and Society 28(3), 801–831 (2003)
32. Barad, K.: Meeting the Universe Halfway: Quantum Physics & the Entanglement of Matter & Meaning. Duke University Press (2007)
33. Herzig, R.: Performance, Productivity, and Vocabularies of Motive in Recent Studies of Science. Feminist Theory 5, 127–147 (2004)
34. Knorr Cetina, K.: Epistemic Cultures: How the Science Make Knowledge. Harvard University Press, Cambridge (1999)
35. Pickering, A.: The Mangle of Practice: Time, Agency, and Science. University of Chicago Press, London (1995)
36. Pickering, A.: The Cybernetic Brain. University of Chicago Press, London (2010)
37. Latour, B.: We Have Never Been Modern. Harvard University Press, Cambridge (1993)
38. Bennett, J.: Vibrant Matter: A Political Ecology of Things. Duke University Press (2009)
39. Braun, B., Whatmore, S.J. (eds.): Political Matter: Technoscience, Democracy, and Public Life. University of Minnesota Press (2010)
40. Callon, M., Lascoumes, P., Barthe, Y.: Acting in an Uncertain World: An Essay on Technical Democracy, trans. Graham Burchell. The MIT Press, Cambridge (2007)
41. Hacking, I.: Representing and Intervening: Introductory Topics in the Philosophy of Natural Science. Cambridge University Press, Cambridge (1983)
42. Latour, B., Woolgar, S., Salk, J. (eds.): Laboratory Life: The Construction of Scientific Facts. Princeton University Press (1986)
43. Latour, B.: Science in Action: How to Follow Scientists and Engineers Through Society. Harvard University Press, Cambridge (1987)
44. Latour, B.: Aramis, or the Love of Technology. Harvard University Press, Cambridge (1996)
45. Latour, B.: Reassembling the Social: An Introduction to Actor-Network-Theory. Oxford University Press (2007)
46. Pickering, A.: Science as Practice and Culture. University of Chicago Press, London (1992)
47. Andersen, C.: Makers: The New Industrial Revolution. Signal, Toronto (2012)
48. Born, G.: Rationalizing Culture: IRCAM, Boulez and the Institutionalization of the Musical Avant-Garde. University of California Press (1995)

A User Experience Design Toolkit

Ioanna Michailidou, Constantin von Saucken, Simon Kremer, and Udo Lindemann

Technische Universität München, Institute of Product Development
{michailidou,saucken,kremer,lindemann}@pe.mw.tum.de

Abstract. User experience design (UXD) is a user-centered and interdisciplinary process, throughout which designers need applicable and feasible methods, tools and criteria. Still only few methods and tools supporting designers in understanding, creating and evaluating user experience systematically are to be found. This paper aims at creating a framework of selected methods, which support designers, even non-UXD-experts, in these activities. The methods come from the fields of product development-engineering, industrial design and interface design and have been applied and adapted in a research project with collaboration with industry. With reference to current state of the art, the methods applied are reviewed and extended with recommendations identified by the researchers. The recommendations should support UXD-practitioners in selecting appropriate, usable and applicable methods, which are most likely to result in positive user experience.

Keywords: DUXU methods and tools, Management of DUXU processes, Story telling.

1 Introduction

The research fields of User Experience (UX) and User Experience Design (UXD) aim at analyzing the users' personal impression and on making the emotional impact of products describable or even measurable. UX refers to an "overall designation of how people have experienced a period of encountering a system" [20] and, according to the ISO definition, it states "a person's perceptions and responses that result from the use or anticipated use of a product, system or service" [9]. We assume that UX in the interaction of a user and a product emerges when the effect of a usage meets the user's psychological motives and needs and fulfills or even exceeds his expectations [22]. UXD is a user-centered and interdisciplinary process and adds important dimensions to the challenge of implementing human-centered design in a mature form. The main distinguishing dimensions of UXD are: UX factors; methods, tools and criteria used in UX work; representation of the UX idea; and UX positioning in the organization [20]. The need for applicable and feasible methods, tools and criteria, in particular, is crucial for the creation of successful but also reproducible products. Still only few methods and tools supporting designers in understanding, creating and/or evaluating UX systematically are to be found.

A. Marcus (Ed.): DUXU 2014, Part I, LNCS 8517, pp. 163–172, 2014.

1.1   Objective

This paper aims at creating a framework of selected methods supporting designers (incl. non-UXD-experts) in analyzing, creating and evaluating UX. The methods come from the fields of product development/engineering, industrial design and interface design. With reference to current state of the art, the methods are reviewed and extended with recommendations and development needs identified by the researchers. The recommendations should support UXD-practitioners in selecting appropriate, usable and applicable methods, which are most likely to result in positive UX.

1.2   Methodology

The study is based on literature review and lessons learned from actual application of methods within a three-year interdisciplinary UXD research project in collaboration with industry. The project goal was the systematical creation and evaluation of UX. The team, consisting of one psychologist, two engineers, one industrial designer, and one human factors expert, investigated, adapted and applied methods from all disciplines in a new development project ("from the scratch"). The project was supervised by UX experts and industrial partners, while the outcomes have also been evaluated in user studies.

2   Results: Methods Selected and Recommendations for Use

Twelve methods have been selected as most effective and applicable. They are presented in this section using following dimensions: design phase of application, goal of application and benefit for UXD. The design process is summarized in three main phases: Analysis (A), Creation (C) and Evaluation (E). The goals of application refer to the literature-based scope of each method. Furthermore, development needs for applying each of the selected methods in the UXD context are suggested by the authors. The main findings of this work are the recommended ways of adapting the methods, in order to make them usable for non-UX-experts with various backgrounds in both academia and industry, and to make their outcomes most likely to enhance a positive UX. In Table 1, the most important results are summarized.

2.1   Mood Board and Overarching Story [17]

Mood boards are typically a collection of abstract media used by designers for personal inspiration and communication with other stakeholders including users. Mood boards are used to promote lateral thinking and help designers refer back to the images when inspiration is needed. Mood boards as tools for communication with non-designers have the advantage of using a shared language getting all stakeholders "on the same wavelength". They are a valuable tool in helping designers to immerse in the user´s world, but also in helping stakeholders to express their emotional needs associated to products. We recommend the use of mood boards to visualize the brand

Table 1.

Method	Phase	Benefits for UXD	Recommendations for UXD
Mood board [17]	A, (E)	Visualizing the vision for the development project in a comprehensive way.	Use of mood boards to visualize the brand image and first development direction, extended by a narration.
Storytelling [4, 19]	A	Collecting user insights with focus on their underlying motives and needs.	Use of Storytelling to collect user insights and documentation/ structuring as story elements [19].
SWOT analysis [24]	A	Analyzing different dimensions of a topic and defining development goals.	Intensive Strength & Opportunity Analysis to define UX-chances (starting points for new positive UX).
Persona [1, 7]	A, (E)	Giving data and statistics a human face.	Creation of market-specific customer profiles based on real data on usage, environment and emotional behavior
Metaphor/Analogy design [16]	C	Anticipating experiences and communicating their emotional impact.	Use of Emotional Mental Models [25] and image-based metaphor representations.
Use scenarios [1, 6]	A, C, E	Promote holistic understanding, derive requirements and insure design targets.	Creating UX Stories, because of their special characteristics which go beyond use scenarios [18, 19].
Requirements list [12]	A, E	Creating measures for the design success.	Extension of requirements list by a UX story visualized as Storyboard [18] and use of Kano-model [12].
TRIZ principles [2]	C	Overcoming contradictions and/or getting inspired by principles and patterns.	Use of UX Principles [26] derived from successful experiences descriptions as inspiration for UXD.
Experience prototypes [5]	C, E	Making the essence of UX visible.	Use of experience prototypes during the whole process, combine different forms (e.g. hardware with UX story).
Function Modelling [12]	A, C	Structuring the product in manageable parts and exploring their relations.	Use of user-oriented and relation-oriented function modeling extended by emotional effects.
Design structure matrix [13]	A	Manage complexity, explore relations, and create function clusters.	UX-related domains, mapping between functions and UX-elements

image and a first development direction in a comprehensive way. Traditionally, a marketing department would provide designers with words and numerical data to work from. Further, we recommend their extension by a narration describing the vision in a more understandable and memorable way ("overarching story").

2.2   Storytelling with Story Elements [4, 19]

Narratives are a helpful tool for supporting communication, collection and compilation of qualitative information. A storytelling approach can be applied during the whole design process to improve the quality of developed concepts regarding UX, as well as to support designers in exploring and communicating their new concept ideas [4]. Narrative methods are commonly applied during the early design phases of situation analysis/field research, mostly in form of real user stories collected through observations and interviews; personas from marketing research; scenarios describing future trends. Storytelling is an appropriate method to collect user insights with focus on their underlying motives and needs, but cannot be used in further development phases unless the results are documented in a useful way. We recommend that the statements obtained from the storytelling sessions should be divided into text blocks and clustered as UX story elements [19]: motives, psychological needs, characters, system components, use cases, key events. Story elements serve as guideline for the interdisciplinary team to structure and summarize its findings and also support the elaboration of (mostly qualitative) requirements.

2.3   SWOT-Analysis and UX Chances [24]

Purpose of a SWOT-analysis is identifying opportunities and risks, analyzing current situation and future developments, identifying strengths and weaknesses. It can be applied as part of product planning or objective analysis and is suitable for strategic as well as operational issues. Its effects involve increased transparency of facts and increased support of the development team in cross-divisional communication and decision making. Particularly important when defining development goals for UXD are the positive aspects of the analysis: strengths and opportunities can serve as starting points/chances for the design of positive experiences. Therefore, we recommend an intensive Strength and Opportunity Analysis to define such UX-chances. Analog to the SWOT-approach, the team analyses the Strengths and Opportunities via appropriate questioning techniques ("What is going well/which are positive experiences?"). Once both fields have been sufficiently illuminated interactions between the two fields are questioned ("How can we use our strengths to exploit the opportunities?"). Results of the analysis are derived UX chances and development goals.

2.4   Persona and Market-Specific Customer Profiles [1, 7]

Personas are fictitious, specific, concrete representations of a customer of a real target group [1], based on behaviors and attitudes of observed real users and representing them throughout the development process [7]. Persona is an excellent method to discuss and prioritize different types of users and their needs in a memorable way and to turn designers' attention on satisfying those customers' needs, making the entire development process more customer-oriented. However, the persona approach can fail due to five main reasons: the persona creation is not accepted/supported by the management; personas appear implausible and are not associated with a methodological approach and use of real data; personas are communicated poorly; the design team has not understood how to use them; their use results into bias and stereotypes. To overcome these difficulties and create a bridge between research and marketing, we suggest creating Customer Profiles with following recommendations:

— create market-specific profiles based on real data
— create a vivid representation in the form of a profile but also show the data they are based on to enhance their conceived validity
— extend real data (e.g. usage and environment data) by findings on emotional behavior and needs
— Customer Profiles should be approved by the management
— their use in next phases (e.g. as UX story characters) should be clearly defined

2.5   Metaphor/Analogy Design and Emotional Mental Models (EMMs) [16, 25]

Human beings understand the world by constructing working models of it in their minds, which are simpler than the entities they represent, known as mental models. Mental models, widely used in usability, are a good approach to influence expectations, although emotional aspects are not considered so far. For the communication and purposeful development of UX stakeholders need to have a shared understanding about the targeted experience. EMMs enrich the concept of mental models in the context of UX [25]. The creation of mental models enhances the usability; EMMs help anticipating the experience and communicating their emotional impact. EMMs enable the capture of emotional responses of people and their explanations and sustain the vision of the design team throughout the design process. For the communication of EMMs image-based metaphor representations focusing on the emotional description of users' motives instead of technologies are recommended.

2.6   Use Scenarios and UX Stories [3, 6, 18]

Anggreeni [3] defines scenarios as "explicit descriptions of the hypothetical use of a product" with three points: Scenarios describe a process or sequence of acts, are formulated from the view point of an actor, which corresponds to a stakeholder and its scope and can range from "narrow" (describing what the product does) to "rich" (describing a larger context of use). Different scenario types can be applied in different design stages, influencing each other and building on each other, as they consist of common elements. Scenarios capture important contextual aspects but miss emotional elements concerning usage over time. The dynamic nature of experiences and temporal aspects of product usage are very important for UXD: indirect experiences can appear before use, e.g. through expectations, as well as extends after usage, e.g. through reflection of previous usage. We recommend creating UX Stories, because of their special characteristics which go beyond use scenarios [18, 19], such as their memorable and understandable narration-format, their specific nature with focus on specific and untypical rather than (proto-) typical situations and on a well-drawn character with known motives and needs rather than an "actor", as well as their personal nature enabling receivers' identification. The UX story bases on user research data collected in the beginning of product development, but can still evolve during the process analog to a requirements list. Both documents accompany the rest of the process as basis for decision making, evaluation and moreover for marketing. Story-building promotes understanding of the interaction and its context holistically, helps identifying qualitative requirements and insuring design targets.

2.7   Requirements List Extended by Storyboard and "Excitement Features" [12]

The aim of a requirements list is to structure and document requirements for task clarification especially at the beginning of the development process but also accompanying during the overall development. The clear documentation of the requirements of a product provides a basis for a complete requirements management; better communication and decision procedures; transparency of priorities and responsibilities; more systematical evaluation and selection of alternative solutions. Traditionally, a requirements list consists of technical, economic or organizational requirements for the life cycle of the product. Because of all these reasons, requirements lists are necessary in UXD projects. Still, they do not capture important UX aspects: contextual and temporal aspects, user motives and goals and interrelations among product attributes or other system components affecting the holistic experience. We therefore recommend extending the requirements list by a UX story visualized as Storyboard [18]. Regarding the requirements prioritization we highly recommend the use of Kano-model [12] to create measures for the design success with emphasis on the features causing customers enthusiasm.

2.8   UX Principles and Patterns [2, 26]

A successful approach to enhance innovation is the "Theory of Inventive Problem Solving-TIPS" [2], developed by G. Altschuller. His approach bases on the claim that successful patented inventions are based on a low number of principles and patterns to overcome contradictions leading to innovation. By analysing a large number of patents (approx. 30000) Altschuller derived 40 innovation principles with examples of successful application to support the creativity process. The approach of overcoming contradictions and getting inspired by principles and patterns can be transferred in UXD: We propose using UX Principles [26] derived from successful experiences descriptions as inspiration for UXD, analog to the use of TRIZ innovation principles. The principles and corresponding examples give helpful recommendations for improving UX aspects.

2.9   Experience Prototypes [5]

"Experience Prototyping" (EP) is a form of prototyping that enables design team members, users and clients to gain first-hand appreciation of existing or future conditions through active engagement with prototypes. EP contributes to design projects in three key ways: Firstly, in understanding essential factors of an existing experience, by simulating important aspects of the whole or parts of the relationships between people, places and objects as they unfold over time. Secondly, EP can provide inspiration, confirmation or rejection of ideas based upon the quality of experience they engender. Thirdly, by enabling others to engage directly in a proposed new experience it supports communication of issues and ideas. For all these reasons we highly recommend the use of EP during the whole design process. Another lesson learned by the application of experience prototypes was that combining different forms of prototypes increased the positive effects: mood boards, UX stories and EMMs can be used besides the hardware prototypes and create a better understanding of UX.

2.10   Function Modeling [12]

Function modeling is a method for analysis and structuring of a product in manageable sub-problems, which are formulated in a solution neutral way. System analysis with identification and description of the system's purpose are in focus, while concrete implementation options are not considered. Positive effects are better dealing with complexity and fewer fixations on existing ideas. There are three types of functional modeling depending on the goal: user-oriented models considering different users during the product life-cycle; flow-oriented considering energy, material and signal conversion; relation-oriented considering relations between functions and depicting connections between useful and harmful functions. Particularly interesting in the UX context are the user- and relation- oriented function models. A user-oriented model can be applied to highlight the differences in the emotional effects caused by the product on different user types. Relation-oriented models are also valuable for visualizing cause-effect relationships and functions useful or harmful to certain emotional effects. By properly adapting the method links such as „caused", „is required for" and „was introduced to avoid" can be used for linking hedonic and pragmatic properties and visualizing the nature (positive/negative) of the relations.

2.11   Design Structure Matrix (DSM) with UX-Related Domains [13]

Matrix-based approaches are widely used for complexity management in many applications in product development, project planning, project management, systems engineering and organization design. Depending on the relations they depict they can be classified in intra-domain matrices (DSMs, in which elements – typically of only one system at a time – and their relationships are mapped), inter-domain matrices (Domain Mapping Matrices-DMMs, linking elements of two different domains), as well as "Multiple-Domain Matrices" (MDMs) as combination. MDM approaches have further been used for managing different types of knowledge configuration and management of multi-project environments. These applications encourage the use of matrix-based approaches in UXD, since similar issues are addressed. To create a positive total UX "soft" aspects, such as user needs and motives need to relate to product functions and characteristics harmoniously. A systematic analysis of those relations can be supported by matrix-based approaches with UX-related domains. Furthermore, UXD practice is user-centered and interdisciplinary and hence challenging to manage; an MDM approach can be beneficial to the UXD-project management.

2.12   UX Evaluation via Needs Fulfillment [10]

Different methods for evaluating UX can be found in literature, depending on the studied period of experience, the types of study and application, the participants and the development phase of application [21]. In our opinion, process-accompanying and continuous, agile testing with user involvement are key aspects concerning UX evaluation. Our approach bases on two claims: that positive UX emerges when users' needs and motives are fulfilled via product usage [22] and that UX can be communicated via experience prototypes (UX stories, mock-ups). Depending on the development phase different types of experience prototypes can be used to communicate the new product idea and needs to be fulfilled to possible users. In early phases, concepts and addressed needs are communicated via a UX story. As the idea becomes more concrete, the UX story is presented in form of a storyboard or accompanies the first physical prototypes. UX stories are a way to create an interaction context, to get certain needs salient and to create a unique experience, since subjects can relive an experience. The needs fulfillment can be tested in questionnaires, where participants are presented relevant items to each need. Early prototypes (e.g. storyboards) can be evaluated within online studies. When testing high fidelity prototypes or, more importantly, the interaction of an integrated prototype, a filed study is preferred. Apart from the qualitative data from the questionnaires, qualitative interview data or customer feedback are very valuable.

3   Discussion: Originality and limitations of this Study

The original findings are the recommendations made by the researchers. The findings are based on the experience of project participants with various backgrounds and are useful for academics and practitioners (because of the research-industry-cooperation), even for non-UX-experts. They reinforce a holistic approach, since most of the selected methods are process-accompanying. The methods are selected because of their suitability for application within complex organizational structures for the design of complex products. Further, some of the methods presented are not used in UXD context so far, while others are known only in specific fields (e.g. interaction design or engineering). The development needs identified would be interesting for the research community.

A limitation of the current study is that the findings are based on lessons learned from one project within a specific frame, so the recommendations are (mostly) valid for application by interdisciplinary teams and preferably during the whole design process. Application in further projects and product categories is planned to support this research. Furthermore, the collection of methods is not exhaustive and should be considered a recommendation rather than a guideline. Future work focuses on creating such a guideline with recommended sequences of methods based on specific project goals.

4   Conclusions

Twelve methods from the fields of engineering, industrial design and HCI are reviewed based on the lessons learned from application in an interdisciplinary UXD project. The researchers identify development needs and recommend adaptations in the use of the methods to support the analysis, creation and evaluation of UX within interdisciplinary teams. The methods presented can be used selectively in the Analysis, Creation or Evaluation phase; on the other hand, the UXD toolkit forces a holistic approach, since the recommended results build on each other. The desired outcomes are: UX chances as development goals; a mood board and a narration describing the vision for the development project; user insights documented as story elements; market-specific customer profiles; a requirements list extended by a UX story visualized as storyboard and highlighted "excitement features"; emotional mental models and experience prototypes describing the new concept; relations depicted in relation-oriented function models and DSMs; evaluation results based on UX stories and experience prototypes. The methods applicability and positive effect on UX ("significantly increased customer insights and design of better UX") was assessed by industry partners, UX experts and prospective users within project studies.

References

1. Adlin, P.: The Essential Persona Lifecycle - Your Guide to Building and Using Personas. Elsevier Inc., Burlington (2010)
2. Altschuller, G.S.: Erfinden: Wege zur Lösung technischer Probleme. Verlag Technik (1986)
3. Anggreeni, I.: Making use of scenarios: Supporting scenario use in product design. Dissertation, Enschede, University of Twente (2010)
4. Brooks, K., Quesenbery, W.: Storytelling for User Experience. O'Reilly Media, Inc. (2011)
5. Buchenau, M., Suri, J.F.: Experience prototyping. In: Proceedings of the 3rd Conference on Designing Interactive Systems: Processes, Practices, Methods, and Techniques. ACM (2000)
6. Carroll, J.M. (ed.): Scenario-based design: Envisioning work and technology in system development, pp. 37–58. Elsevier Science B.V., Amsterdam (1995)

7. Cooper, A., Reimann, R., Cronin, D.: About Face 3 - The Essentials of Interaction Design. Wiley Publishing Inc., Indianapolis (2007)
8. Hawley, M.: Design research methods for experience design (2009), http://www.uxmatters.com/mt/archives/2009/01/design-research-methods-for-experience-design.php (retrieved October 25, 2013)
9. ISO DIS 9241–210:2008. Ergonomics of human system interaction-Part 210: Human-centered design for interactive systems (formerly known as 13407). International Organization for Standardization (ISO). Switzerland (2008)
10. Korber, M., et al.: User experience evaluation in an automotive context. In: 2013 IEEE Intelligent Vehicles Symposium (IV), Gold Coast, Australia (2013)
11. Kumar, V.: 101 Design methods: A structured approach for driving innovation in your organization. Wiley. com (2012)
12. Lindemann, U.: Methodische Entwicklung technischer Produkte: Methoden flexibel und situationsgerecht anwenden, p. 70, 73, 85, 309. Springer, DE (2009)
13. Lindemann, U., et al.: Structural complexity management. Springer (2009)
14. Maguire, M.: Methods to support human-centered design. Human-Computer Studies 55, 587–634 (2001)
15. Mao, J.-Y., et al.: User-centered design methods in practice: a survey of the state of the art. In: Proceedings of the 2001 Conference of the Centre for Advanced Studies on Collaborative Research, vol. 12 (2001)
16. Marcus, A.: Metaphor design for user interfaces. In: CHI 1998 Conference Summary on Human Factors in Computing Systems. ACM (1998)
17. McDonagh, D., Storer, I.: Mood boards as a design catalyst and resource: researching an under-researched area. The Design Journal 7(3), 16–31 (2004)
18. Michailidou, I., von Saucken, C., Lindemann, U.: How to create a user experience story. In: Marcus, A., et al. (eds.) DUXU/HCII 2013, Part I. LNCS, vol. 8012, pp. 554–563. Springer, Heidelberg (2013)
19. Michailidou, I., von Saucken, C., Lindemann, U.: Extending the product specification with emotional aspects: Introducing User Experience Stories. In: International Conference on Engineering Design, ICED 2013, Seoul, Korea (2013)
20. Roto, V., Law, E., Vermeeren, A., Hoonhout, J. (eds.): User Experience Whitepaper (2011), http://www.allaboutux.org/files/UX-WhitePaper.pdf (January 20, 2014)
21. Roto, V., et al.: All about UX (2011), http://www.allaboutux.org (January 20, 2014)
22. Sheldon, K., Elliot, A., Kim, Y., Kasser, T.: What is Satisfying about Satisfying Events? Journal of Personality and Social Psychology 80(2), 325–339 (2001)
23. Thier, K.: Storytelling: Eine Narrative Managementmethode. Springer, Heidelberg (2010)
24. Thompson, J.: Strategic Management: Awareness and Change. Chapman and Hill, London (1994)
25. von Saucken, C., Michailidou, I., Lindemann, U.: Emotional Mental Model. In: The International Conference on Engineering and Engineering Management, Bangong, Thailand (2013)
26. von Saucken, C., et al.: Principles for User Experience Design: Adapting the TIPS Approach for the Synthesis of Experiences. In: Proceedings of the 5th International Congress of International Association of Societies of Design Research, IASDR 2013, Tokyo, Japan (2013)

How Two become One – Creating Synergy Effects by Applying the Joint Interview Method to Design Wearable Technology

Ulrike Schmuntzsch and Lea H. Feldhaus

TU Berlin, Department of Psychology and Ergonomics,
Chair of Human-Machine Systems Office: MAR 3-1, Marchstr. 23, 10587 Berlin, Germany
{usc,lfe}@mms.tu-berlin.de

Abstract. This paper addresses the design of wearable technology and its user acceptance by applying the *Joint Interview Method*. In order to further develop a wearable warning system in form of a glove, five semi-structured joint interviews were held by a trained human factors specialist. Each joint interview consisted of one respondent with an engineering background and one respondent with a psychological or cognitive-science background. In this process, the *Joint Interview Method* revealed two advantages: First, the interviews benefited from the discussion between both participants and, second, it enabled an observation from two different perspectives (i.e. one implementation-oriented view, which focused on the technological capabilities and the other user-oriented view, which focused on human perception and information processing). Both aspects mentioned led to synergy effects. To sum up, the *Joint Interview Method* turned out to be a promising usability approach to explore new technologies' potential and user acceptance and therefore, can be recommended for its use in the process of designing and evaluating wearables.

Keywords: dyadic interview, two-person-interview, user-centered design, user acceptance, smart clothing, wearable warning system, industrial maintenance.

1 Introduction

Technological developments are advancing rapidly while components are getting smaller and more powerful at the same time. As one result, technology is getting closer to the human body and becomes "wearable". This year's International Consumer Electronics Show (CES) held in January 2014 in Las Vegas was focusing on this so-called *wearable technology*. This kind of technology which is usually worn directly on the human body seems to be the next big thing in consumer electronics. At the CES 2014, visitors had the possibility to marvel miscellaneous smart devices such as watches, wrist- and sweatbands, glasses and contact lenses and even jewelry. Most of these devices are designed to give the wearer condensed information gathered from measures of his or her physical and mental state combined with environmental parameters. The majority of these devices are definitely bursting with technical ingenuity, but what manufacturers really need to know is what potential users seek in

A. Marcus (Ed.): DUXU 2014, Part I, LNCS 8517, pp. 173–184, 2014.
© Springer International Publishing Switzerland 2014

smart devices and how these wearables have to be designed in order to convince users to wear those (Gibbs & Arthur, 2014).

Addressing the important issue of user acceptance when designing wearable technology, this paper presents and discusses the *Joint Interview Method* as a promising usability approach which allows evaluating user's opinion in a profound yet efficient way. For this purpose, the paper focuses on the design of a second version of a wearable warning system by applying the *Joint Interview Method*. At the outset, the theoretical background of wearable technology and of usability testing methods, especially the *Joint Interview Method*, is introduced. This is followed by a description of the research design and its implementation in this application context. Later on, findings and the following design process are presented and discussed. This paper concludes with some general advice on how to use the *Joint Interview Method* to design wearable technology.

2   Theoretical Background

2.1   Wearable Technology and Smart Clothing

Currently, wearable technology is having a great deal of attention and there are many attempts to design them in different fields of industry. Some examples are a haptic shoe for visually impaired people guiding their way and warning against obstacles (Saha, 2012), an intelligent curve warning glove for motorcyclists providing warnings by haptic signals (Huth, Biral, Martín & Lot, 2012) or for introducing wearables in industrial contexts a data glove made for hands-free interaction during aircraft maintenance was developed (Nicolai, Sindt, Witt, Reimerdes & Kenn, 2006).

There are many other examples referring to technology that is more or less wearable. Related terms are *smart clothes* or *clothing*, *wearable (computing) technology*, *E-textiles*, *I-wear* and *intelligent garments*. In this paper, the terms *wearable technology* and *wearables* will be used synonymously. Wearable technology aims to develop electronic devices which are wearable. In contrast, smart clothing emphasizes the importance of clothing (Barfield et al., 2001). The components used in wearable technology are conventional and non-textile which oftentimes make them feel bulky and impeding (Cho, Lee & Cho, 2009). In contrast, smart clothing uses textiles in which electronic functions are embedded (Barfield et al., 2001). General examples for electronics becoming wearable are conductive thread, flexible conductor boards or light and flexible sensors. Combining textile characteristics and electronic functionality, users favor smart clothing over wearable technology because of the lightweight design, flexibility, comfort and practicability in terms of washability and robustness (Kirstein, Cottet, Grzyb & Tröster, 2005).

Wearables are numerous and diverse but the main idea is to develop technology for use in practical tasks while releasing the user from having to carry around an extra device such as a tablet or laptop. Another aspect is to enable the user to perform all the necessary tasks without losing focus due to distracting eye movements or interrupting actions. Furthermore, since our world is becoming more and more complex, there is a need for technology that supports its user anytime and anywhere in a personal, unobtrusive and embedded manner (Cho et al., 2009). Focusing on wearable technology, another important aspect to consider is the "wearing comfort". Thereby, three aspects strongly determine the user's well-being and the user's willingness to use a device regularly. These factors are the thermophysiological comfort, the sensorial comfort and the body-movement comfort (Hatch, 1993).

In order to meet these diverse requirements it is essential to involve potential users from an early stage and to develop and test wearables in iterations.

2.2   Usability Engineering Process

A well-known process model to design in iterations and test various kinds of human-machine systems is the *Usability Engineering Lifecycle* according to Deborah Mayhew (1999). This approach consists of three main phases which are named as *requirement analysis, design, testing and development* and *implementation* of the system in an applied setting. Everything revolves around the user's needs in order to facilitate an effective and efficient but also satisfying interaction with the designed product.

After defining user profiles and tasks at the first stage of the *Usability Engineering Lifecycle*, the second stage deals with the iterative design and testing of increasingly advanced prototypes of the future system. Thereby, less than ten potential users per test cycle are sufficient to detect most of the major usability problems and to collect suggestions for further improvements (Nielsen, 2000).

In order to reasonably integrate users in the design process several usability testing methods are at hand (e.g. Sarodnick & Brau, 2006). For instance, observing a user's interaction with a prototype and afterwards asking the user about the experience is an often used combination of methods. Advantages lie in the opportunity of an early detection of usability problems as well as in a selection of ideas for further improvements implemented in a following version of the system. In some cases this combination of methods should be used with caution: High fidelity prototypes, for example, might inhibit the user to express general criticism towards the prototype or its usage. On the other hand, low fidelity paper pencil prototypes, where users might feel less inhibited to express negative thoughts, might lack important physical impressions such as touch. Having this dilemma one should carefully consider how elaborated a prototype has to be and what other options might exist for testing its physical appearance as well.

2.3   The Joint Interview Method

Designing a wearable warning system involves several topics to be considered: On account of its novelty and its closeness to the human body, a participatory design is helpful to identify the needs and doubts of potential users. In this context, semi-structured interviews can be useful (Frieling & Sonntag, 1999). In comparison to a structured interview, a semi-structured interview still captures a predetermined range of issues but ensures flexibility in the topics' arrangement and depth in which they are addressed (Dunn, 2005). Moreover, a semi-structured interview allows a rather natural course of conversation. In this, the interviewees can refer or return to earlier discussed topics thus a topic can be amplified or neglected.

Usually, interviews and user studies are conducted one-on-one: One interviewer asks one respondent. In this case, a different format was chosen: joint interviews. This term is used heterogeneously. Either it means that two interviewers ask one respondent or it refers to the opposite, two interviewees asked by only one interviewer (Arskey, 1996).

In this paper, the term is used if one researcher interviews two respondents at the same time. This constellation has been named differently in the past: *dyadic interview* (Morgan, Ataie, Carder & Hoffman, 2013) and *two-person-interview* (Eliot, 2010). To the authors' knowledge, the *Joint Interview Method* has been scarcely investigated from an explorative design method point of view. Several reasons led to the selection of this method. Because the field of wearables is rather new and has a great potential for innovation, the interviews have an explorative purpose. The respondent's interaction and their sometimes contrary opinions can reveal new theoretical and practical implications to think about. Moreover, the interviewees spur each other to develop and discuss new ideas. Analogically, in usability test sessions a method is used in which two participants are invited to participate simultaneously, interacting with each other. This is also known under the terms *co-discovery method* and *constructive interaction* (Beier & von Gizycki, 2002). In contrast to a focus group, the *Joint Interview Method* avoids biasing group dynamics. One or two dominant group members can control the topic selection which leads to less varied suggestions (Frieling & Sonntag, 1999). Besides, group cohesion makes it hard for one person to have a different opinion on a topic and to express elaborated thoughts about it (Fern, 2001). Therefore, joint interviews offer a rather balanced discussion between two interviewees in which less dominant participants can express their ideas freely.

3   Applying the Joint Interview Method

In order to develop a wearable warning system to support a human operator performing industrial maintenance, this research project used the *Usability Engineering Lifecycle* from Mayhew (1999) which suggests an iterative design process and intensive user involvement. As explained in chapter 2.1, the user-centered approach becomes even more important when designing wearable technology. To choose and implement the appropriate usability method, several aspects have to be considered. As mentioned in chapter 2.2, one should carefully determine how advanced the prototype has to be and how to test its physical appearance. Another crucial aspect is, as mentioned in chapter 2.3, to choose the appropriate form of user involvement to get as much feedback and suggestions as possible, but also to work efficiently and avoid undesirable side effects, e.g. opinion leadership (Frieling & Sonntag, 1999).

Before describing how the *Joint Interview Method* was applied for designing a second version of a wearable warning system, chapter 3.1 briefly introduces the previous prototype which was developed in form of a warning glove.

3.1   Status Quo – The First Version of the Warning Glove

The research project's purpose is to develop a warning system that supports a human operator and reduces human error during maintenance tasks in industrial settings.

Conventional warning systems which are directly attached to a machine often suffer from a lack of what we refer to as *action-specificity*, as signals are not clearly related to the operator's actions and with that do not provide specific instructions to prevent further errors. Furthermore, these warnings are usually given visually and auditory (Wogalter, 2006) excluding the haptic perception.

This research project attempts to avoid both problems by designing a wearable warning system that fits stimulus-response compatibility more appropriately and effectively. Thus, by combining both action-specificity and multimodality including the haptic sense a warning glove was designed and tested against a conventional warning system (Schmuntzsch, Sturm & Rötting, 2012; Schmuntzsch & Feldhaus, 2013). Aiming to minimize body-movement restrictions and maintain natural performance, the first prototype was a glove for the right hand with free fingertips. To directly present multimodal warnings on the glove before or while an operating error took place several electronic devices were attached. Following the given definition of wearable technology and smart clothing from Barfield et al. (2001), as stated in chapter 2.1, the designed warning glove would rather be classified as wearable technology than smart clothing. For transmitting visual warnings, two LED stripes with three red LEDs each were attached. Auditory warnings were given through a small speaker. For tactile warnings two vibrating elements were used. The electronic devices were controlled by an Arduino microcontroller using a wireless XBee connection (Fig 1).

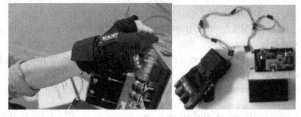

Fig. 1. Warning glove with multimodal devices (left) and glove with Arduino microcontroller and XBee receiver (right)

Using the warning glove, both quantitative and qualitative data was collected in the first study in which the prototype was tested against a conventional warning system. Generally, the warning glove has proven to be an appropriate support to a human operator performing an industrial maintenance task. A trend was observed for reaction times: individuals wearing the warning glove tended to respond quicker to warnings than when using the conventional warning system. This effect was especially commented on tactile and auditory signals. Qualitative interviews revealed that the majority of respondents preferred receiving warnings from the warning glove. However, due to its rigid components which were more attached than incorporated participants mentioned comfort as the main aspect to improve and their feedback clearly gave direction to smart clothing.

Before developing the second version of a wearable warning system another round of iterative user involvement was scheduled to ensure that the new prototype will meet user's requirements. Therefore, due to the benefits mentioned in chapter 2.3, the *Joint Interview Method* was chosen and implemented.

3.2   Research Design and Implementation

To explore the potential of wearables used as warning systems and to seek for user's needs while working with them, a human factors specialist with a psychology background conducted five semi-structured joint interviews. For an effective pairing, the ten participants were selected in consideration of their academic background: One having a social science background, e.g. psychology or cognitive science, the other having a technical background, e.g. mechanical engineering or computer sciences. Merging these differing perspectives, the joint interviews were expected to profit from synergy effects in two respects: First, it should allow for an observation of two different perspectives at once (i.e. one implementation-oriented perspective focused on the technological capabilities and the other user-oriented perspective focused on human perception and information processing). Second, while interacting with each other, the interviewees should inspire each other, building on topics and ideas raised by each other and so stimulating each other's imagination.

During the joint interviews, participants were able to see and touch components and materials which were considered to be used. This permitted the interviewees to develop an accurate impression about the technical components and materials used, to encourage their imagination and to express themselves by pointing at materials.

The interview started with a short introduction of the topic, presenting a maintenance scenario as a possible use case, the first warning glove prototype, and possible components for the new prototype (e.g. OLED-display, warning lights, speaker). Guiding through the conversation, the interviewer asked questions from a set of 15 open-ended questions. The initial topics covered a wide range of aspects such as:

- Possible areas of application and user acceptance (e.g. "In which field of work do you consider the warning glove as a reasonable work support?")
- Specific aspects referring to the wearable's design (e.g. "Can you think of a different wearable fulfilling the same or similar functions?")
- Specific aspects regarding the warnings' characteristics such as the length of warning signals (e.g. "How long should the signal continue?") and the use of word-based warnings versus warning symbols (e.g. "Would you prefer keywords or warning symbols on a display?" and "What sort of keyword would you wish for?").

Starting from a general perspective, participants had the chance to become acquainted with the topic and to develop a mindset including possibilities of wearables in an industrial context before specific characteristics were addressed. Furthermore, the interaction between the interviewees was encouraged by further questions based on previous answers. The semi-structured manner of the interview allowed for a certain level of standardization and subsequent comparability among the answers. Alternatively, there was enough flexibility for the interviewer to explore interesting aspects of the discussion in more detail.

All interviews were video-taped and analyzed. Reoccurring suggestions and differing opinions were summarized. The interviewing time was one hour at most.

4   Results

4.1   Participants

The sample consisted of ten participants (N=10, mean age = 24.8 years, range in age = 23 - 29 years; 6 male and 4 female). All participants were human factors students from the Technische Universität Berlin, either with a bachelor's degree in psychology or in engineering. Participants were recruited by advertisements to the general campus as well as on an internet platform accessible for human factor students. As part of required student assignments, students got credits for participation.

4.2   Findings of the Joint Interview

The findings were rich in content and contrast. Opinions ranged from total rejection to enthusiastic opinions. Of the vast amount of insights which could be gathered, only a certain amount can be mentioned in here. Several theories which should be considered while designing a wearable warning system were mentioned by the participants, e.g. the *stimulus-response compatibility* (e.g. Kornblum & Lee, 1995), the *proximity compatibility principle* (e.g. Wickens & Carswell, 1995), the *cry wolf effect* (e.g. Breznitz, 2013) and the *theory of prospective memory* (e.g. McDaniel & Einstein, 2007). To illustrate the dyadic discussion, the prospective memory was referred to when a rather technical-driven participant mentioned a reminder function build in the glove. His fellow interviewee pointed out that this would support the prospective memory leading to a conclusion that a good application for the warning glove would be given in tasks in which many subtasks are included.

In general, a majority of participants stressed the importance of the task nature. In their opinion a wearable could support a user either when the task has to be done in irregular intervals or when the task is new and the user needs support in his or her learning process (e.g. if the user is an apprentice). Especially, if the task consists of several subtasks a long learning process could be reduced. A recurrent topic was sensors capable of broadening the sensory input of humans and hence the user's perception. Participants suggested perception of magnetic and electric fields, a camera (e.g. an endoscope) attached to the tip of a finger as well as a sensor for heat and weight.

According to the participants, the glove would need to be reliable in order to avoid negative effects such as the *cry wolf phenomenon* (Breznitz, 2013). Furthermore, participants wished for positive feedback. An analogy was drawn between the glove and a build-in car parking assistance: Here, it can be seen how easily people adapt to support signals and use these signals but at the same time why the signals have to be reliable. This marks that a certain routine is important to work efficiently with the warning system. Due to this routine and the immediate feedback, a participant with a rather theoretical background inferred that a consistency between error signals and error-prone situations would assist users to develop a certain sensibility for adverse situations. To conclude the interviewees saw two main opportunities to use the warning glove: First, to use it as an instructional tool and second, to use it as a warning system.

Asked about possible combinations of wearables, one third of the participants asked for data glasses (e.g. *Google glasses*) as well as for earphones to complete the warning glove support. Combined with glasses, the human perception could be enriched with additional data displayed as augmented reality. Participants who asked for earphones thought about sound signals which would only be heard by the user and not by his or her surroundings.

If a glove is already part of protective clothing, a warning glove was considered perfectly feasible. If not so, the majority would prefer for a warning collar in order to have a high degree of freedom in hand action. Maximal closeness to the operator's hand was demanded to fulfil the proximity compatibility principle. This principle states that warning signs and displays showing warning information should be placed together close to the origin of the warning (Wickens & Carswell, 1995).

The major advantage reported by nine out of ten participants is the haptic feedback. Perceived as beneficial is the anonymity especially if several operators are in the surroundings. Additionally, the direct and body-related feedback was emphasized. Moreover, four out of ten interviewees favored a display for a new wearable warning system by. The display should be bigger than the one (0.96") shown as a possible component and if possible it should be a flexible and moveable OLED-display. If the display has to have a fixed positioning than the majority rather preferred a positioning analogically to a watch than on the back of one's hand.

4.3   Insights of the Following Design Process

Generally, the inclusion of the *Joint Interview Method* in the design process of a wearable warning system can be considered beneficial. Due to the participants' discussions new insights were gathered and especially their interaction revealed synergy effects. Furthermore, presenting the maintenance task, the first warning prototype and possible materials for the second version has proven to be stimulating participant's imagination. Many of the ideas gathered in the joint interview were easily applicable.

As mentioned in 4.2, participants asked for a bigger flexible, moveable OLED-display. Due to the still ongoing development of flexible displays and the risks as well as the costs involved in this, a conventional – meaning an inflexible – OLED-display was selected. Nevertheless, the display was exchanged to a 1.5"-display and a watch-like positioning was chosen. The amount of used fabric was decreased. To assure a high degree of hand flexibility, the idea of glove was withdrawn and, as the majority wished for, the idea of a collar was realized. Here, participants asked for a watch-like dimension. Although a high fidelity prototype with microcontrollers was our aim, technical and temporal limitations led to the development of an arm collar with 13cm in width. These microcontrollers are part of the Arduino LilyPad series which are designed for wearables. The idea of additional sensors was not realized since the project focuses on investigating how to design more action-specific warnings and not on the detection of human errors. For positive feedback, green LEDs were integrated next to the yellow and red LEDs for warnings. The warning collar is shown in Fig. 2.

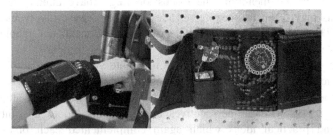

Fig. 2. Warning collar with multimodal devices (left) and the inside of the collar with Arduino LilyPad microcontroller and lithium polymer batteries (right)

5   Discussion

Driven by the project's goal to support human operators while performing maintenance tasks in industrial facilities, a wearable warning system in form of a warning glove was developed and tested. Based on the *Usability Engineering Lifecycle* from Mayhew (1999) this wearable warning system was improved after the consideration of user's feedback. To ensure that the second prototype would meet user's requirements the *Joint Interview Method* was chosen and implemented. Using that method, this paper presents a promising usability method which allows addressing the crucial issue of designing wearable technology and evaluating its user acceptance, a topic also raised at the CES 2014.

In view of the process and its results, applying the *Joint Interview Method*, the project's aim – to create synergy effects – was achieved. First, synergy effects were created by simply interviewing two participants at once. Second, synergy effects also emerged due to the effective pairing of participants one having a rather technical-oriented background and the other one having a psychological background.

According to the first aspect mentioned, having two participants turned the interview more into a dialog between two interviewees rather than a direct face-to-face questioning between one interviewer and one respondent. The interview's atmosphere became more relaxed and both participants stimulated each other so that one idea led to another. Comparing the *Joint Interview Method* with a normal interview, another advantage of the *Joint Interview Method* was found to be timing. While one participant was talking the other one could reflect about the topic profoundly. This led to both a deeper comprehension as well as to more sophisticated ideas regarding the further development of the prototype. Comparing the *Joint Interview Method* with a focus group in which five participants are asked for their opinions at once, a joint interview is less demanding for the interviewer and allows responding individually to each interviewee without strain. Moreover, negative side effects of focus groups such as opinion leadership can be avoided. However, in one of the five joint interview sessions this problem also evolved since one of the interviewees was extremely dominant. In order to equalize the contributions the interviewer then explicitly asked the more silent participant first. With an eye to the participants of a focus group, the situation can be exhausting and frustrating since individuals have to wait for their turn to express their thoughts, while in the meantime the discussion might have already taken another direction. This may result in unexpressed ideas and less active involvement of some individuals. Thus, applying the *Joint Interview Method* facilitates tapping into the individual potential of each interviewee.

According to the second aspect mentioned, interviewing one implementation-oriented participant, focused on the technological capabilities and one user-oriented participant, focused on human perception and information processing allowed for an observation of two different perspectives at once. This led to a combination of theoretical and practical ideas which again complemented each other. Thereby, different roles could be observed: the implementation-oriented participant mostly took the practical part and created lots of ideas whereas the user-oriented one brought in a kind of theoretical skepticism and tried to get to the bottom of the ideas. This in turn sparked new thinking processes and led to more sophisticated concepts expressed by the implementation-oriented participant. In contrast, sometimes the user-oriented participant also underpinned the technical ideas with psychological concepts and developed them further. However, during one session one participant's extreme dominance led to the situation that despite the subtle counteraction of the interviewer the other more psychological-oriented participant secluded herself. Thus, the dialog turned into a monolog and with that the more pragmatic technical-oriented opinion leadership prevailed. Later on, the interviewer tried to balance the dialog, as mentioned above, by asking the rather quiet participant first. However, such a dominant form of opinion leadership happened only once whereas the other interviews were characterized by a balanced and varied dialog.

All in all, it can be stated that the *Joint Interview Method* is helpful for creating synergy effects and supports a user-centered design approach to develop wearables. Although the sample was not representative since all participants were human factors students and thus trained to cooperate interdisciplinary in contexts of human-machine-interaction, the *Joint Interview Method* is considered to be also beneficial in other constellations. Here, participants must be paired effectively and have to be sensitized for interdisciplinary collaboration. Moreover, from our experiences, in order to successfully apply the *Joint Interview Method* it is important to bear certain things in mind: The interviewer must be well-trained and prepared for this task which includes being practiced in interview techniques as well as being aware of group dynamic processes and different personality traits. Furthermore, the interviewer should be open for any directions the interviewees might take even though they wander off the point. During the interviews it became apparent that participants found their way back to the topic without the interviewer's intervention. In fact, it seemed that this deviation led to a deeper understanding and to a development of more sophisticated ideas. Apart from digression the interviewer should also be tolerant if somebody has a calmer mood or says nothing to one or the other aspect.

With regard to promoting the user-centered design of wearables, the *Joint Interview Method* offers a particularly great opportunity for early user involvement. Since physical appearance and touch is of immense importance for wearables, it is highly recommended to not only show paper pencil prototypes but also basic materials such as fabrics and technical components, e.g. OLEDs, speakers and vibrating elements. Because the maintenance scenario, the first warning glove and the materials possible for the second prototype were presented to the participants, the participants were able to develop a certain understanding of the innovative topic "wearable warning systems". As a result, more sophisticated ideas for the second prototype in form of a collar evolved.

6   Conclusion

To sum up, this paper presented and discussed the *Joint Interview Method* as a promising usability approach for designing wearables and evaluating user acceptance. Therefore, the method was used to exemplarily enhance a wearable warning system whose first prototype was a glove whereas the second version turned into a more sophisticated collar. Since one interviewer questions not only one but two interviewees this method facilitates a relaxed and stimulating dialog. Thereby, synergy effects automatically evolve as an inherent part of the *Joint Interview Method* due to the explorative and dyadic character. Finally, from our experiences, applying the *Joint Interview Method* in the design process of wearables can be highly recommended.

Acknowledgments. We thank the German Research Foundation (DFG, Deutsche Forschungsgemeinschaft) for funding this research within the Transregional Collaborative Research Project TRR 29 on Industrial Product-Service Systems – dynamic interdependencies of products and services in production area.

References

1. Arskey, H.: Collecting data through joint interviews. Social Research Update 15, 1–8 (1996)
2. Barfield, W., Mann, S., Baird, K., Gemperle, F., Kasabach, C., Stivoric, J., Bauer, M., Martin, R., Cho, G.: Computational clothing and accessories. In: Barfield, W., Caudell, T. (eds.) Fundamentals of Wearable Computers and Augmented Reality, pp. 471–509. Routledge (2001)
3. Beier, M., Von Gizycki, V. (eds.): Usability. IFIP AICT, vol. 99. Springer, Heidelberg (2002)
4. Breznitz, S.: Cry wolf: The psychology of false alarms. Psychology Press (2013)
5. Cho, G., Lee, S., Cho, J.: Review and reappraisal of smart clothing. International Journal of Human-Computer Interaction 25(6), 582–617 (2009)
6. Dunn, K.: Interviewing. In: Hay, I. (ed.) Qualitative Research Methods in Human Geography, 2nd edn. Oxford University Press (2005)
7. Eliot, S.: David Morgan on the Two-Person Interview. Qualitative-researcher.com (August 31, 2010), http://www.qualitative-researcher.com (retrieved December 12, 2013)
8. Fern, E.F.: Advanced focus group research. Sage (2001)
9. Frieling, E., Sonntag, K.: Arbeitspsychologie. Hans Huber, Bern (1999)

10. Gibbs, S., Arthur, C.: CES 2014: Why wearable technology is the new dress code. The Guardian (2014), http://www.theguardian.com/technology/2014/jan/08/wearable-technology-consumer-electronics-show (retrieved January 8, 2014)
11. Hatch, K.L.: Textile science. West Publishing, Minneapolis (1993)
12. Huth, V., Biral, F., Martín, Ó., Lot, R.: Comparison of two warning concepts of an intelligent Curve Warning system for motorcyclists in a simulator study. Accident Analysis and Prevention 44, 118–125 (2012)
13. Kirstein, T., Cottet, D., Grzyb, J., Tröster, G.: Wearable computing systems – electronic textiles. In: Xiaoming, T. (ed.) Wearable Electronics and Photonics, pp. 177–197. CRC Press, Boca Raton (2005)
14. Kornblum, S., Lee, J.W.: Stimulus-response compatibility with relevant and irrelevant stimulus dimensions that do and do not overlap with the response. Journal of Experimental Psychology: Human Perception and Performance 21(4), 855 (1995)
15. Lieberman, J., Breazeal, C.: Development of a Wearable Vibrotactile Feedback Suit for Accelerated Human Motor Learning. In: Proceedings of the 2007 IEEE ICRA, pp. 4001–4006 (2007)
16. Macefield, G., Gandevia, S.C., Burke, D.: Conduction velocities of muscle and cutaneous afferents in the upper and lower limbs of human subjects. Brain 112(6), 1519–1532 (1989)
17. Mayhew, D.: The Usability Engineering Lifecycle – A Practitioner's Handbook for User Interface Design. Academic Press, San Francisco (1999)
18. McDaniel, M.A., Einstein, G.O.: Prospective memory: An Overview and Synthesis of an Emerging Field. Sage (2007)
19. Morgan, D.L., Ataie, J., Carder, P., Hoffman, K.: Introducing Dyadic Interviews as a Method for Collecting Qualitative Data. Qualitative Health Research 23(9), 1276–1284 (2013)
20. Nielsen, J.: Why you only need to test with 5 users. Nielsen Norman Group (2000), http://www.useit.com/alertbox/20000319.html (retrieved February 5, 2012)
21. Saha, M.K.: Anirudh Sharma Invents Haptic Shoe for the Visually Impaired. MIT Technology Review (2012), http://www.technologyreview.com/tr35/profile.aspx?TRID=1258 (retrieved July 31, 2012)
22. Sarodnick, F., Braun, H.: Methoden der Usability-Evaluation – Wissenschaftliche Grundlagen und Praktische Anwendung. Huber, Bern (2011)
23. Schmuntzsch, U., Feldhaus, L.H.: The Warning Glove: Wearable Computing Technology for Maintenance Assistance in IPS². In: 12th IFAC/IFIP/IFORS/IEA Symposium on Analysis, Design, and Evaluation of Human-Machine Systems, vol. 12(1) (2013)
24. Schmuntzsch, U., Sturm, C., Rötting, M.: How can multimodality be used to design usable interfaces in IPS² for older employees? A Journal of Prevention, Assessment and Rehabilitation 41(1), 3533–3540 (2012)
25. Wickens, C.D., Carswell, C.M.: The proximity compatibility principle: Its psychological foundation and relevance to display design. Human Factors: The Journal of the Human Factors and Ergonomics Society 37(3), 473–494 (1995)
26. Nicolai, T., Sindt, T., Witt, H., Reimerdes, J., Kenn, H.: Wearable computing for aircraft maintenance: Simplifying the user interface. In: 3rd International Forum on Applied Wearable Computing (IFAWC), pp. 1–12. VDE (2006)
27. Wogalter, M.S.: Purposes and Scope of Warnings. In: Wogalter, M.S. (ed.) Handbook of Warnings, pp. 3–9. Laurence Erlbaum Associates, Mahwah (2006)

In-Depth Analysis of Non-deterministic Aspects of Human-Machine Interaction and Update of Dedicated Functional Mock-Ups

Stefano Filippi and Daniela Barattin

University of Udine, DIEGM, Department of Electrical,
Management and Mechanical Engineering, Udine, Italy
{filippi,daniela.barattin}@uniud.it

Abstract. Increasing product complexity makes usability matters more and more important to account for in product development processes. For this reason, tools to design and evaluate interaction are studied and developed day by day. Unfortunately, user non-determinism is difficult to manage. When problems occur during interaction, users can react in several, different ways, depending from their behavioral characteristics. The research described in this paper analyzes non-determinism in depth, characterize situations where it can raise and exploits an existing tool to model and manage it as best as possible.

Keywords: Human-machine interaction, Simulation of non-determinism, Functional mock-up.

1 Introduction

Human-machine interaction is the dialogue between users and products. It describes both user behavior and product functioning, based on executed actions and feedbacks [1]. Its importance has kept increasing in the last thirty years, since products have become more and more complex and this complexity usually leads to poor usability [2]. As the ISO 9241 standard says, usability is "the effectiveness, efficiency and satisfaction with which specified users achieve specified goals in particular environments" [3]. Therefore, interaction design - ID - has become one of the disciplines involved in the product development process [4]. It focuses on the correct interpretation and implementation of the user-product dialogue [5] and allows generating products ready to be used easily and intuitively by the most of the users, accepted since the beginning, free of usability problems [6]. These problems are hard to foresee and manage because of the inner non-determinism of users' behavior. The Norman's model is used to highlights where, when and the reasons why interaction problems could happen [7]. The large variety of users' behavior, depending from many factors like patience, hardness to please, etc., suggests adopting simulation tools for representing interaction to speed up design activities and anticipate reviews in the product development process. The FMUi - functional mock-up for interaction - is a tool for simulating interaction studied and developed by the authors' research group in

A. Marcus (Ed.): DUXU 2014, Part I, LNCS 8517, pp. 185–196, 2014.

the last years [8]. It is involved here in trying to simulate at best non-deterministic interaction issues. All this said, the research described in this paper investigates non-determinism in user-product interaction, aiming at highlighting generic representations of user and product reactions to interaction problems and at finding the best ways to manage them. An updated release of the FMUi is proposed and used to test the results of the research.

Paper structure is as follows. Background section describes current release of the FMUi and some fundamentals of the Norman's model are given. Next section describes the first research activity, consisting in an in-depth analysis of non-determinism during interaction. The limits of the current FMUi and a proposal for an update are described afterwards. Then, an example using the updated FMUi is described. Sections discussing the outcomes of the research and summarizing conclusions and future work close the paper.

2   Background

The research described in this paper exploits a specific tool for the simulation of interaction named Functional Mock Up focused on interaction - FMUi. It has been developed by the authors' research group in the last years and described in [8]. Together with it, the Norman model is used here to describe and validate non-deterministic aspects of interaction [7]. Both of them are introduced in the following.

2.1   The FMUi

The FMUi allows simulating interaction between users and products. It has been derived from the original FMU [9, 10, 11], exclusively focused on technological issues. The FMUi can be used to test and validate interaction design solutions before the concept generation phase. FMUi models are flexible enough to allow easy reconfigurations, so many different design alternatives can be evaluated in short. An FMUi model represents all simple user-product interactions due to the user and the product behavior in every situation. There is a simple interaction when only one action is involved (performed by the user or the product, indifferently). Each simple interaction corresponds to an FMUi block. FMUi blocks contain algebraic equations, Boolean expressions, conditional statements, etc., to elaborate the input data to produce the output. Input data describe user characteristics, but also environmental conditions. User characteristics are ergonomics aspects as height, skill, and memorability, as well as needs/expectations, as desired temperature level, etc. The output allows evaluating the quality of interaction. Output values can be measurements of performances - translation of user needs and expectations in order to make them measurable and comparable against target values - and they are represented as success flag (Yes/No). On the other hand, output can consist of numerical values, percentages, Boolean values, etc. that become known and available only at precise moments and thanks to precise interaction paths. These values can be used as input for further FMUi blocks.

Fig. 1 shows an example of FMUi model. Each block is a black box. Designers do not need to know their content. It is enough to understand how input is transformed into output from a conceptual point of view; this allows designers to build models of interaction by combining blocks together.

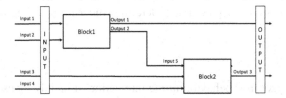

Fig. 1. Example of FMUi model

As an example, the interaction between a user and a magnetic card lock system can be simulated through an FMUi block that reads the card and opens the lock in case of success. The input is composed by the signal coming from the swipe sensor and the orientation of the card during the swiping action. The output consists of a success flag about the correct reading of the card and another value indicating the status of the lock (open/locked). The input and the statements used to compute the output are shown in table 1.

Table 1. Input and output of an FMUi block simulating a magnetic card lock system

INPUT	(Bool)swiping_in_progress, (Bool)card_orientation, (int)lock_number, (int)card_number

OUTPUT	(Bool)success(swiping_in_progress, card_orientation, lock_number, card_number)=
	IF (swiping_in_progress AND card_orientation) THEN
	    IF (lock_number=card_number) THEN success=1 ELSE success=0
	ELSE success=0

	(Bool)lock_status=NOT success

Current release of FMUi shows some limits, mainly regarding its inner determinism. All aspects of a specific interaction must be foreseen in order to build the corresponding FMUi model. Clearly, all of this goes against the simulation of a scenario as dynamic as human-machine interaction is. This is why limits of current release of FMUi are studied in details and updates are proposed, in order to represent and simulate non-determinism at best.

2.2   The Norman's Model

Norman's model describes users' activities in interacting with a system using seven stages [7, 12, 13]. In the first stage, the goals of the interaction are set. The second stage establishes the actions needed to get them. Here the execution gulf takes place. It represents possible misalignment between the actions the user would like to perform and the ones the system seems to make available. Third stage selects the actions to perform among the available ones and fourth stage performs these actions. In the last three stages, the user perceives and interprets the system state after the execution of the actions. Thanks to this, he/she should be able to claim if the goals have been obtained or not. A second gulf is present here, the evaluation gulf. This represents possible problems occurring in interpreting the system state. The two gulfs are used in this research to highlight non-deterministic aspects of interaction.

3   Activities

First activity analyzes user behavior during interaction. It mainly focuses on situations where problems arise, since non-determinism could likely emerge there. This establishes the starting point for highlighting representations of non-determinism to simulate real behavior. Then, these representations are developed and tested thanks to the FMUi. Limits of the current FMUi are highlighted first, in order to highlight current impossibility to implement the representations; after that, the needed modifications are presented. Last activity develops an example to show the exploitation of the new release of the FMUi.

3.1   Analyzing User/Product Behavior

During interaction, a problem arises when what happens does not match the user's problem solving process. In other words, there are discrepancies between the expected results and the real ones. The aim here is to analyze how users react in these cases. Norman's model is used as helping tool. The execution and evaluation gulfs represent the two moments where these discrepancies could arise.

Two different kinds of behavior could happen: the user reacts vs. he/she abandons the task and renounces to get the result he/she aims at. The second case is not considered here, because a renounce does not generate any interaction model. Anyway, the reasons why the user abandons could be interesting and they will be kept into consideration as future work.

The first case is analyzed in detail. In order to solve a problem, user can act in several, different ways. For example, consider a user who wants to close a window. Unfortunately, the window is broken; it allows only being fully opened or tilted in at the top. A user could settle down and set the tilt in position; the window is not close but less air than before flows in. Another user could search for a heavy object to place against the window frame to keep it closed. Another user could move to another room waiting for the windows to be repaired by the maintenance. In the light of the number and heterogeneity of possibilities, the research aims at highlighting interaction models able to summarize the actions the users could undertake.

As a starting point, ten situations where users run into problems are considered. Three interaction experts try to highlight all possible user behavior. The outcomes are analyzed, searching for recurring behavior.

Consider a user interacting with an oven to heat up food. If food remains too cold or becomes too hot after several attempts of temperature setting, the user settles down and eats even if the food temperature is slightly different from the liked one. This is an example of a first recurring behavior. It consists in a voluntary change of the initial user requirements. Hereafter, recurring behaviors will be named representation of non-determinism so the voluntary change of requirements is the first representation of non-determinism. Furthermore, the number of user's attempts to get the result before to change the requirements is an important indicator. This depends from behavioral user's characteristics. If he/she is demanding, this number will be high. On the contrary, a compliant user could limit his/her attempts to one or two before to settle down. Of course, more characteristics determine user's behavior other than the hardness to please; e.g., patience is another one. In the example, a demanding, but impatient, user could make one or two attempts to get the food at the right temperature, as well as the compliant user would do.

Let us consider another example now, consisting in opening a mason jar. After some unsuccessful tries, the user could act differently. He/she could warm it up, in order to exploit thermal strain, or use a knife to punch the cap to let the air flow in the jar and open it thanks to the vacuum disappearance. In both cases, there are heavy changes in the problem solving process. To see the problem solved, user prefers to change strategy instead of modifying the initial requirements. This example shows the second representation of non-determinism considered here. New actions - with related interactions - are added to the user-product dialogue, representing the changes in the problem solving process. Again, user's characteristics determine the nature and number of these actions. In the example, a patient user would likely adopt the warming up solution, while an eager would punch the cap.

Consider now a third example, where the lights in a room are controlled by a motion sensor. The interaction between the user and the product (the lights) could fail because of the morphological characteristics of the user, e.g. he/she is too short. There is no way for the user to understand why interaction fails, so he/she cannot change his/her mind about the constraints or undertake corrective actions (change strategy). The only solution applicable is to change product behavior, instead of user's one. This is the third representation of non-determinism considered in this research. The photocell could be moved or re-calibrated to detect a wider collection of user's morphologies. To avoid false-positive situations (light switched on by the presence of insects, etc.), a two-second interval of continuous presence before to switch on the lights could be required. This amount of time comes from a compromise between the sensor precision (and related cost) and the user's patience, waiting for the lights to be switched on after the entrance in the room and before starting to think about a failure. This shows that user's behavior influences product changes as well.

Finally, of course, sometimes interaction fails and there is no way to get the result, by exploiting any of the previous cases. This must be considered as well, in the definition of the representations.

3.2   Exploiting the FMUi

This section describes the exploitation of the FMUi in modeling the three representations of non-determinism just highlighted. An example of interaction is used to show if they can be already managed using current release of the FMUi or if there is any limitation.

Consider hand washing using a faucet releasing water thanks to a photocell. The FMUi model to simulate interaction is composed by six blocks and its structure is shown in figure 2.

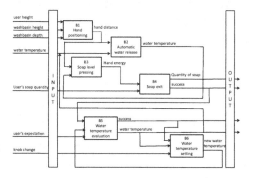

Fig. 2. FMUi simulating the interaction for hand washing

First two blocks model hand positioning and automatic water release. In the hand positioning block, named B1, the user approaches the faucet with his/her hands. This action depends from user's height and washbasin dimensions. In this case, the output is numeric and it becomes known and available only if and when precise conditions happen (the approaching of a user with specific characteristics). Block B2 models the automatic release of water. Given the distance of the user's hands from the faucet, it can release the water or not. Here the only input is this distance. Regarding the output, the water will flow only if the hands are less than 10cm far from the faucet. If yes, the temperature of the water flowing from the faucet is given. This value is known in the system because it corresponds to the aqueduct temperature at the beginning and to the last use of the basin afterwards. Otherwise, a N/A value is given. Blocks B3 and B4 model the interaction with a soap dispenser. B3 represents the hand approaching the dispenser handle. Its input is the hand distance and the output is the force used. In B4, this value determines the quantity of dispensed soap. Another input for B4 is the quantity of soap expected by the user. Thanks to this, B4 can set a yes/no flag representing the success of interaction. If its value is equal to no, in other words if the quantity of dispensed soap does not match the user's expectation, the B3-B4 loop restarts.

Last two blocks manage the water temperature setting. Block B5 simulates user evaluation of temperature of the water flowing from the faucet. The input consists of current temperature, derived from B2, and user's desired one. This can have four values: scalding (more than 50°C), hot (40°C to 49°C), warm (30°C to 39°C) and cold (less than 30°C). The output consists of the success of user evaluation and it informs about current water temperature in order to manage further iterations in case of success equal to no. Block B6 models interaction between the user and the faucet aimed at adjusting water temperature. This block is involved in any case. If there is the need to adjust the temperature because the current one does not match user's expectation, some elaboration happens; otherwise, no actions are taken. If the user feels uncomfortable with current temperature, he/she operates the notched knob to raise or lower it. In this case the input corresponds to the knob change (number of notches), the success flag coming from the previous block, and the water temperature. The output is the new water temperature, looped-back to the previous block for a new evaluation. The number of notches quantifying the user action determines the required variation in the water temperature. Each notch corresponds to two degrees Celsius.

First representation of non-determinism, regarding slight users' changes of mind during interaction due to unsuccessful events, cannot be modeled with current release of FMUi. This because input values describing users' requirements are set at the beginning and cannot be modified on the way. They are somehow external to the model, considered as constants instead of variables inside it. This is considered here as the first limit against modeling non-determinism. It is clearly present in block B5 and B6 of the example. Once the pleasant temperature is set at the beginning, it cannot be changed and this could lead to an infinite number of user's attempts trying to reach it. Of course, this does not correspond to what happens in real life, because soon or later the attempts finish, for several reasons. The impossibility to manage infinite loops represents the second limit of current FMUi. Moreover, main reasons for loops to be finite in real life are closely related to user's characteristics. It is not easy to characterize users from the behavioral point of view. Many aspects must be considered, non-necessarily independent to each other and sometimes varying from situation to situation. Once highlighted, these aspects must be elaborated, and this requires the introduction of interval discretization, etc. Carelessness about users' characteristics is the third limit of current FMUi release to modeling non-determinism.

Second representation of non-determinism, dealing with heavy user's changes in the problem solving process, cannot be modeled using current FMUi as well. Now the FMUi model is static; once defined before starting interaction, it cannot change. All possible alternatives in getting the result of interaction must be planned before to run it. This can be found in the example considering blocks B1 and B2. If the user cannot reach the required distance to let the water flowing from the faucet, hands cannot be washed. Simulation does not allow considering alternatives, as for example the use of a footstool. This static nature of the model is tagged as fourth limit of current FMUi.

Third representation of non-determinism, focused on changes in product behavior aimed at supporting the user at best, would require modifications of the contents of FMUi blocks describing product behavior during the simulation of interaction. Once again, this is not allowed by current FMUi because of the static nature of the model. The impossibility to model product changes on the way is considered as the fifth limit.

The example and the following considerations make clear that in the current release of FMUi everything is strictly deterministic. There is no care to what could happen if an unexpected problem arises. If an action fails - in other words, if the expected result seems to be missing to the user, the FMUi can highlight the unsuccessful state of the dialogue (the success flag is equal to no) but there is no clue about user's interpretation of the error state (evaluation gulf of Norman model) and about his/her possible recovery actions (execution gulf) to proceed towards the final result, the solution of the problem.

3.3   FMUi Update

Once highlighted the limits of current release of the FMUi that prevent modeling non-determinism, this section describes the modifications introduced in order to allow it.

Modeling non-determinism requires the introduction of a supervisor, external to the FMUi model, able to manage any interaction problem. Its introduction comes by exploiting the three representations and eliminates the limits highlighted before. When an interaction problem arises, the supervisor exploits the information present in the model to propose the best solution based on specific behavioral user's characteristics. These characteristics allows the user to be described in order to understand if he/she is disposed to change his/her requirements and the amount of this change, or if he/she could change his/her mind heavier by performing alternative actions to get the goal. This way, the third limit is overcome.

The supervisor contains a counter to manage the number of iterations for loops. This, together with behavioral user's characteristics, allows deciding if one more iteration can be executed instead of exit the loop searching for alternative solutions. Thanks to this, the second limit is gone because infinite loops are not allowed anymore.

The supervisor contains a decision tree. The answers to the questions in the nodes are generated using the information present in the model as the interaction problem arises. The algorithm exploiting this tree works as follows. As soon as any of the success flag in the FMUi model becomes equal to no, the supervisor takes the helm. Based on behavioral user's characteristics and number of interactions of current loop (if any), the first section of the supervisor decides if the user likes to try interaction once again without changing his/her requirements and problem solving process or not. If yes, the counter is incremented and the control comes back to the model; otherwise the FMUi model needs to be changed. The way the changes will happen is decided by the second section of the supervisor, by exploiting the decision tree containing the three representations of non-determinism.

First, the supervisor decides if the user is disposed to change the initial requirements. If yes, the first representation of non-determinism is implemented. The structure of the FMUi has been changed in order to let input parameters act as internal variables. Their values can be changed if required and this eliminates the first limit of current FMUi.

If the user does not like to change requirements, the decision tree goes to the next node, asking for his/her willing to change the problem solving process. If yes, the second representation of non-determinism is implemented. This requires an architectural modification of the FMUi model because new blocks could be added, as well as existing blocks eliminated. A database containing implementations of functions is searched using keywords. These implementations can be considered as sorts of interaction design patterns [14]. The possibility to modify the architecture of the FMUi model once the simulation has started overcomes the fourth limit.

If the user cannot change his/her problem solving process, the only thing to do before to declare the unsuccessfulness of the interaction is to suggest changes in the product the user interacts with. This corresponds to the implementation of the third representation of non-determinism. It comes by modifying the internal structure of the blocks representing the interaction of the product. This way, product behavior changes to support the user problem solving process as best as possible. The supervisor exploits a database of technological design guidelines suggesting how to modify the product. These suggestions allow the blocks of the FMUi model to be changed, so the fifth limit of current release of FMUi goes away as well.

Finally, if behavioral user's characteristics do not allow any other iteration of the interaction and the success flag is still equal to no even after modification to the product behavior, interaction is declared as unsuccessful and simulation ends.

3.4   Exploitation of the Updated FMUi

The hand-washing example described before is involved again here to validate the updated release of the FMUi. The simulation considers a very demanding user regarding the goal to achieve (washed hands) because he is a health fanatic. This makes him disposed to perform many tries and follow different strategies as long as he gets the result. Moreover, recently he burned one hand while cooking, so he requires a precise water temperature. Finally, he is quite compliant on secondary matters not directly related to the final goal or the burn.

• Simulation starts with the user approaching the faucet (block B1) and stopping at a certain distance far from it. In B2, this distance is evaluated as too high for the water to flow so interaction fails and success flag is set to no. This activates the supervisor. Based on behavioral user's characteristics, it determines that the maximum number of attempts to make the water flowing before to do something else will be two. Therefore, the counter is activated and a new iteration, representing a second user's attempt to let the water flow is fired. This attempt fails as well, because the user is still too far. Now the supervisor exploits the decision tree. The option for the user to change the requirements is not available, because the only thing he could consciously do at this point is to leave with his/her hands still dirty but abandons are not considered at the moment, as stated before. Therefore, possible user's changes of mind are taken into account. User's characteristics allow this, because he wants to wash his hands in any case. In other words, he is disposed to change his problem solving process in order to obtain the expected result. Therefore, the FMUi block database is searched for an interaction design solution. The problem is the limited user's height and this is used as keyword. A solution involving a footstool is suggested. The interaction is implemented thanks to two new blocks. One simulated the placement of the footstool close to the faucet and the second the user climbing it. This produces a new user's height, used as input for block B1. A new iteration of blocks B1 and B2 (allowed because when the decision tree is involved the value of the iteration counter is reset) now results in a successful interaction; the water flows from the faucet. Now attention moves to the interaction between the user and the soap dispenser (blocks B3 and B4). One pull of the handle gives a scarce quantity of soap, in user's opinion, so success flag is set to no. The supervisor activates and lets the user try again. No success. Another try, no success again, the quantity is still not enough. The decision tree is involved again. The user seems disposed to accept the soap quantity - he is demanding regarding the result of interaction, the hands washed, and he accepts this tradeoff to be able to get the result, also because his hands are not damaged about the scarce quantity of soap - so the implementation of the first representation of non-determinism comes to the stage. A handful (value expressed in the user's language) of soap will be changed into some drops of it and this is allowed because now the input of the FMUi model acts as internal variables and their values can be changed if required. Last part of the simulation regards the setting of the water temperature. In B5, the user evaluates it; if it does not match his expectations, the success flag is set to no and the supervisor is involved. Once again, the user is disposed to repeat the setting twice. First time water seems too cold. Then the user move the knob of just one notch but this time the temperature is too hot. Then, the decision tree is exploited again. The user cannot wash his hands with water too cold or too hot because of his burn; at the same time, he cannot change something in the problem solving process because he has no idea about how it could change, since the product offers only this way to change temperature. Therefore, the supervisor discards the implementation of both the first and second representations of non-determinism. What remains is the third one, the change of product behavior. The database of technological guidelines is searched, using setting variables as keyword. Proposed solutions focused on automatic setting and setting values closer to each other in order to simplify fine-tuning. An example is the automatic rolling shutter. A two-way button allows moving them in any position, (ideally) without the need to discretize the space. By mapping this example in the case of the faucet, the same two-way button is placed on it. One makes the water warmer, the other colder. Heaters placed in the faucet allow any water temperature to be obtained. Hence, block B4 is modified to reflect this. The number of notches as input is substituted with the button pressed (up or down) and internal data elaboration is changed. Now it manages the pressing of the button up to reach the desired temperature (or not). The success flag indicates if the right way of the button is pressed. Then simulation proceeds. In the first iteration, the success flag is equal to no (the user pressed the wrong way of the button); next iteration has the flag equal to yes and the simulation of the interaction ends with a success.

4   Results and Discussion

The new release of the FMUi avoids the five limits to non-determinism simulation highlighted in paragraph 3.2. The previous release noticed interaction problems but reactions were static. Now, on the contrary, when an interaction problem arises, behavioral user's characteristics are exploited to determine what happens. Initial input values representing user requirements can change, different interaction paths implementing alternative problem solving activities can succeed, or blocks describing product behavior can be modified, reflecting the adaptation of the product to support the user at best. The supervisor performs all of this automatically.

The simulation of interaction generates many interesting pieces of information. Looking at the FMUi model, especially by comparing it before and after the simulation, it contains suggestions about both alternative problem solving processes and product modifications; moreover, some variables as water temperature and user's height are tagged as considerable, so they will be kept into particular account. The same goes for variables describing behavioral user's characteristics. They can be weighted based on the impact/importance they had during the simulation. This stated, the new release of the FMUi is not only a tool to simulate/evaluate human-machine interaction but it is evolving toward being a design aid because it suggests solutions to solve interaction problems.

Some drawbacks must be highlighted as well. Now the block database is quite poor and not structured enough to be easily searched using keywords. Interaction designers and/or evaluators are asked to select the blocks to modify the FMUi model following the suggestions offered by the supervisor. This happens as well for the guidelines aimed at modifying the product. The database of guidelines is enough populated at the moment and the search by keywords works fine. Anyway, human intervention is required to translate the guidelines into modifications of existing blocks.

Another important drawback is the exclusive selection of one representation of non-determinism at a time. For example, a technological modification of the product in order to support better the problem solving process could imply a different strategy in solving the problem by the user. This contemporaneity cannot be managed by the new release of the FMUi.

Last negative aspect regards the use and management of the variables collecting behavioral user's characteristics. Now they are considered quite orthogonal and separated, while in real life they very often influence each other. Moreover, values of these variables are considered as constants during the simulation of interaction and once again, this does not find correspondence in the real life. A user can start interacting with something quite patiently, but suddenly he/she can become impatient because of inner or outer causes.

5   Conclusions

The research described in this paper has dealt with non-deterministic issues of human-machine interaction and their applications into a dedicated simulation tool named functional mock-up for interaction - FMUi. Norman's model helped in highlighting where, when and why users could change their mind while solving problems in interacting with products. The research has studied what could happen if interaction problems arise and generated three ways to explicate non-determinism, named representations. These allowed highlighting some limits in the current release of the FMUi that prevent it to be used for simulating non-determinism. A new release of FMUi has been proposed, where all limits seem overcome. Its characteristics and functioning have been described using an example.

Future work will focus on the new FMUi. Specifically, structure and functioning of the supervisor need to be further validated; the database of the FMUi blocks must be structured and populated while the database of the guidelines needs modifications in order to apply structural changes to existing blocks in an automatic way. Moreover, the reasons why users could abandon interaction must be kept into consideration as source of information to improve the human-machine dialogue. Variables describing the user from the behavioral point of view need to be further investigated, by taking into account any relationship/dependence among them and associating weights to define mutual importance. Weights could derive from the resources needed to accomplish them; e.g., fewer resources, more importance. The same attention should be placed to the variables representing the output of the FMUi model. Interaction goodness is not addressed now; the model is only able to say if interaction drives to a success or not.

References

1. Dix, A.: Human-Computer Interaction. Pearson Education (2004)
2. Hertzum, M., Clemmensen, T.: How do usability professionals construe usability? Int. J. Hum.-Comput. Stud. 70, 26–42 (2012)
3. ISO 9241-11. Ergonomic Requirements for Office Work with Visual Display Terminals (VDTs)-—Part 11: Guidance on Usability (1994)
4. Lee, G., Eastman, C.M., Taunk, T., Ho, C.H.: Usability principles and best practices for the user interface design of complex 3D architectural design and engineering tools. Int. J. Hum.-Comput. Stud. 68, 90–104 (2010)
5. Hertzum, M.: Images of usability. Int. J. Hum.-Comput. Interact. 26, 567–600 (2010)
6. Koca, A., Funk, M., Karapanos, E., Rozinat, A., van der Aalst, W.M.P., Corporaal, H., Martens, J.B.O.S., van der Putten, P.H.A., Weijters, A.J.M.M., Brombacher, A.C.: Soft Reliability: an Interdisciplinary Approach with a User-System Focus. Qual. Reliab. Eng. Int. 25, 3–20 (2009)
7. Norman, D.A., Draper, S.W.: User Centered System Design; New Perspectives on Human-Computer Interaction. L. Erlbaum Associates Inc., Hillsdale (1986)
8. Filippi, S., Barattin, D., Ferrise, F., Bordegoni, M., Cugini, U.: Human in the loop: a model to integrate interaction issues in complex simulations. In: Marcus, A. (ed.) DUXU/HCII 2013, Part I. LNCS, vol. 8012, pp. 242–251. Springer, Heidelberg (2013)
9. Zorriassatine, F., Wykes, C., Parkin, R., Gindy, N.: A survey of virtual prototyping techniques for mechanical product development. Proceedings of the Institution of Mechanical Engineers, Part B: Journal of Engineering Manufacture 217, 513–530 (2003)
10. Ferrise, F., Bordegoni, M., Cugini, U.: Interactive Virtual Prototypes for testing the interaction with new products. Comput. -Aided Des. Appl. 10, 515–525 (2013)
11. Enge-Rosenblatt, O., Clauß, C., Schneider, A., Schneider, P.: Functional Digital Mock-up and the Functional Mock-up Interface – Two Complementary Approaches for a Comprehensive Investigation of Heterogeneous Systems. In: Proceedings 8th Modelica Conference, Dresden, Germany, March 20-22, pp. 748–755 (2011)
12. Norman, D.: The Design of Everyday Things: Revised and Expanded Edition. Basic Books (2013)
13. Ag. Ibrahim, A. A., Hunt, A.: An HCI Model for Usability of Sonification Applications. In: Coninx, K., Luyten, K., Schneider, K.A. (eds.) TAMODIA 2006. LNCS, vol. 4385, pp. 245–258. Springer, Heidelberg (2007)
14. Gangemi, A.: Ontology design patterns for semantic web content. In: Gil, Y., Motta, E., Benjamins, V.R., Musen, M.A. (eds.) ISWC 2005. LNCS, vol. 3729, pp. 262–276. Springer, Heidelberg (2005)

Grammatical Analysis of User Interface Events for Task Identification

Yonglei Tao

School of Computing and Information Systems,
Grand Valley State University,
Allendale, MI 49401, USA
taoy@gvsu.edu

Abstract. Modern window-based applications are event-driven. User interface events carry valuable information about user behavior and are considered as an important source of data for usability evaluation. Aspect-oriented techniques provide an effective way to capture user interface events. However, it is insufficient to analyze event traces based on the information carried within events themselves. We describe a grammatical approach to analyzing event traces and identifying user tasks in the context of a task model. We also describe a proof-of-concept experiment to demonstrate its feasibility. Our approach paves the way for automatic support for task identification and therefore is beneficial to user interface evaluation that relies on task-based usability data.

Keywords: Automatic Support for Usability Evaluation, Analysis of User Interface Events, Aspect-Oriented Programming.

1 Introduction

Modern window-based applications are event-driven. User interface events are generated within a window-based application as natural products of its normal operation. Such events carry valuable information about user behavior with respect to the application's user interface and are considered as an important source of data for usability evaluation [1]. Because they are extremely voluminous and rich in detail, it is indispensible to provide automatic support for tracing and analyzing user interface events [2].

Instrumentation is a common technique for event tracing. It typically requires the developer to insert code at specific locations in the target application in order to capture useful information during execution. Instrumentation code tends to be distributed throughout the application; hence, manual instrumentation is inflexible when changes in user interface design arise frequently in the development process. Several publications in the literature propose to use aspect-oriented techniques to perform instrumentation [3-6]. Aspect-oriented techniques provide an effective way to modularize instrumentation code that would otherwise be scattered over an application, making it possible to trace user interface events in a non-intrusive

A. Marcus (Ed.): DUXU 2014, Part I, LNCS 8517, pp. 197–205, 2014.

manner. More importantly, aspect-oriented instrumentation promises better adaptability to user interface evolution [4]. In order to provide automatic support for event tracing, aspect-oriented code is developed independent of the target application. While being capable to capture events of interest, it is insufficient to analyze them based on the information carried within events themselves [1, 3].

In this paper we describe a grammatical approach to analyzing event traces with the intent to identify user tasks. We also describe a proof-of-concept experiment to demonstrate that this approach can be realized in an automatic manner. Usability evaluation is to determine to what extent the user interface under consideration allows users to accomplish their tasks effectively and efficiently; in many ways, its success depends task-based usability data [2, 12]. As such, automatic support for task identification is beneficial as an effective way to provide the needed usability data.

The rest of this paper is organized as follows. Section 2 covers related work. Section 3 provides background information about the problem under consideration. Section 4 introduces our approach to analyzing event traces in order to identify user tasks and section 5 describes a proof-of-concept experiment about our approach. Finally section 6 concludes this paper.

2   Related Work

User interface events occur in a window-based application and its run-time environment when the user interacts with the application via its user interface [1]. A range of techniques are available for tracing user interface events. Manual instrumentation is especially inflexible with an evolving user interface. Recent publications in the literature have revealed potential benefits with using aspect-oriented techniques to provide automatic support for event tracing [3-6]. Most of them attempt to capture events across well-defined boundaries in the target application and its run-time environment. While user interface events are identifiable with an appropriate means, they tend to include a lot of data that reflect low-level activities within the target application. Our approach is to focus on events that result from inter-component communication in a window-based application, which are more relevant to user-level activities and therefore more amenable to analysis [4].

Usability evaluation is task-based [10]. In order to support usability evaluation, it is crucial to have the ability to identify tasks that users performed from event traces [2]. However, an accurate interpretation of event traces requires contextual information beyond what automatic tools are able to capture in an application-independent manner [1, 3]. Supplementary information is needed for analyzing event traces. To that end, techniques are developed to align event traces with additional data obtained through other methods, for example, digital video recording [5, 7].

As reported in [8, 9], event traces can be analyzed according to observable patterns of usage of a user interface. A task description, such as the task model used in Hierarchical Task Analysis (HTA), is typically considered as a way of discovering and documenting requirements for user interface design [10]. Since such a task description shows the expected sequences of user actions, it is also used as a basis to interpret event traces for usability evaluation [12]. Moreover, a grammar-based task description provides a convenient way to map event traces into user tasks in order to serve various purposes [13, 14]. We take a similar approach to enabling automatic support from event tracing to analyzing.

3   Capturing User Interface Event

Most window-based applications are structured according to the Model-View-Controller (MVC) architecture. In the MVC architecture, the model manages application data, the view is responsible for visual presentation on the screen, and the controller handles input from the user. By encapsulating them into separate components, the impact of changes in the user interface is isolated and minimized. More importantly, the three components must communicate to carry out the application's functionality; separating them also exposes user interface events, making them identifiable within the application.

AspectJ is an aspect-oriented extension to the Java programming language [15]. It provides a construct, called aspects, to modularize processing elements that would otherwise span multiple modules. One can define an aspect to describe when it should act and what it should do; for example, reporting what is going on when certain method calls are made. We use aspects to trace events that occur across boundaries of the MVC architecture. Ignoring low-level events, such as those that appear between the application and its run-time environment, effectively reduces the amount of analytical effort without loss of relevant information.

Here, we use a window-based application in Java, called AccountManager, as an example. Briefly, this application allows the user, that is, a bank customer, to manage each of his/her bank accounts in a separate window. In the window for an account, it displays the account balance as a text and as a bar graph, and also includes a text field and two buttons, where the former allows the user to enter an amount and the latter to withdraw and deposit the input amount, respectively. In addition, this application shows the total assets held in all of the customer's accounts as a pie chart. Although this application does not provide many features typically available in a banking application, it involves various interaction mechanisms and multiple windows that are sufficient for us to investigate issues of interest.

Event traces captured by aspect-oriented instrumentation is not immediately usable because they come with some irrelevant details. We built a preprocessor to extract useful information from event traces. Fig. 1 shows a segment of the preprocessed event traces that were captured as a user was using the AccountManager application. We have removed timestamps and irrelevant information, such as hash code values for some objects, from the original data. Note that the only application-specific element in the sample data is the word "Deposit"; it is the text associated with a push button to describe what it does and extractable from the event generated when the user clicks the button. But application-specific information is not available with events from other screen elements.

```
JTextField Gained Focus
Key 1 Typed in JTextField
Key 0 Typed in JTextField
Key 0 Typed in JTextField
JButton Deposit Clicked
Dialog Confirmation returned YES_OPTION
AssetPieChartView Updated
AccountBarGraphView Updated
AccountTextView Updated
```

Fig. 1. A segment of preprocessed event traces

Individual events shown in Fig. 1 result from user actions; however, they do not carry enough information on their own to allow their meanings to be appropriately interpreted. For example, the three key events indicate what the user did, but it is not clear what the user intended to accomplish on the basis of the information they carry within them alone. We have to take into consideration events that precede and succeed the three events to understand user's intention. Evidently, contextual information plays a crucial role in analyzing event traces. Since contextual information spreads across multiple events, it is necessary to analyze event traces at a higher level of abstraction, that is, the level of user tasks.

Furthermore, although it is possible to reason about the task that the user intended to perform from events shown in Fig. 1, those events themselves do not reveal how they can be combined as a unit at a higher level of abstraction. Consequently, additional sources of data need to be included in order to identify user tasks from event traces [1].

4   Identifying Tasks from Event Traces

User interface events result from user actions, such as clicking on a toolbar button and pressing a key, as well as system responses, such as updating the screen display and bringing up a message box. Whereas the former are observable actions that users perform, the latter correspond to users' cognitive actions because they have to perceive the state change of the user interface in order to proceed. Hence, event traces reflect action sequences that users perform for task completion.

Hierarchical Task Analysis (HTA) is a structured technique to analyze activities that users perform to accomplish their tasks [10]. In HTA, a task is broken down into subtasks and subtasks continue to be decomposed until appropriate user actions are determined, thus creating a hierarchical model for the task. Fig. 2 shows the textual representation of an HTA task model for making a transaction in the above-mentioned application. In Fig. 2, the intended task consists of subtasks 3 and 4 as well as user actions 1, 2, and 5, subtask 3 in turn consists of user actions 3.1 and 3.2, and subtask 4 consists of user actions 4.1 and 4.2. Here, user actions are both observable and cognitive. Fig. 2 also includes four plans to specify in what order and under what conditions user actions are performed. Plans illustrate possible scenarios for the user to complete a task.

```
0. Make Transaction
    1.  Select Account
    2.  Enter Amount
    3.  Select Transaction Type
        3.1 Click "Deposit" Button
        3.2 Click "Withdraw" Button
    4.  Confirm Action
        4.1 Click "Yes" Button
        4.2 Click "No" Button
    5.  View Updates

Plan 0: do 1-2-3.1-4.1-5
Plan 1: do 1-2-3.1-4.2-5
Plan 2: do 1-2-3.2-4.1-5
Plan 3: do 1-2-3.2-4.2-5
```

Fig. 2. A task hierarchy

HTA is often used to analyze requirements and investigate user needs. It allows the developer to find user activities that are to be supported by a system and therefore is considered as a critical component in user interface design. An HTA task model is also used to understand an existing user interface for redesign and evaluation purposes since it is the model that user interface design originates from. Hence, even though individual events do not carry sufficient information on their own, their roles in task completion can be appropriately interpreted in the context of a relevant task model.

```
<Make Transaction> ::= "Focus" <Input> <Action>
                        <Confirmation> <View>
<Input> = <KeyIn> | <KeyIn> <Input>
<KeyIn> = "0"|"1"|"2"|"3"|"4"|"5"|"6"|"7"|"8"|"9"
<Action> ::= "Deposit" | "Withdraw"
<Confirmation> ::= "Yes" | "No"
<View> ::=  "ViewUpdate" | "ViewUpdate" <View>
```

Fig. 3. A BNF grammar

User actions with respect to the user interface of an interactive application are grammatical in structure [10]. Grammars can be used to analyze the structure of event traces and subsequently to identify user tasks. We define a BNF (Backus-Naur Form) grammar according to the HTA task model in order to analyze event traces.

As shown in Fig. 3, a BNF grammar involves a set of rewriting rules. Symbols that appear on the left-hand side of the ":: =" symbol are non-terminals, such as <Input> and <View>. Symbols that appear only on the right side are terminals, such as "Focus" and "Deposit", which correspond to user interface events. One of the non-terminals, such as <Make Transaction>, is selected as the start symbol. Rewriting rules define the way in which non-terminals on the left can be composed of terminals and non-terminals on the right. Fig. 3 shows how a BNF grammar can be used to describe the syntactic structure of those events that result from actions the user performed to complete the <Make Transaction> task.

Note that the BNF grammar in Fig. 3 can be derived from the HTA task model in Fig. 2 in a systematic manner, except that the rule for non-terminal <KeyIn> is a common way to describe a numerical value (for simplicity, we show in this example only the part of rules for a whole number).

Using BNF grammars offers a number of significant benefits as a way to identify tasks from event traces. BNF grammars give a precise, yet easy to understand syntactic description for event traces. Also they allow an efficient parser to be constructed automatically. Such a parser makes it possible to map event traces to user tasks in context.

5   An Experiment

We have conducted a proof-of-concept experiment to inspect the practical aspect of the approach described above. Roughly, we used two open source programs, Lex and Yacc, as the basic components to build a prototype of an event analyzer. Our goal is to use the event analyzer to process event traces and obtain relevant data to support task-based usability evaluation.

Fig. 4 shows what components that the event analyzer is made of and how these components work together to achieve the overall functionality.

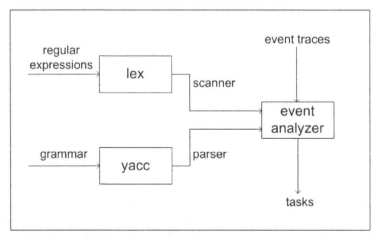

Fig. 4. A prototype for event processing

Lex is a lexical analyzer generator [16]. We specify the lexical structure of event traces using regular expressions. Lex takes our regular expressions as input and constructs a scanner for lexical analysis. Such a scanner is able to match strings in event traces and convert them to tokens that denote user actions; for example, mapping the "JButton Deposit Clicked" event shown in Fig. 1 into the "Deposit" token shown in Fig. 3. Note that this scanner produces a sequence of tokens for further processing.

Yacc is a parser generator [16]. We use a BNF grammar to specify the syntactic structure of a token sequence. Yacc takes our grammar as input and builds a parser for syntactic analysis. Such a parser uses grammar rules to analyze a token sequence and identify user tasks; for example, recognizing the token sequence resulting from the event trace shown in Fig. 1 as the "Make Transaction" task according to the grammar shown in Fig. 3. Output from this parser is a sequence of task identifiers that can be directly used for usability evaluation.

Our event analyzer is a script that uses Lex to construct a scanner from the given regular expressions and Yacc to create a parser from the given BNF grammar, and then combines them to process event traces. As a consequence, this event analyzer is able to take the preprocessed event traces as input and produce tasks and task sequences as output.

Note that our regular expressions and BNF grammar are defined according to a task model for the user interface under evaluation; they provide contextual information for event trace analysis. Since they are made available as input, the event analyzer is able to process event traces in an application-independent manner and therefore has the potential to serve the needs of usability evaluation for various window-based applications.

6   Conclusion

While user interface events from window-based applications can be captured with aspect-oriented instrumentation, the lack of contextual information within the recorded events poses a challenge for mapping them into user tasks. We describe a grammatical approach to analyzing event traces in the context of an HTA task model. An HTA task model is developed to facilitate user interface design; therefore, it is readily available when the user interface is evaluated. Such a model provides essential information that allows event traces to be appropriately interpreted.

The central element in our approach is to derive a BNF grammar from a task model and use it to recognize user tasks from event traces. A model-based grammar allows an efficient parser to be constructed and subsequently integrated into a task analyzer to identify user tasks from event traces.

Information about tasks and task sequences makes it possible to collect basic measures, such as the time to complete certain tasks, percent of task completion, number of erroneous action sequences, and usage of certain functions, and use them for usability evaluation [1, 12]. It also allows the developer to step through individual tasks for a close examination over user actions.

We conducted an experiment to investigate the feasibility of our approach. In this experiment, we built a prototype of an event analyzer from two basic components, a scanner and a parser. Such an event analyzer has the ability to create these components as needed according to application-specific input (i.e., regular expressions and grammars), making it possible to adapt to the needs of event trace analysis for a wide range of window-based applications. Hence, our approach paves the way to provide automatic support for usability evaluation that relies on task-based usability data.

Our approach has been successfully applied to analyze event traces obtained from a small but relatively comprehensive window-based application. Although the experimental results were largely satisfactory, there are still a few issues to be addressed, such as the need to find an adequate solution to identify all erroneous event sequences, which will be the focus of our future research effort.

References

1. Hilbert, D.M., Redmiles, D.F.: Extracting Usability Information from User Interface Events. Computing Surveys 32(4), 384–421 (2000)
2. Ivory, M., Hearst, M.: The State of the Art in Automating Usability Evaluation of User Interfaces. Computing Surveys 33(4), 470–516 (2001)
3. Hartman, G.S., Bass, L.J.: Logging Events Crossing Architectural Boundaries. In: Costabile, M.F., Paternó, F. (eds.) INTERACT 2005. LNCS, vol. 3585, pp. 823–834. Springer, Heidelberg (2005)
4. Tao, Y.: Toward Computer-Aided Usability Evaluation for Evolving Interactive Software. In: Proceedings of the International Workshop on Reflection, AOP and Meta-Data for Software Evolution, the 21st European Conference on Object-Oriented Programming, Berlin, Germany (2007)
5. Bateman, S., Gutwin, C., Osgood, N., McCalla, G.: Interactive Usability Instrumentation. In: Proceedings of SIGCHI Symposium on Engineering Interactive Computing Systems, pp. 45–54. ACM Press, Pittsburgh (2009)
6. Shekh, S., Tyerman, S.: An Aspect-Oriented Framework for Event Capture and Usability Evaluation. In: Maciaszek, L.A., González-Pérez, C., Jablonski, S. (eds.) ENASE 2008/2009. CCIS, vol. 69, pp. 107–119. Springer, Heidelberg (2010)
7. Kim, J.H., et al.: Tracking Real-Time User Experience (TRUE): A Comprehensive Instrumentation Solution for Complex Systems. In: Proceedings of the 27th International Conference on Human Factors in Computing Systems, pp. 443–451. ACM Press (2008)
8. Cook, J.E., Wolf, A.L.: Automating Process Discovery through Event-Data Analysis. In: Proceedings of International Conference on Software Engineering. ACM Press (1995)
9. Olson, G.M., Herbsleb, J.D., Rueter, H.H.: Characterizing the Sequential Structure of Interactive Behaviors through Statistical and Grammatical Techniques. Human-Computer Interaction Special Issue on ESDA 9 (1994)
10. Dix, A., Finlay, J., Abowd, G.D., Beale, R.: Human-Computer Interaction, 3rd edn. Pearson, Prentice-Hall (2004)
11. Pew, R.W., Mavor, A.S. (eds.): Human-System Integration in the System Development Process: a New Look. The National Academies Press, Washington, DC (2007)
12. Lecerof, A., Paterno, F.: Automatic Support for Usability Evaluation. IEEE Transactions on Software Engineering 24(10) (1998)

13. Srinivasan, S., Amir, A., Deshpande, P., Zbarsky, V.: Grammar-Based Task Analysis of Web Longs. In: Proceedings of International Conference on Information and Knowledge Management. ACM Press, Washington, DC (2004)

14. Asimakopoulos, S., Dix, A., Fildes, R.: Using Hierarchical Task Decomposition as a Grammar to Map Actions in Context: Application to Forecasting Systems in Supply Chain Planning. International Journal of Human-Computer Studies 69(4), 234–250 (2011)

15. Miles, R.: AspectJ Cookbook. O'Reilly Media, Inc. (2005)

16. Niemann, T.: Lex & Yacc Tutorial. ePaperPress,
http://epaperpress.com/lexandyacc/

Model-Based User Interface Development
for Adaptive Self-Service Systems

Enes Yigitbas, Holger Fischer, and Stefan Sauer

University of Paderborn, s-lab – Software Quality Lab,
Zukunftsmeile 1, 33102 Paderborn, Germany
{eyigitbas,hfischer,sauer}@s-lab.upb.de

Abstract. Self-service systems are complex technical systems and provide products and services for the end user. Due to heterogeneity of the users of such systems the usability of the user interfaces is of great importance. The user interfaces have to be adapted or adapt itself to the various skills and preferences of the users. Due to the monolithic system architecture of existing self-service systems, a simple and flexible usage of the user interface is often restricted. The development of adaptive user interfaces involves challenges for developers that are addressed partially by frameworks like the CAMELEON Reference Framework (CRF). However, no concrete approaches to support the development of flexible and adaptive user interfaces for distributed self-service systems exist in industry. In this paper we describe an integrated model-based approach for the development of adaptive user interfaces.

Keywords: Model-Driven Software Development, User Interface, Usability, Models, Self-Adaptiveness, Self-Service Systems, Model-Based User Interface Development.

1   Motivation

User interface development (UID) is an important aspect in today's system development industry; as the result – the user interface (UI) – represents the way the users perceive the system. They focus on the usability of a system and are satisfied if the system meets their expectations and needs as well as it is suitable for their tasks. However, the establishment of usability activities and human-centered design (HCD) as part of the development process still remains to be a challenge although various approaches have been worked out to integrate these aspects in the software development [1], [2], [3].

In this paper we concentrate on self-service systems. Currently, existing systems support services in the fields of entertainment, information, finance and banking, travelling or postal services. The focus in the development of such systems lies on the functionality and security. However, self-service systems are complex technical systems that provide products and services for the end users. Compared to the use of a computer during every day work, the time of using such a system is typically really

A. Marcus (Ed.): DUXU 2014, Part I, LNCS 8517, pp. 206–213, 2014.
© Springer International Publishing Switzerland 2014

short, often only a few minutes. Due to heterogeneity of the users of such systems the usability of the user interfaces is of great importance. The user interfaces have to be either adaptable or even self-adaptive to the various skills and preferences of the users. Due to the monolithic system architecture of existing self-service systems, simple and flexible usage of the user interface is often restricted. The development of adaptive user interfaces involves challenges for developers that are addressed partially by frameworks like the CAMELEON Reference Framework (CRF) [4]. However, concrete solutions for supporting the development of flexible and adaptive user interfaces for distributed self-service systems do not exist in industry. In this paper we describe an integrated model-based approach for the development of adaptive user interfaces.

The paper is structured as following: First, the authors present some necessary background information and related work in the areas of self-adaptation and model-based development. Thereafter, the authors describe an example scenario, which shows the main challenges for developing flexible user interfaces for distributed self-service systems. Based on this example scenario a methodology concerning the model-based approach on developing adaptive user interfaces is described. In the end, the authors conclude with a summary and a critical reflection.

2   Background

Focusing on the topic of model-based user interface development of adaptive self-service systems multiple topics have to be taken into account: The possibilities and different levels of adapting a system and frameworks for addressing the part of model-based development including aspects of adaptation.

2.1   Adaptation

Developing software with a user interface is getting more and more interactive and complex. Some years ago, domain specialists built their own software to use the computer as a tool to do some sort of calculations. Today, computer experts build software for domain specialists supporting them to do their tasks more effective and with greater efficiency. Therefore, the computer experts have to gain lots of domain knowledge to create an adequate user interface. Having self-service systems in mind, the time the users spend on the system is rather short. Therefore, the interface must be very simple which is in some cases restricted due to the amount of information, existing necessary processes or the heterogeneity of the users (e.g. young people, older people, people with special needs). An alternative exists in creating user interfaces with a certain level of adaptation. Thereby, we would like to distinguish between and define three levels of adaptation, which differs in the way of who is initiating the process of adaptation – the user or the system:

- **Adaptable UIs** (*manual adaptation*). The user is able to customize respectively individualize the user interface (e.g. arranging information fields in a dashboard (*layout adaptation*), creating shortcuts for often used tasks or views (*navigation adaptation*)).

- **Adaptive UIs** (*semi-automatic adaptation*). Due to some sort of authentication, the system is able to recognize the user and support him with suggestions (e.g. Amazon's recommendation system about potential products of interest (*content adaptation*)). It would also be possible that the systems notice if the user has some difficulties in achieving his goal. Therefore, the system would be able to support the user with suggestions concerning alternative workflows. All the time, the user is able to decide whether or not to accept a suggestion of the system.
- **Self-adaptive UIs** (*automatic adaptation*). Self-adaptive UIs are based on systems with its own 'intelligence'. These systems are equipped with some kind of sensors. Due to a knowledge base or even a learning mechanism a system is able to analyze the kind or the behavior of a user in front of it. Thus, it automatically changes some parts or even the whole UI (e.g. adjusting the physical height of a display depending of the size of the user (*hardware adaptation*), switching to audio guidance for blind people (*input/output adaptation*), reacting to the emotional status of the user by placing the coupon input at the end of a task (*business process adaptation*), rearranging the navigation according to the cultural heritage (*context adaptation*), supporting user with interaction problems (*workflow adaptation*)).

Working in the field of self-adaptive systems, some new research questions arise which have to be discussed. In the past, software ergonomics addressed the topics of reducing the cognitive learning effort of a user. In addition, heuristics like 'user control and freedom' have been defined. Due to the fact that self-adaptive systems are trying to automatically react on context parameters, it has to be ensured that the systems always react in the same way. Having a new different adaptation of the workflow or layout of the UI every time the user uses a self-service system, he will be confused or even unsatisfied. Furthermore, the lost of control will also end up in the same way.

Trying to address such issues, it is necessary to have a software development methodology that also supports usability activities and concepts. Therefore, this paper focuses on model-based UI development.

2.2   Model-Based Development

Model-based development methods have been discussed in the past for various individual aspects of a software system and for different application domains. This applies to the development of the data management layer, the technical functionality or for the development of a user interface [5].

The CAMELEON Reference Framework (CRF) [4] provides a unified framework for model-based and model-driven development of user interfaces. There are already different kinds of work such as [6] or [7] which propose a model-based development of user interfaces. These approaches mainly focus on model-based development and their technological implementation. However, aspects of self-adaptive software systems for increasing the flexibility of user interfaces for heterogeneous user groups are not sufficiently integrated with the model-based development process.

Existing architectural concepts for self-adaptive systems such as the MAPE-K by Kephart and Chess [8] and the 3-layer reference architecture of Kramer and Magee [9] describe the logical concepts for the implementation of adaptive software. Based on the MAPE-K approach existing frameworks like Rainbow by Garlan et al. [10] or StarMX by Asadollahi et al. [11] provide a more refined architecture for implementing self-adaptive systems. Geihs et al. develop a framework for the development of self-adaptive and reconfigurable software based on the distributed software architecture of the EU project MUSIC [12]. The focus is in particular on the creation of adaptive mobile applications that offer location-based services to the user.

In our approach for model-based user interface development for adaptive self-service systems, we follow a development methodology that integrates several aspects of a software system, such as functionality, the user interface as well as adaptation. Model-based approaches in the field of self-adaptive systems have to be combined with ideas from the field of model-based development of user interfaces. For this, however, different challenges and issues have to be considered, which can be derived from the following example scenario from the area of ticket sales.

3   Example Scenario

If we think of a scenario (see Figure 1) with a distributed, networked multi-channel system, in which the ticket purchase is carried out by the use of different channels, we can see that different interaction interfaces are available. In this scenario the ticket purchase is first prepared on a home PC entering the reservation dates (date or time for round-trip). In transit the user is available to book additional services (luggage service, seat reservation, hotel reservation at destination) via smartphone. Finally, the printing of the ticket from the ticket machine is done.

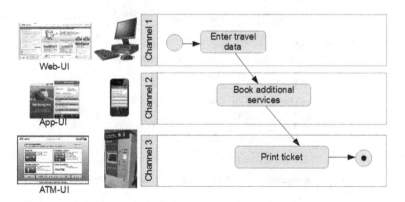

Fig. 1. Example scenario

In existing self-service systems integration of additional channels (Smartphone, Tablet, etc.) with new interaction modalities to interact with a self-service system is often not sufficiently supported. Therefore it is necessary to develop flexible and easy to use user interfaces to improve the monolithic architecture towards a multi-channel system offering

- distributed business and interaction processes enabling different interaction modalities (e.g. graphics, speech, gestures),
- multi-platform capability for integration and usage of heterogeneous devices,
- adaptation of system functionality and user interfaces.

Based on the described example scenario, one can find summarized that there is a need for an integrated model-based development approach in the area of self-service systems. This should include different aspects of a software system, such as functionality, the user interface as well as adaptation and provide a suitable development process for industry.

4 Method and Result

In cooperation with an industrial partner we develop a new methodology for the model-based development of user interfaces for distributed self-service systems. To meet the above described requirements, we are pursuing in our methodology a model-based development approach based on the CAMELEON Reference Framework (CRF). The CRF is an established reference architecture for model-based development of user interfaces which emerged as part of the European CAMELEON project (Context Aware Modelling for Enabling and Leveraging Effective interaction) [4]. Essentially, this framework consists of four different layers (see Figure 2).

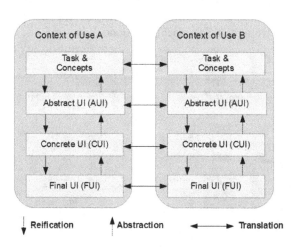

Fig. 2. CAMELEON Reference Framework [4]

The top layer Task & Concepts includes a task model that is used for the hierarchical description of the activities and actions of individual users of the user interface. The abstract user interface (AUI) is described in the form of a dialogue model that specifies the user's interactions with the user interface without regard to a specific technology. The actual display of the user interface is performed by the concrete user interface (CUI), which is represented by a presentation model. The lowest layer of the framework is the final user interface that is eventually generated for the target platform of a particular terminal. The vertical dimension describes the path from abstract to concrete models. Here, a top-down approach is followed, in which the abstract descriptions of relevant information about the user interface are enriched to more sophisticated models through model-to-model transformations (M2M). Subsequently, the refined models are interpreted or transformed (model-to-code transformation, M2C) to produce the final user interface (FUI). On the horizontal level, the possibility of adapting the model is shown depending on the current context.

For supporting the analysis and design phase in the development of distributed, adaptive user-interfaces we have designed a target architecture which pays special attention to aspects of adaptation and integrates them into the model-based development process for user interfaces. Figure 3 shows the target architecture of our solution based on the CAMELEON approach. At the level of conceptual modeling (Computation Independent Model, CIM) a task model and a user model (representing different user groups or individuals) are created as input for the creation of an abstract model of the user interface at the level of platform-independent modeling (Platform Independent Model-PIM).

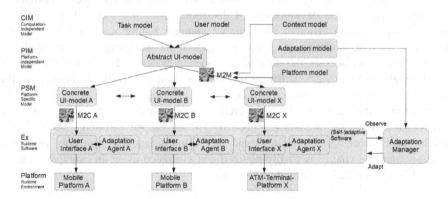

Fig. 3. Target Architecture

Another conceptual model describes the context of use in the form of contextual factors, such as the localization of the user (context model). This model is used together with a platform model to implement the model-to-model transformation from the abstract user interface model (Abstract UI-model) into the concrete user interface model (Concrete UI-model) at the level of platform-specific modelling (Platform-Specific Model, PSM). This translation step should be supported by the use of appropriate tools. The concrete user interface model consists of a set of coupled partial models for the respective platforms. With the aid of specific generators and interpreters required for a concrete platform, a suitable user interface is then generated from the respective sub-model, which can then be run on this platform. For increasing the usability of the final user interfaces different HCI Patterns or guidelines can be integrated in the generation step.

This model-driven development approach will also support the dynamic adaptation of the user interface at runtime. For this purpose, an adaptation model is created in addition to a monitoring concept that describes the adaptation of the user interface (as well as the functionality coupled thereto). From the resulting adaptation models the adaptation manager is derived. This is a software component that observes the adaptable software and controls the adaptation according to the adaptation model. It is contemplated to supplement the Adaptation Manager by dedicated sub-components or Adaptation Agents. The latter interoperate on the respective platform instances and are responsible for the adaptation of the user interfaces and their coupled functionality. Looking at the example scenario from the previous section (see Figure 1), there are different adaptation components for each device. For example, in the transition from channel 1 to channel 2 the adaptation component of the smartphone should ensure in cooperation with the adaptation manager that functionality and presentation of specific characteristics and requirements of smartphones are adjusted so that irrelevant or inappropriate information from the web interface (additional offers advertisements, logos etc., which take up much space) are hidden.

To achieve the objectives described in the example scenario, we first examined today's self-service systems in terms of their user interfaces and architectures. Based on the results of the requirements analysis, a model based development approach is designed to support the development of distributed user interfaces of modern self-service systems in an efficient and reliable manner. Future work will include the development of a modeling language to support the modeling of distributed and adaptive user interfaces in the area of self-service systems. To support the model-based development process, software tools are needed to effectively implement the development tasks. In addition to an editor for creating and editing models in the specified modeling language, tools for creating an executable user interface from the concrete user interface models are needed. The developed solution - model-based development process, architecture and operation/interaction concept, modeling language and tool chain - is finally realized and evaluated using an example scenario like in Figure 1 in the form of a demonstrator.

5   Conclusion

This paper presents a concept for the efficient development of adaptive user interfaces for self-service systems in a distributed multi-platform environment. In this paper we have referred to an example scenario from practice, from which requirements for the development of adaptive interactive self-service systems were derived. Based on the requirements a model-based approach for the implementation of adaptive flexible user interfaces was presented for interactive self-service systems. For this purpose we extended the CAMELEON reference framework to the aspect of adaptation. For the planning of the technical implementation, we are currently in the process - on the basis of the performed analysis of relevant use cases and common architectures and interfaces in the area of self-service systems - to develop appropriate adaptation models that can be integrated into the model-based development of user interfaces.

References

1. Seffah, A., Desmarais, M.C., Metzker, E.: HCI, Usability and Software Engineering Integration: Present and Future. In: Seffah, A., Gulliksen, J., Desmarais, M.C. (eds.) Human-Centered Software Engineering – Integrating Usability in the Development Process, pp. 37–57. Springer, Berlin (2005)
2. Lallemand, C.: Toward a Closer Integration of Usability in Software Development: A Study of Usability Inputs in a Model-Driven Engineering Process. In: Proceedings of the 3rd ACM SIGCHI Symposium on Engineering Interactive Computing Systems EICS, pp. 299–302. ACM, New York (2011)
3. Fischer, H., Nebe, K., Klompmaker, F.: A Holistic Model for Integrating Usability Engineering and Software Engineering Enriched with Marketing Activities. In: Kurosu, M. (ed.) Human-Centered Design, HCII 2011. LNCS, vol. 6776, pp. 28–37. Springer, Heidelberg (2011)
4. Calvary, G., Coutaz, J., Thevenin, D., Limbourg, Q., Bouillon, L., Vanderdonckt, J.: A Unifying Reference Framework for Multi-target User Interfaces. In: Interacting with Computers, pp. 289–308 (2003)
5. Hussmann, H., Meixner, G., Zuehlke, D. (eds.): Model-Driven Development of Advanced User Interfaces. SCI, vol. 340. Springer, Heidelberg (2011)
6. Link, S., Schuster, T., Hoyer, P., Abeck, S.: Modellgetriebene Entwicklung grafischer Benutzerschnittstellen (Model-Driven Development of Graphical User Interfaces). i-com 6(3), 37–43 (2008)
7. Botterweck, G.: A Model-driven Approach to the Engineering of Multiple User Interfaces. In: Kühne, T. (ed.) MoDELS 2006 Workshops. LNCS, vol. 4364, pp. 106–115. Springer, Heidelberg (2007)
8. Kephart, J.O., Chess, D.M.: The Vision of Autonomic Computing. Computer 36(1), 41–50 (2003)
9. Kramer, J., Magee, J.: Self-managed Systems: An Architectural Challenge. In: Proceedings of 2007 Future of Software Engineering (FOSE 2007), pp. 259–268. IEEE Computer Society, Washington, DC (2007)
10. Garlan, D., Cheng, S.-W., Schmerl, B.: Increasing System Dependability Through Architecture-based Self-repair. In: de Lemos, R., Gacek, C., Romanovsky, A. (eds.) Architecting Dependable Systems. LNCS, vol. 2677, pp. 61–89. Springer, Heidelberg (2003)
11. Asadollahi, R., Salehie, M., Tahvildari, L.: StarMX: A Framework for Developing Self-managing Java-based Systems. In: Proceedings of the 2009 Workshop on Software Engineering for Adaptive and Self-Managing Systems (SEAMS 2009), pp. 58–67 (2009)
12. Geihs, K., Reichle, R., Wagner, M., Khan, M.U.: Modeling of context-aware self-adaptive applications in ubiquitous and service-oriented environments. In: Cheng, B.H.C., de Lemos, R., Giese, H., Inverardi, P., Magee, J. (eds.) Software Engineering for Self-Adaptive Systems. LNCS, vol. 5525, pp. 146–163. Springer, Heidelberg (2009)

User Experience Evaluation

Usability Evaluation of Mobile Passenger Information Systems

Shirley Beul-Leusmann[1,2], Christian Samsel[3], Maximilian Wiederhold[3], Karl-Heinz Krempels[3], Eva-Maria Jakobs[1], and Martina Ziefle[2]

[1] Textlinguistics & Technical Communication/ HCI Center,
RWTH Aachen University, Germany
[2] Communication Science/ HCI Center, RWTH Aachen University,
[3] Information Systems, RWTH Aachen University, Germany
{s.beul-leusmann,e.m.jakobs}@tk.rwth-aachen.de,
{beul-leusmann,ziefle}@comm.rwth-aachen.de
{samsel,wiederhold,krempels}@dbis.rwth-aachen.de

Abstract. Public transportation becomes increasingly diverse because of innovation in transport modalities and a large number of service providers. For facilitating passengers' comfort, intermodal passenger information systems are required, which combine data of different providers and transport modes. Therefore, context sensitive mobile applications are promising solutions to supporting passengers at every stage of their trip. Crucial for the success of these applications is their usability. In this paper, a prototype of an intermodal passenger information system is investigated in a usability evaluation and tested in comparison to the leading mobility application in Germany. Both iOS apps were evaluated with a questionnaire using the system usability scale (SUS) in a lab setting (n=20) and in a field test (n=20). Additionally, participants of the field test were interviewed retrospectively about app and setting. The user feedback was beneficial in learning about users' expectations towards information retrieval procedure in and functionalities of a passenger information system. The usability evaluation basically revealed easy to improve usability problems, but also a trust issue and the need for a participatory component in public transportation, probably by integrating social media.

Keywords: mobile applications, smartphone app, travel information, passenger information system, usability, evaluation methods.

1 Innovating Public Transportation

Current trends in urbanism foster sustainable and green city designs for enhancing dwellers' quality of life [1]. In this context, transportation plays a notably role because emissions still grow in this industrial sector [2]. One strategy of mitigating the pollution is to enlarge public transportation and simultaneously reduce the number of rides with personal vehicles. To achieve this hoped-for emission decrease, the ridership in public transportation must be raised significantly [3].

A. Marcus (Ed.): DUXU 2014, Part I, LNCS 8517, pp. 217–228, 2014.

For providing public transportation across an urban region, three levels of activity must be considered according to the transportation expert Paul Mees [4]: (a) On the *strategic level* system objectives are set, for instance funding sources, transportation modes etc. (b) On the *tactical level* the objectives are transferred into system-wide service strategies, for example defining the route network, drives, timetables etc. (c) Then, the tactic is translated to the *operational level*. There, day-to-day-operations are carried out such as training personnel, selling tickets, designing and distributing passenger information.

The image of public transportation emerges by the interaction of multiple factors; but predominantly by passengers' experience of consuming public transportation services. Therefore, even slight improvements on the operational level can contribute to accomplish a higher customer satisfaction. For this, it is necessary to identify shortcomings, which impair their comfort.

According to [5] and [6], passengers are highly frustrated when using public transportation because of lacking information provided by transit agencies. Travel information often seems incomprehensible to passengers; for instance understanding timetables overtaxes many people. Furthermore, they have no real-time information about the actual position of the vehicle they are waiting for. As a consequence, they do not know about its progress on its route and also not about delays, which causes frustration. Hence, introducing interactive information systems with real-time passenger information is a promising solution and a common passenger request. They can be realized using information and communication technologies (ICT). In particular, the proliferation of mobile Wi-Fi and the increasing prevalence of smartphones shift the focus strongly on mobile passenger information systems (PIS) realized as smartphone apps [3]. They can offer passengers the opportunity of easy and rapid information access and will advance to the position of passengers' daily companions [7].

Crucial for the success of these services are two factors: a) the quality of the provided information in terms of comprehensiveness and completeness and b) the systems' usability. For achieving this comfort improvement, passengers must award a "perceived usefulness" to these apps (according to the technology acceptance model of [8]). Hence, passengers' perspective must be thoroughly integrated during the iterative development of a passenger information system for accomplishing the best possible user experience.

2   Related Work

Recent work about passenger information systems is wide-ranging because various disciplines grapple with these services: Engineers address technical issues such as the development of primary-context models and ontologies [9] or dynamic personalization in multi-channel data dissemination environments [10]. Mobility experts deal with generic models of transport management systems including components for traffic regulation support and user information [11]. Especially, real-time data consideration is of major importance for assisting passengers en-route [12].

In the last decade, many pilot projects have presented their prototypes: One example is the TUTPIS application, which accompanies passengers at every stage of their trip and offers them personalized, real time information services (e.g. timetables, connection search, electronic ticketing) [13]. Another promising initiative is the UbiBus project, in which an ubiquitous system for public transport assistance uses context information [14]. Its core is an intelligent transportation system application, which supplies travel information on onboard displays, is available on the web and as a smart phone app. The latter delivers information about the current location of a bus or its progress on its route respectively.

Besides information distribution for public vehicle use, attention is also drawn to pedestrian navigation in multimodal routing services. For instance, Yu and Lu [15] created an initial prototype considering walking as a transport mode, which assesses travel modes by a defined criteria set. Their approach uses dynamic information about real-time and historic traffic data to facilitate precise estimations. In addition, Baus et al. [16] present a pedestrian navigation system for indoor and outdoor use, which can automatically adapt to location changes and display directions on different devices. Creating an intermodal information system also requires indoor navigation features. While passengers change modes at transit points, they often must route themselves through buildings in a short time period. Rehrl et al. [17] are aware of this problem and, therefore, propose an electronic guide, which generates a hierarchical model of the transit point complex and gives user instructions using visual aids (e.g. maps). According to a study investigating pedestrians' informational requirements, landmarks are the most valuable navigation cues and are way more important than street names or distance information [18]. Chowaw-Liebman et al. [19] and Heiniz et al. [20] have used this finding as a basis for developing a turn-by-turn approach for navigation inside large complexes of buildings (e.g. airports).

When surveying the latest research on passenger information systems, the majority of research initiatives focuses on technical aspects. Only few research activities were dedicated to HCI topics. Human factors experts work on user-centered application concepts: they study user behavior to design intuitively usable passenger information systems (see [21]). Especially, displaying travel information on mobile (small screen) devices is challenging why evaluating different presentation formats is necessary, for instance with paper prototyping [22]. In [4] and [23], Wirtz et al. conduct user tests to evaluate a passenger information system. The collected data was analyzed to investigate patterns and reference objects for gaining a deeper understanding of the media net surrounding a lately launched application.

Regarding user diversity, few empirical studies have been carried out on user groups' particularities. The ongoing demographic change shifts attention on elderly who are increasingly considered in the development of electronic devices and services (see [24]). Schaar and Ziefle [25] found that age is a notable factor in the acceptance of passenger information systems. This age effect underlies travel expertise and also technology experience. Another relevant user group are passengers with restricted mobility. Heck et al. [26] propose a concept for providing information about handicapped accessible routing using a hotline and a website. In this approach, most types of disabilities are considered; user profiles can be personalized.

Still missing are user test studies with passenger information systems to collect authentic user feedback. For this, an evaluation with a lab setting seems insufficient because it does not represent realistic using conditions. Therefore, an additional field test is necessary.

3   Empirical Study

The presented study deals with the usability evaluation of an exemplary intermodal passenger information system, which emphasizes guiding passengers in intermodal scenarios throughout the whole journey.

3.1   Evaluated Application[1]

A passenger information system is created following the guiding principle of gamification. The main conceptual idea is to design passenger information similarly to navigation aids in complex video games (e.g. World of Warcraft). There, the information provision is portioned according to situation-specific gamer needs (cascading information), which supports keeping gamers' actions focused on the objective, for instance completing the current level [27].

An intermodal trip is regarded as a quest game conceptualized as a chain of single tasks, which is displayed in a turn-by-turn-like user aid. Passengers gradually solve these tasks (get on bus, change mode etc.) until they reach their destination. Information is only given in order to reach the next intermediate target. The prototype is realized as an iOS 6 app, whose GUI basically consists of three different views: planning, selecting and assisting (see Figure 1).

Fig. 1. Screenshots of views displayed in the prototype during an intermodal journey: a) plan view, b) selection view, c) assistance view (bus), d) assistance view (pedestrian)

The *plan view* displays a search mask for entering a trip's starting point (*From*), destination (*To*), a date selector (*Time*), and a search button (*Plan!*) (see Fig. 1,

---

[1] For more information about the approach (e.g. functions, view design, back-end realization, implementing etc.) see [27].

screenshot a). Using the virtual keyboard passengers can insert, for example, an address for start and/or destination. Furthermore, the current geolocation can be used as a starting by tapping a green position icon, which appears while interacting with the *From* text field. Two scenarios can be serviced: planning a route or rescheduling an active trip. The actions in the former lead to the selection view, in which feasible itineraries are listed; the ones in the latter to the first listed itinerary implying that this is the optimum route.

The *selection view* is displayed as a table (see Fig. 1, screenshot b). On top of it, starting and destination are described. Subsequently, the possible itineraries are listed; each providing time of departure and arrival, trip duration, required transportation modes (icon-based visualization), vehicle /route identifier (e.g. bus number).

On the *assistance view* the trip is segmented into steps, which are drawn in a map (see Fig. 1, screenshot c). Progress on the route is visualized as well as starting points of each step (position markers). When walking is the proposed transportation mode, a *compass* functionality – inspired by quest games – gives passengers information about the direction of their destination (rotatable green arrow). The displayed text refers to the actual transport mode: While walking, the turn-by-turn assistance is provided. The name of the road the pedestrian is supposed to walk down is given as well as the distance this step covers. Moreover, the absolute and the relative direction are presented via map. While being on a transit stage, the current mode depicted by an icon and informational labels are shown. They incorporate details such as vehicle type, transit route, departure and arrival time, starting point as well as destination of step. Finally, a progress bar conveys information regarding time about the total progress on the chosen route.

3.2   Evaluation Methodology

The described prototype was tested in comparison to the DB Navigator, which is the most popular mobility application in Germany [28]. The test covered a leading scenario and three tasks which test participants had to tackle by interacting with the apps. The scenario was used to communicate participants the nature of the test and to give the tasks an overall framing (participant is a student with an iPhone owning a student ticket and using public transportation frequently).

After reading the scenario, the task processing began. All tasks focused on the apps' primary functionality routing. For lowering the cognitive load, task instructions were handed over only after completing or terminating the previous task.

Task 1 required a routing from the actual position to a bus stop: *It is 09:18 a.m. at the 3rd of August 2013. You are running through an unknown street. You have to go to the Audimax, a university building, to write an exam. The exam will start at 10:00 a.m. Use your app to find information about a bus ride to your exam. Use the integrated functionality to find your actual location.*

Task 2 was about routing from a bus stop to an address: *It is 03:03 p.m. at the 3rd of August 2013. Your performance during the exam was more or less successful. You are having a late lunch with your girlfriend Claudia and have to plan a trip from the Pontstrasse, Aachen to the home improvement store because you have to buy material* *for fixing a shelf for Claudia. The home improvement store is located in Roermonder Strasse 177, Aachen. You are again pressed for time because later you have an important appointment. Use your app to reach your destination by bus as quickly as possible.*

Task 3 was dedicated to routing between two addresses: *It is 17:13 p.m. at the 3rd of August 2013. After you have carried out all tasks you have promised to Claudia you must rush to your family to help them preparing a birthday party. At the moment, you are at Claudia's place in Oppenhoffallee 143, Aachen. Your parents live in Burtscheid, a suburb of Aachen, in the street Birkengrund 10, Aachen. You have to be there at 06:00 p.m. to set up a pavilion for the guests. You have to hurry because the weather forecast has announced 88% brollability. Use your app to reach your destination by bus as quickly as possible.*

All participants had to execute all tasks on both apps. The experimental design considered position effects: 50% of the test participants started with the prototype and used afterwards the DB Navigator, the other 50% vice versa.

Experimental Setting. Both applications were evaluated using an iPhone 4s. The test was carried out in two conditions: The first was an indoor laboratory setting in which participants were sitting at a desk in an office. The second was a field setting in which participants had to solve the test outdoor while walking (see Figure 2).

Fig. 2. Left: Test participant interacting with the prototype in the lab setting. Study manager documents the interaction using a screen camera, video camera, and a stopwatch. *Right:* Test participant interacting with the prototype in the field test. Only voice is recorded.

The latter condition refers to a current societal phenomenon: Many people deal with ICT-related multi-tasks in their everyday life. For instance, they interact almost all the time and everywhere with their smartphones, even while walking on the road. Passenger information systems foster this behavior because they are frequently consulted when information about public transportation is urgently needed, e. g. when immediately re-scheduling a trip. In such stressful situations, moving (rushing) to an entry of the public transportation system (bus stop etc.) often happens.

During the test, participants were instructed to "think aloud" (spontaneous commenting on interaction). Verbal comments were digitally recorded. In the lab, the interaction was additionally recorded with a screen record software. Due to technical restrictions this was not applicable for the field setting. For compensating this, additional retrospective interviews were carried out with field test participants. After all, participants' feedback was collected with a questionnaire consisting of six sections: (1) demographic data, (2) mobility profile, (3) technology use, (4) assessment of DB Navigator, (5) assessment of the prototype, (6) overall rating.

The usability of both apps was measured with a questionnaire using the System Usability Scale (SUS) [29]. It is an easy-to-apply ten-item scale, in which users are asked to indicate the degree of (dis)agreement to several statements on a 5-point Likert scale from 1 ("strongly disagree") to 5 ("strongly agree"). The overall scale gives a global view of subjective usability assessments. The maximum score on the SUS is 100 points. For avoiding any biases, the items are alternated between positive and negative ones (see Table 1):

Table 1. System Usability Scale (SUS) [29]

System Usability Scale	
1	I think that I would like to use this system frequently.
2	I found the system unnecessarily complex.
3	I thought the system was easy to use.
4	I think that I would need the support of a technical person to be able to use this system.
5	I found the various functions in this system were well integrated.
6	I thought there was too much inconsistency in this system.
7	I would imagine that most people would learn to use this system very quickly.
8	I found the system very cumbersome to use.
9	I felt very confident using the system.
10	I needed to learn a lot of things before I could get going with this system.

Sample. 40 test participants took part in the user test (20 lab condition: Table 2; 20 in field test: Table 3). In total, the sample consisted of young adults (20-32 years old, 50% male/ 50% female). All test persons were well educated (university students, university graduates) and predominantly worked in technology-related professions.

Table 2. Sample description of the laboratory setting n = 20

Age	Gender	Profession
M = 23.9	Male = 11	20 students (mostly technology-related/
SD = 2.7	Female = 9	technical study programs)

Table 3. Sample description of the field setting n = 20

Age^2	Gender	Profession
M = 26.1	Male = 9	14 students (mostly technical study programs)
SD = 3.8	Female = 11	6 university graduates (scientific staff)

---

[2] One participant did not specify his/her age.

About their daily mobility they stated to be multimodal and use public transportation often (19 using bus daily). 34 test persons were using smartphones (no use: 2, missing data: 4). Concerning mobility apps, 38 stated to know the DB Navigator and 30 to use it (in addition: 8 Öffi users, 7 Navigon users, 37 Google Maps users[3]). The DB navigator's popularity was regarded as a problem because user experience influenced the results of performance tests. However, this experience had also a positive effect on assessing the prototype's quality by eliciting focused improvement suggestions.

3.3   Results

Participants' overall SUS rating of the evaluated apps differs in 3.9 points. The DB Navigator gained averagely 79.6 points out of 100 possible (SD = 14.9). In comparison, the prototype received a rating of 75.7 points (SD = 14.7). Carrying out the test with the prototype took 14 seconds longer compared to the DB Navigator. When working with the prototype, participants spent averagely 103 seconds on completing one task during the lab condition, 117s in the field. When interacting with the DB Navigator, 90 seconds were required in the mean to solve one task at the lab and 102s in the field (for details, see Figure 3).

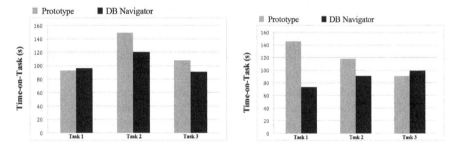

Fig. 3. Left: Time-on-task of lab setting (s). *Right:* Time-on-task of field setting (s).

Regarding the average duration for processing a task (time-on-task), a wide difference between lab and field condition becomes apparent: participants were dealing longer with the tasks during the field condition.

Besides the usability assessment using the SUS, participants gave a detailed feedback on prototype's visualization and features by writing down comments in the questionnaire and uttering them during the interviews. Many positive comments were made on the prototype in general. It was simply structured, minimalistic designed and quickly to learn. One participant stated: *"I really liked that the app was designed so minimalistic: only two [text] fields and a button. This means I just start this widget and have no access barrier at all." (DB_5_23_m)*. In addition, they acknowledged the door-to-door routing, the icon-based choice of transportation mode, the integrated map and the step-by-step support during the journey. One participant identified a

---

[3] Many participants stated they did not differentiate between app and website Google Maps.

disadvantage of the latter: *"You can zoom in [the map], this was nice. But you could not enlarge the map to see the whole route in a glance. There was also no list view of all steps, which had to be tackled successively. It would be nice to add this [overview] function. [...] Maybe just [... display] what I need, but I want to have the option [at least]."* Further negative comments addressed missing features or information. Test participants criticized the lacking comfort when mentioning that a tool to set arrival/departure time was missing, no auto-complete was offered in the text fields, no selection of surrounding bus stops was automatically provided or that a default setting of the territory was lacking (e.g. displayed data related to actual position, not to whole country). One female said: *"I had the impression that [the DB Navigator] retrieves more [results] with less information than the prototype. It suffices to insert a street name and it detects the street in the correct city [automatically]."* (QBMI_6_30_f)

Regarding the *size of the map*, participants were pleased. The majority stated it was sufficient and useful for maintaining orientation during the trip. However, problems while scrolling were observed because a swiping functionality was accidentally activated which opened a superior menu. Also zooming (pinch-to-zoom) was reported as a little challenging. The *quality of icons* was rated as comprehensive, except for two icons (train and bus), which appeared too similarly. Marking icons was intuitively usable, but its meaning was unclear. Finally, the color code was criticized: a dark blue marking on a black icon fully covers the icon. Participants also liked the idea of having *information about the overall progress* during their trip. The majority opted for implementing a progress bar. Some people reported that it was not obvious to them, which progress was visualized in the prototype – distance, time, or number of turns within the turn-by-turn assistance.

Moreover, difficulties were mentioned which are common for small screen device applications, for example a too large proximity of (navigation) elements. Besides, the interaction was assessed as too slow because reactions evoked by tipping on interactive elements (e.g. buttons) occurred comparing to other apps relatively late. Deleting text from the text fields did not work as in other iOS apps. Concerning the transportation mode choice, participants could not intuitively understand the meaning of the marker ('chosen' or 'excluded'?). Many error reports occurred. Technical problems of the location-based service were mentioned.

4   Discussion and Conclusion

Both apps received relative similar scores on the SUS, which is amazing because the prototype is only a demonstrator, and by far not as sophisticated as the DB Navigator is. This rating could result from the composition of the sample, which is not representative for the whole workforce. The young participants showed according to their study programs/jobs a high technology-affinity. They might have overlooked technical problems and less serious design problems. For a sound assessment of the prototype, further studies should involve older people with lower technology-affinity. Besides, the prototype needs to be improved with regard to system reliability (e.g. wheel to set time/date not working properly) and arrangement of navigation elements (e.g. too close proximity of buttons).

Interestingly participants uttered requirements concerning the information retrieval procedure. They were expecting an intelligent, context aware passenger information system, which would offer assistance, not only information. For instance, they supposed the app to consider their actual position and the surrounding region when proposing routes, in best case all alternatives within one list. Concerning the turn-by-turn assistance of the prototype, participants highly appreciated the small amount of information including the visual aids given in each step, but opted for an additional overview functionality, probably a large map and/or a list view. They uttered this request, but could not give a comprehensible reasoning. This raises the question to which extent users trust the displayed information and which features a passenger information system must offer to be the ideal daily mobility broker.

Finally, all these presented endeavors tend to enhance passengers' comfort and, finally, to increase ridership in public transportation. However, the overall impact of passenger information systems should be examined. A study on decision-making reveals that innovating passenger information does not lead to a "substantial behaviour change (certainly in terms of mode choice)" [31]. Therefore, the perceived usefulness of public transportation must be increased, probably by adding a participatory component. Foth and Schroeter [32] investigated the daily journey of commuters and envisioned a "digitally augmenting of the public transport environment" in terms of using electronic devices and interactive services for creating a unique, enjoyable and meaningful user experience. Similarly, Camacho, Foth and Rakotonirainy [3] are aiming at an image modernization of public transportation. They propose extending the service portfolio, for instance providing free Wi-Fi access or location-based services (tour guides). Passengers can consume these new services, but can also become active themselves, for example when sharing information about seat availability via social media.

In conclusion, passenger information systems can contribute to a modernized image of public transportation and enhance passengers' comfort. Thus, system designers must identify and consider user requirements concerning interaction design, layout and range of functions at an early stage within the design cycle. They must take trust-related aspects into account as well as innovative participatory components such as social media features. Finally, user experience must be generated and communicated early to empower passengers' confidence in any novel application.

Acknowledgements. We thank our participants for spending time on our user tests (especially during dusk and rain) and our research interns Saskia de Luca and Niloofar Jafarian Suraki for their support. Finally, we thank the anonymous reviewers for their helpful feedback on our proposal. This research was funded by the German Ministry of Economics and Technology (reference number 01 ME 12052).

References

1. Low, N., Gleeson, B., Green, R., Radovic, D.: The Green City. Sustainable Homes. Sustainable Suburbs. UNSW Press, Sydney (2005)
2. Chapman, L.: Transport and Climate Change: A Review. J. Transp. Geog. 15, 354–367 (2007)

3. Camacho, T.D., Foth, M., Rakotonirainy, A.: Pervasive Technology and Public Transport: Opportunities Beyond Telematics. Pervasive Computing 12(1), 18–25 (2013)
4. Mees, P.: Transport for Suburbia: Beyond the Automobile Age. Earthscan, London (2010)
5. Caulfield, B., O'Mahony, M.: An Examination of the Public Transport Information Requirements of Users. IEEE Transactions on Intelligent Transportation Systems 8, 21–30 (2007)
6. Papangelis, K., Sripada, S., Corsar, D., Velaga, N., Edwards, P., Nelson, J.D.: Developing a real time passenger information system for rural areas. In: Yamamoto, S. (ed.) HIMI/HCII 2013, Part II. LNCS, vol. 8017, pp. 153–162. Springer, Heidelberg (2013)
7. Wirtz, S., Jakobs, E.-M., Beul, S.: Passenger Information Systems in Media Networks – Patterns, Preferences, Prototypes. In: Proceedings of the IEEE International Professional Communication Conference, pp. 131–137. IEEE Press, New York (2010)
8. Davis, F.D.: Perceived Usefulness, Perceived Ease of Use, and User Acceptance of Information Technology. MIS Quarterly 3(13), 319–339 (1989)
9. Lee, D., Meier, R.: Primary-Context Model and Ontology: A Combined Approach for Pervasive Transportation Services. In: Proceedings of the 5th annual IEEE International Conference on Pervasive Computing and Communications, pp. 419–424. IEEE Computer Society, Washington, DC (2007)
10. Goto, K., Kambayashi, Y.: A New Passenger Support System for Public Transport Using Mobile Database Access. In: Proceedings of the 28th International Conference on Very Large Data Bases, pp. 908–919. Morgan Kaufmann, San Francisco (2002)
11. Ezzedine, H., Bonte, T., Kolski, C., Tahon, C.: Intermodal Transportation System Management: Towards Integration of Traffic Management System and Users Information System. In: Proceedings of the IMACS Multiconference on Computational Engineering in Systems Applications, pp. 972–979. IEEE Press, New York (2006)
12. Garcia, C.R., Candela, S., Ginory, J., Quesada-Arenciba, A., Alayon, F.: On Route Travel Assistant for Public Transport Based on Android Technology. In: Proceedings of the Sixth International Conference on Innovative Mobile and Internet Services in Ubiquitous Computing, pp. 840–845. IEEE Press, New York (2012)
13. Hannikainen, M., Laitinen, A., Hamalainen, T., Kaisto, I., Leskinen, K.: Architecture of a Passenger Information System for Public Transport Services. In: Proceedings of the Vehicular Technology Conference, vol. 2, pp. 698–702. IEEE Press, New York (2001)
14. Vieira, V., Caldas, L.R., Salgado, A.C.: Towards an Ubiquitous and Context Sensitive Public Transportation System. In: 2011 4th Proceedings of the International Conference on Ubi-Media Computing (U- Media), pp. 174–179. IEEE Press, New York (2011)
15. Yu, H., Lu, F.: Advanced Multi-Modal Routing Approach for Pedestrians. In: Proceedings of the 2nd International Conference on Consumer Electronics, Communications and Networks (CECNet), pp. 2349–2352. IEEE Press, New York (2012)
16. Baus, J., Krüger, A., Wahlster, W.: A Resource-Adaptive Mobile Navigation System. In: Proceedings of the 7th International Conference on Intelligent User Interfaces, IUI 2002, pp. 15–22. ACM, New York (2002)
17. Rehrl, K., Leitinger, S., Bruntsch, S., Mentz, H.-J.: Assisting Orientation and Guidance for Multimodal Travelers in Situations of Modal Change. In: Proc. of 8th Int. IEEE Conf. on Intelligent Transportations Systems, pp. 407–412. IEEE Press, New York (2005)
18. May, A.J., Ross, T., Bayer, S.H., Tarkiainen, M.J.: Pedestrian Navigation Aids: Information Requirements and Design Implications. Personal and Ubiquitous Computing 7(6), 331–338 (2003)

19. Chowaw-Liebman, O., Christoph, U., Krempels, K.-H., Terwelp, C.: Indoor Navigation Approach Based on Approximate Positions. In: Proc. of the Int. Conf. on Indoor Positioning and Indoor Navigation (IPIN), pp. 15–17. IEEE Press, New York (2010)
20. Heiniz, P., Krempels, K.-H., Terwelp, C., Wüller, S.: Landmark-based Navigation in Complex Buildings. In: Proceedings of the International Conference on Indoor Positioning and Indoor Navigation (IPIN), pp. 1–9. IEEE Press, New York (2012)
21. Sanghoon, B.: An Advanced Public Transportation Systems Application: Feasibility Study of Bus Passenger Information Systems Operational Test in the Town of Blacksburg. In: Proceedings of the 6th Vehicle Navigation and Information Systems Conference 1995, Conjunction with the Pacific Rim TransTech Conference 'A Ride into the Future', pp. 408–413. IEEE Press, New York (1995)
22. Keller, C., Korzetz, M., Kühn, R., Schlegel, T.: Nutzerorientierte Visualisierung von Fahrplaninformationen auf mobilen Geräten im öffentlichen Verkehr, pp. 59–68. Oldenbourg Wissenschaftsverlag GmbH, München (2011)
23. Wirtz, S., Jakobs, E.-M.: Improving User Experience for Passenger Information Systems. Prototypes and Reference Objects. Transactions on Professional Communication 56(2), 120–137 (2013)
24. Karim, N.A., Nwagboso, C.: Assistive Technologies In Public Transport: Meeting The Needs of Elderly and Disabled Passengers. In: Proceedings of International Conference on Information and Communication Technologies: From Theory to Applications, p. 69. IEEE Press, New York (2004)
25. Schaar, A.K., Ziefle, M.: Potential of e-Travel Assistants to Increase Older Adults' Mobility. In: Leitner, G., Hitz, M., Holzinger, A. (eds.) USAB 2010. LNCS, vol. 6389, pp. 138–155. Springer, Heidelberg (2010)
26. Heck, H., Bühler, C., Becker, J.: ÖPNV-Reiseassistenz für mobilitätsingeschränkte Menschen. In: Proc. of 1st German Ambient Assisted Living Conference. VDE, Berlin (2008)
27. Samsel, C., Beul-Leusmann, S., Wiederhold, M., Krempels, K.-H., Ziefle, M., Jakobs, E.-M.: Cascading Information for Public Transport Assistance. In: Proceedings of the 10th International Conference on Web Information Systems and Technologies (WEBIST 2014). INSTICC, Barcelona (in press, 2014)
28. Statista GmbH: App Monitor Deutschland. Technical Report, Hamburg (November 2012)
29. Brooke, J.: SUS: a quick and dirty usability scale. In: Jordan, P.W., Thomas, B., Weerdmeester, B.A., McClelland, I.L. (eds.) Usability Evaluation in Industry. Taylor and Francis, London (1996)
30. Lyons, G.: The Role of Information in Decision-Making with Regard to Travel. IEE Proceedings IET Intelligent Transport Systems 153(3), 199–212 (2006)
31. Foth, M., Schroeter, R.: Enhancing the Experience of Public Transport Users with Urban Screens and Mobile Applications. In: Proceedings of the 14th International Academic MindTrek Conference, pp. 33–40. ACM, New York (2010)

SCENE: A Structured Means for Creating and Evaluating Behavioral Nudges in a Cyber Security Environment

Lynne Coventry[1], Pam Briggs[1], Debora Jeske[1], and Aad van Moorsel[2]

[1] Psychology & Communication Technology Lab, Northumbria University,
Newcastle-upon-Tyne, UK
[2] Head of Computing Science, Newcastle University, Newcastle-upon-Tyne, UK
{lynne.coventry,p.briggs,debora.jeske}@northumbria.ac.uk,
aad.vanmoorsel@newcastle.ac.uk

Abstract. Behavior-change interventions are common in some areas of human-computer interaction, but rare in the domain of cybersecurity. This paper introduces a structured approach to working with organisations in order to develop such behavioral interventions or 'nudges'. This approach uses elements of co-creation together with a set of prompts from the behavior change literature (MINDSPACE) that allows resesarchers and organisational stakeholders to work together to identify a set of nudges that might promote best behavioral practice. We describe the structured approach or framework, which we call SCENE, and follow this description with a worked example of how the approach has been utilised effectively in the development of a nudge to mitigate insecure behaviors around selection of wireless networks.

Keywords: stakeholder involvement, user-centred design, user experience, management of design, methodology, MINDSPACE framework, decision-making, nudging.

1 Introduction

The cyber security community is increasingly concerned with changing the security behaviors of individual Internet users. In a 2013 survey of UK organizations across different sectors, 93% of large organizations reported having a security breach in the previous year, and 87% of small businesses. 36% of the worst breaches were attributed to "inadvertent human error" including accidental leakage of confidential information (pwc, 2013). A National Cyber Security Association (NCSA, 2012) survey of small businesses in the US, conducted in 2012, suggested a cyber security disconnect where 47% of companies believed a data breach would have no impact on their business, yet 87% did not have a formal written Internet security polity and 69% did not even have an informal one. Finally, 18% said they would not even know if their computer network was compromised. This leaves us with a situation where many companies do not have security policies which outline the online behaviors they

A. Marcus (Ed.): DUXU 2014, Part I, LNCS 8517, pp. 229–239, 2014.

expect from their employees, and for those that do, employees do not always comply with that policy. This problem is further compounded by the increased use of mobile devices that blur the boundaries between personal and work-related use. Mobile technology users typically lack the expertise to effectively protect themselves (Ho et al 2010; Furman et al 2012), thus the rise of Bring Your Own Device (BYOD) practices in the workplace can leave many businesses open to cyber security attack.

There are a number of human behaviors which are required to maintain cyber security. A review of the websites dedicated to raising awareness of cyber security issues has resulted in the following list of required requirements of users . Each of these requirements has multiple behaviors associated with it. This makes studying cyber security behaviors difficult as we are not talking about a single behavior.

- Use strong passwords and manage them securely.
- Use security software including anti-virus, anti-spyware and firewalls, and ensure they are up-to-date.
- Always run the latest and official version of software (including operating system). Update as soon as update released..
- Log out of sites when you finish, disconnect from the internet and switch off your computer.
- Only use trusted and secured connections, and devices (including Wi-Fi)
- Only use trusted and secure sites and services and connect securely
- Stay informed about scam/phishing risks (knowledge, common sense, intuition) and try to avoid them
- Always opt to provide the minimal amount of personal information needed for any online interaction and keep your identity protected.
- Be aware of your physical surroundings to prevent theft and shoulder surfing etc.
- Report suspicious or criminal online activities to the authorities

To address the human component of cyber security we need to understand the factors which affect the cyber security behaviors of individual internet users. A significant research literature documents the efficacy of behavior change interventions in other domains (Abraham & Michie, 2008). However, only a small number of researchers have considered behavioral approaches to address the cybersecurity issues (Blythe, 2013; Pfleeger & Caputo, 2012). Little is currently known and much needs to be understood if we are to be effective in changing vulnerable behaviors in order to lower cyber-security threats. In particular, we lack the following:

- Reliable behavioral data on individual users' cybersecurity behaviors.
- Research on the factors influencing an individual's cybersecurity practices or lack thereof.
- A theory of human behavior or how to change human security behavior with validated predictive power.
- Agreement between stakeholders on the size of the problem, the risks and the necessary behaviors required.

Traditional thinking in the organizational sphere is that insecure behaviors simply reflect poor awareness of key security policies and practices. Many organizations implement awareness training as a solution (Leach, 2003). Mainstream information security awareness programs are typically top-down, and try to bring about changes in individual behavior by introducing an expert who delivers relevant information using various media and approaches (Ashford, 2012). However, awareness training is not always effective (Schneier, 2013). This suggests that while awareness is necessary (and may change intentions) it is rarely sufficient as a means of engineering behavior change. We present a structured methodology that allows us to work with organizational stakeholders to identify vulnerabilities and develop relevant technology-based, behavior change interventions (based on theories of behavior) that may prove more effective than simple training.

Telling people how they should behave does not always have an effect on how they actually behave. This certainly applies to security policy compliance (Bulgurcu et al., 2010). Factors such as willpower, motivation, risk perception, cost and convenience are often more important than a lack of knowledge. Various models of behavior exist that identify factors that influence behavior - and some have been applied to the cybersecurity context. These include threat avoidance theory (Liang, 2010), the theory of planned behavior (Burns & Roberts, 2013), deterrence theory, protection motivation theory and the health belief model (Davinson & Sillence, 2010). While such developments offer promise, researchers have yet to fully exploit these behavior models as a basis for developing cybersecurity interventions. Theories tend to assume that people behave reasonably and make good use of all the information available to them when deciding between choices and that people consider the implications of their choices. This may not always be the case and research into decision making suggests that people are subject to a number of cognitive shortcuts and biases when making a decision about how to behave at any particular point in time (Gilovich, Griffin and Kahneman 2002). While we may intend to act in a particular way we may not always act according to that intention.

People can, however, be persuaded to act in particular ways when technologies are designed with user behavior in mind. While we are addressing cyber security behaviors, persuasive technology has been applied to many domains relevant to HCI including ecommerce and mobile health apps. Such persuasive technology (Fogg 2003) is based on three principal assumptions: that a person is motivated to change, that they have the ability to change and that there is an effective environmental trigger (cue to action) for the desired behavior to happen. Thaler and Sunstein (2008) popularized this idea that people can be nudged towards a particular choice or behavior by the careful design of cues in the environment, recognizing that people do not make decisions in a vacuum. They make them in an environment where many features, noticed and unnoticed, can cue their decisions.

Their goal is to show how 'choice architectures' can be designed to help nudge people towards make better choices without forcing certain outcomes upon anyone. The tools they highlight are: effective defaults, designing for error, understanding mappings, giving feedback, structuring complex choices, and creating incentives. We should note that these are concepts that human computer interaction practitioners are already familiar with, as they have been traditionally associated with designing for ease of use. Note, too, that nudging is already common within the ecommerce domain - the example in Figure 2 shows how choice can be presented to dissuade people from the free version towards paying for the upgrade. The "Upgrade Now" option is bright green and highlighted, where as "download now" is dark grey with "No Thanks" written below. Both serve as cues towards the upgrade option.

Fig. 1. A nudge towards paying for a premium version of security software (http://www. lavasoft.com/products/ad_aware_free.php#)

1.1   MINDSPACE and Nudging

The MINDSPACE framework (Dolan et al., 2012) is a useful framework for drawing together a number of the 'influencing factors' that have been identified across different economic and psychological models of behavior change. MINDSPACE has been used by the UK government's Behavioral Insight Team to create policies and inform practice in the field. Each of the nine influencers in the framework has been shown to be effective in influencing behavior and decision making. There is overlap between the factors summarised in Nudge and MINDSPACE. The influencing factors identified in MINDSPACEare as follows:

1. **Messenger:** We are influenced by the person and/or method by which the message is delivered (Hayes, 2008).
2. **Incentives**: We are influenced by the rewards and punishments (losses) we receive. This includes our evaluation of the cost of behaving appropriately and the cost of the consequences if we do not. For instance, Herath and Rao (2009) found that the severity of the punishment has a negative effect on security behaviors.
3. **Norms:** We are influenced by the behaviors demonstrated by influencial others, such as senior managers, colleagues and family (Leach, 2003).
4. **Defaults:** We go with the flow of preset options. The default option will be chosen more often (Thaler & Sunstein, 2008).

5. **Salience**: We are attracted by what is either novel or particularly relevant to ourselves (Lamy, Leber, & Egeth, 2004).
6. **Priming**: Our acts are influenced by sub-concious cues (Kay et al, 2004). For instance green represents safety and red represents danger in many cultures.
7. **Affect:** Our emotional associations influence our behavior (Hareli & Rafaeli, 2008). For example, initial emotions formed when visiting a new and unfamiliar shopping websites can influence whether or not a visitor to these sites will disclose information (Li, Sarathy, & Xu, 2011).
8. **Commitments**: We seek to be consistent with our public statements and reciprocate the acts of others (Shore & Wayne, 1993).
9. **Ego**: We act in ways that make us feel better about ourself.

We believe the MINDSPACE framework provides a useful tool to keep the many different potential influencers in mind when developing technology based nudges. For example, using messenger effects and social norms the example in Figure 2 could be further enhanced by adding that 99% of customers choose the upgrade.

Lack of an evidence base to determine what will effectively change peoples' security behaviors has led us to develop an approach, based on MINDSPACE, for working interactively with companies to identify their current security behavior problems and identify possible technology based nudges. These nudges would allow us to influence security behaviors at the specific point in the interaction where decisions relevant to security must be made.

This is a general approach that can be used to identify different problems and solutions may not necessarily involve technology. However, in our work, the focus is on redesigning the technology to persuade people to follow a secure path. We assume that, while people may intend to act securely, their primary goal is very rarely security and therefore it is important to influence decisions at the point the decision has to be made. The goal of our approach is therefore to help organisations identify their most pressing problems (in the form of scenarios) and the most appropriate behavioral design interventions for them.

1.2   Approach

Our iterative behavior design approach - with the acronym SCENE - involves stakeholders in (i) Scenario elicitation; (ii) Co-creating nudges; (iii) Election of nudge(s) for further development; (iv) Nudge prototyping and (v) Evaluation of prototype(s) - (See Fig. 1).

Three important points are worth noting in terms of the application of this methodology. First, every stage utilises numerous stakeholders. This ensures that the solution focuses both on the needs of the end users as well as on the various other individuals directly or indirectly involved or affected by any changes in procedures. Second, the methodology is not a one-time cycle. Instead, the process provides a methodological framework for carefully assessing proposals for change in defaults, settings, and choice architecture based on numerous established practices and findings (Thaler & Sunstein, 2008; Johnson et al., 2012). Thirdly, we believe that the sense of

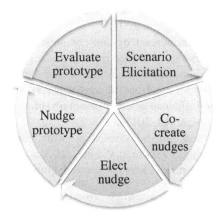

Fig. 2. Five stages in the development and evaluation of a behavioral nudge

joint ownership of security problems at work can be increased by involving stakeholders in the fashion we envision in our framework.

Scenario Elicitation. In this first stage, the aim is to capture poor security behaviors within the organization and understand more about the context for these behaviors. To achieve this, we carry out a group workshop (or series of workshops for larger organizations) where the eventual output is in the form of a security-related scenario or set of scenarios that can feed into the second stage in order to prompt thinking about behavior change. Our contention is that the company benefits from an open discussion of the behaviors which occur within the organization and an open discussion about why users act the way they do. This requires trust within the organization to ensure that these behaviors can be revealed and no blame will be attributed. Participants may be unaware of problematic behaviors. Managers may become aware that their Information Security Policy is too restrictive and employees are utilizing workarounds to optimize productivity. The act of taking part in this process can thus improve awareness of inappropriate behaviors and their consequences. Researchers can provide a back-ground on known user behaviors and vulnerabilities, but the organizational stakeholders should provide information on relevant information systems, usage modes and security behaviors, as well as the relevant security controls, the vulnerabilities of the system and the threats to which the vulnerabilities expose the organization and users.

Output: Identification of selected security scenario(s) where a behavioral change intervention would be beneficial for the organization.

Co-create Using MINDSPACE Workshop. In the second stage, all parties come together in a co-creation activity in which they brainstorm how the different influencing factors from MINDSPACE (described above) could be used to change vulnerable behaviors in the selected scenario(s). Thus a scenario can be reviewed in terms of whether or each of the MINDSPACE influencers would be fruitful to be exploited through "nudges" in order to instill more secure behaviors. The workshop allows for an open, uncritical discussion of the problem and allows participants the opportunity to explore a number of different perspectives. The very act of taking part in the process will have made users more aware of how their security behavior may be influenced.

Output: A list of nudge possibilities.

Elect Nudge for Development. In the third stage, participants assess the nudge(s) generated and elect one or more for implementation. All parties can contribute to this prioritization process and consider whether these approaches have been tried before (generally or within this company) and whether they practically possible within the scenario and company. In addition, different stakeholders can independent prioritize which nudge they would support. We use a rating scheme to demonstrate the level of support for a proposed solution (as low agreement may reduce the chances that the nudge will be adopted in its final form by all the stakeholders). It is also a means to assess communication and commitment to the process across the board.

Output: Agreement on nudge to employ and its initial design.

Nudge Prototype. In this fourth stage, the final nudge or intervention is developed in detail. In doing this we are involved in creating the choice architecture (Thaler & Sunstein, 2008) which can take many different forms – e.g. an application prototype or particular form of communication. We know that the work context may attenuate the effectiveness of a nudge (if cyber security compliance is onerous it can lead to productivity loss) and so consideration of the work context is vital to ensure nudges do not interrupt the work flow unduly.

Output: A prototype intervention.

Evaluation of Nudge. In the fifth stage, the new nudge prototype is evaluated. It is important to use quick evaluations as part of the prototype process and feedback early to developers if the suggested nudge does not appear to be effective. Researchers and practitioners need to formulate clear success criteria, capture baselines and to record change in self-reports and actual behavioral changes. These data then serve as a means to assess the extent to which the intervention had a reliable and noticeable effect on behaviors. When the evaluation has shown a significant group difference in relation to the behaviors exhibited by the experimental group that was subject to the intervention compared to the control group, the intervention can be rolled out to further groups or applied to a larger sample. Care must be taken to ensure that the intervention is appropriate for all groups.

Output: Roll out and evaluation of intervention to add to evidence base.

2   Piloting the Framework

Any framework also needs to prove itself in practice. In this section we briefly outline an initial evaluation of the framework, in terms of its general effectiveness in generating useful nudges in our own organizations - addressing known security problems for university staff and students (see Jeske et al., 2014; Turland et al., 2014 for a more detailed description of the resulting nudge application). The development of nudges in the university context followed the SCENE methodology, as follows:

Scenario elicitation: This was undertaken by a research team consisting of psychologists, computer scientists, mathematicians and security experts who worked for two universities in the North East of England, working with other university users. The team identified several scenarios relating to security vulnerabilities, including USB use, failure to update security software on personal computers and the use of social media. A particular scenario around the use of personal computers to carry out (sometimes confidential) work in public places, using insecure public wireless networks was identified as a particularly promising. The use of insecure wireless networks creates a number of security vulnerabilities that can be exploited (man in the middle, spoofing, hacking, e.g., Herzberg & Jbara, 2008). Human biases (e.g., selecting the first, familiar networks) can also be exploited to mislead individuals to utilize the wrong wireless access points (Ferreira et al., 2013).

Co-creation: The team explored the wireless scenario in more detail, looking at current systems and the defaults that might lead the user to make insecure choices. Using the MINDSPACE framework, a number of potential nudges were identified, with the most promising of these listed in Table 1.

Table 1. Application of MINDSPACE influencers for nudge development

	Influencers	Description of possible nudges (for chosen scenario)
	Messenger	Warning messages should come from a trusted provider not generic, perhaps from the university. Perhaps a celebrity should be used to deliver warning messages.
	Incentives	When connected to unsecure network hamper productivity by reminding people they are on an unsecured network (negative). Provide free printing to students using a secure network.
Criteria chosen	Norms	Tell the user the % of people who lost/infected data within the company that have used that network. Tell the user of the % of people using the preferred network.
	Defaults	Present most secure as first option – order list by Security.
	Salience	Prompt 'Not a secure network' etc. Trusted network list produced by company.
	Affect	Use of emotive colors. Mark insecure networks as red.

Election of a nudge for development: Ideas were collated in a spread sheet and sent to each workshop participant a week later. Given time for reflection, participants could then elect their top three ideas. The research team also assessed which of the potential nudges were technically feasible.

Nudge prototyping: Our final decision was to develop a prototype application that would change the presentation of wireless networks available to the user. We created a trusted network list, which would be managed by the chief security officer of a company in tandem with an application that would nudge users towards this 'white list' by changing the menu order of available wireless networks (change default list) and to color code the options available using colors with affective associations (red=danger, green=safe). This nudge was developed as a new app for the Android platform (see Turland et al., 2014 for technical details).

Evaluation: A laboratory-based evaluation was conducted to determine whether the application effectively improved security decisions. The two manipulations (menu order and color) were assessed independently and in combination in a study in 67 students were asked to connect to a wireless network The results of the nudge prototype suggested that color could be a very effective nudge (see Jeske et al., 2014 for a full description of the evaluation method and results).

Next steps: We believe the best way to solve cybersecurity issues is to research how and why people make decisions, and then design products, services and places to nudge people to make better decisions in the future. In addition, using this process over time and across various security scenarios, organizations can develop a stakeholder-informed and needs-based nudge decision model that provides them with a procedural framework for their independent and continuous improvement. We have presented the methodology to several SME's, who have previously asked for technical support as a result of a security breach, and are currently starting to utilize this process with these companies to help prevent further breaches.

3   Conclusion

The use of a framework based on behavioral change literature and in the area of cyber security is still relatively novel (see Pfleeger & Caputo, 2012; Siponen, 2000). The fact that our framework considers the importance of co-creation in the design of nudges acknowledges the role that users increasingly play in the security decision-making process. Another benefit of the model is that our framework is not context specific, which makes it more readily transferable to other settings. For instance, our approach can be used to evaluate if an interface is optimized to achieve the intended behavior. We therefore believe that this framework can make an important contribution to cybersecurity, HCI and awareness initiatives. In conclusion, we believe this methodology can help practitioners and academics to develop a strong evidence base for different interventions at the same time as achieving practical results for organizations.

Acknowledgements. This research is supported by EPSRC Grant EP/K006568 Choice Architecture for Information Security, part of the GCHQ/EPSRC Research Institute in Science of Cyber Security. We would also like to acknowledge the support of several colleagues from Computing Sciences at Newcastle University and the HCII reviewers for their suggestions.

References

1. NCSA (2012). 2012 NCSA / Symantec National Small Business Study. National Cyber Security Alliance, Symantec, JZ Analytics (October 2012)
2. Abraham, C., Michie, S.: A taxonomy of behavior change techniques used in interventions. Health Psychology 27(3), 379–387 (2008)
3. Ashford, W.: IT security awareness needs to be company-wide, says (ISC)^2 (2012), http://www.computerweekly.com/news/2240163342/IT-security-needs-to-be-company-wide-says-ISC
4. Blythe, J.M.: Cyber security in the workplace: Understanding and promoting behavior change. In: Proceedings of CHI Italy Doctoral Symposium, Trento, September 1-10 (2013)
5. Bulgurcu, B., Cavusoglu, H., Benbasat, I.: Information security policy compliance: A study of rationality-based beliefs of information security awareness. MIS Quarterly 34(3), 523–548 (2010)
6. Burns, S., Roberts, L.: Applying the Theory of Planned Behavior to predicting online safety behavior. Crime Prevention and Community Safety 15(1), 48–64 (2013)
7. Davinson, N., Sillence, E.: It won't happen to me: Promoting secure behavior among internet users. Computers in Human Behavior 26(6), 1739–1747 (2010)
8. Dolan, P., Hallsworth, M., Halpern, D., King, D., Metcalfe, R.: Influencing Behavior: The MINDSPACE way. Journal of Economic Psychology 33, 264–277 (2012)
9. Ferreira, A., Huynen, J.-L., Koenig, V., Lenzini, G., Rivas, S.: Socio-technical study on the effect of trust and context when choosing wifi names. In: Accorsi, R., Ranise, S. (eds.) STM 2013. LNCS, vol. 8203, pp. 131–143. Springer, Heidelberg (2013)
10. Fogg, B.J.: Persuasive Technology: Using computers to change what we think and do. Morgan Kaufman (2002)
11. Furman, S.M., Theofanos, M.F., Choong, Y.-Y., Stanton, B.: Basing Cyber security Training on User Perceptions. IEEE Security and Privacy, 40–49 (March/April 2012)
12. Furnell, S., Rajendran, A.: Understanding the influences on information security behavior. Computer Fraud & Security, 12–15 (March 2012)
13. Gilovich, T., Griffin, D., Kahneman, D.: Heuristics and Biases: The Psychology of Intuitive Judgement. Cambridge University Press (2002)
14. Hareli, S., Rafaeli, A.: Emotion cycles: On the social influence of emotion in organizations. Research in Organizational Behavior 28, 35–59 (2008)
15. Hayes, D.: Does the messenger matter? Candidate-media agenda convergence and its effect on voter issue salience. Political Research Quarterly 61, 134–146 (2008)
16. Herath, T., Rao, H.R.: Encouraging information security behaviors in organizations: Role of penalties, pressures and perceived effectiveness. Decision Support Systems 47, 154–165 (2009)
17. Herzberg, A., Jbara, A.: Security and identification indicators for browsers against spoofing and phishing attacks. ACM Transactions on Internet Technology 8(4). Article 16, 36 (2008)

18. Ho, J.T., Dearman, D., Truong, K.N.: Improving users' security choices on home wireless networks. In: Symposium on Usable Privacy and Security, SOUPS (2010)
19. Jeske, D., Coventry, L., Briggs, P., van Moorsel, A.: Nudging whom how: IT proficiency, impulse control and secure behavior. Paper submitted to "Personalizing Behavior Change Technologies" Workshop, Toronto, Canada (April 27, 2014)
20. Johnson, E.J., Shu, S.B., Dellaert, B.G.D., et al.: Beyond nudges: Tools of a choice architecture. Marketing Letters 23, 487–504 (2012)
21. Kay, A.C., Wheeler, S.C., Bargh, J.A., Ross, L.: Material priming: The influence of mundane physical objects on situational construal and competitive behavioral choice. Organizational Behavior and Human Decision Processes 95(1), 83–96 (2004)
22. Lamy, D., Leber, A., Egeth, H.E.: Effects of task relevance and stimulus-driven salience in feature-search mode. Journal of Experimental Psychology: Human Perception and Performance 30(6), 1019–1031 (2004)
23. Leach, J.: Improving user security behavior. Computers & Security 22(8), 685–692 (2003)
24. Li, H., Sarathy, R., Xu, H.: The role of affect and cognition on online consumers' decision to disclose personal information to unfamiliar online vendors. Decision Support Systems 51, 434–445 (2011)
25. Li, Y.: Theories in online information privacy research: A critical review and an integrated framework. Decision Support Systems 54, 471–481 (2012)
26. Liang, H.: Understanding security behaviors in personal computer usage: A threat avoidance perspective. Journal of the Association for Information Systems 11(7), 394–403 (2010)
27. Pfleeger, S.L., Caputo, D.D.: Leveraging behavioral science to mitigate cybersecurity risk. Computers & Security 31, 597–611 (2012)
28. Pwc. 2013 Information Security Breaches Survey. Survey conducted by pwc for UK government Business and Innovation Department (2013), http://www.pwc.co.uk/assets/pdf/cyber-security-2013-technical-report.pdf
29. Schneier, B.: Security Awareness Training. Schneier on Security (2013), https://www.schneier.com/blog/-archives/2013/03/security_awaren_1.html (retrieved November 26, 2013)
30. Shore, L.M., Wayne, S.J.: Commitment and employee behavior: Comparison of affective commitment and continuance commitment with perceived organizational support. Journal of Applied Psychology 78(5), 774–780 (1993)
31. Siponen, M.T.: A conceptual foundation for organizational information security awareness. Information Management & Computer Security 8(1), 31–41 (2000)
32. Thaler, R.H., Sunstein, C.R.: Nudge. Improving Decisions About Health, Wealth and Happiness. Penguin (2008)
33. Turland, J., Jeske, D., Coventry, L., Briggs, P., Laing, C., van Moorsel, A., Yevseyeva, I.: Nudging secure wireless network. Developing an application for wireless network selection for android phones. Conference paper, Mobile HCI, Conference, Toronto (September 2014)

Attempts to Quantitative Analyze for the Change of Human Brain Activity with Physical and Psychological Load

Hiroaki Inoue[1], Shunji Shimizu[1], Hiroyuki Nara[2], Takeshi Tsuruga[3],
Fumikazu Miwakeichi[4], Nobuhide Hirai[5], Senichiro Kikuchi[6], Eiju Watanabe[6],
and Satoshi Kato[6]

[1] Tokyo University of Science, SUWA, Japan
Jgh12701@ed.tus.ac.jp, shun@rs.suwa.tus.ac.jp
[2] Hokkaido University, Japan
nara@ssc.ssi.ist.hokudai.ac.jp
[3] Hokkaido Institute of Technology, Japan
tsuruga@hit.ac.jp
[4] The Institute of Statistical Mathematics, Japan
miwake1@ism.ac.jp
[5] Tokyo Medical and Dental University, Japan
nobu@nobu.com
[6] Jichi Medical University, Japan
{skikuchip,psykato}@jichi.ac.jp, eiju-ind@umin.ac.jp

Abstract. Recently, Japan (also world-wide countries) has become aged society, and a wide variety welfare device and system have been developed. Various companies are trying to enter the welfare device and system. Successful cases of the attempt are rare. There are several problems. For example, it is difficult to sell to the user because it does not known the effect. Thus, the direction of development is hard to determined. Because there is no evaluation method is the main cause of those. Evaluation of welfare system and device are limited only stability, intensity and partial operability. So, evaluation of usefulness is insufficient. Therefore, we will attempt to establish the standard to evaluate usefulness for objectively and quantitatively on the basis of including non-verbal cognition. In this paper, we measure load of sitting and standing movement to use Electoromyogram (EMG) and 3D Motion Capture and set a goal to establish objective evaluation method. We think that establishing objective evaluation method is necessity to develop useful welfare device. We examined possibility of assessing load and fatigue from measuring brain activity to use Near Infra-Red Spectroscopy (NIRS). The idea of universal design is widespread in welfare device and system. Measuring requires verification of all generations. But, we performed to measure younger subjects as a first step. We think that younger subjects were observed the significant difference, because they had enough physical function. Considering younger subjects as a benchmark is appropriate for creating evaluation method.

Keywords: Evaluation, Movement, Exercise, 3D Motion Capture, NIRS, EMG, Care, Welfare Technology, Usefulwelfare device evaluation, Evaluation method.

A. Marcus (Ed.): DUXU 2014, Part I, LNCS 8517, pp. 240–249, 2014.
© Springer International Publishing Switzerland 2014

1   Introduction

With the increasing aging population in Japan and world-wide countries, welfare systems and device are rapidly developing, and various devices are manufactured based on the increased popularity of welfare device and system. Also, the market of welfare device and system is expanding. However, the evaluation method is limited respectively to stability, strength and a part of operability for individual system or device. It means that evaluation methodology for usefulness of them was not established. Therefore, we will attempt to establish a   standard to evaluate the usefulness for objectively and quantitatively on the basis of cognition such as physical load, reduction of fatigue and postural stability. Especially, in considering universality, it is necessary to measure human movement in daily life. Movement was not measured by using particular device, but routinely-performed movement in daily life.

So, we examined the possibility of evaluation by measuring physical load due to activities of daily living with using 3D Motion Analysis System [1] and EMG [2]. Also, we looked into the possibility of quantitative evaluation of tiredness and load on the basis of brain activity using NIRS [4]. Also, we consider that physical and psychological load are linked to cognition including non-verbal cognition. In this paper, the purpose of experiments is to evaluate motion focusing on sitting and standing movement, which is usually done in our life by using 3D Motion Analysis System, EMG, NIRS. We consider that human feel physical and psychological load during life motion. We tried to measure physical load by using 3D Motion Analysis System, EMG. Additionally, we tried to measure non-verbal cognition about psychological load by using NIRS.

Subjects were healthy males in twenty, because the elderly people who have various types of disease is inept in quantitative evaluation.

2   Experimental Method

2.1   Evaluation by Using 3D Motion Analysis and EMG

We simultaneously measured 3D position and muscle potential of subject during task by using 3D Motion Analysis System (nac IMAGE TECHNOLOGY Inc. products-MAC3DSYSTEM [1]) and EMG (KISSEI COMTEC Inc. products-MQ16 [2]).

Regarding to measuring 3D position, 8 Infrared cameras were placed around subject, and 27 makers of the body surface were set on the basis of Helen-Hayes Hospital Marker set (Figure 1). In measuring muscle potential, measurement regions were tibialis anterior muscle, gastrocnemius muscle, quadriceps femoris muscle, hamstring, flexor carpi ulnaris muscle, extensoe carpiulnaris muscle, triceps branchii, latissimus dorsi muscle of the right side of the body   because these muscle were deeply associated with standing and sitting movement. Also, wireless measurement was used so that subject was constrained as little as possible. As sampling frequency, 3D Motion Analysis System was 100Hz, and EMG was 1kHz.

Subjects were three males aged twenty. They were asked to read and sign an informed consent regarding the experiment.

In this experiment, subject repeated one series of movements, which was to transfer from chair to seat face of welfare device (IDEA LIFE CARE Co. Ltd products-NORISUKEsan [3]) and opposite one with alternating between standing and sitting, at five times per one measurement. Seating face of welfare device, which was designed to assist transfer movement, was manipulated by simple method and appeared on the top of chair.

Subjects were heard buzzer every one second and kept a constant motion of speed to satisfy certain measuring conditions. Also, they transferred from seat face to chair or conversely every 8 seconds with consideration for movement of elderly persons.

Fig. 1. Experimental View of 3D motion Analysis and EMG

Operation of welfare device was performed by the operator other than subject.

2.2   Evaluation by Using NIRS

We measured brain activity during motion with the purpose of establishing evaluation method based on generality (Figure 2).

Subjects were six males aged twenty. They were asked to read and sign an informed consent regarding the experiment. Measurement apparatus was NIRS (SHIMADZU CO. Ltd products-FOIRE3000 [4]). Measurement region was at right and left prefrontal cortex.

1. Measuring brain activity during transfer with standing position (task1). At this measurement, the subjects used welfare device to perform transferring in a standing position. In this measurement, subject sat on seating face of welfare device appeared on the top of chair after raising hip until kneeling position. Also, subject performed inverse transferring from seating face to chair. Time design was rest (5 seconds), task (10 seconds), and rest (5 seconds). This time design was repeated 30 times. Rest time is to stabilize the brain activity. In the measurement NIRS,

2. Measuring brain activity during transfer with half-crouching position (task2). At this measurement, the subjects used welfare device to perform transferring in a half-crouch position. In this measurement, the subjects sat on seating face of welfare device appeared on the top of chair after raising hip until kneeling position. Also, the subject performed inverse transfer from seating face to chair. Time design was rest (5 seconds), task (10 seconds) and rest (5 seconds). This time design was repeated 30 times. In experiments of task1 and task2, the operation of welfare device was performed by an operator other than subject. Before this measuring, subjects adjusted to transferring by use of welfare device.

3. Measuring brain activity during keeping a half-crouch position   (task3). The subjects performed two tasks at this measurement. During task3-1, subject sat on seating face of welfare device with eyes open. During task3-2, they kept a half-crouch position.

Subjects alternated task3-1 and task3-2. Also, subjects took resting time between two types of motion with eyes close. Therefore time design was rest (5 seconds), task3-1 (10 seconds), rest (5 seconds), task3-2 (10 seconds) and rest (5 seconds). This time design was repeated 15 times.

2.3   Brain Activity Measurements When the Load Was Applied to the Subjects

We have performed measuring brain activity in the case where no load is applied to subject. In previous experiment, load of subjects were derived from only standing and sitting movement. In this experiment, we added the weight as additional load. As load, there are some cases which are no load, 5kg and 10kg. Subjects wear a backpack containing the weight. And Subjects performed standing and sitting movement. Task design was same with previous experiments.

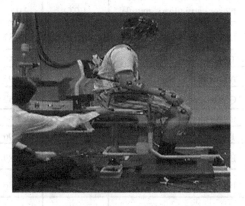

Fig. 2. Experimental View of NIRS

3   Experimental Result

3.1   Evaluation by Using 3D Motion Analysis and EMG

Figure 3 shows the result of transferring which was measured by 3D motion analysis and EMG. In Figure 3, middle trochanter is the height of midpoint between right and left trochanter from the floor. Trunk angle is the forward slope of trunk. Also, following terms are arectifying voltage wave for each eight muscles, which are Tibialis anterior muscle, Astrocnemius muscle, Quadriceps femoris muscle, Hamstring, Triceps brachii muscle, Etensor carpi ulnaris muscle, Flexor carpi ulnaris muscle and Latissimus dorsi muscle.

Next, analysis was performed by extracting muscle potential during standing and sitting movement from the measuring result with reference to middle trochanter and trunk angle and calculating value of interal during movement. Table 1 shows the ratio of value integral with welfare device to one without device. Also, we compared moving distance of median point between using welfare device and not. Table 2 shows the comparison results in a manner similar to Table 1.

Table 1. Comparison of Integral EMG

muscle	Region	Subject1	Subject2	Subject3
Standing	Tibialis anterior muscle	0.37	0.49	0.64
	Astrocnemius muscle	0.83	0.78	0.97
	Quadriceps femoris muscle	0.66	0.36	0.81
	Hamstring	1.90	0.50	1.07
	Triceps brachii muscle	1.07	3.34	1.01
	Etensor carpi ulnaris muscle	1.08	1.31	0.96
	Flexor carpi ulnaris muscle	1.07	0.89	0.85
	Lattissimus dorsi muscle	0.98	0.87	1.20
Sitting	Tibialis anterior muscle	0.50	0.59	0.80
	Astrocnemius muscle	1.01	0.92	0.94
	Quadriceps femoris muscle	0.49	0.57	0.85
	Hamstring	2.16	1.60	0.96
	Triceps brachii muscle	0.89	0.96	1.07
	Etensor carpi ulnaris muscle	0.79	0.89	0.86
	Flexor carpi ulnaris muscle	0.79	0.86	0.95
	Lattissimus dorsi muscle	1.16	1.18	0.93

3.2   Evaluation by Using NIRS

As the common result of all subjects, oxy-Hb tended to increase during task and to decrease in resting state. Therefore, it was thought that change of hemoglobin density due to task was measured. Figure. 7, Figure. 8 and Figure. 9 show trend of the channel in which significant different was shown. Analysis was performed via one-sample t-test [5,6,7,8,9] by a method similar to previous researches [5,6,7,8,9]. In this analysis, it was necessary to remove other than change of blood flow due to fatigue. So, our method was mainly focused on resting state to compare with the 1st trial and another trials of brain activity.

In task1, 1 and 2, each of sample data for analysis was 4 seconds after the task (Figure. 4). In task 3, sample data was 4 seconds during task (Figure. 5).

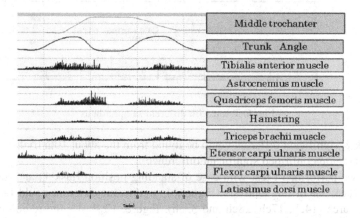

Fig. 3. Result of 3D Motion Analysis and EMG

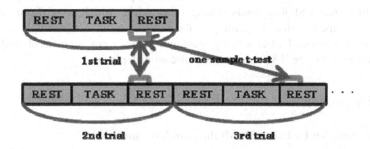

Fig. 4. T-test of sample-data of task1 and 2

In the t-test of the same task, we performed t-test with first time trial and other trial which was from second times to thirty times, and examined relationship the number of trials and significant differences.

In task 1, significant different could be found from the about 10th trials. Figure. 10 shows the region confirmed significant difference.

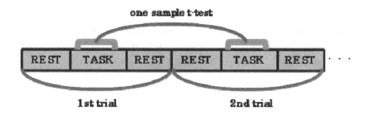

Fig. 5. T-test of sample-data of task3

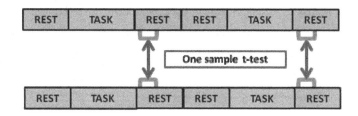

Fig. 6. T-test with different sample-datas

In task 2, significant different could be found from the about 10th trials too. Figure. 11 shows region confirmed significant difference.

Next, we performed t-test with case of standing position (task 1) and half-crouch position (task 2). In this analysis (Figure.6), significant different could be found at prefrontal area (14ch, 17ch, 28ch and 32ch). Figure. 12 shows the region confirmed significant different.

Also, two types of motion which was sitting and keeping a half-crouching position were repeated alternatively in task 3. At first, we performed t-test using 4 seconds during first trial and 4 seconds during other trials, which were from second to fifteenth in same position. Regarding to the analysis result using sample data during sitting position and half-crouching position, there were significant different at Prefrontal area. Figure. 13 confirms a significant difference.

4   Discussion

4.1   Evaluation by Using 3D Motion Analysis and EMG

From the analysis result, it was shown that value of integral was decreased by using assistive apparatus for transfer. Especially, there was remarkable decrease in value of integral at tibialis anterior muscle, quadriceps femoris muscle. On the other hand, it was shown to be minor decrease in one at upper limb and muscles of the back. Also, moving distance of barycentric position was decreased by the use of welfare device.

On the ground of this result, it was thought to be due to difference in height between chair and seating face of welfare device. Therefore, it was thought that the use of assistive apparatus is useful to lighten burden on lower limb. Thus, it is contemplated that muscle load during standing and sitting movement was decreased and reduced centroid fluctuation to lower the possibility of turnover.

Even if subjects performed daily movements of standing and sitting with the use of assistive equipment, it was shown that the integral of muscle potential and distance of centroid change was decreased. Therefore, it was proved that there is the possibility of evaluation of daily performance except for movement with welfare device.

4.2   Evaluation by Using NIRS

In this experiment, we tried to measure quantitatively the physical and psychological strain on the basis of brain activity. Also, we think that brain activity disclose human cognitive including non-verbal. As a result, it was shown that there were differences at brain activity due to number of trials and postural. In this time, analysis was performed via one-sample t-test using sample of brain activity in resting state during task or after task. Hence, analysis method was to remove disturbance such as body motion and angular variation of neck to the extent possible although there was the possibility to measure skin blood flow. Therefore, it was thought that strain due to tasks was quantitatively measured by being recognized significant differences.

Also, in previous research, it was reported to decrease in activity in the brain around #10, 11 [10], as the result of measuring brain activity during Advanced Trial Making Test using PET [11]. Therefore, this result came out in support of previous research in no small part.

Of course, it is necessary to increase number of subject at the present stage. In addition, there are problems associated with experiment, number of subject, method and measured region. However, in terms of being recognized significant differences at brain activity due to movement, it was thought to show useful result in evaluating quantitatively daily movements.

5   Conclusion and Future Work

In this experiment, our purpose was to evaluate quantitatively physical load with focusing on standing and sitting movement which was part of daily movements using 3D motion analysis system and EMG.

As the result, it was shown that the integral of lower-limb muscle, such as tibialis anterior muscle and gastrocremius muscle, significantly decreased by the use of welfare device.

Also, it was reported that there is a positive correlation between anteversion angle of body trunk and movement duration in previous research [12]. But, our experiment method was to estimate the possibility of falling in rising from a sitting position by calculating moving distance of median point. And, it was confirmed that the possibility of falling was decreased by using device.

Next, we tried to measure physical and psychological load quantitatively on the basis of brain activity. And there were significant differences due to number of trials, holding position. In this experiment, analysis method was to remove disturbance such as body motion and angular variation of neck to the extent possible by using the measurement result in resting state as sample. Therefore, it was thought to show the useful result in evaluating quantitatively load due to movement task by being recognized difference in brain activity caused by number of trials, substance of task and holding position.

Main purpose in this study is to evaluate physical load and fatigue quantitatively. So, we tried to evaluate change of muscle load due to difference of motion by simultaneous measuring with 3D motion analysis System and EMG quantitatively.

However, evaluation of psychological load is necessary, too. In terms of using welfare device, prolonged use must be taken into account. In this case, it is important to consider not only physical load but also psychological load due to prolonged use from standpoint of developing welfare device and keeping up surviving bodily function.

Also, in previous research, separation between physical and psychological load has been performed. But, our view is that there is correlation with physical and psychological load. So, we tried to measure psychological load including physical one based on brain activity and quantitatively evaluate both load.

For the future, our aim is to establish method of discussing useful of welfare device by evaluating load involved in other daily movements with increasing number of subjects.

References

1. Shinoda, Y., Watanabe, Y., Mito, Y., Watanuma, R., Marumo, M.: Consideration of feature extraction based on center of gravity for Nihon Buyo dancer using motion capture system. In: SICE Annual Conference 2011, Tokyo, Japan, pp. 1874–1878 (2011)
2. Yamaguchi, Y., Ishikawa, A., Ito, Y.: Development of Biosignal Integration Analysis System for Human Brain Function and Behavior. Organization for Human Brain Mapping, China, pp. 329–336 (2012)
3. Inoue, H., Shimizu, S., Takahashi, N., Nara, H., Tsuruga, T.: Fundamental Study for Evaluation of the Effect due to Exercise Load. In: Assistive Technology, Bio Medical Engineering and Life Support 2011, Japan, CD-ROM (2011)
4. Watanabe, E., Yamashita, Y., Ito, Y., Koizumi, H.: Non-invasive functional mapping with multi-channel near infra-red spectroscopic topography in humans. Heurosci. Lett. 205(1), 41–44 (1996)
5. Takahashi, N., Shimizu, S., Hirata, Y., Nara, H., Miwakeichi, F., Hirai, N., Kikuchi, S., Watanabe, E., Kato, S.: Fundamental Study for a New Assistive System during Car Driving. In: Proc. of International Conference on Robotics and Biomimetics, DVD-ROM, Tenjin, China (2010)
6. Takahashi, N., Shimizu, S., Hirata, Y., Nara, H., Inoue, H., Hirai, N., Kikuchi, S., Watanabe, E., Kato, S.: Basic study of Analysis of Human Brain Activities during Car Driving. In: Smith, M.J., Salvendy, G. (eds.) Human Interface, HCII 2011, Part I. LNCS, vol. 6771, pp. 627–635. Springer, Heidelberg (2011)

7. Shimizu, S., Takahashi, N., Nara, H., Inoue, H., Hirata, Y.: Fundamental Study for Human Brain Activity Based on the Spatial Cognitive Task. In: Hu, B., Liu, J., Chen, L., Zhong, N. (eds.) BI 2011. LNCS (LNAI), vol. 6889, pp. 218–225. Springer, Heidelberg (2011)

8. Shimizu, S., Takahashi, N., Nara, H., Inoue, H., Hirata, Y.: Basic Study for Human Brain Activity Based on the Spatial Cognitive Task. In: The Third International Conference on Advanced Cognitive Technologies and Applications, Italy, pp. 148–151 (2011)

9. Shimizu, S., Takahashi, N., Inoue, H., Nara, H., Miwakeichi, F., Hirai, N., Kikuchi, S., Watanabe, E., Kato, S.: Basic Study for a New Assitive System Based on Brain Activity associated with Spatial Perception Task during Car driving. In: Proc. International Conference on Robotics and Biomimetics, Thailand, pp. 2884–2889 (2011)

10. Watanabe, Y.: Molecular/neural mechanisms of fatigue, and the way to overcome fatigue. Folia Pharmacological Japonica 129, 94–98 (2007)

11. Kuratsune, H., Yamaguti, K., Lindh, G., Evengard, B., Hagberg, G., Matsumura, K., Iwase, M., Onoe, H., Takahashi, M., Machii, T., Kanakura, Y., Kitani, T., Langstrom, B., Watanage, Y.: Brain Regions Involved in Fatigue Sensation: Reduced Acetylcarnitine Uptake in to the Brain. Neuroimage 17, 1256–1265 (2001)

12. Maruta, K.: The influence of Seat Angle on Forward Trunk Inclination During Sit-to-Stand. Journal of Japanese Physical Therapy Association 31(1), 21–28 (2004)

Measuring Confidence in Internet Use: The Development of an Internet Self-efficacy Scale

Mary Joyce and Jurek Kirakowski

School of Applied Psychology,
University College Cork, Ireland
{m.joyce,jzk}@ucc.ie

Abstract. With the Internet distinguished across so many environments today, the need to measure how individuals relate to the Internet has become an extremely important aspect of Human-Computer Interaction research. However, the measurement of users' confidence with using the Internet is a poorly researched topic. This concept of confidence with using the Internet is known as Internet self-efficacy, described as a person's belief in their personal capabilities to achieve specific goals with the Internet [1]. Only a small number of studies [2, 3] have actually attempted to measure Internet self-efficacy through the use of psychometric scales. Regrettably, these attempts have produced unsatisfactory means of measuring Internet self-efficacy. Such issues include the failure to follow methodologies for the measurement of self-efficacy, wording of statements representing constructs other than Internet self-efficacy, and references to computer rather than Internet related tasks. One of the aims of this research was to develop a statistically reliable scale which measures Internet self-efficacy. This paper focuses on outlining the development of the Internet Self-Efficacy Scale.

Keywords: Internet, Self-Efficacy, Measurement, Scale Development, Validity, Gender differences, Age factors.

1 Introduction

With an ever-increasing number of people accessing the Internet worldwide, the measurement of individuals' interactions with the Internet is of paramount importance in Human-Computer Interaction (HCI) research. However, the measurement of individuals' confidence in their ability to use the Internet is a poorly researched topic. Only a small number of studies [2, 3] have actually attempted to measure individuals' confidence with using the Internet through the use of psychometric scales. To make the situation even less satisfactory, these studies failed to employ appropriate methodologies for the measurement of this construct, also known as self-efficacy. These attempts have thus produced unsatisfactory means of measuring Internet self-efficacy and have raised issues that serve to obfuscate rather than clarify. As a result,

A. Marcus (Ed.): DUXU 2014, Part I, LNCS 8517, pp. 250–260, 2014.
© Springer International Publishing Switzerland 2014

the validity of such scales is questionable and unsatisfactory for use in HCI research as they stand.

The primary aim of this research was to develop a statistically reliable and psychometrically valid scale which accurately measures Internet self-efficacy. In order to do so, guidelines for the development of self-efficacy scales were taken into consideration. With this in mind, this paper outlines briefly the fundamental background from self-efficacy literature as it pertains to the development of the Internet self-efficacy scale. Following this, the three main issues in previous Internet self-efficacy literature are reviewed. The paper concludes with a brief outline of the newly developed Internet Self-Efficacy Scale.

1.1   Definition of Self-efficacy

Self-efficacy is defined by Bandura as "beliefs in one's capabilities to organize and execute the courses of action required to produce given attainments" (p. 3) [4]. Only slight variations of this definition of self-efficacy exist in the literature, and most self-efficacy researchers are in agreement with Bandura's proposed definition.

1.2   Theoretical Models of Self-efficacy

As Bandura has been hailed 'the father of self-efficacy', and with little or no conflicting evidence for his self-efficacy definition, it is hardly surprising that to date, there has been just one known theoretical model of self-efficacy proposed. Put forward by Bandura [5] himself in one of his first influential articles documenting the concept of self-efficacy, he suggests that self-efficacy expectations derive from four sources of information: performance accomplishments (more recently referred to as enactive mastery experience), vicarious experience, verbal persuasion, and physiological states.

1.3   Characteristics of Self-efficacy

The construct of self-efficacy has a number of distinctive characteristics. These features are extremely important in the study of self-efficacy as they provide a point of comparison with other psychological constructs and have four implications for how self-efficacy should then be measured [6].

Firstly, self-efficacy focuses on judgments of perceived capabilities to perform a task or activity rather than focusing on personal qualities such as physical or psychological traits and characteristics [7]. Second, self-efficacy perceptions are domain, context and task specific. Bandura [4] outlined that self-efficacy beliefs are multidimensional and should be measured in terms of "judgments of capability that may vary across realms of activity, under different levels of task demands within a given activity domain, and under different situational circumstances......This requires clear definition of the activity domain of interest, and a good conceptual analysis of its difference facets, the types of capabilities it calls upon, and the range of situations in which these capabilities might be applied" (p. 42). Thirdly, self-efficacy is dependent on a mastery criterion of performance rather than on a normative criterion. Using an example of self-efficacy in terms of exam performance; individuals might rate how well they performed in an exam at a specific level of personal performance rather than how better they performed than their peers. Fourthly and finally, self-efficacy beliefs are typically assessed prior to engaging in a particular task or activity so that self-efficacy may be conceptualized as a forethought process within self-regulation models [6].

In addition to the characteristics of self-efficacy as suggested by Zimmerman and Cleary [6], Bandura [4] put forward that efficacy beliefs vary on several dimensions that have important performance implications. These three dimensions of self-efficacy are (a) level, (b) generality, and (c) strength:

(a) The level of self-efficacy refers to its dependence on the difficulty level of a particular task. Perceived efficacy of different individuals may range from the ability to achieve simple task demands to extremely difficult demands within a particular domain;

(b) Generality refers to the transferability of personal efficacy judgments across tasks or activities. Individuals may feel efficacious across a wide range of activities or their efficacy beliefs may be limited to specific domains of functioning;

(c) Strength refers to the magnitude of one's conviction that they can complete the specified task.

1.4   Self-efficacy Measurement

Self-efficacy is measured through the use of psychometric scales. Many psychometric scales, such as those used in the measurement of attitudes, require participants to indicate whether they agree or disagree with a statement. However, for the measurement of self-efficacy, Bandura [4] argues persuasively that individuals should be asked to rate the strength of their belief to complete specific activities in the domain in question on a self-rating interval scale instead of "agreeing" or "disagreeing" with the statement. The items presented to respondents should be phrased in terms of can do rather than will do because can is a judgment of capability whereas will is a statement of intention. Furthermore, Bandura suggests that the standard methodology for the measurement of self-efficacy should present participants with a 100-point scale to measure strength of belief, ranging in 10-unit intervals from 0 ('Cannot do') through intermediate degrees of assurance, 50 ('Moderately certain can do'); to complete assurance, 100 ('Certain can do').

Self-efficacy Measurement Principles. Bandura's self-efficacy scales assume the following principles:

1) Self-efficacy scales should be unipolar; scales should range from 0 to a maximum strength (100 is the general maximum strength recommended by Bandura). Self-efficacy scales should not include negative numbers because a judgment of complete incapability (0) has no lower graduations.

2) Scales which "use only a few steps should be avoided because they are less sensitive and less reliable" (p. 44) [4] as suggested by Streiner and Norman [8]. Bandura [4] also advocates that the inclusion of too few steps "loses differentiating

information because people who use the same response category would differ if intermediate steps were included" (p. 44).

3) Preliminary instructions are given to participants which establish the appropriate mind-set that participants should have when rating the strength of belief in capability. People are asked to judge their operative capabilities as of now, and not their potential capabilities or their expected future capabilities [9].

Scoring Self-efficacy. Bandura [4] outlines that there are two formats which can be used to measure self-efficacy strength. The first involves what Bandura [4] refers to as a "dual-judgment format" (p.44) where respondents first indicate whether or not they can complete the outlined task. Only for tasks which they indicate they can complete, do respondents then rate the strength of their perceived efficacy using the self-rating 0-100 scale. The second method which Bandura describes as the "single-judgment format" (p.44), invites respondents to rate the strength of their perceived efficacy on all items presented in the scale. The method utilizing the single-judgment format is recommended by Bandura [4] as he suggests that this format provides "essentially the same information and is easier and more convenient to use" (p. 44). When participants complete rating their efficacy strengths, the efficacy strength scores are then summed and divided by the total number of statements. This then indicates the strength of self-efficacy in the domain in question. Finally, "a measure of efficacy level can be extracted by selecting a cutoff value below which people would judge themselves incapable of executing the activities in question" (p. 44) [4].

2   Internet Self-efficacy

Self-efficacy was earlier defined as "belief's in one's capabilities to organize and execute the courses of action required to produce given attainments" (p.3) [4]. Thus, Internet self-efficacy can be identified as "a person's belief in their personal capabilities to achieve specific goals with the Internet" [1]. Principal failings in Internet self-efficacy research to date stem from a lack of clarity regarding how self-efficacy in general is conceptualized. Issues include:

— the failure to follow methodologies for the measurement of self-efficacy
— the wording of statements as representative of something other than Internet self-efficacy
— the inclusion of items representing computer related tasks rather than Internet related tasks.

The most significant of these issues has been the failure to follow fundamental principles for the measurement of self-efficacy.

2.1   Incorrect Self-efficacy Measurement Methods

As earlier outlined, Bandura [4] advocates that individuals should be asked to rate the strength of their belief to complete specific activities in the domain in question on a self-rating interval scale instead of 'agreeing' or 'disagreeing' with the statement. However, many studies (e.g. [2], [3], and [10]) fail to incorporate such guidelines in the development of their self-efficacy scale. For example, Eastin and LaRose [2] developed an Internet self-efficacy scale in which items for the scale were informed by Compeau and Higgins' Computer Self-Efficacy Scale [11], findings from the Graphic, Visualization and Usability Center's Tenth Annual Survey [12], and Nahl's [13] study on perceived self-efficacy. Items from these scales were adapted in line with the definition of Internet self-efficacy offered by Eastin and LaRose, and were phrased to represent judgments of ability to use the Internet to produce overall attainments, rather than accomplishing specific Internet tasks. The final instrument consisted of eight items and participants were invited to indicate on a 7 point Likert-type scale whether they agreed or disagreed with each of the statements. There is a fundamental measurement issue with the scale as it would seem that levels of agreement with a statement are being obtained rather than information about individual's beliefs in their capabilities to achieve specific goals on the Internet.

Similarly, there are measurement issues present in Torkzadeh and Van Dyke's [3] self-efficacy scale. Torkzadeh and Van Dyke developed a self-efficacy instrument to measure the perception of individual's ability to interact with the Internet while also exploring the multidimensional nature of Internet self-efficacy. The authors set out to achieve such tasks by extending previous research on computer self-efficacy into the domain of the Internet. In order to successfully measure Internet self-efficacy, an extensive review of the literature on self-efficacy and information processing was carried out. This review generated a list of 24 items which were subsequently reviewed by five practitioners and four academics. Some of the items on the list were reworded following this review but all 24 original items were retained for purposes of analysis. Individuals were required to indicate their level of agreement with each statement on a 5-point Likert type scale. As with Eastin and LaRose's [2] study, there are concerns with such measurement methods. Participants were required to indicate their level of agreement with each statement on a 5-point Likert type scale. As earlier outlined, Bandura [4] argues persuasively for the use of a self-rating interval scale to measure self-efficacy instead of 'agreeing' or 'disagreeing' with the statement. Bandura's methodologies were not applied in this study and the results generated from this study again tell us more about one's level of agreement with the statements in the scale than about their perception of capability to use the Internet.

2.2   Unsuitable Wording of Statements

In addition to measurement issues, there have also been issues with the wording of statements in previous research ([2] and [10]). For example, in Eastin and LaRose's [2] study, there are concerns about the statements being representative of items which depict Internet self-efficacy. While the authors offer a definition of Internet self-efficacy based on Bandura's general definition of self-efficacy, it is difficult to understand how the statements generated for Eastin and LaRose's scale correspond with this definition. For example, one of the items included in the scale is 'I feel confident describing functions of Internet hardware'. This statement refers to describing information about Internet hardware; something an Internet user would not need to know about to determine feelings of confidence about using the Internet. A second example of this in Eastin and LaRose's scale is the statement 'I feel confident explaining why a task will not run on the Internet' which is more representative of the ability to articulate computer issues than depicting feelings of Internet self-efficacy.

Other examples of this issue exist in Eachus and Cassidy's [10] study. Examples of statements in their study include 'I am not really sure what a modem does' and 'Using ftp to upload web pages to a server is quite complicated'. These statements tell us more about an individual's reflection on their knowledge of how the Internet works rather than their confidence about using the Internet. Thus, as with Eastin and LaRose's scale items, such statements are unrepresentative of feelings of Internet self-efficacy.

2.3   Inclusion of Non-internet Related Tasks

Similar to the issue of unsuitably worded items to denote feelings of Internet self-efficacy is the issue where self-efficacy items are included which describe computer related tasks instead of Internet related tasks. For example, in Torkzadeh and Van Dyke's [3] study, a list of 24 items was generated to develop a self-efficacy instrument which measured perception of individual's ability to interact with the Internet. However, some of the included items refer to computer, rather than Internet related tasks. Examples of such items include 'I feel confident scanning pictures to save on the computer' and 'I feel confident playing an audio CD on my computer'. These examples refer to activities that an individual may carry out on a computer but are activities that one does not require the Internet for, nor indeed would use the Internet for. Thus, the validity of such items as representative of feelings of Internet self-efficacy is questionable.

2.4   Addressing Issues in Previous Research

In order to develop a valid and statistically reliable scale which measures Internet self-efficacy, it was important that the issues highlighted above were addressed. With this in mind, it was important to ensure that the Internet self-efficacy scale followed appropriate methodologies for the measurement of self-efficacy to ensure correct measurement of self-efficacy beliefs. Additionally, it was of critical importance to ensure that items on the scale refer to Internet related tasks and that statements were worded in an appropriate manner to capture feelings of Internet self-efficacy. Finally, it was important to obtain a varied sample of Internet users with varying levels of experience to ensure a representative Internet user sample. Keeping these issues in mind, the development of the Internet self-efficacy scale is now briefly described.

3   Development of the Internet Self-efficacy Scale

As earlier outlined, Bandura's [4] theoretical model of self-efficacy is the theoretical model and framework which was followed for the development of the Internet

Self-Efficacy Scale (ISES). However, little empirical research is available in general investigating Bandura's [4] four proposed sources as influential in self-efficacy. Thus, this research first sought to clarify Bandura's [4] sources theory in Internet self-efficacy research. Additionally, the other issue under investigation in this research concerns the measurement of self-efficacy. Bandura [9] proposed guidelines for the creation of self-efficacy scales and the measurement of self-efficacy beliefs. This research identified flaws in these current measurement methods and sought to resolve such issues with a particular focus on the area of Internet self-efficacy. Thus, both of the outlined issues were investigated in detail where each issue was individually addressed at different stages in the development of the ISES.

3.1   Sources of Internet Self-efficacy

The four sources of self-efficacy as put forward by Bandura [4] are mastery experience, vicarious experience, verbal persuasion and physiological states. However, there is an apparent lack of concrete evidence to support the hypothesis that self-efficacy beliefs are influenced by these four sources across varying self-efficacy domains. While extensive research has been completed in areas such as academic self-efficacy and these four sources have been confirmed to be influential in this particular domain, no known research to date has examined Bandura's [4] proposed sources as influential in feelings of self-efficacy in a domain such as the Internet. With this in mind, it was important to investigate these sources in the current domain of interest (the Internet) to determine if these sources had any effect on Internet self-efficacy scores.

3.2   Format of Questionnaire

The questionnaire, consisting of four main sections, was distributed to 176 students studying Psychology in University College Cork, Ireland. The first section of the questionnaire asked for information about how frequently participants performed specific tasks on the Internet (mastery experience) and invited participants to indicate how frequently they perform a list of major Internet activities on a 5 point scale with the following response anchors: Never, Rarely, Sometimes, Frequently, Very frequently. The second section asked for information on acquaintances and their use of tasks on the Internet (vicarious experience) by asking participants to indicate on a 5 point scale how many Internet users they knew personally who performed the listed Internet activities. The response anchors for this question were: No-one I know, Very few people I know, Some people I know, A lot of people I know, Everyone I know. The subsequent section requested information about how much help and encouragement was available to participants should they encounter difficulties using the Internet (verbal persuasion). Participants were asked to indicate how much encouragement they would receive from others if they encountered difficulty with the listed activities. There were five response anchors: None at all, Very little, Some encouragement, A fair amount, A large amount. Finally, the fourth section requested information on people's level of confidence in performing various tasks on the

Internet (self-efficacy) by asking participants how confident they felt they can do each of the listed activities, as of now. The five response anchors were: Not at all confident, Slightly confident, Somewhat confident, Very confident, Extremely confident. Physiological states were not investigated as a predictor of Internet self-efficacy as the focus of this research is on stable predictors of self-efficacy. As self-efficacy is concerned with beliefs which are more concerned with trait characteristics, rather than state characteristics, it was deemed inappropriate to evaluate individuals' state characteristics such as their mood and feeling when determining feelings of Internet self-efficacy. Furthermore, Bandura [4] outlines that somatic indicators are particularly relevant in domains that involve physical accomplishments. As the Internet is not concerned with physical accomplishments, it was decided that it was unnecessary to measure physiological states when evaluating Internet self-efficacy.

3.3   Results

In order to determine if the three variables (mastery experience, vicarious experience and verbal persuasion) were significant predictors of self-efficacy scores, regression analyses were carried out on the data. A multiple regression analysis was carried out for each of the individual Internet tasks. The results demonstrated that the first independent variable (mastery experience) was a significant predictor of self-efficacy scores across all Internet tasks, achieving a significant p value of <.001. The second variable (vicarious experience) was a significant predictor of self-efficacy for some tasks. The verbal persuasion variable was the least significant predictor of self-efficacy scores achieving significance on just one task. The total variance explained by the model as a whole ranged from 18% to 41% indicating that about a quarter to a third of the variability in Internet self-efficacy scores is predicted by mastery experience, vicarious experience and verbal persuasion. Mastery experience made the strongest unique contribution to explaining self-efficacy scores when the variance explained by the other independent variables in the model was controlled for.

3.4   Conclusion

The results of the multiple regression analysis suggest that the proposed model is not a satisfactory predictor model of Internet self-efficacy. Across all tasks, only one of the independent variables (mastery experience) was a consistently significant predictor of self-efficacy scores. Results of post-hoc comparisons demonstrated that correlations for mastery experience and self-efficacy were the only variables which achieved medium to strong correlation values. Correlation values between the other variables were weak with low significance levels suggesting little or no relationship between the variables. As a result, it can be concluded that mastery experience is the only strong predictor of self-efficacy scores.

3.5   Scale Refinement

Following on from the previous analysis, refinements to the scale were necessary. Information which would inform the item pool for the Internet self-efficacy scale had been collected at multiple points throughout the course of this research. Data which was collected in the early stages of scale development (outlined above) was also taken into consideration when finalizing the items for inclusion in the final scale. During that data collection, a participant noted that while the listed Internet activities incorporated shopping and buying items on the Internet, no activity encapsulated the selling of items. Thus, a new activity (e-commerce) was created for inclusion in the final scale.

Additionally, the response options were also revised after the previous data collection. Response options in the scale described above involved five response items for self-efficacy measurement. However, it was felt that five response options may have been too few options to do justice to nuances of self-efficacy. This was further highlighted by a large number of responses obtained for options one and five at the extreme ends of the scale. As a result, it was decided to increase the number of response options from five to seven options to best capture feelings of Internet self-efficacy.

4   Scoring Internet Self-efficacy

Earlier in this paper, Bandura's [4] methods for scoring self-efficacy were outlined in detail. Bandura put forward the dual-judgment format and the single-judgement format for measuring the strength of self-efficacy beliefs. Bandura further suggested that the preferred method is the latter for which respondents' rate the strength of their perceived self-efficacy for all items presented on the scale and when this is complete, the efficacy scores are summed, and then divided by the total number of statements to give an average self-efficacy score. In other words, average self-efficacy over all the tasks, regardless of how often they are done. This will hereafter be referred to as Bandura's self-efficacy score. However, scoring self-efficacy in this manner only gives the researcher limited information about the way in which individuals formulate their self-efficacy beliefs. Keeping the findings of this research in mind (that mastery experience is highly correlated with self-efficacy), it was decided that it would be important to incorporate people's scores on mastery experience, with their self-efficacy scores, to give a 'true' self-efficacy score. In doing so, individuals are providing further information which can be used to extract a clearer identification of their 'true' self-efficacy scores.

In order to do so, it is imperative that researchers collect two elements of information from participants: the first part invites respondents to indicate how often they complete each of the Internet tasks on a 5-point scale. In the second part, participants' are invited to rate how confident they feel that they can perform each of the ten listed Internet tasks 'as of now' on the 7-point response scale. With this information obtained for each participant, a formula was devised to obtain an overall self-efficacy score for each individual hypothesizing a multiplicative relationship between mastery experience and self-efficacy. Thus, respondents who rate themselves high on self-efficacy for tasks which they do not perform often score within a middle range compared to those with high self-efficacy and high frequency. Similarly, those who rate themselves low on self-efficacy but high on frequency are in a middle range in comparison to those who score low on both self-efficacy and frequency. The multiplicative relationship mutually accentuates the two effects which have been shown to be correlated in earlier parts of this research. Using this formula to measure self-efficacy results in possible scores ranging from 0 – 100 where 0 indicates an extremely low self-efficacy score and 100 indicates an extremely high self-efficacy score.

4.1   Gender Differences

Many studies [14-16] have investigated gender difference with technology in an effort to better understand how males and females interact with it. However, the evidence for gender differences in how confident individuals feel about using the Internet is conflicting. This disparity in the evidence quite likely results from the issues with Internet self-efficacy research outlined earlier in this paper.

The results of the analyses in the present study found no significant differences in Internet self-efficacy scores between the males and females. Effect sizes for the differences between the sexes are so small as to be negligible.

4.2   Age Differences

While there has been speculation about gender differences in Internet self-efficacy, little research has investigated age differences in Internet self-efficacy. This research hypothesized that there may well be a division in groups between those who have grown up within a readily accessible Internet environment (digital natives) and those who have had to learn about this new technology (digital immigrants). Age differences in Internet self-efficacy scores were found in the current analyses. Participants aged 25-34 years obtained the highest scores on Internet self-efficacy while participants aged <18 years obtained the lowest scores. Additionally, for participants increasing in age beyond 44 years, Internet self-efficacy scores started to decrease with age. The differences between the groups were significantly different. What was surprising was the low Internet self-efficacy scores achieved for the youngest age group (<18 years). However, the number of participants in the sample for this age group was extremely small (n = 11) so these results must be interpreted with caution. Further exploration of Internet self-efficacy in this age category is thus necessary.

5   Conclusion

Following extensive testing and analyses of the Internet Self-Efficacy Scale, the final scale consists of 10 items where confidence in ability is rated on a seven point scale.

The construct validity of the questionnaire is at least positively commendable and the authors hope that other researchers interested in Internet self-efficacy will be challenged enough by our results to want to adopt our scales in their research.

References

1. Joyce, M.: Development of a general internet attitude scale and internet self-efficacy scale (Unpublished doctoral dissertation). University College Cork, Ireland (2013)
2. Eastin, M.S., LaRose, R.: Internet self-efficacy and the psychology of the digital divide. Journal of Computer Mediated Communication 6(1), 1–8 (2000)
3. Torkzadeh, G., Van Dyke, T.P.: Development and validation of an Internet self-efficacy scale. Behaviour& Information Technology 20(4), 275–280 (2001)
4. Bandura, A.: Self-efficacy: the exercise of control. W.H. Freeman, New York (1997)
5. Bandura, A.: Self-efficacy: toward a unifying theory of behavioural change. Psychological Review 84(2), 191–215 (1977)
6. Zimmerman, B.J., Cleary, T.J.: Adolescents' development of personal agency: the role of self-efficacy beliefs and self-regulatory skill. In: Pajares, F., Urdan, T. (eds.) Self-efficacy Beliefs of Adolescents, pp. 45–70. Information Age Publishing, Greenwich (2006)
7. Zimmerman, B.J.: Self-efficacy and educational development. In: Bandura, A. (ed.) Self-efficacy in Changing Societies, pp. 202–231. Cambridge University Press, Cambridge (1995)
8. Streiner, D.L., Norman, G.R.: Health measurement scales: a practical guide to their development and use. Oxford University Press, New York (1989)
9. Bandura, A.: Guide for creating self-efficacy scales. In: Pajares, F., Urdan, T. (eds.) Self-efficacy Beliefs of Adolescents, pp. 307–337. Information Age Publishing, Greenwich (2006)
10. Eachus, P., Cassidy, S.: Development of the web users self-efficacy scale (WUSE). Issues in Informing Science and Information Technology 3, 199–209 (2006)
11. Compeau, D.R., Higgins, C.A.: Computer self-efficacy: development of a measure and initial test. MIS Quarterly 19, 189–211 (1995)
12. Graphics, Visualization and Usability Center, GVU's tenth annual survey. GVU Centre, Georgia Institute of Technology, Atlanta (1999), http://www.cc.gatech.edu/gvu/user_surveys/survey-1998-10/
13. Nahl, D.: Affective monitoring of Internet learners: perceived self-efficacy and success. Journal of American Society for Information Sciences 33, 200–209 (1996)
14. Tsai, C.-C., Lin, C.-C.: Taiwanese adolescents' perceptions and attitudes regarding the Internet: exploring gender differences. Adolescence 39(4), 725–734 (2004)
15. Hargittai, E., Shafer, S.: Differences in actual and perceived online skills: the role of gender. Social Science Quarterly 87(2), 432–448 (2006)
16. Dutton, W.H., Blank, G.: Next generation users: the Internet in Britain. Oxford Internet Survey, Oxford Internet Institute, University of Oxford (2011)

Customer Journey Mapping of an Experience-Centric Service by Mobile Self-reporting: Testing the Qualiwall Tool[*]

Inka Kojo[1], Mikko Heiskala[2], and Juho-Pekka Virtanen[3]

[1] Aalto University, School of Engineering, Department of Civil and Structural Engineering, Built Environment Services (BES) Research Group, P.O. Box 14100, FI-00076 Aalto, Finland
[2] Aalto University, School of Science, Department of Computer Science and Engineering, P.O. Box 15400, FI-00076 Aalto, Finland
[3] Aalto University, School of Engineering, P.O. Box 14100, FI-00076 Aalto, Finland
{inka.kojo,mikko.heiskala,juho-pekka.virtanen}@aalto.fi

Abstract. A focus on the user experience and user-centric perspective are considered to be essential in today's product and service development processes. Technological advancements during the last two decades have made user studies based on digital, mobile self-reporting possible. The goal of this study is to report on our experiences using a mobile self-reporting tool called Qualiwall for the customer journey mapping of an experience-centric service. The results indicate that the Qualiwall tool is especially suitable for mapping the customer experiences because it enables the collection of rich, real-time and in-situ data; however, it also possesses certain disadvantages. To arrive at more general conclusions, future research will focus on piloting the Qualiwall tool in other service-related user research situations as well.

Keywords: Service experience, customer journey mapping, mobile self-reporting.

1 Introduction

A focus on the user experience and user-centric perspective are considered to be essential in today's development processes, whether discussing products, services or places [1-3]. A number of research methods attempt to provide temporal user data by emphasising immediate user participation and self-reporting or self-documentation. The participatory design viewpoint sees users as "creative people who can participate directly in the design process when given the appropriate tools and encouragement" [4]. Self-documentation refers to participatory research methodologies where the

---
[*] This research was supported by the Academy of Finland CoE-LaSR, the Centre of Excellence in Laser Scanning Research (project number 272195), the Finnish Funding Agency for Innovation, the EUE program (project number 2141226) and the UNME program (project number 21138913).

A. Marcus (Ed.): DUXU 2014, Part I, LNCS 8517, pp. 261–272, 2014.

research participants report their own behaviour to the researchers [4]. The benefits of this approach include providing the most direct approach to user-experience annotation and affect detection [5].

Several methods and tools such as design probes [4] and diary studies exist for the purpose of self-reporting. Diaries refer to a class of methods such as experience-sampling, event-sampling and daily diary studies [6] whose features and characteristics appear to generally overlap [7-9]. Initially, these methods were conducted as pen-and-paper studies. However, because of technological advancements during the last two decades, conducting user studies using digital, mobile self-reporting tools has become possible. In fact, diary methods begin to address the limitations of participation using manual methods [7].

This has enabled the performing of real-time self-reporting studies. Real-time data gathering concerns "asking the questions in close temporal proximity to the event of interest" [10]. The benefits of using real-time research methods include the ability to acquire, for instance, higher-quality data by limiting the issue of questions having multiple meanings, reducing problems relating to memory and estimation and facilitating access to episodic details [10]. Initially, users participated in these surveys using manual tools, typically paper and pencil [7]. However, conducting user studies using more customised digital mobile and digital real-time self-reporting methods has become possible.

The goal of this study is to report our experiences using Qualiwall, a mobile self-reporting tool for the customer journey mapping of an experience-centric service. The case service was the Finlandia Trophy 2013 International Figure Skating Competition event held in Espoo, Finland over the course of a weekend in October 2013.

In this paper, we first discuss the evolution of mobile self-reporting applications and the methodological background related to user studies of experience-centric services and customer journey mapping. Next, the Qualiwall tool and its capabilities are presented, and the research design is explained. Finally, the results are viewed and a discussion and conclusions are given along with possible future research avenues and developments.

2   Background

2.1   Evolution of Self-reporting Applications

The concept of utilising mobile devices for experience-sampling by self-reporting dates back over three decades. Originally, the technology used in mobile self-reporting studies was based on using the features of mobile phones or other devices such as voice-mail [11], picture capturing, video recording, text and multimedia messaging, email [12-14] and instant messaging [15]. In addition, tailor-made, research situation specific applications have been developed [13, 16-17].

An early example of a generic mobile self-reporting application is the Experience Sampling Program (ESP), which is a system that operates on Palm Pilot handheld computers [18]. It has been reported that the ESP was already in use in the late 1990s [19]. Subsequently, numerous projects were established where mobile devices, mostly early smartphones, were used for mobile experience sampling. These projects included Mobile Probes [13], which ran on Nokia smartphones, and MyExperience [20-21]. Later examples included Contextual Activity Sampling System Query (CASS-Q) [22] and Ohmage [23].

Throughout this development, the main benefits of using mobile devices in experience sampling, which include the collection of real-time data [20], passive data collection using various sensors that the devices are equipped with [23], inclusion of images [13], and customisability of surveys performed [21], have remained roughly the same. In addition to research projects, a large number of tools exist on the market designed for experience sampling using contemporary smartphones. Listings of these applications are also available [9, 24-25]. These products range from applications with Internet survey-type functionality [26] to tools developed purely to conduct experience sampling [27]. Typically, the experience sampling applications are available on both Android and iOS operating systems.

2.2   Experience-Centric Services and Customer Journey Mapping

User or customer experience has become a relevant topic in a number of fields of research and industry, one of which is service design. As previously stated, the importance of the customer experience as it pertains to customer satisfaction and loyalty has long been recognised by service organisations [3]. Thus, customer experience has been viewed as the core of many service organisations [28-29] by delivering "experience-centric services", which refers to services where organisations proactively craft the customer experience to create distinctive product and service offerings [30].

The customer experience has been defined as "all aspects of the end-user's interaction with the company, its services and its products" [31]. Thus, the customer experience includes three elements, the user, the product or service and the context of use [32], and examines the wider relations that exist between these elements to better understand the individual's personal perceptions at a given moment [33]. A customer experience occurs when "a customer has any sensation or acquires knowledge from some level of interaction with the elements of a context created by a service provider" [34].

Customer journey mapping is used to understand a customer's behaviour, feelings, motivations and attitudes while using a service. The customer journey includes all activities and events related to the delivery of the service from the customer's perspective. It is an emotional and physical journey that the customer experiences. The steps of the customer journey can involve anticipation of and arrival at an experience, departure, and savouring. In contrast, a touchpoint is a concept relating to customer journeys; it shows up whenever a customer "touches" a service and can occur across multiple channels and at various points in time [3].

Experience-centric services are designed to engage customers in a personal, memorable way emotionally, physically, and/or intellectually. The particularly personal nature of the customer experience in experience-centric services appears to make self-reporting especially promising as a user-study methodology. Experiences are personal and take place in-situ. Self-reporting via smartphone applications appears especially promising as a research approach for mapping customer journeys of experience-centric services. Smartphones are widespread and are often the main personal computing device of a person. Studies conducted using a self-reporting application on a person's personal phone is relatively unobtrusive and causes limited adverse effects to the service experience relative to, for example, self-reporting via pen-and-paper or via a dedicated, extra research device that the person would need to carry around.

3   Methodology

3.1   The Qualiwall Tool

The Qualiwall tool is a research platform for administering and conducting self-reporting studies via mobile devices. The development of the Qualiwall tool originally began in 2011 as a student project. The Android operating system was chosen as the platform because it appeared to offer the largest software ecosystem, especially in mid-priced smartphones. The know-how for Android application development was also available in the team. However, other platforms may be included in the future.

The Qualiwall tool has been divided into two main components: the client software, which runs on Android OS smartphones and tablets, and the server software, which runs on an online web server. The work is divided between these components such that the client is purely an answering tool for self-reporting, and the server side software is used to create the surveys and process the results. In Figure 1, we see how the server's users access the server and create surveys that are subsequently sent to the mobile users. The answer data from the mobile users is then sent to the server and downloaded by the server users. The server application operates over the network connection, where the mobile application must be downloaded and installed separately. There can be several server users and mobile users accessing the server simultaneously.

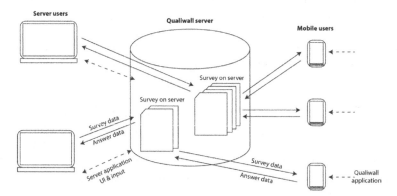

Fig. 1. The Qualiwall server with both server and mobile users

The Qualiwall tool includes a set of prebuilt tools for building surveys. These tools include the very basic question types found on most online survey tools and traditional survey forms: a short and long free response-style answer, checkbox and radio-button selections, choosing a single alternative from a given set of possible answers, and a zero to five star rating. In addition to the basic questions, photos and video can be captured. The researcher can also record the GPS positions of the users when an answer is recorded or make the questions available for answering at certain times or physical locations.

In the Qualiwall tool, the users and the publicity of the surveys are controlled individually. Surveys can be available to anyone or to a limited group of users. In both cases, the survey can either be open or closed, making it available to the users or not. An individual survey in the Qualiwall tool is divided into pages as shown in Figure 2. The pages are entities that can be tied to times and places and can contain several individual questions of different types. Using the page structure, more complex surveys can be built; the user may be tasked to move between different locations, each having a specific set of questions to answer at each location. In a similar fashion, the user may be required to complete a certain set of tasks at a certain time during the day.

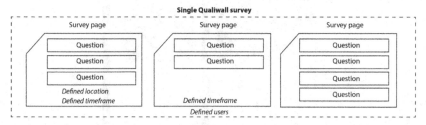

Fig. 2. Single survey with defined users, showing pages with defined locations and or time-frames, and questions on pages

A Qualiwall survey can be closed when desired, ignoring all subsequent responses. Alternatively, an analysis can be begun immediately after the first answers arrive. In the analysis process, the data can be sorted, for instance, according to the answers given, by different respondent ids, or by data types. Subsequently, the results can be exported from the Qualiwall system in a digital format for further analysis using tools such as affinity diagrams.

3.2   Research Design

To report our experiences using the Qualiwall tool, we conducted a study at the Finlandia Trophy Espoo 2013 International Figure Skating Competition. Figure skating is an aesthetic, competitive sporting event and is a good example of an experience-centric service. Self-reported data using the Qualiwall tool was collected from participants chosen by convenience-sampling from Aalto University students and staff and Finlandia Trophy staff. The participants were mostly first-time visitors to a figure skating event. While this naturally skews results towards first timers who form only a portion of the event's audience, omitting regular visitors, this does not affect the evaluation of the tool and research approach, which was the goal of the study. For a comprehensive study of the customer journeys at such an event, the participant sampling should attempt to cover all customer segments.

The seven participants received free tickets to the Finlandia Trophy and were given brief instructions on how to install and use the Qualiwall tool. No personal assistance was given. The participants attended the Finlandia Trophy figure skating event and self-reported their experience using the Qualiwall client software.

The participants first answered a short background survey using the Qualiwall tool. They were subsequently asked to map each touchpoint they considered relevant for their service experience before, during, and after attending the event to capture the whole customer journey. For each touchpoint, the participants created a note that consisted of a photo, the name of the touchpoint, and an evaluation on a one to five star scale indicating how positive their experience of the touchpoint was and how well it met their expectations. The participant could also leave an open comment on the note. Two screenshots from the survey for each touchpoint are shown in Figure 3.

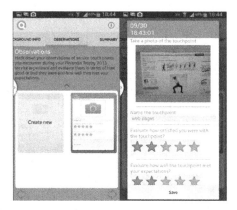

Fig. 3. Screenshots of touchpoint evaluation

To offer a comparison point to the Qualiwall self-reported data, an additional participant was instructed to compose a similar customer journey map of his experience using smartphone photos and his own notes without Qualiwall-support and another (an experienced ethnographer) collected ethnographic notes of his experiences at the event.

4   Results

In total, the seven participants who used the Qualiwall tool submitted a total of 110 notes. Two of the seven participants who used the Qualiwall tool for self-reporting had only completed the background survey and did not map any touchpoints. The other five participants mapped varying numbers of touchpoints. One participant mapped 58 touchpoints over the course of two days of attendance at the event. Another participant had logged 31 touchpoints during a single visit. The other three had mapped between 4 and 7 touchpoints during a single visit.

Table 1. A number of touchpoints identified from the data

Event website	Half of the journeys included a visit to the event website. Generally, the participants were dissatisfied with the website. It failed to create excitement prior to the event, and information was hard to find.	
Tickets	Many of the participants had mapped the tickets as a touchpoint and were satisfied with them. They included the relevant info.	
Venue entrance, outside	The venue entrance was considered uninviting, and many wondered why there were so few event posters outside.	
Venue entrance, inside	A small number of participants complained about uncomfortable crowding immediately after entering the venue hall. The area was filled with people buzzing around the many sales booths and info desks.	
Finding the seats	Almost every participant reported difficulties in finding their seats. They complained about poor signage and "temporary" signs printed on A4-paper.	
Watching the show	Everyone reported on the competition and performances positively and rated them highly.	
Eating	Another repeated observation was related to eating. The experiences were rated as average, with a few commenting on "ice hockey food". The event hall is home to a professional ice hockey team.	

As the event took place in a relatively confined space and time, the data analysis was completed more efficiently because of the small sample of participants. Based on six customer journeys (one person visited the event over the course of two days), we could identify a number of similar patterns and experiences involving the same touchpoints. Thus, the observations began to saturate on certain issues. These issues are discussed in Table 1 with examples. It is not an exhaustive list of issues or touchpoints found from the data but, rather, is meant to illustrate the potential of the Qualiwall tool for mobile self-reporting of service experiences.

Table 2. Examples of data from smartphone and pen-and-paper and ethnographic notes

		Touchpoint	
		Finding seats	*Watching the show*
Data collection method	*Qualiwall*	*Entrance was smooth; finding the seats a small adventure.*	*The program was better than I expected, and you could see the performances well.*
	Pen-and-paper and smartphone camera	*We arrived, our tickets were scanned, and we are in! But where do we go? We see the action in front of us and get in; there are some stores, but we want to see the skaters, so we go straight into the grey curtains. A security guy stops us and asks for the tickets. We show them, and he said that our seats are on the third floor (how can I know that?). We walk to our seats on the third floor, wondering where 500 is. The signs say 400 only.*	*The ice dance presentation starts, the skaters interact and dance following the music. Is a very nice show, we are enjoying it and our daughter also. She stands up to do some jumps and turns and then she seats to watch the skaters again. It is very dynamic and in comparison to the previous parts, where everyone seemed to be doing the same routine and very rigidly, here all the couples and all the music styles are different and they dance!*
	Ethnographic notes	*We get lost, but a volunteer notices and asks if she can help us to our seats. This is great. I feel like they want to take care of us and let us have a good time. We find our seats and sit down.*	*The skaters appear and the competition starts. I have never been to a skating event before and am surprised how much the experience resembles classical ballet. The experience is much more intense than seen from the TV, although we are sitting high up. I was expecting the contrary. The charisma of the performers comes through; the performances really are of a high quality. Music and skating are well balanced. This is good!*

The participant who took notes using a pen, paper, and a smartphone camera generated a total of 22 of recordings. The participant who took ethnographic notes reported three pages (1500 words) worth of observations and included a number of images. These data were compared to the data collected using the Qualiwall tool. We illustrate this comparison in Table 2, which shows examples of the two touchpoints "finding seats" and "watching the show" from the viewpoint of data collected with the Qualiwall tool, pen-and-paper and smartphone camera and ethnographic notes. It shows that when compared to the other data collection methods, the textual data acquired using the Qualiwall tool is meagre relative to the data collected using the other methods.

5   Discussion and Conclusions

Several software tools for mobile self-reporting, which take advantage of the cameras included in mobile devices and GPS, have been developed in the past. They appear to be promising tools for user studies of experience-centric services because they support in-situ self-reporting of "fresh" customer experiences. They can also provide rich data for the purposes of customer journey mapping. However, doing self-reporting during an experience-centric service may interfere with the actual experience, though other methods of data collection, such as outsider observations and post-hoc interviews, do not necessarily capture the "true" experience.

In the experiment presented in this study, a number of participants were asked to be in the audience of a figure skating competition and document their experiences using the Qualiwall tool. For comparison, one of the participants took notes with pen-and-paper and another took notes as an ethnographer. All of the participants using the Qualiwall tool were able to use the application, and their answers were successfully transmitted to the server. The Qualiwall tool allowed for the frequent, real-time mapping of touchpoints.

The Qualiwall self-reports, the paper-and-pen customer journey, and the ethnographer's notes contained observations of similar issues. It appears that even with this relatively small sample of participants, a saturation occurred around the main issues related to the service experience. The tools used did not appear to have any significant effect on what observations the participants made. However, there are a number of clear differences in the textual data participants reported: the ethnographic notes and post-hoc-constructed customer journey map provide richer and more verbose textual data in comparison to the data collected by the Qualiwall tool. This may have been caused by the difficulty of writing longer texts using a smartphone. The ethnographer and pen-and-paper customer journey mappers were instructed to observe their experience and take notes and photographs using their smartphones, but they used a computer to compile their notes after the event, which most likely made writing easier. Thus, it appears that smartphones and tablets are not the best tools for generating extensive textual data.

In all of the methods, the notes were taken during the event, but in the cases of the pen-and-paper and the ethnographic notes, the textual data were edited by the participants after the event. Given the available data, it is impossible to draw conclusions on whether this created any differences in the observations. The subsequent editing of the notes may enable a reflection on the experience, which may slightly modify the results. One of the benefits of using the Qualiwall tool was that the answer's creation time can be confirmed from the server, and it is possible to verify whether or not all the answers are created in-situ. With pen-and-paper notes, this determination cannot be made.

When analysing at the answers obtained with the Qualiwall tool, at least two issues can be noted. First, two of the participants mapped a significantly higher number of touchpoints than the other participants. It is difficult to say what caused this difference. Perhaps these two participants were more motivated in the study than the other participants. Another explanation might be that the other participants considered much fewer touchpoints to be significant to their service experience and only mapped those they were instructed to map. Second, a number of the participants did not return any answers from the event. This may have been caused by a number of reasons including a lack of motivation or time, not going to the event, not having a smartphone at the event, or forgetting the task due to immersion with the experience. The reasons may also be related to the Qualiwall tool and its usability. It is possible that the use of a smartphone application in the given situation was viewed as too laborious. There may also be technical reasons such as a battery becoming depleted or unknown software errors caused by different hardware configurations. Finally, it is also possible that there was a problem in the definition of the task, and the participants were not able to clearly distinguish the touchpoints from the event. Unfortunately, these questions cannot be answered based on the currently available data.

When looking at the results from existing research, we can see that similar observations have been made: the collection of large data amounts from live situations is well facilitated by mobile experience sampling [20,22], but gathering longer text answers may be difficult with these methods [22]. The research community has already drawn a number of conclusions from past experiences with mobile experience sampling, highlighting the need for multi-platform, customizable experience sampling system [35]. These development considerations and observations correlate with our experiences and current development goals.

Future research will focus on piloting the Qualiwall tool to study other experience-centric services to identify more generalisable results relating to the suitability of Qualiwall tool for customer journey mapping and service design in general.

Acknowledgements. We are grateful for the Finlandia Trophy organisation for sponsoring free tickets for the participants and for the opportunity to do the research. We thank also the anonymous research participants.

References

1. Alexander, K.: The Application of Usability Concepts in the Built Environment. Journal of Facilities Management 4, 262–270 (2006)
2. Bilgram, V., Brem, A., Voigt, K.-I.: User-centric Innovations in New Product Development – Systematic Identification of Lead Users Harnessing Interactive and Collaborative Online-tools. International Journal of Innovation Management 12, 419–458 (2008)
3. Zomerdijk, L., Voss, C.: Service Design for Experience-Centric Services. Journal of Service Research 13, 67–82 (2010)
4. Mattelmäki, T.: Applying Probes – From Inspirational Notes to Collaborative Insights. CoDesign 1, 83–102 (2005)
5. Yannakakis, G.N., Hallam, J.: Ranking vs. Preference: A Comparative Study of Self-reporting. In: D'Mello, S., Graesser, A., Schuller, B., Martin, J.-C. (eds.) ACII 2011, Part I. LNCS, vol. 6974, pp. 437–446. Springer, Heidelberg (2011)

6. Ohly, S., Sonnentag, S., Niessen, C., Zapf, D.: Diary Studies in Organizational Research: An Introduction and Some Practical Recommencations. Journal of Personnel Psychology 9, 79–93 (2010)
7. Bolger, N., Davis, A., Rafaeli, S.: Diary Methods: Capturing Life as it is Lived. Annual Review of Physchology 54, 579–616 (2003)
8. Conner, T.M., Lehman, B.J.: Getting Started – Launching a Study in Daily Life. In: Mehl, M.R., Conner, T.S. (eds.) Handbook of Research Methods for Studying Daily Life, pp. 89–107. The Guilford Press, New York (2012)
9. Kubiak, T., Krog, K.: Computerized Sampling of Experiences and Behavior. In: Mehl, M.R., Conner, T.S. (eds.) Handbook of Research Methods for Studying Daily Life, pp. 124–143. The Guilford Press, New York (2012)
10. Schwartz, N.: Why Researchers Should Think "Rea-Time": A Cognitive Rationale. In: Mehl, M.R., Conner, T.S. (eds.) Handbook of Research Methods for Studying Daily Life, pp. 22–42. The Guilford Press, New York (2012)
11. Palen, L., Salzman, M.: Voice-Mail Diary Studies for Naturalistic Data Capture Under Mobile Conditions. In: Conference on Computer Supported Cooperative Work, CSCW 2002, pp. 87–95. ACM, New York (2002)
12. Iversen, O.S., Nielsen, C.: Using Digital Cultural Probes in Design with Children. In: Conference on Interaction Design and Children, IDC 2003, pp. 154–155. ACM, New York (2003)
13. Hulkko, S., Mattelmäki, T., Virtanen, K., Keinonen, T.: Mobile Probes. In: 3th Nordic Conference on Human-Computer Interaction, NordiCHI 2004, pp. 43–51. ACM, New York (2004)
14. Andrews, L., Russell-Bennett, R., Drennan, J.: Capturing Affective Experiences Using the SMS Experience Sampling (SMS-ES) Method. International Journal of Market Research 53, 1–27 (2011)
15. Fetter, M., Gross, F.: PRIMIExperience: Experience Sampling via Instant Messaging. In: Conference on Computer Supported Cooperative Work, CSCW 2011, pp. 629–632. ACM, New York (2011)
16. Hutchinson, H., Mackay, W., Westerlund, B., Bederson, B., Druin, A., Plaisant, C., Beaudouin-Lafon, M., Conversy, H.E., Hansen, H., Roussel, N., Eiderbäck, B., Lingquist, S., Sundblad, Y.: Technology Probes: Inspiring Design for and with Families. In: The SIGHI Conference on Human Factors in Computing Systems, CHI 2003, pp. 17–24. ACM, New York (2003)
17. Langdale, G., Kay, J., Kummerfeld, B.: Using an Intergenerational Communications System as a 'Ligh-Weight' Technology Probe. In: Extended Abstracts on Human Factors in Computing Systems, CHI EA 2006, pp. 1001–1006. ACM, New York (2006)
18. Experience Sampling Program, http://www.experience-sampling.org/about.shtml
19. Fischer, J.E.: Experience-sampling tools: a critical review. In: 11th International Conference on Human-Computer Interaction with Mobile Devices and Services, Mobile-HCI 2009, p. 9. ACM, New York (2009)
20. Consolvo, S., Harrison, B., Smith, I., Chen, M.Y., Everitt, K., Froehlich, J., Landay, J.A.: Conducting in Situ Evaluations for and with Ubiquitous Computing Technologies. International Journal of Human-Computer Interaction 22, 103–118 (2007)
21. Froehlich, J., Mike, Y.C., Consolvo, S., Harrison, B., Landay, J.A.: MyExperience: A System for In Situ Tracing and Capturing of User Feedback on Mobile Phones. In: 5th International Conference on Mobile Systems, Applications and Services, MobiSys 2007, pp. 57–70. ACM, New York (2007)

22. Muukkonen, H., Inkinen, M., Kosonen, K., Hakkarainen, K., Vesikivi, P., Lachmann, H., Karlgren, K.: Research on Knowledge Practices with the Contextual Activity Sampling System. In: 9th International Conference on Computer Supported Collaborative Learning, CSCL 2009, pp. 385–394. International Society of the Learning Sciences (2009)
23. Ramanathan, N., Alquaddoomi, F., Falaki, H., George, D., Hsiel, C., Jenkins, J., Ketcham, C., Longstaff, B., Ooms, J., Selsky, J., Tangmunarunkit, H., Estrin, D.: Ohmage: An Open Mobile System for Activity and Experience Sampling. In: IEEE 6th International Conference on Pervasive Computing Technologies for Healthcare, pp. 203–204 (2012)
24. Market Research in the Mobile Word: Quick Review of Mobile Apps for Qualitative Research, http://www.mrmw.net/news-blogs/295-a-quick-review-of-mobile-apps-for-qualitative-research
25. Conner, T.S.: Experience Sampling and Ecological Momentary Assessment with Mobile Phones (November 2013),
http://www.otago.ac.nz/psychology/otago047475.pdf
26. iSurvey, https://www.isurveysoft.com/
27. Metricwire, https://metricwire.com/
28. Pine, B.J., Gilmore, J.H.: The Experience Economy: Work is Theater& Every Business a Stage. Harward Business Press, Massachusetts (1999)
29. Haeckel, S.H., Carbone, L.P., Berry, L.L.: How to Lead the Customer Experience. Marketing Management 12, 18–23 (2003)
30. Voss, C., Roth, A.V., Chase, R.B.: Experience, Service Operations Strategy, and Services as Destinations: Foundations and Exploratory Investigation. Production and Operations Management 17, 247–266 (2008)
31. Alben, L.: Quality of Experience: Defining Criteria for Effective Interaction Design. Interactions 3, 11–15 (1996)
32. Battarbee, K.: Co-Experience: Understanding User Experience in Social Interaction. Doctoral dissertation, University of Art and Design Helsinki, Helsinki (2008)
33. McNamara, N., Kirakowski, J.: Functionality, Usability, and User Experience: Three Areas of Concern. Interactions 13, 26–28 (2006)
34. Pullman, M.E., Gross, M.A.: Ability of Experience Design Elements to Elicit Emotions and Loyalty Behaviors. Decision Sciences 35, 551–578 (2004)
35. Batalas, N., Markopoulos, P.: Considerations for Computerized In Situ Data Collection Platforms. In: 4th ACM SIGCHI Symposium on Engineering Interactive Computing Systems, EICS 2012, pp. 231–236 (2012)

Evaluation of Tablet PC Application Interfaces with Low Vision Users: Focusing on Usability

Cínthia Costa Kulpa and Fernando Gonçalves Amaral

Federal University of Rio Grande do Sul, Porto Alegre, Brazil
cinthia.kulpa@gmail.com, amaral@producao.ufrgs.br

Abstract. This article described the results of a qualitative research by analyzing a focus group, on the accessibility of Tablet PC application interfaces regarding the digital inclusion of low vision users, which brought evidence of the need for studies on how those users view, recognize and interpret the information presented by this new technology, with the purpose of making it possible to provide better usability of those interfaces. For such, it presents the themes involved such as: mobile technologies, low vision disability and accessibility, leading on to discussions on the digital inclusion of those users.

Keywords: Tablet PC, low vision, accessibility, usability.

1   Introduction

The significant evolution of mobile technologies has broadened the options of resources and strategies for digital inclusion, since they allow for interaction to take place anytime, anywhere, free of time and space limitations, as they are connected to wireless networks and integrate mobility, communication and processing power [1].

This way results in flexible groupings to occur, where age and location become more relevant, with people interacting according to their interests, needs and curiosity; producing a growing number of users of virtual environments through mobile technologies and the broadening of   the diversity in their profiles.

The Tablet Personal Computer (TPC), a computer in the shape of an electronic clipboard with virtual keyboard and touchscreen is the technology most widely implemented in teaching institutions worldwide among the currently available mobile technologies [2] and [3]. At present, the TPC is deemed the best form of presenting information through text, image, video and audio applications [2]. Moreover, it offers users applications that allow for real time interactivity by navigating in the virtual environment, make notes, research terms, interact with other users, among other possibilities.

However, as the amount of applications developed for TPC grows, there is also increasing use of such applications by different user profiles, bringing to evidence difficulties in performing tasks, that leads to loss of data, reduced productivity and even full rejection of this new technology by those users, since those applications do not include in their interfaces accessibility for different users that considers their

A. Marcus (Ed.): DUXU 2014, Part I, LNCS 8517, pp. 273–284, 2014.
© Springer International Publishing Switzerland 2014

personal traits, behavior, needs, discourse, as well as disabilities and limitations brought on by the physical environment or technological barriers [4].

Although accessibility is increasingly present in virtual environments, it is not yet explored by applications for TPC, in comparison with existing computer systems, since there are few applications for this technology, and also because the development of such applications involves significant periods of time and investment. In some cases of applications for TPC, the use of the Universal Design is seen, but "Universal Design based projects do not ensure compliance and accessibility to all persons in the same manner due to the broad diversity of disabled and non-disabled persons, and due to the situations in which those persons find themselves" [5].

The demographic census of 2010 [6], shows that 24% of the population have disabilities with degrees of severity investigated. Among the disabilities pointed out, low vision comprises 18.3% of the Brazilian population, that is, 35 million Brazilians are diagnosed as having low vision disability. Those data point towards the pressing need for research and studies on the development of the new applications for TPC aimed at providing accessibility for these users, and indicating the likelihood of them being TPC users if some particularities or adjustments were to be observed [5].

From the information presented above, it can be noticed that there is a need to investigate the use of applications developed for TPC by persons with Low Vision disability, taking into consideration better usability and ensuring accessibility for those users

2   Mobile Technologies

For an interface to serve a person with low vision to provide accessibility, it is of no use that developers makes use only of the World Wide Web guidelines that are available and always updated to build interfaces; they must learn what possibilities those users have, their traits, expectations and needs. Otherwise, that interface will always be bound by the Universal Design recommendations, which seeks to include the highest number of users through generalized actions. In that case of differences not being considered, it creates obstacles for users with low vision, since they will have to adapt to the interfaces that are imposed, limiting the use of their functional vision and setting the threshold of possibilities at the lower level.

Moreover, a technological revolution has been taking place in the world, affecting, among other areas, education, not only with the advent of the first TPC (2010), but also the expansion and massification of that technology. The need to produce efforts that would result in knowledge and information to assist the development of applications for TPC with adequate accessibility and usability for persons with low vision has become inevitable and conclusive.

The market currently offers several types of mobile technologies, more commonly known as mobile devices aimed at corporate and general consumers [7]. The TPC is classified as a computer, as well as being called a personal mobile device, which is integrated to a large interactive screen, is in the shape of a clipboard and has access to the wireless virtual environment. It features a touchscreen that, by touching with the finger tips or using a specially designed pen for it, activates its functionalities and is the main entry device to browse around this platform. It is considered to be a new concept, that stands out with its capability of allowing users to write using a pen directly onto the screen.

The first TPC was created by Apple Inc. and was launched in 2010, called the iPad. Since then, several similar models have appeared, which goes to prove it has been accepted by the general public.

There are two operational systems for TPC: Android and iOS. The Android operational system was launched by Google through a partnership with companies from varied fields of activity and is defined as an Open Source platform for mobile devices that makes use of Java programming language and allows for developers to access the system application framework whenever they wish to build an Android application. The iOS is Apple's mobile operational system and is restricted to Apple devices only [8].

Some of the differences between the TPC and other technologies is that it makes it easy to access and display text and presentations, youngsters are prepared for this technology, it integrates trends, is increasingly affordable, there is software being designed that is suited for this technology and the device is adjusted to the profile of youngsters concerning technological cognition and Human-Computer Interaction.

3   Human Computer Interaction

The graphic interface is the visible part of the software to the users, through which they communicate with the system to perform tasks. Visual perception is attained when the users manage to "intuitively" handle the visual representation that is configured in the relation between what the developer wishes to inform and what the user perceives from that information [9].

Interface is not only the image that appears to the users, it is a set of interface entities that relate with the application or system entities and that results in the users not even noticing that they are interacting with the system [10]. Therefore, user interfaces cannot be thought of without considering the human being who will be using them and relating with the computer. To be able to understand how this effective communication takes place it is necessary to learn about the human-computer interaction.

Human-Computer Interaction (HCI) involves topics such as design, assessment and implementation of interactive computer systems focused on the use by people, besides being concerned with the main phenomena that involve this relation: human-computer [11]. These studies are concerned with producing systems with better usability, effectiveness, utility, security and that are more functional. This way, it can be stated that the term "systems" refers to the hardware, software and the entire computational environment, either through the use or affected by the use of this technology [12].

HCI encompasses a multidisciplinary view to assist in improving acceptability by analyzing different points of view and taking into account different human factors. Thus, this human-machine interaction relation is unique and individual, since each user carries an exclusive experience according to their traits, expectations, life and culture [13].

The development of graphic interfaces must make use of knowledge related to HCI in order to project a graphic interface that will assure not only adequate functionality of the system, but its usability as well.

Usability refers to how fast users can learn how to use something, its efficiency, satisfaction, easy memorization and the level of propensity to mistakes [14]. It can be classified as a characteristic quality in the use of programs and applications by indicating an agreement between interface, user, task and environment [13].

And it is through usability aims that makes it possible to identify problems when using a graphic interface Those aims concern effectiveness, efficiency, security, utility, learning capability and memorization capability. In addition to those aims, there are the aims that result from user experience. Even so, they are not clearly measurable, since they indicate that an interface must be satisfactory, pleasant, fun, interesting, useful, motivational, esthetically appealing, creativity inducing, rewarding, emotionally adequate.

Recognizing and understanding the balance between the usability aims and those resulting from user experience becomes very important, with the types of aims established depending on who will be the users of the system being developed, in addition to their context of use, capabilities and objectives [11].

4   Low Vision

Low vision is defined as a severe loss of sight that cannot be corrected through clinical or surgical treatment or with conventional glasses; and it is related to the visual capacity a person has located between 20/40 and 20/200, after correction [5].

Such severe loss leads to an important hindrance of visual function, but it is not characterized as blindness. The hindrance that occurs may be related to the reduction of visual acuteness, adaptation to light or darkness and differentiating colors. However, this condition does not prevent the person from planning or performing tasks using their sight[15].

People with low vision are in an intermediate position between the reality of people who can see normally and total visually disabled people. Since they have limitations that make it impossible for them to perform certain functions, they are not treated as someone with normal sight. However, they are not considered to be blind, since they have a residual sight that allows them to perform some tasks perfectly well. This marginal condition leads to a social exclusion level that is much stronger than the exclusion of people who are blind or have normal sight [16].

The "Convention on the Rights of Persons with Disabilities", adopted by the UN in 2006, came about to defend, promote and ensure conditions of life with dignity and emancipation of citizens of the world who have some form of disability. Among the principles of that convention, are included the person's independence, individual autonomy, full and effective participation and inclusion in society, respect for the difference, equal opportunities for men and women, and accessibility.

5   Accessibility

Accessibility in the virtual environment, for a person with low vision disability, goes far beyond the search for information, it is the possibility to include that person in society in general, since it eliminates communication barriers. And, according to the UN Convention for the rights of persons with disabilities, if there is no accessibility it means there is discrimination, condemnable under the moral and ethical view, and punishable in the form o law. This way, all States Parties undertake to promote inclusion on equal bases with other persons, as well as providing access to all existing opportunities to the population in general [6].

There are several guidelines to assist developers in the pursuit of accessibility in the virtual environments. Nevertheless, it can be observed that the vast majority of interfaces developed is aimed at users in general, and do not take into account those users who have some form of disability. Concerning the cutting edge technologies, such as TPC, there are no guidelines that include users with low vision disability, making accessibility difficult to this type of system by those users, and as a consequence, hindering their digital inclusion.

Digital inclusion involves overcoming several barriers that involves the development of solutions for the diversity of the human potential by making information and communication accessible, usable and useful for everyone. The solutions for those challenges must be built by and with the players involved [18]. Strategies and solutions must be outlined to make possible the construction of a digital society for everyone that promotes the full exercise of citizenship and educational inclusion based on the human rights.

6   Research Methodology

In order to gain an initial understanding of the interaction of low vision users with TPC and its application interfaces, in addition to identifying and analyzing likely usability problems in such interaction, a qualitative research with a focused group was chosen. Since this type or research is not representative regarding the stratified population, it was used to seek the generation of data to feed quantitative researches that will allow to perform a future triangulation of both results.

The 5 participants were chosen for having low vision disabilities regardless of each one's diagnosis and etiology, taking into account only the functional vision that would make it possible to handle and choose their actions on the TCP not requiring the support of assistive technologies.

In order that they all could interact among themselves at the same dialog level, it was established that the participants should be aged between 18 and 28 and inserted within the academic context. They were members of the Incluir Program at UFRGS, which supports actions that favor the inclusion of persons with disability in higher education. All the participants were familiar with the computer technologies:

A script was used that contained open questions presented by the moderator who carried out the interview. Initially, each participant was handed and read to a term of free and clarified consent explaining the objective of the research and their participation rights. The script was created with questions that would lead the study to its closure naturally, as presented in Table 1 below:

Table 1. Questions Covered in the Interview

Type of Question	Question
Introductory	What is the diagnostic of your visual disability?
	Talk about your functional vision
Transitional	What do you think of the Tablet PC?
	Have you used a Tablet PC?
Directional	Please turn it on
	Which elements in the initial interface are perceived?
	Try to change the TPC configurations to be able to use it according to your profile
	Try to navigate in the Virtual Environment
Of Closure	Talk about the ease of use
	Did you feel secure using a Tablet PC?
	What were the difficulties perceived
Final	Would you like to complement with any impression?

The chosen location was a meeting room at UFRGS, with indirect lighting, with the participants positioned around a table. They were handed a TPC with the operational system Android 3.1 and a 10.1 inch screen with several applications in the initial interface (Fig. 1).

Fig. 1. Initial Interface with Applications

The interview was recorded on video and audio, with the information being later transcribed, analyzed and interpreted, as presented in the final considerations of this paper.

7   Research

It was first requested of the participants to talk about the diagnostic of their disability and how they classified their functional vision. All that information was relevant, despite all of them having complied with the research selection criteria, since it is the functional vision that determines the quality of sight and gives them autonomy in their actions. Furthermore, since sensitivity to light was one of the characteristics that could interfere in the interview results, it was possible to adjust the position in the environment of the participants who indicated this characteristic.

Of the five participants, three are sensitive to light, one has "poor functional vision" (quoted from the participant) which made many autonomous actions inviable. All five participants wanted to have a TPC, as they imagined it a being an alternative technology for reading and navigating in the virtual environment without the difficulties perceived in other devices. Only one participant had the opportunity of handling a TPC before this interview, but he added that the experience lasted only a few minutes.

They were asked to turn on the TPC. In the beginning, none of them managed to perform the action, not even together, without the intervention of the moderator. The on/off button is fitted to side of the product (Fig. 2) with the volume button next to it, both with the same texture and color of the product, and the on/off button must be pressed and held for a few seconds to be activated. The indication that it is turning on is provided by sound and moving image, but two participants pressed the volume button together with the on/off button, muting it and making it impossible for the participants to identify that is was on. Additionally, they did not perceive the moving image because it was too quick.

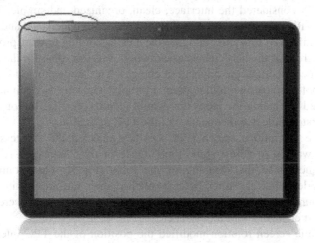

Fig. 2. Location of the On/Off Button

As to the colors and shapes of the application icons located on the initial interface, the color contrast was considered strong, but they could not understand the details in most of them or identify what was written below each one, since the font was too small. The camera icon was clearly identified, as was the Facebook icon (Fig. 3) that in addition to being located immediately on the interface, all five perceived the white, "f" over the blue background. The distance observed between the participants' eyes and the TPC interface was of 3cm to 10cm.

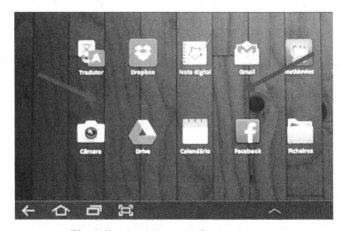

Fig. 3. Facebook Icon and Camera Icon

They noticed the lack of an expanded legend for the icons, since there it the name of the application just below them and activation is done by touching, not with a mouse. They all considered the interface, clean, organized and simple. They noticed that the icons with a ¼ of the screen in size were easier to understand and identify.

They were all asked to try to configure the TPC according to their profile from the "Definitions". Two of the participants asked where was the zoom for the initial screen to be able to better follow the navigation choices. The moderator told them that the system does not have its own initial zoom. For approximately five minutes they were all concentrated in finding the icons that would identify the "Definitions", and in the end the moderator indicated the location of the TPC definitions.

Once in the definitions screen (Fig. 4), they selected the "Accessibility" item because they wanted to adjust some tools. Once in the "Accessibility" screen, the participants questioned the meaning of the tools (Fig.5). They found the terms difficult to understand, and after being explained their meanings with the existing tutorial, the found that they were not the accessibility resources they were looking for, such as contrast change, zoom font size, etc.

The automatic screen rotation modified the position of the TPC interface several times due to the movement the participants made to better adapt the viewing of information, which led them to lose the point they were focusing on and having to start the action from the beginning. The moderator indicated the path to turn off the selection of that tool.

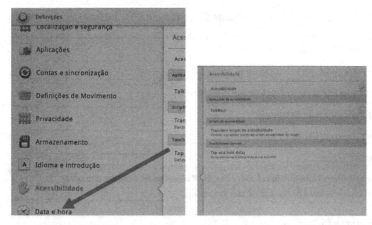

Fig. 4. Definitions of Configuration and Accessibility Tools

To navigate in the virtual environment, it was necessary to indicate the icon. In the initial interface, they did not find the zoom feature, it was only perceived once they had chosen a site th navigate. They considered the "new page tab" easy to understand and intuitive due to the contrast between the white fonts on the black background and the shape, but the size of the font prevented them from reading what was written. They were pleased with the contrasts, zoom and readability of the information on the sites.

As to the questions related to the closure of the interview, it was decide to place the statements in a table (Table 2) to related them with the usability goals referred to in this paper. Following the presentation of Table 2, the results and authors' considerations will be presented.

Table 2. Statements and Usability Goals

Statements	Action Stage
"this is difficult"	Interaction Intuitive
"it will be no use trying to use this kind of technology"	
"I found a button, pressed it and nothing happened"	
"oh, this button must be held and I think it turned on because it vibrated"	
"application distribution is good, clean"	Learning Capability and Memorization Capability
"I would need to know the icons beforehand to be able to memorize the shapes of these ones"	
"The contrast would help me more., but it can't have too much contrast"	
"I can't identify what this is and have no idea of what it is"	
"can I click here?"	
"to expand do I have to go to configurations?"	

Table 2. (*continued*)

"where are the configurations?"	
"the contrast is good, but it is difficult to arrive here"	
"it does not give any security in choosing the action"	Effectiveness
"words of difficult understanding"	And
"that is not the accessibility I wanted to find!"	Efficiency
"translate this!"	
"the screen position change when I move the TCP is not good, because it undoes my mental image related to the path I was following"	Security And Protection
"I need help to lock it"	Against Mistakes
"the first time round it is difficult, but worse is to find out on my own"	
"how long would it take me to learn?"	
"some things here are accessible, but how do I get to these accessible things?"	Trust
"it's a matter of lack of autonomy"	Autonomy
"too intuitive"	
"it's too sensitive"	

8   Results

According to the statements given, it was possible to map the usability goals that could help with better navigation by considering each one of the problems perceived by that user.

The difficulties found to turn on the TPC occurred due to the formal oversimplification of the product components. It would be possible to improve this interaction by simply modifying one element in these components, such as texture, button color or shape, together with the automatic response to user action (in this case "press the button"). Interaction with users could be taken into account without interfering with the formal aspect of the product and its components. In this case, it resulted in frustration of and questioning by the user of his or her autonomy.

The initial interface proved to have optimistic learning and memorization qualities, since the participants appreciated the lay out of the elements and their contrasts. The possibility of using the zoom tool in this page could better help them to choose the applications, the application icons could have the option of increasing their size to make readability easier, or the legends below the icon could have larger sized fonts. Such improvement could reduce the search for the applications and increase the certain choices by these users.

The accessibility resources present in the TPC were seen as "lacking efficiency" and not at all "effective", since they did not perform what they were apparently proposed to do, communication of their objectives did not have an accessible language, did not meet the expectations of the participants and caused disappointment. The lack of resources such as zoom, increase font and contrast in the item "accessibility", led to questioning about where those resources are actually located. They could be highlighted in the initial interface, thus ensuring a minimum navigation in the system with security, initiative and sureness of action. In this case, it was noticed that the insecurity caused by the uncertainty about the actions was present throughout the interview.

The participants finished the interview with a rather different idea of the TPC from the initial one. They all questioned the adaptation time they would require to gain a minimum interaction with the product. It was observed that there was a lack of autonomy in this interaction.

9   Conclusion

The objective of this research was to list the issues related to the digital inclusion or persons with low vision disability in the new technologies. The intention of gathering the data that would point to possible problems in this interaction was only attained through the effort and patience of the participants involved.

Considering the significant figure of 35 million persons with low vision who could be benefiting from cutting edge technologies, such as TPC, so that they may be included in the digital and educational media, it can be noticed that there is a need for more actions that would consider them within the scope of not only existing technologies, but also where new technologies are concerned.

With an understanding of how persons with low vision disabilities communicate with their surroundings, what their expectations are and the actual limitations imposed by the physical, digital, and especially social media, it is possible to intervene in favor of the quality of life of those persons through the use of the accessible competences and possibilities.

A proposal for the future is to further the studies on this interaction by composing researches that are representative of the population of users with this trait through individual interviews based on the usability tests and user experience.

References

1. Hassan, M.H., Al-Sadi, J.A.: New Mobile Learning Adaptation Model. International Journal of Interactive Mobile Technologies (iJIM) 3(4) (2009) ISSN: 1865-7923
2. Madan, V.: 6 Reasons Tablets are ready for the classroom. McGraw-Hill Higer Education eLabs. Mashable Tech, NY (2012),
   http://mashable.com/2011/05/16/tablets-education/
   (acess: April 04, 2012)
3. Ismail, I., Idrus, R.M., Ziden, A.A., Rosli, M.: Adoption of Mobile Learning Among Distance Education Students in Universiti Sains Malaysia. International Journal of Interactive Mobile Technologies (iJIM) 4(2) (2010) ISSN: 1865-7923

4. Nielsen, J.: Connected Devices: How We Use Tablets in the U.S. The Nielsen Company (2011),
   `http://blog.nielsen.com/nielsenwire/online_mobile/connected-devices-how-we-use-tablets-in-the-u-s/` (acess: October 02, 2012)
5. Kulpa, C.C.: A contribuição de um modelo de cores na usabilidade das interfaces computacionais de usuários de baixa visão., UFRGS, Originalmente apresentada como Dissertação de Mestrado, Porto Alegre – RS (2009)
6. IBGE (Instituto Brasileiro de Geografia e Estatística), Censo Demográfico 2010: Resultados Gerais da Amostra, Rio de Janeiro: Ministério do Planejamento, Orçamento e Gestão (2012)
7. Scolari, C.A., Aguado, J.M., Feijó, C.: Mobile Media: towards a definition and taxonomy of contents and applications. International Journal of Interactive Mobile Technologies (iJIM) 6(2) (2012) ISSN: 1865-7923
8. Apple Inc. Develop apps for ipad, `https://developer.apple.com/ipad/sdk/` (acess: May 15, 2012)
9. Preece, J., Rogers, Y., Sharp, H.: Design de Interação: além da interação homem-computador". Bookman, Porto Alegre (2005)
10. Kouroupetroglou, C., Tektonidis, D., Koumpis, A., Ignatiadis, I.: Mainstreaming of Mobile Assistive Technology: Experts' Thoughts and Opinions. International Journal of Interactive Mobile Technologies (iJIM) 6(1) (January 2012)
11. SIGCHI, "Human Factors in Computing Systems". In: Bauersfeld, P., Bennett, J., Lynch, G. (eds.) Proceedings ACM CHI 1992 Conference, Monterey, CA, May 03-07 (1992)
12. Rocha, H.V., Baranauskas, M.C.C.: Design e avaliação de interfaces humano-computador. NIED/UNICAMP, Campinas (2003)
13. Cybis, W., Betiol, A.H., Faust, R.: Ergonomia e Usabilidade: Conhecimento, Métodos e Aplicações. Novatec, São Paulo (2007)
14. Nielsen, J., Loranger, H.: Usabilidade na Web: projetando Websites com qualidade. Elsevier, RJ (2007)
15. Faye, E.E.: El Enfermo com Déficit Visual – experiência clínica em adultos y niños. Editorial Científico – Médica, Barcelona (1972)
16. Paschoal, C.L.L.: Educação visual. Instituto Benjamin Constant, Área da Deficiência Visual, Rio de Janeiro. Originalmente apresentada como Dissertação de Mestrado (1993)
17. Lima, N.M.: Legislação Federal Básica na Área da Pessoa Portadora de Deficiência. Compilação. Brasília: Secretaria Especial dos Direitos Humanos, Coordenadoria Nacional para Integração da Pessoa Portadora de Deficiência, Sistema Nacional de Informações sobre Deficiência (2007)
18. Baranauskas, M.C.C., Souza, C.S.: Desafio 4: Acesso participativo e universal do cidadão brasileiro ao conhecimento, Computação Brasil, Porto Alegre, vol. 23, Set./Out. (2006)

Relationship between Elements of the Usability and Emotions Reported after Use: A Mexican Case

Irma Cecilia Landa-Ávila[1] and Lilia Roselia Prado León[2]

[1] Maestría en Ergonomía con orientación en Diseño,
Universidad de Guadalajara, Guadalajara, MEX
clandavila@gmail.com
[2] Centro de Investigaciones en Ergonomía,
Universidad de Guadalajara, Guadalajara, MEX
aililpleon@gmail.com

Abstract. This paper presents the study of Mexican users of design software to find out if there is any relationship between any of the elements of usability and emotions reported after using said product.

A usability test was conducted with inexperienced users who had to perform three tasks in sequential order, under a spoken protocol. After each task, participants responded to the SMEQ mental effort questionnaires, the ASQ satisfaction questionnaire and used the PrEMO tool to report their emotions and feelings while using the software. Subsequently, video recordings of the tests were reviewed to find the level and quality of completed tasks and the number of errors.

We found that there is a relationship between some of the usability metrics and the emotions of the users, which is manifested more significantly between subjective usability metrics. The perception of the perceived mental effort turned out to be the element with the biggest relationship to the reporting of emotions, however, this relationship appears to affect both positive and negative emotions and some assumptions point to factors such as the sudden increase in the complexity of a task, which increases the force with which negative emotions are reported.

Keywords: Web Usability, User's Emotions, Mexican Usability Test, Software Design.

1 Introduction

The importance of emotions as an integral element of the user experience is being widely considered in current studies of Human Computer Interaction (HCI). It is, however, considered a secondary aspect. The role of the elements of usability such as efficiency, effectiveness and satisfaction still positions itself as the most important and reliable for the study of the use of products.

Emotions during product use have been considered in recent studies such as in Brave and Nass (2002) who have described some emotion metrics and their

A. Marcus (Ed.): DUXU 2014, Part I, LNCS 8517, pp. 285–295, 2014.
© Springer International Publishing Switzerland 2014

application at a more theoretical level. Other approaches have shown that humans are more efficient and have managed to solve creative problems when they are happy (Hirt, ER et alt, 1996) and that emotion is linked to acceptance and user satisfaction and can greatly impact purchase intentions (Erevelles, 1998 S. Martino, et alt 2006).

Many professionals in cognitive studies argue that it is impossible to act or think without entering (at least subconsciously) into our emotions. Until recently, HCI research tended to focus on the ease of use of the cognitive system, in which the topics of greatest interest were related to ease of use, efficiency, ease of learning and error handling. These cognitive factors are certainly of great importance to HCI, but the feelings of users interacting with the system are equally important, as stated Barnes and Thagard (1996) in their study. They argued that emotions interact together with knowledge in order to achieve a certain goal.

The objective of this study is to discover whether there is any relationship between the traditional elements of usability (effectiveness, efficiency and satisfaction) of a piece of design software with emotions reported by inexperienced users after using the product.

2   Background

2.1   Usability

The International Organization for Standardization (ISO) has defined usability from two perspectives. The first one is in the ISO / IEC 9126, which states: "Usability refers to the ability of software to be understood, learned, used and being attractive to the user, within specific conditions of use". This definition emphasizes the internal and external product attributes, which contribute to its functionality and efficiency. In contrast, in the ISO / IEC 9241 we find the following: "Usability is the degree to which a product can be used by specified users to achieve specified goals with effectiveness, efficiency and satisfaction in a specific context of use".

In their study Bevan and Macleond (1994) found that the nature of the scope required in the study of usability depends on the context of use of the product. Bevan said that usability is a feature of the system as a whole, that is "the quality of its use in a certain context.

In the study by Frøkjær, Hertzum and Hornbæk's (2000), correlations between the three aspects of usability are analyzed. They found that the correlation between effectiveness and efficiency it is so weak, that it cannot be used for practical. They determined that those three measurements should be considered as an independent aspect of usability, but all must be included and evaluated in the test.

Sauro and Dumas (2009) conducted a review of the most common satisfaction tests. Among the reviewed instruments, the scale of the Subjective Mental Effort Question (SMEQ) showed the best performance, it was easy to learn and highly correlated with other measurements, so their suggestions pointed at its use on other post-test scales.

In the study, Lewis (1991) concluded that the three items in the ASQ questionnaire can greatly condense the results of post-test assessments by adding up the results.

Another conclusion was that ASQ is sensitive enough to be used in usability studies, and that its concurrence validity in each of the scenarios was equally good.

For this study, a usability test was performed with voice protocol, and at the end of each task the SMEQ and ASQ questionnaires will be applied. Subsequently, the level and quality with which a task was completed will be recorded, in addition to the number of errors; allowing us to offer a comprehensive assessment of usability.

2.2   Emotions

Emotion is a psychophysiological reaction to certain stimuli related to needs, goals or individual concerns. Emotions are affected by innate and learned influences, with invariant features and others that depend on the group or culture to which they belong (Levenson, 1994).

While evoked emotions are idiosyncratic, there are universal patterns that can be identified in the essential process of how these emotions are evoked. Usually, the duration of an emotion lasts merely seconds or minutes (Ekman, 1994), so reporting of emotions must be performed immediately after they are generated.

In the field of HCI, the interpretation of emotions focuses on emotional responses (feelings) that are assigned to an interface during and after their use. It is believed that emotions are intentional, because they comprise and involve a relationship between the person experiencing it and a particular object (Frijda, 1994).Also, people are able to identify the object causing the emotion (Ekman 1992).

2.3   Usability and Emotions

The role of emotions in HCI studies begins to establish the need for instruments capable of measuring with the same rigour as other mechanisms from which traditional usability metrics are obtained. It is said that an emotion always includes evaluating how the use of an object can harm or benefit a person (Arnold, 1960) and that evaluation is always immediate and direct in a positive or negative sense.

In the study by Agarwal and Meyer (2009) compared the difference that existed between the tools to measure emotions verbally and nonverbally. They established beforehand that verbal tools had some limitations, including the fact of dependence on language, and users having to remember how they felt and ascribe a term to it. Meanwhile nonverbal methods attempt to capture unconscious emotional responses and incorporate a certain amount of vagueness appropriate for the study of emotions. They concluded that a positive user experience cannot be expressed only in terms of usability metrics and that it is valuable to study emotions, because they supplement the evaluation of interfaces, since it allowed them to know whether there were differences with standard usability metrics that they would not notice.

2.4   Methods for Measuring Emotions

Emotions are entities of multiple components. In relation to that, tools for reporting emotions can be classified into one of four classes with respect to the measurement components. (Table 1)

Table 1. Measuring Instruments and recorded components

Requirements	Measuring Instruments			
	Emotional expression	Psychological Reactions	Feelings	Subjective
Set product emotions	-	-	+	+
Found emotions	+	+	+	
Transcultural	-		-	+
Equipment / experience			+	+

It is observed that no instrument is capable of measuring all four components. Despite this shared drawback there is a kind of instrument that has some important advantages over the others: the instruments of self-reporting (subjective), they are capable of measuring a mixture of emotions beyond the basic emotions, such tools are in turn subdivided into verbal and nonverbal methods.

PrEMO. The acronym of Product Emotion Measurement is an instrument specifically designed to measure the emotions of any product. Developed by Pieter Desmet (2005), it is based on 14 animations of a cartoon character, seven of them pleasant (desire, pleasant surprise, inspiration, fun, admiration, contentment and fascination), and seven unpleasant (anger, contempt, disgust, unpleasant surprise, dissatisfaction, disappointment and boredom).In the validation process, two emotions failed the test, so they were removed from the instrument.

It measures various and mixed emotions and does not require participants to verbalize their emotions, avoiding excessive mental effort, since it was designed to be fast and intuitive to use. The visual display is accompanied by a body animation of a character and a sound that lasts approximately one second. Participants are required to report their emotional response to the twelve animations by interacting and placing each of them on a scale of five values ranging from 0 for no feeling to 4 for a strong feeling.

3   Methodology

3.1   Participants

Recruitment was used to obtain participants for convenience. The exclusion criteria were being older than 18 and not having previous experience with design software.

It featured a sample of 32 participants (11 men and 21 women, mean age of 21 years and a standard deviation of 3.9).

3.2   Materials

The test was conducted in a room with two computers, one for the use of the software, in which the user performed the tasks of the test, and a program that allowed videotaping the test for later review; in the computer the PrEMO tool for reporting emotions was installed.

Reporting PrEMO Emotions
To report emotions, the PrEMO system was installed on a computer with internet connection. The tool consists of a character showing 12 different emotions, which should be evaluated through a 5-point scale by the participants after each task, the range was from 0 if no emotion was felt and it goes up to 4 if they felt it strongly.

SMEQ Scale
It is also known as the effort grading scale. After each task the moderator conducted the Spanish version of the SMEQ questionnaire. This scale has a range of 1 to 150 and nine labels from "not at all difficult to do" to "extremely difficult to do."

ASQ Scale
Self-reported satisfaction questionnaire, it was performed at the end of each of the tasks comprising 3 statements regarding satisfaction with the time taken to perform the task, the ease with which it is performed and help to do so. Here, the participant could respond by using a scale that ranges from 1 for strongly agree until 7 for strongly disagrees.

Time
Each of the tasks was assigned a maximum time for completion, a stopwatch signaled when the time was up.

Number of Errors
After the test, a review of each of the usability tests was performed and a count of detected errors was made. An error was considered as any action that did not respond to the user's intention. It was not considered wrong to follow an order, to conduct a search or to visually scan the interface.

Level and Quality Completed Tasks
A checklist for each of the tasks was made. This list was made according to a subdivision by individual actions, which were assigned a score relative to the complexity they had. Each task could have a score 100 if it had been fully completed with quality and accuracy.

Support for Tasks
Aid was provided for each item, in which some instructions concerning the tasks are listed, participants were delivered a full-scale model of the design that they had to make.

3.3   Tasks

The test was made of three tasks, which should always be made in the same order, due to the learning that participants could obtain from the preceding task.

- Task 1: In the first task the participant had to make a red square of 8 cm and a blue circle of 5 cm in diameter. The maximum time to complete the task was 3 minutes.
- Task 2: The second task was to make a business card, this design required to make rectangles, enter text in specific sizes and place some elements that were provided as input. The maximum task time was 6 minutes.
- Task 3: For the third task the participant was asked to do a poster. Some of the specific actions that had to be done were making boxes, changing colours, copying items, changing size, writing text, and making blueprints. The maximum task time was 10 minutes.

3.4   Procedure

At the beginning of the session participants were informed about the dynamics of the test, permission to videotape the test was requested and an initial questionnaire that collected demographic data was applied, also one for similar design software.

Each of the tasks was explained just before beginning, task aids were given and questions concerning the task were answered. Questions regarding how to do it using software were not answered.

The participants that were performing the task had to talk out loud at all times and they had to mention the actions performed or intended to perform. If participants showed little verbal activity, the moderator made some questions during the course of the tests.

At the end of the task or the maximum end time the ASQ and SMEQ questionnaires were delivered. Immediately thereafter, the PrEMO tool was used for reporting the emotions of each of the tasks, the participants had unlimited time to assign a value to each of the characters used.

Once task 3 concluded, a final questionnaire was administered in which participants were asked about their overall perception and satisfaction with the software. The test had a maximum duration of 45 minutes.

Subsequently, a review of each of usability test for a count of errors per task was conducted. Also, a complete checklist regarding the level and quality of completed tasks was made.

4   Results

The results of the usability tests showed the following results in each of the following areas:

4.1   Efficiency

The metrics considered for efficiency were time and perception of perceived mental effort. Due to the characteristics of the test, each task was analyzed independently. The results are shown in Table 2.

Table 2. Time results and SMEQ by task

Test Tasks	Time			SMEQ		
	Minimum	Maximum	Mean	Minimum	Maximum	Mean
Task 1	79 seg.	300 seg	155 seg. SD 35.9	0	15	28 SD 25.9
Task 2	360 seg.	360 seg.	360 seg. SD 0	10	142	58 SD 35.95
Task 3	298 seg.**	600 seg.	578 seg SD 74.61	20	150	79 SD 34

**All minimum results of task 3 were obtained with participants who decided to abandon the task.

4.2   Effectiveness

For the effectiveness metrics, two metrics were considered, the number of errors and the level and quality of completed tasks.

Table 3. Results of errors, level and quality of completed tasks

Test Tasks	Mistakes			Level and quality tasks		
	Minimum	Maximum	Mean	Minimum	Maximum	Mean
Task 1	0	8	3.2. SD 2.12	0	100	55.4 SD 29.9
Task 2	1	13	6.1 SD 2.9	0	60	30.5 SD 17.2
Task 3	2	21	10.1 SD 4.9	0	48	18.9 SD 12.9

4.3   Satisfaction

Satisfaction was reported by users through the ASQ scale, the scale value of 1 was assigned to "strongly agree" for satisfaction, and 7 stood for "strongly disagree." (table 4).

Table 4. Percived satisfaction results (ASQ)

2	Usability Satisfaction			Time satisfaction			Material support satisfaction		
	Minimum	Maximum	Mean	Minimum	Maximum	Mean	Minimum	Maximum	Mean
Task 1	1	7	3.88 SD 1.8	1	7	4.97 SD 1.8	1	7	5.41 SD 1.8
Task 2	1	7	3.38 SD 1.9	1	7	4.84 SD 1.7	1	7	5.31 SD 1.8
Task3	1	7	2.56 SD 1.9	1	7	2.59 SD 2	1	7	3.03 SD 2.1

4.4 Relationship between the Elements of Usability

Data was analyzed to find whether there is a relationship between the various metrics that make up usability. The results obtained from the tasks are presented using a bivariate correlation analysis in Table 5, where the three most significant relationships are shown (significant at the 0.01 level correlations).

Table 5. Obtained Correlations with the usability elements

Test Tasks	Related elements		
	Element	In relation with	Coefficient
Task 1	Mistakes	Time	0.764
	Quality and completed tasks level	Time	-0.723
	Satisfaction usability	Perceived mental effort	0.672
Task 2	Satisfaction usability	Perceived mental effort	0.790
	Satisfaction time	Satisfaction usability	0.611
	Satisfaction time	Perceived mental effort	0.495
Task 3	Satisfaction usability	Perceived mental effort	0.600
	Satisfaction time	Satisfaction usability	0.490
	Satisfaction time	Perceived mental effort	0.440

4.5 Emotions

The PrEMO study yielded a report of the emotions per task. In Table 6 the 3 main emotions expressed by participants are listed.

Table 6. Main task emotions expressed by participants

Test Tasks	More strongly emotions factors reported by users		
	Emotions	Scale Value (Frecuency)	Average
Task 1	Fascination	0 (2) + 1 (5) + 2 (6) + 3 (11) + 4 (8)	2.59
	Joy	0 (7) + 1 (7) + 2 (1) + 3 (10) + 4 (7)	2.09
	Satisfaction	0 (6) + 1 (6) + 2 (8) + 3 (6) + 4 (6)	2
Task 2	Fascination	0 (4) + 1 (5) + 2 (4) + 3 (13) + 4 (6)	2.38
	Dissatisfaction	0 (6) + 1 (4) + 2 (10) + 3 (5) + 4 (7)	2.09
	Hope	0 (11) + 1 (2) + 2 (8) + 3 (5) + 4 (6)	1.78
Task 3	Dissatisfaction	0 (6) + 1 (4) + 2 (5) + 3 (7) + 4 (10)	2.34
	Fascination	0 (2) + 1 (6) + 2 (11) + 3 (7) + 4 (6)	2.28
	Hope	0 (6) + 1 (6) + 2 (5) + 3 (9) + 4 (6)	2.09

4.6   Value of the Elements of Usability and Emotions

The analysis of the correlation data, detected the following relationships between the elements of usability and emotions. Table 7 shows the three main task relationships between the elements of usability and emotions reported by users.

Table 7. Primary relationships of usability and emotions elements

Test Tasks	Related elements		
	Element	Emotions	Coefficient
Task 1	Level and quality tasks	Satisfaction (+)	0.660
	Satisfaction usability	Disgust (-)	0.510
	Level and quality tasks	Dissatisfaction (-)	-0.468
	Level and quality tasks	Pride (+)	446
	Satisfaction of time	Disgust (-)	0.444
Task 2	Satisfaction usability	Sadness (-)	0.672
	Perceived mental effort	Sadness (-)	0.666
	Perceived mental effort	Shame (-)	0.650
	Perceived mental effort	Disgust (-)	0.599
	Satisfaction usability	Dissatisfaction (-)	0.589
Task 3 **	Number of mistakes	Pride (+)	-0.457
	Perceived mental effort	Satisfaction (+)	-0.445
	Number of mistakes	Joy (+)	-0.435 *
	Number of mistakes	Satisfaction (+)	- 0.372 *

* Significant correlation at the level 0.05   ** In task 3 were detected only four relations

5   Conclusion

This study allowed us to analyze the results of a usability test and report emotions of users towards a piece of design software.

The first part of the analysis of the results shows that there is a rather weak relationship between some usability metrics such as satisfaction with the ease of use and time (ASQ Questionnaire) and perceived mental effort (SMEQ questionnaire).

The relationship between the number of errors and time, as well as the one concerning the level and quality of task completion time, is worth noting. These two relationships are the only ones considered objective metrics such as time and error count, which suggests that relationships between any methods of self-reporting made after using the product are more frequent.

Similarly, we can assert that the relations of objective metrics were only detected in the first task, in which the time for completion is less, probably because with an increasing time of task completion, the participant loses track of time and that stops it from being a crucial factor that is reflected in the methods that use self-reporting.

Also, the relationship between traditional usability metrics and emotions yields little conclusive results that would allow us to establish the anatomy of the relationship.

Again we find that over 71% of the relationships found were produced with usability metrics, such as the self-reported perceived mental effort and perceived satisfaction that it takes to complete a task, it may be that once the participant externalized some aspects of the test, s/he makes a general assessment of the experience with the use of the product, which is replicated in the other self-reporting tools.

In the second task we can note that relations with greater significance are expressed in negative emotions, although usability metrics were very similar to the ones in task number three, but varied considerably in comparison with the first task, especially concerning the mental effort perceived. This sharp increase in the complexity of the task seems to have had a strong negative impact on the emotions of the users, a phenomenon that is not seen in the third task, because despite being considered an extremely difficult task to do, participants reported emotions such as pride or satisfaction, emotions likely to be associated with the fact that they had completed the usability test in full.

We can state that if there is a relationship between some of the metrics that make up usability and emotions of the users, this is observed more significantly in subjective measurements belonging to self-reporting, where the perception of mental effort turned out to be one of the elements that bears a closer relation to the report of emotions. This relationship appears to affect both emotions, positive and negative, and some assumptions suggest that other factors are the ones that increase negative emotions, such as the sudden increase in the complexity of the task.

6   Discussion

The relationship of the elements of usability with emotional factors has mixed and somewhat ambiguous results that prevent us from establishing its invariance.

The tendency of emotions to show a more pronounced relationship to subjective measurements scales as the ASQ or SMEQ allows us to raise the possibility that the relationship occurs not because of the use of the product. Rather, the externalization of users of any judgment, under any method of self-reporting, is the variable that we must pay more attention to.

There is a need for studies in which self-reporting instruments are controlled. A possible effect derived from the order of delivery of the tools must be considered. In this study, the SMEQ questionnaire recorded the strongest relationships with emotions, and it was the first method used. The variable of the order of delivery of the questionnaires must be considered and one must rethink the relationships found as a result of that.

Similarly, the context of the users must be considered in order to enhance the contribution of the study's findings. Testing expert users, who have used software as a tool would help to determine the evolving relationship between emotions and usability or, alternatively, whether the relationships are fleeting and random.

The relationship between the elements of software usability and emotions reported by users should be explored in order to clarify these questions.

References

1. Arnold, M.B.: Emotion and personality. Colombia University Press, New York (1960)
2. Agarwal, A., Meyer, A.: Beyond usability: evaluating emotional response as an integral part of the user experience. In: CHI 2009, Extended Abstracts on Human Factors in Computing Systems, pp. 2919–2930 (2009)
3. Bevan, N.: Measuring usability as quality of use. Software Quality Journal 4, 115–150 (1995)
4. Barnes, A., Thagard, P.: Emotional decisions. In: Proceedings of the Eighteenth Annual Conference of the Cognitive Science Society, University of California, pp. 426–429 (1996)
5. Bevan, N., Macleod, M.: Usability measurement in context. Behaviour and Information Technology 13, 132–145 (1994)
6. Brave, S., Nass, C.: Emotion in human-computer interaction. In: Jacko, J., Sears, A. (eds.) Handbook of Human-computer Interaction, pp. 251–271. Lawrence Erlbaum (2002)
7. Desmet, P.: Measuring emotion: development and application of an instrument to measure emotional responses to products. Funology, 111–123 (2005)
8. Desmet, P.M.A.: Faces of Product Pleasure: 25 Positive Emotions in Human-Product Interactions. International Journal of Design 6(2), 1–29 (2012)
9. Erevelles, S.: The role of affect in marketing. Journal of Business Research 42, 199–215 (1998)
10. Ekman, P.: An Argument for Basic Emotions. Cognition and Emotion 6, 169–200 (1992)
11. Ekman, P.: Moods, emotions, and traits. The nature of emotions, fundamental questions, pp. 56–58. Oxford University Press, Oxford (1994)
12. Frijda, N.H.: Varieties of affect: emotions and episodes, moods, and sentiments. The nature of emotion, fundamental questions, pp. 59–67. Oxford University Press, Oxford (1994)
13. Frøkjær, E., Hertzum, M., Hornbæk, K.: Measuring Usability: Are Effectiveness, Efficiency, and Satisfaction Really Correlated? In: Proceedings of the ACM CHI 2000 Conference on Human Factors in Computing Systems, pp. 345–352. The Hague, The Netherlands Press, New York (2000) (preprint version)
14. Hirt, E.R., Melton, R.J., McDonals, H.E., Harackiewicz, J.M.: Processing goals, task interest, and the mood-performance relationship: A mediational analysis. Journal of Personality and Social Psychology (1996)
15. Levenson, R.: Human emotion: a functional view. In: The Nature of Emotion, pp. 123–126. Oxford University Press (1994)
16. Lewis, J.: Psychometric evaluation of an after-scenario questionnaire for computer usability studies: The ASQ. SIGCHI Bulletin 23(1), 78–81 (1991)
17. Sauro, J., Dumas, J.: Comparison of Three One-Question, Post-Task Usability Questionnaires. In: CHI 2009 (2009)
18. Sauro, J., Lewis, J.: Correlations among Prototypical Usability Metrics: Evidence for the Construct of Usability. In: CHI 2009 (2009)

Experimental Research in Applying Generative Design and 3D Printers in User Participating Design

Lin-Chien James Lee and Ming-Huang Lin

National Chiao Tung University, Institute of Applied Arts, Taiwan
lin_chien2001@yahoo.com.tw, ludwiglin@mail.nctu.edu.tw

Abstract. This research applied an open structure of generative design in order to provide parametric sliders for users to adjust a digital model under the designer's plan. Moreover, the design outcome can be printed immediately using 3D printing technology, to experiment with users' preferences and see the effects of generative design in modifying pattern, regular/irregular and detail transformations on a product. Three types of feature modification on i-phone4 case were chosen as simulations by 3 design experts. Five experienced and five young designers were asked to manipulate a digital generative design model as they want. Then 2D rendering images and 3D printed mockups were presented for subjects to compare with their original design. The result demonstrated that experienced and young designers both can recognized their work in 3D print mockups. Experienced designers can use the limited tool to make distinct outcomes for more satisfaction form tan subjects. Young designers expected to obtain 3D printed mockup to help their design decision in design process.

Keywords: Generative design, Design process, Grasshopper.

1 Introduction

As aided tool, s computer and software help designers rapidly verify ideas through 2D or 3D models rapidly. Nowadays minimalism has becomes a representation of Apple's style and the imitation of followers has led products to look the same. Customers tend to focus on accessories to add personality in their product shapes. The trend of 3D printing such as MakerBot's thingiverse(www.makerbot.com) free platform, it has opened a door for users to make almost anything themselves and share their creations with others in open space. Many hardware and software companies in different industries are aware of the trend, from the auto industry's BMW to the mobile industry's Nokia both of whom have announced that they will develop open source component and data for customers to make parts of their own. As a leading software company, Autodesk kept developing free and easy to use 3D software app, the 123D series, on pad devices in order to satisfy non-the demands of users without a design background. This trend could contribute to 3D print and generative design related software support. In the design profession, the rises of cheap 3D printers in recent years have led designers to be able to make design decisions through real models in the early stages of the design process. Furthermore, generative design

A. Marcus (Ed.): DUXU 2014, Part I, LNCS 8517, pp. 296–307, 2014.
© Springer International Publishing Switzerland 2014

offers the user an excellent pattern design tool. However, has the new developed tool and interface been accepted by designers? Could it fulfill the demands of design job? These are the concerns of this research.

1.1   Background

In a previous study, Cooperative Generative Design Method (CGDM) was proposed. It demonstrated that industrial designers and generative designers working together could help each other focus on what they are good at. An industrial designer could concentrate on shape grammar definition and think about what kind of shape or style they like to add to products. On the other hand, the generative designer's duty is to define the solution space given current conditions, such as electronic and engineering demands, then considering shape grammar to build up digital parametric models on Rhino software as platform and Grasshopper plugin as interface. Then the industrial designer could manipulate sliders or input parameters to control the digital model to acquire the perfect shape that they want. The results got many positive feedbacks. This research is based on it to explore more advanced experiments.

1.2   Purpose

3D printer rapid prototype technique was used in this research to explore the accuracy of representation in 2D rendering pictures and 3D printing models when a designer is dealing with shape thinking and expression. Moreover, patterns on the back surface of handset cover were defined as design details. Computer generated random calculated patterns and human controlled pattern generative models were proposed to test out of computer random calculated shapes or human controlled shapes which one was suitable to represent designers' idea.

2   Related Works

2.1   Mass Customization and User Participation

Mass customization and user participation related researches had achieved a lot in the B2C field by management scholars. Piller, F. and Walcher, D., 2004, used Toolkit software to allow hundreds of customers to participate in choosing watch styles. Users could follow steps to select many kinds of dial plates, indicators, belts, colors, textures and materials. They used quantitative research and statistical methods to prove that target groups would pay more for purchasing their participated results. However, the process was still featured on a computer screen where the groups would select a designed module and combine the parts together. There was still a question whether the final product and screenshot were the same as the customer's imagination while they are using Toolkit. This research invited users to participate in a real design process to discover the users' though process when they were manipulating generative digital models and compared 2D rendering and 3D printing outcomes to know which one is close to users' imagination. The current question in customization is that when users have a chance to choose their own design does the meaning and story of the design though process from designer remain?

2.2   CGRM

Dav, Singh V. and Gu, N. 2012, compared Cellular automata, Genetic algorithms, Shape grammars, Lindenmayer systems and Swarm intelligence through background technique, design point of view and system constructive factors. They proposed an integrated generative design structure, according to Dav, Singh V., because conceptual demands are different in varied design situations, from up to down or from down to up, a flexible generative technique can be used to get better results. The point of view is similar to this research.

Hsiao S.W., 2010, Hsiao, K.A. and Chen, L.L., 2006, Chen, K.S. 2006, Lin, M.H, 2003, inspected shape structure through genetic algorithm, components, morphing and Kansei engineering individually. Their stimulations are rough 2D or 3D components database. Subjects could not adjust details as real as design jobs. However, generative design tools offered designers a chance to check shape changes directly. It made research and experiments closer to real design situations. This research proposed an agent-based model that generative designer following design experts' shape grammar to build up generative digital models for industrial designers to manipulate. Currently, CGDM is more suitable for applying in shape refine processes for routine design job. For concept extend process of non-routine design jobs, CGDM process needs to be reorganized and test.

2.3   3D Printer

3D printing is not new technique, there were some scholars and engineers devoted to computer-aided manufacturing who used digital models to produce real objects directly while computer aided design was still in its early stage. Consequently, the rapid prototype technique has been developing to this today, many companies developed their own material and methods to produce things, such as Stereolithography apparatus (SLA), Selective laser sintering (SLS), Fused deposition modeling (FDM) and so on. Most of the technique patents were held by companies. Yan. X. and Gu. P. 1996, indicated that in early stages 3D printers meant those machines which contain special powders and nozzles that went through slice paths layer by layer from digital models to eject special glue for bounding to become object. Due to expensive components and patents of materials, only few large companies and specific industries such as the automotive and toy industries were able to afford RP equipment. In recent years, FDM technique patents have expired, moreover, open source has incited users to make a machine themselves through internet opened components lists to reduce the cost. 3D printing has become a symbol to realize the dream of ordinary family.

3   Case Study-CGDM for iPhone4 Cover

This research executed two experiments by applying Grasshopper to construct two kinds of generative digital models in different iPhone4 cover shape for subjects who could adjust the parameters according to their preference. In order to analyze the feedback differences between individual subjects individually, while they were adjusting the structural and irregular texture details and comparing 2D rendering and 3D print results. Further, the aesthetic feel of random computer generated design and human manipulation between the different groups of subjects were discovered through experiments.

3.1   iPhone4 Cover Shape Grammar

This research invited three design experts with 10 years of experience each to participate. They discussed the design process of the main body and detail refinement and chose the iPhone cover as a suitable example to conduct the experiment. The shape grammar and solution space of the iPhone cover which drives the generative model to assemble with iPhone were defined at the same time. After that, the generative designer followed the definitions to construct generative digital models and leave wide range parameters to control shapes. The generative models then were delivered to design experts to setup appropriate parameters and restraint.

The iPhone shape continued Apple's style of taking a rounded square as its basic feature. Design experts all agreed that parametric adjustments of width, length and corner radius are fundamental in main body control. Then other conditions were added such as raised or indented (convex or concave) curves, symmetry or asymmetry. After three design experts manipulated the generative digital model, back surface adjustments were added in. As a result three generative digital models can be described as:

a.   Main body structure-
   1.   Three parameters controlling width, length and depth
   2.   Three parameters became a group to control upper curves for adjusting raised/indent, symmetry/asymmetry, the other three parameters are the same, controlling the curve on the right side.
   3.   The curvature of the corner was manipulated by 2 parameters.
   4.   The back surface was constructed using three curves: left, middle and right curve. Each curve contained three parameters to adjust the height of the upper,   middle and lower point of the curve.
b.   Random pattern details
   1.   Hollow patterns were constructed by vonoroi function in Grasshopper.
   2.   The number (1-30) of holes could be adjusted by parametric slider.
   3.   The shapes of holes are randomly calculated by computer algorithm.
   4.   The width and thickness of the wire frame could be adjusted while the shape and numbers of holes are changed.
   5.   The radius of the hole corner can be controlled by parametric slider.

c.   Human controlled patterns-
  1. Users can set up the number (1-30) and position of points as they want.
  2. The coverage of holes can be controlled by parametric slider.
  3. The width and thickness of the wire frame can be adjusted while shape and numbers of holes are changed.
  4. The degree of hole curve can be adjusted by parametric slider.

3.2   Solution Space Definition

This research separated the iPhone cover features into main body and details. The iPhone handset had to be fit into the cover seamlessly and generative models must be able to be used by an iPhone4 and iPhone5. The situation is similar with the inside-out design in the previous CGDM study. Therefore, the iPhone handset digital model was first build up as reverse engineering process. Then following with shape grammar, (See 3.1), the generative designer built up a generative model which width, length and corner radius could be adjusted by parametric sliders. After that, 3D digital models were translated to a 3D printer to produce a real model for ensuring that the virtual models' size was real. (See Figure 01-03)

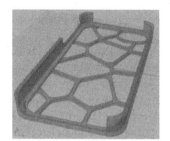  

Fig. 1.   **Fig. 2.**   **Fig. 3.**

2D digital model and 3D Printed mockup for i-phone case

3.3   CGDM Example Modeling

According to the definitions shape grammar from design experts (see 3.1), the generative designer built up the iPhone cover digital model which was controlled by three groups of parametric sliders, upper length, right width and corner round. (See Figure   04) L and W sliders controlled the total length and width. L1, L2 and L3 sliders decided the shape of the left, middle and right at top of the cover. The same as W1, W2 and W3, the right side shape was controlled by these 3 sliders. R1 and R2 controlled the shape of the corner. The top and bottom, right and left shapes were symmetry in this case. Because Grasshopper is Rhino plugin sliders cannot be shown on digital models directly. All parametric sliders were placed on their relative position for users to understand the location of the shape they were adjusting.

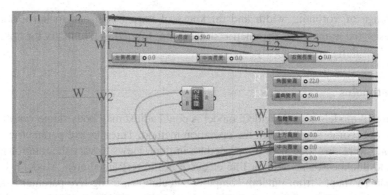

Fig. 4. Interface of i-phone case digital generative model

The back surface shape was structured using 3 curves through 9 points. (See Figure 05). Adjusting La, Lb, Lc, Ma, Mb, Mc and Ra, Rb, Rc sliders the height of the left, middle and right curves on the back surface would be changed. They also had been placed in relative position.

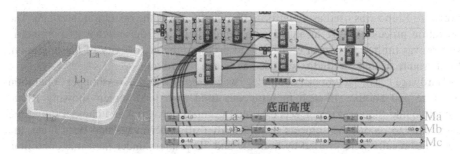

Fig. 5. Back surface interface of CGDM digital model

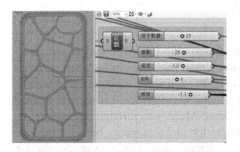

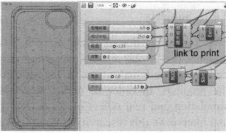

Fig. 6. Details adjusted details UI   **Fig. 7.** Human controlled details UI

Details adjustments were controlled by two kinds of generative models. The first model was the random parametric inputs model. (See Figure 06). Users could decide the number of holes, the width and thickness of the wire frame, then drag the slider to adjust the random number to choose a shape they want. The other human controlled model   required users to move, add or delete points in Rhino. (See pic.07). Then effect range of voronoi, width and thickness of wire frame had to be decided. In these cases, the numbers of parametric sliders were limited in five to six for observing subjects' thinking process easily.

3.4   Stimulus

Three digital models were provided: model A could adjust mail body shape variation for subjects to become familiar with the operation method. Three to five parametric sliders as a group were provided with the procedure in three views to vary the ratio of length, width and thickness, also straight line or curve in the restrained area. Model B1 could select pattern shapes from random computer calculations, using five parametric sliders to choose the numbers of patterns, random shape types, wire frame width and thickness and radius of pattern corners. Model B2 required subjects to add, delete or move points in Rhino program in order to decide the numbers of patterns and its location by human control, then a Grasshopper generated pattern would surfaces immediately.

3.5   Equipment

Software-Rhino was used as a platform, Grasshopper was the operation interface. The operation processes were arranged with three views and the number of parametric sliders was limited to five in each view to decrease the complexity of the operation. Furthermore, Camtasia Studio was used as screen record tool.

Hardware- An Notebook computer was used as the Grasshopper operation interface and another 15-inch monitor was used as extend screen showing Rhino model. While the experiment was executed Camtasia program and camera ran at the same time to record the subjects' actions. After all experiments had been done, the outcomes results were printed by both 2D and 3D printers under the same condition, then the results were compared.

3.6   Subjects

Five forth-year design students with basic Rhino training (two males and three females, age 20-22) and five designer with more than five years of experience (three males and two females, age 33-38) were invited. iPhone4 users were preferred but not the required, in order to realize how the feedback difference between computer simulation and real object effect design decision. Moreover, through questionnaires and interviews this research explored the recognition and acceptance between random computer generated and human manipulated shapes, also offering suggestions for further studies.

3.7   Experiment Process

First demonstrated the mission, explained the interface and model construction theorem for five minutes, then the subjects based on three provided digital prototype adjusted main body variation and two different details for iPhone covers in ten minutes. In that period, subjects could suspend the time to ask questions anytime, then after explanation, the experiment continued. If the experiment duration were over or less than 10 minutes, the experiment kept going until the subject was satisfied with the outcome then the time was recorded. An interview was held for 10-15 minutes after the end or the experiment. After all 10 subjects finished the experiments, the 2D and 3D rendering was printed out by KeyShot and RealFun3D printers respectively under same conditions. After one week, thirty rendered pictures and real models were provided separately to the 10 subjects, they were asked to choose the one they liked and find out their own design. Also the differences among shape imagination, 2D simulation and physical product in design process were discussed.

4   Results

The two groups both agreed the main body generative model could easily help check rough shapes, and the interface was quite easy to understand. Comparing the 2D rendered and 3D printed outcomes, the two groups both admitted that the real model could help to make design decision accurately in the concept stage if it was provided earlier. Some design students expressed that the 2D render plus the 3D print was enough to demonstrate and check their ideas. If they could have their real design models immediately after the experiment, they might change their design again. Most experienced designers understood that concept idea, 2D rendered picture and 3D printed model have gaps because their purposes are different. Although the source digital model of 2D render and 3D print was the same, they usually spent more time in materials, lighting, reflection …etc. effects to make the pictures "overly realistic" on purpose. They treated it as a kind of advertisement to attract the clients' eyeball.

Comparing the two groups of more than five years experienced designers and four years design training students, the design though process and difference in purpose made the outcomes totally different, although the generative model had restrained the shape variation in a limited solution space. Experienced designers tend to think about how to manipulate the digital model to create the shape they want, even though sometimes the system revealed unexpected shapes. Most of the subjects tried the unexpected shape and checked the outcome then went back to their original ideas. Furthermore, many experienced designers submitted demands to add more parameters in order to make the shape have different shape grammar. It demonstrated that if industrial designers were involved in the early shape grammar stage, this system would be extended in a large scale containing varied kinds of shape styles.

4.1   Generative Model Experiments Results

The average main body generative model adjustment time of the five experienced designers was eight minutes and thirty seconds, the five design students' average time was six minutes and thirty seconds. All subjects manipulated parametric sliders from the top view to check the shape then went to perspective view to confirm details.

In the random computer pattern generative model experiment, the designers and design students spent seven minutes and thirty seconds, and eight minutes and five seconds in average time on adjusting models respectively. Many designers focused on hiding the camera wire frame or assimilating it with patterns. On the other hand, most design students focused on the aesthetic of the pattern to adjust the shape and size of holes. In the human controlled pattern experiment, the average operational time of the designers were six minutes and ten seconds, the students was thirty minutes five seconds. All the designers spent most of their time on moving, adding or deleting points to confirm the direction of the shape. Most of them chose to deviate from the original shape. However, the students tended to spent more time on shape details, sometimes they restarted again because they were unsatisfied the outcome.

The two groups both expressed that the interface was easy to use and suitable for basic shape variations during interviews after the experiments. There were subjects in both groups that suggested adding more parametric sliders to change shape grammar because it was difficult to produce regular geometry shape in current generative model. Moreover, the cover shape grammar became three or five points grabbed the handset, or some irregular blocks extruded out of the cover.

4.2   2D Rendering Interview Results

Because the back surface possessed features of the main body and was difficult to be displayed on picture, the front view and other different perspective rendering were printed to assist the interview. All designers recognized their own design, however, there were two students' whose results looked similar. Figure 8 and 9, both from the designer group, displayed the most popular curve surface main body shape. They both got 5 votes in ten subjects. Figure 10, from the student group, was the best of the random computer generated design. Figure 11, from the designer group, shows the favorite human controlled generative model of ten subjects. Subjects indicated that comparing the aesthetic of texture shapes or the propotion, a specific shape from random variations of handset covers could be recognized easily.

Fig. 8.   **Fig. 9.**   **Fig. 10.**   **Fig. 11.**

Most popular main body shapes   Most popular rendom design from students and human controled design from designer

4.3   3D Print Interview Results

Figure 12 displays some results from 3D printer. Figure 13 shows the front and back of the favorite iPhone covers, all from the group of designer, produced by three generative models. All subjects could recognize their own design immediately from 3D printed models. And they confessed that the back curve surface and two side curves made the main body model looked outstanding and easy to hold. That was the reason they chose it. On the other hand, the back surface thickness and the special circle texture made those two get more votes from the irregular pattern generative models.

Fig. 12. 3D printed results   **Fig. 13.** Favorite iPhone covers

5   Discussions and Suggestions

This research utilized practical methods to explore generative design combined with 3D print techniques for applying it to specific shape details of product design operative process. It compared the design decision difference from simulated and real design representation tools between different levels of designers. The results demonstrated that current interface and function of submitted generative models are suitable for basic design shape variations. If there were appropriate platform or data transfer methods the experiment could be executed by ordinary users. As a touchstone, this research did evoke the designers' interest in shape grammar and proposed more demands on shape variations. Although the design students did not reveal requirement of shape grammar, they expressed that combining 2D rendered pictures and 3D print models could help to present ideas accurately and efficiently, even though the 3D print model quality was poor. Moreover, 3D print models rapidly fixed the gap between imagined shapes and 2D renderings to young designers. It helped them deal with uncertain shape details to make design decisions before they waste time and money in CNC procedure to produce the final model.

Different level of designers revealed different idea in to applying 2D rendering and 3D printing. Design students believed rapid real model could help with idea presentation and confirmation of rough concepts. Though designers were interested in 3D printing and had the urge to buy their own design produced by a3D printer, a designer manager expressed that the generative design application and process this research proposed could be applied inside design departments to reach agreements rapidly. However, if an unfinished concept was produced using rough 3D printing and handed to non-design departments it might cause misunderstanding and disturb the design direction.

This research combined the advantages of 3D print and CGDM, with the help of generative designer, industrial designer could focus on the meanings and variations of shapes then demonstrate the idea and usability. However, the platform is currently limited to specific professional programs. Users must learn Rhino manipulation first, it would be even better if designers could understand Grasshopper programming principles. It would help in working with generative designer seamlessly. Also, generative designers must communicate with industrial designer frequently during the CGDM process in order to understand the real and potential demands.

References

1. Amant, R.: User Interface Affordances in a Planning Representation. Human-Computer Interaction 14(3), 317 (1999)
2. Baecker, R.M., et al.: Readings in Human-Computer Interaction: Toward the Year 2,000, pp. 51–60. Morgan Kaufmann Publish Human-Computer Interaction (1995)
3. Bentley, P.J., Corne, D.W.: An introduction to creative evolutionary systems. In: Creative Evolutionary Systems, pp. 1–77. Morgan Kaufmann, San Francisco (2002)
4. Bowman, D.A., Kruijff, E., LaViola Jr., J.J., Poupyrev, I.: 3D User interface: theory and practice. Addison Wesley, Canada (2005)
5. Cardella, M.E., Atman, C.J., Adams, R.S.: Mapping between design activities and external representations for engineering student designers. Design Studies 27, 5–24 (2006)
6. Cedermann, C., Ermanni, P., Kelm, R.: Dynamic CAD objects for structural optimization in preliminary aircraft design. Aerospace Science and Technology 10, 601–610 (2006)
7. Chen, K.H., Chang, T.Y.: A Study on the Cognitive Thresholds of Formal Styles. Concurrent Engineering 14(3), 207–218 (2006)
8. Chien, S.F.: Supporting information navigation in generative design systems. Ph.D. Dissertation, School of Architecture, Carnegie Mellon University, Pittsburgh, PA (1998)
9. Dorest, K., Cross, N.: Creativity in the design process: co-evolution of problem solution. Design Studies 22(5), 425–437 (2001)
10. Fischer, T., Burry, M., Frazer, J.: Triangulation of generative form for parametric design and rapid prototyping. Automation in Construction 14(2) (2005)
11. Fischer, T., Fischer, T.: Toolmaking for digital morphogenesis. International Journal of Design Computing (2003)
12. Gero, J., Maher, M.L.: Computational models of creative design (Conference collections), Sydney, Australia (1995)
13. Hartson, H.R.: Human-computer interaction: Interdisciplinary roots and trends. The Journal of Systems and Software 43, 1 (1998)
14. Heisserman, J.: Generative geometric design and boundary solid grammars. Ph.D. Dissertation, Department of Architecture, Carnegie Mellon University, Pittsburgh, PA (1991)
15. Hsiao, K.A., Chen, L.L., Wang, C.F., Tsang, H.T.: Fundamental Dimensions of Affective Responses to ProductShapes. International Journal of Industrial Ergonomics (2006)

16. Hsiao, S.W., Chiu, F.Y., Lu, S.H.: Product-form design model based on genetic algorithms. International Journal of Industrial Ergonomics 40, 237–246 (2010)
17. Hix, D., Hartson, H.R.: Developing User Interface: Ensuring Usabulity Through Product and Process. Wiley, New York (1993)
18. Zeisel, J.: Inquiry by design: Tools for environment-behavior research. Cambridge University Press, Cambridge (1981)
19. Jun, H., Gero, J.: Emergence of shape semantics of architectural shapes. Environment and Planning B: Planning and Design 25, 577–600 (1998)
20. Kalay, Y.E.: Principles of computer-aided design: Computability of design. Wiley-Interscience Publication, New York (1987)
21. Lin, M.H.: Affective and Communicational Effect in Product Design- a Case Study Based on Alessi Kettles. The Science of Design 49(6), Issue No. 156, 77–84 (2003)
22. Lin, M.-H., Lee, L.-C.: An Experimental Study for Applying Generative Design to Electronic Consumer Products. In: Marcus, A. (ed.) DUXU/HCII 2013, Part IV. LNCS, vol. 8015, pp. 392–401. Springer, Heidelberg (2013)
23. Jackson, M.: Representing structure in a software system design. Design Studies 31, 545–566 (2010)
24. Monica, E.C., Cynthia, J.A., Robin, S.A.: Mapping between design activities and external representations for engineering student designers. Design Studies 27, 5–24 (2006)
25. Prats, M., Lim, S., Jowers, I., Garner, S.W., Chase, S.: Transforming shape in design: observations from studies of sketching. Design Studies 30, 503–520 (2009)
26. Piller, F., Walcher, D.: Value Creation by Toolkits for User Innovation and Design: The Case of theWatchMarket. Journal of Product Innovation Management 21(6), 401–415 (2004)
27. Piller, F., Walcher, D.: Toolkits for idea competitions: a novel method to integrate users in new product development. R&D Management 36(3) (2006)
28. Pratt, M.J., Anderson, B.D., Tanger, T.: Towards the standardized exchange of parameterized feature-based CAD models. Computer-Aided Design 37, 1251 (2005)
29. Sato, T., Hagiwara, M.: IDSET: Interactive Design System using Evolutionary Techniques. Computer-Aided Design, 367–377 (2001)
30. Shea, K., Aish, R., Gourtovaia, M.: Towards integrated performance-driven generative design tools. Automation in Construction 14 (2005)
31. Shneiderman, B.: Designing the User Interface, 4th edn. Addison-Wesley, New York (2005)
32. Sivam, K.: A practical generative design method. Computer-Aided Design 43, 88–100 (2011)
33. Singh, V., Gu, N.: Towards an integrated generative design framework. Design Stusy 33, 185–207 (2012)
34. Sinha, R., Liang, V.C., Paredis, C.J.J., Khosla, P.K.: Modeling and Simulation Methods for Design of Engineering Systems. Journal of Computing and Information Science in Engineering 1, 84–91 (2001)
35. Stiny, G.: Introduction to shape and shape grammars. Environment and Planning B 7, 343–351 (1980)
36. Stiny, G., Gips, J.: Shape Grammars and the Generative Specification of Painting and Sculpture. The Best Computer Papers of 1971, 125–135 (1972)
37. Yan, X., Gu, P.: A review of rapid prototyping technologies and systems. Computer-Aided Design 26(4), 307–316 (1996)
38. Ye, X., Liu, H., Chen, L., Chen, Z., Pan, X., Zhang, S.: Reverse innovative design— an integrated product design methodology. Computer-Aided Design 40, 812–827 (2008)

Building a Semantic Differential Scale as Tool for Assisting UX Evaluation with Home Appliances

Vanessa Macedo[*] and Caio Marcio Silva

Instituto de Pesquisa para o Desenvolvimento LACTEC, Curitiba, Brazil
{vanessa.macedo,caio.silva}@lactec.org.br

Abstract. This paper presents the development process of a semantic differential scale, to support the UX evaluation with home appliances, specifically, generating a database of Portuguese adjectives related to the interaction with home appliances. We performed a survey with three fonts: users and designers perception about home appliances usage; perception from researchers on home appliance UX, towards efficiency; and marketing search, examining disclosure materials of a home appliance manufacturer. Then, we performed a data analysis from hierarchies, binary matrix of correlation and antonyms generation. After the method application, the research resulted in 20 adjectives, which can assist the UX evaluation with home appliances.

Keywords: Semantic Differential Scale, Home Appliance, User Experience.

1 Introduction

Home appliances are products developed to help individuals on accomplishing daily activities. These products provide several interfaces of usage; sometimes by user control panel, sometimes by interacting with three-dimensional interfaces, such as handles, doors, knobs, and so on [1]. In addition, home appliances are products designed for the domestic environment, where different users can share them [2]. These users can vary on age, familiarity with technology, physical and mental abilities, desires and goals [3]. Despite this variety of users, tasks and features, home appliances should provide intuitive use in every possible situation [4].

With regarding this need for intuitive use provided by home appliances, User Experience (UX) studies become paramount. By taking into account the UX, the designer plan the home appliance focusing on the user and its real needs, comprehensions and abilities [5]. Evaluating the UX is a path for understanding the user and all experiences that he/she engages with a product. An experience is not only the interaction itself; thinking about the product, using other times, experiences with similar products, and other aspects also composes the UX.

In order to operationalize the UX evaluation, professionals have been developing many methods and tools for measuring the User Experience [6]. Vermeeren *et. al.* [7] verified that questionnaires and scales are the most popular tools among industry and

---

[*] Corresponding author.

A. Marcus (Ed.): DUXU 2014, Part I, LNCS 8517, pp. 308–317, 2014.

academy professionals. Scales allow the self-report of an experience and utilize predefined measures, generating easy to analyze data.

Semantic differential scales are versatile tools, first developed decades ago by Osgood. et. al. [8] but still employed in several fields of knowledge, supporting the measurement of a series of aspects. This scale presents opposite adjectives in pairs, connected by a certain space (it can be a line, likert scale, or even a blank space), in which the user marks the level of approximation based on a determined idea.

By literature review, we observed that authors [9;10] have developed studies on this tool's usage for specific contexts, such as the sound evaluation inside aircrafts. Given the lack of proper tools for UX evaluation with home appliances, we developed a database for constructing semantic differential scales for this scope.

This study's main goal was developing a proposal of a semantic differential, generating a database of adjectives collected specifically for the user experience evaluation with home appliances. The tool here presented can be adapted for different home appliances categories and it allows application on different stages of usage, such as pre, during and post interaction.

We applied a method divided into three phases: Questionnaire 1, about home appliances characteristics, answered by users and designers; Questionnaire 2, regarding perceived efficiency, responded by UX experts; and, Marketing Search, examining disclosure materials of a manufacturer. Then, was performed a data analysis using hierarchies, binary matrix of correlation and antonyms generation by researchers.

The study resulted into 39 adjectives in the first cut, and 20 adjectives in the final cut. We developed the entire research in Brazil, utilizing Portuguese adjectives. Nevertheless, we present a suggested translation for the usage of this research's results by other UX professionals, assisting the user experience evaluation with home appliances.

2   User Experience Evaluation

User experience (UX) is every aspect resultant from the interaction between an artifact and an individual, whether before, during or after usage. In UX, authors consider that those interactions occur in a context [11], taking into account that external factors also modifies the experience, as well as social and cultural contexts. Given that user experience as a knowledge field is still recent, there is a variety of concepts about what exactly is UX, as is observed by Rebelo et. al. [12].

Preece et. al. [13] consider that usability is a part of user experience, in which UX is a broader perspective of the entire experience, and usability considers aspects such as efficiency and effectiveness. Thus, the user experience contemplates not only the usability itself, but also all the aspects that composes the satisfaction. The user experience is unique, since each individual has its own repertoire of knowledge, skills and expectations.

The user experience study and evaluation supports the user centered design (UCD), enabling the creation of systems centered on humans. UCD aims the developing of intuitive artifacts, allowing ease of usage, satisfaction during interaction and diminishing amount of resources spent on training and support. In order to evaluate the user experience, usability experts and UX experts performs UX studies, using specific methods, dimensions and metrics, enabling the comprehension and measurement of various aspects about the user experience with an artifact.

Many authors [14, 15, 16, 6, 7] present tools, methods and metrics for evaluating user experience, human factors and usability. However, the UX evaluation can result in a large amount of data. The UX expert has to consider multiple variables for the UX evaluation method selection, such as time to execute the method, participants required, need for specific software and hardware, location, among other aspects [17]. During the developing process, is common to follow schedules and deadlines, so is wise to anticipate which kinds of data the evaluation methods will result in, always paying attention on how will be the analysis of those data [6].

Questionnaires and surveys are popular methods, because they are easy to apply and allow fast analysis [15]. Questionnaires follow standards, which means that results are comparable, facilitating data analysis. In the research applied by Vermeeren *et. al.* [7], the authors observed that many professionals (from industry and academy) apply questionnaires on their routines of UX evaluations; 42 of the 93 selected methods from the research collect UX data via questionnaires. The authors also states that questionnaires are one of the most versatile research tools.

Many questionnaires use scales to allow different possibilities on aswering, but also utilizing predefined measures. The Semantic Differential, scope of this research, was developed by Osgood, Suci & Tannenbaum [8], and aims to measure the reaction of individuals through bipolar scales, ie, opposite adjectives [8]. Given its application versatility, the literature presents a variety of derivations of this scale, such as the Differential Emotion Scale, developed by Izard [18] and the AttrakDiff of Hassenzahl, Burmester & Koller [19]. However, even with its versatility, the UX expert should select proper adjectives for the semantic differential, considering type of audience that will respond, the product evaluated type and the scope of each survey.

Osgood *et. al.* [8] observes that words helps measuring a series of aspects, dimensions and meanings. Therefore, once the user has contact to a certain experience, the semantic differential helps evaluating multiple dimensions by presenting opposite pairs of adjectives, connected by a likert scale or even a continuous line, in which the user marks the approximation for each pair, as the Figure 1 illustrates. The semantic differential main goal is to measure the affective meaning on some experience. Pereira concludes that the semantic differential it is a tool that enables the registering, quantifying and comparing meanings by various individuals, in one or many situations, in a specific moment or multiple instances, by one or a set of scales [20 *apud* 9].

Fig. 1. Examples of semantic differential scales with likert scale (left) and with continuous line (right). Source: The authors.

Pereira [20] conducted a survey of adjectives to apply in the Semantic Differential in Portuguese, verifying high levels of accuracy using this tool on Portuguese. Considering the context of specifying the type of product evaluated in order to develop specific tools, Andrade *et. al.* [10] designed a semantic differential for evaluating aircraft interior sounds, and Neves [9] developed a Semantic Differential for evaluating UX with washing machines during a long period of usage. This procedure included the following steps: market research, brainstorming, collecting adjectives from literature, consolidation and classification of adjectives, adjectives selection, preparation of pairs of adjectives and preparation of questionnaires. Even though Neves developed a research specific tool for evaluating user experience with washing machines, the adjectives resulted from the study may not be applicable for home appliances in general. Therefore, this research inserts in this scope.

2.1   Home Appliances and User Experience Evaluation

Home appliances are products used by various kinds of people: people with varying ages, from young to older persons; with various levels of physical abilities; individuals with different levels of familiarity with technologies, and so on [21]. In addition, home appliances, like washing machines and ovens, are products used in a domestic context, where different users can share them. Therefore, home appliances in general must provide an effective and efficient usage, regardless the user abilities and repertoire.

Han *et. al.* [1] points out that hybrid products are those composed by union between software and hardware elements. In this sense, home appliances enable interactions with user control panel, as well with hardware interfaces, such as sockets, grooves, doors, handles, etc. Thus, home appliances are hybrid products, implying in evaluations that embraces this characteristic.

Another particularity about home appliances is the relatively long period of usage, which characterize them as durable goods. These various stages of usage allow different situations, as well as different user experiences, creating challenges for its evaluation. Freudenthal [2] highlights that home appliance usage can be representative of user self-sufficiency, i.e., elderly being able to perform daily activities by themselves, and at the moment the home appliance impose some barrier for usage, the user can feel a lack of independence, needing to recur for help.

Some few authors have been considering the user experience provided by home appliances. A perceived trend on these studies is the focus on usage by elderly, i.e, Higgins & Glasgow [3], Sandhu [22] and Hong & Ono [23]. Even though the literature presents specific tools for evaluating UX with some particular product category (i.e., Game Engagement Questionnaire [24] and Service User Experience Questionnaire [25]), we still have not found any specific tool for evaluating UX with home appliances, sustaining the reasons for this research.

3   Method

In order to create a Portuguese adjectives database for semantic differentials to evaluate UX with home appliances, we applied a method composed by the following three phases:

1. Questionnaire with users and designers, collecting adjectives related to home appliances;
2. Questionnaire with user experience experts that work with home appliances, regarding perceived efficiency;
3. Marketing search, examining disclosure materials of a home appliances' manufacturer.

The first questionnaire was both printed and digital, stating for the respondent to list at least ten adjectives, positive or negative, that he/she consider as a home appliance characteristic. This first phase intended to collect what adjectives users tend to relate when they think about home appliances. Thirty-two home appliances users and 32 home appliances designers (total: 64) answered the questionnaire 1. The second questionnaire asked which adjectives seven user experience experts and eight designers specialized on home appliances relate with efficiency of usage. This second questionnaire aimed on gathering words related with positive aspects of home appliances usage, adding the UX experts view. Brazilian individuals answered both questionnaires in Portuguese.

The third and last method phase was the research on disclosure materials provided by the marketing team of a home appliance manufacturer. In this phase, we aimed to verify which adjectives the manufacturers use to communicate with the target audience. This research used a retailer website, verifying various home appliances of a same brand, contemplating different categories (such as ovens, refrigerators and dishwashers). For the website selection, we selected five Brazilian retailer, choosing the one with a larger number of different home appliances categories of a specific brand. The chosen brand manufactures home appliances for Brazilian market, being a ramification of a multi international company.

In the purpose for adjectives reduction to representative words, we used spreadsheets and debates between three researchers. The spreadsheet helped eliminating repeats, and debates enabled the discussion on synonyms and non-representative words. When the number of words reached <40, we made a correlation matrix. The matrix presents all adjectives in alphabetical order on the first column and first row. With this matrix, the researchers evaluated the correlation of all adjectives between one another using binary values. We marked "1" if both adjectives were synonyms or strongly correlated, and "0" if the adjectives were antonyms or without direct relation. In instance: "automatic" and "technological" are closely related, so we marked "1"; "Simple" and "Loud" did not present correlation, so we marked "0". The matrix allows us to verify which adjectives are more representative (higher number of incidences), and which adjectives are more distinguished (lower number of incidences). The Figure 2 illustrates the correlation matrix.

	Automatic	Noisy	⋮	Simple	Technological
Automatic	1	0	-	1	1
Noisy	0	1	-	0	0
...	-	-	-	-	-
Simple	1	0	-	1	0
Technological	1	0	-	0	1

Fig. 2. Correlation Matrix example. Source: The authors.

4   Results and Discussion

The data research, composed by the three phases, generated 930 input data. After filtering repeats, the collecting resulted in 214 different adjectives. The questionnaire 1 resulted in Ninety-two adjectives and 343 entry data resulted. The second questionnaire produced 149 adjectives and 400 entry data. The marketing search enable us to raise 81 adjectives and 187 entry data. The adjectives with highest incidence per questionnaire are "Beautiful" from questionnaire 1, "Practical" from questionnaire 2, and "Easy" from Marketing Research. By curiosity, we highlight some unusual adjectives: "cautious", "ethereal", "stinky", "Chinese" and "Oneiric". We observed a higher plurality of different adjectives on the questionnaires responded by the 32 designers. It is important to clarify that we performed the research entirely in Portuguese, presenting on this document a suggested translation, made with dictionary aid.

Then, we arranged the 214 adjectives in a spreadsheet for reduction of similar or unrepresentative made by three individuals. All the adjectives were read by the researchers and debated about the meaning and possible synonyms, reducing for 25 adjectives from the first phase, 15 from the second phase and 22 from the third phase. We gathered the adjectives from all three phases in a same list, performing again the reduction by strong synonyms and non-representative words, resulting in 39 adjectives (that satisfies the previously established cutting line). There are both positive and negative adjectives in this 39-item list. We did not consider composed terms, such as "easy to clean".

The 39 adjectives, ordered by incidence on the three questionnaires, were: practical, beautiful, modern, economical, easy, efficient, durable, resistant, secure, fragile, heavy, noisy, functional, spacious, simple, technological, fast, clean, innovative, elegant, intuitive, smart, large, silent, useful, robust, expensive, light, reliable, ergonomic, clean, compact, complex, comfortable, ecological, cheap, difficult, automatic and flexible.

Those 39 adjectives are, therefore, the database resulted from this research. However, in order to select the most representative adjectives, we used the correlation matrix. After creating the correlation matrix with the 39 adjectives, we made a sum of correlation incidences. We selected the higher frequency (20) and divided by 2, resulting in 10, which was the cutting line. Therefore, applying this cutting line, we selected 22 adjectives (in alphabetical order): automatic, comfortable, easy, ecological, economical, efficient, elegant, ergonomic, expensive, fast, flexible, functional, innovative, intuitive, modern, practical, reliable, secure, simple, smart, technological and useful. At last, we searched for antonyms for each of the 22 adjectives.

We observed that from the six adjectives with higher incidence in questionnaire 2 (answered regarding efficiency), five made into the final cut (22 adjectives). This evidences that the approach with UX Experts showed to be quite useful and relevant.

Comparing the first cut, 39 adjectives, with the 30 positive adjectives collected by Neves [9], eighteen adjectives were present in both researches; twelve adjectives from Neves did not coincide with the collect adjectives from this research; and twenty-one adjectives that we collected were not present on Neves study [9]. We present this comparison with Table 1.

Table 1. Comparison on collected adjectives between this research and Neves [9]. Source: The authors.

Adjectives collected both by this research and by Neves [9]	Adjectives collected only by this research	Adjectives collected only by Neves [9]
1)Automatic, 2)beautiful, 3)comfortable, 4)difficult, 5)ecological, 6)economical, 7)efficient, 8)ergonomic, 9)innovative, 10)smart, 11)clean (cleaning), 12)modern, 13)practical, 14)resistant, 15)secure, 16)silent, 17)simple, 18)technological	19)Cheap, 20)clean (aesthetics), 21)compact, 22)complex, 23)durable, 24)easy, 25)elegant, 26)expensive, 27)fast, 28)flexible, 29)fragile, 30)functional, 31)heavy, 32)intuitive, 33)large, 34)light, 35)noisy, 36)reliable, 37)robust, 38)spacious, 39)useful	I)Pleasant, II)neat, III)controllable, IV)dynamic, V)stimulating, VI)easy to clean, VII)easy to use, VIII)honest, IX)strong, X)multifunctional, XI)organized, XII)surprising

Even though some adjectives are represented by other synonyms in our 39-list, we point out some methodology differences that may be the reasons for these differences. Neves [9] accepted the usage of composed expressions, and this research considered only adjectives. In addition, this research considered the user experience as a whole on the adjective collecting, not dividing into dimensions or categories, activity that Neves performed (division between functionality, usability and pleasure, each category composed by 10 adjectives). In one way, Neves was able to balance three aspects of UX through the selected adjectives, on the other hand, by not dividing the adjectives, we used only those more representative. So, if, for instance, the respondents on this research consider the "usability" aspect as the most important, this aspect will be more represented by the final adjectives. It is possible to recognize that, comparing our results (on home appliances in general) with Neves' results (towards washing machines) the most contemplated categories are usability and functionality. We also highlight that Neves' research [9] was performed taking into account only one category, and in this study we considered home appliances as a whole.

5   Conclusions

User experience is a growing area, each time more recognized by professionals and industry. In this context, tools that helps UX evaluation become relevant, supporting professionals on quantifying subjective aspects and operationalizing evaluation tasks. Semantic differential scales are versatile tools used for evaluating a certain experience or meaning, through the usage of opposite adjectives pairs. It is a tool developed several decades ago, but still stays current, facilitating the user experience evaluation.

However, since the semantic differential scale is fundamentally based on words and meanings, the application on different languages implies on adapting. Pereira [20] verified that semantic differential scale can be a successful tool if used in Portuguese. Based on Pereira [20] and many collecting activities, Neves [9] generated a semantic differential scale for evaluating long term UX with washing machines. After examining these two studies - one with a wide overview, and other with a very specific approach - we detected the possibility for creating a middle term collection of adjectives for semantic differential scales: the scope for home appliances in general.

The three phases of the applied method enabled us to collect adjectives from various sources: users, designers, UX experts and manufacturer. Designers provided a large variety of adjectives, contributing with different synonyms of many relevant aspects of UX with a home appliance. The collecting with User Experience Experts, even though resulted in a smaller number on variety, was paramount for detecting elementary words and meanings. Raising adjectives from users and marketing materials was fundamental on choosing words that are representative and part of the user's vocabulary.

The adjectives reduction was a challenging step: it was important to reduce into representative adjectives, and still not leave behind relevant meanings from the UX with a home appliance. The correlation matrix supported us on verifying which adjectives had most correlation with one another. However, debating with other researchers was indispensable to compose a list of adjectives that contemplate many home appliances' aspects. The researcher's participation was also important on turning the adjectives into antonyms, enabling the further application on semantic differentials.

It was possible to select a first group of adjectives, with 39 adjectives, and a second group, with 20 adjectives. We presented both groups on this document, allowing professionals to choose if they prefer the larger or smaller group of adjectives.

Comparing with the literature, we consider that the collected adjectives from this research were representative and applicable for various home appliances categories. For further studies, we indicate the verification if the translation here presented is valid for other cultures, highlighting that we developed this study in Brazil, on Portuguese. We also suggest the application of these adjectives in a comparative manner using different home appliances. With this study, is important to check if all adjectives are applicable for all home appliances categories, or if it is more adequate to select specific adjectives from the 39-item list for each application.

References

1. Han, S.H., Yun, M.H., Kwahk, J., Hong, S.W.: Usability of consumer electronic products. International Journal of Industrial Ergonomics 28, 143–151 (2001)
2. Freudenthal, A.: The design of home appliances for young and old consumers. Delft University Press, Delft (1999)
3. Higgins, P.G., Glasgow, A.: Development of guidelines for designing appliances for older persons. Work 41, 333–339 (2012)
4. Hurtienne, J.: Image Schemas and Design for Intuitive Use. Exploring New Guidance for User Interface Design. Thesis (PhD in Engineer) - Technische Universität Berlin, Germany – (2011)
5. Eijk, D.V., Kuijk, J.V., Hoolhorst, F., Kim, C., Harkema, C., Dorrestijn, S.: Design for usability: practice-oriented research for user-centered product design. Work 41, 1008–1015 (2012)
6. Tullis, T., Albert, B.: Measuring the user experience: Collecting, Analyzing, and Presenting Usability Metrics. Morgan Kaufmann, San Francisco (2008)
7. Vermeeren, A.P.O.S., Law, E.L.-C., Roto, V., Obrist, M., Hoonhout, J., Vaananen-Vanio-Mattila, K.: User Experience Evaluation Methods: Current State and Development Needs. In: NordiCHI 2010 (Proceedings), out. 16-20 (2010)
8. Osgood, C.E., Suci, G.J., Tannenbaum, P.H.: The measurement of meaning. University of Illinois, Urbana (1957)
9. Neves, A.B.: Experiência cronológica do design de Eletrodomésticos. Master Thesis. Programa de Pós-graduação em Design UFPR (2011)
10. Andrade, A.L., Cruz, R.M., Paul, S., Bitencourt, R.F.: Construção de escalas de diferencial semântico: medida de avaliação de sons no interior de aeronaves. Avaliação Psicológica 8(2) (2009)
11. Krippendorff, K.: The semantic turn: a new foundation for design. Taylor & Francis, Boca Raton (2006)
12. Rebelo, F., Noriega, P., Duarte, E., Soares, M.: Using virtual reality to assess user experience. Human Factors 54(6), 964–982 (2012)
13. Preece, J., Rogers, Y., Sharp, H.: Interaction Design: beyond human computer interaction. John Wiley & Sons, London (2002)
14. Stanton, N.A., Hedge, A., Brookhuis, K., Salas, E., Hendrick, H.: Handbook of Human Factors and Ergonomics Methods. CRC Press, Boca Raton (2005)
15. Dumas, J.S., Salzman, M.C.: Usability Assessment Methods. Reviews of Human Factors and Ergonomics 2, 109–140 (2006)
16. Karwowski, W.: International Encyclopedia of Ergonomics and Human Factors, 2nd edn. Taylor & Francis, Boca Raton (2006)

17. Annett, J., Stanton, N.A. (eds.): Task Analysis. Taylor & Francis, London (2000)
18. Izard, C.D.: Human Emotions. Plenum Press, New York (1977)
19. Hassenzahl, M., Burmester, M., Koller, F.: AttrakDiff: Ein Fragebogen zur Messung wahrgenommener hedonischer und pragmatischer Qualitat. In: Szwillus, G., Ziegler, J. (eds.) Mensch and Computer 2003, Stuttgart, Germany, September 7-10 (2003)
20. Pereira, C.A.A.O.: Diferencial semântico: uma técnica de medida nas ciências humanas e sociais. Ed. Ática, São Paulo (1986)
21. Naumann, A.B., Hurtienne, J., Israel, J.H., Mohs, C., Kindsmüller, M.C., Meyer, H.A., Hußlein, S.: Intuitive Use of User Interfaces: Defining a vague concept. In: Harris, D. (ed.) Engineering Psychology and Cognitive Ergonomics, HCII 2007. LNCS (LNAI), vol. 4562, pp. 128–136. Springer, Heidelberg (2007)
22. Sandhu, J.: Design for the elderly: user-based evaluation studies involving elderly users with special needs. Applied Ergonomics 24(1), 30–34 (1993)
23. Hong, S.-H., Ono, K.: An investigation for integrated user interface of home appliances based on user's cognitive structure. In: IASDR 2009, International Association of Societies of Design Research, Proceedings, Seoul (2009)
24. Brockmyer, J.H., Fox, C.M., Curtiss, K.A., Mcbroom, K.M., Burkhart, E., Pidruzny, J.N.: The development of the Game Engagement Questionnaire: A measure of engagement in video game-playing. Journal of Experimental Social Psychology 45, 624–634 (2009)
25. Väänänen-Vainio-Mattila, K., Segerståhl, K.: A Tool for Evaluating Service User eXperience (ServUX): Development of a Modular Questionnaire. In: User Experience Evaluation Methods in Product Development (UXEM 2009). Workshop in Interact 2009 Conference, Uppsala, Sweden (August 25, 2009)

Evaluating Quality and Usability of the User Interface: A Practical Study on Comparing Methods with and without Users

Caio Marcio Silva[1,*], Vanessa Macedo[1], Rafaela Lemos[2], and Maria Lúcia L.R. Okimoto[2]

[1] Instituto de Pesquisa para o Desenvolvimento LACTEC and Universidade Federal do Paraná UFPR, Curitiba, Brasil
[2] Universidade Federal do Paraná UFPR, Curitiba, Brasil
{vanessa.macedo,caio.silva}@lactec.org.br,
rafaelalemos.dgn@gmail.com, lucia.demec@ufpr.br

Abstract. This paper aimed to verify the suitability of the methods "Rehearsal Technique" with users and "Heuristic Evaluation" in the evaluation process of the usability of appliance's control panel, during the product development process. Both methods were applied with the same goal, identify usability issues with emphasis on information design, and with the same product, a functional prototype of a washing and drying machine's control panel. The heuristic evaluation was applied by three analysts, and the rehearsal technique, applied with ten participants. Each of the methods resulted on usability issues, which were evaluated by criticality and related to design fields. It was concluded that the heuristic evaluation allowed the verification of broader usability problems, early detecting about 85% of the issues identified on the rehearsal technique. However, the rehearsal technique enabled the identification of user feedback, as well as actual behaviors, and confirming some usability issues. Therefore, it is indicted the consideration of heuristic evaluation as a helpful strategy on evaluation of usability, not only as a preliminary evaluation for the usability test.

Keywords: user experience, home appliance, usability assessment.

1 Introduction

Assessing products usability is a subject discussed in the literature and also in the context of research and development in some companies. In this sense, Maguire (2001) [11] points out some benefits of a good usability system, such as increased productivity, reduced number of errors during the interaction, the decrease of necessary support and training, as well as improvement of accepting the product. As a consequence of this, there is an improvement of the way in which the company is seen by the user. Methods, with emphasis on usability, are: discussed by authors (Karwowski et. al., 2011; Dumas & Salzman, 2006) [10], [4], presented in "manuals"

---

* Corresponding author.

A. Marcus (Ed.): DUXU 2014, Part I, LNCS 8517, pp. 318–328, 2014.

(Stanton et. al., 2005) [15]; and indicated by standards (ISO 16982:2002) [8]. However, there is a constant concern to identify low-cost methods, fast to be applied and that result in valid data [12]. In this direction, this research intends to help professionals in the field of usability and user experience to select methods for evaluation of products control panels, from the comparative reporting involving two different evaluation methods: one of them with no user involvement (Heuristic Evaluation) and the other with users involvement (Interaction Rehearsal Technique). The object of study was a graphic user interface of a washing and dryer machine.

It aimed to make a comparison between the results of these two methods. Thus, both methods were applied with the same interface and the same purpose: to identify usability issues with emphasis on information design. The results were compared, verifying the appropriateness of the methods for the following evaluation criteria: performance time, number of usability problems identified; criticality of the raised usability problems, and number of usability problems for the information design.

2   Usability Evaluation

Regarding methods with emphasis on usability and related topics, Dumas & Salzman (2006) [4] present methods for evaluating products divided into four categories: (i) inspection methods (heuristic evaluation and cognitive walkthrough), (ii) usability testing, (iii) self-report methods (questionnaires, interviews and focus groups), and (iv) methods of observation (ethnography). Maguire (2001) user-centered design, setting as methods for evaluation: participatory assessment; dynamic assessment; heuristic evaluation; controlled testing with users; satisfaction questionnaires; assessment of metal loading; analysis of critical incidentes; and post-experience interviews.

For choosing a usability method, many factors must be taken into account. Stanton & Young (1999) [14] suggest that it should be considered the project developmental stage, available resources and time, in addition to the analysts' skills, access to end users and the necessity of data for the project. Anett & Stanton (2000) point out issues that must be raised for the selection of the usability method, such as: "how deep should the analysis be?"; "what existing tools to provide support for the use of the method?"; "how reliable and valid is the method?", among other questions.

Also in this context, Roto et. al. (2009) [12] conducted a survey with professionals in UX. It was found that professionals who came from industry show more concern about the resources required for implementation of the method than professionals from academia, as well as the speed and ease of application. They also report that qualitative methods are preferred when the product is in the early stages of the development process, seeking to present constructive data to the design team. Moreover, Tullis & Albert (2008) [16] emphasize the need of presenting numerical data to customers at the time of the usability report, making quantitative data a necessity. In this context, it is essential that the usability and UX professional is aware of costs, time and recruitment for applying the methods, as well as the method speed to detect key points of usability problems.

From the literature review, there is a high number of usability methods directed and/or applied to the human computer interaction [6], not being identified a method developed specifically for evaluating the usability of home appliances. Thus, this research was based on general methods, which can be applied in different contexts for different types of products (systems and product with three-dimensional interface). Given the research of Roto et. al. (2009) [12], which highlights usability testing, and of Dumas & Salzman (2006) [4], with emphasis on the evaluation by a specialist, there is the motivation to check the positive aspects and caveats of these two methods.

However, there are many variables in usability testing highlighted by Tullis & Albert (2008) [16], such as: number of observers, systematization of data tabulation (synchronous, asynchronous, both), application of thinkaloud, moderator interventions, support systems for use (instruction manuals, quick guide, instructional videos), use of specialized software for data tabulation, insertion of pre and post interaction questionnaires, among others. Faced with these choices which influence costs and resources for the implementation, it was decided to choose, among the possibilities for usability test, the Interaction Rehearsal Technique. This procedure was selected for having less statistical, technical accuracy (for example: materials, control of variables, number of involved analysts), as well as for allowing an evaluation from the potential users interaction with the product.

Just like Usability Testing has some variants, the assessment by expert also presents alternatives; either the number of experts who will carry out the activity, the type of material that will be used (heuristic, checklist) and the way the activity will be performed (cognitive walkthrough or traditional scan). Still within the same category of review by an expert, there are other options, such as the types of used heuristics, golden rules, principles of dialogue and ergonomic criteria.

The heuristics proposed by Nielsen (1994) suggest aspects to be followed by the developed interfaces. They are: visibility of system status; match between system and the real world; user control and freedom; consistency and standards; help users recognize, diagnose, and recover from erros; error prevention; recognition rather than recall; flexibility and efficiency of use; aesthetic and minimalist design; and help and documentation. The golden rules proposed by Shneiderman & Plaisant (2004) [13], are the following: strive for consistency, enable frequent users to use shortcuts, offer informative feedback, design dialog to yield closure, offer simple error handling, permit easy reversal of actions, support internal locus of control and reduce short-term memory load. There are also the dialogue principles proposed by ISO 9241-11 (1998) [8], which are: suitability for the task, self-descriptiveness, controllability, conformity with user expectations, error tolerance, suitability for Individualization and suitability for learning.

In addition to these authors, there are others who contemplate aspects for evaluation of interfaces from the inspection by experts, among them, Bastien & Scapin (1993) [2]. The authors argue that the interfaces should be developed from some ergonomic criteria which can subsequently be elements for evaluation, such as: conduction; workload; explicit control; adaptability; errors management; uniformity/consistency; and meaning of codes denominations, as well as compatibility. Given this literature review, it was created a table summarizing the topics discussed here and the principal authors.

Table 1. Synthesis of authors raised for the literature review

Area	Authors
UX / Usability Methods	Karwowski (2011);
	Dunas and Salzan (2006);
	Tullis and Albert (2008);
	Roto et. al. (2009)
DCU / Human Factors Methods	Stanton et. al. (2005);
	ISO 16982:2002;
	Maguire (2001);
	Stanton and Young (1999);
	Annett and Stanton (2000).
Heuristics / Recommendations	Nielsen (1994);
	Shneiderman and Plaisant (2004);
	ISO 9241-10:1998;
	Bastien and Scapin (1993);

3   Method

This study was conducted in four stages. The first step one consisted in the literature review. In step two, the heuristic evaluation by three usability analysts was performed. In step three, the interaction rehearsal technique was performed. Finally, in step four the analysis of results and report writing was done.

In order to provide ways of direct comparison, it was selected the same artifact to be evaluated with heuristic and from the interaction rehearsal technique; it is a control panel of a washing and dryer machine. It aimed to carry out such assessments with the artifact in development, simulating a formative evaluation. For this, it was used an Adobe "flash" file, simulating smaller analysis cycles of the control panel, from tests with functional prototype. However, even without operating the machine. This kind of prototype, in the context of the development of graphical interfaces for home appliances, is one of the most faithful ones, when compared to the prototypes on paper and interactive guides. In it, audible and visual feedback can be more faithfully reproduced.

3.1   Heuristic Evaluation

For the heuristic evaluation, three professionals of usability with products were recruited, with different levels of training. It was then requested that these professionals made individual evaluations, based on Nielsen's heuristics (1994) and on the ergonomic criteria of Bastien & Scapin (1993) [2], completing a worksheet, exemplified in Table 1, and they were free to choose how to lead the heuristic evaluation. This evaluation guides were the present items in the columns of the available spreadsheet: criticality, which is how critical the problem is and needs to be priority to be modified; the description of the problem, pointing the problem to the developer; the Heuristic or Ergonomic Criterion infringed, who moved the problem description, the area, that directs which development team will be responsible for a solution/improvement for the usability problem, and the impact, which indicates what is the size of usability negatively influenced by this usability problem.

Table 2. Example of the usability problems spreadsheet

Criticality	Problem description	Violated Ergonomic Criterium or Heuristic	Area	Impact
Problem criticality (high/médium/low).	Succint description of identified problem.	Indication of the heuristic violated by the problem.	Relation between the usability problem and one of the three areas: graph, information and interaction.	Delimitation of what dimension(s) of usability can be impacted (satisfaction, efficiency and effectiveness).

3.2   Interaction Rehearsal Technique

After the heuristic evaluation, the interaction rehearsal technique was performed, composed of ten sessions with voluntary users. The participants were chosen according to schooling, so that 50% of the participants had a college degree and 50% had incomplete college degree. Among these, 60% were male and the rest (40%) female. The ages of the participants were concentrated in the range of 21 to 30 years, except for one participant who was in the range of 41 to 50 years. The graduation area of the participants was varied, as examples: engineering, college student, psychology and design.

Each session lasted on average 40min. The interaction rehearsal technique, although with no statistical rigor as data capture and sample selection, aimed to investigate the relationship between users and the artifact under study and, from this, identify usability problems related not only to use but also regarding the design of interfaces.

In the first step, the demographic questionnaire aimed to capture data as education, gender, occupation and age group, while the inspection of familiarity sought to ascertain whether the user had knowledge about the use of this category products. Through this tool, it was investigated if the user had ever had contact with washing and dryer machines, if he/she has such a product in his/her home and what is the frequency of use. After questioning "pre interaction" it started the Step 2 - Rehearsal Technique. At first, the user was placed in front of the product and the moderator, in turn, encouraged the participant to verbalize the meaning of each function of the graphic user interface and its mode of use, even with no physical contact with the interface. Still in this step without tactile interaction, two tasks were also presented to the user. After the utterance of these tasks, the participant was encouraged to submit their mental model from the verbalization of the steps taken to complete them.

The rehearsal was pursued by tactile interaction, composed by presenting four scenarios, addressing tasks with distinct features like: use of "hypoallergenic" function; use the function "delay start"; using a reduced amount of clothing; and use the function "drying", without washing. Finally, it was presented a translated and adapted version of the satisfaction questionnaire after use QUIS (Questionnaire for User Interface Satisfaction).

All the ten sessions were observed by a usability analyst, who performed a synchronous tab. After the session, the data were reviewed and, after these ten sessions, the data and report were sent to two other analysts, responsible for synthesis usability problems. The identified problems were organized into three groups: initial exploration, tasks mental model and tasks, as shown in Table 2. Each behavior obtained a frequency (sum of the number of participants who performed the particular behavior), and from this number, were generated usability issues for those behaviors often equal to or greater than three.

Table 3. Example of spreadsheet of recording behaviors in Interaction Rehearsal Technique

Behavior	P1	P2	...	P10	Frequency	Usability Problem
Initial Exploration						
Mental Model						
Tasks						
Comments						

The usability problem frequency was also related to criticality: usability problems with frequency less than or equal to four were considered low criticality; usability problems often five and six were considered average criticality; and usability problems often more than or equal to seven were classified as high criticality.

4   Results

4.1   Results of the Heuristic Evaluation

As it was mentioned in the method, the Heuristic Evaluation was performed by three usability analysts; here named "A1", "A2" and "A3". The analyst "A1" identified fourteen usability problems, being five of average criticality and nine of low criticality. The analyst "A2" also found fourteen usability problems, of which eight were low criticality and six average criticality. Finally, the analyst "A3" appointed eleven usability problems, among them, five of average criticality and six of low criticality. These data are presented in Table 1.

Table 4. Number of usability problems identified by the three analysts in the Heuristic Evaluation

	A1	A2	A3
Low criticality	9	8	6
Average criticality	5	6	5
High criticality	0	0	0
Total of usability problems	14	14	11

The usability problems verified by the three analysts were grouped into a spreadsheet for a total twenty-five distinct usability problems. Therefore, the incidence of the same usability problem was observed in the evaluation of more than one analyst. Four usability problems of low criticality and two of average criticality were also detected by two analysts. Regarding the agreement of the three analysts in usability issues, a total of four issues were observed, two of which were classified as average criticality and two as low criticality. Divergence was seen in the classification of criticality in just two usability issues, prevailing the classification by the analyst(s) with most experience in this area. Regarding the runtime and analysis of heuristic evaluation, each analyst reported having developed the heuristic evaluation in part time work (four hours) and it was computed a bout of work for data analysis, accounting for the entire eight working hours, requiring three analysts and a final evaluator.

Among the problems that concordance of two or more analysts (total of ten) were found, it appears that the most violated heuristics were: "Communication", with four incidences of problems with compliance, "Conduction and Control" and "User Freedom", both with two incidences. Among the three areas of categorization of usability problems identified in the heuristic evaluation, information design was categorized in all ten problems, interaction design was related to six problems and, finally, graphic design displayed in four problems. Regarding impacted dimensions, efficiency was pointed at eight problems, followed by satisfaction, pointed at four usability issues, and effectiveness, in turn, occurring in three usability problems: as presented in Table 4.

Table 5. Violated heuristics, related areas and dimensions impacted on issues of agreement among analysts

Violated heuristic	**Related area**	**Impacted dimension**
Communication (4)	Information (10)	Effectiveness (3)
Workload (1)	Interaction (6)	Efficiency (8)
Conduction (2)	Graph (4)	Satisfaction (4)
Compatibility of system – real world (1)		
Control and freedom for the user (2)		
Consistency and standards (1)		

4.2   Results of Interaction Rehearsal Technique

With respect to technological familiarity of the ten participants, seven have a washing machine in their homes, two participants use collective laundries and one participant does not use this type of product. It was found that 7 participants use the product from one to four times a week, while 3 participants use the washing machine rarely. These three participants, one had never used a washing machine or clothes dryer.

The interaction rehearsal technique was tabbed from the verification of users' behaviors, both errors as hits during the execution of the task presented. A matrix has been developed for the recognition of functions of the graphic user interface, related to the exploration stage with no tactile interaction. For this phase, it was observed that the functions of lower scores were: "lock panel" (4/10 hits); "rinse" (5/10 hits); "spin" (5/10 hits) and "unlock door "(5/10 hits).

Forty-four (44) behaviors were identified in the ten sessions of the interaction rehearsal. The behaviors which obtained frequency equal to or greater than three were transcribed into a format of usability problems. This procedure resulted in a total of fourteen (14) different usability problems. It was noted also that two distinct behaviors can result in a same usability problem.

With respect to criticality of the issues raised in the interaction rehearsal, it was verified four usability problems of high criticality (frequency greater than or equal to 7), two of average criticality (frequency of 5 or 6), and eight of low criticality (frequency of 3 4). The most related area to usability issues raised in usability rehearsal was the "Info", with twelve issues. The other two areas considered, Interaction and Graphics, were associated with six usability problems each. The four usability problems, classified as high criticality are related to "Info" and "Graph" areas.

4.3   Comparison between Heuristic Evaluation and Interaction Rehearsal Technique

The fourteen (14) usability problems verified in the interaction rehearsal were compared to the twenty-five (25) usability problems observed in the heuristic evaluation, in order to identify if the application had concordance between the two methods. Twelve (12), of the fourteen (14) usability issues of interaction rehearsal, had already been detected in the heuristic evaluation, of which nine (9) were recorded with consent of two or more analysts. Thus, the heuristic evaluation raised thirteen (13) usability issues which were not observed in the test interaction.

It was found that the two (2) usability problems raised just in the interaction rehearsal technique refers to the understanding specific functions that the product has. They are: "Lack of clarity of function 'Delay Start'", which, although doesn't clearly appear as a usability problem in heuristic evaluation, is related to another aspect verified in the same rating on the poor visibility of the operating mode "Delay Start" and "Lack of clarity of 'Spin' function", which was not identified in the inspection without user.

About comparing criticality of usability problems raised from the two methods, it was observed that only one usability problem classified as low criticality in the interaction rehearsal technique obtained in a different heuristic criticality rating (average). The four usability issues of high criticality of interaction rehearsal technique were classified differently in the heuristic evaluation, two low and two average criticality. Attributed to this divergence of criticality to the fact that the heuristic evaluation, criticality was referring to interference in the completeness of the task, the test of interaction, criticality was generated from the frequency of the behavior.

Regarding the time required for the application of this method, for each session it's added a twenty minute period for reviewing post session data. For the tabulation of data, observers demanded eight (8) hours for organization and unification of data, while two analysts have ordered about half a period (four hours). Thus, the interaction rehearsal technique was performed and analyzed in approximately 22 hours in total (not running) demanding: one moderator, one observer, two analysts and ten participants.

It was observed that, both in the heuristic evaluation as in the interaction rehearsal technique, the "Information" area was the most affected, obtaining similar results between the two methods of application. The other two areas (graphic and interaction) also obtained similar results in both assessments. Thus, it is understood that both methods were able to identify the areas of the project development which need improvement. As an illustration of this abstract data comparison, it's given the Figure 1.

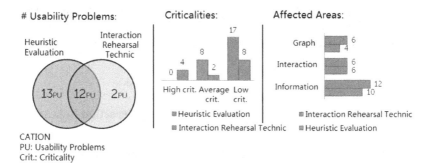

Fig. 1. Comparison of results between usability problems from the heuristic evaluation and the interaction rehearsal technique (Source: the authors)

The interaction rehearsal technique provided data from several users comments, regarding the use, the preference of functions and also the visibility and legibility of elements of the control panel. However, since these comments were not reflected in behavior, they were not counted as usability problems. Thus, the interaction rehearsal technique yielded no data directly related to legibility of elements.

5   Discussion and Final Considerations

From this research, a similarity of results from the application of heuristic rating and interaction rehearsal technique was observed, however, it was also found that the heuristic evaluation enabled a comprehensive look at the usability problems while testing possible interaction investigate in more detail the positioning of users regarding the identified problems. Thus, it summarizes this scenario with the prospect that the heuristic evaluation allowed visiting different usability problems (horizontal approach), while the interaction rehearsal technique approached fewer problems, but with more details (vertical approach).

Here, representative methods were selected for the use in industry and also in the academy, going against the placement of Roto et. al. (2009) [12] and Dumas & Salzman (2006) [4]. The selection of both methods applied took into consideration the variables presented in ISO 16982:2002 [7], since the product used is an adaptation of the existing system, is a well-understood prototype - given the high fidelity representation of the final product panel - and was able to simulate a product under development. Regarding the presentation of both numeric data such as qualitative commented by Tullis and Albert (2008) [16], it was found that both methods made possible the production of numeric data.

Another aspect observed in the application of both methods is the suggestion of improvements. The heuristic evaluation tends not only to detect problems, but also to suggest ways to fix or improve the interaction as a whole, going against the positioning of Dumas et. al. (2004) [3] as the "positive" reviews of usability. Regarding the heuristics of Nielsen (1994), the golden rules of Shneiderman & Plaisant (2004) [13], the principles of ISO 9241-11 (1008) [8] and the recommendations of Bastien & Scapin (1993) [2], it was found that the analysts used frequently the heuristics and recommendations of Nielsen and Bastien & Scapin.

The heuristic evaluation showed well evaluated for number of generated usability problems, for the analysis of criticality and for the execution time and analysis. The interaction rehearsal technique proved to be more appropriate in capturing actual behavior, investigating user opinions and reviewing and verifying user understanding about the new features. Both methods were not biased by the level of fidelity prototype, indicating that this type of prototype is suitable to conduct evaluations of the control panel during product development.

For the application of the heuristic evaluation, it must be considered the importance of not applying only with a specialist. The worksheet for capturing usability problems proved to be a useful low-cost alternative. The interaction rehearsal technique requires a bigger number of individuals who, even having a value less technical time, shall be accompanied by a moderator and an observer for each session. As this study did not account for costs, because it is voluntary, we consider the "time of application of the method". In this respect, we have that the interaction rehearsal technique demands more time not only for the sessions, but also for the data analysis.

Given the above, we raise the following relationships between these two methods. The heuristic evaluation can be applied at an early stage of evaluation of interface, even before planning a Usability Testing. The results of this Heuristic evaluation would help guide the scenarios, the tasks and the focus of evaluation on a Interaction Rehearsal Technique or Usability Testing. In this view, these two methods are complementary, checking some different problems and reasons levels of criticality from the interaction rehearsal technique. However, if the purpose of the usability study is to develop a broad sweep in finding usability problems, regardless of the degree of development of the artifact, it is suggested heuristic evaluation as an appropriate alternative, and less costly. However, the application of both methods, especially in the heuristic evaluation, it is important to pay attention to the choice of professionals with experience (theoretical and practical) in the area to perform the activity, since this is a method that directly depends on the expert.

References

1. Annett, J., Stanton, N.A. (eds.): Task Analysis. Taylor & Francis, London (2000)
2. Bastien, J.M.C., Scapin, D.L.: Ergonomic criteria for the evaluation of human-computer interfaces. Tech. Rep. n. 156. Rocquencourt, France: Institut National de Recherche en Informatique et en Automatique (1993)
3. Dumas, J.S., Molich, R., Jeffries, R.: Describing usability problems: Are we sending the right message? Interactions 11(4), 24–29 (2004)
4. Dumas, J.S., Salzman, M.C.: Usability Assessment Methods. Reviews of Human Factors and Ergonomics 2, 109–140 (2006)
5. Hackos, J.T., Redish, J.C.: User and task analysis for interface design. John Wiley & Sons, Inc., Nova York (1998)
6. Hartson, H.R., Andre, T.S., Williges, R.C.: Criteria for evaluating usability evaluation methods. International Journal of Human-Computer Interaction 10, 145–181 (2003)
7. International Organization for Standardization, ISO TR 16982:2002, Ergonomics of human-system interaction - Usability methods supporting human-centred design (2002)
8. International Organization for Standardization, ISO 9241-11:1998, Ergonomic requirements for office work with visual display terminals (VDTs) - Part 11: Guidance on usability (1998)
9. Jones, M., Marsden, G.: Mobile Interaction Design. John Wiley & Sons Ltd., West Sussex (2006)
10. Karwowski, W., Soares, M.M., Stanton, N.A. (eds.): Human Factors and Ergonomics in Consumer Product Design, Uses and Applications. CRC Press, Boca Raton (2011)
11. Maguire, M.: Methods to support human-centred design. Int. J. Human-Computer Studies 55, 587–634 (2001)
12. Roto, V., Obrist, M., Mattila, K.V.V.: User experience evaluation methods in academic and industrial contexts. In: Proceedings of the Workshop on User Experience Evaluation Methods UXEM 2009 (INTERACT 2009), ACM, Uppsala (2009)
13. Shneiderman, B., Plaisant, C.: Designing the UserInterface: Strategies for Effective Human-Computer Interaction. Addison Wesley, Boston (2004)
14. Stanton, N.A., Young, M.S.: A Guide to Methodology in Ergonomics: Designing for human use. Taylor & Francis, Londres (1999)
15. Stanton, N.A., Salmon, P.M., Walker, G.H., Baber, C., Jenkins, D.P.: Human factors methods: a practical guide for engineering and design. Ashgate, Cornwall (2005)
16. Tullis, T., Albert, B.: Measuring the user experience: Collecting, Analyzing, and Presenting Usability Metrics. Morgan Kaufmann, San Francisco (2008)

Multicultural Text Entry: A Usability Study

Cristina Olaverri-Monreal[1], Maria Lúcia L.R. Okimoto[2], and Klaus Bengler[1]

[1] Technische Universität München, Germany
{olaverri,bengler}@lfe.mw.tum.de
[2] Federal University of Paraná, Brazil
lucia.demec@ufpr.br

Abstract. A detailed study of cultural differences can facilitate the process of introducing a product into a particular market. Such an analysis can be used to decide to what extend a global design of a product needs to be considered and which subsequent measures related to localization or adaptation to a specific target culture need to be taken. In the particular case of text entry input methods to interact with electronic systems, consideration of cultural preferences could lead to a better usability and user experience. Cognitively demanding multimodal interaction with an interface might be reflected in an increased error rate or a decreased typing speed, factors that affect the success and accuracy of a task. We examine in this paper cultural differences through a cross cultural electronic system to determine the degree to which they can affect the ease of use in textual input methodology. Results indicated that users' performance varied depending on the selected language to perform the tasks.

Keywords: text input method, cultural differences, target culture.

1 Introduction

Effective methods for text entry on devices that are gaining in popularity such as Tablet PCs, smart phones or devices for the electronic reading of documents remain a problem [1]. Therefore, several studies have been dedicated to compare how well the performance of a particular device serves user needs, as well as how pragmatic and learnable the device is depending on the environment where the device in question is used [2]. In a non-mobile context, it has been shown that the text entry speeds of a keyboard are rarely exceeded by other input modalities-not even by handwritten testing do the speeds compete, implying a reduced screen visibility due to the positioning of the hand can have a powerful impact on speeds [3]. In a mobile context some areas of active text entry research include methods for mobile phones and wearable computers [4-6] and also methods that support different writing systems [7]. In this intercultural context, a detailed study of cultural differences can facilitate the process of introducing a product into a particular market. Such an analysis can be used to decide to what extend a global design of a product needs to be considered and which subsequent measures related to localization or adaptation to a specific target culture need to be taken [8, 9]. In the particular case of text entry input methods to interact

A. Marcus (Ed.): DUXU 2014, Part I, LNCS 8517, pp. 329–339, 2014.

with electronic systems, consideration of cultural preferences could lead to a more efficient usability and a more positive user experience. Cognitively demanding multimodal interaction with an interface might be reflected by an increased error rate or decreased typing speed, both of which are factors that affect the success and accuracy of a task. Therefore in this paper we examine the effectiveness and efficiency of different text input methods according to the ISO 9241-11 [10] and its associative cultural aspects through a cross cultural electronic system. For this purpose, we developed an electronic framework to automatically collect data from different countries with different input methods and then post process it. Afterwards we selected the data relevant for the input modalities hardware keyboard and virtual keyboard and performed the pertinent statistical analyses.

2   Data Collection

To perform the study we used an electronic Lenovo device connected to a computer monitor for better visibility that enabled the text entry through different modalities. To acquire the required data we relied on the Limesurvey tool [11]. The system is implemented in PHP and supports the researcher in the task of designing online surveys [12]. As Limesurvey is based on an open source application, we tailored the electronic system to serve our purpose and designed a survey in the following languages: English, German, Spanish and Portuguese.

2.1   Survey Design

In the design process of the survey, we set question groups with a common title that represented related questions, all appearing together on the same page. Six question groups were related to personal information such as age, gender, profession, native language as well as other known languages of the participant, familiarity with keyboard layouts for several languages, frequency of use of different devices (i.e. laptop, pc, tablets), frequency of use of different input modalities (i.e. keyboard, touchpad, mouse, digital pen), first and second language selection for the experiment and two selected input modalities to be tested (i.e. hardware keyboard, virtual keyboard, touchpad, digital pen). After making sure that the selected input modality was connected, we showed to the participants relevant question groups according to the selected languages and input modalities. Consequently, different typing tasks consisting of several strings were displayed to the test subject in two languages and two input modalities selected. The grade of difficulty was determined by the string length and the order of the characters: in task 1 a short sentence with 16 characters; in 2 a longer sentence with 256 characters; in 3 a sequence of 39 unordered characters and in task 4 a longer sequence of 91 unordered characters. Figure 1 shows a screenshot of a typing task in Portuguese to be entered by the user through a virtual keyboard.

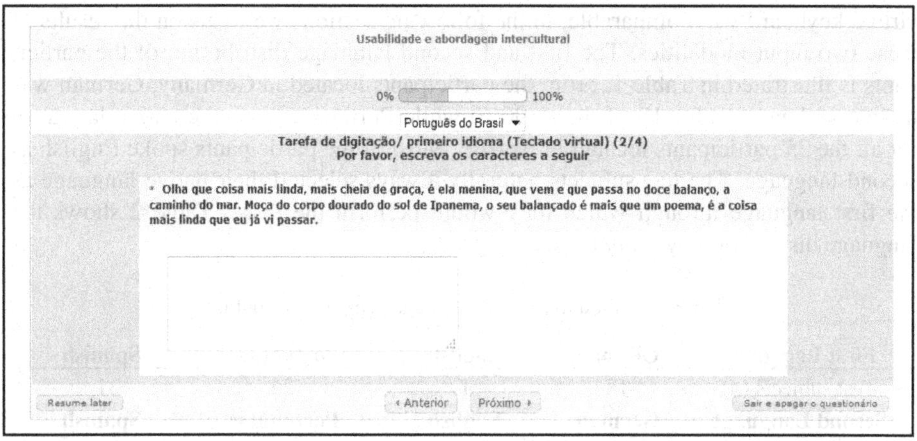

Fig. 1. Typing task in the selected language Portuguese to be performed using a virtual keyboard

2.2   Experiment Setting

A total of 51 test subjects between 21 and 62 years, (mean=27.39, SD=11.65) in Brazil and in Germany were asked to enter several strings with varying levels of difficulty in their languages of preference to acquire comparative empirical data related to different entry methods. They had been previously instructed and were thus already familiar with the system. An electronic visual display was used to perform the tasks. The user had control capabilities by touching the screen, by writing on it with a digital pen or by using an external keyboard. Handwriting recognition software enabled to verify if the text was accurate. Additionally, an external monitor was connected to the system. To determine the impact of the user's culture on the input modality as well as to study potential different strategies to enter text between Germany and Brazil, we contrasted the use of one or another input methods measuring the following usability metrics average Task Completion Time (TCT) to measure the amount of effort required to enter the text and number of spelling errors to determine the effectiveness with which users completed a specified task.

3   Descriptive Data Analysis Results

From the total number of test subjects that participated in the study we excluded 6 records from the analysis, as these individuals did not complete all required questions. Our final sample comprised therefore 45 participants. We analyzed our information collection through descriptive statistics. Most of the test subjects selected hardware keyboard as the input device for entering the information with 38 participants (84% of all 45 participants), followed by a total of 29 test subjects that selected virtual keyboard as input device (64%). 13 test subjects selected digital pen (29%) and 7 touchpad (15%). As the percentage of test subjects that selected hardware keyboard and virtual keyboard was comparable, in the following sections we focus on the results of these two input modalities. The first and second language distribution of the participants is illustrated in Table 1. From the participants located in Germany, German was the native language for 18 of them (90%) while Portuguese was the native language for all the 25 participants located in Brazil.   Most of the participants spoke English as second language. The test subjects naturally always selected their native language as the first language through which they would perform the tasks. Table 2 shows the language distribution by input device selected.

Table 1. First and second language sample distribution

First Language	German	English	Portuguese	Spanish
Test subjects (n)	18	1	25	1
Second Language	**German**	**English**	**Portuguese**	**Spanish**
Test subjects (n)	1	40	0	4

Table 2. Language distribution by input device selected

First Language	German	English	Portuguese	Spanish
Hardware keyboard	15	1	21	1
Virtual keyboard	11	1	16	1
Touchpad	0	0	7	0
Digital pen	10	0	3	0
Second Language	**German**	**English**	**Portuguese**	**Spanish**
Hardware keyboard	1	33	0	1
Virtual keyboard	1	24	0	4
Touchpad	0	7	0	0
Digital pen	0	13	0	0

3.1   Hardware Keyboard as Input Modality

Task Completion Time. 38 participants selected hardware keyboard to perform the tasks. Table 3 and the boxplots in Figure 1 indicate the average Task Completion Time (TCT) to measure the amount of effort users needed to enter the text requested in the four tasks in the languages that were selected by the user as a first and a second language.   Significant differences are indicated. Results regarding the first language selected show that the TCT for the first task was comparatively lower than for the other three tasks. The higher number of strings to be entered for tasks 2 and 4 was reflected in the TCTs.   We performed an independent-samples t-test to compare the time to perform a task in first language German and first language Portuguese conditions with a significance level = 0.05. Results showed that significant differences in TCT existed between Brazilian and German participants in all the tasks, specifically being that the typing speed for Brazilians was lower than for Germans. This could be due to the existence of additional characters that need to be typed in letters with accents. Regarding the second language selected to perform the tasks, statistically significant differences could be found between English and Spanish in task 3. The sample contained only one person who spoke German as second language.

Table 3. TCT median values in seconds with the hardware keyboard for the first and second language

First Language	German	Portuguese	t	df	p-value	English	Spanish
Task 1	18.74	36.92	-2.8668	21.012	0.0092	9.66	10.42
Task 2	78.53	126.38	-2.4704	27.529	0.0199	102.73	127.72
Task 3	37.26	63.03	-3.5308	29.64	0.0013	50.67	51.49
Task 4	61.62	136.13	-4.7266	22.275	9.932e-05	87.25	85.28
Second Language	**German**	------------				**English**	**Spanish**
Task 1	11.96	NA				19.14	17.32
Task 2	123.87	NA				106.81	155.76
Task 3	51.12	NA	3.8318	13.022	0.002072	63.86	42.21
Task 4	85.28	NA				83.76	85.87

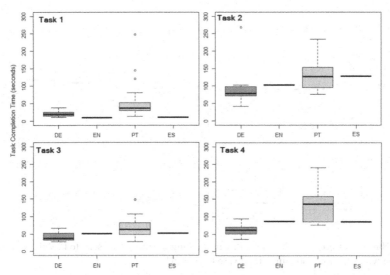

Fig. 2. Average Task Completion Time (TCT) to measure the amount of effort users needed to enter the text requested in the four tasks in the language that was selected by the user as first language with the input modality "hardware keyboard"

Number of Spelling Errors. Table 4 and boxplots in Figure 2 shows the number of errors with the hardware keyboard for the first and second language. Significant differences are indicated. No misspellings could be detected in the first task. Test subjects, who selected German as first language made more errors than people who selected Portuguese as a first language by performing the second task— therein, creating a difference that was statistically significant.

Table 4. Median values of errors with the hardware keyboard for the first and second language

First Language	German	Portuguese	t	df	p-value	English	Spanish
Task 1	0	0				0	0
Task 2	11	2	8.6291	26.337	3.734e-09	5	3
Task 3	0	2	-6.2265	33.949	4.41e-07	0	6
Task 4	3	5	-4.2566	30.293	0.0001849	0	3
Second Language	**German**	------	**t**	**df**	**p-value**	**English**	**Spanish**
Task 1	0	NA	2.9584	13.403	0.01079	1	0
Task 2	1	NA				11	2.5
Task 3	0	NA				2	4.5
Task 4	3	NA				2	1

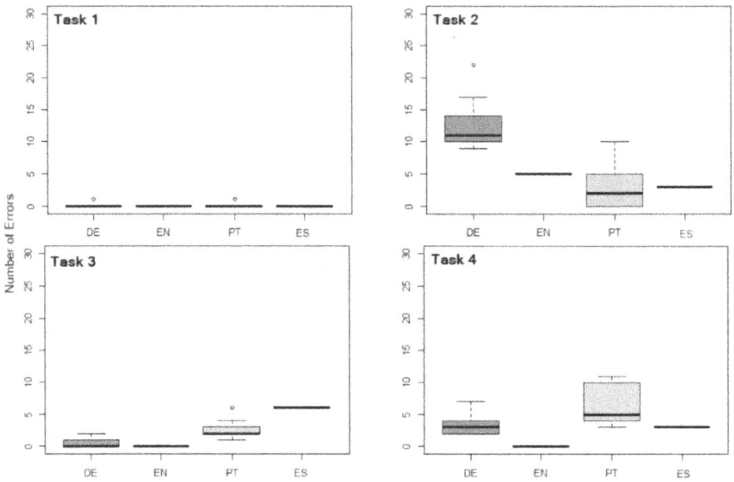

Fig. 3. Number of errors in the four tasks in the language that was selected by the user as first language with the input modality "hardware keyboard"

3.2   Virtual Keyboard as Input Modality

Task Completion Time. As shown in Figure 3 and table 5 the time required to enter the given strings from task 2 through the virtual keyboard was quite slow in comparison to the other methods. Additionally, the TCT to complete the tasks 1, 2 and 3 for test subjects that selected German as a first language was in average longer than for subjects that selected Portuguese as a first language. Statistically significant differences are indicated. Only 4 persons selected Spanish as second language. Figure 4 shows a high variability outside the upper quartiles for Spanish in task 1 caused by an outlier.

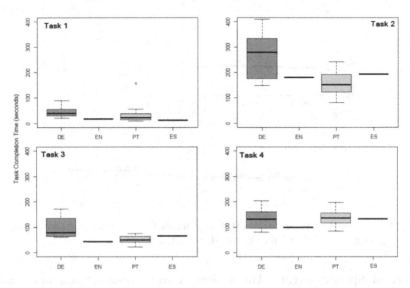

Fig. 4. Average Task Completion Time (TCT) to enter the text requested in the four tasks in the language selected as first with the input modality virtual keyboard

Table 5. TCT median values in seconds with the virtual keyboard for the first and second language

First Language	German	Portuguese	t	df	p-value	English	Spanish
Task 1	40.12	22.14				16.98	12.20
Task 2	278.96	151.76	3.7249	13.642	0.00235	180.50	193.95
Task 3	78.10	50.19	3.6943	11.929	0.00309	42.92	65.28
Task 4	131.34	136.04				99.45	132.49
Second Language	**German**	--------------	**t**	**df**	**p-value**	**English**	**Spanish**
Task 1	12.77	NA				20.84	26.53
Task 2	176.93	NA				197.21	318.60
Task 3	64.61	NA				65.87	72.31
Task 4	93.72	NA				123.40	124.42

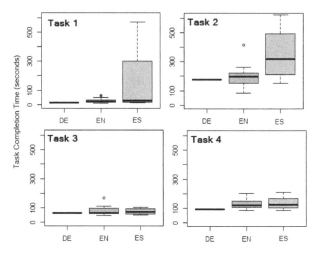

Fig. 5. Average Task Completion Time (TCT) to enter the text requested in the four tasks in the language selected as second with the input modality virtual keyboard

Number of Spelling Errors. The number of errors from subjects who selected German as first language and the other subjects in task 2 were statistically significant (Table 6, Figure 5). Regarding the selected second language, in task 4 an outlier produced a high variability outside the upper quartiles for Spanish: one person made 45 errors (Figure 6). Significant differences existed in task 3 for English and Spanish.

Table 6. Median values of errors with the virtual keyboard for the first and second language

First Language	German	Portuguese	t	df	p-value	English	Spanish
Task 1	0	0				0	0
Task 2	25	1.5	13.8554	12.677	4.975e-09	1	0
Task 3	0	2	-4.0019	24.581	0.000505	0	4
Task 4	3	6	-2.7285	17.616	0.01398	1	1
Second Language	**German**	--------------	**t**	**df**	**p-value**	**English**	**Spanish**
Task 1	3	NA				0	0
Task 2	0	NA				3	3.5
Task 3	0	NA	-3.201	3.617	0.0378	1	5.5
Task 4	11	NA				1	3

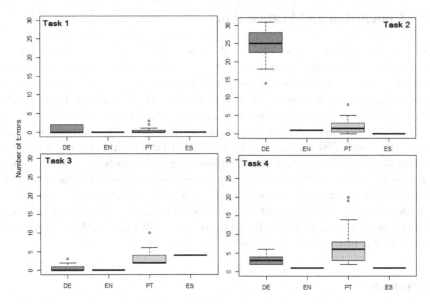

Fig. 6. Number of errors in the four tasks in the language selected as first with the input modality virtual keyboard

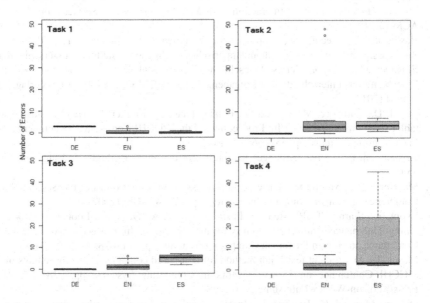

Fig. 7. Number of errors in the four tasks in the language that selected as second with the input modality virtual keyboard

4   Conclusion and Future Work

Results from our data analysis showed that users' performance varied depending on the language selected by the user to perform the tasks and depending on the input modality. Comparative results regarding hardware and virtual keyboard showed that the time required to enter information in a computer through a virtual keyboard was longer than with hardware keyboard for German native speakers. Brazilians however, performed better with the hardware keyboard only in task 2 that consisted in entering a long string with 256 characters. The number of errors with both input modalities was similar except for the task 2 in German, where the number of errors was lower than with the virtual keyboard. Regarding the performance with English as a second language, there were no conclusive results produced. The number of errors and time to accomplish the tasks depended on the selected language regardless of whether or not this was the native language. In future work we will aim for a bigger sample size to make further inferences about the selected population.

References

1. Scott, J., Izadi, S., Rezai, L.S., Ruszkowski, D., Bi, X., Balakrishnan, R.: RearType: text entry using keys on the back of a device. In: Proceedings of the 12th International Conference on Human Computer Interaction with Mobile Devices and Services, pp. 171–180. ACM (2010)
2. Haslbeck, A., Pecot, K., Popova, S., Eichinger, A., Bengler, K.: Menschliche Zuverlässigkeit bei der alpuhanmerischen Eingabe mittels unterschiedlicher Eingabemedien. Book Series Menschliche Zuverlässigkeit bei der alphanumerischen Eingabe mittels unterschiedlicher Eingabemedien, vol. 2146, pp. 87–97. VDI-Verlag, Düsseldorf (2011)
3. Vogel, D., Cudmore, M., Casiez, G., Balakrishnan, R., Keliher, L.: Hand occlusion with tablet-sized direct pen input. In: Proceedings of the SIGCHI Conference on Human Factors in Computing Systems, pp. 557–566. ACM (2009)
4. Kristensson, P.O.: Five challenges for intelligent text entry methods. AI Magazine 30(4), 85 (2009)
5. MacKenzie, S.: Mobile text entry using three keys. In: Proceedings of the Second Nordic Conference on Human-computer Interaction, pp. 27–34. ACM (2002)
6. Lyons, K., Starner, T., Plaisted, D., Fusia, J., Lyons, A., Drew, A., Looney, E.: Twiddler typing: One-handed chording text entry for mobile phones. In: Proceedings of the SIGCHI Conference on Human Factors in Computing Systems, pp. 671–678. ACM (2004)
7. Masui, T.: An efficient text input method for pen-based computers. In: Proceedings of the SIGCHI Conference on Human Factors in Computing Systems, pp. 328–335. ACM Press/Addison-Wesley Publishing Co. (1998)
8. Olaverri-Monreal, C., Bengler, K.: Impact of cultural diversity on the menu structure design of Driver Information Systems: a cross-cultural study. In: Proceedings IEEE Intelligent Vehicles Symposium, pp. 107–112 (2011)
9. Olaverri-Monreal, C., Bengler, K., Breisinger, M., Draxler, C.: Markup Languages and Menu Structure Transformation during the Internationalisation process of Driver Information Systems. Localisation Focus 9(1), 4–12 (2010)

10. ISO, W.: 9241-11. Ergonomic requirements for office work with visual display terminals (VDTs). The international organization for standardization (1998)
11. LimeSurvey, LimeSurvey (2014), http://www.limesurvey.org/en/
12. Team, L.: LimeSurvey Manual. In: Book LimeSurvey Manual. Series LimeSurvey Manual (2014)

Subjective and Objective Assessment of Mashup Tools

Tihomir Orehovački[1] and Toni Granollers[2]

[1] University of Zagreb, Faculty of Organization and Informatics
Pavlinska 2, 42000 Varaždin, Croatia
`tihomir.orehovacki@foi.hr`
[2] University of Lleida, Polytechnic School, GRIHO Research Group
C. de Jaume II, 69, 25001 Lleida, Spain
`tonig@diei.udl.cat`

Abstract. Mashup tools are platforms that enable end users to combine components from multiple sources and thus create, deploy, and share their own web applications. The aim of this paper is to present and discuss the findings of two empirical studies on evaluation of mashup tools by means of subjective and objective measuring instruments. In the first study, data were gathered with the employment of SUS post-use questionnaire and Tobii eye-tracking device, and in the second, by applying the retrospective thinking aloud method. The analysis of collected data uncovered strengths and weaknesses of evaluated mashup tools. In addition, the relevance that users assign to quality in use attributes in the context of mashup tools has been determined.

Keywords: Mashup Tools, Subjective and Objective Evaluation, Post-use Questionnaire, Eye-tracking, Retrospective Thinking Aloud, Empirical Findings.

1 Introduction

Mashup tools are specific breed of Web 2.0 applications [16] that integrate disparate components, such as RSS/Atom feeds, services, content provided by third parties, or widgets, which are readily available on the Web. They are meant for the development of novel situational applications, services, or functionalities in a value-adding fashion. Requiring no programming skills from their users, mashup tools are online development environments that enable everyone to create their own web applications. In that respect, they represent shift from product-oriented software development to consumer-oriented composition [14]. Malinga et al. [13] distinguish four types of mashup tools. Process-oriented mashup tools enable users to simulate business procedures [7] and integrate assorted processes [8] in an enterprise. Data-oriented mashup tools facilitate the aggregation of data from heterogeneous remotely hosted online sources. Knowledge management mashup tools improve the interaction among members of the organization. Interface-oriented mashup tools help users to develop interactive input menus and query result filters. Hoyer and Fischer [9] have categorized mashup tools into two main groups. Consumer mashup tools enable individuals to create mashups in the form of personalized web portals that combine data elements from more than one source

A. Marcus (Ed.): DUXU 2014, Part I, LNCS 8517, pp. 340–351, 2014.

(e.g. news, weather forecast, e-mails, etc.) and display them on a simple graphical interface. This individualized browser start pages are frequently referred to as front-end [22] or presentation layer [21] mashups. Enterprise mashup tools are intended for the development of applications that integrate various resources from multiple sources deployed in an enterprise ecosystem.

Evaluation plays an important role in a lifecycle of every web application. Although literature offers various models and methodologies dealing with the evaluation of web sites [15][20] and Web 2.0 applications [17][18], approaches addressing the assessment of mashup tools are less common. This paper reports findings of two empirical studies in which mashup tools were evaluated by means of subjective and objective measuring instruments.

The remainder of the paper is structured as follows. Brief overview of current advances in the assessment of mashups is contained in the next section. Results of conducted studies are presented in the third and the fourth section. Concluding remarks and future research directions are provided in the last section.

2   Background to the Research

Recent research on the assessment of mashups was focused on exploring diverse aspects of their quality and usability. Drawing on recent standard [11] aimed for evaluating different facets of software quality, ergonomic criteria introduced by Bastien and Scapin [2], and usability guidelines for Web design, Insfran et al. [10] proposed the Mashup Usability Model in which usability has been decomposed into following six sub-characteristics: appropriateness recognisability, learnability, operability, user error protection, user interface aesthetics, and accessibility. Koschmider et al. [12] emphasize that selection of quality metrics depends on the type of mashups. The same authors argue that presentation and extraction mashups should be evaluated in terms of consistent graphical representation, data mashups have to meet metrics meant for the assessment of efficiency in modularization and connectivity, functionality mashups need to satisfy metrics related to accessibility of disparate mashed data and the composition itself, flow mashups should address metrics intended for evaluating connectivity, availability of components, and error rates, client- and server-side mashups have to comply with metrics related to efficient security policies and right management, while the quality of enterprise mashups should be measured in terms of availability, error rates, popularity, user rating, and comments. Quality of the mashup can be observed from the perspective of heterogeneous components that constitute it [5] as well as from the aspect of the final composition [19]. In that respect, Cappiello et al. [4] developed the model which enables evaluation of following quality dimensions: data quality (accuracy, timeliness, completeness, availability, and consistency), presentation quality (usability and accessibility), and composition quality (added value, component suitability, component usage, consistency, and availability). Nevertheless, results of a systematic mapping study [6] suggest that there is still a need for empirical research addressing the assessment of security, usability, and reliability of mashups.

Contrary to the aforementioned, studies related to the evaluation of tools aimed for the development of mashups are rather scarce. For that reason we initiated a research which was comprised of two experimental studies. The objective of the first study was to determine to what extent measuring instruments meant for evaluating the usability of websites are suitable for the assessment of consumer mashup tools. The purpose of the second study was to identify a set of quality in use attributes which users find relevant in the context of interaction with front-end mashup tools. Findings of both studies are described in more detail in the following two sections.

3   First Study

Participants. Ten subjects ranging in age from 19 to 34 years (M = 26.00, SD = 5.696) were recruited for the first study. The sample was composed of 70% male and 30% female students from the Polytechnic School at the University of Lleida in Spain. At the time when the study was carried out, the majority of participants (50%) were in the second year of a graduate programme, 40% of them were second-year undergraduate students, while 10% of them were enrolled in the third year of an undergraduate programme. Most of respondents (60%) had at least very good knowledge of using Web 2.0 applications. Study participants had been loyal users of Facebook, YouTube, Twitter, and Wikipedia (80%, 40%, 30%, and 30% of them, respectively, used those popular Web 2.0 applications at least between once and twice a day).

Measures. Users' performance in executing scenario tasks was examined with five disparate metrics. Task efficiency is the estimated amount of minutes needed to complete the task. Task completion refers to the ratio of number of tasks attempted and total number of tasks. Task effectiveness denotes the product of task completion and the extent to which goals of the task have been reached. Task productivity represents the proportion of task effectiveness and task efficiency. Number of fixations is total quantity of relatively stable positions of users' eyes per task. Perceived usability of both mashup tools (Netvibes and Protopage) was explored with System Usability Scale (SUS) [3] post-use questionnaire.

Apparatus. With an aim to create a comfortable environment, the study was conducted in a GRIHO usability lab. Data on participants' eye movements as well as their efficiency and effectiveness in completing scenario tasks were recorded with Tobii T60 eye tracker which is a 15-inch LCD display (96 dpi) with a screen resolution of 1280x1024 pixels and a sampling rate of 60 Hz. The collected data were analyzed with Tobii Studio 3.2 and Morae 3 software. The SUS was administrated online using the KwikSurveys questionnaire builder. Responses to the items were scored on a five point Likert scale (1- strongly disagree, 5 – strongly agree).

Procedure. The study was composed of two main parts: the execution of predefined tasks and the completion of the online questionnaire. Upon arriving at the lab, the participants were welcomed and briefly introduced about the usability evaluation study which was followed by the explanation of the equipment to be used. The participants were then asked to complete an informed consent form. At the beginning of the tasks performance session, the form containing a list of fifteen representative tasks (see Appendix) was given to the participant. The eye-tracker was then calibrated to the participant with a short 9-point procedure during which he or she watched a circle moving on the screen. When the eye calibration succeeded, Tobii Studio launched the mashup tool in Internet Explorer web browser. The experimenter left the room while the participant started working on tasks. Data recording commenced when the participant began reading the task, and ended when the participant either completed or cancelled the task. Each participant went through the calibration procedure and tasks solving session twice – first with Netvibes and then using the Protopage. After completing all the tasks with both mashup tools, the participants were asked to fill out the post-use questionnaire. At the end of the study, respondents were debriefed, and thanked for their participation. The duration of the experiment was between 30 minutes and one hour.

Findings. The first study adopted a within-subjects design contrasting two consumer mashup tools. Taking into account the results of Shapiro-Wilk Tests which uncovered that at least one of the variables in a pairwise comparison violates the assumption of normality in data ($p < .05$), differences between evaluated mashup tools were explored by means of Wilcoxon Signed-Rank Tests.

Mean values of the time-on-task metric are presented in Table 1. Overall, the participants have spent significantly more time ($Z = -2.805$, $p = .005$, $r = -.63$) on completing all scenario tasks by means of Netvibes (Mdn = 22.865) than when they employed Protopage (Mdn = 11.855) for the equivalent purpose. More specifically, the participants were significantly more efficient ($Z = -2.803$, $p = .005$, $r = -.63$) in adding widgets to the tab entitled Business when they were using Protopage (Mdn = 1.075) than when they performed the same task with Netvibes (Mdn = 2.445). As a follow up, the analysis of recordings revealed that participants had difficulties in finding functionality for adding widgets to the Netvibes. On the other hand, the participants had to invest significantly less time ($Z = -2.191$, $p < .05$, $r = -.49$) to personalize the Google Maps widget on Netvibes (Mdn = .400) because during the execution of the identical task with Protopage (Mdn = 1.365) they could not figure out how to change the default location displayed in the widget. Data analysis also uncovered that participants were significantly less efficient ($Z = -2.805$, $p = .005$, $r = -.63$) in changing the background image on Netvibes (Mdn = 3.090) than completing the equivalent task on Protopage (Mdn = .450). The rationale behind this finding is that participants were unable to find the specified background theme in a timely manner. It was also found that Netvibes (Mdn = 2.425) does not support changing the tab color which is the reason why the participants needed significantly less time ($Z = -2.803$, $p = .005$, $r = -.63$) to complete the eleventh task with Protopage (Mdn = .190). The participant were significantly more efficient ($Z = -2.805$, $p = .005$, $r = -.63$) in sorting widgets when they were using Protopage (Mdn = .240) than when they were performing the identical task with Netvibes (Mdn = .775). In addition, the participants invested significantly less time ($Z = -2.599$, $p < .01$, $r = -.58$) in changing the background image to the default value on Protopage (Mdn = .225) than when they were doing the same on Netvibes (Mdn = 1.040). Finally, the participants spent significantly more time (Z = -2.312, p < .05, r = -.52) on logging out from Netvibes (Mdn = .195) than completing the equivalent task with Protopage (Mdn = .140). All the aforementioned effects are large in size.

There was no significant difference (Z = -.912, p = .362) between two mashup tools in terms of the extent to which the participants succeeded to complete all scenario tasks. Since Protopage (Mdn = 0) does not provide the functionality of changing the interface language, the participants were significantly more successful (Z = -2.828, p = .005, r = -.63) in completing the identical task with Netvibes (Mdn = 1). On the other hand, the participants were significantly more effective (Z = -2.000, p < .05, r = -.45) in personalizing the weather widget on Netvibes (Mdn = 1) than when they were in doing the same on Protopage (Mdn = 1). Given that participants experienced difficulties in adding news feed for Esport3.cat website on Protopage (Mdn = 0.75), they were significantly more successful (Z = -2.070, p < .05, r = -.46) in completing this task on Netvibes (Mdn = 1). It was also found that participants were significantly more effective (Z = -2.000, p < .05, r = -.45) in customizing the Google Maps widget on Netvibes (Mdn = 1) than they were in executing the same task on Protopage (Mdn = 0). Taking into account that participants were unable to change tab color on Netvibes (Mdn = 0), they were significantly more effective (Z = -3.162, p < .005, r = -.71) in completing this task on Protopage (Mdn = 1). Finally, the participants were significantly more successful (Z = -2.449, p < .05, r = -.55) in changing the background image to the default value when they were using Protopage than when they were employing Netvibes for the equivalent purpose. The effects related to the fifth, sixth, and eighth task are medium in size while remaining reported effects are large in size.

Table 1. Average values of task efficiency and task completion metrics for selected mashup tools

Tasks	Task Efficiency *		Task Completion **	
	Netvibes	Protopage	Netvibes	Protopage
Task 1	0.63	0.70	1.00	1.00
Task 2	0.85	0.68	1.00	1.00
Task 3	1.92	1.74	0.80	0.00
Task 4	3.09	1.20	0.90	1.00
Task 5	0.61	0.86	1.00	0.60
Task 6	1.68	1.74	1.00	0.65
Task 7	1.68	2.18	0.85	0.80
Task 8	0.58	1.31	0.80	0.40
Task 9	3.12	0.49	0.70	0.90
Task 10	0.56	0.27	1.00	0.90
Task 11	2.50	0.23	0.00	1.00
Task 12	0.95	0.25	0.90	1.00
Task 13	1.53	1.09	0.90	0.75
Task 14	1.78	0.23	0.30	0.90
Task 15	0.31	0.14	1.00	1.00
* A lower value means a better result, ** A higher value means a better result				

Considering the values shown in Table 2, the participants were significantly more effective when they were performing all scenario tasks with Netvibes (Mdn = .775) than when they were doing the same by means of Protopage (Mdn = .680). More specifically, the participants could complete the third task significantly more accurately ($Z = -2.828$, $p = .005$, $r = -.63$) when they were using Netvibes (Mdn = 1) than they did when they were interacting with Protopage (Mdn = 0). On contrary, the participants were significantly more effective ($Z = -2.724$, $p < .01$, $r = -.61$) in completing the fourth task with Protopage (Mdn = 1), than they were with Netvibes (Mdn = .660). Moreover, Wilcoxon Signed-Rank Test revealed that participants were significantly more effective ($Z = -3.162$, $p < .005$, $r = -.71$) in executing the fifth task by means of Netvibes (Mdn = 1) than when they were working on the identical task with Protopage (Mdn = 0). According to results of data analysis, the participants could complete the sixth task significantly more accurately ($Z = -2.070$, $p < .05$, $r = -.46$) when they employed Netvibes (Mdn = 1) than when they applied Protopage (Mdn = .625) for the equivalent purpose. It was also found that participants were significantly less effective ($Z = -2.646$, $p < .01$, $r = -.59$) in executing the eighth task using the Protopage (Mdn = 0) than when they were solving the identical task with Netvibes (Mdn = 1). On the other hand, the participants were able to complete the eleventh task significantly more accurately ($Z = -3.000$, $p < .005$, $r = -.67$) by means of Protopage (Mdn = 1) than they were with Netvibes (Mdn = 0). Finally, the participants were significantly less effective ($Z = -2.070$, $p < .05$, $r = -.46$) in performing the thirteenth task with Protopage (Mdn = .625) than when they used Netvibes (Mdn = 1) for the equivalent purpose. Effects related to the third, fourth, fifth, eighth, and eleventh task are large in size while effects referring to sixth and thirteenth task are medium in size.

According to the mean values of task productivity presented in Table 2, the participants were in general 50.97% more productive in completing all scenario tasks when they were using Protopage than when they were applying Netvibes for the same purpose.

Table 2. Average values of task effectiveness and task productivity metrics for selected mashup tools (note that a higher value means a better result)

Tasks	Task Effectiveness		Task Productivity	
	Netvibes	Protopage	Netvibes	Protopage
Task 1	1.00	1.00	1.58	1.44
Task 2	1.00	1.00	1.17	1.47
Task 3	0.80	0.00	0.42	0.00
Task 4	0.56	1.00	0.18	0.83
Task 5	1.00	0.00	1.63	0.00
Task 6	1.00	0.55	0.60	0.32
Task 7	0.70	0.68	0.42	0.31
Task 8	0.80	0.10	1.39	0.08
Task 9	0.60	0.90	0.19	1.83
Task 10	0.80	0.90	1.44	3.40
Task 11	0.00	0.90	0.00	4.00
Task 12	0.90	1.00	0.95	3.95
Task 13	0.90	0.63	0.59	0.57
Task 14	0.30	0.40	0.17	1.75
Task 15	0.90	1.00	2.95	7.06

An analysis of collected data revealed that the evaluated mashup tools differ significantly (Z = -2.293, p < .05, r = -.51) in terms of the overall number of fixations that were recorded during the implementation of all fifteen tasks. Results of Wilcoxon Signed-Rank Tests presented in Table 3 indicate that participants were significantly more effective in carrying out the fourth, ninth, eleventh, twelfth, and fifteenth task

Table 3. Average number of fixations per task for evaluated mashup tools (note that a lower value means a better result)

Tasks	Overall number of fixations		Z	p	r
	Netvibes	Protopage			
Task 1	47.12	52.35	-.357	.721	N/A
Task 2	65.71	52.10	-1.274	.203	N/A
Task 3	145.39	135.74	-.051	.959	N/A
Task 4	244.08	91.67	-2.293	.022	-.51
Task 5	44.49	62.49	-.561	.575	N/A
Task 6	143.79	140.77	-.663	.508	N/A
Task 7	126.95	168.08	-.561	.575	N/A
Task 8	47.04	102.97	-2.191	.028	-.49
Task 9	228.58	38.64	-2.803	.005	-.63
Task 10	37.30	20.72	-1.682	.093	N/A
Task 11	184.40	17.55	-2.803	.005	-.63
Task 12	68.52	19.28	-2.803	.005	-.63
Task 13	103.37	81.88	-1.274	.203	N/A
Task 14	139.28	17.51	-2.599	.009	-.58
Task 15	22.37	11.16	-2.395	.017	-.54

Table 4. Perceived usability of selected mashup tools

SUS Items	Netvibes	Protopage
I think that I would like to use this mashup tool frequently.	3.10	3.00
I found the mashup tool unnecessarily complex	3.10	2.90
I thought the mashup tool was easy to use.	3.40	3.60
I think that I would need the support of a technical person to be able to use this mashup tool.	2.50	2.20
I found the various functions in this mashup tool were well integrated.	3.30	3.10
I thought there was too much inconsistency in this mashup tool.	2.70	2.60
I would imagine that most people would learn to use this mashup tool very quickly.	3.50	3.70
I found the mashup tool very cumbersome to use.	2.60	2.40
I felt very confident using the mashup tool.	3.00	3.40
I needed to learn a lot of things before I could get going with this mashup tool.	2.50	2.10
SUS Score	57.25	61.50

when they were using Protopage than when they were interacting with Netvibes. On contrary, the participants have made significantly less fixations when they were working on the eighth task in Netvibes than when they were performing the identical task by means of Protopage. All reported effects are large in size.

According to the values presented in Table 4, Protopage was perceived as more usable mashup tool than Netvibes. Given that SUS scores of both Netvibes and Protopage are below the acceptable threshold [1], their usability should be improved. Nevertheless, the selected mashup tools do not differ significantly (p > .05) in terms of responses to particular SUS items nor in the context of the overall SUS scores.

Gaze plots, heat maps, and clusters which represent the distribution of fixations made by all participants during the execution of the first task are shown in Figure 1. The aforementioned illustrations imply that in the case of Netvibes the participants had difficulties in finding a login form while in the context of Protopage their attention was interfered with advertisements and comics which were displayed on the home page.

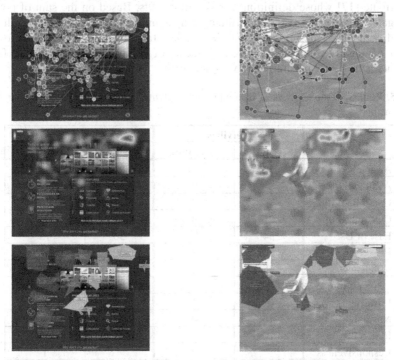

Fig. 1. Gaze plots, heat maps, and clusters (top to bottom) illustrating the distribution of fixations in the first task (left: Netvibes, right: Protopage)

4   Second Study

Participants. A total of 110 respondents (84.55% male, 15.45% female), aged 20.25 years (SD = .960) on average, were involved in the second study. At the time when the study took place, majority (90%) of research subjects were enrolled in the second year of an undergraduate programme at Faculty of Organization and Informatics, University of Zagreb in Croatia. All of them had been frequent users of social networking site Facebook and video podcasting service YouTube (90.91% and 82.73%, respectively, had been using those Web 2.0 applications at least between once and twice a day). Most of students (95.45%) had at least good knowledge of interacting with Web 2.0 applications.

Procedure. During one semester students were asked to employ mashup tools as Personal Learning Environments, that is, for receiving updates on heterogeneous educational artifacts created and integrated with various Web 2.0 applications. At the end of the semester, participants had to deliver a critical review of the used mashup tools in the form of a written report. Considering the specificities of the Retrospective Thinking Aloud method, a two-phase analysis of qualitative data was carried out. Firstly, positive and negative statements related to particular mashup tool were extracted from the reports. Thereafter, each statement was assigned to the quality in use attribute [17] whose definition it most closely fits. Based on the sum of positive and negative statements, a set of attributes that should be considered when evaluating the quality in use of mashup tools was determined. In addition, drawing on the overall number of negative statements allocated, the most common issues users are facing when interacting with mashup tools were identified.

Table 5. Results of the analysis of data collected applying the Retrospective Thinking Aloud (RTA) method

Attributes	Netvibes		Protopage	
	Strengths	Weaknesses	Strengths	Weaknesses
Aesthetics	36	10	20	25
Availability		4	4	4
Controllability	3	4	3	1
Customizability	25	4	13	5
Ease of Use	54	13	56	13
Effectiveness	20	3	30	4
Efficiency	9	2	10	
Learnability	8	7	5	7
Loyalty	1	1	3	1
Navigability	16	4	18	7
Reliability	10	4	7	4
Responsiveness		2		1
Satisfaction	26	6	29	4
Uniqueness		23	1	23
Usefulness	7		12	1

Findings. With the employment of the RTA method the participants generated the set of 613 statements related to the strengths (69.49%) and weaknesses (30.51%) of evaluated mashup tools. Majority of statements were related to the following quality in use attributes: ease of use (22.19%), aesthetics (14.85%), satisfaction (10.60%), effectiveness (9.30%), customizability (7.67%), uniqueness (7.67%), and navigability (7.34%). Statements on weaknesses of selected mashup tools were mostly attached to the uniqueness (24.60%), aesthetics (18.72%), ease of use (13.90%), learnability (7.49%), navigability (5.88%), satisfaction (5.35%), and customizability (4.81%). On the other hand, strengths that were reported in majority of cases were assigned to the ease of use (25.82%), aesthetics (13.15%), satisfaction (12.91%), effectiveness (11.74%), customizability (8.92%), and navigability (7.98%). The results of data analysis presented in Table 5 indicate that Protopage (47.39%) has better ratio of strengths and weaknesses than Netvibes (40.47%).

5   Conclusion

The objective of the work presented in this paper was to examine consumer mashup tools from subjective and objective perspective. For that purpose, two empirical studies were carried out. Results of the first study imply that objective metrics have a higher level of validity than subjective ones. In that respect, metrics of task efficiency, completion, effectiveness, and productivity can be used to determine the significant difference among mashup tools. On the other hand, mashup tools cannot be compared and ranked by mean values of responses to the SUS post-use questionnaire items.

Findings of the second study suggest that each front-end mashup tool should: be simple to operate (ease of use); have an attractive interface (aesthetics); meet users' expectations (satisfaction); enable users to execute tasks accurately and completely (effectiveness); be distinctive among other mashup tools (uniqueness); be customizable to users' specificities (customizability); have intuitive user interface (navigability); enable users to quickly become proficient in using its interface functionalities (learnability); be dependable, stable, and bug-free (reliability); enable users to quickly complete tasks (efficiency); be beneficial in a specified context of use (usefulness); allow use without registration and enable signing in with existing user account (availability); give users full freedom in carrying out tasks (controllability); encourage visitors to become regular users (loyalty); and react promptly to users' actions (responsiveness).

The aforementioned set of attributes will be used as a basis for our future work which will be focused on the development of a measuring instrument that would enable the assessment of all relevant pragmatic and hedonic facets of the quality in use in the context of mashup tools. With an aim to explore the robustness of findings presented in this paper and to draw generalizable sound conclusions, further studies will be carried out during which heterogeneous groups of users will evaluate various types of mashup tools.

References

1. Bangor, A., Kortum, P., Miller, J.: Determining What Individual SUS Scores Mean: Adding an Adjective Rating Scale. Journal of Usability Studies 4(3), 114–123 (2009)
2. Bastien, J.M., Scapin, D.L.: Ergonomic Criteria for the Evaluation of Human-Computer Interfaces. Technical Report no. 156. INRIA, Rocquencourt (1993)

3. Brooke, J.: SUS: a "quick and dirty" usability scale. In: Jordan, P.W., Thomas, B., Weerdmeester, B.A., McClelland, I.L. (eds.) Usability Evaluation in Industry, pp. 189–194. Taylor and Francis, London (1996)

4. Cappiello, C., Daniel, F., Koschmider, A., Matera, M., Picozzi, M.: A Quality Model for Mashups. In: Auer, S., Díaz, O., Papadopoulos, G.A. (eds.) ICWE 2011. LNCS, vol. 6757, pp. 137–151. Springer, Heidelberg (2011)

5. Cappiello, C., Daniel, F., Matera, M.: A Quality Model for Mashup Components. In: Gaedke, M., Grossniklaus, M., Díaz, O. (eds.) ICWE 2009. LNCS, vol. 5648, pp. 236–250. Springer, Heidelberg (2009)

6. Cedillo, P., Fernandez, A., Insfran, E., Abrahão, S.: Quality of Web Mashups: A Systematic Mapping Study. In: Sheng, Q.Z., Kjeldskov, J. (eds.) ICWE Workshops 2013. LNCS, vol. 8295, pp. 66–78. Springer, Heidelberg (2013)

7. De Vrieze, P., Xu, L., Bouguettaya, A., Yang, J., Chen, J.: Process-Oriented Enterprise Mashups. In: Proceedings of the Workshops at the 4th International Conference on Grid and Pervasive Computing, pp. 64–71. IEEE, Geneva (2009)

8. Fichter, D., Wisniewski, J.: They Grow Up So Fast: Mashups in the Enterprise. Online 33(3), 54–57 (2009)

9. Hoyer, V., Fischer, M.: Market Overview of Enterprise Mashup Tools. In: Bouguettaya, A., Krueger, I., Margaria, T. (eds.) ICSOC 2008. LNCS, vol. 5364, pp. 708–721. Springer, Heidelberg (2008)

10. Insfran, E., Cedillo, P., Fernández, A., Abrahão, S., Matera, M.: Evaluating the Usability of Mashups Applications. In: Proceedings of the 8th International Conference on the Quality of Information and Communications Technology, pp. 323–326. IEEE, Lisbon (2012)

11. ISO/IEC 25010:2011. Systems and software engineering – Systems and software Quality Requirements and Evaluation (SQuaRE) – System and software quality models (2011)

12. Koschmider, A., Hoyer, V., Giessmann, A.: Quality Metrics for Mashups. In: Proceedings of the Annual Research Conference of the South African Institute of Computer Scientists and Information Technologists, pp. 376–380. ACM, Bela-Bela (2010)

13. Malinga, M., Gruner, S., Koschmider, A.: Quality and usability of mashup tools: criteria and evaluation. In: Proceedings of the Annual Research Conference of the South African Institute of Computer Scientists and Information Technologists, pp. 154–159. ACM, East London (2013)

14. Nestler, T.: Towards a mashup-driven end-user programming of SOA-based applications. In: Proceedings of the 10th International Conference on Information Integration and Web-based Applications & Services, pp. 551–554. ACM, Linz (2008)

15. Olsina, L., Rossi, G.: Measuring Web Application Quality with WebQEM. IEEE Multimedia 9(4), 20–29 (2002)

16. Orehovački, T., Bubaš, G., Kovačić, A.: Taxonomy of Web 2.0 Applications with Educational Potential. In: Cheal, C., Coughlin, J., Moore, S. (eds.) Transformation in Teaching: Social Media Strategies in Higher Education, pp. 43–72. Informing Science Press, Santa Rosa (2012)

17. Orehovački, T., Granić, A., Kermek, D.: Evaluating the Perceived and Estimated Quality in Use of Web 2.0 Applications. The Journal of Systems and Software 86(12), 3039–3059 (2013)

18. Pang, M., Suh, W., Hong, J., Kim, J., Lee, H.: A New Web Site Quality Assessment Model for the Web 2.0 Era. In: Murugesan, S. (ed.) Handbook of Research on Web 2.0, 3.0, and X.0: Technologies, Business, and Social Applications, pp. 387–410. IGI Global, Hershey (2010)

19. Picozzi, M., Rodolfi, M., Cappiello, C., Matera, M.: Quality-Based Recommendations for Mashup Composition. In: Daniel, F., Facca, F.M. (eds.) ICWE 2010 Workshops. LNCS, vol. 6385, pp. 360–371. Springer, Heidelberg (2010)
20. Seffah, A., Donyaee, M., Kline, R.B., Padda, H.K.: Usability measurement and metrics: A consolidated model. Software Quality Journal 14(2), 159–178 (2006)
21. Young, G.O.: The Mashup Opportunity – How To Make Mone in The Evolving Mashup Ecosystem. Forrester Research (2008), http://mdc.jackbe.com/enterprise-mashup/sites/default/files/Forrester_The_Mashup_Opportunity_May2008_0.pdf
22. Zhao, Z., Bhattarai, S., Liu, J., Crespi, N.: Mashup Services to Daily Activities – End-user Perspective in Designing a Consumer Mashups. In: Proceedings of the 13th International Conference on Information Integration and Web-based Applications and Services, pp. 222–229. ACM, Ho Chi Minh City (2011)

Appendix

Please complete the following tasks with Netvibes first and then by means of Protopage:

1. Log in with the predefined username and password.
2. Create three new tabs: Business, News, and Fun.
3. Change the interface language to Spanish. If it is already in Spanish, change it to English.
4. Add following widgets to the Business tab: To Do List, Weather, and Calendar.
5. Personalize the Weather widget in a manner that it displays the weather in Barcelona.
6. Add following widgets to the News tab: CNN.com and Esport3.cat.
7. Add following widgets to the Fun tab: Facebook and Google Maps.
8. Personalize the Google Maps widget in a manner that it displays the map of London.
9. Change the background image to Coffee Beans.
10. Change the title of the page to Lleida.
11. Change to color of the News tab to purple.
12. Sort widgets on Business tab in following order: Calendar, To Do List, Weather.
13. Delete all three tabs and the title of the page.
14. Change background image to the default value.
15. Log out and press ESC.

Usability Analysis of Smartphone Applications for Drivers

Manuela Quaresma and Rafael Gonçalves

LEUI Laboratory of Ergodesign and Usability Interfaces,
Pontifical Catholic University of Rio de Janeiro (PUC-Rio),
Rua Marquês de São Vicente, 225 – 711F, 22451-900, Rio de Janeiro, RJ, Brazil
mquaresma@puc-rio.br, rafaelcirinogolcalves@gmail.com

Abstract. This article shows the results of a benchmarking conducted of four different GPS navigation apps intended to be used while driving. The analysis was based on usability guidelines for smartphones and safety guidelines for the use of in-vehicle information systems (IVIS). The analysis aimed to observe and compare the main issues and solutions related to the use of these apps in a very particular context of use (driving a vehicle). The results demonstrate that, although there are some good interface solutions, there are potentially dangerous issues to a specific context of use that can lead to driver distraction.

Keywords: GPS app design, usability, driver distraction.

1 Introduction

It's not surprising that the use of smartphones is in vogue in the communication market. Since 2008, with the arrival of the iPhone and its revolution in the model of interaction with the mobile platform, the development in this area has grown wildly. According to statistics from a survey conducted by Google in partnership with Ipsos Institute [1], in just one year, the number of smartphones in Brazil has nearly duplicated - from 14% in 2012 to 26% in 2013.

This boom of sales was accompanied by a significant increase of the number of applications available in the major App Stores (Apple App Store, Google Play, Windows Phone Store and Blackberry World). However, the development of this area and sale's growth do not necessarily mean product quality in terms of interface design.

Nowadays, there are several smartphone apps designed to be used while driving, to guide the driver along the way he should go or for give information about the traffic jams, or warn about the events that are occurring in traffic (such as accidents, constructions, etc.), and many other services. It can be seen that, day after day, new applications are being developed for use in vehicles.

A. Marcus (Ed.): DUXU 2014, Part I, LNCS 8517, pp. 352–362, 2014.
© Springer International Publishing Switzerland 2014

2   Problem

As can be seen in most GPS navigation apps available in the App Stores, much of the information presented on displays has small size to be read while driving, even more considering vehicle's vibration. Other issues, such as the visual demand required for the completion of data entry tasks and the lack of standardization and compatibility with the user expectation and with operating systems seem to be problematic [2], as well as the number of actions needed to interact with the application while driving. All these problems can lead to potential driver distractions, impairing road safety.

According to the U.S. National Highway Traffic Safety Administration [3], driver distraction can be defined as "a specific type of inattention that occurs when drivers divert their attention that occurs when drivers divert their attention away from the driving task to focus on another activity". This distraction can occur in different ways, according to the following categories:

Visual Distraction – Task that require the driver to look away from the roadway to visually obtain information (like app's visual interfaces);

Manual Distraction – Tasks that require the driver to take a hand off the steering wheel and manipulate the device(Like the data entry by touchscreens and physical buttons);

Cognitive Distraction – Tasks that require the driver to avert their mental attention away from the driving task.

Burns [4] points out that both multifunction devices (products with multiple functions on a single display with few controls) or portable technologies most often overlook the user's needs, capabilities and limitations, preventing the effective integration between the system and the user. The author believes that mobile devices can become the road safety's biggest problem.

Due to its portability and the fact that a smartphone can be used in any situation or location, they can't be disconnected from the context of use, which means that very often users don't have time or appropriate environment to perform certain tasks, requiring a system adequacy to the context in which it will be used. Further, Clark [5] and Wroblewski [6] also argue that the experience of using a mobile device is similar to operate any device with one hand and one eye seeing a big blur, which means that distractions are very constant during the interaction and, in most of cases, users don't pay attention to details.

Despite the different possibilities of use and scenarios, many authors [11, 8, 5, 9, 10, 6] affirm that due to the difficulty to interact with small screens, low processing speed, high effort to navigate on smartphones, the tasks performed with them should be as brief, focused and simple as possible. For the authors, much of the usability issues found in apps are closely related to hardware limitations. Such limitations impose themselves during the apps' development stages being definitive factors for the choice of the interface elements.

When smartphones are used outdoors, there are many factors that impair the interaction with the interface, both directly and indirectly. Common examples are: the display glare due the sunlight or the distraction caused by the driving task.

Wroblewski [6] states that good apps should be prepared to the interaction in the real world, considering their actual context of use since users are not locked in rooms reserved for doing certain task.

3   Methodology

This study aimed to conduct a comparative analysis (benchmarking) of some the most popular GPS navigation systems in Brazil based on usability guidelines for mobile devices and guidelines for the driver's safety with the use of in-vehicle information systems (IVIS). The chosen applications were: a) TomTom Brazil, b) iGO Primo Brazil, c) Sygic Brazil and d) Waze (navigation function).

For the analysis the following methodology was used:

1. Extensive literature review of books on usability in mobile interfaces [5-8, 10, 11], aiming to collect for principles and design guidelines;
2. Literature review of governmental documents and notices, and reports and books on recommendations for IVIS [3, 12-16], also with the purpose of gathering standards and guidelines on road safety;
3. Collection of guidelines for the development of mobile applications from human interface design guides [17-20];
4. Analysis and consolidation of all emerging guidelines from the literature review and guides, using a bottom-up approach like the Affinity Diagram [21];
5. Benchmarking of the applications based on the consolidated guidelines.

3.1   Consolidation of Emerging Guidelines for Smartphones Apps for Drivers

Due to the large amount of information collected in the literature review, a specific tabulation was needed to enable a direct analysis of similar guidelines from different sources – for example, comparing the two publications that talk about the navigation in menus. Also, because of the discrepancy between the subcategories defined by different sources and together with the amount of data (many of them with the same information), the Affinity Diagram was chosen as the most suitable technique, from a bottom-up approach.

The Affinity Diagram technique is a fast and efficient activity for treatment of a large amount of information, with the basic purpose of grouping similar items. For Barnum [21], the technique consists of a series of steps, which should preferably be performed in group, such as: 1) collect information and write them on sticky notes; 2) put all of the sticky notes up on a wall or whiteboard in random order; 3) organize the sticky notes by grouping the ones that are somehow related or similar – preferably without dialogue among the team; 4) when the grouping has finished, team members must label the categories of each group of sticky notes; 5) With labeled groups, they should be placed in a logical hierarchy, subjecting one group to another, if relevant, or dividing them.

For a better understanding, initially each guideline was selected according to the table of usability principles developed by Quaresma [22]. Once the guidelines were selected by principles, the sticky notes were regrouped into groups of thematically similar subjects – like for example, navigation or inputs by gestures; and then a hierarchy of themes was made by subdividing larger groups and subordinating smaller groups. Finally, the guidelines were consolidated in groups by the union of those that had recurrent content between the different sources.

The process to consolidate the emerging guidelines was conducted in three stages. In the first stage, all guidelines from books on usability in mobile interfaces and human interface design guides were grouped. In the second stage, driver safety guidelines for the use of IVIS were grouped too. In the final stage, the two groups were merged, considering the proximity and adaptation of content.

3.2   Definition Criteria for Apps Analysis

For the apps comparative analysis a table was created with categories of guidelines defined in the consolidation (Table 1), which were used as criteria to analyze and compare screen by screen of each application. It was highlighted both the items that don´t meet the criteria, as well as positive items that exceed the expectations regarding the guidelines' rules.

Table 1. Guidelines categories used as criteria for apps analysis

Guideline Categories	Description
1. Context	Guidelines that focus on the environment, circumstance and the way the users interact with their smartphones, taking into account the basis of mobility principles;
2. Content	Guidelines focused on selecting the information to be presented in a mobile platform, considering the importance, volume and adaptation of information and its presentation timing;
3. Information Architecture	Guidelines related to the general structure of an application and organization of its content, following the major systems of information architecture – organization, navigation, labeling and search;
4. Screen Layout	Guidelines related to screens setup, layout of graphical and textual elements on the screen and their adaptations to the screen sizes;
5. Maps	Guidelines related to the use of maps displayed for geolocation and other purposes;
6. Charts	Guidelines focused on recommendations for the use of charts;
7. Forms	Guidelines concerning the use of forms in the mobile platform;
8. Dialogs	Guidelines regarding the communication outputted by the system to the user;
9. Entry Methods	Guidelines related to user's inputs and his interaction with graphic elements, considering the tools of data entry, such as keyboards, gestures or several sensors;
10. System Functions	Guidelines concerning specific tools and issues of mobile context, such as autosave or integrated devices - GPS, camera and accelerometer.

4   Results

The applications were compared based on the main sections of driver interaction while driving: route guides (maps), main menu and address data entry. Thus, the conclusions could be drawn about the interfaces design, considering well designed solutions, isolated failures and problems in common.

4.1   Route Guides

In this section, the main issues found were about the clarity of the information on the map, the quality of interaction with it, the legibility of icons, navigation and map shortcuts. When comparing the clarity of the map information of the four applications, it is evident that the systems (a) and (d) show maps and information more efficiently (Fig. 1 and Fig. 4), due to their simplicity and their care with the amount of graphic elements. Noteworthy the system (d) that uses well placed transparencies so that the elements do not interfere with information about the route, keeping the driver's attention on the main information (Fig. 4). In contrast, the system (c) presents a complex and confusing screen, without a proper indication of interaction elements (Fig. 3).

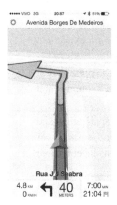 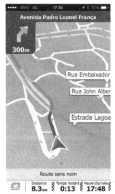  

Fig. 1. Route Guide, System (a)   **Fig. 2.** Route Guide, System (b)   **Fig. 3.** Route Guide, System (c)   **Fig. 4.** Route Guide, System (d)

Regard to the interaction with the map, it is noticeable that all four systems have issues regarding recognition of the interaction elements. Systems (a) and (d) present issues for novice users, due to the fact that the system (a) does not use navigation affordances to find the main menu, requiring a direct tap on the map. The button to access the main menu of system (d) shows an unclear icon for those unfamiliar with the app visual identity (Fig. 4). The main issue with system (b) in this point is related to an inconsistency in button icons, since they vary according to what is selected in the main menu – basic, custom or full menu (Fig. 2 and Fig. 11). While the system (c) presents an issue due the difficulty to distinguish the elements of interaction from the route guide information (Fig. 3).

As for the legibility of icons, the system (d) stands out from others by having map icons well designed, ensuring good legibility during interactions (Fig. 4). This becomes clear when compared to the system (c), which has exactly legibility issues considering the size and design of its icons. These issues may impair the system comprehensibility (Fig. 3).

In the category map navigation, the systems present a very similar operation, allowing a pan view on the map and offering a button to return to the vehicle position – except system (a), which for security reasons does not allow this type of functionality (pan view interaction) in the route guide. The main difference between them is that the system (d), unlike the others (Fig .5 and Fig. 7), has a button with a target icon to return to the point of view to vehicle location on the route (Fig. 9), symbol very common in this type of application.

Fig. 5. Map Navigation, System (c)

Fig. 6. Map shortcuts, System (a)

Fig. 7. Map shortcuts, System (b)

Fig. 8. Map shortcuts, System (c)

Fig. 9. Map shortcut, System (d)

Finally, analyzing the shortcuts on the maps, as can be seen most applications underuse this tool, offering very basic functions for map interaction, like pan view, zoom and compass (Fig. 7-9). Only system (a) offers shortcuts with really relevant functions that need quick access – music functions, mute switch, day/night colors and 2D/3D vision (Fig. 6).

4.2   Main Menu

In this section, the issues found are directly related to the amount of menu options and the way it is presented to the user, taking into account the information architecture and screen layout.

In terms of amount of menu options, the applications offers between 5 and 8 options per screen, thereby minimizing the use of scroll and keeping the good standards of usability. The only ones that differ from this pattern are the system (d), displaying four options (Fig. 13) – since it is not classified as an advanced GPS system, and system (b) with a total of 28 options in the full menu, providing several unnecessary options competing with the driving task. Even though the latter system provides two other types of menu – basic and custom (Fig. 11), interfaces designed for the interaction while driving must not allow the user to deal with so many options. This kind of issue forces the driver to spend precious time scrolling to find what he is searching.

Fig. 10. Main Menu,   **Fig. 11.** Main Menu,   **Fig. 12.** Main Menu,   **Fig. 13.** Main Menu,
System (a)   System (b)   System (c)   System (d)

In terms of menu layout, the systems have adopted two different ways to present the information: springboard menus – used by systems (d) and (b) (Fig. 11 and Fig. 13), and the list menus – used by systems (a) and (c) (Fig. 10 and Fig. 12). However, only (a) and (d) have made better use of the chosen type of menu, adapting themselves to their different needs, handling well with the icons size and ensuring good text legibility (Fig. 10 and Fig. 13). These factors were not correctly handled by the other two, once the system (c) does not fill all the available space of the cells (using small characters) (Fig. 12) and (b) uses two lines of text in its cells, having to reduce the size of the icons without using a consistent pattern for the system (Fig. 11).

The last point of this section is related to <u>the quick access of the route guide</u> for times of emergency. The analysis concluded that only the systems (a) and (d) have a shortcut that allows direct access to the of the route guide at any point in system hierarchy (Fig. 10 and Fig. 13). The others require the user to use the back button several times until he can reach the map, which can be harmful if a maneuver information is required (Fig. 11 and Fig. 12), beyond the fact that this can become the interaction unnecessarily harder.

4.3   Address Data Entry

For this section the issues observed were mainly related to the process of the task completion and the adaptation of the data entry methods to the user's needs.

As for the <u>process of address data entry</u>, this is a very hard task for any driver to perform with the vehicle in motion. Good solutions are associated to lower amount of interactions that the user must perform to achieve his goal (entering the address). Although systems do not have a significant difference, the systems (a) and (d) have a shorter process in terms of the amount of screens to interact for data entry. These systems suppress unnecessary screens and information to the user, such as the screen of the selected target presented by the system (b) (Fig. 14) or the screen for choosing between "Drive to" or "Walk there" requested by the system (c) (Fig. 15).

Fig. 14. Destination point view, System (b)   **Fig. 15.** Select Action Screen, System (c)   **Fig. 16.** Route information System (b)

Finally, about the methods of data entry, most apps use the default keyboard system, with the exception of (b), which uses proprietary keyboard due to its dynamic search filter. Although they use similar systems, the apps consider users' needs in different ways. A well-executed solution was observed in the system (b), with its dynamic filtering of possible keys related to the text being written, limiting the choice of characters to be typed (Fig. 19-20). Another good example is the fact of system (a) changes the keyboard to a numeric system similar to a phone keyboard (Fig. 18), making it easier to entry the address numbers. The applications (d) and (c) are flawed in this aspect due to the fact of not having predictive text (Fig. 23) and not clearing the fields after an address data entry (Fig. 21-22), respectively. In system (d) the task of address data entry is even harder, once that the user needs to type the full address to be found in the system database (Fig. 23-24), which means a waste of time and great effort while driving.

Fig. 17. Street Name Entry Screen, System (a)

Fig. 18. Street Number Entry Screen, System (a)

Fig. 19. Custom keyboard, System (b)

Fig. 20. Address Selection Screen, System (b)

Fig. 21. Street Name Entry Screen, System (c)

Fig. 22. Street Number Entry Screen, System (c)

Fig. 23. Address Data Entry Screen, System (d)

Fig. 24. Address Selection Screen, System (d)

5   Conclusions

It is a fact that the growth of the smartphone market, combined with an improvement of the input data and geolocation technologies, provides a development of applications targeted for use in vehicles. The main issue is that this kind of application can distract the driver instead of help him during driving task, once the context of use and the design principles are not considered in its conception.

This research aimed to conduct benchmarking with four applications for drivers that work as GPS navigation systems – TomTom, iGO Primo, Sygic, and Waze, considering the usability guidelines for smartphones and those for safety in use of

IVIS. This study presents some usability and safety issues found in each application and their consequences when compared to other solutions that better attends user needs. The research concluded that even if the systems are not dedicated for driving context, it is important to minimize the effort for both comprehension and performing of the tasks. This way, it is possible to design better interfaces and more adapted to deal with the challenges inherent in driving context.

This research is part of an ongoing study on usability of smartphones applications developed for use in vehicle. The next steps intends to make similar studies with other categories of applications for drivers, in order to investigate the issues that impair the driving task and reach a consensus on recommendations of safety and usability for this type of application and interaction (driver-smartphone).

Acknowledgements. To CNPq for financing the PIBIT grant.

References

1. Google, & Ipsos. Our mobile planet,
   http://www.thinkwithgoogle.com/mobileplanet/en/
2. Quaresma, M.: Assessment of visual demand of typical data entry tasks in automotive navigation systems for iPhone. WORK: a Journal of Prevention 44, 6139–6144 (2012)
3. National Highway Traffic Safety Administration: Visual-Manual NHTSA Driver Distraction Guidelines for In-Vehicle Electronic Devices (2013)
4. Burns, P.: Strategies for Reducing Driver Distraction from In-Vehicle Telematics Devices: A Discussion Document - Transport Canada (2003),
   http://www.tc.gc.ca/eng/roadsafety/tp-tp14133-menu-147.htm
5. Clark, J.: Tapworthy: Designing Great iPhone Apps. O'Reilly Media, Sebastopol (2010)
6. Wroblewski, L.: Mobile First. A Book Apart, New York (2011)
7. Nielsen, J., Budiu, R.: Mobile Usability. New Riders, Berkley (2012)
8. Fling, B.: Mobile Design and Development: Practical Concepts and Techniques for Creating Mobile Sites and Web Apps (Animal Guide). O'Reilly Media, Sebastopol (2009)
9. Gafni, R.: Usability Issues for Wireless Devices. Issues in Informing Science and Information Technology (IISIT) 6, 755–769 (2009)
10. Ginsburg, S.: Designing the iPhone User Experience: A User-Centered Approach to Sketching and Prototyping iPhone Apps. Addison-Wesley Professional, Boston (2010)
11. Neil, T.: Mobile Design Pattern Gallery. O'Reilly Media, Sebastopol (2012)
12. Alliance of Automobile Manufactures: Statement of Principles, Criteria and Verification - Procedures on Driver Interactions with Advanced In-vehicle Information and Communication Systems, Washington DC (2006)
13. Japan Automobile Manufacturers Association, Guidelines for in-vehicle display systems, Tokyo (2004)
14. Commission of the European Communities: Recommendations on safe and efficient in-vehicle information and communication systems: update of European statement of principles on human machine interface. European Union (Official Journal 2008/653/EC), Brussels (2008)
15. Stevens, A., Cynk, S.: Checklist for the assessment of in-vehicle information systems, Wokingham (2011)

16. Harvey, C., Stanton, N.A.: Usability Evaluation for In-Vehicle Systems. CRC Press, Boca Raton (2013)
17. Apple: iOS Human Interface Guidelines,
    `https://developer.apple.com/library/ios/documentation/`
    `UserExperience/Conceptual/MobileHIG/index.html`
18. Google: Android Design Guidelines,
    `http://developer.android.com/design/index.html`
19. Microsoft: Design Library for Windows Phone,
    `http://msdn.microsoft.com/en-us/library/windowsphone/`
    `design/hh202915v=vs.105.aspx`
20. RIM: Blackberry Key Principles,
    `https://developer.blackberry.com/devzone/design/bb10/`
    `key_principles.html`
21. Barnum, C.M.: Usability Testing Essentials: Ready, Set..Test! Morgan Kaufmann, Burlington (2011)
22. Quaresma, M.: Usability evaluation of in-vehicles information systems: an ergonomic study of GPS navigation systems (D.Sc. Thesis) Departamento de Artes e Design, Pontifícia Universidade Católica do Rio de Janeiro, Rio de Janeiro (2010)

Eye Tracking Insights into Effective Navigation Design

Andrew Schall

SPARK Experience, LLC Bethesdsa, Maryland, USA
andrew@sparkexperience.com

Abstract. An intuitive and easy to navigate interface is the cornerstone to good user experience (UX). Usability issues often arise from navigation that has been poorly designed, often because of the organization, placement, visual design, or terminology used. Current methods for measuring the effectiveness of navigation are limited to observable behaviors and verbal feedback from participants. Eye tracking is becoming an increasingly common tool in UX testing, in part to discover new ways to optimize navigational elements. This paper addresses how eye tracking can be used to understand the effectiveness of commonly used navigational elements in interface design.

Keywords: Eye tracking, usability, user experience, navigation, menu systems, interface design.

1   Introduction

How many times have you become lost while navigating through an interface? An intuitive and easy to navigate system is the cornerstone to good user experience. Nearly all digital products have some sort of menu system that must be navigated in order to complete a task. Usability issues often arise from navigation that has been poorly designed, usually because of the organization, placement, visual design, or terminology used. According to the International Standards Organization, usability refers to "the extent to which a product can be used by specified users to achieve specified goals with effectiveness, efficiency and satisfaction in a specified context of use." [1] Jeffrey Rubin also includes the following usability objectives [2]:

- Usefulness - product enables user to achieve their goals - the tasks that it was designed to carry out and/or wants needs of user.
- Effectiveness (ease of use) - quantitatively measured by speed of performance or error rate and is tied to a percentage of users.
- Learnability - user's ability to operate the system to some defined level of competence after some predetermined period of training. Also, refers to ability for infrequent users to relearn the system.
- Attitude (likeability) - user's perceptions, feelings and opinions of the product, usually captured through both written and oral communication.

A. Marcus (Ed.): DUXU 2014, Part I, LNCS 8517, pp. 363–370, 2014.
© Springer International Publishing Switzerland 2014

For the purposes of this paper, navigation design will be primarily discussed on the basis of effectiveness (ease of use), efficiency, and learnability.

The evaluation of usability often takes place in a usability test whereby participants are asked to perform a series of tasks using a system. Usability tests can include a variety of metrics to assess usability [3] including think-aloud protocol, observable behaviors (i.e. mouse movements, clicks, etc.), and self reported measurements such as post experience surveys. Qualitative data from these measurements can result in understanding common behavior patterns, self-reported feelings (i.e. frustration), and relative easy of use. Quantitative data can include time to task completion, number of clicks or key presses, error rate or recovery, etc. These metrics can be very effective in measuring the performance of navigational elements, however they are limited to what a user actually does and what they selectively self report to the study facilitator.

In trying to understand what users decide to pay attention to we can't always rely on the participants to accurately tell us. Participants are terrible at self-reporting where they looked. For the most part, this is due to our eyes often moving involuntarily and the limits of our short-term memory. Guan et al.[4] measured the extent to which participants did not discuss elements that they in fact visually attended to. They labeled these as omissions. Participants had omissions 47% of the time, meaning that almost half of the time they did not mention elements that they looked at. Omissions may have occurred because participants forgot about seeing the elements, or perhaps simply because they just didn't think or care to mention them. It should also go without saying that a researcher can't simply ask a participant if they noticed a certain on-screen element. This action draws the participant's attention directly towards something that they may or may not have originally seen. This inherently and irreversibly biases the participant and no confident answer can be obtained. Eye tracking provides an objective running commentary of where the individual looks without any need for participants to verbalize what they have seen. Eye tracking can be a complementary tool combined with traditional usability testing methods to not only understand what a user is doing, but also where they look while completing tasks[5]. Even the most intuitive navigation structure is useless if users never notice it.

2   Effectiveness (Ease of Use)

Effectiveness is the completeness and accuracy with which users achieve specified goals. It is determined by looking at whether the user's goals were met successfully and whether all work is correct [6]. Effectiveness is the driving force behind successful task completion and helping users to complete their goals. Navigation is often the primary way for users to be able to access information and to get from one function within a system to another. Applications today use a variety of navigational elements to help users accomplish their tasks. Many of these elements build off of more traditional designs such using dropdown menus with increasing complexity. The effectiveness of these menu systems is determined by whether a user can locate and use the navigation option they are seeking and take them to the expected location.

2.1   Dynamic Menu Systems

Dynamic menu systems, such as fly-outs and dropdowns, have become commonly-used navigation paradigms. These menus have the benefit of allowing users quick access to content without the need to fill up the valuable screen real estate with navigational elements. While these may be beneficial, dynamic menu systems also have their share of usability problems.

According to Cooke [7], researchers have found that before people fixate a specific menu item, they first visually "sweep" the menu. Next, users view the first one or two items on the menu. Then users glance at items at the bottom of the menu and finally, at the middle of the menu.

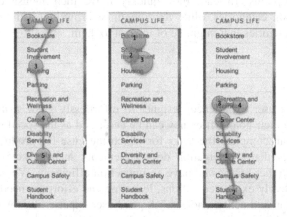

Fig. 1. Before users fixate a specific menu item, they first visually "sweep" the menu. Next, they view the first one or two items on the menu. Then they glance at items at the bottom of the menu and finally, at the middle of the menu.

To improve visual search efficiency, user interface designers can take advantage of this behavior. Important navigation items within the menu should be placed at the very top of the list, and items of least relative importance should be placed towards the middle.

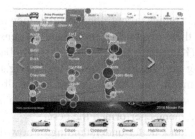

Fig. 2. In a pilot study of Edmunds.com, several participants scanned the columns quickly and had difficulty locating Land Rover, even though columns were structured in alphabetical order

Fig. 3. The sub navigation options are not displayed until the user hovers over the primary navigation

Many news websites require users to hover over each of the primary navigation options to see the sub navigation options. Presenting both the primary and secondary navigation in a horizontal format can negatively impact users' ability to effectively scan the menu options. Users may hover over a category and then only scan the immediate sub navigation below, and they do not start at the very beginning of the sub navigation options. Instead, they quickly move their mouse over additional primary navigation categories while they continue browsing. This causes users to often miss sub categories that might be of interest to them.

3   Efficiency

It is the job of a user experience designer to effortlessly guide a user through an interface to reach their goal. Efficiency can be described as the speed (with accuracy) in which users can complete the tasks for which they use the product [5]. Whitney Quesenbery states that, "Navigation design elements such as keyboard shortcuts, menus, links and other buttons all have an impact on efficiency. When they are well-designed, with clearly expressed actions, less time and effort are needed for the user to make navigation and action choices." A good user experience is when a user does not have to spend a significant amount of time locating, evaluating and using the navigation. Jakob Nielsen puts it this way:

It may seem like people should look at global navigation more than a quarter of the time, but think of it as you would a lifejacket stored under your seat on an airplane. You may confirm its existence during the safety instruction presentation, but you are not going to put it on, inflate it, and wear it just in case you need to evacuate. Nor will you repeatedly look to make sure it's still there during your flight. But you know where it is if you need it. You ignore it when you don't. That's the way it is with Web site menus. [8]

There have been few studies about the optimal viewing position of primary navigation elements, and there does not seem to be a consensus on which format has the best user experience (Kingsburg and Andre, 2004; Kalbach and Bosenick, 2003; DeWitt, 2010). Kingsburg and Andre [9] found that navigation times were slightly faster when the primary menu was located on the left. Kalbach and Bosenick [10] found no evidence that vertical left-located menus were significantly faster and concluded that top-aligned menus performed the best.

DeWitt [11] sought to gain a better understanding of how the placement of primary navigation impacted a user's experience. They studied the eye-tracking behaviors of 147 participants across 15 navigational menus. They found that designing a vertical or horizontal menu does not seem to impact how quickly users can locate the desired item within the menus, although vertical menus run the risk of requiring page scrolling which slows down navigation.

Users are accustomed to seeing the sub navigation in close proximity to the primary navigation either in a horizontal or vertical format. In the Kingsburg and Andre study, navigation performance was best when the secondary and tertiary menus were placed together. User experience problems arise when users cannot easily identify the sub navigation elements on a web page.

Task performance is a key way to measure the efficiency and effectiveness of a navigation system. Users need to be able to quickly identify navigational elements, understand what they mean, and be able to keep track of where they are. Time to first fixation is a useful way to measure the amount of time it takes before a user notices navigational elements on the page. We can tell exactly how quickly they notice elements and the relationship between when they notice other screen elements.

We can also analyze the specific elements within a given area, such as the number of links within a set of navigation items that the user looks at before deciding which one to click on. We can then measure the time it takes from noticing a navigational element to how long before the element is clicked. Task performance can be significantly slowed if users are forced to read through a long list of links before finding the one they want to click on.

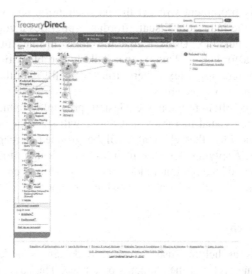

Fig. 4. Participants would scan the long list of links looking for keywords that would help them get to the information they were seeking

The quantitative capabilities provided by eye tracking allow researchers to accurately report on how quickly a participant noticed a navigational element and then how much time elapses before they make a select from the menu. It is also possible to track the number of fixations that occur within a navigational element and also the duration of the fixations prior to an element being clicked.

4   Learnability

Menu systems, no matter how complex, should be designed in a way so as to be intuitive to the user. The labeling and terminology used in a navigational interface can negatively impact ease of learning if it does not match the user's mental model. Eye tracking can often identify issues associated with poor labeling when there are a relatively high number of fixations and high fixation duration of a link label. Regressive saccades are a common fixation movement that can indicate that a user did not see a link that they were expecting to find, or they are evaluating and/or reevaluating the meaning of a given set of links, possibly due to a lack of cues. Goldberg [13] suggests that optimal scanning patterns include long saccades, short scanpaths, and few fixations in a small area of focus.

4.1   Visual Affordance

With any new interface users need to quickly gain an understanding of which elements on the screen can be used to navigate. Users often spend only a few seconds taking in all of the elements of the page. Within these few seconds, they are establishing a mental floor plan of the interface. During this short time, elements that are the most visually prominent will get the most attention and will help shape the user's perception of the interface. Visual affordance provides a cue to the user that a certain element is clickable. Users frequently miss in-line links when there is insufficient visual affordance. This is particularly problematic when links are embedded within paragraphs of text where users typically scan the information very quickly and often skip over large areas.

Interface designers often rely on the Gestalt principles, which are time-tested methods that shape the visual hierarchy that a user will see. For example, the law of similarity reflects the idea that elements will be grouped perceptually if they are similar to each other. Applying Gestalt principles to the design of navigation can help highlight the presence of navigational elements and provide a cue for users to know which elements are related to each other and which are not.

4.2   Visual Hierarchy

Eye tracking excels at helping user experience designers understand how users perceive the visual hierarchy of the elements on a page. The navigational elements of an interface are in direct competition for the user's attention and can often take a backseat to other content. This can often result in users not noticing navigational elements and consequently not understanding how to get to the information they seek. It is critical for navigation to be designed in a way where it is easy to find and is consistent from screen to screen. This consistency will help users to learn to use the interface faster and to make navigational elements predictable, however ultimately less prominent compared with the rest of the content.

The redesign of the San Francisco Police Department's website significantly altered users' eye gaze patterns. Much of the content and layout in the redesign changed, with the exception of the right column navigation.

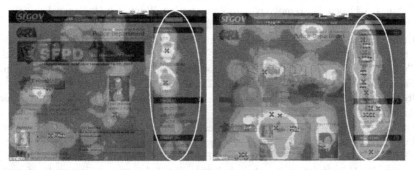

Fig. 5. Original (left) and modified (right) versions of the San Francisco PD website (Courtesy, EyeTools, 2005)

However, the design changes led to large changes in user behavior in the right column, as evidenced by both the eye tracking and click data. 64% of participants clicked on the right navigation on the redesigned page whereas only 14% of participants clicked on the right navigation on the old design. Participants looked at the new right navigation longer and more often, indicating that they read more in that area, despite no change to the design or content of the right navigation. A change on one part of the page can impact other, unrelated elements on the page. The right navigation bar was used completely differently on the new re-designed website because the content to the left of it changed [14].

Interfaces with clear visual affordances for representing navigational elements and a visual hierarchy that highlights navigation where users expect to see it can significantly increase effectiveness, efficiency, and learnability.

5 Conclusion

Creating a usable navigation design is a critical element of a positive user experience. This paper discussed how eye tracking could be a valuable addition to studies that focus on evaluating the usability of navigational elements. Usability attributes specific to navigation were addressed including effectiveness, efficiency, and learnability. Eye tracking can help provide quantitative measurements for each of these attributes and does not rely on the highly subjective nature of either the study participant or facilitator. Eye tracking can provide deeper insights that would not be possible to obtain by think-aloud or self-reporting techniques. As eye tracking becomes a more ubiquitous tool in user research, we can expect more attention to be paid to not only how users interact with an interface, but also how they view it.

References

1. ISO 9241-11.1998, Ergonomic requirements for office work with visual display terminals (VDTs) – Part 11: Guidance on usability (1998)
2. Rubin, J., Chisnell, D.: Handbook of usability testing. Wiley Pub., Indianapolis (2008)
3. Nielsen, J.: Usability engineering. Academic Press, Boston (1993)
4. Guan, Z., Lee, S., Cuddihy, E., Ramey, J.: The Validity of the Stimulated Retrospective Think-Aloud Method as Measured by Eye Tracking. In: Grinter, R., Rodden, T., Aoki, P., Cutrell, E., Jeffries, R., Olson, G. (eds.) Proceedings of the SIGCHI Conference on Human Factors in Computing Systems 2006, pp. 1253–1262. ACM Press, New York (2006)
5. Romano Bergstrom, J., Schall, A.: Eye tracking in user experience design. Morgan Kaufmann Publisher (2014)
6. Quesenbery, W.: What Does Usability Mean: Looking Beyond 'Ease of Use' - Whitney Interactive Design (2001), http://www.wqusability.com/articles/more-than-ease-of-use.html (accessed: February 1, 2014)
7. Cooke, L.: How do users search web home pages? An eye-tracking study of multiple navigation menus. Technical Communication 55(2), 176–194 (2008)
8. Nielsen, J., Pernice, K.: Eye Tracking Web Usability. New Riders, Berkeley (2010)
9. Kingsburg, J.R., Andre, A.D.: A comparison of three-level Web menus: Navigation structures. In: Proceedings of the Human Factors and Ergonomics Society Annual Meeting (2004)
10. Kalbach, J., Bosenick, T.: Web page layout: A comparison between left- and right-justified site navigation menus. Journal of Digital Information 4(1) (2003)
11. Dewitt, A.J.: Examining the order effect of website navigation menus with eye tracking. Journal of Usability Studies 6(1), 39–47 (2010)
12. Sibert, J.L., Gokturk, M., Lavine, R.A.: The Reading Assistant: Eye gaze triggered auditory prompting for reading remediation. In: Proceedings of the Thirteenth Annual ACM Symposium on User Interface Software and Technology, pp. 101–107. ACM Press, NY (2000)
13. Goldberg, J.H., Kotval, X.P.: Eye movement-based evaluation of the computer interface. In: Kumar, S.K. (ed.) Advances in Occupational Ergonomics and Safety, pp. 529–532. ISO Press, Amsterdam (1998)
14. Edwards, G.: Eyetracking a Navigation Bar – How Many Elements Are Read (2007)

Changing Paradigm – Changing Experience?

Comparative Usability Evaluation of *Windows 7* and *Windows 8*

Tim Schneidermeier, Franziska Hertlein, and Christian Wolff

Media Informatics Group, University of Regensburg,
Universitätsstraße 31, 93051 Regensburg, Germany
{Tim.Schneidermeier,Christian.Wolff}@ur.de,
Franziska.Hertlein@stud.uni-regensburg.de

Abstract. With the introduction of MS *Windows 8, Modern UI / Metro Design* was established as a new design paradigm for interaction. In this paper, we evaluate the usability of *Windows 8* in comparison with *Windows 7* with respect to effectiveness, efficiency and satisfaction. Our test was conducted on three sample rates with differing experience on MS *Windows* systems. The findings concerning each of the three dimensions are presented as well as results for the overall usability.

Keywords: comparative usability evaluation, flat design, *Windows 8*.

1 Introduction

In October 2012 Microsoft introduced its latest update for its operating system (OS), *Windows 8*. It was released with a major change in its interaction paradigm, differing widely from its predecessors. *Windows 8* is designed as a multi-platform OS, being operable on PCs as well as touch-based tablet devices. Microsoft`s approach is aiming at an seamless experience on different devices. Yet the main challenge for the success of *Windows 8* will be to add additional benefits – whether by functionality or usability in a workspace environment. In this paper, we present a usability study comparing *Windows 7* as a representative of the traditional WIMP (windows, icons, menu, pointers) interaction paradigm and *Windows 8* in terms of efficiency, effectiveness and user satisfaction. The study was conducted based on typical operating system tasks which were collected by asking users about typical tasks they have to complete on a regular basis. Both operating systems were tested by 24 participants, divided in three groups according to their experience with *Windows*. We also wanted to see if there is a connection between the prior experience with *Windows* and the way the participant interacts with *Windows 8*.

2 Object of Investigation: *Windows 7* and *Windows 8*

The *look and feel* as well as the interaction style of the new *Windows* user interface at the same time differ in many ways from its predecessors and yet are quite similar in

A. Marcus (Ed.): DUXU 2014, Part I, LNCS 8517, pp. 371–382, 2014.

other respects: Instead of the familiar desktop surface known since the beginnings of *Windows* (*Windows 1.0* 1985), the newly introduced start screen in *Metro Design / Modern UI* (figure 1) gives an overview of selected apps. These are represented by tiles and vary from colored shapes with a logo to dynamic content showing a preview of the app data (photos, weather data etc.).

Fig. 1. *Windows 8*'s start screen in *Metro Design*

2.1   Flat Design vs. Skeuomorphism

The skeuomorphic design language in *Windows 7* (and older versions) is based on a realistic representation of real world objects, using shadows, light reflection, color gradients etc. as design tools (Grossman 2013). The objects in *Windows 8* (e.g. tiles, buttons etc.) on the contrary are designed with simple shapes, no color gradients and no kittenish details. The *flat design* should provide a clearly structured two-dimensional *look and feel* (see figure 2).

Fig. 2. Icons for "Video"; left image: skeuomorphism; right image[1]: *flat design*

---

[1] The *Windows 8*'s tile for "Video" is now styled according to (*ISO 18035:2003*, 2008).

2.2   Full Screen vs. *Windows*

Based on the WIMP paradigm starting a program or double-clicking a folder in *Windows 7* will open a new window showing the selected content. The users can manipulate these windows in different ways (e.g. resizing, dragging); to terminate a software the user can just close the window the application is running in. The interaction in *Windows 8* uses slightly different rules: Starting an app by clicking on a tile in the start screen will open the app in full screen mode, closing an app won't work by clicking in the right top corner, instead you have to click at the border above and drag it down (alternatively one can use the new *Windows 8* task manager). Working with multiple windows simultaneously in *Windows 7* allows you to customize the desktop to your needs: you can just drag the windows and position them according to your preferences. Operating in full screen mode in *Windows 8* is not that customizable. Yet there is still a possibility to show at least a limited number of apps at the same time: An app can be snapped at the right or left border, so that it won't use the whole space. If another app is opened, it uses the remaining space.[2]

2.3   Desktop View

Even though *Windows 8* is introducing a new interaction style, the familiar desktop view can still be found "behind" the start screen. It can be opened by selecting the corresponding tile on the start screen. Like any other app in *Windows 8* it will run in full screen mode. The surface is almost the same as known from previous *Windows* releases, but is missing the start button to trigger the well known start menu[3] in the lower left corner, which is replaced by the newly introduced vertical toolbar *charms*. The *charms* bar can be activated throughout shortcuts or the OS hovering above one of the right corners (on touch-based devices it is reached with a swipe gesture from right to left). The *charms* menu provides five items to the user: *Search, Share, Start, Devices* and *Settings*. While some features provide the same functionality throughout the system, others are app-sensitive, i.e. the provided functions vary whether they are activated on the start screen or within an app. For example, clicking on the Start item within an application will lead to the *Windows 8* start screen, using the same element on the start screen the application last used will be displayed (Microsoft, 2014a).

3   Study Design

The goal of this study was to compare the usability for standard tasks using *Windows 7* and *Windows 8*. We have chosen a user-based over an expert-based

---

[2] The version of *Windows 8* tested in this study only provides the possibility to snap two apps in the proportion 1:3. The latest update *Windows 8.1* allows for displaying up to four apps at once (Microsoft, 2014a).

[3] In *Windows 8.1* a start button is re-introduced, which offers e.g. power options or a device manager (Microsoft, 2014b).

evaluation to get more realistic results. To measure the usability each participant had to complete six tasks on both systems. In addition to measuring the overall usability we were interested in whether prior experience in using *Windows 7* had any influence on using *Windows 8*. As the latter introduces a new interaction paradigm, we wanted to find out if there is a correlation between using *Windows 8* with and without any prior experience with older versions of the OS in terms of efficiency, effectiveness and user satisfaction. The test participants therefore were divided in groups with different levels concerning their expertise with *Windows*.

3.1   Measuring the Usability

Usability is measured by effectiveness, efficiency and user satisfaction (*ISO 9241*, 1998). Effectiveness was measured by whether a user was able to successfully complete a task (task success score / task completion rate, Sauro & Lewis 2012, p. 12), efficiency by the number of interaction steps (mouse clicks) and time per task. The task success score also allowed us to distinguish whether a task was completed without help or with an additional advice from the test supervisor. We used Morae[4] (TechSmith, 2013) to record the data during the test sessions.

To measure the individual user satisfaction we used the *AttrakDiff2*, a questionnaire developed to measure the user experience (Hassenzahl, Burmester, & Koller, 2008). It is based on 28 bipolar, seven-stage items. The antonyms of the *AttrakDiff2* questionnaire can be mapped onto four scales: pragmatic quality, hedonic quality (stimulation), hedonic quality (identity) and attractiveness. The tool provides a result visualization, where the rated products are positioned according to a pragmatic and hedonic axis. A product with a position in the top right corner can be seen as most pragmatic and hedonic and therefore offers a good user satisfaction. (User Interface Design GmbH, 2013)

For interpreting the results, we used a paired *t*-test. This test is suited for evaluating data of one control sample but two products. The paired *t*-test is a one-sample *t*-test executed with the difference of two measured values by person (Sauro & Lewis, 2012, p. 63ff). This approach should show whether the arithmetical means are significantly different. The null hypothesis is accordingly that no difference of the means exists. Although we had less than 30 participants, the paired *t*-test can nevertheless produce correct *p*-values (Sauro & Lewis 2012, p. 68). All tests are based on a significance level $\alpha=0.05$.

3.2   Conducting the Study

We conducted the usability study with three groups of participants differing in their experience with the *Windows* OS (see table 1).

---

[4] Software to conduct, record and analyze data for usability studies.

Table 1. Test persons and their *Windows* experience

experience-level	number of users
up to *Windows 8*	10
up to *Windows 7*	10
no *Windows* experience	4

Even though we took a lot of effort, we weren't able to find a sufficient number of participants with no prior *Windows* experience. The ones who took part in the study were all Linux users with little or no expertise in *Windows*, which probably means that they had significant general ICT expertise. All participates were between 18 and 28 years old and students.

Table 2. Test tasks

Task number	Description
1	Checking emails using a browser
2	Text processing
3	Organizing files in folders
4	Changing default values
5	Installation of new software
6	Shutting down the device

To identify typical tasks for the study we conducted a survey asking about frequent tasks users have to accomplish on a regular basis. Based on the results we identified six tasks for our study design (see table 2). The user tests were conducted within one month at the usability lab of the *Media Informatics Group*, University of Regensburg (see figure 3). The participants were asked to accomplish all tasks on both OS, *Windows 7* and *Windows 8* using the same 13" *Samsung* ultrabook.

Fig. 3. Test environment

After the initial welcome, the test procedure was explained to each participant. Additionally, all participants were introduced to the *Thinking aloud* method and kindly asked to communicate their thoughts and feelings during the test session (Lewis 1982, Nielsen Norman Group, 2014). In order to prevent any influence on the test results based on sequence of the test, the order in which the OS had to be used was randomized. Each test session followed the same sequence: After editing the six tasks on OS A the participants were asked to fill out the *AttrakDiff2* questionnaire and continue with OS B.

4   Results

In the following, we present the main results for the three dimensions of our test, effectiveness (task success score), efficiency (mouse clicks / completion time) as well as overall user satisfaction (*AttrakDiff2*).

4.1   Effectiveness

Figure 4 shows the number of people needed help to complete a task. One can see at first glance that more help was needed while using *Windows 8*. In general, only in five cases help had to be provided to the participants completing the tasks 1, 2, 4 and 5 using *Windows 7*. Considerably more help had to be given when the participants were using *Windows 8*. Task 3 could only be completed by eight out of 24 people – five of them were actual *Windows 8* users. Changing the wallpaper (task 4) seemed to be very easy at all. For the other four tasks, between three and eight test participants needed help. The test conductor helped during the tests of *Windows 8* altogether 40 times.

It is obvious that the editing of task 3 in *Windows 8* is the most difficult task: The test subjects had to select five favourite pictures out of a folder and copy it in a new one, which they had to create and rename. The problems here may be due to the use of the *Windows 8's Photo app*. Most of the test participants used this application to have a look at the pictures. The behaviour of the application is similar to the *File Explorer* combined with the *Windows Photo Viewer*, which are known from *Windows 7*. That is why the functions of these applications, for example creating a new folder and copying pictures, were expected in the new *Windows 8*-application, but the application doesn't offer these. To do so, users have to change to the desktop. Several participants realized this only with clues given by the test supervisor. Before they could finish the task in the desktop environment, they had to close the *Photo app* or at least minimize it. This was because of the use of the full screen the second huge problem for solving task 3.

The help, which had to be provided for solving task 4, has similar reasons: Changing the wallpaper is a function offered amongst others in the *File Explorer*, so the test persons looked for it at this position. But to solve this task, they had to use the option offered in the desktop environment.

Eight people needed help during the editing of task 6 (shutting down the device). To find this option in *Windows 8*, you have to call the *charms* bar. The option "shut down" can be found in the category *Settings*.

Because we wanted to know whether there is a significant difference in the quantity of providing help, we executed a paired t-test. The null hypothesis was: While working on *Windows 8* help has to be provided as often as while working on *Windows 7*. The test results show that this null-thesis has to be refused (t=-5.7171, df=23, p=0.0000) and more help had been provided during testing *Windows 8*.

All tasks could be solved, no matter in which system they were edited. But it is clear that more *Windows 8* users needed help during the test in *Windows 8* than *Windows 7* users during testing *Windows 7*. Therefore, *Windows 8* can be judged to be less effective than *Windows 7* in that respect.

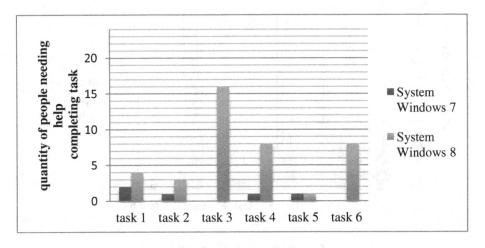

Fig. 4. Task success score for both systems

4.2   Efficiency

Summarizing the time which was needed for solving all six tasks, it can be seen that all groups testing *Windows 7* are very close to each other in comparison with the testing of *Windows 8*. The results of the average total time testing *Windows 7* are: *Windows 7* users 7:25 minutes, the group of *Windows 8* users 7:46 minutes and the persons with least *Windows* experience 8:34 minutes.

Solving the tasks in *Windows 8*, *Windows 7* users needed 14:35 minutes, the user of other systems 14:59 minutes and the active *Windows 8* users only 9:04. It is interesting that the time of *Windows 7* users and not *Windows*-users are very close together and that the *Windows 8* users have a clear advance. Thus we have to reason that prior experience in handling *Windows* systems is no immediate advantage for working with *Windows 8*. Task 5 required most time in both systems. During this task, software needed to be downloaded and installed. This caused a waiting time which is part of the time displayed in fig. 5. An examination of the total time needed for all tasks with the paired t-test shows that the time the *Windows 8* users needed differs significantly from the time of the *Windows 7* users (t = 3.5906, df = 9, p = 0.005834).

The *Windows 8* users needed almost 6 minutes less than the rest for finishing the tasks in *Windows 8*. During the test in *Windows 7*, the *Windows 7* users couldn't reach a similar result. Therefore it is assumed that experience in handling *Windows 8* can raise the efficiency considerably.

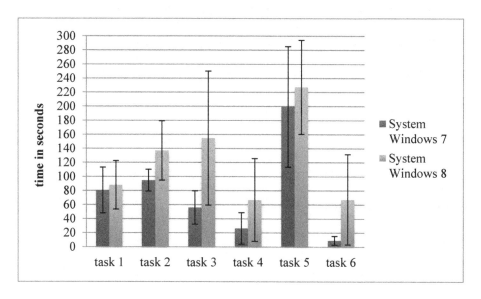

Fig. 5. Average time of all test participants

Figure 5 shows the average time of all test results. It is apparent that every task in *Windows 8* on average took more time than in *Windows 7*. Only one out of ten *Windows 8* users could beat his own *Windows 7* task time using *Windows 8* needing less time in every task. But the paired t-test shows that the null hypothesis, editing the tasks in *Windows 8* needs more time than in *Windows 7*, could not be rejected because of the inequality of the variance (t = -1.2855, df = 9, p = 0.2307).

As a second variable for measuring the efficiency, the sum of clicks was taken. Unfortunately, results logged by Morae were erroneous: In nine tests, zero clicks per task were counted, mainly during the tests in *Windows 8*. Fig. 6 gives the results for the remaining tests. These results support the findings of the time analysis: Task 3 and task 6 show the most explicit difference between both systems. And in *Windows 8*, every edited task on average needs more clicks to finish than in *Windows 7*.

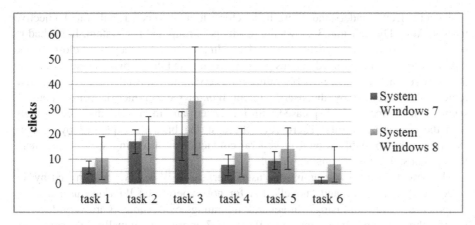

Fig. 6. Average mouse clicks of all test participants

4.3 User Satisfaction

The results of the AttrakDiff2 questionnaire (see figure 7) show that the users see clear difference in handling *Windows 7* and *Windows 8*. Especially the benchmarking of the pragmatic quality is very different. The automatically derived analysis of AttrakDiff2 states that *Windows 7* "assists its users optimally", while the "hedonic value is only average" and has "clearly room for improvement". In general, *Windows 7* can said to be "practice oriented".

Windows 8's user interface is rated as "neutral". It is more hedonic than *Windows 7* but in return less pragmatic. The *AttrakDiff2* results show that there is room for improvement in both dimensions, but definitely more in the pragmatic one. The confidence interval of *Windows 8* on the pragmatic axis has the broadest range. This could be explained with the participants' different experience in operating *Windows 8*: The groups didn't agree about the pragmatics of the system. The detected results in pragmatic and hedonic quality differ significantly. As *Windows 8* still is a quite novel product, less possible overall experience might be one explanation for this.

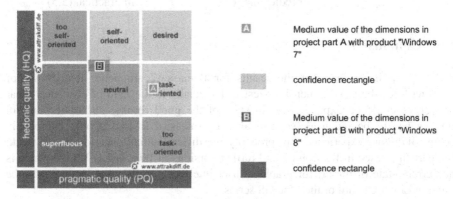

Fig. 7. Results of *AttrakDiff2*

To get a deeper understanding we had a closer look at some strongly rated adjective pairs in AttrakDiff2. Table 3 shows the results per group and per system. Items had to be rated on a scale ranging from 0 to 7, depending on whether they were closer to the left or the right item in the adjectives pairs. We converted the displayed result scales so that now seven is the best possible rating for every item. Especially the very negative review of *Windows 8* by the users without *Windows* experience is conspicuous. It seems as they were very displeased with the system and the results disagree strongly with the remaining results. There could be a strong bias not explained by missing experience, but possibly rooted in general convictions concerning specific products. We did not study this dimension, though.

The new direction in designing the user interface of *Windows 8* is mirrored by the adjectives "innovative" and "novel", but for not experienced *Windows* user also by "impractical" and "confusing". In general, the ratings of *Windows 8* are very different for the three groups. In comparison, *Windows 7* is rated as equally "pleasant" and "good" by both *Windows*-experienced groups. In the opinion of the last group, it is also "straight forwards" and "clearly structured" – according to them the clear opposite of *Windows 8*. In general, there was a stronger agreement among the three groups in rating *Windows 7* than in *Windows 8*. According to AttrakDiff2, both good results, but *Windows 7* is closer to an ideal user satisfaction.

Table 3. Highest rated items in the *AttrakDiff2* adjective pairs

user group	tested system	
	Windows 7	*Windows 8*
Windows 7-user	practical (6.1)	innovative (5.8)
	pleasant (6)	challenging (5.5)
	good (6)	attractive (5.4)
Windows 8-user	pleasant (6.2)	novel (5.9)
	manageable (6.1)	creative (5.9)
	good (6.1)	presentable (5.8)
No *Windows*-user	straight forwards (6.25)	confusing (6.25)
	clearly structured (6)	unpleasant (5.75)
	predictable (6)	impractical (5.5)

5   Conclusion

Summing up it is clear that the results for *Windows 7* are better than those for *Windows 8* for the three dimensions tested. Especially in the field of efficiency clear differences could be exposed. But in spite of the good results, one of the control samples has to be reconsidered critically: It was hard to find people completely lacking *Windows* experience, but probably the differentiating criterion is too weak: The paradigm used in *Windows 7* and further versions of *Windows* is WIMP which is the current state of the art for graphical user interfaces on PCs and can e.g. also be found in Linux Ubuntu or the Mac OS series.

Even if the persons in the control sample never have used or even seen a *Windows* product before the test (which is unlikely given the strong market position of the *Windows* family of products), they also should not have used any other operation system based on the WIMP paradigm. If they had, they know how to handle windows, interact with icons and menus by clicking with a mouse from a similar system to *Windows 7*. So actually the control sample should be labelled "users with no WIMP-experience", but to find people to join them was not in the realm of possibility for this study – more than 30 years after the market introduction of GUI systems this hardly comes as a surprise. Hence *Windows 7* has an advantage of familiarity during the test, because of its widely spread paradigm.

Before the testing phase, we had suspected that *Windows 8*'s split interface would disturb novel users, but this could not be confirmed. Changing between desktop and tile environment was confusing at first, because users didn't expect to find the desktop after the surprising new start screen. But after a short familiarisation phase it was accepted and not longer recognized as a problem. For example, during task 5, installation of software (*Adobe Reader XI*, not as app version) *Windows 8* changes automatically from the download of the installation file in the *Internet Explorer* app to the desktop where the installation dialog appears. Most of the users did not notice the automatically change of the environment. Working with two interaction paradigms in one system does not appear as a problem according to our test.

The biggest criticism of *Windows 8* was the missing start button, a fact well reflected in popular online discussions of the problem.[5] Many users claimed at the beginning of a task that they would now call the start menu over the start button to start the handling of the task. Because they could not use this function any longer, they had to find different ways to start. Many of the possibilities offered were also available in *Windows 7*, but test subjects were used to the start button, hence they didn't have alternatives on their mind. With the disappearance of the start button in *Windows 8*, Microsoft has removed an important initial point for operating the system. There was a lot of public criticism on Microsoft for this decision, so Microsoft decided to put a new version of the button back in the desktop in *Windows 8.1*.

Because of the suitability of *Windows 8* for touch devices, apps in full screen and the *charms* bar are an important feature. Both caused many problems during the test: As described above, changing or closing apps running in full screen mode was difficult for many users. They did not see any obvious possibilities and spent much time on searching a way out. The hint of changing the cursor appearance when the user hovers over the upper border was not enough to provoke a drag gesture from the top to a middle position. Similar problems with hidden functions occurred with the *charms*. Novel users did not know how to let the hidden bar appear and stay fixed. It fist seemed kind of random how the users tried to activate the *charms* bar with their mouse movements. But after a while, this feature was apprehended and could be used in a controlled way by the test subjects.

---

[5] The quite specific query "*Windows 8*" "missing start button" yields 200,000 hits in *Google*.

After the analysis of the control samples' data, the hypothesis that *Windows 8* is more usable than *Windows 7* could not be confirmed. The differences between the results of each part of the usability analysis are quite remarkable. Because *Windows 7* is a representative of the WIMP paradigm and *Windows 8* is built on its own new interaction paradigm, WIMP has to be seen as more usable than the paradigm introduced in *Windows 8*. It is open, though, whether this finding might change with longer experience phases for the new interaction style.

References

1. Hassenzahl, M., Burmester, M., Koller, F.: Der User Experience (UX) auf der Spur: Zum Einsatz von www.attrakdiff.de. In: Brau, H., Diefenbach, S., Hassenzahl, M., Koller, F., Peissner, M., Röse, K. (eds.) Usability Professionals, pp. 78–82. German Chapter der Usability Professionals Association, Stuttgart (2008)
2. ISO. Information technology – Icon symbols and functions for controlling multimedia software applications (ISO 18035:2003). International Standards Organization, Geneva (2003)
3. ISO. Ergonomic requirements for office work with visual display terminals (VDTs), Part 11, Guidance on usability (ISO 9241-11:1998E). International Standards Organization, Geneva (1998)
4. Microsoft. Search, share, print, and more (2014a),
   `http://windows.microsoft.com/en-gb/windows-8/charms-tutorial`
   (retrieved January 19, 2014)
5. Microsoft. Start screen (2014b), `http://windows.microsoft.com/en-gb/windows-8/start-screen-tutorial` (retrieved January 19, 2014)
6. Nielsen Norman Group. Thinking Aloud: The #1 Usability Tool (2014),
   `http://www.nngroup.com/articles/thinking-aloud-the-1-usability-tool/` (retrieved January 22, 2014)
7. Sauro, J., Lewis, J.R.: Quantifying the User Experience. Elsevier/Morgan Kaufmann, Amsterdam (2012)
8. TechSmith. Morae (2013), `http://www.techsmith.com/morae.html` (retrieved October 09, 2013)
9. User Interface Design GmbH. AttrakDiff (2013),
   `http://attrakdiff.de/sience-en.html` (retrieved January 20, 2014)

Applying the User Experience Questionnaire (UEQ) in Different Evaluation Scenarios

Martin Schrepp[1], Andreas Hinderks[2], and Jörg Thomaschewski[3]

[1] SAP AG, Walldorf, Dietmar-Hopp-Allee 16, 69190 Walldorf, Germany
[2] RMT Soft GmbH & Co. KG, Carl-Zeiss-Str. 14, 28816 Stuhr, Germany
[3] Hochschule Emden/Leer, Constantiaplatz 4, 26723 Emden, Germany
martin.schrepp@sap.com, andreas@hinderks.org,
joerg.thomaschewski@hs-emden-leer.de

Abstract. A good user experience is central for the success of interactive products. To improve products concerning these quality aspects it is thus also important to be able to measure user experience in an efficient and reliable way. But measuring user experience is not an end in itself. Several different questions can be the reason behind the wish to measure the user experience of a product quantitatively. We discuss several typical questions associated with the measurement of user experience and we show how these questions can be answered with a questionnaire with relatively low effort. In this paper the user experience questionnaire UEQ is used, but the general approach may be transferred to other questionnaires as well.

Keywords: User Experience, Usability, Questionnaire, Pragmatic Quality, Hedonic Quality.

1   Introduction

To create successful products or services it is necessary to ensure that the product has a sufficiently high user experience. Different users or different groups of users may judge the same product quite differently concerning its user experience, for example because they have different needs or different abilities or skills to use the product. An efficient and inexpensive method to conduct such measurements is thus the usage of validated questionnaires. But before such a complex multi-dimensional construct like user experience can be measured in a meaningful way, it is very useful to clearly understand the meaning of the concept.

A well-known definition of user experience is given in ISO 9241-210 [1]. Here, user experience is defined as "a person's perceptions and responses that result from the use or anticipated use of a product, system or service". Thus, user experience is seen as a holistic concept that includes all types of emotional, cognitive or physical reactions concerning the concrete or even only the assumed usage of a product. This is a quite general and abstract definition that is not helpful at all if we want to get an idea on how to measure this quality aspect of a product.

A. Marcus (Ed.): DUXU 2014, Part I, LNCS 8517, pp. 383–392, 2014.
© Springer International Publishing Switzerland 2014

A different interpretation (which we adopt in this paper) is to define user experience as a set of distinct quality criteria [2] that includes classical usability criteria, like efficiency, controllability or learnability, and non-goal directed or hedonic quality criteria [3], like stimulation, fun-of-use, novelty, emotions [4] or aesthetics [5]. This has the advantage that it splits the general notion of user experience into a number of simple quality criteria, which describe distinct and relatively well-defined aspects of user experience that can be measured independently.

The measurement of user experience is not an end in itself. In fact, several different and quite natural questions can be the reason behind the wish to measure the user experience of a product quantitatively:

- *Continuous improvement by measuring the user experience of new versions:* Has the redesign of the product improved user experience compared to the previous product version? This question can be answered relatively simple by a statistical comparison of two measurements.
- *Comparison to the direct competitors in the market*: How good is the user experience of the product compared to the direct competitors in the market? This is similar to the question above, since here only the direct competitors, i.e. a special group of products, are of interest for a comparison.
- *Test if a product has sufficient user experience*: Does the product fulfill the general expectations of users concerning user experience? Such general expectations of users are formed by their usage of products that they frequently use. To answer this question it is thus necessary to compare the measured user experience of the product to results of other established products, for example from a benchmark data set containing quite different typical products.
- *Determine areas of improvement*: What should be changed in order to improve the user experience of the product? This question cannot be answered directly by a quantitative measurement of user experience. To answer this question, a connection of product features to the measurement is required.

We will discuss these different facets of user experience measurement using the example of the user experience questionnaire (UEQ) [6, 7].

2   Construction of the User Experience Questionnaire (UEQ)

The main goal of the UEQ is to allow a fast and immediate measurement of user experience. The UEQ considers aspects of pragmatic and hedonic quality [6, 7].

The original German version of the UEQ was created 2005 by a data analytical approach in order to ensure a practical relevance of the constructed scales, which correspond to distinct quality aspects. An initial item set of 229 potential items related to user experience was created in brainstorming sessions with usability experts. This item set was then reduced to an 80 items raw version of the questionnaire by an expert evaluation.

The 80 items raw version was used in several studies focusing on the quality of interactive products, including e.g. a statistics software package, cell phone address books, online-collaboration software or business software. In these studies 153 participants answered the 80 items. Finally, the scales and the items representing each scale were extracted from this data set by principal component analysis [6, 7].

The reliability (i.e. the consistency of the scales) and validity (i.e. the scales really measure what they intend to measure) of the UEQ scales was investigated in 11 usability tests with a total number of 144 participants and an online survey with 722 participants. The results of these studies showed a sufficiently high reliability of the scales (measured by Cronbach's Alpha). In addition, a number of studies [7, 8], showed a good construct validity of the scales.

The user experience questionnaire contains 6 scales with 26 items:

- Attractiveness: Overall impression of the product. Do users like or dislike is? Items: annoying / enjoyable, good / bad, unlikable / pleasing, unpleasant / pleasant, attractive / unattractive, friendly / unfriendly.
- Perspicuity: Is it easy to get familiar with the product? Items: not understandable / understandable, easy to learn / difficult to learn, complicated / easy, clear / confusing.
- Efficiency: Can users solve their tasks without unnecessary effort? Items: fast / slow, inefficient / efficient, impractical / practical, organized / cluttered.
- Dependability: Does the user feel in control of the interaction? Items: unpredictable / predictable, obstructive / supportive, secure / not secure, meets expectations / does not meet expectations.
- Stimulation: Is it exciting and motivating to use the product? Items: valuable / inferior, boring / exiting, not interesting / interesting, motivating / demotivating.
- Novelty: Is the product innovative and creative? Items: creative / dull, inventive / conventional, usual / leading edge, conservative / innovative.

Attractiveness is a pure valence dimension. Perspicuity, Efficiency and Dependability are pragmatic quality aspects (goal-directed), while Stimulation and Novelty are hedonic quality aspects (not goal-directed). Figure 1 shows the assumed scale structure of the UEQ.

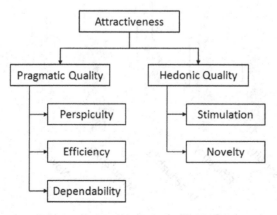

Fig. 1. Assumed scale structure of the UEQ

The questionnaire together with some information concerning its application and an Excel-Tool for data analysis is available free of charge under www.ueq-online.org. For semantic differentials like the UEQ it is of course important that participants read the items in their natural language. Thus, several language versions were constructed and validated (for example, English, Spanish [9], Portuguese [10], etc.). For German there is also a version for children and teenagers available [13] that uses a simplified language. These versions are also available under www.ueq-online.org [12].

Applying the UEQ does not require much effort. Usually 3-5 minutes [11] are sufficient for a participant to read the instruction and to complete the questionnaire. Analyzing the data can be done quite efficiently with the provided Excel-sheet.

3   Continuous Improvement by Measuring the User Experience of New Versions

Most software products undergo a number of redesigns during their lifetime. Typically a more or less complete first version is delivered and then refined based on customer feedback in a number of release cycles. A quite natural question is if the user experience of a revised version is better or at least comparable (for example, if the new version offers more functions and is more complex) to the previous version.

With a questionnaire like the UEQ it is quite simple to answer such questions. All one needs to do is to collect data from a representative sample of users and to compare both versions concerning the single scale means.

Figure 2 shows the results of the UEQ for two versions (a newer and an older version containing the same business functionality) of a business software product. For both versions, participants of a usability test completed the UEQ after they had finished their tasks in the test (20 participants for new version A and 19 participants for old version B).

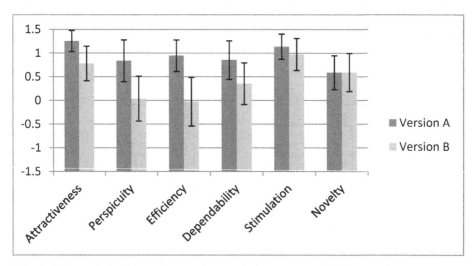

Fig. 2. UEQ result for two product versions. Error bars represent the 95% confidence intervals

Is seems that version A performs better than version B for all scales except novelty. But is this difference significant or only a more or less random deviation? Especially with smaller samples it is absolutely necessary to check if the observed differences are also statistically significant. If the scale mean of version A is higher than the corresponding scale mean of version B and the error bars do not overlap it is immediately clear that version A shows a significantly better result. However, the reverse statement is not true, so even if the error bars overlap (as in this example), the difference can still be significant − in this cases it is necessary to perform a classical significance test. For the example above such a test shows that the differences are despite the small sample size significant for Attractiveness and the pragmatic scales Perspicuity, Efficiency and Dependability at the 5% level.

Based on this simple possibility to compare two product versions it is straightforward to establish a continuous monitoring of user experience for a product. An example of an implementation of such a process is described in [11]. The availability of a quantitative measure for user experience also helps to define clear goals concerning the expected user experience of new or refined products.

4   Comparison to the Direct Competitors in the Market

Often is it not only the goal to be good, but to be better than the direct competitors in the market. The question if a new product outperforms competition with respect to user experience is related to the previous question. The only problem here is to collect data concerning the user experience of competitor products. With classical on premise software this is in most cases impossible due to practical problems to access users of the competitor products. For modern web-based applications this if often much simpler, since in many cases at least product demos are available on the web.

As an example we show a first evaluation of the currently available services for web automation. The three investigated services are *IFTTT* (www.ifttt.com), *Zapier* (www.zapier.com) and *We Wired Web* (www.wewiredweb.com). The basic function of these products is to connect different web services by user defined rules. It is, for example, possible to store a photo as file in a Dropbox when it is posted on Facebook. A rule is defined by a trigger associated with a channel (Facebook) and an action (store the photo in the Dropbox) that is fired when the trigger is activated (photo is posted).

82 students of the University of Applied Sciences Emden/Leer evaluated the services as part of a practical task with the UEQ. Each student had to use one of these web services to solve three different problems with the service, i.e. had to define three different rules. This forces the students to get familiar with the service and to get a realistic impression concerning its user experience. After this phase each student had to evaluate the service he or she used with the simplified German version [14] of the UEQ.

Figure 3 shows the results for the three services.

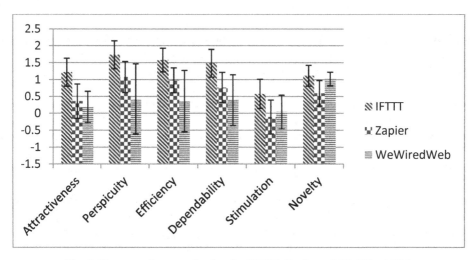

Fig. 3. User experience evaluation for IFTTT, Zapier and We Wired Web

All three services offer quite similar functionality and interaction concepts. But their evaluation by students shows quite different results concerning user experience. Obviously IFTTT outperforms the other two services, especially with respect to pragmatic quality aspects.

The effort for such a comparative evaluation of different competing solutions is quite limited. As long as an access to the solutions is available or if it is possible to contact a sufficiently large sample of users, such an evaluation can be done in a couple of days. Suggestions on how to plan and perform such evaluations can be found in [14].

5   Test If a Product Has Sufficient User Experience

If a new product is launched, a typical question is if the user experience of the product is sufficiently high to fulfill the general expectations of users. Such expectations of users are formed during their interaction with other typical software products. These products must not belong to the same product category. For example, the everyday experience of users with modern web sites and modern interactive devices, like tablets or smartphones, has also heavily increased the expectations concerning the user experience of professional software, for example business applications, in the last couple of years.

Thus, the question if the user experience of a new product is sufficient can be answered by comparing the results for the product with the results of a large sample of other commonly used products, i.e. a benchmark data set.

For the UEQ such a benchmark was developed in the last couple of years [11]. The benchmark contains data from 163 product evaluations with the UEQ. These evaluated products cover a wide range of applications. The benchmark contains complex business applications (98), development tools (4), web shops or services (37), social networks (3), mobile applications (13), and a couple of other (8) products.

In total 4818 responses of subjects are contained in the benchmark. The number of respondents per evaluated product varied from extremely small samples (3 respondents) to huge samples (722 respondents). The mean number of respondents per study was 29.56 (std. deviation 73.5).

Many evaluations were done as part of usability tests, so the majority of the samples was in the range of 11 to 20 respondents (53%). The samples with more than 20 respondents (20%) were usually collected as online evaluations. Of course the studies based on tiny samples with less than 10 respondents (27%) do not carry much information. It was thus checked if these small samples had an influence on the benchmark data reported in the rest of this section. Since the results do not change much if studies with less than 11 respondents are eliminated, it was decided to keep them in the benchmark data set.

Since the benchmark data set contains currently only a quite limited number of evaluation results it was decided to limit the feedback per scale to 5 categories:

- *Excellent*: In the range of the 10% best results.
- *Good*: 10% of the results in the benchmark data set are better and 75% of the results are worse.
- *Above average*: 25% of the results in the benchmark are better than the result for the evaluated product, 50% of the results are worse.
- *Below average*: 50% of the results in the benchmark are better than the result for the evaluated product, 25% of the results are worse.
- *Bad*: In the range of the 25% worst results.

The following table shows the connection of these categories to the scale means for the 6 UEQ scales.

Table 1. Benchmark intervals for the UEQ scales

	Att.	Eff.	Per.	Dep.	Sti.	Nov.
Excellent	≥ 1,72	≥ 1,64	≥ 1,82	≥ 1,6	≥ 1,50	≥ 1,34
Good	≥ 1,50 < 1,72	≥ 1,31 < 1,64	≥ 1,37 < 1,82	≥ 1,4 < 1,6	≥ 1,31 < 1,50	≥ 0,96 < 1,34
Above average	≥ 1,09 < 1,50	≥ 0,84 < 1,31	≥ 0,90 < 1,37	≥ 1,06 < 1,40	≥ 1,00 < 1,31	≥ 0,63 < 0,96
Below average	≥ 0,65 < 1,09	≥ 0,50 < 0,84	≥ 0,53 < 0,90	≥ 0,70 < 1,06	≥ 0,52 < 1,00	≥ 0,24 < 0,63
Bad	< 0,65	< 0,50	< 0,53	< 0,70	<0, 52	< 0,24

The benchmark is also included in the data analysis sheet and is automatically calculated together with the other statistics.

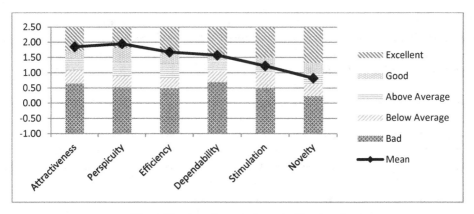

Fig. 4. Benchmark graph form the Excel tool

With the availability of a benchmark it is relatively easy to decide if a new product has sufficient user experience to be successful in the market. It is sufficient to measure the user experience with a large representative sample of users. A comparison of the results for the different scales with the results of the products in the benchmark allows then conclusions regarding the relative strengths and weaknesses of the product. However it must be noted that the general expectations concerning user experience grew over time. Since the benchmark contains also data from established products, a new product should reach at least the Good category in all scales.

6   Determine Areas of Improvement

Collecting quantitative data concerning user experience with a questionnaire like the UEQ is quite efficient. But this efficiency also has some drawbacks. We only get high level data concerning the scales of the UEQ, but the question which product features needs to be improved in order to increase user experience sometimes cannot be answered directly. If we compare these high level data with the results of a usability test, the situation is quite different. A usability test typically identifies a number of concrete problems, i.e. points that should be changed, but does not provide a good impression on how users feel about the product (especially since usability tests cause a lot of effort and can only be performed with a small sample of users).

However, with a questionnaire like the UEQ it is possible to make at least educated guesses about the areas where improvements will have the highest impact. For an evaluated product, the UEQ shows a pattern of 6 measured user experience qualities. From this pattern it is possible to make at least some assumptions where to look for improvements.

The evaluation of IFTTT shown in Figure 3 can serve as example. It shows good values (in the sense of the benchmark) concerning all pragmatic quality scales. Users seem to have the impression that it is easy to understand, efficient to use and offers a controllable interaction. On the other hand, the value for stimulation is not really encouraging, so if effort is spent to increase the user experience of IFTTT it is quite clear that this effort should try to increase the fun of use of the service. A different pattern can be seen for product version B in Figure 2. Here it is quite clear that designers and developers first need to focus on an improvement of the pragmatic quality, especially efficiency and perspicuity.

7   Discussion

Obviously, a good user experience improves the chances of a product in the market. The UEQ offers the possibility to evaluate the user experience of a product quickly and efficiently. This simple and fast data collection with the UEQ offers the possibility to measure not only the current version of a product, but to establish a continuous measurement of different product versions for quality control. Another scenario that is possible due to this efficient measurement is to compare a product with its direct competitors to get information on the comparative position of the product.

The described benchmark offers an additional possibility to get an idea if the current user experience of a product is sufficient, by comparing it to a large number of different established products. Of course the benchmark offers just a high level impression about the position of a product in the market and should ideally be extended by a comparison to the direct competitors to get a clearer picture.

Clearly the efficiency of the UEQ has also the drawback that only high level information about strength and weaknesses of a product are provided. But since the different scales of the UEQ describe distinct quality aspects of an interactive product, some conclusions on concrete improvements are usually possible. This allows setting up special test activities that can help to get more detailed information about the problematic areas.

References

1. DIN EN 9241210, 2011-01, Ergonomics of human-system interaction - Part 210: Human-centred design for interactive systems. Beuth, Berlin
2. Preece, J., Rogers, Y., Sharp, H.: Interaction design: Beyond human-computer interaction. Wiley, New York (2002)
3. Hassenzahl, M.: The effect of perceived hedonic quality on product appealingness. International Journal of Human-Computer Interaction 13, 479–497 (2001)
4. Norman, D.: Emotional Design: Why We Love (Or Hate) Everyday Things. Basic Books, Boulder Colorado (2003)
5. Tractinsky, N.: Aesthetics and Apparent Usability: Empirical Assessing Cultural and Methodological Issues. In: CHI 1997 Electronic Publications (1997), http://www.acm.org/sigchi/chi97/proceedings/paper/nt.htm
6. Laugwitz, B., Schrepp, M., Held, T.: Konstruktion eines Fragebogens zur Messung der User Experience von Softwareprodukten. In: Heinecke, A.M., Paul, H. (eds.) Mensch & Computer 2006 – Mensch und Computer im Strukturwandel, pp. 125–134. Oldenbourg Verlag (2006)

7. Laugwitz, B., Held, T., Schrepp, M.: Construction and evaluation of a user experience questionnaire. In: Holzinger, A. (ed.) USAB 2008. LNCS, vol. 5298, pp. 63–76. Springer, Heidelberg (2008)

8. Laugwitz, B., Schubert, U., Ilmberger, W., Tamm, N., Held, T., Schrepp, M.: Subjektive Benutzerzufriedenheit quantitativ erfassen: Erfahrungen mit dem User Experience Questionnaire UEQ. In: Brau, H., Lehmann, A., Petrovic, K., Schroeder, M. (eds.) Usability Professionals, pp. 220–225 (2009)

9. Rauschenberger, M., Schrepp, M., Cota, M.P., Olschner, S., Thomaschewski, J.: Efficient measurement of the user experience of interactive products - How to use the User Experence Questionnaire (UEQ). Example: Spanish Language Version. International Journal of Interactive Multimedia and Artificial Intelligence 2(1), 39–45 (2013)

10. Pérez Cota, M., Thomaschewski, J., Schrepp, M., Goncalves, R.: Efficient Measurement of the User Experience. A Portuguese Version. In: DSAI 2013 Software Development and Technologies for Enhancing Accessibility and Fighting Info-exclusion, Vigo, Spain, November 13-15 (2013)

11. Schrepp, M., Olschner, S., Schubert, U.: User Experience Questionnaire Benchmark - Praxiserfahrungen zum Einsatz im Business-Umfeld. In: Brau, H., Lehmann, A., Petrovic, K., Schroeder, M. (eds.) Usability Professionalspp, pp. 348–353 (2013)

12. UEQ, http://www.ueq-online.org ((last visited: January 20, 2014))

13. Hinderks, A., Schrepp, M., Rauschenberger, M., Olschner, S., Thomaschewski, J.: Konstruktion eines Fragebogens für jugendliche Personen zur Messung der User Experience. In: Brau, H., Lehmann, A., Petrovic, K., Schroeder, M. (eds.) Usability Professionals 2012, pp. 78–83 (2012)

14. Rauschenberger, M., Thomaschewski, J., Schrepp, M.: User Experience mit Fragebögen messen. Durchführung und Auswertung am Beispiel des UEQ. In: Brau, H., Lehmann, A., Petrovic, K., Schroeder, M. (eds.) Usability Professionals 2013, pp. 72–76. German UPA e.V., Stuttgart (2013)

Online Psychometric Design (OnPsyD) Tool

Shiny Verghese[1], Paul van Schaik[2], and Steve Green[2]

[1] Gulf University for Science and Technology, Mishref, Kuwait
[2] Teesside University, Middlesbrough, United Kingdom
moncy.s@gust.edu.kw, {p.van-schaik,s.j.green}@tees.ac.uk

Abstract. This paper discusses the architecture, and design of a research tool for online psychometrics. A few limitations of the current web-based tools available for psychometric research are discussed and the need for the OnPsyD Tool is laid. We provide a description of the database structure, and the architecture of the questionnaire presentation manager. The focus for OnPsyD Tool in this paper is the design of an extensible software architecture. Hence, new question types, extensions to existing question types, design style of questionnaires, and appearance of questions could be adapted easily. The paper concludes with a brief note on its limitations and extensions.

Keywords: online psychometrics, extensible database, design parameters for online questionnaires.

1   Introduction

The growing popularity of psychometric testing has penetrated every walk of life. In contemporary society, where technology is rapidly spreading, the traditional method of testing through pen(cil) and paper is being converted to online test administration. There is a plethora of research available on the advantages of online administration of questionnaires. In this research, a distinction is to be made between psychometric questionnaires and factual questionnaires or surveys. The former are, for example, used to measure customers' perceived quality of (online or offline) services and to measure users' interaction experience with a website in terms of flow experience [12]. Compared to the popularity of web-based surveys, there is very little research available to aid the design of online psychometric questionnaires and to ensure sound measurement. Because psychometric questionnaires do not measure factual information, it is more likely that the responses given are influenced by external factors, such as the presentation design of the particular questionnaire that is being administered. For example, research has shown a significant impact of presentation format on response quality [14] [15] and substantial differences in information-processing style between western and eastern cultures [10], with potential implications for using psychometrics in any domain. Empirical research is therefore needed to develop knowledge in particular for the presentation of online psychometrics. Therefore, a technical system is required to support research on design parameters in online psychometrics.

A. Marcus (Ed.): DUXU 2014, Part I, LNCS 8517, pp. 393–401, 2014.
© Springer International Publishing Switzerland 2014

With a plethora of survey tools available currently, an obvious question might be why there is a need for another one. In contrast to the available survey software tools, OnPsyD Tool is developed solely for research and hence gives researchers access to source code to add more functionalities and contribute to a repository of psychometric data collected with the tool. This paper describes the architecture details of the software.

Human-computer interaction (HCI) is the study of interaction between people (users) and computers. After the inception of psychometrics in the early 1900s, it was during the late 1970s, that psychometric questionnaires started to be used to measure the quality of human-computer interaction [5]. For example, research by Ahuja and Webster [1] led to the identification of two distinct scales to measure disorientation and perceived ease of use. Factor structure and psychometric properties such as reliability, validity and sensitivity [6] were confirmed through empirical research on these scales. In another study conducted by Davis and Wiedenbeck [2], a new scale to measure flow, defined as a psychological state of a person to feel cognitively efficient or motivated and happy [9] during Web use, was developed. Research by van Schaik and Ling [12] [13] [14] established the psychometric properties of these scales in empirical studies measuring the quality of human-computer interaction. The recommendation of this research focused on investigating a comprehensive set of design parameters and experimental manipulations of web site parameters to demonstrate sensitivity of measures and quality of human-computer interaction [14]. Accordingly, the OnPsyD Tool will provide a framework for this research.

2   Problem Statement

Various research studies demonstrate how usability science, along with other research in HCI, can benefit from the application of psychometrics in our daily life such as assessment, information search, and diagnostics. However, the way psychometric instruments are presented on-line and respondents' interaction with on-line instruments can influence measurement [12] [14]. Because psychometrics models human psychological characteristics, it is important for instruments administered on-line to be sound and standardize in terms of measurement. Very little research exists in online psychometrics that addresses psychometric measurement in human-computer interaction through web applications or mobile applications. Large-scale empirical research is required to develop a comprehensive understanding of online psychometrics. This research addresses the following problems through the development of the OnPsyD Tool. First, existing software tools do not offer good support for experimenting with visual design in questionnaires. Second, there is a lack of separation between content, style and design of online questionnaires is prevalent in existing software tools.

3   Architecture

3.1   General Software Description

The focus of the development of the OnPsyD Tool is on the design of an extensible software architecture. OnPsyD Tool will be available as a research tool for online psychometrics. The visualization of questionnaire items remain separated from the questionnaire content. This separation allows researchers to efficiently create experiments to test the effect of presentation style across a range on content. One of the main tasks is the storage of questionnaires. As questionnaires contain items from a shared list, one questionnaire item could be a part of one or more questionnaires. The same questionnaire exists with different presentation styles. The response for each questionnaire item is stored in a database according to different design parameters. The implementation of the different modules of the OnPsyD Tool is based on the MVC (Model View Controller) architecture. The model represents data and the rules that govern access to and updates of this data. In enterprise software, a model often serves as a software approximation of a real-world process. The view renders the contents of a model. It specifies exactly how the model data should be presented. If the model data changes, the view must update its presentation as needed. The controller translates the user's interactions with the view into actions that the model will perform [3].

3.2   Questionnaire Items

A questionnaire item contains an item *stem* and a *response* part. The attribute description is the item *stem* that is composed of full sentences, phrases or single words. The *response* part is the measure that describes the degree of the attribute description and varies according to different response formats, such as rating scales (e.g. Likert scales) or binary anchored phrases (e.g., yes-no, agree-disagree). The response part is involved in item presentation and response collection. There are different question types such as

- bipolar scales, in particular semantic differential;
- graded/discrete response format such as a Likert scale;
- visual analogue scale or continuous scale;
- pictogram question, where pictures represent textual alternatives;
- matrix question, where multiple questions have the same alternatives as their response.

Due to the similarity of the structure of different questionnaire item types, object-oriented concept of inheritance is used to model their similarities and their differences in an integrated fashion. The UML representation for the class Question is provided in Figure 1. Thus, variations in the structure of existing items and addition of new questionnaire items are incorporated without much change to the software design. The UML represents the structure of the questionnaire item that could be represented with different design patterns. The architecture of separating content and style allows an item to adapt to different presentation styles. Response formats each have their own advantages and disadvantages. For example, research has identified advantages of discrete and visual analogue formats for Likert and semantic differentials [12] [4]. Allowing the a questionnaire item to adapt to different presentation styles through the OnPsyD Tool supports further research on response formats in a systematic and efficient way.

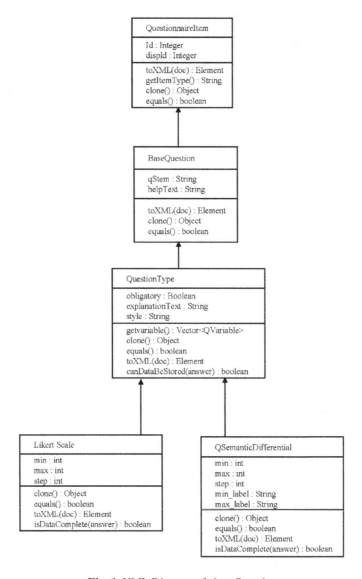

Fig. 1. UML Diagram of class Question

3.3   Responses

The other focus of the software design is on the storage of responses. The user's response to each item is stored into the database as it is completed. The mapping of the user's response is very important. Every response recorded for an item will be associated with the item itself along with the type of response format, the presentation style and the questionnaire that was administered. The response will also record the response time. However, this will be achieved through client-side implementation, depending on the loading of the page and the response to the questionnaire items subsequently.

3.4   Design Parameters

For the initial implementation stages of OnPsyD Tool, only a limited set of design parameters is included in the architecture. However, a comprehensive set of design parameters will be implemented and made available for research purposes. Important parameters include response format, questionnaire layout, and interaction mechanism.

Response format. Different types of response format have already been mentioned in Section 3.2. These formats will be recorded in the database with unique identification number, to enable mapping between the questionnaire item, visual representation and the response.

Questionnaire layout. There are different ways of partitioning questionnaires for on-line presentation [11]. Implementation in the functionality module will include design of questionnaires according to each presentation layout. However, in the database, each layout will be recorded with a unique identification to enable mapping between layouts, items used and the different response formats for the items. Research reported by van Schaik and Ling [14] investigated the presentation of online psychometric questionnaire as whole form (all items in one page) and as single item presentation (one item per page). However, a large-scale empirical analysis is required to investigate various questionnaire layout presentations, and hence the implementation of the OnPsyD Tool will be of significant importance.

Interaction mechanism. Interaction mechanisms, such as direct and indirect, can be distinguished. For example, in direct interaction, users can immediately select from a set of visible options (e.g., radio buttons), whereas in indirect interaction users can choose from a set that will become visible when interacting with the control (e.g., drop-down list). Possible interaction mechanisms for different response formats will be stored in the database along with their unique reference number. This will enable mapping between questionnaire item, its response format, the interaction mechanism and finally the questionnaire layout. Empirical analysis on the data collected may exhibit effects that could be of importance for the quality of responses in online psychometrics.

3.5   Presentation Manager

A web-based presentation manager integrated with the database will administer the questionnaires. For example, the presentation manager will map and store the different presentation styles, items for the questionnaire and the design parameters such as response formats into the database of a questionnaire that has been designed. Further, the manager will administer the designed online psychometric questionnaire through the Web. The presentation manager will also facilitate collecting responses back into the database. Finally, the presentation manager will facilitate the export of responses and other related data for data analysis by statistical software (e.g. SPSS).

4   Implementation

The software for the OnPsyD Tool is divided into subprojects to ensure the capability to re-use components. In addition, the model-view-controller architecture significantly reduces time involved in developing the user interface. The main components are

- Users Module – the module to creating administrators and users
- Functionality Module – the module for the core functionalities like creating questionnaires according to various design parameters
- Web Module – the module to administer the questionnaire online
- Database – the module to store data: user details, questionnaire details, design parameters and responses

4.1   Users Module

The Users Module manages two different kinds of user, administrators with administrative privileges and other registered users who can participate in experiments, as part of online-psychometrics research. The login session for administrators to create and administer research experiments is web-based. Registered users will be invited via email and registered with unique user-id and password. The participation of the users in research experiments will also be web-based in either controlled (e.g. lab) or un-controlled (e.g. home) environments. The users will be first required to agree to participate through an online consent form before the start of the experiment. Participants will be able to exit from an experiment any time.

4.2   Functionality Module

This module is the core of the OnPsyD Tool. Since the tool's focus is separation of questionnaire visualization from its content, the functionality module contains the necessary implementation. One of the main tasks is the storage of questionnaire. The mapping between questionnaire items, design parameters and questionnaire is coded and stored in the database. The functionality module also facilitates presentation of questionnaires according to different layouts. Furthermore, the module supports the export of database data collected in psychometrics experiments to formats (e.g., csv) for analysis by statistical software (e.g. SPSS).

4.3   Web Module

The web module facilitates administration of questionnaires and collection of responses. Client side implementation will include collection of general data such as screen resolution, optional IP address, and operating system details.

4.4   Database

The initial design for the OnPsyD Tool is illustrated in Figure 2. This initial design comprises of tables such as user details, the questionnaire layout, questionnaire items, the questionnaire itself, and response format. Foreign key references between entities enable mapping of required data for empirical analysis.

4.5   Current Stage of Implementation

The implementation of the OnPsyD Tool is in the initial stages. Currently, the User Module and the database design have been partially implemented. Once completed, the tool will be deployed on a Web server and the source code will be published online for reference and use as a research tool.

5   Results

As noted above, the important effort here is to produce a flexible research tool with an extensible architecture. With very little research available currently, it is expected that OnPsyD Tool will help increase research in the study of design parameters for online psychometrics. Eventually, psychometrically sound instruments with design features that help bring out the best results in terms of measurement will contribute immensely to the field of HCI and the practical application of sound online psychometrics.

Contribution to HCI. The important aim of developing psychometric scales, is to help make "IT products better suited for human" [8]. Hence, design parameters that affect online rating scales are of prime importance in research. Furthermore, the tool will facilitate storage of data that can help in analyzing and determining utility as one of the factors for new or existing scales. Utility is the degree of usefulness for which a scale is developed [8]. Besides, the database modelling enables data collection from experiments conducted in different (social and geographical) settings. This will help to establish the generalizability of results. Although the focus of HCI has always been on user interaction, the field of HCI recently is contributing to designing new tools and techniques that improve usability [7]. Hence, OnPsyD Tool will be a unique knowledge contribution to the field of HCI and online Psychometrics.

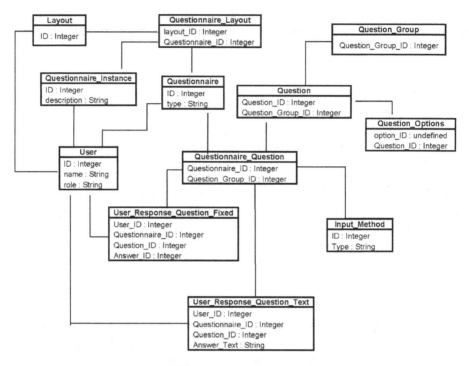

Fig. 2. Database Design

6   Limitations

OnPsyD Tool has been designed as a research tool. Hence, currently, there is no intention to integrate data analysis capabilities (e.g. statistical data analysis). However, if required, this facility could be integrated later on. Further, no skip logic or branching rules for questionnaire items are implemented. If required, in future, the database, because it is extensible, will be able to accommodate this functionality.

7   Future Work

On successfully implementing and testing the OnPsyD Tool the plan is to extend the same to mobile technologies.

References

1. Ahuja, J.S., Webester, J.: Perceived disorientation: an examination of a new measure to assess web design effectiveness. Interacting with Computers 14(1), 15–29 (2001)
2. Davis, S., Wiedenbeck, S.: The mediating effects of intrinsic motivation, ease of use and usefulness perceptions on performance in first-time and subsequent computer users. Interacting with Computers 13(5), 549–580 (2001)

3. Eckstein, R.: Java Docs (2007),
   http://www.oracle.com/technetwork/articles/javase/index-
   142890.html (retrieved 2014 from Oracle)
4. Funke, F., Ulf-Dietrich, R.: Why semantic differentials in web-based research should be
   made from visual analogue scales and not from 5-point scales. Field Methods 24(3), 310–
   327 (2012)
5. Kirakowski, J., Claridge, N., Whitehand, R.: Human centered measures of success in web
   site design. In: Proceedings of the Fourth Conference on Human Factors and the Web
   (1998)
6. Lewis, J.R.: Psychometric Evaluation of the PSSUQ Using Data from Five Years of
   Usability Studies. International Journal of Human-Computer Interaction 14(3), 463–488
   (2002)
7. Li, F., Jagadish, H.V.: IEEE Data Eng. Bull. 35(3), 1–9 (2012)
8. Lindgaard, G., Kirakowski, J.: The Tricky Landscape of Developing Rating Scales in HCI.
   Interacting with Computers 25(4), 271–277 (2013)
9. Moneta, G.B., Csikszentmihalyi, M.: The effect of perceived challenges and skills on the
   quality of subjective experience. Journal of Personality 64(2), 275–310 (1996)
10. Nisbett, R.E., Peng, K., Choi, I., Norenzayan, A.: Culture and systems of thought: holistic
    versus analytic cognition. Psychological Review 108(2), 291–310 (2001)
11. Norman, K., Friedman, Z., Norman, K., Stevenson, R.: Navigational Issues in the Design
    of On-Line Self-Administered Questionnaires. Behaviour & Information Technology
    20(1), 37–45 (2001)
12. van Schaik, P., Ling, J.: Using on-line surveys to measure three key constructs of the
    quality of human–computer interaction in web sites: psychometric properties and
    implications. International journal of Human Computer Studies 59(5), 545–567 (2003)
13. van Schaik, P., Ling, J.: Five psychometric scales for online measurement of the quality of
    human-computer interaction in web sites. International Journal of Human-Computer
    Interaction 18(3), 309–322 (2005)
14. van Schaik, P., Ling, J.: Design parameters of rating scales for web sites. ACM
    Transactions on Computer-Human Interaction 14(1), 4 (2007)
15. van Schaik, P., Ling, J.: An Experimental Analysis of Experiential and Cognitive
    Variables in Web Navigation. Human-Computer Interaction, 199–234 (2012)

Comparing Effectiveness, Efficiency, Ease of Use, Usability and User Experience When Using Tablets and Laptops

Werner Wetzlinger, Andreas Auinger, and Michael Dörflinger

University of Applied Sciences Upper Austria, Campus Steyr
{werner.wetzlinger,andreas.auinger}@fh-steyr.at,
michael.doerflinger@outlook.com

Abstract. Initially perceived as a consumer device, in recent years tablets have become more frequently used in business contexts where they often replace laptops as mobile computing devices. Since they follow different user interaction paradigms we conducted a study comparing effectiveness, efficiency, ease of use, usability and user experience when using tablets and laptops in typical private and business tasks. To measure these characteristics we used the task completion rate, the task completion time, the Single Ease Question (SEQ), the Software Usability Scale (SUS) and AttrakDiff. Results indicate that there is a difference between effectiveness, efficiency and the users' assessment of the devices. Users can carry out tasks more effectively and efficiently on laptops, but rate tablets higher in perceived usability and user experience, indicating that a pleasant and meaningful experience depends on more characteristics than work-related qualities such as effectiveness and efficiency.

Keywords: usability, user experience, satisfaction, ease of use, AttrakDiff.

1 Motivation

In recent years tablets have reached a considerable market penetration.[1, 2] In comparison to more established devices like laptops they rely on touch based controls, are smaller and consequently lead to different user interactions. These different interaction paradigms have also led to different usage scenarios. Laptops have always been used in work contexts and people are therefore used to carrying out work related tasks with them (e.g. writing emails or scheduling meetings). Tablets are primarily designed for the consumer market and are mostly used at home (e.g. as media consumption device or as companion to television viewing and other living-room activities) [3] However, studies show that the adoption rate is also surging in the business context. Especially IT and business professionals use tablets extensively and do so for private as well as work related tasks [4]. This is especially true for mobile workers (e.g in customer relations, sales and management) [2]. Furthermore there is a tendency to use private devices to access work related applications and services [4]. Yet despite the growing adoption rate in business and consumer areas, there is still

A. Marcus (Ed.): DUXU 2014, Part I, LNCS 8517, pp. 402–412, 2014.

little comparative research with focus on usability aspects. Ozok et al. [5] conducted a study in 2008 comparing tablets and laptop on a number of tasks, but the usability of modern tablets has improved heavily in the last years. We therefore conducted a pilot study to examine the differences between these two device types taking into consideration their different application areas. We also wanted to examine different evaluation concepts and metrics. Since laptops are often used in work- and task-related contexts, we considered usability as defined by the ISO as "the extent to which a product can be used by specified users to achieve specified goals with effectiveness, efficiency, and satisfaction…"[6] as an appropriate characteristic for the comparison. Nonetheless, especially in the consumer market, this work and task-related perspective has been broadened by focusing on the whole user experience which incorporates further needs and emotions such as enjoyment, fun, excitement or appeal when using a device or system[7]. Since tablets are a typical consumer product we also considered user experience as an interesting metric.

We therefore decided to conduct a study comparing the two devices on usability and user experience metrics when performing typical tasks in a private and business context. To gain experience carrying out the experiment we started with a small scale pilot study with eight participants. The results will be used as lessons learned for a following study with more participants.

The remainder of the paper is structured as follows: In chapter 2 we describe the methodology of the study. Chapter 3 contains the results of the user tests and the limitations of the study. In chapter 4 we draw conclusions and point out future work.

2 Methodology

The evaluation compares tablets and laptops based on a number of metrics. Since we wanted to compare these devices based on user performance metrics derived from the field of usability [U] as well as perceived qualities by users, we defined effectiveness [U1], efficiency [U2], ease of use [U3], usability [U4] and user experience [UX] as relevant evaluation criteria. Furthermore, we adopted a 2-step approach by using metrics that were measured after every task and metrics that were measured for the devices after completing all tasks.

- **Task oriented metrics:** These post-task metrics were measured for every task after the participant had completed the task.
  - **Effectiveness [U1]:** Effectiveness was measured using the task completion rate by observing how many attempts participants needed and rating the attempts using a 4-step scoring model. A task was considered "easy" (step 1) if it was completed on the first attempt and "hard" (step 2) if it was completed on the second attempt. The task was considered not successfully completed if the participant had to be assisted (step 3) or failed (step 4).
  - **Efficiency [U2]:** Efficiency was measured using the task completion time. We compared the user performances based on the mean, the maximum and minimum completion time.
  - **Ease of Use [U3]:** To measure task-performance satisfaction, we used the Single Ease Question (SEQ) "Overall, how difficult or easy did you find this

task?" The question was asked after the completion of every task and participants had to rate the difficulty on a 7-step Likert scale from *"very difficult"* to *"very easy"*. This question was chosen, because it performs as well as other, more complicated measures of task-difficulty like the Subjective Mental Effort Questionnaire (SMEQ) or the Usability Magnitude Estimation (UME) [8]. Owing to the low number of participants we used the mean instead of the median to compare the difficulty of the tasks.

- **Device oriented metrics:** These post-study metrics were measured for every device after the participant had completed all tasks on the specific device.
  - **Usability [U4]:** Overall perceived usability using a device was measured using the Software Usability Scale (SUS) questionnaire [9]. SUS also provides a reliable global measure of system satisfaction. The questionnaire consists of 10 items that are answered using a 5-step Likert scale reaching from *"strongly disagree"* to *"strongly agree"*. It was chosen, because it is a reliable and valid measure of perceived usability [10, 11] and is widely applied, which allows for a comparison with existing results and products. The questionnaire was answered once for every device after carrying out all tasks on the respective device, because it is designed as a post-study questionnaire.
  - **User Experience [UX]:** User experience was measured using *AttrakDiff* [12], which contains 28 bipolar items that are rated on a 7-step scale to determine *"pragmatic quality"*, *"hedonic quality (stimulation)"*, *"hedonic quality (identity)"* and *"attractiveness"* of the devices. AttrakDiff was chosen, because the reliability of its subscales measured using Cronbach's Alpha coefficient is higher (between .73 and .90) [12] than the reliability of the User Experience Questionnaire (UEQ) (between .65 and .89) [13]. The questionnaire was answered once for every device after answering the SUS questionnaire.

Since all these metrics are based on measurable user performances (effectiveness, efficiency) or the users' perceptions of the capabilities of the devices to achieve certain goals (ease of use, usability, user experience), we had to define a number of tasks to be carried out. To ensure an objective comparison we included the most frequently executed tasks from the private as well as the business context. We determined these tasks by comparing and analyzing existing studies. Since the results of all studies referenced to similar tasks we defined the following tasks for our pilot study:

- **Business context**
  - **Task 1: Writing an email**: Participants had to open an email client, create a new email, add a specific recipient, a subject and content, insert a certain picture and send the email.
  - **Task 2: Creating a calendar entry**: Participants had to open a calendar app, create a new appointment, choose a date, the time and the duration, define a location, save the appointment and reopen it to add a reminder, switch to month-view and move the appointment to another day.
- **Private context**
  - **Task 3: Browsing and filling out forms**: Participants had to open a web browser, enter a specific URL, fill out a form completely and send the form.

— **Task 4: Finding and gathering information**: Participants had to open a web browser, research the address of a certain hotel and find out the route to this location.

Participants had to carry out all four tasks using an iPad 2 running iOS 5.1.1 and an Acer Laptop (Aspire 5740) running Microsoft Windows 7. These devices were chosen because at the time of the study the iPad was the top-selling tablet with iOS being the leading tablet platform[1, 14] while Windows was the leading platform on desktops and laptops.[15] To ensure participants were experienced in using the devices they had to have used them in a private or business context at least occasionally in the previous three months and had to be familiar with the standard applications *"Mail"* (iOS), *"Calendar"* (iOS) and *"Outlook"* (Windows). As web browsers *"Google Chrome"* (laptop) and *"Safari"* (iPad) were used, but the particular functionality of the browsers was not crucial for task fulfillment.

Eight people (7 men and 1 woman between 22 and 37 years old) participated in the study. Four participants began carrying out the tasks by using the iPad, four used the laptop first.

3   Results

In the following sections we lay out the results of the user tests in respect to the 5 chosen metrics.

3.1   Effectiveness

Participants had problems completing task 1 on the tablet. One participant completed the task on the second attempt, 2 participants needed assistance, one participant failed completely. Nobody had problems using the laptop. All other task did not lead to considerable problems or differences (see Fig. 1).

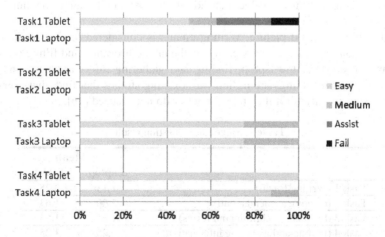

Fig. 1. Task Performance Rates results

3.2   Efficiency

Efficiency was measured by the task completion time. Fig. 2 illustrates the results using the mean time in seconds represented by the columns, as well as the minimum and maximum time needed using error bars. Participants who failed to complete a task were not considered in this analysis.

Comparing each task on the two devices results shows that all tasks were carried out faster on the laptop. In case of task 1 the difference in mean time was high (35.9%), because three participants had trouble completing the task. All other tasks were only slightly faster on the laptop (task 2 4.1%, task 3 16.2%, task 4 11.2%).

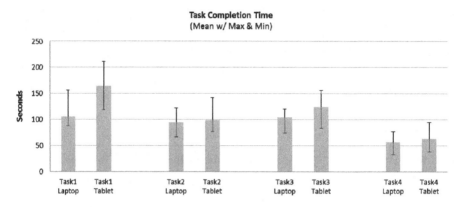

Fig. 2. Task Completion Time results

3.3   Ease of Use

Ease of Use was measured using the Singe Ease Question (SEQ). Answers were rated on a 7-step Likert scale from 1 (very easy) to 7 (very difficult). Table 1 summarizes the results using the mean value instead of the median because the number of participants was so low.

Results show a mixed picture. Writing emails is considered harder on the tablet, creating calendar entries is slightly easier on the tablet, browsing and filling out forms is slightly easier using the laptop, finding and gathering information is considered equally easy. These findings are in line with existing studies that find, that users tend to rate tasks more difficult if they take longer or do not succeed [16].

Table 1. Singe Ease Question results

	Mean	
	Laptop	Tablet
Task 1 (Writing Email)	1,13	3,25
Task 2 (creating a calendar entry)	2,00	1,63
Task 3 (browsing and filling out forms)	1,25	1,63
Task 4 (finding and gathering information)	1,25	1,25

3.4   Usability

Usability was measured using the Software Usability Scale (SUS). It consists of ten items that participants had to rate on a 5-step scale. The resulting SUS score was higher for the tablet (82.5) than the laptop (75) resulting in an overall higher perceived usability of the tablet (see Table 2 and Table 3).

Table 2. SUS-Score of the laptop

System Usability Scale	Strongly Disagree			Strongly Agree		
75% SUS Score:	1	2	3	4	5	Mean
I1 I think I would like to use this software product frequently.	0	0	0	2	6	4,750
I2 I found the product unnecessarily complex.	3	2	2	1	0	2,125
I3 I thought the product was easy to use.	0	1	1	3	3	4,000
I4 I think I would need Tech Support to be able to use this product.	6	1	0	0	1	1,625
I5 I found the various functions in this product were well integrated.	1	1	2	2	2	3,375
I6 I thought there was too much inconsistency in this product.	3	3	2	0	0	1,875
I7 I imagine that most people would learn to use this product very quickly.	0	1	4	2	1	3,375
I8 I found the product very cumbersome to use.	4	3	1	0	0	1,625
I9 I felt very confident using this product.	1	0	1	2	4	4,000
I10 I need to learn a lot about this product before I could effectively use it.	4	1	1	1	1	2,250

Table 3. SUS-Score of the tablet

System Usability Scale	Strongly Disagree			Strongly Agree		
82,5% SUS Score:	1	2	3	4	5	Mean
I1 I think I would like to use this software product frequently.	0	0	1	0	7	4,750
I2 I found the product unnecessarily complex.	2	6	0	0	0	1,750
I3 I thought the product was easy to use.	0	2	0	1	5	4,125
I4 I think I would need Tech Support to be able to use this product.	7	0	0	0	1	1,500
I5 I found the various functions in this product were well integrated.	0	2	1	4	1	3,500
I6 I thought there was too much inconsistency in this product.	6	2	0	0	0	1,250
I7 I imagine that most people would learn to use this product very quickly.	1	0	2	1	4	3,875
I8 I found the product very cumbersome to use.	5	2	1	0	0	1,500
I9 I felt very confident using this product.	1	0	1	2	4	4,000
I10 I need to learn a lot about this product before I could effectively use it.	6	2	0	0	0	1,250

Furthermore the tablet was also considered to be less complex (I2), easier to learn (I7) and more consistent (I6).

Results from I3 (I thought the product was easy to use) seem to contradict the results from the Singe Ease Question (SEQ) in section 3.3. Table 1 shows that using the mean of all answers to the SEQ the laptop is perceived as easier. When asked in I3 of the SUS about ease of use, participants rate the tablet as easier to use. This is true not only for the mean value, but also the median.

3.5   User Experience

To measure user experience, we used *AttrakDiff [12],* which evaluates devices based on the four dimensions *"pragmatic quality"* (PQ), *"hedonic quality - identity"* (HQ-I), *"hedonic quality - stimulation"* (HQ-S) and *"attractiveness"* (ATT).

- Pragmatic quality (PQ): A quality of a product that describes whether its functions are appropriate to achieve certain goals (e.g. practical)
- Hedonic quality - identity" (HQ-I): A quality of a product that describes whether its attributes can satisfy the human need to be perceived by others in a certain way (e.g. presentable or stylish)
- Hedonic quality - stimulation (HQ-S): A quality of a product that describes whether it can fulfill the human need to improve personal skills and knowledge (e.g. creative).
- Attractiveness" (ATT): A general positive or negative assessment of the appeal of a product.

Within these four dimensions the devices had to be rated based on 7 word pairs using a 7-step scale. Fig. 3 illustrates the results for every word pair using the mean rating of all participants.

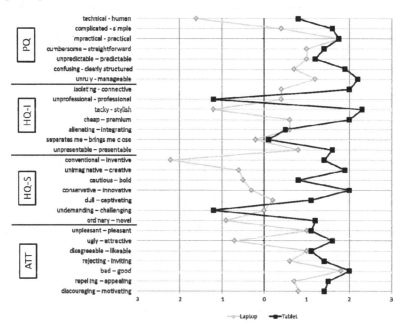

Fig. 3. Mean ratings of word pairs

The results show that the tablet scores higher in nearly all word pairs. Consequently, using the mean value of the including word pairs, the tablet scores higher in all four dimensions of AttrakDiff (see Fig. 4).

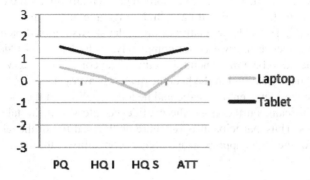

Fig. 4. Mean values of all four AttrakDiff dimensions

Furthermore, there is an influence between these dimensions. Pragmatic quality and hedonic quality are independent and both influence attractiveness. Therefore AttrakDiff compares the devices based on these two dimensions and positions them in a two-dimensional portfolio (see Fig. 5), which consists of nine areas. Products that have a high pragmatic as well as hedonic quality are desired. If the pragmatic quality is average or low products are considered to be too self-oriented. If the hedonic quality is average or low the product is too focused on task fulfillment.

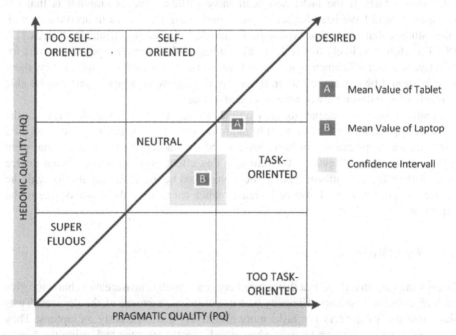

Fig. 5. Pragmatic and hedonic quality of tablets (A) and laptops (B)

Products are represented in this portfolio using the mean value and a confidence interval. The confidence interval is calculated using t-tests and a significance level of 0.05. A small confidence interval indicates that participants agree on the rating of the product. Consequently, the rating is also more likely to really apply to the product.

Results for the tablet show that it has a high pragmatic quality and is considered to be *"task-oriented"*. The hedonic quality of the tablet shows a mixed picture. It is also high, but the confidence interval is not completely in the high area ("desired"). The laptop is considered to be a more neutral product. The confidence interval reaches the top area in pragmatic quality, but the hedonic quality is average.

These differences between pragmatic and hedonic qualities of the two products are statistically significant. Furthermore, the confidence interval of the tablet is smaller for both qualities. Thus, participants agree more on the qualities of the tablet, whereby the assessment of the tablet applies with a higher probability to the actual product.

3.6   Limitations

Since this was only a pilot study to evaluate the chosen metrics and methods, the sample size serves as a limitation. Eight users are not a sufficiently high number to ensure valid results for such quantitative metrics.

The results for the metric *"effectiveness"* are very similar for all tasks. With the exception of task 1 on the tablet every task was carried out with very few problems. This is an indicator that the tasks may have been too easy.

Consequently, the results for the metric *"efficiency"* also just show a high variance for this one task. If the tasks had been more difficult, the assumption is that the variances would have been higher. Nevertheless these results are in accordance with other studies that show that typing performance is lower on virtual keyboards [17, 18]. Therefore it is likely that if the tasks had required more user inputs the results for effectiveness and efficiency would have been worse on the tablet. Consequently, these aspects should be considered when designing the follow up study in order to be able to reach a fair balance between the tasks and devices.

Finally, results do depend not only on the device but also on the platform and the software applications used. We tried to minimize this effect by utilizing the most used platforms and applications for both devices and only accepting participants that were regular users of both devices. To minimize this effect even further, different device types with different platforms and applications could be used. The familiarity with the device and platform could also be increased when users bring their own device to the experiment.

4   Conclusions

Results indicate that there is a difference between actually measureable characteristics such as effectiveness and efficiency and the users' assessment of the devices. Tests show that users can carry out tasks more effectively and efficiently on laptops. They also rate them as easier on laptops when asked directly after the task using the Single

Ease Question. However participants rated tablets higher in usability when asked after performing all tasks.

Furthermore, despite the problems in carrying out tasks the user experience in the sense of pragmatic quality, hedonic quality (stimulation and identity) and attractiveness (AttrakDiff) is rated higher for tablets, indicating that a pleasant and meaningful experience depends on more characteristics than work-related qualities like effectiveness and efficiency.

Another interesting aspect is the difference between post-task and the post-study metrics about difficulty. Answering the Singe Ease Question (Overall, how difficult or easy did you find this task?) after every task participants rated the laptop as easier to use (using the mean of all answers). However, in the post-study System Usability Score (SUS) questionnaire in item 3 (I thought the product was easy to use) participants rated the tablet as easier. Since this difference is small and there are a number of limitations to the study, this aspect should be examined in another study with a higher number of participants.

Since in this pilot study there seems to be a discrepancy between effectiveness, efficiency and ease of use after carrying out the tasks and the results of the post-study System Usability Scale, we want to analyze this aspect further. In a follow-up study we want to eliminate the limitations of this pilot study and investigate whether and how a higher attractiveness of a device influences peoples' ratings of task-related usability aspects in post-task and post-study evaluations.

References

1. Huberty, K., Holt, A., Moore, J., Devgan, S., Meunier, F., Gelblum, E., Devitt, S., Lu, J., Chen, G., Shih, S., Kim, S., Yoshikawa, K.: Tablet Landscape Evolution: Window(s) of Opportunity. Morgan Stanley Research (2012)
2. iPass: The iPass Global Mobile Workforce Report, http://www.ipass.com/wp-content/uploads/2013/03/ipass_mobile-workforce-report_q1_2013.pdf
3. Mueller, H., Gove, J.L., Webb, J.S.: Understanding Tablet Use: A Multi-Method Exploration. In: Proceedings of the 14th Conference on Human-Computer Interaction with Mobile Devices and Services (Mobile HCI 2012), pp. 1–10. ACM (2012)
4. International Data Group: iPad for Business. Survey (2012), http://www.idgconnectmarketers.com/wp-content/uploads/2012/01/iPad-Survey.pdf
5. Ozok, A.A., Benson, D., Chakraborty, J., Norcio, A.F.: A Comparative Study Between Tablet and Laptop PCs: User Satisfaction and Preferences. International Journal of Human-Computer Interaction 24, 329–352 (2008)
6. ISO: Ergonomic requirements for office work with visual display terminals - Part 11: Guidance on usability (1988)
7. Hassenzahl, M., Tractinsky, N.: User experience - a research agenda. Behaviour& Information Technology 25, 91–97 (2006)

8. Sauro, J., Dumas, J.S.: Comparison of three one-question, post-task usability questionnaires. In: Olsen Jr., D.R., Arthur, R.B., Hinckley, K., Morris, M.R., Hudson, S.E., Greenberg, S. (eds.) Proceedings of the 27th International Conference on Human Factors in Computing Systems, pp. 1599–1608. ACM, New York (2009)
9. Brooke, J.: SUS - A quick and dirty usability scale. In: Jordan, P.W., Thomas, B., Weerdmeester, B.A., McClelland, A.L. (eds.) Usability Evaluation in Industry, pp. 189–194. Taylor and Francis, London (1996)
10. Bangor, A., Kortum, P.T., Miller, J.T.: An Empirical Evaluation of the System Usability Scale. International Journal of Human-Computer Interaction 24, 574–594 (2008)
11. Lewis, J.R., Sauro, J.: The Factor Structure of the System Usability Scale. In: Kurosu, M., et al. (eds.) Human Centered Design, HCII 2009. LNCS, vol. 5619, pp. 94–103. Springer, Heidelberg (2009)
12. Hassenzahl, M., Burmester, M., Koller, F.: AttrakDiff: Ein Fragebogen zur Messung wahrgenommener hedonischer und pragmatischer Qualität. In: Szwillus, G., Ziegler, J. (eds.) Mensch & Computer 2003, vol. 57, pp. 187–196. Vieweg+Teubner Verlag, Wiesbaden (2003)
13. Laugwitz, B., Held, T., Schrepp, M.: Construction and Evaluation of a User Experience Questionnaire. In: Holzinger, A. (ed.) USAB 2008. LNCS, vol. 5298, pp. 63–76. Springer, Heidelberg (2008)
14. Good Technology: Good Technology Device Activations Report Q4 (2012), http://media.www1.good.com/documents/Good-Q4-Device-Activations.pdf
15. Net Applications, http://www.netmarketshare.com/
16. Sauro, J., Lewis, J.: Correlations among Prototypical Usability Metrics: Evidence for the Construct of Usability. In: Olsen Jr., D.R., Arthur, R.B., Hinckley, K., Morris, M.R., Hudson, S.E., Greenberg, S. (eds.) Proceedings of the 27th International Conference on Human Factors in Computing Systems, pp. 1609–1618. ACM, New York (2009)
17. Kim, J.H., Aulck, L., Bartha, M.C., Harper, C.A., Johnson, P.W.: Are there differences in muscle activity, subjective discomfort, and typing performance between virtual and conventional keyboards? In: Proceedings of the Human Factors and Ergonomics Society 56th Annual Meeting, pp. 1104–1108. SAGE, Boston (2012)
18. Lee, S., Zhai, S.: The performance of touch screen soft buttons. In: Olsen, D.R. (ed.) Proceedings of the 27th International Conference on Human Factors in Computing Systems, CHI, pp. 309–318. ACM, New York (2009)

Heuristic Evaluation

Heuristics for Evaluating the Usability of Mobile Launchers for Elderly People

Muna S. Al-Razgan, Hend S. Al-Khalifa, and Mona D. Al-Shahrani

Information Technology Department, College of Computer and Information Sciences,
King Saud University, Riyadh, Saudi Arabia
{malrazgan,hendk}@ksu.edu.sa

Abstract. Touch based mobile phone launchers are programs used by elderly people to ease their use of mobile phones. Despite their varieties in the mobile phone market, little has been done to evaluate their applicability to the target users. In this paper we describe a systematic approach to convert design guidelines and recommendations for touch-based phones into heuristics targeting elderly people. Then an assessment of the heuristics is carried out by creating personas and conducting usability evaluation.

Keywords: Heuristics evaluation, usability, elderly people, touch-based mobile phones, personas.

1 Introduction

Mobile phone world is advancing with new technologies emerging each day. New, small and thin phones with new features and applications are being developed constantly. These phones are built with sophisticated features that hinder senior adults from using them. As the number of elderly people has increased [1], this fact signals the need for designing mobile phones targeting senior adults.

Previous studies have been conducted to evaluate the effectiveness of mobile phones in general e.g. [2], however mobile applications usability evaluation is still new area to research. A recent study in [3] presented a set of broad heuristics for mobile devices. Another more specific study evaluated existing iOS mobile applications for diabetes management and spotted drawbacks to avoid in designing such mobile applications [4]. The usability of mobile applications differs from regular software applications in issues related to context, connectivity, screen size and resolution, text and data entry methods. In [5] the authors proposed a general framework for conducting usability test for mobile applications.

From the research that we had reviewed and our own experience with elderly people, older adults are the people who are limited by some level of disability with an age of 50 and above [6]. These people require special attention in developing easy to use mobile phones. Therefore, there is a need to propose a corresponding set of heuristic that consider the specific needs of elderly people while interacting with touch-based mobile phones.

A. Marcus (Ed.): DUXU 2014, Part I, LNCS 8517, pp. 415–424, 2014.
© Springer International Publishing Switzerland 2014

In this paper, we introduce a new set of proposed heuristics for evaluating the usability of touch-based mobile phone launchers for elderly people. To our knowledge, no empirical research exists addressing the evaluation of touch based mobile launchers. Hence, our research will focus exclusively on the usability of elderly touch-based mobile launchers. These proposed heuristics were evaluated by usability evaluators to elicit feedback on the adequacy of our heuristics as will be illustrated in the paper.

2   Methodology

The process we used to develop usability heuristics for touch-based mobile phones for elderly followed these main steps:

— Convert previous guidelines into usability problems, and
— Group similar usability problems into categories.

Firstly, we converted guidelines that we had defined previously in our earlier publication [7], to usability problems, and combined similar ones under one category.

Secondly, we translated usability problems into heuristics that provide guidelines on how they can be avoided. The translated heuristics were also inspired by other heuristics that were adapted for older adults and the heuristics for Touch-based Mobile Devices (TMD) heuristics [5]. In addition, we have checked if any of the usability problems fit into the heuristics presented in [6][8] or do we need to develop a new heuristic.

After doing the previous systematic steps, we wrote the proposed heuristics as interrogative sentences, this is because interrogative sentences are more intuitive for answering and scoring compared to declarative sentences [6]. Then we elaborated our heuristics into list of questions.

Following the above process we came up with a list of newly proposed heuristics evaluation for touch-based mobile devices for elderly people, as illustrated in table 1. The heuristics are classified into three sections: (1) look and feel, (2) interaction, and (3) functionality.

Table 1. Touch-based Mobile Heuristics Evaluation for elderly people

Look And Feel:
1. Make Elements on the page easy to read
1.1. Is the font large enough for older adults?
1.2. Is there any option to enlarge the font size?
1.3. Are the text and background colors have good contrast?
1.4. Is it possible to customize colors?
1.5. Is the amount of text minimized; is the only necessary information presented?
1.6. Does color choices allow for easy readability?

Table 1. (*continued*)

2. Easy Recognition and accessibility
2.1. Are the icons clear, understandable and labeled?
2.2. Are labels described clearly?
2.3. Can the most important or frequently needed functions accessed directly?
2.4. Is the keypad separated into numbers and letters for data entry?
2.5. Is data entry process easy for elderly?
2.6. Are there any visual cues in the launcher that help the elderly know there is more content in a page?
3. Make clickable items easy to target and hit
3.1. Is it obvious which item is clickable and which is not?
3.2. Are buttons large enough to easily see the image or text on them?
3.3. Is there enough space between buttons to prevent hitting multiple or incorrect buttons?
3.4. Is buttons size adequate to finger touch?
3.5. Do buttons and icons enlarge when the rest of the text size is increased?
3.6. Is the image on a button or an icon easy to predict what does it do?
4. Use the elderly language and culture; minimize technical terms
4.1. Does the launcher use words that majority of older adults are familiar with?
4.2. Does the options/information have logical sequence?
4.3. Are the icons familiar to elderly?
Interaction:
5. Provide clear feedback on actions
5.1. Is there audio/visual/haptic confirmation when tapping?
5.2. Is there an option to enable them?
5.3. Are error messages descriptive, and did they provide a solution to the elderly for recovery?
5.4. Are confirmation messages clear?
5.5. Does the launcher keep elderly informed about what is going on, through appropriate feedback?
6. Provide preferable gesture for elderly
6.1. Does the launcher use tap gestures for most of the actions?
6.2. Is the object has more than one gesture to perform actions?(e.g. it has tap and drag gesture on the same object)
6.3. Does the launcher use scrolling gestures in order to view more content?(what is the usability problem you think it will be getting from this heuristic)
6.4 Do gestures of launcher work correctly and smoothly?

Table 1. (*continued*)

7. Provide elderly with information on launcher/elderly status
7.1. Does the elderly know where is he and what can he do next?
7.2. Is the elderly aware when the launcher turns off or gets an error that causes it to stop working?
8. Use conventional interaction items
8.1. Are items usage is the same from section to section within the launcher?
8.2. Does the launcher apply consistent format?
9. Ergonomics design
9.1. Are Items placed in recognizable positions?
9.2. Do the items in the elderly interface fit the natural posture of the hand and finger?
<u>**Functionality:**</u>
10.Provide functions that reduce the elderly memory load
10.1. Does the launcher support or provide shortcuts for direct access to the most frequent functions or items?
10.2. Does the launcher provide supports to remember functions easily?
10.3. Does the launcher group similar functions in one place? (example, {call, contact list, write text message in one group}, {camera, pictures, videos in another group})
10.4. Are the important functions always available (call, turn-off, etc)?
11.Elderly does not feel lost or stuck (Elderly control and freedom)
11.1. Does the main navigation menu exist consistently in all pages?
11.2. Does clicking the back button always go back to the previous page that the elderly comes from?
11.3. Does the launcher provide emergency exits to leave unwanted state and is it clearly pointed?
12.Prevent error from occurrence
12.1. Does the graphical interface design and the organization help prevent errors?
12.2. Is there confirmation message for critical actions such as deletion?
12.3. Are the important functions placed at top of the screen to avoid mistake touches?
13.Provide necessary information and settings
13.1. Does the launcher show level of battery, time and date, signal of contact/Wi-Fi/3G?
13.2. Are the default settings of mobile phone available to the elderly in an easy way?(e.g. change ringtone)

3   Assessing Heuristic Performance

We devised and conducted an experimental study aimed at assessing the appropriateness of the proposed heuristics.

3.1   Participants and Materials

The evaluation entailed four senior undergraduate students who have studied HCI course and conducted usability evaluation before.

Three launchers and three applications from Android market, as shown in table 2, were tested.

Table 2. List of Android Launchers and their description

Launcher	Description
Big Launcher[1]	A simple and easy-to-read interface designed for seniors and low vision people
Phonotto[2]	A basic touch screen launcher for senior people includes the main functions of regular phone of calling, address book, and send/receive text messages.
EasyPhone[3]	An android application that provides extra large font for dial, call log, contact, and SMS. The aim is for low vision people such as elderly.
Liv+[4]	A large smart application operates with only four buttons navigational buttons for simple use for elderly people
Oldroid[5]	A basic elderly application where the administrator can monitor the setting of the phone through its website and will be synchronized automatically.
Georgie[6]	An application has OCR function that display text in larger fonts and offers an audio for listening.

We also developed two personas based on our knowledge in interacting with elderly people and from our previous experiment and research we reviewed [6]. These two personas represent different gender in addition to their ability to read and write.

Persona -1-, female, 61 years old, mother of six grandchildren. She lives with her son, and studies at the Literacy school. She can read and write but with mistakes. She

---

[1] http://www.biglauncher.com/
[2] https://play.google.com/store/apps/details?id=com.gammapps.SimplePhone&hl=en
[3] https://play.google.com/store/apps/details?id=com.orange.labs.easyphone&hl=en
[4] https://play.google.com/store/apps/details?id=com.livlivsolutions.skin&feature=search_result
[5] www.oldroid.net
[6] http://www.engadget.com/2012/07/16/georgie-app-offers-up-android-features-and-voice-guided-menus-visually-impaired/

has a mobile phone with physical keyboard, but has not used a touch-based mobile phone before. She wear glasses when reading, she suffers from blood pressure, and hearing impairment. She has arthritis, so sometimes tapping on the screen is a problem.

Persona -2-, male, 76 years old, grandfather of seven children. He lives with his wife in the lower floor and his son with his children in the upper floor. He cannot read or even write. He has diabetes and suffers from memory impairment, and short temper. He uses a mobile phone with physical keyboard, and thinks that the new technology is difficult and he is not willing to learn it.

3.2   Procedure

To assess the performance of our proposed heuristics, the evaluation procedure followed the following protocols:

Orientation Session. This entailed welcoming the evaluators and explaining in detail the goals of the study and testing procedure. A training session was also conducted to explain the list of heuristics and how to assess them. The evaluators were asked to impersonate the two personas and write their observations [6]. Evaluation scripts were prepared in advanced and distrbuted among the evalutors.

Evaluation Session. The usability evaluators conducted the usability evaluation on each of the six Android launchers to identify usability problems, and prioritize them according to Nielson's five-point Severity Ranking scaled from 0-4, where 0-indicates no problem, 1- cosmetic problem, 2- Minor problem, and 4- catastrophic [9] . More explanation of the rating is presented in table 3. Also in order to avoid order effect, the sequence of launchers evaluation was counterbalanced for each evaluator.

Table 3. Severity Ranking Scale (SRS) borrowed from (adapted from [3])

Rating	Description
0	I don't agree that this is a usability problem at all
1	Cosmetic problem only. Need not be fixed unless extra time is available on project
2	Minor usability problem. Fixing this should be given low priority
3	Major usability problem. Important to fix, so should be given high priority
4	Usability catastrophes. Imperative to fix this before product can be released

Debriefing Session. After the usability evaluators have sent the evaluation results, they were asked to describe the experience of the process, i.e. strengths and limitations of using the heuristics to evaluate the launchers [10] [6]. Table 4, shows the asked questions.

Table 4. Debriefing session questions

What are the strength and limitation of these heuristics?
Which heuristics are most useful?
Which heuristics are difficult to understand?
Does the heuristics cover all usability problems in these launchers?
Are these heuristics easy to understand?(in general)

4   Discussion and Results

The data collected after conducting the usability evaluation were analyzed both quantitatively and qualitatively.

Quantitatively, after receiving the heuristics severity rating by each usability evaluator, we combined the results and came up with the following findings:

Most of the heuristics were rated as "no problem" by the evaluators. However, couple of them has varied severities. To further carry out the analysis, we had counted the severity rating by each evaluator for all of our proposed heuristics to measure how effective our proposed heuristics were.

Table 5. Parentage of Severity Ranking Scale (SRS)

Severity ranking scale	%
No problem	61%
Cosmetic	3%
Minor	9%
Major	12%
Catastrophe	16%

As depicted in Table 5, we noticed that 61% of evaluators had no problems when evaluating the six applications, which means that the available applications took into consideration the important criteria when designing elderly software. However, we noticed that the catastrophic rating (16%) comes second in the severity list, although the evaluators were experts; this signals an alarm about the usability of the available applications for elderly people.

Table 6 shows the proposed heuristics and their corresponding usability problems found in the launchers. The look and feel category has the highest number of catastrophic issues which raise the importance of look and feel features for elderly, especially of their declining ability of low vision, and difficulties to recognize icons when their size is small. Functionality comes second in the number of usability problems. A launcher has to contain all the important functionality the elderly needs to make it easy to handle and attractive to use. The least number of problems was found in the interaction category, which indicates the impact of recent attention of the literature toward the increase elderly populations by designing launchers with good user experience that addresses elderly needs.

Furthermore to carry in-depth investigation of the problems found with the proposed heuristics, we discuss next the issues with highest rating (major and catastrophic).

In heuristic 1.1 "is there any option to enlarge the font size?" and 1.4 "Is it possible to customize colors?" evaluators indicted that changing the text font or color using the installed launcher is not possible and required the changes to be done through the device setting. Examples of these launchers include "Olddriod, Liv+, Georgie, Phonotto (free version)". This issue will not be easy for the elderly to figure out, which is considered a major problem among the examined launchers.

In heuristic 2.1 "Are the icons clear, understandable and labeled?" evaluators pointed that some launchers placed text on top of icons. Designers have to take into consideration the specific needs of the elderly, if they cannot read; they need to present the launcher in two format (text, and image) icons, which can be set by the care giver based on the elderly ability. Also, for heuristic 2.6 "Are there any visual cues in the launcher that help the elderly know there is more content in a page?", evaluators, indicated that the user has to press + sign or tap arrows to know if there is more content in the page.

In heuristic 3.5 "Do buttons and icons enlarge when the rest of the text size is increased?" the experts stated that this option is not available in most of the launchers under investigations. Since our focus is on the heuristics not the specific launchers, we suggest the importance of enabling these features for elderly, especially with their declining ability of vision, difficulties to recognize icons when their size is small.

Table 6. Proposed heuristics and corresponding usability problems

Description of heuristics	Number of usability problem
Look And Feel:	
1. Make Elements on the page easy to read	
1.1. Is there any option to enlarge the font size?	10
1.4. Is it possible to customize colors?	14
2. Easy Recognition and accessibility	
2.1. Are the icons clear, understandable and labeled?	8
2.6. Are there any visual cues in the launcher that help the elderly know there is more content in a page?	8
3. Make clickable items easy to target and hit	
3.5 Do buttons and icons enlarge when the rest of the text size is increased?	14
Interaction:	
5. Provide clear feedback on actions	
5.2 Is there an option to enable them?	8
Functionality:	
12. Prevent error from occurrence	
12.2 Is there confirmation message for critical actions such as deletion?	11
Provide necessary information and settings	
13.2 Are the default settings of mobile phone available to the elderly in an easy way?(e.g. change ringtone)	10

In heuristic 5.2 "Is there an option to provide clear feedback on actions" the experts stated that this statement is not available in most of the examined launchers.

In heuristic (12.2 and 13.2) "Is there confirmation message for critical actions such as deletion?" and "Are the default settings of mobile phone available to the elderly in an easy way? (e.g. change ringtone)". These two heuristics are not available in the launchers that have been tested, such as when an elderly delete a message or a contact by mistake; there is no warning of his/her action. However, elderly people need it since they mostly have memory shortage or their hands are shaking, which might lead them to accidently pressing the delete button by mistake. The elderly has to be warned before completing any action by presenting a message along with sound.

The last heuristic was concerned about the default setting of the phone. Default phone settings are not available via the examined launchers which create a problem. As elderly will not be able to figure out how to change the ring tone from the phone settings, a launcher has to contain all the important functionality the elderly needs and make it easy to access.

Qualitatively, after finishing the evaluations we asked the usability evaluators for their input about the heuristics by answering table 4 questions. The evaluators stated that the heuristics covered the important needs for elderly people; which were the aim of our research. They also indicated that the heuristics were understandable, easy and simple especially for the "Look and feel & interaction" category, as these show the importance of launchers appearance and the impact of the first impression to attract the elderly. However, one of the evaluators stated that some heuristics targeted specific functions without explaining the use of it to the elderly.

The evaluators also described some limitations of the heuristics. They mentioned that they could include some questions for the types of elderly who can read/write and those who cannot. Because some of the questions were not useful for the case of persona 2, and one evaluator said that "some questions like (is there any option to change font size, or customize colors) need to be in two parts" to help the evaluator to measure its availability and then its easiness for the elderly.

Other evaluators stated that the heuristics are missing the evaluation of "Responsive time" while using specific functions. As we know elderly usually require more time to do specific functions because of their limited abilities to learn new technology and their hesitation of making mistakes. For this reason we eliminated measuring the response time in our usability evaluation.

5   Conclusion

To recap, our study presented a proposed set of 13 heuristics which cover the usability of touch based mobile launchers designed for elderly people. These heuristics can be further used as guidelines when designing any launcher targeting elderly people.

Future direction of this research is to design a touch-based mobile phone launcher that covered the proposed heuristics. In addition, we will implement the launcher to address elderly Arab people cultural needs. We will also carry a user centered testing to evaluate our proposed launcher and adjust it according to the elderly needs.

Acknowledgement. The authors would like to thank Elham Alsobky, Manahel Al Twaim, Moneerah Al-Mohsin, and Ibtihal Al-musallam for conducting the evaluation. This project is supported by grant no. D-C-12-117 from King Abdulaziz City for Science and Technology.

References

1. Plaza, I., Martín, L., Martin, S., Medrano, C.: Mobile applications in an aging society: Status and trends. J. Syst. Softw. 84(11), 1977–1988 (2011)
2. Connors, A., Sullivan, B.: W3C. Mobile Web Application Best Practices (2008), http://www.w3.org/TR/mwabp/
3. Osais, Y.: Appropriating Usability Heuristics. In: Safari. Safari Books Online, pp. 1–14 (2011)
4. Martin, C., Flood, D., Sutton, D., Aldea, A., Harrison, R., Waite, M.: A Systematic Evaluation of Mobile Applications for Diabetes Management, pp. 466–469 (2011)
5. Zhang, D., Adipat, B.: Challenges, Methodologies, and Issues in the Usability Testing of Mobile Applications. Int. J. Hum. Comput. Interact. 18(3), 293–308 (2005)
6. Chisnell, D.E., Redish, J.C.G., Lee, A.M.Y.: New Heuristics for Understanding Older Adults as Web Users 53(1), 39–59 (2006)
7. Al-Razgan, M.S., Al-Khalifa, H.S., Al-Shahrani, M.D., AlAjmi, H.H.: Touch-Based mobile phone interface guidelines and design recommendations for elderly people: a survey of the literature. In: Huang, T., Zeng, Z., Li, C., Leung, C.S. (eds.) ICONIP 2012, Part IV. LNCS, vol. 7666, pp. 568–574. Springer, Heidelberg (2012)
8. Pinelle, D., Street, U., Hall, G.: Heuristic Evaluation for Games: Usability Principles for Video Game Design, pp. 1453–1462 (2008)
9. Nielsen, J.: Usability inspection methods. In: Conference Companion on Human Factors in Computing Systems, pp. 413–414. ACM (1994)
10. Masip, L., Granollers, T., Oliva, M.: A Heuristic Evaluation Experiment to Validate the New Set of Usability Heuristics. In: 2011 Eighth Int. Conf. Inf. Technol. New Gener, pp. 429–434 (April 2011)

Heuristic Inspection to Assess Persuasiveness:
A Case Study of a Mathematics E-learning Program

Eric Brangier[1] and Michel C. Desmarais[2]

[1] Université de Lorraine – Metz, PErSEUs EA 7312, Psychologie Ergonomique et Sociale pour
l'Expérience Utilisateurs - BP 30309 Île du Saulcy - 57006 Metz, France
[2] Polytechnique Montréal, Département de génie informatique et génie logiciel, C.P. 6079,
succ. Centre-Ville, Montréal, Québec H3C 3A7, Canada
Eric.Brangier@univ-lorraine.fr,
michel.desmarais@polymtl.ca

Abstract. This research extends existing heuristic inspection with criteria grids to include emotional and persuasiveness factors. We first review the existing criteria and categorize them into four major groups, aligned along a historic perspective of HCI. Hence, we find criteria that fall into (a) accessibility, (b) usability, then (c) affective, and finally (d) persuasive categories. In the second part of the paper, we focus on heuristic inspection based on persuasive criteria. We show their importance and apply them to the example of an e-learning platform for college mathematics. Results of the heuristic inspection of the persuasive factors are reported along with their prescribed recommendations.

Keywords: Persuasive technology, Heuristic inspection, Ergonomics criteria, E-learning.

1 Heuristic Inspection and the Evaluation of HCI

The field of ergonomics has produced numerous guidelines to measure the quality of interfaces. But in the field of persuasive technology, the idea to evaluate persuasion is not yet commonplace. Our approach is to define guidelines to measure and assess the persuasive dimensions of user experiences. These guidelines provide heuristics on persuasion that experts in User Experience can use during the evaluation and design processes.

A heuristic is a general principle that can guide a design decision or be used to assess the quality of a design decision in an existing interface. Heuristic evaluation has been developed as a method for conducting the assessment of a system using a set of simple and general heuristics. The general idea behind heuristic evaluation is that user experience (UX) specialists independently assess interfaces to identify potential problems. Heuristic evaluation is best used as a cost and time effective evaluation technique. However, existing criteria grids typically do not address persuasion factors in interfaces. Hence the goal to develop a method of heuristic inspection dedicated to persuasion.

A. Marcus (Ed.): DUXU 2014, Part I, LNCS 8517, pp. 425–436, 2014.
© Springer International Publishing Switzerland 2014

The influence of emotional and persuasive factors towards the success and failure of user interfaces is gaining stronger recognition. In addition to the recent explosion of social and commercial web sites that need to attract and retain their user base, e-learning applications is another family of applications that rely on their effectiveness to engage their users in a learning process. We focus on one such application to demonstrate the proposed persuasion criteria grid and evaluate its capacity to help suggest improvements to the e-learning application interface. This application is a self-regulated exerciser in college mathematics. Students are left completely free to use this exerciser or not, and therefore the potency of its user interface to motivate and convince the student to use it paramount in this context.

2   Heuristic Inspection Framework: From Accessibility Criteria to Usability, Pleasure and Persuasiveness Criteria

The use of criteria for heuristic inspection of user interfaces can be traced back over the last 50 years of so of technology evolution [1]. Fig. 1 schematically illustrates the historical co-evolution.

Early criteria in the 1960s were defined for making computers accessible to individuals with special needs. The criteria addressed a set of psychophysiological and biomechanical constraints adapted to physiological or mental human characteristics. A recent example of well known accessibility criteria is the Web Content Accessibility Guidelines from W3C/WAI.

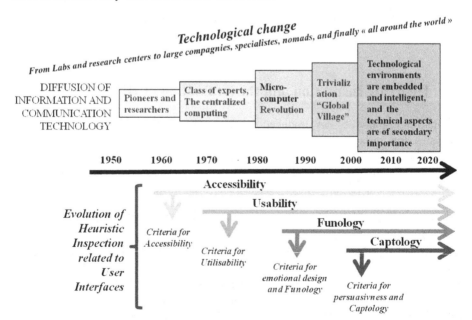

Fig. 1. Criteria for heuristic inspection and the development of information and communication technologies

The 1970's saw the emergence of usability concerns. They were eventually cast into standards such as ISO 9241-11, and in design and evaluation heuristics such as [4, 9, 12].

The evaluation criteria of standards and heuristics aimed to provide design guidelines and evaluation tools. They specifically aim to empower the user to perform tasks in an efficient and fluent manner. However, they did not address the affective and emotional dimensions of HCI, in particular factors that affect user engagement and motivation to use an application such as aesthetics, social value and prestige, social interaction, sense of accomplishment, self expression, and learning.

Interestingly, the affective and emotional criteria are sometimes at odds with usability criteria. For example, aesthetics can influence the mood of a user and positively affect his likeliness to buy a product on a site, but the positive effect may be offset if the aesthetic is emphasized at the expense of usability.

The persuasive dimension addresses the motivational factors of HCI. Fogg [3] defines persuasion as "An attempt to change attitudes or behaviors or both (without using coercion or deception)" (Fogg, 2003, p. 15). Persuasive technology aims to capture the user's attention and to maintain the will to interact. A long list of design patterns and principles can be deployed to help tunnel user behaviour towards specific target either witin a human-computer interaction [3] or a computer mediated human-human interaction [11].

The next section addresses the goal of evaluating, through the use of a criteria grid, the quality and effectiveness of an interface.

3   Heuristics to Inspect Persuasion in Interfaces

Effective persuasion rests upon motivational and cognitive factors. We first review the theoretical foundations of the persuasive mechanisms at stake and then describe the criteria that derive from this framework.

3.1   Persuasion Indicators and Persuasive Technology Means

Oinas-Kukkonen & Harjumaa [11] define four types of persuasive design means. They are the support means for the (a) task, (b) interaction dialog, (c) social interaction and (d) credibility.

- **Task support**. To bring the user towards the target behaviour, task support should be provided through interface facilitators, which can take the form of attractive icons and images, personalized messages, repeated messages and a suggestive sequence of interactions. Task support design principles are:

— Reduction: streamline the steps towards the desired behaviour.
— Tunneling: progressively constrain the path to the desired behaviour.
— Tailoring and personalization: adapt the information displayed to user needs, interest, personality or context of use.
— Self-monitoring: monitor progress towards desired goal and provide support when

- Simulation: provide simulations to allow observation of the causal relationship of a given behavior.
- Rehearsal: allow the user to repeat a given behaviour

- **Dialog support.** Techniques to initiate dialog and forster its continuation:

- Praise: positive feedback in words, images, symbols or sound.
- Rewards: reward desired behaviour.
- Reminders: provide continuous reminder or desired behaviour.
- Suggestion: display timely and relevant behaviour suggestions.
- Similarity: use similarity with established system.
- Liking: attractive look.
- Social role: associate a social role to the system.

- Social support. Facilitate interaction with like-minded people and avoid contact with people of diverging values. Social support encourages behaviour rationalization, in particular for situations of cognitive dissonance.

- Social learning: allow users to observe peer behaviour of peers and learn about social conducts and their consequences.
- Social comparison: allow user to compare their behaviour with other and foster perseverance.
- Normative influence: leverage social pressure to induce target behaviours.
- Social facilitation: leverage the tendency of individuals to initiate and persist in desired behaviours if they feel observed or if a peer is also involved in parallel conduct.
- Cooperation: leverage the natural tendency of individuals to collaborate.
- Competition: leverage the natural tendency of individuals to compete.
- Recognition: provide a group or an individual a public recognition of merit for their behaviour.

- **System credibility.** Credibility is key to social influence. A system that provides incorrect information or, for some reason, loses its credibility can be permanently disabled to exert any kind of persuasion.

- Trustworthiness: induce a perception of good intention, high moral values, and unbiased communication.
- Expertise: perception as a knowledgeable and competent source of information.
- Third-party endorsement: show that the system has outside support.
- Surface: the visual look must support the impression of competence.
- Real-world feel: show that an organisation and a team is behind the system.
- Authority: make references to authoritative sources.
- Verifiability: allow information to be cross-verified..

3.2   Persuasiveness Criteria Grid

The above framework is behind the Nemery, Brangier and Kopp [8, 9] criteria grid for persuasion inspection. The grid rests on the general technique of inspection. To inspect the usability of a product, whether a user interface or any artefact designed to be used by some user, is to make a judgement about its ability to be effective, efficient, error-tolerant, easy to learn and satisfying. This judgement is made by experts in ergonomics or HCI. Inspections are often the method of choice to quickly target usability issues and find the proper corrections to bring to the design of an application. As a result, the guidelines purpose is to measure the persuasive dimensions involved in interface, to help experts to evaluate the interface using these criteria.

The Persuasiveness criteria grid [8, 9] follows from the review of 164 papers in the field of captology and PT. Eight criteria were deemed sufficient to encompass the persuasiveness factors: credibility, privacy, personalization, attractiveness, solicitation, initiation, commitment and ascendency [6]. These criteria are grouped under static and dynamic categories (see Table 1):

- Static criteria are prerequisite elements to establish a fertile context within which a dynamic process of persuasion can be launched. These elements pro-mote the acceptance of a persuading process.
- Dynamic criteria are involved in a process designed to engage the user in a series of planned and ordered persuasive steps in which the temporal factor is critical. At each step of the behavioral changes, elements of the interface bring the user to commit to greater levels of engagement.

4   A Case Study for the Criteria Grid

In an effort to assess the Persuasiveness criteria grid, we analyze an e-learning application using this grid. The software over which the grid is applied is designed as a drill and practice learning environment on the topic of college mathematics. We will refer to it as the Exerciser. The Exerciser was inspected by the two authors who are HCI and e-learning experts. In the final communication, we will provide insights on the application of the grid.

4.1   The Application Domain: College Mathematics for Freshman Engineers

Mathematics is often a source of difficulty in the first year of an engineering program. To help newly enrolled students ensure they have the expected mastery of all prerequisites in math for the first year courses, Polytechnique Montreal developed the Exerciser which contains over 1000 exercices [5]. All of the approximately 1000 newly enrolled students were invited to test their knowledge with an online test and they were thereafter invited to use the Exerciser if they wished. No other incentive to use it was given.

In its first deployment in the spring-summer of 2012, only a few tens of students used it, from a few minutes up to over 100 hours for a few cases. The high rate of students who did not pursue over a few minutes led us to consider that it was a good case to apply persuasive technology to encourage students using the Exerciser more extensively.

Table 1. The eight persuasive interactions criteria of Nemery et al. (2011)

	Criteria	Definitions	Sub-criteria
Static criteria	**Credibility**	is the ability of the interface to inspire confidence and to make the user confident in the veracity of its information. Credibility is based on reputation and notoriety.	*Trustwothiness.* *Expertise.* *Fidelity.* *Legitimity.*
	Privacy	refers to the protection of personal data and the preservation of personal integrity and security of the interaction. It also refers to protection against loss, destruction or inadvertent disclosure of this data.	*Safeness.* *Law respect feeling.* *Confidentiality.*
	Personalization	refers to the concept of customization of the interface to the needs of the user. The customization can be a greeting, a promotion, or any means to achieve a more personal interaction with the user. It may also rely on group membership.	*Individualization.* *Group membership.*
	Attractiveness	is the use of aesthetics (graphic, art, design) to capture the attention of the user, to support the interaction and create a positive emotion. The animation, colors, menus, drawings, video films are designed to catch and maintain the interest of the user.	*Emotional attraction.* *Call to action.* *Tunneling design.*
Dynamic criteria	**Solicitation**	is the first of the four dynamic criteria. It refers to the initial stage which aims to swiftly attract and challenge the user to initiate the relationship. The interface attempts by words, graphics, or any form of dialogue, to suggest a behavior and induce action through minimal influence.	*Allusion.* *Suggestion.* *Teasing.*
	Initiation	refers to elements of the media that entice the first user-initiated actions. The user's attention is captured and, through his own initiative, encouraged to realize the first engaging action. The user is caught in a gradual engagement process.	*Priming.* *First action guidance.*
	Commitment	means that system further involves the user in a process. Several queries and incentives regularly and gradually engage the user. The electronic media will induce more intensive and regular behavior.	*Repeated request.* *External negative factor avoidance.* *Increased cost.*
	Ascendency	is an expression of the completion of the engaging scenario. The user has unequivocally accepted the logic and goals of the media. The interaction is characterized by induced pleasure and possibly by the relief of internal discomfort. Ascendency is closely related to the concept of immersion in the video game field and it implies a high level of repetition and regularity of interaction, and sometimes emotional involvement in the story that results in dependence and game character identification. Users develop emotional attachment and cannot envision themselves without these products, or would feel a substantive negative effect in case of loss.	*Prescription of repetition.* *No-limit interaction.* *Pressure released.*

4.2   Exerciser Interface Screens

The Exerciser interface is composed of eight types of screens:

— Welcome page,
— Confidenciality agreement and consent,
— General explanation page,
— Exercise pages (1040 exercises shown between 2 to 5 at a time),
— A dialog window for the solution to each exercise,
— Class notes (equivalent to approx. 150 pages in print); navigation from a topic of
   the class notes to the corresponding exercises, and back, is available throughout the
   notes,
— Summary results page showing completed exercises,
— Online help page.

These eight screen types were inspected with the persuasion criteria grid in order to
identify strong and weak features (fig. 2 and 3).

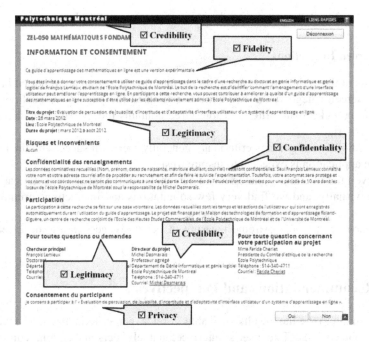

Fig. 2. Some good examples of persuasion issues of the Exerciser

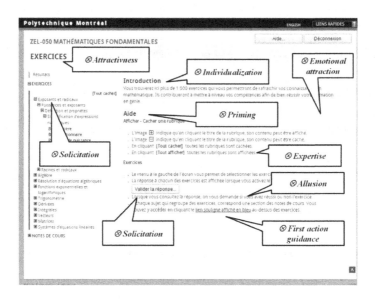

Fig. 3. Some bad examples of persuasion issues of the Exerciser

4.3   Screen Inspections

The results of the eight screen categories persuasion inspection are reported in table 2. For each screen category, the two experts estimated the persuasive quality over the eight criteria and 23 sub-criteria. Table three contains the global compilation along the eight criteria.

The credibility and privacy criteria are generally met with success by the Exerciser [2].   The application is expected to inspire trust.

However, the interactive dialog is not personalized, the interface is not particularly attractive visually, and we find very few solicitations and interactions priming.   The prospects of engaging the user to interact are weak.

Ascendency, the most extreme measure of persuasiveness, does not appear to be present at all.

5   Recommendations and Perspectives

Table 3 summarizes the results of Table 2 on a per criteria basis. It reveals the weaker points of the Exerciser's interface, namely personalization, commitment, initiation, attractiveness, and solicitation. Table 4 lists some of the specific problems and their corresponding remedial recommendations that follow from the inspection results.

Table 2. Results of the inspecction with the persuasive criteria grid for all eight screen types.s

		Screens	Welcome	Consent	Introduction	Exercise	Answer	Course	Score	Help	Total Yes (+)	Total No (−)
Static criteria	Credibility	Trustworthiness	Yes	Yes	Yes	Yes	Yes	Yes	Yes	Yes	8	0
		Expertise	Yes high	Yes	Yes	Yes	Yes	Yes	Yes	No	7	1
		Fidelity	Yes	Yes	Yes	Yes	No	Yes	Yes	No	6	2
		Legitimity	Yes	Yes	Yes	Yes	No	Yes	Yes	No	6	2
	Privacy	Safeness	Yes	Yes	Yes	No	No	No	Yes	No	4	4
		Law respect feeling	Yes	Yes	Yes	No	No	No	Yes	No	4	4
		Confidentiality	Yes	Yes	Yes	No	No	No	Yes	No	4	4
	Personalization	Individualization	No	No	No	No	No	No	Yes low	No	1	7
		Group membership	No	No	No	No	No	No	No	No	0	8
	Attractivity	Emotional attraction	No	No	No	No	No	No	No	No	0	8
		Call to action	Yes low	No	No	Yes low	No	No	No	No	2	6
		Tunneling design	No	No	No	No	No	No	No	No	0	8
Dynamic criteria	Solicitation	Allusion	No	No	No	Yes low	No	No	Yes low	Yes	3	5
		Suggestion	No	No	No	No	No	No	Yes low	Yes	2	6
		Teasing	No	No	No	No	No	No	No	No	0	8
	Initiation	Priming	No	No	No	No	No	No	Yes low	No	1	7
		First action guidance	No	No	No	No	No	No	No	No	0	8
		Repeated request	No	No	No	No	No	No	No	No	0	8
	Commitment	External negativ factor avoidance	No	No	No	No	No	No	No	No	0	8
		Increased cost	No	No	No	No	No	No	No	No	0	8
		Prescription of repetition	No	No	No	No	No	No	No	No	0	8
	Ascendency	No-limit interaction	No	No	No	No	No	No	No	No	0	8
		Pressure released	No	No	No	No	No	No	No	No	0	8
		Total Yes (+)	8	7	7	6	2	4	11	3	48	
		Total No (−)	15	16	16	17	21	19	12	20		136

Table 3. Globalization of the scores of each persuasive criteria (Ascendancy is not relevant in the case of educational interfaces)

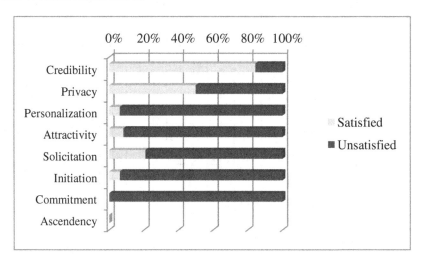

We claim that, akin to the heuristic inspection of an interface's usability, persuasion can be subjected to heuristic inspection and that the results will help guide the design of persuasive interfaces. Through iterative prototyping, they allow the development of more effective persuasive technology, especially in the early stages of development, when prototypes are too rudimentary for user testing.

E-learning applications are well suited applications for leveraging persuasiveness. Engaging the student in a learning process can definitely benefit from persuasive technology principles. We rely on inspection grid to assess the persuasiveness of e-learning systems and apply it over an existing e-learning environment to gather concrete experience on how appropriate it is in the specific context of e-learning.

Table 4. Some recommendations stemming from the persuasion inspection

General ideas	Examples
Personalization: Improve the customization aiming to adapt the interface to the needs of individual ownership from the user. The customization includes all actions aimed at characterizing a greeting, a picture, a badge or a context to achieve a closer approach the user. As any users, the learner want services tailored to their needs and learning.	A lack of customization may cause a lack of interest in interaction. A personalized welcome will challenge the user. Give the user the ability to select the characteristics of its screens makes the user more receptive to influences. A proposal that reflects and complements previous exercises will be experienced as a personalized proposal.

Table 4. (*continued*)

Attractiveness: Improve the use of aesthetics (colors, graphic, art, design) to capture the attention of the user, to support the interaction and create a positive emotion. Persuasive design could motivate users towards specific actions.	The animation, colors, menus, drawings, video films are designed to catch and maintain the interest of the user. The conformity between the text and images reinforce attractiveness. The use of a virtual agent could increase the seduction of the user.
Solicitation: Improve the first stage, which aims to briefly attract and challenge the user to start exercises. The invitation sets up the beginning of the relationship and the dialogue between the user and web exercises.	When broadly disseminated, the first personalized message increases the probability of initiating the first action from the user. Highlight attractive messages for the website to encourage users to click on a link… and learn math.
Initiation/Priming: Improve elements of the media that triggers the persuasive influence. These elements may take the form of piloting the first steps. With initiation, the first action is done without coercion or perception,	Organize interactions where the user is caught in a process that grabs him gradually. Complete simple exercises, which give you congratulations, badges or social awards.
Commitment: Improve the capacity of the system continues to involve user through an engaging process. It is the set up of action sequences or predetermined situations.	Organize queries, questions, exercises, messages regularly and gradually which involve the user. Repeat to the user to get in touch with other students in order to strengthen the information on a social network related to math.

References

1. Brangier, E., Bastien, J.-M.-C.: Ergonomie des produits informatiques: faciliter l'expérience utilisateur en s'appuyant sur les notions d'accessibilité, utilisabilité, émotionnalité et d'influençabilité. In: Vallery, G., Zouinar, M., Leport, M.-C. (eds.) Ergonomie, Conception, de Produits et Services Médiatisés, PUF, pp. 307–328 (2010)
2. Brangier, E., Desmarais, M.: The design and evaluation of the persuasiveness of e-learning interfaces. International Journal of Conceptual Structures and Smart Applications 1(2), 38–47 (2013); Special Issue on Persuasive Technology in Learning and Teaching
3. Fogg, B.J.: Persuasive Technology: Using Computers to Change What We Think and Do. Morgan Kaufmann, San Francisco (2003)
4. Jordan, P.W.: An introduction to usability. Taylor & Francis, London (1998)
5. Lemieux, F., Desmarais, M.C., Robillard, P.-N.: Motivation et analyse chronologique des traces d'un exerciseur pour l'auto-apprentissage. Sciences et Technologies de l'Information et de la Communication pour L'Education et la Formation, STICEF (2013) (accepted)

6. Némery, A., Brangier, E.: Criteria grid for persuasive interfaces (2011), http://www.univ-metz.fr/ufr/sha/2lp-etic/Criteres_ Persuasion_Interactive-2.pdf (retrieved October 2013)

7. Némery, A., Brangier, E., Kopp, S.: Proposition d'une grille de critèresd' analysesergonomiques des formes de persuasion interactive In B. David, M. Noirhomme et A. Tricot (Eds). In: Proceedings of IHM 2010, International Conference Proceedings Series, pp. 153–156. ACM, New York (2010)

8. Némery, A., Brangier, E., Kopp, S.: First validation of persuasive criteria for designing and evaluating the social influence of user interfaces: justification of a guideline. In: Marcus, A. (ed.) Design, User Experience, and Usability, HCII 2011, Part II. LNCS, vol. 6770, pp. 616–624. Springer, Heidelberg (2011)

9. Nielsen, J.: Heuristic Evaluation. In: Neilsen, J., Mack, R.L. (eds.) Usability Inspection Methods. John Wiley & Sons, Inc., New York (1994)

10. Oinas-Kukkonen, H.: Behavior Change Support Systems: A Research Model and Agenda. In: Ploug, T., Hasle, P., Oinas-Kukkonen, H. (eds.) PERSUASIVE 2010. LNCS, vol. 6137, pp. 4–14. Springer, Heidelberg (2010)

11. Oinas-Kukkonen, H., Harjumaa, M.: Persuasive Systems Design: Key Issues, Process Model, and System Features. Communications of the Association for Information Systems 24(1), 485–500 (2009)

12. Scapin, D.L., Bastien, J.M.C.: Ergonomic criteria for evaluating the ergonomic quality of interactive systems. Behaviour and Information Technology 16, 220–231 (1997)

Design as a Tool for Managing Risks and Vulnerabilities Regarding Artifacts of Public Safety

Walter F.M. Correia, Sérgio Ximenes da Silva, Fábio F.C. Campos,
Marina L.N. Barros, and Marcelo Márcio Soares

Federal University of Pernambuco, Av. Prof. Moraes Rego, Center of Arts and
Communication, Cidade Universitária, Recife – PE, Brazil
ergonomia@me.com, {sergioxim,fc2005,marinalnbarros}@gmail.com,
marcelo2@nlink.com

Abstract. It is on man's interaction with the environment, taking into account all objects whether or not they are natural that design is focused. However, the relationship between the quantity and quality of what is produced and the creative processes of design do not always bring about the responses that the end user wants. This paper puts forward a proposal for designing a tool that may contribute to design methodologies for evaluating the safety of artifacts the use of which are restricted in the activity of Law Enforcement by Managing their Risks and Vulnerabilities. The paper sets out to include the knowledge of an expert in this subject area who is working on the risks and vulnerabilities that are present so as to obtain the most appropriate artifact possible for the demand proposed. The process of making such artifacts adequate and selecting them is permeated by such a large number of factors that they can only be matched, in amount, to the number of possible combinations between pieces of a chessboard. Hence the importance of producing a scale of values by using a rational and practical tool.

Keywords: Design, End User, Design methodologies, Safety of Artifacts, Public Safety, Risks, Vulnerabilities, Scale of Values.

1 Introduction

In general, when considering such methodologies as those of Cross, Roosenburg, Archer Jones, Gero, Lobach, Briggs and Burdek, one observes that their steps and design techniques are, at bottom, grouped into the following four main phases: Exploration of the Problem; Generating and Selecting Alternatives; Evaluating Artifacts; Presenting the Solution. (VASCONCELOS & NEVES, 2009).

The needs of people today are usually anchored on being consonant with their professional and private activities, family relationships, leisure, sports, i.e. not necessarily with issues of safety, warranty against direct and indirect attacks on their lives. This is because to guarantee this, there is the presence of the state, whose obligation it is to ensure that citizens have a dignified and safe life.

A. Marcus (Ed.): DUXU 2014, Part I, LNCS 8517, pp. 437–444, 2014.
© Springer International Publishing Switzerland 2014

Article 1 of the Brazilian Constitution of 1988, in its sole paragraph, states: "all power emanates from the people, who exercise it through elected representatives or directly under this constitution". The article in question draws attention to the ownership of the exercise of power by exemplifying that the holder of power is the people. However, the exercise of that power occurs via the representatives of the people in the sense of formally establishing a Democratic State of Right and, therefore, of the sovereignty of the people.

It is precisely because of this, we have a set of different needs and aspirations to which great attention must be paid, namely that which comes from the Activity of Law Enforcement. This is because it is this which, nowadays, is responsible for upholding peace and resolving disputes, since this activity is directly engaged in life or death battles.

It is within this framework that the designer must serve by seeking to meet the most demanding needs arising from the Sector of Law Enforcement such that it may satisfy not only the large-scale production of artifacts that applies to all users and regards them as equal but also by bringing to the forefront concepts and procedures that enable the end user's increasingly specific needs to be externalized. This should be dealt with as being one and the same for everyone.

Hence a new need arises within the design process: using expert knowledge in the process of data collection in an attempt to list its main features, resulting in formulating a scale of values that should be prioritized so as to achieve results that are more specific and appropriate to the demand coming from the activity of Law Enforcement.

This research study seeks to obtain an aspect of the visual perception of the real space of Pernambuco/Brazil, concerning the items of equipment for individual use in the activity of public safety, the focus being on police vehicles. This will be done by working on the absence of a fit-for-purpose methodology of analysis for selecting, purchasing and distributing them. These will be analyzed from different perspectives by means of interviewing users directly and filming and photographing situations in which they are used. The vehicles are used in various operating environments that have the lowest and highest risk for the police. "Risk" is understood as a possibility that may occur from an event that may cause major or minor injury. Aspects such as ergonomics, usability and liability will be addressed.

2   Theoretical Background

Design refers not only to the aesthetic appearance of products; it is geared towards well-being in people's lives.

There are very different specialties in the field of design: interior design, fashion, industrial design, etc. Another specialty which is very relevant is that of the Design of Vehicles, a concept presented by the Portuguese researchers Donato Nappo and Stefania Vairelli in their book "Design of Vehicles": "This is the study of the formal and aesthetic evolution of vehicles, from their origins to the present day. It is a chronological narration that precedes and crosses the world of wheeled transport that ends up joining those who, with their ingenuity, managed to make history by determining the most significant developments and stages around the world".

Public safety, on the other hand is a concept linked to the legal provision of Safety, duly allocated in our Magna Carta, the Federal Constitution of 1988 in article 6 on social rights, together with education, health, work, housing, leisure, social security, the protection of motherhood and childhood as well as assistance to the destitute.

In the light of the principle of Human Dignity that guides the concept of public security, the renowned commentator on Law Rogerio Greco states: "Even the vilest, most hateful man, the cruellest and most cold-hearted criminal is a bearer of this value".

It is clear that in both concepts (design and public safety) there is a common factor: a plurality of disciplines and related issues that act as automatons on an assembly line, in which each of the concepts and disciplines is responsible for a portion of the whole and on which they have a direct influence on the final result should they be relegated to oblivion. Thua what they require is not special attention, but a just one to the correct coorect degrre that is applicable to each factor.

It is, in this diversity, that design is present as an element that creates, adapts and links artifacts to the specific needs of the users responsible for conducting the activity of public safety, and it is there that the Design of Public Safety is found.

Through the Designer of Public Safety, potentialities that were dormant because of the lack of dedication and knowledge will have been developed.

3   Research Methodology

The Tool for Managing Risks and Vulnerabilities proposed starts with a specialist in the area in question making a direct evaluation (such as the end user, for example, policemen who constantly use vehicles in different situations).

First of all, the risks and vulnerabilities present must be listed. Then, they should be explained, put on a scale and subdivided into groups by functionality and relevance.

From then, the Likert scale and the GUT table are applied. At the end there should be a cross-check between the Likert Scale and the GUT Table and the most relevant markings applied on the Table of Scaled Values.

Hence there will be a Guideline by functionality of the aspects of risks and vulnerabilities considered the most important to be worked on. On using this Guideline, the main goal is achieved: that of obtaining an artifact that is best fitted for the demand initially proposed.

Questions about financial and time viability must be dealt with in a secondary analysis because they imply technical and administrative issues.

Some topics listed in the guidelines are specific to police cars and these alone, since they are the focus of this case study. The fact that the Tool for Managing Risks and Vulnerabilities can be used on any public safety artifact means that new risks and vulnerabilities present in these other artifacts be listed and that they need to be evaluated. This should be done by using the knowledge of another expert in the field for that other object to be evaluated. The list of risks and vulnerabilities varies depending on the artifact to be evaluated. For example, if the object is a building such as the Arts and Communication Center of the Federal University of Pernambuco and the demand is for organic safety, by using the tool, the risks and vulnerabilities present using the knowledge of safety experts and end users, and in addition to determining what core values are to be worked out, they can be scaled and differentiated, for example, by finding out whether students are more at risk than teachers.

3.1   Development of the Tool through the Case Study

Situation Map of Risks and Vulnerabilities. On using police vehicles as a case study, the first step should be to list the risks and vulnerabilities and place them on a Situation Map of Risks and Vulnerabilities. Those listed must be related to the performance of the activity to be studied. They should be divided into groups by affinity, which is to be understood as those that have similar characteristics that a priori individualize the related risks and vulnerabilities and this may relate items precisely because they do not fit into any other existing group. The subdivision into groups allows for ease of observation and quantification when implementing the next steps of the tool. At this stage of application of the tool to the case study, six different groups were identified that have components which are interconnected by functionality such as protection against external threats or availability of an adequate place to allocate artifacts or the possibility of interference in the space so that to create room for moving around in it.

Table 1. The table with this step is available in the annex to the dissertation for the whole project. (Table 1 – Situation Map of Risks and Vulnerabilities Present in the Use of Vehicles. Source: The Author (2013)).

Situation Map of Risks and Vulnerabilities Present in Use of Vehicles.		
Affinity groups	**No. of needs order.**	**Risks and Vulnerabilities.**
Group 1	1	A lockable compartment with bars to transport detainees.
	2	Radio Communicators.

After drawing up the list of risks and vulnerabilities, all factors must be exemplified one by one as per the examples below:

(1) Lockable compartment with bars (fit for humans at the back of the vehicle) to transport detainees.

This is what is usually called in Portuguese the "jail-cage "in the car, only suitably adapted. Instead of transporting those arrested and detainees in the trunk of the vehicle or in the back seat without any structure to contain them except for hand-cuffs, they can be transported safely (both with regard to themselves and the police officers who are escorting them). In one case in 2005, two policemen transported a prisoner in the back seat properly handcuffed behind his back when they stopped at a house to pick up his documents. While one officer was out of the car, the prisoner brought his hand-cuffed hands under his legs and grabbed the gun of the officer who was in front, in the driver's seat. After much struggle between the two of them, the police officer managed to retrieve his pistol and contained the prisoner. He almost lost his life. This is to make no mention of when the vehicle is involved in accidents, a time when a prisoner in the boot is likely to be severely injured.

Likert Scale. For this, we consider the risks and vulnerabilities related to a police vehicle, duly listed in the previous step of developing the tool. Each aspect will be evaluated according to what the user considers is more important or less important to safe-guard life. After quantifying this perception of importance what will be highlighted are the aspects considered as being the most significant ones to be worked on and as being indispensable in the daily routine. Such items scored at level 5 will be related to the scores given later from the GUT tool which will be developed in the next step for managing risks and vulnerabilities.

The table with this step is available in the annex to the dissertation for the whole project. (Table 7 - Grading the level of risk and vulnerability using the Likert Scale. Source: The Author (2013)).

G.U.T. Tool. Considering the levels of severity/ gravity (damage wreaked by the situation), urgency (minimizing the time to resolution) and trend, the GUT tool actions regarding the risks and vulnerabilities by priority level will be listed.

The table with this step is available in the annex to the dissertation for the whole project. (Table 13 - Requirements to be prioritized through the tool GUT Source: The Author (2013)).

Data Analysis. In this step a cross-check is made between the risks and vulnerabilities marked as most significant on the Likert Scale and GUT tool. Based on such cross-checking, there will be a real stratification of the aspects that are considered the most important ones which will enable values to be concentrated that result in a Guideline for scaling priority values when assessing the quality of a police car which will be worked on in the next step for managing risks and vulnerabilities.

The table with this step is available in the annex to the dissertation for the whole project. (Table 14 - Data Analysis. Source: The Author (2013)).

4   Results

4.1   Guideline for Scaling Priority Values When Assessing the Quality of a Police Car

If the methodology proposed is followed, the result will be a Guideline with a list of priority values when assessing the level of quality of a police vehicle (the object worked on as a case study). The result is realistic as to the needs of the object demanded since it arises from observations made by an expert in the area and follows a logical process of gathering and correlating data. The proposed model is not restricted to police vehicles but can be used for other artifacts.

Table 2. The table with this step is available in the annex to the dissertation for the whole project. (Table 15 - Guide Line Scheduling Priority values when assessing the quality of a police car. Source: The Author (2013)).

Guide Line for Scaling Priority values when assessing the quality of a police car.		
Affinity groups	**No. of needs order.**	**Risks and Vulnerabilities.**
Group 1	1	A lockable compartment with bars to transport detainees.

Risks and vulnerabilities listed in the final guideline above, resulting from the application of the management tool, are the ones that should be considered when assessing the level of the fitness-for-purpose of a police vehicle for the desired activity. The final decision should be based on the response to the demand for police vehicles and serve as guides for defining the artifacts to be worked on as a priority as they were defined as most important ones founded on the knowledge of experts in the field.

5   Conclusion

5.1   Initial Considerations

No methodology for evaluating the effectiveness of restricted use equipment in the activity of public safety was found that takes into account the knowledge of experts in the data collection phase in the design process. To some extent, methodological submission to empiricism takes place.

It was not verified that there was a process of individualizing equipment with a view to adjusting them to the professional and thus reducing the possibility of failure in the performance of his/her activities.

5.2   Compliance with the Objectives of This Study

Risks and vulnerabilities proved to be an efficient means of development for the applicability of the management tool for interventions in restricted-use artifacts in the activity of public safety, specifically in police vehicles.

The methodological processes of Design are benefited from the inclusion of expert knowledge in the development stage of the product, otherwise, a deficit in the safety of the end product might arise.

The transfer of knowledge from experts in the form of guidelines for the design process proved to be of paramount importance for the correct intervention of the designer, or at least for a more appropriate tweaking of the proto-design of artifacts.

5.3   Contributions to the Design

Design methodologies usually do not put into the phase of collecting data, expert knowledge on the subject that one wishes to tackle.

Regarding police cars, the procedures allocated are arranged empirically, with studies and assessment processes being restricted to the methodologies of manufacturers which are geared to the average consumer. With the proposed tool, there is a strengthening to the designer for the process of creating and developing artifacts focused on the activity of public safety, thereby facilitating and strengthening the development of this professional activity.

5.4   Recommendations for Future Work

Because the dynamics of the theme worked on, relevant aspects require further developments that may eventually become part of a differentiated whole, comprising important procedural changes in the activity of public safety.

Suggestions for what future research studies might tackle include aspects such as:

- Establishing a Standard (an NBR, the acronym in Portuguese for a Brazilian Regulatory Standard) about specific aspects in police cars such as the control of sirens, indicative lighting and radio.
- The creation of a specific methodology, focused on assessing artifacts for restricted use in the activity of public safety.
- Testing the tool on equipment that is not related to the activity of public safety.

5.5   Final Remarks

Currently, there are investments in public safety in the State of Pernambuco/ Brazil in respect of purchasing the latest equipment such as a thermal camera for use in helicopters, the trucks of Integrated Control and Command Center used in the Confederations Cup in 2013 and later to be used during the World Cup football in 2014, the fully automated anti-bomb robot, special vehicles used in tactical units, boats and helicopters. However, as regards police vehicles, in general, submission to empiricism occurs regarding the necessary adjustments, which are not set out in a methodological tool for this purpose.

The tool proposed enables efforts and resources to be allocated more precisely, resulting in savings of time and fostering a better adaptation of artifacts to the user, as it should be, assuming an interaction where the user has to adapt him/herself to the minimum extent possible to the artifact in order to survive the hazards present in his/her working environment.

It was found that there are no in-depth studies on causes that led to incidents to do with public safety equipment.

For the activity of public safety, comfort and security are interdependent and the link is design. The process of selecting and making artifacts fir for purpose is permeated by so many factors that can only be matched in number to the amount of possible combinations beweem pieces of a chessboard. Hence the importance of producing a scale of values using a rational and practical tool that will assist in developing safer artifacts.

References

1. BRASIL. Constituição, Constituição da República Federativa do Brasil. Brasília, DF, Senado (1998)
2. Greco, R.: Atividade Policial: aspectos penais, processuais penais, administrativos e constitucionais, 4ª edn. Impetus, Niterói (2012)
3. Nappo, D., Vairelli, S.: Design de Viaturas – a evolução do design dos veículos de estrada. Lisma, Tradução Silvia Steiner (2006)
4. Vasconcelos, L.A.L.: Uma Investigação em Metodologias de Design. Recife, Monografia (Graduação) – Universidade Federal de Pernambuco / Departamento de Design (2009)

Enhancing Usability Engineering in Rural Areas Using Agile Methods

Rüdiger Heimgärtner[1], Alkesh Solanki[2], and Bernd Hollerit[3]

[1] Intercultural User Interface Consulting (IUIC), Germany
[2] Continental Engineering Services GmbH, Germany
[3] University of Tokyo, Japan
ruediger.heimgaertner@iuic.de,
alkesh.solanki@conti-engineering.com,
hollerit@gmail.com

Abstract. Usability engineering is all about developing usable products and/or services for a certain user group in a specific context. In this paper, we present some ideas about how to enhance usability engineering in rural areas (i.e. for users in rural contexts) taking agile methods into account. First, rural areas, rural users and rural products are illustrated. We elucidate the cultural, technological and social differences and the specifics of rural areas. Then, we look at the most important steps according to the standard user-centered design process defined in ISO 9241-210 in order to identify possible challenges and implications for usability engineering in rural areas. Finally, we analyze how usability engineering profits by using agile methods in this context.

Keywords: Rural, Agile, HDI, Developing Countries, Newly Industrialized Countries, User-Centered Design, ISO 9241-210, Culture, HCI, Approach, Process, Structure, Intercultural, Intercultural User Interface Design, Standard, Usability Engineering, Intercultural Usability Engineering.

1 Rural Areas in the World

1.1 Developing and Newly Industrialized Countries

A developing country, also called a less-developed country (LDC),[1] is a nation with a lower living standard, underdeveloped industrial base, and a low Human Development Index (HDI) relative to other countries. The HDI is a composite statistic of life expectancy, education, and income indices used to rank countries into stages of human development. Figure 1 shows that India is a newly industrialized country with an HDI between industrialized and developing countries. The challenges of newly industrialized countries also affect developing countries because they lack even more than newly industrialized countries. Africa is the continent with the lowest average HDI even if almost all ranges of HDI are represented.

---

[1] Cf. URL=http://en.wikipedia.org/wiki/
Developing_country_-_cite_note-1, last access 2014-02-24.

A. Marcus (Ed.): DUXU 2014, Part I, LNCS 8517, pp. 445–452, 2014.

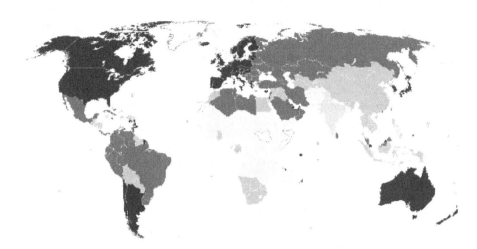

Fig. 1. 2013 UN Human Development Report Quartiles (cf. United Nations Human Development Index (HDI) rankings for 2012, URL=https://data.undp.org/dataset/Table-1-Human-Development-Index-and-its-components/wxub-qc5k, last access 2014-02-24). The lighter the areas in Figure 1, the lower the HDI ranking implying more and/or larger rural areas.

The economy of newly industrialized countries (NIC) has not yet reached developed country status but has, in a macroeconomic sense, outpaced their developing counterparts. Moreover, these nations are undergoing rapid economic growth (usually export-oriented). Ongoing industrialization is an important indicator of a NIC. NICs usually share some common features, including a switch from agricultural/rural to industrial economies, large national corporations operating on several continents, strong capital investment from foreign countries, political leadership in their area of influence as well as rapid growth of urban centers and population.

In this paper, the challenges for rural areas are exemplified by India because:

- India is the largest newly industrialized country of the world (1,237 billion inhabitants)[2]
- The per capita income of India is the lowest in the G8+5 countries.
- With the lowermost HDI of the G8+5 countries, India has the maximum potential for human resource development.
- According to a Goldman Sachs review of emerging economies, by 2050 the largest economies in the world will be as follows: China, USA, India, Brazil, and Mexico.[3]

---

[2] URL=https://www.google.de/search?q=einwohner+indien&oq=einwohner+indien&aqs=chrome..69i57j0l5.3003j0j4&sourceid=chrome&espv=210&es_sm=93&ie=UTF-8, last access 2014-02-26.

[3] URL=http://web.archive.org/web/20110810095039/http://www.chicagobooth.edu/alumni/clubs/pakistan/docs/next11dream-march%20%2707-goldmansachs.pdf, last access 2014-02-26.

- In 2013, the Indian government invested 73175 INR in the development of rural areas regarding infrastructure, education and employment because 70% of India's population lives in rural areas.[4]
- A good portion of related work for HCI design in rural areas was researched in Namibia (cf. [1]), whose HDI is slightly higher than that of India.

1.2   Characterization of the Rural Areas in India

Electricity is available mostly everywhere in India. Rural areas are also mostly remote regions which suffer bad accessibility and are not very well connected to other economic centers. Mobile communication is available all over the country. In addition to the mainstream media, the rural development ministry of Indian government is investing in every new and emerging electronic media (radio, television, internet, social media and electronic library). Official websites are available in English and Hindi. E-government is available in all rural areas of India. This results in less corruption, more transparency and a revolution in mobile communication which ensures that people are accessible everywhere, since almost everybody in rural areas has a mobile phone with internet access. From the 1,237 billion inhabitants in total in India, there are:

- 904.56 million telephone subscribers (wireless and landline),
- 29.08 million land lines,
- 875.48 million cell phones.[5]

Amenities in the Following Areas Are Provided through Projects

- Water,
- Electricity,
- Construction and village maintenance,
- Village linked tourism,
- Streets,
- Integrated Rural Hub,
- Drainage,
- Rural Market,
- Solid Waste Management,
- Agri - Common Services Centre,
- Skill development,
- Warehousing,
- Development of economic activities,
- Any other rural-economy based project,
- Village street lighting,
- Telecommunications

---

[4] URL=http://www.rural.nic.in/sites/downloads/annual-report/
MoRDEnglish_AR2012_13.pdf, last access 2014-02-26.

[5] URL=http://en.wikipedia.org/wiki/
Telecommunications_statistics_in_India_-_cite_note-
trai_subnumbers-6, last access 2014-02-24.

Rural Products. E-governance products, public information booths (internet activated), rural libraries might all have internet connections, providing m-commerce, e-commerce, m-banking, e-banking, communication (apps, chat, messages), information (news, databases), social media (facebook, google+) (cf. [2]) and mobile phones (cf. [1]). In addition, there is a tool for bridging the digital divide in rural India (cf. [3] and [4]).

User Groups. Rural users must work to live. Therefore, they do not have time to speak with the designer or test the product. In addition, they are often illiterate or not well educated, do not have good knowledge of English and speak only Hindi or a local language and therefore, they are not able to express their expectations and needs clearly. Rural users are not tech savvy and do not have formal computer education.

1.3   Challenges in Rural Areas in India

Accessibility to the user is not easy (great distances, no direct connectivity to rural areas, knowledge of local languages or translator necessary). HCI designers must have enhanced capabilities and skills such as being more flexible, pragmatic and empathic in order to understand the expectations and the needs of rural users. In addition, there are many other general challenges in designing HCI for rural areas (cf. [5], [6], [7], [8], [9], [10], [11], [3], [12], [13], [14], [15]) and in "designing in the wild" (cf. [16], [17], [18], [19]). In addition, in rural areas, bridging digital diversity is a fundamental political concern of "repairing worlds" (cf. [20]).

1.4   Approaches and Methods to Tackle the Challenges for HCI Design in Rural Areas

Several techniques must be applied such as "designing in the wild" (i.e. "in situ design", cf. [19]) or reframing HCI thinking by taking indigenous perspectives into account (cf. [21]). Motivated by the identified challenges for HCI design in rural areas, a growing number of researchers focus on adapting or discovering new approaches and methods with which to tackle the problems of using participatory design (cf. [22]) at genius loci (cf. [5]). Furthermore, several testing methods have been adapted to "oral" rural users (cf. [23]) such as digital story telling (cf. [24]), using oral repositories (cf. [25]) or 3D visualizations of indigenous knowledge (cf. [26]). Before we add the concept of agile methods to this solution portfolio, we analyze the implications of the challenges in rural areas to usability engineering.

2   Usability Engineering Challenges in Rural Areas

Let us now analyze the standard HCI development process in ISO 9241-210 (cf. [27]) concerning its use in rural contexts. Figure 2 shows an overview of the user-centered HCI design process. The process consists of various steps which will be analyzed concerning their use in HCI design for our purpose (cf. also [28]). First, we examine the weaknesses in every process step, then we define and recommend   implementing agile methods to improve the HCI design process for its application in rural areas. In addition, ISO 9241-210 refers also to the seven dialog principles defined in ISO 9241-110, which should be applied in human computer interaction design. They should be analyzed with regard to their applicability as general dialog principles in rural contexts. However, that is beyond   the focus of this paper.

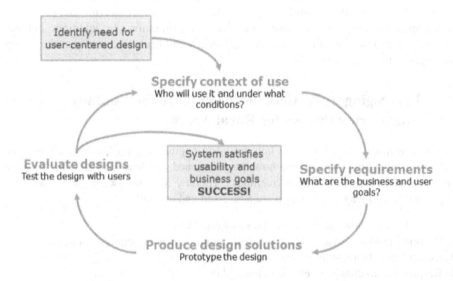

Fig. 2. User-Centered Design Process following ISO 9241-210

2.1   Understanding the Context of Use and Specifying User Requirements

We propose user-centered design for rural areas in particular, as the potential clients might not be familiar with computer software. In order to increase the willingness to adapt to new technologies, the design has to meet high usability standards. Furthermore, "watching what the users do rather than listening to what the users   say" becomes even more applicable in the case of rural users because what they say is not exactly what they want or they must have. Here agile methods can be very supportive (cf. section 3 about leveraging agile methods). In this context, also secondary users (for example, local volunteers) can be contacted to obtain a better understanding and access to the primary user and his context of use and his user needs in order to determine the user requirements.

2.2   Producing Design Solutions and Evaluation

Evaluation and re-evaluation of the design has to be performed after every iteration until the users are satisfied with their user experience. New users testing a re-design might encounter problems that have not been discovered during earlier tests and we must address them. Hence, in the rural context we must use unconventional methods such as disseminating messages through folk and traditional art forms, direct contact programs like rallies, door to door campaigns, village level meetings, film shows and videos[6] to achieve a greater involvement of users during the design the product and also enabling the users to give meaningful feedback during the formative and summative evaluation of the prototypes and the final product. Hence, in rural contexts, it is even more efficient to apply agile principles (cf. section 3, (i) and (ii)): For instance, seeing the low-fidelity prototype as a living specification and preferring communication in place of comprehensive documentation. In addition, outdoor outreach mode is a most impressive medium of communication to transport the proper messages to the rural public.

3   Leveraging Agile Methods to Optimize the Usability Engineering Process for Rural Areas

Let us now direct our analysis to how usability engineering profits from using agile methods in the rural context and how the mentioned challenges in section 2 can be met and resolved using agile methods. Thereby the following principles and implications of the agile manifesto are addressed and applied:[7]

1. Individuals and interactions over processes and tools,
2. Working products (user interfaces) over comprehensive documentation,
3. Customer collaboration over contract negotiation,
4. Responding to change over following a plan.

The agile manifesto even supports "designing in the wild" / "in situ design" because the designer is locally on the spot living with the users. In such a rural context the agile manifesto can be lived literally: live requirements development, in situ design thinking, continuous integration and "just in time" deliveries. Also the evaluation feedback loop is fully integrated in the live process.

In fact, in situ design even pushes the agility of the whole process to a level higher than the one defined by the current agile process. Therefore, agile principles are necessary in usability engineering in rural areas because they support the principles of usability engineering and the necessary flexibility to in-situ design in rural areas covering the following aspects with ease:

- many deliveries/releases,
- live user feedback,
- collection, description and comprehension of user needs in short iterative cycles,
- permanent clarification of conflicting user needs and specification of user requirements,
- continuous integration, testing and evaluation.

---

[6] Cf. URL=http://www.rural.nic.in/sites/downloads/annual-report/ MoRDEnglish_AR2012_13.pdf, last access 2014-02-26.

[7] Cf. URL=http://agilemanifesto.org/, last access 2014-02-24.

4   Conclusion

This agile HCI design process for rural areas represents a new approach by combining the best practices of the current HCI design process defined in ISO 9241-210 with the elements of the paradigms of "designing in the wild" and agility. Living this process, the UI designers will better understand the user needs in rural areas and accommodate the frequent changes for design. In addition, the approach reduces the development time dramatically by continuous live feedback loops.

References

1. Bidwell, N., Winschiers-Theophilus, H., Koch Kapuire, G., Rehm, M.: Pushing Personhood into Place: Situating Media in the Transfer of Rural Knowledge in Africa. Int. Journal of Human-Computer Studies 69(10), S 618–S 631 (2011b); Special Issue on Locative Media
2. Bidwell, N.J., et al.: Please call ME. NU 4EVER: Callback & Social Media Sharing in Rural Africa. In: Proceedings of The 10th International Workshop on Internalisation of Products and Systems, Kuching, Malaysia (2011)
3. Das, R.K., Patra, M.R., Mahapatra, S.C.: e-grama: a tool for bridging the digital divide in rural India. In: Proceedings of the 2nd International Conference on Theory and Practice of Electronic Governance, pp. 361–366. ACM, Cairo (2008)
4. Design, I.B.: Low cost self-diagnosis tool for rural India, http://indian-bydesign.wordpress.com/2010/05/06/product-feature-low-cost-self-diagnosis-tool-for-rural-india/ (May 6, 2010)
5. Bidwell, N.J., Browning, D.: Pursuing genius loci: interaction design and natural places. Personal Ubiquitous Comput. 14(1), 15–30 (2010)
6. Marshini, C., Tucker, W., Blake, E.: Developing locally Relevant Software Application for Rural Areas: South African Example, Proceedings. In: SAICSIT (2004)
7. Maunder, A., Marsden, G., Tucker, W.: Evaluating the relevance of the 'Real Access' criteria as a framework for rural HCI research. In: Proceedings of CHI-SA, 2006, pp. 57–79 (2006)
8. Sandhu, J.S., Altankhuyag, P., Amarsaikhan, D.: Serial hanging out: rapid ethnographic needs assessment in rural settings. In: Jacko, J.A. (ed.) Human-Computer Interaction, HCII 2007, Part I. LNCS, vol. 4550, pp. 614–623. Springer, Heidelberg (2007)
9. Zhao, J.: ICT4D: Internet adoption and usage among rural users in China. Knowledge, Technology & Policy 21(1), 9–18 (2008)
10. Walker, K., et al.: A resource kit for participatory socio-technical design in rural kenya. In: CHI 2008 Extended Abstracts on Human Factors in Computing Systems, pp. 2709–2714. ACM, Florence (2008)
11. Abdelnour-Nocera, J., Dunckley, L.: Sociotechnical research and knowledge communication in community-centred systems design: a technological frames perspective. International Journal of Web Based Communities 4(4), 476–490 (2008)
12. Sukumaran, A., et al.: Intermediated technology interaction in rural contexts. In: CHI 2009 Extended Abstracts on Human Factors in Computing Systems, pp. 3817–3822. ACM, Boston (2009)
13. Bidwell, N.J., et al.: Designing with mobile digital storytelling in rural Africa. In: Proceedings of the SIGCHI Conference on Human Factors in Computing Systems, pp. 1593–1602. ACM, Atlanta (2010)

14. Oreglia, E., Liu, Y., Zhao, W.: Designing for emerging rural users: experiences from China. In: CHI 2011 Proceedings of the 2011 Annual Conference on Human Factors in Computing Systems. ACM (2011)
15. Liu, J., et al.: How socio-economic structure influences rural users' acceptance of mobile entertainment. In: Proceedings of the SIGCHI Conference on Human Factors in Computing Systems, pp. 2203–2212. ACM, Atlanta (2010)
16. Button, G.: Cognition in the Wild, Edwin Hutchins. Comput. Supported Coop. Work 6(4), 391–395 (1997)
17. Dourish, P., et al.: Security in the wild: user strategies for managing security as an everyday, practical problem. Personal and Ubiquitous Computing 8(6), 391–401 (2004)
18. Marshall, P., et al.: Rethinking 'Multi-user': An in-the-wild study of how groups approach a walk-up-and-use tabletop interface. In: Conf. Hum. Fact. Comput. Syst. Proc. Conference on Human Factors in Computing Systems - Proceedings, pp. 3033–3042 (2011)
19. Rogers, Y.: Interaction design gone wild: striving for wild theory. Interactions 18(4), 58–62 (2011)
20. Jackson, S.J., Pompe, A., Krieshok, G.: Repair worlds: maintenance, repair, and ICT for development in rural Namibia. In: Proceedings of the ACM 2012 Conference on Computer Supported Cooperative Work, pp. 107–116. ACM, Seattle (2012)
21. Abdelnour-Nocera, J., et al.: Re-framing HCI through Local and Indigenous Perspectives. In: Campos, P., Graham, N., Jorge, J., Nunes, N., Palanque, P., Winckler, M. (eds.) INTERACT 2011, Part IV. LNCS, vol. 6949, pp. 738–739. Springer, Heidelberg (2011)
22. Winschiers-Theophilus, H., et al.: Being participated: a community approach. In: Proceedings of the 11th Biennial Participatory Design Conference, pp. 1–10. ACM, Sydney (2010)
23. Gorman, T., et al.: Adapting usability testing for oral, rural users. In: CHI 2011 Proceedings of the SIGCHI Conference on Human Factors in Computing Systems, pp. 1437–1440. ACM, Vancouver (2011)
24. Reitmaier, T., Bidwell, N.J., Marsden, G.: Situating digital storytelling within African communities. International Journal of Human-Computer Studies 69(10), 658–668 (2011)
25. Reitmaier, T., et al.: Communicating in designing an oral repository for rural African villages (2012)
26. Jensen, K.L., et al.: Putting it in perspective: designing a 3D visualization to contextualize indigenous knowledge in rural Namibia. In: Proceedings of the Designing Interactive Systems Conference, pp. 196–199. ACM, Newcastle Upon Tyne (2012)
27. DIN, DIN EN ISO 9241-210 Ergonomische Anforderungen der Mensch-System-Interaktion Teil 210: Prozess zur Gestaltung gebrauchstauglicher Systeme. BeuthVerlag, Berlin (2010)
28. Schoper, Y., Heimgärtner, R.: Lessons from Intercultural Project Management for the Intercultural HCI Design Process. In: Marcus, A. (ed.) DUXU/HCII 2013, Part II. LNCS, vol. 8013, pp. 95–104. Springer, Heidelberg (2013)

Serious Games and Heuristic Evaluation –
The Cross-Comparison of Existing Heuristic Evaluation
Methods for Games

Natalia Jerzak[1,2] and Francisco Rebelo[2,3]

[1] Consortium Euromime, Poitiers, France
njerzakpl@gmail.com
[2] Ergonomics Laboratory, Faculdade de Motricidade Humana -Universidade de Lisboa,
Portugal
[3] Centre for Architecture, Urban Planning and Design (CIAUD) Universidade de Lisboa,
Portugal
frebelo@fmh.utl.pt

Abstract. Learning by playing has been a desire in the educational domain. The use of serious games may offer the possibility to learn and train at the same time the learner is playing. It makes us consider the serious games as an important research area that can have huge implications in the way the new generations are learning, getting experience, practice knowledge, gain skills, train their habits and reactions. There are many heuristics available in the area of video games, several are presenting repetitive aspects, some are isolated up to the point of reaching contradictory outcomes. The main purpose of this article is to define the nature of serious games and the process of evaluating game. We are taking as the references existing heuristics for games together with their weaknesses and strengths. In order to approach the problem we grouped together and present the most important HEs for games and complied three sets of heuristic evaluation to identify the areas of tangency.

Keywords: heuristic evaluation, serious games, simulators, usability evaluation, design guidelines, video games, computer games, HCI.

1   Introduction

When considering the serious games as dispositive, that can be used with educational and training purpose, we should assure that the used games are satisfying the educational and training needs. This need makes us think about the importance of conducting a formal evaluation of serious games. Our intention in the future is to build fundaments for holistic, complete, easily applicable, comprehensive method that will take into account the nature of serious games.

There are two main objectives of this research paper. Firstly, the paper discusses the concept of "serious games". It will be followed by discussion of the advantages of using serious games and illustrate the possibilities of appliance. Secondly, we will

A. Marcus (Ed.): DUXU 2014, Part I, LNCS 8517, pp. 453–464, 2014.

discuss Heuristic Evaluation (HE) for games. Heuristic evaluation has proven to have a very huge potential and to be a valuable assessment method. This research work has extensively presented the existing heuristic evaluation in the area of the games together with their analysis, advantages, limitations and stating the possibilities of applying them into the concept of serious games. We are also presenting the matrix - the cross-comparison of the most cited HEs with their areas of tangency.

2   Serious Games

2.1   Concept of Serious Games

What is exactly a serious game? Can the game framework serve a serious educational purpose? This is the main critics that are presented around the idea of serious games. At first, usage of terminology, serious game, might seem to be mutually exclusive. Indeed, the term serious game can be seen as an oxymoron or as a tautology combining contradictory terms, game - an engaging and amusing activity with seriousness of content and context.

Clark C. Abt [1] already in 1970 presented the richness of the concept of the game that can be in favor for serious games. The main aspects presented in his book were both formally describing the rules of the game and motivation of the players. The games are effective tools for teaching and training for students due to their highly motivating nature and effective way of transferring the concept and facts. Games can create *"dramatic representations of the real problem"* in which students can take realistic roles in order to solve given problems by developing strategies, taking decisions, receiving fast feedback on the progress towards the set goal. What is more games can serve as the tool of evaluating performance and prevent students from taking a risk of solving the problem in real world together with the costs of conducting errors [1].

According to Michael & Chen, the first and main goal of serious game is the educational and training role: meeting specific educational purpose, specific learning aspects, specific training objective offered in many new forms rather than simple entertainment [2]. What is more learning in the game environment is not a hard "work". Learning is based and achieved by solving the problems, experiments and exploration, all the aspects that are keeping the learners active and interested [3].

For the purpose of this research we consider serious games as: specialized learning and training tools that can be used to enrich the process of learning, training, habit creation and the attitude change. It is offered in varied forms and at the same time it uses the main characteristic of game and entertainment factor in order to reach specific educational and training purposes.

2.2   Application and Advantages

There are many classifications of Serious Games. Games can be created for many reasons among which are health, training, education, science, research, production, work and marketing/publicity. The interested group in applying them can include government together with NGOs, defense/military, healthcare, marketing & communication, education, corporate and industry. Serious Games can be seen from other points such as sociability: allowing collaboration and/or competition and by number of players: single player, multiplayer components and tournaments or massive-online games and simulators. It is also crucial to include hardware in the classification e.g. if the game is available on all type of platforms or is limited to only one e.g., portable consoles, personal computers, tablets, mobiles, XBOX 360, WII etc.

There is the consensus that serious games are the potential tools designed to have the educational impact. Firstly, thanks to using serious games we can raise students engagement and motivation [4-5]. Secondly, the solutions offered by implementing serious games are suitable for even beginners within the computer-mediated system; moreover, they allow students to take more active role in their education [6].

In addition, the games are providing a special feeling of accomplishment during the play, sense of triumph that encourages the immersion in the learning process [7]. Games are improving problem solving, critical thinking, and allow collaboration, socialization with other players [8]. Serious games are perfect method of assessing the knowledge of the students and they allow receiving the immediate feedback on player's performance. There is very strong visible emotional connection between a student and learning material that allow students to do the meaningful choices [9]. Ideally all those characteristics should be presented in school but they are usually ignored or limited [10]. Serious games allow the learners to experience the situations that are normally hard to be experienced in real-life situations because of many limitations such as time, space, safety etc. We cannot ignore the fact that simulations and serious games are allowing the gamers to experience the situation that normally, because of safely and cost-effective reasons, would be impossible. The idea behind the serious games is to intentionally create the learning bridge between the experience of daily life and learning styles [11-12] and provide the situated learning that is long lasting compared to standard learning. What is more, according to many studies, students are preferring games and simulators over the standard class exercises [13].

There was a wide study conducted by Conolly [14] and his colleges in which they revisited the available literature on serious games - they found almost 130 papers presenting the empirical evidences of the significant impact of serious games. The most important areas of the impact that were identified are in the area acquisition of the knowledge, understanding the content and essential rise in motivation and affection. Additionally, it was stressed that we should not perceive the games as the remedy for all the problems and the only good solution; we should distinguish the benefits of using it in the areas of higher-level thinking and social skills. Games can be of great value especially in certain fields like in healthcare [14].

Primack together with his colleges collected and review the wide selection of available studies that are focusing on the impact of video games in healthcare – huge effectiveness of serious games in patient treatment, phobias treatment and acquisition of clinical knowledge and skills by medical personnel [15]. The researchers identified 38 papers in clinical studies. Among health-topics the common topics were asthma, strokes, physical activities and cancer. The results of his studies have proven a significant and positive impact of games in the clinical settings.

3   Heuristic Evaluation for Games

Heuristics Evaluation (HE) has become an extensively acknowledged method of usability evaluation in software development and a current, widely accepted and used method of usability evaluation and inspections. Usability inspections methods are playing important role in the designing a well-structured, effective, learning and training tool such as video game. HE are qualitative method used by the experts in evaluating given problems. HE is the method of finding the usability problems so that they can properly attended and resolved by implementing evaluators who are inspecting and examining given system, software or product [16]. That is why, HE can be perceived as more subjective method than the other usability inspections methods because it is strongly embedded in the skills of the evaluators and their experience [17]. It is possible that those characteristics might have a negative impact but while implementing skilled evaluators into the process of evaluation we can easily find the problems, potential areas of conflicts and inconsistency in the serious games. That is why conducting the heuristic evaluation can be a valuable and significant in the serious game design process from the evaluation the game at its concept stage through game prototype up to final serious game.

Nowadays serious games are considered as fast growing field with varied areas of implementations. There are several heuristics evaluations in the area of games but they are partially applicable or not applicable to serious games' nature. We have decided to present different sets of heuristics created for evaluating games (Table 1.).

Table 1. Heuristic Evaluation for games

Author	Description
Malone, 1982	Set of heuristics for instructional games with the emphasize on challenges and fantasies that can foster the curiosity development and have the impact on learning outcomes. The first HE encouraging to use games in learning and teaching [18].
Federoff, 2002	Proposed a complete set of heuristics that were divided into three groups, game interface, game mechanics and game play. The limitation could be seen in applicability only at the preliminary stage of game design and not covering properly the emotional features of the games and immersion [19].
Desurvire, Caplan, Toth, 2004	Heuristics to Evaluate Playability (HEP). HEP consists of game play, game mechanics, game usability and introduced new class: game story. HEP was a method that was including the narrative plot of the game and the character development during the game play as an important factor. The limitation can be connected with applicability only at the preliminary stage and generalization that could lead to problems with objectivity [20].

Table 1. (*continued*)

Korkonen, Koivisto, 2006	Set of heuristics to measure playability for the mobile games that include the specifications and limitations of used platform such as power battery limits or size of the screen [21].
Korkonen, Koivisto, 2007	Extended version of previous heuristics for mobile games that additionally included the multi-player dimension [22].
Jegers, 2008	Usability and playability heuristics designed for persuasive games: games that are using one of the three characteristics: i) mobile and place/time independence, ii) social interactions and iii) integration between physical and virtual worlds. Proposed heuristics are focusing on the aspects that have not been covered before by other heuristics in the area of game development such as involving interactions between the players and with the game environment [23].
Pinelle, Wong, Stach, Gutwin, 2009	Usability heuristics for networked multiplayer games - Networked Game Heuristics (NGH). The heuristics were build after detailed examination of the reviews of multiplayer games that are available online. It was the first set of heuristics that was derived from real problem of network games reported by the end users in the game portals: GameSpy and GameSpot [24].
Desurvire, Wiberf, 2009	Game usability heuristics (Play) that was covering the areas of game play, skill development, tutorials, strategy and challenges, game story, immersion, coolness and usability and game mechanics. Play was initially refining the proposed list of heuristics HEP by the following dimensions: multiple types of games and genders. Those features made PLAY applicable mostly at the early stage of game development [25].
Omar, Jaafar, 2010	Playability heuristics for Educational Games including five issues: interface, pedagogical/educational, multimedia, content and playability. It the first available heuristic that was treating the educational aspect as a main objective of games. This set of heuristics was treating the educational features is very general way and not covering the features connected with serious games [26].

4   Matrix of Cross Comparison of HEs for Games

4.1   Methodology and Results

In order to reach the global view of the related works we have decided to analyze in details three set of heuristics for games and video games by cross-comparison:

- Federoff, M.A.: Heuristics and usability guidelines for the creation and evaluation of fun in video games [19].

- Desurvire, H., Caplan, M., Toth, J.: Using heuristics to evaluate the playability of games [20].
- Desurvire, H., Wiberg, C.: Game Usability Heuristics (PLAY) for Evaluating and Designing Better Games [25].

The outcomes are presented in the table below (Table 2.). With the mark "X" we mark the presence of a certain feature. For the sake of clearness he have grouped the features in three distinguished categories:

- Game Play - grouping all the issues connected with the playability of the game;
- Learning and Entertainment - issues connected with fun and learning;
- Usability and Game Mechanics issues together.

It is allowing us to clearly observe the areas of tangency between the sets.

Table 2. Cross-comparison of three sets of HE in the area of games

	Federoff	Desurvire, Caplan, Toth	Desurvire, Wiberg
I Game Play			
1. Game story			
The player feels as though the world is going on whether their character is there or not.	X	X	X
The player is interested in the story line. If possible, the story experience relates to player's real life and grabs their interest.	X	X	X
If there is a game story, the player should discover it as the part of the game play.	-	X	-
If there is a game story, the player is eager to spend time thinking of the possible outcomes.	-	X	-
2. Enduring the play			
The game does not put the unnecessary burden, fatigue, or feeling of discomfort for the player by varying activities and pacing during the game. Players shouldn't be burdened with tasks that don't feel important.	-	X	X
The player should not be penalized respectively for the same failure.	-	X	X
Game play is long, enduring and interesting for the player.	-	-	X
The player experiences fairness of outcomes.	X	X	-

Table 2. (*continued*)

3. Challenge, Strategy and Pace			
The game is paced in order to apply pressure but without frustrating the player. The game should increase the players' skills at an appropriate pace as they progress through the game.	X	X	X
The game is easy to learn but is harder and challenging to master.	X	X	X
The game challenges are triggering the positive game experience rather than a negative one.	-	X	X
If possible, the game provides different difficulty levels (levels of challenge for different learning activities and for different players)	X	-	-
The players are interested enough to continue playing rather than quitting the game.	-	X	X
4. Consistency in Game World			
The game world reacts to the players and remembers their passage through it.	-	X	X
Changes the player makes in the game world are persistent and noticeable if they back-track to where they've been before.	-	X	X
The Artificial Intelligence (AI) is visible to the player, reasonable, balanced with the player's actions yet unpredictable.	X	X	-
The game should imply mode in the game play but it should be perceived by the player as modeless.	X	X	-
5. Goals			
The game learning goals are clear for the player. The game is presenting overriding, clear goals (both short and long term) early throughout the game play.	X	X	X
The game gives the meaningful rewards that are immersing the player more deeply into the game by moving the player to a higher level or unlocking special achievements. Players should be rewarded appropriately for their effort and skill development during the learning process. If possible, the rewards are increasing the player's capabilities and expanding their ability to customize.	X	X	X
The player is taught skills early that he is expected to use/practice the skills later on during the game play, or right before the new skill is needed.	X	X	X
6.Variety of Players and Game Styles			
The game play is balanced without definite way to win (single optimal winning strategy) but there are multiple paths to win the game.	X	X	X
The first players' actions are obvious and should result in immediate and positive feedback.	-	X	X

Table 2. (*continued*)

7.Players Perception of Control			
The player has the sense of control and influence onto the game world (like their actions matter and they are shaping the game world).	X	X	X
The player should feel a sense of control over their characters or units and their movements and interactions in the game world.	X	X	X
The players should feel a sense of control over the actions that they take and the strategies that they use and that they are free to play the game the way that they want (not simply discovering actions and strategies planned by the game developers).	X	X	X
Allow player to build the content in the game.	-	X	-
II Learning and Entertainment			
1. Learning			
Shortens the learning curve by following the trends set by the gaming industry to meet users' expectations.	X	X	X
2.Emotional Connection			
The player is developing the emotional connection with the game world and/or game characters (player should feel emotionally involved in the game).	-	X	X
The game transports the player into a level of personal involvement emotionally (e.g., scare, threat, thrill, reward, punishment) and viscerally (e.g., sounds of environment).	-	X	-
3.Coolness & Humor			
The player finds the game fun with no repetitive or boring tasks.	-	-	X
The game is enjoyable enough for the player to be eager to replay it again or replay some specific learning activities.	X	X	-
4. Immersion			
The game utilizes visceral, audio and visual content to further the players' immersion in the game.	X	-	X
III Usability and Game Mechanics			
1. Documentation and Tutorial			
The game provides the interesting and absorbing tutorial that mimics the game play. Players can be taught to play the game through tutorials or initial levels that are giving the feeling of playing the game.	X	X	-
The player does not need to access the tutorial in order to play.	-	-	X
The player does not need to read the manual or documentation in order to play.	X	X	X

Table 2. (*continued*)

2. Status and Score			
Upon initially turning the game on the player has enough information to get started to play.	X	X	X
Mechanics/controller actions have consistently mapped and learnable responses.	X	X	X
Game controls are consistent within the game and follow standard conventions.	X	X	X
A player should always be able to identify their score/status, learning outcomes and goals in the game without interfering the game play.	X	X	X
3. Feedback			
Provide appropriate audio/visual/visceral feedback (music, sound effects, controller vibration) to stir a particular emotions.	X	X	X
Game provides feedback and reacts in a consistent, immediate, challenging and exciting way to the players' actions.	X	X	X
Use sounds to provide the meaningful feedback.	X	-	-
4. Burden on the player			
The game has varied difficulty levels or tasks so that the players has greater challenge as they develop mastery.	X	-	X
The game controls are basic enough to learn quickly, yet if necessary can be expandable for advanced options for advanced players.	X	X	X
5. Screen Layout			
Art is recognizable to the player and speaks to its function.	X	X	X
The player experiences the user interface as consistent (in controller, color, typographic, dialogue and user interface design). Learning objects and tasks might be varied but all menu instructions, tips or error messages are appearing in the same place on the screen.	X	X	X
The interface should be as non-intrusive to the player as possible.	X	X	-
Make the menu layers well-organized and minimalist to the extent the menu options are intuitive.	X	X	-
6. Error Prevention			
The players are able to play and get involved quickly and easily with tutorials, and/or progressive or adjustable difficulty levels (if the game gives the options to change the level).	X	X	X
The players should be given learning context sensitive during the game play so that they are not stuck and need to rely on a manual for help.	-	X	X

Table 2. (*continued*)

The players should feel a sense of control over the game shell (can easily turn the game off and on, and be able to save games in different states).	X	X	X
Upon initially turning the game on the player has enough information to get started to play.	-	X	X
The players' error is avoided, players should not be able to make errors that are detrimental to the game and should be supported in recovering from errors.	-	-	X
Provide means for error prevention and recovery through the use of warning messages.	X	-	-

5   Conclusions and Future Work

Serious games are providing an engaging, interesting experience, motivation and self-reinforcement during learning and training. We should not be forgetting it is not remedy for all, the wise implementation of serious games can really trigger the positive impact on learner. When combined together with standard form of training and teaching we can acquire the effect of synergy and create appealing, thought-provocative, inspirational ambient.

It is bound that serious games will be fully integrated into the learning process in the future and specialized training simulations will become an important and integral part of the curriculum as a practical workshops and great assessing method to check the progress of student's knowledge in action.

In order to achieve that we should ensure that used games are meeting our objectives. Heuristic Evaluation has proven to be a very valuable method of assessment. In order to reach the global view of the related works we have decided to analyze the different set of heuristics for games and video games. The outcome of this paper is the cross-comparison between the different heuristics. We have chosen the most relevant HE for the scope of the project, in order to identify uncovered areas and the strong points of each HE. We need to stress out that existing heuristics are not dealing with seriousness and learning features present in the concept of serious games. We noticed the lack of specially established heuristics evaluation methods applicable for the concept of serious games, among which are:

- player's concentration: responses to stimuli, maintaining attention, different responses to workload, distraction and stress;
- social interactions - providing the opportunities for social interactions (competition, cooperation);
- learning content - different types of learning content on different level of games;
- players' immersion - encouraging deep experience yet effortless and natural;
- features concentrated on specialized training games and simulators e.g. for military, air force, firefighters that have specific purposes of training habits, attitudes, behaviors, reactions and other specific learning outcomes.

After conducting a systematic literature revision we have identified the most citied articles, key concepts and principal heuristics evaluations for games with the intention of analyzing the uncovered areas relevant to serious games. In the future it will allow us to conceptualize, develop and introduce a brand new HE for serious games.

References

1. Abt, C.C.: Serious Games. Viking Press, New York (1970)
2. Michael, D.R., Chen, S.L.: Serious Games: Games That Educate, Train, and Inform. In: Education, pp. 1–95. Muska & Lipman/Premier-Trade (October 31, 2005)
3. Edery, D., Mollick, E.: Changing the game. how video games are transforming the future of business, p. 218. Ft Press (2009)
4. Lim, C.P., Nonis, D., Hedberg, J.: Gaming in a 3D multiuser virtual environment: Engaging students in Science lessons. British Journal of Educational Technology 37, 211–231 (2006)
5. Kim, B., Park, H., Baek, Y.: Not just fun, but serious strategies: Using meta-cognitive strategies in game-based learning. Computers & Education 52, 800–810 (2009)
6. Martin, S., Diaz, G., Sancristobal, E., Gil, R., Castro, M., Peire, J.: New technology trends in education: Seven years of forecasts and convergence. Computers & Education 57, 1893–1906 (2011)
7. Prensky, M.: Digital game-based learning. Computers in Entertainment 1, 21 (2003)
8. Klopfer, E., Yoon, S.: Developing games and simulations for today and tomorrow's tech savvy youth. TechTrends 49, 33–41 (2004)
9. Johnson, L., Adams, S., Cummins, M.: NMC Horizon Report - 2012. In: Higher Education Edition, vol. 2012, p. 42 (2012)
10. Klopfer, E., Osterweil, S., Salen, K., Groff, J., Roy, D.: Moving Learning Games Forward. Flora 3, 58 (2009)
11. Proserpio, L., Gioia, D.A.: Teaching the Virtual Generation. Academy of Management Learning & Education 6, 69–80 (2007)
12. Vahey, P., Tatar, D., Roschelle, J.: Using handheld technology to move between the private and public in the classroom. In: Ubiquitous Computing: Invisible Technology, Visible Impact, pp. 187–210 (2006)
13. Chin, J., Dukes, R., Gamson, W.: Assessment in Simulation and Gaming: A Review of the Last 40 Years. Simulation & Gaming 40, 453–568 (2009)
14. Connolly, T.M., Boyle, E.A., MacArthur, E., Hainey, T., Boyle, J.M.: A systematic literature review of empirical evidence on computer games and serious games. Computers & Education 59, 661–686 (2012)
15. Primack, B.A., Carroll, M.V., McNamara, M., Klem, M.L., King, B., Rich, M., Chan, C.W., Nayak, S.: Role of Video Games in Improving Health-Related Outcomes. American Journal of Preventive Medicine 42, 630–638 (2012)
16. Nielsen, J.: Paper versus computer implementations as mockup scenarios for heuristic evaluation. In: Proceedings of the IFIP Tc13 Third interational Conference on Human-Computer Interaction, pp. 315–320. North-Holland Publishing Co. (1990)
17. Mack, R., Nielsen, J.: Usability inspection methods. ACM SIGCHI Bulletin 25, 28–33 (1993)

18. Malone, T.W.: Heuristics for designing enjoyable user interfaces: Lessons from computer games. In: Thomas, J.C., Schneider, M.L. (eds.) Proceedings of the 1982 Conference on Human Factors in Computing Systems, pp. 63–68. Ablex Publishing Corporation, Norwood (1982)
19. Federoff, M.A.: Heuristics and usability guidelines for the creation and evaluation of fun in video games. Chemistry & Biodiversity 1, 1829–1841 (2002)
20. Desurvire, H., Caplan, M., Toth, J.: Using heuristics to evaluate the playability of games. In: Human Factors and Computing Systems, CHI 2004, p. 1509 (2004)
21. Korhonen, H., Koivisto, E.M.I.: Playability heuristics for mobile games. In: Proceedings of the 8th Conference on Human-computer Interaction with Mobile Devices and Services, ACM (2006)
22. Korhonen, H., Koivisto, E.M.I.: Playability heuristics for mobile multi-player games. In: Proceedings of the 2nd International Conference on Digital Interactive Media in Entertainment and Arts, pp. 28–35. ACM (2007)
23. Jegers, K.: Investigating the Applicability of Usability and Playability Heuristics for Evaluation of Pervasive Games. In: Third International Conference on Internet and Web Applications and Services, ICIW 2008. IEEE (2008)
24. Pinelle, D., Wong, N., Stach, T., Gutwin, C.: Usability heuristics for networked multiplayer games. In: Proceedings of the ACM 2009 International Conference on Supporting Group Work, p. 169. ACM (2009)
25. Desurvire, H., Wiberg, C.: Game Usability Heuristics (PLAY) for Evaluating and Designing Better Games: The Next Iteration. In: Ozok, A.A., Zaphiris, P. (eds.) Online Communities. LNCS, vol. 5621, pp. 557–566. Springer, Heidelberg (2009)
26. Omar, H., Jaafar, A.: Heuristics evaluation in computer games. In: 2010 International Conference on Information Retrieval & Knowledge Management (CAMP), pp. 188–193. IEEE (2010)

Towards the Development of Usability Heuristics
for Native Smartphone Mobile Applications

Ger Joyce and Mariana Lilley

School of Computer Science, University of Hertfordshire, Hatfield,
Hertfordshire, AL10 9AB, United Kingdom
gerjoyce@outlook.com, m.lilley@herts.ac.uk

Abstract. This paper reports on initial work in the identification of heuristics that may be most usefully applied in the heuristic evaluation of native smartphone applications. Given the prevalence of such applications, this work seems pertinent, particularly as it also seems under-represented in the literature. Once defined, the heuristics were developed further based on the quantitative and qualitative feedback received from sixty Human-Computer Interaction experts in eighteen countries. The resulting heuristics could be beneficial to HCI researchers and educators, and could also potentially expedite and cut the cost of smartphone application usability evaluations for HCI practitioners.

Keywords: Usability, Heuristic Evaluation, Smartphone, Mobile Application.

1 Introduction

The ability to quickly learn, use and be satisfied with native smartphone applications is vital to users [1]. To meet this goal, a usability evaluation should be employed during the development phase of the mobile application. Otherwise, design considerations specific to native smartphone applications may not be taken into account, which in turn could lead to difficult-to-use applications, frustrated users and lost revenue [2]. Detailed platform-specific guidelines are available from Apple, Google, Microsoft and BlackBerry, yet their focus tends to be on style and design issues, not on usability issues. Furthermore, some of these guidelines can be too extensive, especially for enterprise-class native smartphone mobile applications built across iOS, Android, Blackberry and Windows mobile operating systems.

Research has also shown that traditional usability methods cannot be readily applied to the usability evaluation of native smartphone applications as traditional usability methods does not, among other issues, consider applications built for small screens nor environments far less constant than desktop applications. These types of issues present significant challenges for usability experts [3]. Consequently, when considering our options for defining usability methods for native smartphone applications, we were faced with two options:

A. Marcus (Ed.): DUXU 2014, Part I, LNCS 8517, pp. 465–474, 2014.
© Springer International Publishing Switzerland 2014

1. To create completely new usability evaluation paradigms for native smartphone applications;
2. To modify well-known, tried-and-tested usability methods, proven over many years of research.

Maintaining the benefits of a low-cost, effective, relatively fast usability inspection method, such as a Heuristic Evaluation [4], would seem to be an interesting idea to adapt for the mobile panorama. While existing heuristics may be used for evaluations of native smartphone applications, these tend to be too generic and their applicability to the domain may be limited which, in turn, may impair any evaluation that uses them. To this end, the applicability of each of traditional heuristics to the mobile panorama was considered, and then tailored to the usability inspection of native smartphone mobile applications. Furthermore, where gaps were identified, new heuristics were created.

The Heuristic Evaluation method, created by Nielsen and Molich and later modified for the web by Nielsen in 1994, offers the potential for a relatively inexpensive, effective method of usability inspection. This method became popular after studies revealed that the method found more usability problems when compared to other methods [5]. Indeed, the technique has since been applied in a range of domains, albeit with changes to the heuristics used; the heuristics were originally created for desktop interfaces, not native smartphone mobile applications which tend to be task-driven, are displayed on small screens with different methods of user input, and are typically used within constantly changing contexts and environments. As new products develop the need for the development of heuristics tailored to these new products becomes apparent [1].

2   Literature Review

To understand how a Heuristic Evaluation may be applied to the mobile panorama, an analysis of one hundred and five peer-reviewed papers in the field of usability evaluation was conducted. The literature review found that heuristics tailored to native smartphone mobile applications were under-represented in the literature. Indeed, much of the work does not fully target native smartphone mobile applications.

Initially, the history of the field of usability was researched from the time it first became considered. Papers such as "Designing for usability: key principles and what designers think" [6] were written to examine the issue of usability with desktop-based applications. Other studies defined sets of usability principles, including those in "Cognitive engineering principles for enhancing human-computer performance" [7] and "Heuristic Evaluation of user interfaces" [4].

Following general research into the initial interest in usability, research for this work began to funnel toward native smartphone application usability with the reading of papers such as "Three Facets of Usability in Mobile Handsets" [8], which recognized that the standard usability methods in use then and now did not work well within the mobile domain. Following this observation, papers such as "Heuristic Evaluation and Mobile Usability: Bridging the Realism Gap" by Po et al. [9] started to call for future research into adapting traditional usability methods, specifically

Nielsen's heuristics, for the mobile domain. Two notable works emerged from the call by Po et al., namely "Appropriating and Assessing Heuristics for Mobile Computing" by Bertini et al. [10] and more recently "Usability Heuristics for Touchscreen-based Mobile Devices" by Inostroza et al. [11]. The teams of researchers led by Enrico Bertini and Rodolfo Inostroza produced noteworthy papers in their quest to adapt Nielsen's heuristics for the mobile domain.

However, the heuristics defined within each paper are not directly applicable to the usability evaluation of native smartphone applications. This is because the heuristics from Bertini et al. tend to concentrate on the operating system, the loss of the mobile device, and the ergonomics of the mobile device. This resulted in just several of the nine heuristics aimed at the mobile software, resulting in important areas not being included. On the other hand, while the paper from Inostroza et al. concentrates fully on smartphone application heuristics, not the device. Yet, the authors changed only one heuristic and added another based on Nielsen's traditional heuristics. While, the author's mention that the definitions of the heuristics differed from Nielsen's even if the heuristics had the same titles, this approach could potentially be ambiguous to HCI experts that have worked with Nielsen's heuristics. The author's subsequently report that the number of usability problems found in an experimental study was not significant in comparison to those found using Nielsen's heuristics. Consequently, the evidence would appear to suggest that native smartphone mobile application heuristics:

- Should be more applicable than Nielsen's heuristics to the mobile domain;
- Should not have the same heuristic title as Nielsen's heuristics.

3 Approach

Based on this research and using Nielsen's heuristics as a point of reference, a set of eleven heuristics applicable to the evaluation of native smartphone mobile applications was devised. An important aspect of this work was to subject the set of eleven heuristics developed to a review by HCI experts and researchers.

We sent emails to one hundred and twenty HCI experts requesting their participation in a review of the newly-defined heuristics. The emails addresses were those of authors of papers read during the literature review. This allowed the experts to rate the heuristics through the use of a five-point Likert scale displayed under each heuristic on a custom-built survey. An area for free text comments was also included. We then analyzed the quantitative and qualitative feedback received from the HCI experts that took part in the review, refining the heuristics based on the feedback.

4 Initial Set of Native Smartphone Mobile Application Heuristics

The initial set of heuristics based on the literature, prior to the application of HCI expert feedback follow. We refer to these as **S**martphone **M**obile **A**pplication heu**R**is**T**ics ("SMART") for purposes of differentiation from other sets of heuristics:

SMART1: Provide immediate notification of application status – Ensure the mobile application user is informed of the application status immediately and as long as is necessary.

SMART2: Use a theme and consistent terms, as well as conventions and standards familiar to the user – Use a theme for the mobile application to ensure different screens look alike. Also create a style guide from which words, phrases and concepts familiar to the user will be applied consistently throughout the interface, using a natural and logical order. Use platform conventions and standards that users have come to expect in a mobile application such as the same effects when gestures are used.

SMART3: Prevent errors where possible; Assist users should an error occur – Ensure the mobile application is error-proofed as much as is possible. Should an error occur, let the user know what the error is in a way they will understand, and offer advice in how they might fix the error or otherwise proceed.

SMART4: Use a welcome mat for first-time users – A welcome mat displaying the main features and how to interact with the application allows first-time users to get up-and-running quickly, after which they can explore the mobile application at their leisure.

SMART5: Employ a simplistic, focused, glanceable, visually pleasing, intuitive interface – Main interfaces should be easy-to-learn whereby next steps are obvious, focused on one task, be simple to the point of only having the absolute necessary elements to complete that task which will allow access to vital information while users are interrupted frequently and are themselves mobile, yet the interface should still be attractive and memorable.

SMART6: Design a clear navigable path to task completion – Users should be able to see right away how they can interact with the application and navigate their way to task completion.

SMART7: Allow configuration options and shortcuts – The mobile application should allow configuration options and shortcuts to the most important information and frequent tasks, including the ability to configure according to contextual needs.

SMART8: Cater for diverse mobile environments – Diverse environments consist of different types of context of use such as poor lighting conditions and high ambient noise are common ailments mobile users have to face every day. Cater for these potential issues, for example by allowing users to change interface brightness and sound settings.

SMART9: Facilitate effortlessness input – Mobile devices are difficult to use from a content input perspective. Ensure users can input content accurately by displaying keyboard buttons that are as large as possible, as well as allowing multimodal input.

SMART10: Make good use of sensors – Utilize the complex sensors available as much as possible to provide users with a more interesting and stimulating experience.

SMART11: Create an aesthetic and identifiable icon – An icon for a mobile application should be aesthetic and identifiable as this is what a user sees when searching the device interface for the application they wish to launch and when scanning through app stores it will be the first item they see before the application title, description and screenshots.

5 HCI Expert Survey

The review of the heuristics was held through the use of a custom-built online survey (see Figure 1). Prior to the survey, the participants were informed of the gap identified in the literature that prompted the research and subsequent creation of the heuristics.

Fig. 1. HCI expert survey

The participants were asked to rate each of the eleven heuristics developed using a five-point Likert Scale from 1 (Not Useful) to 5 (Very Useful). Sixty HCI experts from eighteen countries took part in the review; forty-six of the reviewers were HCI researchers, with the remainder being primarily HCI practitioners and HCI educators.

6 HCI Expert Survey Results

The heuristics were well-received by the reviewers. The free text comments received were also very insightful. The modes received in the survey for each heuristic were:

Table 1. Modes for each heuristic

Heuristic	Mode (1 – Not Useful to 5-Very Useful)
SMART1	5
SMART2	5
SMART3	5
SMART4	3
SMART5	5
SMART6	5
SMART7	4
SMART8	4
SMART9	4
SMART10	3
SMART11	5

We used a centered stacked bar chart to display the review results as a standard stacked bar chart does not have a common baseline [12] (see Figure 2). By removing Likert scale responses equal to 3 (Neutral) a central line is created. This separates positive and negative responses, allowing the results to be clearly visualized [13].

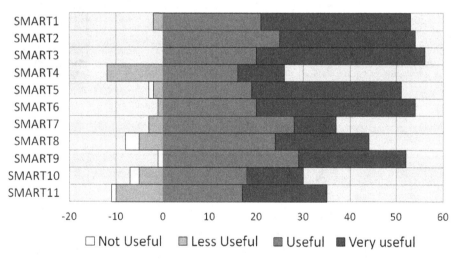

Fig. 2. HCI expert survey quantitative results

As can be seen in Figure 2, the vast majority of HCI experts rated the SMART heuristics either "Useful" or "Very Useful". However, the results also clearly show that a number of HCI experts deemed SMART heuristics 4, 8, 10 and 11 less useful without modification. Based on their comments, modifications were made to the heuristics.

7   Modifications to Initial Set of Heuristics

Changes to SMART4 were to use the term *overlay* which is more commonplace than *welcome mat*, as well as an addition to the definition as a HCI expert mentioned that overlays should be available also for later use. This certainly makes sense where a power user has discovered a lot of the features they wish to use, and would like to see the overlay to learn more features.

For SMART8 "Cater for diverse mobile environments", the HCI experts pointed out that there are too many contexts to be able to cater for them all. While this is true, much can be done to cater for the most common mobile contexts. Other HCI experts pointed out that it was the responsibility of the operating system to adjust screen and sound settings to the environment.

Moving onto SMART10, several HCI experts pointed out that sensors and other smartphone features such as the camera and sensors may not be needed for standard applications and may only be needed for certain applications such as context-aware applications and that the heuristic title sounded as if sensors must be used. This would mean that evaluators would need to highlight the lack of sensor use as a problem even if the application did not require their use. However, rather than remove this heuristic, it was instead modified as a call-to-action to consider using the camera and sensors to lessen users' workloads where possible.

There were no comments specifically about creating an aesthetic and identifiable icon, yet it can be seen from the results that some HCI experts did not deem SMART11 as important. As the majority of HCI experts felt this heuristic was either useful or very useful, it was decided to leave the heuristic as is.

Finally, while SMART5 was deemed 'Useful' / 'Very Useful' by most HCI Experts, several experts commented on the need to create separate heuristics from this single heuristic. To this end, SMART5 was broken up into:

— SMART5: Each interface should focus on one task;
— SMART6: Design a visually pleasing interface;
— SMART7: Intuitive interfaces make for easier user journeys.

The initial heuristics SMART6 to 11 were therefore re-numbered SMART8 to 13.

8   Final Native Smartphone Mobile Application Heuristics

Following the aggregation, analysis and implementation of quantitative and qualitative feedback received during the HCI expert survey, the final set of SMART heuristics for the usability evaluation of smartphone-deployed mobile applications were defined as:

SMART1: Provide immediate notification of application status – Ensure the mobile application user is informed of the application status immediately and as long as is necessary. Where appropriate do this non-intrusively, such as displaying notifications within the status bar.

SMART2: Use a theme and consistent terms, as well as conventions and standards familiar to the user – Use a theme for the mobile application to ensure different screens look alike. Also create a style guide from which words, phrases and concepts familiar to the user will be applied consistently throughout the interface, using a natural and logical order. Use platform conventions and standards that users have come to expect in a mobile application such as the same effects when gestures are used.

SMART3: Prevent errors where possible; Assist users should an error occur – Ensure the mobile application is error-proofed as much as is possible. Should an error occur, let the user know what the error is in a way they will understand, and offer advice in how they might fix the error or otherwise proceed.

SMART4: Display an overlay pointing out the main features when appropriate or requested – An overlay pointing out the main features and how to interact with the application allows first-time users to get up-and-running quickly, after which they can explore the mobile application at their leisure. This overlay or a form of help system should also be displayed when requested.

SMART5: Each interface should focus on one task – Being focusing on one task ensures that mobile interfaces are less cluttered and simple to the point of only having the absolute necessary elements onscreen to complete that task. This also allows the interface to be glanceable to users that are interrupted frequently.

SMART6: Design a visually pleasing interface – Mobile interfaces that are attractive are far more memorable and are therefore used more often. Users are also more forgiving of attractive interfaces.

SMART7: Intuitive interfaces make for easier user journeys – Mobile interfaces should be easy-to-learn whereby next steps are obvious. This allows users to more easily complete their tasks.

SMART8: Design a clear navigable path to task completion – Users should be able to see right away how they can interact with the application and navigate their way to task completion.

SMART9: Allow configuration options and shortcuts – Depending on the target user, the mobile application might allow configuration options and shortcuts to the most important information and frequent tasks, including the ability to configure according to contextual needs.

SMART10: Cater for diverse mobile environments – Diverse environments consist of different types of context of use such as poor lighting conditions and high ambient noise are common ailments mobile users have to face every day. While the operating system should allow the user to change the interface brightness and sound settings, developers can assist users even more for example by allowing them to display larger buttons and allowing multimodal input and output options.

SMART11: Facilitate easier input – Mobile devices are difficult to use from a content input perspective. Ensure users can input content more easily and accurately by, for instance displaying keyboard buttons that are as large as possible, as well as allowing multimodal input and by keeping form fields to a minimum.

SMART12: Use the camera, microphone and sensors when appropriate to lessen the users' workload – Consider the use of the camera, microphone and sensors to lessen the users' workload. For instance, by using GPS so the user knows where they are and how to get there they need to go, or by using OCR and the camera to digitally capture the information the user needs to input, by allowing use of the microphone to input content which would save the user from having to type on the small keyboard.

SMART13: Create an aesthetic and identifiable icon – An icon for a mobile application should be aesthetic and identifiable as this is what a user sees when searching the device interface for the application they wish to launch and when scanning through app stores it will be the first item they see before the application title, description and screenshots.

9   Conclusion and Future Work

The traditional heuristic method is an inexpensive, highly effective and intuitive method of usability inspection. However, much of Nielsen's and Molich's traditional heuristics are too general for the evaluation of applications that have emerged after these heuristics were first created in 1990, such as native smartphone mobile applications.

In this work, Nielsen's and Molich's heuristics as well as findings from the HCI literature were used as a basis for the development of thirteen heuristics tailored to the inspection of native smartphone mobile applications. Initial results were very encouraging, as the heuristics developed as part of this work received positive reviews from a group of sixty HCI experts in eighteen countries.

Much of the literature has evolved based on expert reviews and empirical studies. The next stage of this work will be to empirically evaluate the usage of the heuristics. It is hoped that this work will contribute towards the development of a set of usability heuristics for native smartphone applications that can be applied widely by HCI researchers, educators and practitioners.

Acknowledgments. The authors are grateful to the sixty HCI experts that participated in the heuristics review and to the School of Computer Science, University of Hertfordshire for providing funding.

References

1. Rogers, Y., Sharp, H., Preece, J.: Interaction Design: Beyond Human - Computer Interaction. John Wiley & Sons (2011)
2. Coursaris, C.K., Kim, D.J.: A Meta-Analytical Review of Empirical Mobile Usability Studies. Journal of Usability Studies 6(3), 117–171 (2011)
3. Bernhaupt, R., Mihalic, K., Obrist, M.: Usability Evaluation Methods for Mobile Applications. In: Lumsden, J. (ed.) Handbook of Research on User Interface Design and Evaluation for Mobile Technology. IGI Global (2008)
4. Nielsen, J., Molich, R.: Heuristic evaluation of user interfaces. In: Proceedings of the SIGCHI Conference on Human Factors in Computing Systems, pp. 249–256 (1990)
5. Jeffries, R., Miller, J.R., Wharton, C., Uyeda, K.: User interface evaluation in the real world: a comparison of four techniques. In: Proceedings of the SIGCHI Conference on Human Factors in Computing Systems, pp. 119–124 (1991)
6. Gould, J.D., Lewis, C.: Designing for usability: key principles and what designers think. Communications of the ACM 28, 300–311 (1985)
7. Gerhardt-Powals, J.: Cognitive engineering principles for enhancing human-computer performance. International Journal of Human-Computer Interaction 8, 189–211 (1996)
8. Ketola, P., Röykkee, M.: The three facets of usability in mobile handsets. In: CHI 2001 Workshop: Mobile Communications: Understanding Users, Adoption & Design (2001)
9. Po, S., Howard, S., Vetere, F., Skov, M.B.: Heuristic evaluation and mobile usability: Bridging the realism gap. In: Brewster, S., Dunlop, M.D. (eds.) Mobile HCI 2004. LNCS, vol. 3160, pp. 49–60. Springer, Heidelberg (2004)
10. Bertini, E., Gabrielli, S., Kimani, S.: Appropriating and assessing heuristics for mobile computing. In: Proceedings of the Working Conference on Advanced Visual Interfaces, pp. 119–126 (2006)
11. Inostroza, R., Rusu, C., Roncagliolo, S., Jimenez, C., Rusu, V.: Usability Heuristics for Touchscreen-based Mobile Devices. In: Proceedings of the Ninth International Conference on Information Technology: New Generations (ITNG), pp. 662–667. IEEE, Las Vegas (2012)
12. Robbins, N.B.: Creating More Effective Graphs. John Wiley & Sons (2012)
13. Petrillo, F., Spritzer, A.S., Freitas, C.D.S., Pimenta, M.: Interactive analysis of Likert scale data using a multichart visualization tool. In: Proceedings of the 10th Brazilian Symposium on Human Factors in Computing Systems and the 5th Latin American Conference on Human-Computer Interaction, pp. 358–365 (2011)

Common Industry Format (CIF) Report Customization for UX Heuristic Evaluation

Llúcia Masip, Marta Oliva, and Toni Granollers

University of Lleida, Jaume II 69, 25001 Lleida, Spain
{lluciamaar,oliva,tonig}@diei.udl.cat

Abstract. The ISO/IEC 25062:2006 standard presents the Common Industry Format template for the user test results. This standard only considers usability results of a specific evaluation technique: the user test. Nowadays, more aspects apart from usability are considered to get a product quality. In addition, other evaluation methodologies are also very used and different types of results can be obtained (formative/summative and qualitative/quantitative). This research proposed how to adapt the Common Industry Format report for the heuristic evaluation methodology and considering more aspects apart from usability.

Keywords: CIF, ISO/IEC 25062:2006, customization, heuristic evaluation, UX.

1 Introduction

The Common Industry Format (CIF) for Usability Test Reports is a template for reporting usability test that provides a standardized document to be used by companies and User eXperience (UX) practitioners when documenting usability evaluations. This international standard is intended to be used for: (i) Reducing training time for UX practitioners: an individual only needs to learn to use one form regardless of how many companies he or she works for [1]. (ii) Increasing the communication between vendors and purchasing organizations sharing a common language and expectations [1]. (iii) Providing a guide for expert and non-expert organizations [1]. (iv).Providing a comparable report with other similar ones. (v) Presenting a useful template that can be used in the results of all different and specific cases.

Besides CIF template is the best contribution to standardize usability test reports, it presents three challenges in order to be applicable in real context. The first challenge is the applicability of these kinds of reports in more facets than usability. Usability is the most considered facet in the development process of an interactive system, but up to now other facets have been emerging [2]. Therefore, it is necessary to consider in the CIF report the chance of adapting the results of a test according to other facets such as security, emotional, cross-cultural, among other.

Second challenge is concerning the final purpose of the CIF report. As is explained in "Audience" section of the standard [1], the information that the CIF shows is

A. Marcus (Ed.): DUXU 2014, Part I, LNCS 8517, pp. 475–483, 2014.
© Springer International Publishing Switzerland 2014

summative because it tries to present a summary of the results. However, these days, and bearing in mind the competitive sector, much more specific information should be provided to reach more details about the identification of problems. Therefore, the CIF should also include formative information. Furthermore, CIF template has been thought for reporting user tests. But the number of methodologies for improving an interactive system is wide extensive, then CIF template should be customized for reporting more evaluation methodologies. This is the third challenge.

In summary, the main goal of this communication is to present the adaptation of the CIF template to the three challenges introduced above and considering the heuristic evaluation as the methodology to get UX evaluation results. In the following section our methodology to carry out a heuristic evaluation is presented. Then, a comparison between the user test and heuristic evaluation is detailed. Following this section, the state of the art about some CIF customizations are presented. Later, the differences applied in the CIF template updating some sections of the standard report. Afterwards, how to get this new template using our web-based resource called Open-HEREDEUX is described [10]. Finally, conclusions and future work are explained.

1.1   Our Methodology for UX Evaluations Based on Heuristics

Heuristic Evaluation (HE) was created by Johnson, Ravden and Clegg [3] but it was promoted by Nielsen and Molich [4] only one year later. The methodology is divided into three main steps: the organization of the evaluation, the evaluation of the heuristics and the extraction of results. In the first step, the administrator of the evaluation should select the best heuristics for the specific interface, should choose who will be the evaluators of the interactive system and he or she should determine the severity factors that evaluators will use to score each heuristic (by default Nielsen's scale [4] is considered in the heuristic evaluation). In the second step, each evaluator scores each heuristic using the severity factors selected previously. Once all evaluators have scored all heuristics, results are taken. Usually in the third step, qualitative and formative results are obtained according to the scores of the evaluators and the observations that they made in the scoring process.

However HE is one of the most used methodologies, it presents some deficiencies that induce a slower and more expensive process. Two are the most relevant: (i) The first deficiency is the non-existence of a repository or library containing specific guidelines (heuristics) saved in. Usually, whoever plans to carry out a heuristic evaluation needs to review the literature, select different sources of heuristic lists and, then, elaborate manually the most appropriate sets of heuristics to determine the best guidelines for every specific interactive system.

(ii) Another relevant deficiency appears at the end of the process, when obtaining the evaluation results. HE traditionally presents qualitative and formative results according to the evaluator's scores and their observations during the scoring process. However, quantitative and summative results are sometimes achieved because the scientific community aims for objectivity [5] which cannot be obtained using qualitative results.

Then, one of our main goals is to solve the heuristic evaluation deficiencies defining a methodology that semi-automates some parts of the heuristic evaluation. Our new proposal includes the repository of information, the heuristic suggestion process, the realization of the evaluation and the extraction of UX results in a standard report.

A repository of information is essential for reaching an optimum process for suggesting heuristics. Therefore, heuristics are the most valuable data that should be related to the components, features, functionalities and UX facets. Using this relation and considering that an interactive system is defined through components, functionalities, features and UX facets, the selection of the most suitable heuristics for a system is evident. [6]

Regarding the suggestion for heuristics, our new proposed methodology solves one of the main deficiencies of the heuristic evaluation methodology. It details for the suggestion of the best heuristics for a specific interactive system using different considerations such as different goals for design or evaluation, different types of heuristics according to the receiver [7], financial constraints (such as the UX degree [8]) and the possibility of documenting conflicting heuristics [9]. Then, these two first stages of the methodology provide the needed conditions to facilitate the evaluation process per se. This stage is not really automatic or optimized but due to the consideration of the rest of the methodology, the scoring of each heuristic becomes a very easy step.

Finally, the last part of the methodology is the extraction of results. Our methodology proposes the automatic process to get the results and also the automatic downloaded report. The most general goals of this automatic downloaded report are: to facilitate the interpretation of these results to improve the specific interactive system, and to compare these results in the possible following evaluations of improved versions and other systems, for instance systems from rivals. We are working on the definition of different UX measures to solve this gap.

In this paper we will focus on the presentation of the UX evaluation results using the heuristic evaluation and presenting the results through the ISO/IEC 25062:2006 standard (Software engineering -- Software product Quality Requirements and Evaluation (SQuaRE) -- Common Industry Format (CIF) for usability test reports). Thus, the next section presents the main difference between user test (technique used in the CIF report) and heuristic evaluation (our base to propose a new UX evaluation methodology based on heuristics).

1.2   User Test vs. Heuristic Evaluation

User test and heuristic evaluation are the most used methodologies to improve the product quality [11]. The most important differences among both methods are detailed in the following paragraphs.

Regarding the classification of usability evaluation methodologies, the most used and general classifications are: inquiry, test and inspection evaluation methodologies [12] [13]. User test is a test evaluation methodology where representative users work on typical tasks using the system (or the prototype) and the evaluators use the results to see how the user interface supports the users doing their tasks. On the other hand, heuristic evaluation is an inspection technique performed by usability specialists that examine usability aspects (from a preselected list of guidelines or heuristics) of a user interface.

Another important difference is concerning the stakeholders of the methodology. User test is prepared by a project manager but it is performed by real end users. In contrast, heuristic evaluation is also prepared by a project manager but it is performed by expert users. Therefore, heuristic evaluation needs expert users understanding those that know very well the heuristic evaluation methodology and/or the interactive system.

In addition, the specific execution of both techniques presents a main difference. User test introduces tasks that users have to perform to get the usability problems of the product. The evaluators of the heuristic evaluation do not need tasks. They usually freely explore the interface for detecting as many problems as possible considering the heuristics of the evaluation.

The execution costs of both techniques are considerably different. Usually, the budged of heuristic evaluation is cheaper than user test, mainly because heuristic evaluation does not need end users. The time to recruit users represents the mainly part of the user test budget. So, only for this reason user test is considered as one of the most expensive techniques. Table 1 summarizes the differences among both methodologies.

Table 1. User test vs heuristic evaluation

Methodology	Type	Users	Procedure	Budget
User test	Test	End and real users	Task oriented	Expensive
Heuristic evaluation	Inspection	Expert users	Free navigation	Cheap

2   CIF Customization

Certainly, there are few references about how to customize, adapt or modify the CIF for a specific real context of use. The National Institute of Standards and Technology [14] changed some sections and information of the CIF template to adapt it forvoting systems. In the same way, another customization done by the same institute is in the electronic health sector [15]. Furthermore, a research to adapt the CIF to the heuristic evaluation methodology is presented in [16]. Using the heuristics evaluation methodology some formative results appear in the CIF report. However, the most informative report is the one presented in [17].

Due to the three of the needed improvements, an adaptation of the CIF report is proposed. Next table presents the current sections of the CIF template and checked with those changed in our proposal. Then more details about the changes done in each section are described.

Table 2. The updated sections of the CIF

CIF section		Is it changed?
Executive summary		No
Introduction	Full product description	No
	Test objectives	No
Method	Participants	**Yes**
	Context of product use in the test	**Yes**
	Participant's computing environment	No
	Test administrator tools	No
	Experimental design	**Yes**
	Usability metrics	**Yes**
Results	Data analysis	**Yes**
	Presentation of results	**Yes**

2.1 Method Section

The information regarding the evaluation process is described. The changed sections of the CIF report here detailed are: participants, context of product use in the test, experimental design and usability metrics.

Participants. In this section of the CIF template, information about the users is required. Printed version of the standard includes end users whom did the test. Information about their specific profile is asked for. In our proposal, this section needs to include to different user profiles: End users: If the UX would be considered, the end user should be included in the development process of an interactive system. For this reason, the end user who is not an expert in the methodology based on heuristics is considered in the report. Therefore, the novelty is not in the consideration of the end user in the report but the consideration of the end user in the methodology used for achieving formative results. Furthermore, end users will provide information about their likes and feeling to get results for the emotional UX facet. Expert users: Expert users are those users who know the methodology that is used to evaluate the interactive system. For instance, interface designers, UX researchers or project managers. The users are the traditional evaluators proposed in the heuristic evaluation.

In our methodology, this information is obtained from two pre-evaluation questionnaires that each evaluator should fill in before starting the evaluation. The CIF reports this information in two different tables. The table referring to the end users includes information about gender, age, education, computer experience and product or interactive system experience. The table referring to the expert users presents gender, age, education, computer experience, years in HCI and the number of evaluations done.

Context of Product Use in the Test. In this section, CIF template includes different subsection. Our focus is in the subsection called "Tasks". There, many details about the tasks that users have to perform are described.

Tasks subsection was removed in our proposal because heuristic evaluation methodology does not use tasks. End users and expert users use the interactive system freely.

Experimental Design. In the same way as the last point, this section has a subsection called "Participant task instructions". So for the same reason commented above, the subsection called "Participants task instructions" was also removed.

Usability Metrics. The CIF template calls this section as "Usability metrics" and metrics for effectiveness, efficiency and satisfaction are proposed.

Bearing in mind our approach towards the UX, our proposal calls this section "UX metrics". In addition, the metrics for effectiveness, efficiency and satisfaction have been substituted by new ones. (We are working on these UX metrics.)

2.2 Results Section

This section describes how the results of the evaluation are provided.

Data Analysis. In this section, the CIF template proposes to present enough detail to allow replication of the data analysis methods by another organization if the evaluation is repeated. Specifically, it details the data collection (the differences between the data that was planned to be collected and the data that was actually collected), the data scoring (the mapping between the data values that were collected and the values used in further analysis) and data reduction (the method used to compute the measure of central tendency and to characterize the variation in the data). Finally, the statistical analysis used to analyze the data is explained in detail.

Severity factors used to score each heuristics are presented in our proposal. Heuristic evaluation uses impact and frequency defined by Nielsen as the severity to score the heuristics. Therefore, the results analysis is based on the scorings of each heuristic per each evaluator using these severity factors.

Presentation of Results. CIF template proposes specific tables for every usability metric and for every end user. Obviously, if the metrics to analyze the UX are changed, the presentation of the results is also modified.

Qualitative and formative results are presented in our proposal as an improvement list for the interactive system. This improvement list includes the whole set of violated heuristics. Furthermore, quantitative and summative results are shown through the UX measures. These quantitative and summative results enable the comparison of different versions of the same interactive system and it permits comparison among the same types of interactive systems.

3   How to Get the CIF Template through Open-HEREDEUX

Then, based on the heuristic evaluation methodology, OPEN-HEREDEUX is presented as a solution to consider the UX in an interactive system design or evaluation process. OPEN-HEREDEUX is the short name for our proposal: "OPEN HEuristic Resource for Designing and Evaluating User eXperience". Figure 1 shows the Open-HEREDEUX overview. Open-HEREDEUX is available on this url: www.grihotools.udl.cat/openheredeux.

Open Repository (Fig 1- 1) is provided with all the necessary information to achieve the set of heuristics as complete and minimum as possible.

Adviser of heuristics is the second component (Fig 1- 2). It intends to be a tool whose objective is to propose, for a specific interactive system, the most appropriate list of heuristics to be used. It is suitable for such usages as recommendation principles in a design phase or as evaluation principles in a UX evaluation based on heuristics. Therefore, heuristic suggestions can be used either as a list of recommendations to design a specific interactive system or as an input for the next, and third, component: Scorer of heuristics, which is in charge of carrying out the realization of the evaluation (Fig 1- 3). Finally, Results Analyzer is the last component. It provides quantitative/qualitative and formative/summative data interpretation (Fig 1- 4).

New CIF template report is obtained by Result Analyzer component. It provides the report in an editable and standard format file. The main tasks that the project manager can carry out using Results Analyzer are: (i) Download the new report. (ii) Upload the previous downloaded (or not) report for saving it in Open Repository. (iii) Download the previous uploaded report.

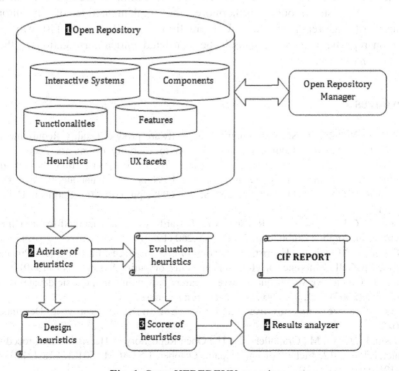

Fig. 1. Open-HEREDEUX overview

In reference to qualitative and formative results, a list of improvements according to the evaluators' observations and heuristics scored incorrectly will be achieved. They are the ones that designers should apply to the interactive system to improve it. Apart from qualitative and formative results, quantitative and summative ones should be presented because these will attempt to show the UX degree for every interactive system [8]. If quantitative and summative results are achieved, UX experts will have a standard method or a possible certification to compare evaluations and see which interactive system provides users with the best experience. Quantitative results will get an objective measure that is impossible to obtain due to the subjectivity of qualitative results.

4   Conclusions and Future Work

CIF report is a very useful document to present quality results but it should be customized to enable the better description in different context of use. We proposed the customization of the CIF template in three ways: the adaptation to the heuristic evaluation methodology, the consideration of more aspects apart from the usability and the proposal of summative/formative and qualitative/quantitative results in the report.

Our customized proposal do not change the essence of the CIF template report, it only includes and changes some sections and subsection to provide with an added value to UX result report. Furthermore, the implementation of an automatic generation of this report provides UX practitioners with a very fast way to get evaluation reports. This process could be translated into a certification of the UX evaluation in the near future.

References

1. ISO/IEC 25062:2006 Software engineering. Software product Quality Requirements and Evaluation (SQuaRE). Common Industry Format for usability test reports (2006)
2. Masip, L., Oliva, M., Granollers, T.: User experience specification through quality attributes. In: Campos, P., Graham, N., Jorge, J., Nunes, N., Palanque, P., Winckler, M. (eds.) INTERACT 2011, Part IV. LNCS, vol. 6949, pp. 656–660. Springer, Heidelberg (2011)
3. Johnson, G.I., Clegg, C.W., Ravden, S.J.: Towards a practical method for user interface evaluation. Applied Ergonomics 20(4), 255–260 (1989)
4. Nielsen, J., Molich, R.: Heuristic evaluation of user interfaces. In: CHI 1990: Proceedings of the SIGCHI Conference on Human Factors in Computing Systems, NY (1990)
5. Neil, J.: Qualitative versus quantitative research: Key points in a classic debate. Research methods (2007), http://wilderdom.com/research/QualitativeVersusQuantitativeResearch.html (last visit: December 19, 2012)
6. Masip, L., Oliva, M., Granollers, T.: The Open Repository of Heuristics. In: Procedings of Interaccion 2012, Elche, Alicante, Spain, October 3-5. ACM (2012); 978-1-4503-1314-8/12/10 (Copyright 2012)

7. Masip, L., Granollers, T., Oliva, M.: A Heuristic Evaluation Experiment To Validate The New Set of Usability Heuristics. In: Proceedings of 8th International Conference on Information Technology: New Generations, Las Vegas (2011); 978-0-7695-4367-3/11 © 2011 IEEE

8. Masip, L., Granollers, T., Oliva, M.: User Experience Degree and Time Restrictions as Financial Constraints in the evaluation methodology based on heuristics. Accepted paper in 6th Latin American Conference on Human Computer Interaction (2013)

9. Masip, L., Martinie, C., Winckler, M., Palanque, P., Granollers, T., Oliva, M.: A design process for exhibiting design choices and trade-offs in (potentially) conflicting user interface guidelines. In: Winckler, M., Forbrig, P., Bernhaupt, R. (eds.) HCSE 2012. LNCS, vol. 7623, pp. 53–71. Springer, Heidelberg (2012)

10. Masip, L., Oliva, M., Granollers, T.: OPEN-HEREDEUX: open heuristic resource for designing and evaluating user experience. In: Campos, P., Graham, N., Jorge, J., Nunes, N., Palanque, P., Winckler, M. (eds.) INTERACT 2011, Part IV. LNCS, vol. 6949, pp. 418–421. Springer, Heidelberg (2011)

11. "UPA, Salary Survey" Usability Professional's Association (2009),
    http://usabilityprofessionals.org/usability_resources/
    surveys/2009salarysurvey_PUBLIC.pdf

12. Nielsen, J., Mack, R.L.: Usability Inspection Methods. John Wiley & Sons, New York (1994) ISBN: 0-471-01877-5

13. Dix, A., Finlay, J., Abowd, G., Beale, R.: Human-Computer Interaction. Prentice Hall (2009)

14. National Institute of Standards and Technology. Voluntary Voting System Guidelines Recommendations to the Election Assistance Commission. Modified CIF template for voting system test laboratories- (August 2007)

15. Schumacher, M., Lowry, S.: Customized Common Industry Format Template for Electronic Health Record Usability Testing. National Institute of Standards and Technology Interagency/Internal Report (NISTIR) – 7742 (November 16, 2010)

16. von Baggo, K., Johnston, L., Burmeister, O.K., Bentley, T.: Common Industry Format: Meeting Educational Objectives and Student Needs? In: Masoodian, M., Jones, S., Rogers, B. (eds.) APCHI 2004. LNCS, vol. 3101, pp. 521–530. Springer, Heidelberg (2004)

17. Formative Test Reports. Journal of Usability Studies 1(1), 27–45 (November 2005)

Evaluating the Usability on Multimodal Interfaces:
A Case Study on Tablets Applications

Edvar Vilar Neto[1] and Fábio F.C. Campos[2]

[1] UFPE, Informatics Center, Recife-PE, Brazil
[2] UFPE, Department of Design, Recife-PE, Brazil
excvn@cin.ufpe.br, fc2005@gmail.com

Abstract. Usability has become the main quality attribute on the development of digital devices. Meanwhile, the new interaction paradigms represent a great challenge for usability. Traditional methods for usability evaluation may not be appropriated to the nature of these new interaction models. This paper introduces a new set of usability heuristics for multimodal paradigm, specially multitouch and speech-based interaction. We analyzed traditional usability heuristics, characteristics of multitouch and speech-based interaction, and guidelines for developers, aiming to reach a satisfactory result. A comparative case study between our proposal and Nielsen's heuristics is then conducted.

Keywords: usability heuristics, new usability, multimodal interaction.

1 Introduction

Usability has become a relevant topic in the literature of human-computer interaction. The ISO/IEC standard defines usability as the capability that an interactive system offers the users, allowing them to perform tasks effectively, efficiently and satisfactorily, in a specified context of use. Currently, evaluating usability can be considered a key point of user-centered technologies [1]. In general, there are two methods of usability evaluation: user tests and inspection. User tests are powerful methods to identify usability problems, but they can be very expensive and time-consuming because it requires collecting users to testing application in specified physical places [2]. Heuristic evaluation is a method of usability inspection often used because it is performed by experts, which makes it cheaper, easy to be executed and able to find many usability problems. By this method, expert evaluators systematically inspect and evaluate a user interface according to usability principles or heuristics [2-4]. Usability inspections are well documented and many publications describe their use and methods. Meanwhile, most of them focus on traditional interaction paradigms, such as WIMP (Windows, Icons, Menus and Pointers). However, there are many others interaction styles, which possess very different characteristics when compared with traditional paradigms. Some new interaction paradigms are already present for many people. Devices such as computer tablets have multitouch and speech-based interaction, i.e. a multimodal interaction. According to IDC (International Data Corporation), the number of tablets sold in

A. Marcus (Ed.): DUXU 2014, Part I, LNCS 8517, pp. 484–495, 2014.

2013 must overcome desktops (growth of 48,7% compared to a decline of 4,3%, respectively). These devices have a relatively new interaction style, and hence, a great challenge to traditional usability methods [5].Therefore, designers and developers will probably adapt the traditional usability literature to create ad hoc methods, many of which are incompatible and incoherent. Thus, it is extremely important to review whether conventional methods of usability evaluation possess a satisfactory and consistent performance for this emerging scenario, and also investigate ways to contribute to a new usability [6]. In this paper, we introduce a new set of heuristics for multimodal interaction focused on tablet applications. In the next section we show concepts of multimodal paradigm. Then, we describe the process that we used to develop the heuristics. We analyse traditional usability heuristics, characteristics of multitouch and speech interaction, and guidelines for developers, aiming to reach a satisfactorily result. Finally, we compare the new set generated with Nielsen's Heuristics in a case study.

2   Multimodal Interaction

Multimodal interactions refer to a combination of inputs and outputs of several sensory modalities (hearing, smell, taste, touch, sight) as part of a more natural computer communication. We can have, for example, inputs and/or outputs via voice, exploring our sensory variety in parallel or sequentially, as part of an interaction that promotes complementary or redundant information to the user [7-10]. Just recently, multimodal interaction systems have gained a maturity level that allows them to be widely applied. However, there is no specific model or interaction style for an appropriate integration among different emerging modalities. Multimodal interfaces still represent a big challenge in technical and human factors terms, which can affect the traditional usability concepts [10-12].

Nevertheless, there are many opportunities to be explored. Multimodal platforms have potential to create powerful user interfaces and channels of interaction. The use of different modalities can demand less cognitive load from the user as well as bring a better recognition performance and interpretation of inputs by the system. In the same way, information provided from the system can be better adapted for people and the context of use whether several outputs are available. The development of multimodal platforms has provided this, mainly by combining the use of multitouch gestures and speech [11-14]. Multitouch technologies allow people to experience more freedom within a simpler and more coherent way of interaction. This interaction provides richer inputs from users into interactive system when compared with single-touch interfaces. However, in spite of its capacity to bring a fuller interaction control, designing gesture-based intuitive interfaces for complex systems is more difficult [15, 16]. According to Norman, gestures are not natural. Cultural factors can hinder the understanding of certain gestures in different places in the world. Thus, gesture-based interfaces require feedbacks and these are only possible with elements of conventional interfaces, such as menus, popups, tutorials and other forms of feedback from Graphical User Interfaces (GUI) [17]. However, this statement only reinforces that this type of interaction is converging to multimodal nature. According to Pfleging, users do not have great difficulties in controlling commands with gestures. Actually, they have a high concordance of movements between them [11]. This, combined with other types of interaction such as speech-based, can enhance the user experience. Speech recognition transforms spoken words from users to readable inputs for machines. These inputs allow systems to identify what people are talking and convert the spoken words from users into commands, and then produce outputs which can also be spoken [14]. Though there are still many challenges with regard to the efficient use of this modality, speech interactions can reduce the amount of interaction time when compared to others mechanisms, allowing people to focus on primary tasks. Other advantages of using speech include reduced learning time (because it is a natural method of communication) and, consequently, increased work productivity [14, 18, 19].

3   Compiling Usability Heuristics for Multimodal Interaction

To reach the new set of multimodal heuristics, we followed a similar method proposed by Rusu [20]. We have gathered some traditional usability heuristics from the usual literature, characteristics of multitouch and speech-based interaction, and some guidelines for developers. The following steps were conducted:

- Step 1: an heuristics review was done from the literature;
- Step 2: characteristics of multitouch and speech interaction were surveyed;
- Step 3: guidelines for developers from iOS, Android and Microsoft Surface documentation were examined;
- Step 4: a crossing between them was performed and the new set of heuristics was compiled.

These steps made it possible to understand this scenario and the current relationship between the new paradigm and conventional usability heuristics. After the last step, a case study with expert evaluators is executed, comparing our proposal with a traditional set of heuristics.

3.1   Step 1 – Heuristic Review

At first, a critical review of the most usual heuristics was performed. For this, we have listed three traditional sets of heuristics from the traditional literature, which are: Nielsen's Heuristics, Norman's Principles of Usability, and the 8 main Ergonomic Criteria by Bastien and Scapin (table 1) [21-23]. With the heuristics at hand, we could note that Nielsen's heuristics included the others into their criteria. That indicates its generic nature and how it can be considered sufficient when compared with the conventional literature. Because of this, we will take Nielsen's heuristics as a starting point to generate new heuristics.

Table 1. Some traditional usability heuristics

Nielsen's Heuristics	Norman's Principles	Ergonomic Criteria by Bastien and Scapin
Visibility of system status	Use both knowledge in the world and knowledge in the head.	Guidance
Match between system and the real world	Simplify the structure of tasks	Workload
Consistency and standards	Get the mappings right	Adaptability
Error prevention	Exploit the power of constraints, both natural and artificial	Error management
Recognition rather than recall	Design for error	Consistency
Flexibility and efficiency of use	When all else fails, standardize.	Significance of codes
Aesthetic and minimalist design		Compatibility
Help users recognize, diagnose, and recover from errors		
Help and Documentation		

3.2   Step 2 – Characteristics of Multitouch and Speech Interaction

In general, multi-touch gestures-based devices – such as cell phones, tablets and tabletops – have common shared characteristics that make it possible for them to be included in the same category. However, they can differ in some aspects. Mobile devices can be categorized by their reduced screen size, processing power and limited memory, and because their buttons possess more than one functionality. Others characteristics in relation to user interaction are: used mainly with hands, wireless, support to internet connection and possibility of adding new application [24, 25]. Considering this scenario, Inostroza and collaborators proposed a set of heuristics focused on touchscreen-based mobile devices. The study focus mainly on touch-based phones and it is based on Nielsen's heuristics. The heuristics are: (1) visibility of system status; (2) match between system and the real world; (3) user control and freedom; (4) consistency and standards; (5) error prevention; (6) minimize the user's memory load; (7) customization and shortcuts; (8) aesthetic and minimalist design; (9) help users recognize, diagnose and recover from errors; (10) help and documentation; and (11) physical interaction and ergonomics [26]. Apted and collaborators exposed specific characteristics of tabletops: collaborative interaction, context of use, orientation, tabletop size, human reach, use of table area, clutter and limited inputs. The authors conduct an extension of the guidelines proposed by Stedmon and collaborators, resulting in a set of heuristics for interaction evaluation on tabletops: (1) design independently of table size; (2) support reorientation; (3) use large selection points; (4) minimize human reach; (5) use large selection points; (6) manage interface clutter; (7) use table space efficiently; and (8) support private and group interaction [27]. Multitouch-based devices as tablets are a midway between mobile devices and tabletops. Thus, it is critical to consider these three classes when generating heuristics for a larger class of multitouch-based interfaces. We reached for the general characteristics of multitouch interaction: (1) Gestures-based interaction; (2) Context of use is important; (3) Orientation can change; (4) Human range can be considered; (5) Use of screen area; (6) Content can be organized; (7) Limited inputs; (8) Reduced processing power and memory; (9) Connectivity; (10) Expandability; (11) Possibility of collaborative interaction.

Speech-Based Interaction. Robbe proposed a study of speech and gesture interaction for general public. According to the author, linguistics constraints can be easily assimilated by users in a multimodal environment since they do not generate restrictions on semantic expressions of the users, which may lead to side effects from users [28]. In a later study, Robbe and collaborators noticed that the users understood the linguistic limitations that they should fulfill progressively when they interacted with a multimodal environment. Another result showed that the restrictions did not reduce significantly the efficiency of the interaction, but they could be interfered in multimodal interaction [29].According to Stedmon and collaborators, people use shorter commands and without relative terms when they are confronted with a machine, because they think that it is not capable to understand complex inputs. This can take more time when compared to a human-human interaction, since users ended up repeating commands to complete the task. Another study conducted by the same authors shows that, in spite of people generally using longer and more complex speeches in human-human interaction, the time used to perform tasks and the number of commands are shorter. As a result of this study, we can take the following criteria: (1) more generic and general vocabulary; (2) speech for simpler and direct tasks; and (3) speech should be an alternative input [30]. This way, we note that speech restrictions do not interfere with the efficiency of the interaction. However, a more generic and freer vocabulary can be more appropriate for a multimodal interaction. It also suggests that speech can be offered along with other input methods, allowing more flexibility to users and enhancing a multimodal interaction nature.

3.3   Step 3 – Guidelines from Developer Documentations

Because of the recent nature of multimodal paradigm, collecting data from developer documentations can be considered a good way of analyzing multitouch and speech-based models. This way, we have collected the main guidelines for designing and developing of multitouch devices, such as smartphones, tablets, and tabletops. It is important to remember that these devices also have speech-based interaction. Thus, we gathered guidelines from Android, iOS and Microsoft Surface documentations. We called each guideline as follow (table 2) [31-33]: These criteria will guide us when making a correlation between traditional heuristics and multitouch and speech interactions in the next step.

Table 2. Design and interaction guidelines for developers, divided by initials and colors

Android Guidelines	iOS Guidelines	Microsoft Surface Guidelines
Android Design Principles (ADP)	iOS Design Principles (IDP)	Surface Design Principles (SDP)
	iOS Interaction Guidelines (IIG)	Surface Interaction Design Guidelines (SID)
		Surface Visual & Motion Design Guidelines (SVMD)
		Surface Sound Design Guidelines (SSD)
		Surface Language & Text Design Guidelines (SLTD)
		Surface Input Methods (SIM)

3.4   Step 4 – Compiling Usability Heuristics for Multimodal Interaction

In this step, we crossed the developer guidelines gathered with Nielsen's heuristics and the characteristics surveyed, and then we compared the result in order to generate new heuristics for multimodal interaction. We have the first crossing in table 3.

Table 3. Crossing between Nielsen's Heuristics and Developer Guidelines

Nielsen's Heuristics (NH)	Developer Guidelines
NH1	ADP1, ADP9, ADP15, IDP4, IIG4, IIG12, IIG20, SDP5, SPI4, SPI6, SVMD8
NH2	IDP1, IDP5, IIG6, IIG16, SDP3, SVMD3, SSD2, SSD3
NH3	ADP7, IDP6, IDP4
NH4	ADP11, ADP13, IDP2, IDP6, IIG5, IIG15, IIG21, IIG27, SSD4
NH5	IIG26
NH6	ADP4, ADP10, ADP16, IIG5, IIG7, IIG8, IIG22, IIG24, IIG25, SIM2
NH7	ADP3, ADP15, SID1, SID3, SIM2
NH8	ADP5, ADP6, ADP8, ADP12, ADP17, IIG1, IIG2, IIG3, IIG5, IIG14, IIG17, IIG23, IIG28, IIG29, IIG30, SDP1, SDP2, SVMD4, SVMD5, SVMD6, SVMD7, SSD1, SLTD
NH9	ADP7, IIG26
NH10	

In table 4, we did a combination, crossing the developer guidelines with the characteristics raised in Step 2. When we look at these crossing, we can observe that two of Nielsen's heuristics were not filled by any developer's guideline. At the same time, some guidelines were not put into any these heuristics, which can mean there are specific elements that traditional usability heuristics cannot cover. Some of these developer guidelines were placed in the tablet 4 and others filled both crossings. That suggests a combination and complementation between both analyses. This way, table 5 shows which elements were filled by developer guidelines and tablet 6 shows the correlation between them.

As a result of the analyses above, we compiled a new set of heuristics for multimodal interaction: (1) Visibility and feedback; (2) Compatibility; (3) Control and freedom; (4) Consistency; (5) Error prevention; (6) Minimum actions; (7) Flexibility of use; (8) Organized content; (9) Error management; (10) Direct manipulation; (11) Changes of orientation; and (12) Human range. In order to validate the set of heuristics for multimodal interaction proposed, in the next section we performed a case study comparing it with Nielsen's heuristics.

Table 4. Crossing between Characteristics of Multitouch and Speech Interaction and developer guidelines

Characteristics of Multitouch Interaction	Developer Guidelines
Gestures-based interaction	ADP02, IDP3, IIG21, SID2, SIM1
Context of use is important	
Orientation can change	IIG18, SVMD1
Human range can be considered	IIG19, SIM1
Use of screen area	
Content can be organized	ADP17, IIG1, IIG2, IIG3, IIG10, IIG14, IIG23, IIG28, IIG29, IIG30, IIG31, SDP2, SDP4, SID5, SVMD2
Limited inputs	IIG7, SIM2
Reduced processing power and memory	
Connectivity	ADP10, IIG9, SIM2
Expandability	
Possibility of collaborative interaction	SID1
Characteristics of Speech Interaction	Developer Guidelines
More generic and general vocabulary	IIG6
Speech for simpler and direct tasks	SSD1
Speech should be a input alternative	IDP4

Table 5. Heuristics and characteristics filled by guidelines

Nielsen's Heuristics	Multitouch characteristics	Speech Characteristics
NH1	Gestures-based interaction	More generic and general vocabulary
NH2	Orientation can change	
NH3	Human range can be considered	Speech for simpler and direct tasks
NH4	Content can be organized	
NH5	Limited inputs	Speech should be an input alternative
NH6	Connectivity	
NH7	Possibility of collaborative interaction	
NH8		
NH9		

Table 6. Correlation between Nielsen's heuristics and multitouch/speech characteristics

Nielsen's Heuristics	Multitouch characteristics	Speech Characteristics
Visibility of system status		Speech should be an alternative input
Match between system and the real world		More generic and general vocabulary
Recognition rather than recall	Limited inputs, Connectivity	
Flexibility and efficiency of use	Possibility of collaborative interaction	
Aesthetic and minimalist design	Content can be organized	Speech for simpler and direct tasks

4   Case Study

We conducted a case study comparing the new set of usability heuristics focused on multimodal interaction and the Nielsen's heuristics. The goal of that comparison is to verify whether a traditional method of usability inspection is appropriate to this contemporary paradigm and whether specific heuristics are more adequate (table 7).

Table 7. Nielsen's and multimodal heuristics

Nielsen's Heuristics (NH)	Multimodal Heuristics (MH)
NH1-Visibility of system status	MH1-Visibility and feedback
NH2-Match between system and the real world	MH2-Compatibility
NH3-User control and freedom	MH3-Control and freedom
NH4-Consistency and standards	MH4-Consistency
NH5-Error prevention	MH5-Error prevention
NH6-Recognition rather than recall	MH6-Minimum actions
NH7-Flexibility and efficiency of use	MH7-Flexibility of use
NH8-Aesthetic and minimalist design	MH8-Organized content
NH9-Help users recognize, diagnose, and recover from errors	MH9-Error management
NH10-Help and Documentation	MH10-Direct manipulation
	MH11-Changes of orientation
	MH12-Human range

To this end, 12 designers divided into 3 groups performed heuristic evaluations on three tablet applications. The device used was an Acer Iconia B1 tablet, which runs Android OS 4.1, and the following applications were evaluated: Google (4.2.122 version), Facebook (1.2.336 version) and UOL News (2.3.1 version). The groups were divided as follows: MH Group – used multimodal heuristics; NH – used Nielsen's heuristics; and a control group (CG) – that worked freely. Before each evaluation, a set of heuristics to be used was explained as well as the scenario of each application. Each evaluator found usability failures individually. After that, they classified each failure according to the violated heuristic, and then they attributed a degree of severity using a scale from 0 to 4. The set of usability heuristics for multimodal interaction has more criteria than Nielsen's. That probably occurs because there are specific interaction elements in this paradigm. However, most of these (MH1 to MH9) have some equivalence to Nielsen's heuristics and can be considered an extension of these, being better adapted to the use context of multimodal interfaces.

4.1   Results

A total of 123 problems were found in all three applications by the 12 evaluators. The majority of problems were identified by the group that used multimodal heuristics, who also attributed a higher average severity. We can divide them all as follow:

- 13 problems found by both groups (10,57%);
- 25 problems found by MH and NH (20,33%);
- 26 problems found by MH and CG (21,14%);
- 14 problems found by NH and CG (11,38%);
- 55 problems found only by MH (44,72%);
- 19 problems found only by NH (15,45%);
- 12 problems found only by CG (8,94%).

Table 8 shows the numbers of problems divided by heuristics and their average severity.

Table 8. Number of problems divided by heuristics

MG Group			NG Group			CC
Heuristics	Number of problems	Average severity	Heuristics	Number of problems	Average severity	
MH1	12	2,13	NH1	13	1,62	
MH2	11	2,45	NH2	6	1	
MH3	6	3	NH3	10	1,5	
MH4	7	2,14	NH4	3	0,67	
MH5	1	4	NH5	6	2	
MH6	9	2,33	NH6	1	2	
MH7	2	2	NH7	3	1,33	
MH8	29	2,66	NH8	1	1	
MH10	8	2,52	NH10	2	3	
MH11	3	2,75				
MH12	4	3,63				
Total	92		Total	45		38
Average severity		2,55	Average severity		1,53	2,19

Besides finding more problems, the MH group attributed a higher average severity in its evaluation (2,55 compared to 1,53 from NH group, that used Nielsen's and 2,19 from control group – CC). Table 9 shows only the number of problems and average severity in equivalent heuristics between MH and NG groups. Nevertheless, we still have a total of 113 problems found and most of them were still found by MH group.

The severity average from MH group decreases in this case (2,49 compared to 2,55), but it still higher than others groups. This supposed superiority might have occurred because the set of heuristics used by MH group is better adapted for the interaction paradigm in question.

In relation to the problems found only by NG group, they were categorized in the following heuristics: *NH1-Visibility of system status* (7 problems), *NH2-Match between system and the real world* (3 problems), *NH3-User control and freedom* (4 problems), *NH5-Error prevention* (3 problems), *NH7-Flexibility and efficiency of use* (2 problems), and *NH10-Help and Documentation* (2 problems). Only *NH10-Help and Documentation* has no any equivalent heuristic in multimodal set. Nonetheless, in the multimodal heuristic *MH8-Organized content* are mentioned help solutions through tutorial layers on the interface. Thus, it is likely that evaluators from MH group have ignored these problems found only by NH group.

Table 9. Number of problems divided by equivalent heuristics

MG Group			NG Group			CC
Heuristics	Number of problems	Average severity	Heuristics	Number of problems	Average severity	
MH1	12	2,13	NH1	13	1,62	
MH2	11	2,45	NH2	6	1	
MH3	6	3	NH3	10	1,5	
MH4	7	2,14	NH4	3	0,67	
MH5	1	4	NH5	6	2	
MH6	9	2,33	NH6	1	2	
MH7	2	2	NH7	3	1,33	
MH8	29	2,66	NH8	1	1	
			NH10	2	3	
Total	77		Total	45		38
Average severity		2,49	Average severity		1,53	2,19

5 Conclusions

Usability on digital devices has become an essential tool in developing new products and systems in recent decades. It is often cited as a success factor and a useful differential in the market. However, there are many challenges when traditional usability methods are confronted with new interaction paradigms. This paper presents a contribution for a new usability through a new set of usability heuristics for multimodal interaction focused on multitouch and speech. These heuristics have had a better performance when compared to a traditional set of heuristics on tablets applications. As conclusions from the case study we can emphasize:

- The use of more and better-adapted heuristics in the use context of multimodal paradigm has better performance;
- The new set of heuristics are still more adequate when only compared to equivalent heuristics to the Nielsen's;
- The NH group has not had a significant result when compared with the CC group.

It is possible that the lack of significant differences between the use of any usability criteria and Nielsen's heuristics occurs because the latter are widely known by most professionals and academicians in the area. Whereas the better performance of the set of multimodal heuristics probably occurs because there are substantial differences between a traditional interaction style – in which Nielsen's heuristics were founded – and a new interaction paradigm – in which the present work focused on. Thus, we can conclude that the use of more and better-adapted heuristics in a specific context of use had a better performance when compared with a traditional set of heuristics. This reinforces our hypothesis that we need to think in a new usability, which is capable to work with the new challenges that the new interaction paradigms bring. As future work, we intent to conduct a new case study with less experienced participants in order to verify the performance of the new set of heuristics for multimodal heuristics in this scenario. We will also perform similar studies with other emerging interaction paradigms, as well as explore other related disciplines.

Acknowledgments. The authors would like to thank all the experiment participants. And a special thanks to Elis Damasceno for helping in the grammar review.

References

1. International Organisation for Standardisation, Software Ergonomics Requirements for office work with visual display terminal (VDT), ISO 9241, Geneva (1998)
2. Chan, A.J., Islam, M.K., Rosewall, T., Jaffray, D.A., Easty, A.C., Cafazzo, J.A.: Applying usability heuristics to radiotherapy systems. In: Radiotherapy and Oncology, vol. 102, p. 5 (January 2012)
3. Kevin, B., Saul, G., Carl, G.: Heuristic Evaluation of Groupware Based on the Mechanics of Collaboration. Journal (2001)
4. Rusu, C., Roncagliolo, S., Tapia, G., Hayvar, D., Rusu, V., Gorgan, D.: Usability Heuristics for Grid Computing Applications. Journal, 53–58 (2011)
5. IDC Forecasts Worldwide Tablet Shipments to Surpass Portable PC Shipments in 2013, Total PC Shipments in 2015 (May 28, 2013) (press release)
6. Peter, T., Robert, D.M.: Introduction to the new usability. ACM Trans. Comput.-Hum. Interact. 9, 69–73 (2002)
7. Anja, B.N., Ina, W., Jörn, H.: Multimodal interaction: A suitable strategy for including older users? Interact. Comput. 22, 465–474 (2010)
8. Charles, R., Angus, F., Tobias, H.: Enabling Multimodal Mobile Interfaces for Interactive Musical Performance. Journal (2013)
9. Coutaz, J., Nigay, L., Salber, D., Blandford, A., May, J., Young, R.M.: Four easy pieces for assessing the usability of multimodal interaction: the CARE properties. Journal, 115–120 (1995)
10. Wechsung, I., Engelbrecht, K.-P., Kühnel, C., Möller, S., Weiss, B.: Measuring the Quality of Service and Quality of Experience of multimodal human–machine interaction. Journal on Multimodal User Interfaces 6, 73–85 (2012)
11. Bastian, P., Stefan, S., Albrecht, S.: Multimodal interaction in the car: combining speech and gestures on the steering wheel. Journal (2012)
12. Julie, R., Stephen, B.: Gesture and voice prototyping for early evaluations of social acceptability in multimodal interfaces. Journal (2010)

13. Schalkwyk, J., Beeferman, D., Beaufays, F., Byrne, B., Chelba, C., Cohen, M., Kamvar, M., Strope, B.: "Your Word is my Command": Google Search by Voice: A Case Study. Journal, 61–90 (2010)
14. Zhang, H., Wei Lieh, N.: Speech recognition interface design for in-vehicle system. Journal (2010)
15. Gilles, B., Rg, M., Ller,Eric, L.: Design and evaluation of finger-count interaction: Combining multitouch gestures and menus. Int. J. Hum.-Comput. Stud. 70, 673–689 (2012)
16. Oscar Kin-Chung, A., Chiew-Lan, T.: Multitouch finger registration and its applications. Journal (2010)
17. Donald, A.N.: Natural user interfaces are not natural. Interactions 17, 6–10 (2010)
18. Charles, J., Sorin, D.: Speech interfaces based upon surface electromyography. Speech Commun. 52, 354–366 (2010)
19. Dominique, K., Philippe, B., Christine, R., Margot, P., Manuel, G.: Fran, ois, R.,Ludovic Le, B.: Reducing user linguistic variability in speech interaction through lexical and syntactic priming. Journal (2012)
20. Rusu, C., Roncagliolo, S., Rusu, V., Collazos, C.: A Methodology to Establish Usability Heuristics. Journal, 59–62 (2011)
21. Bastien, J.M.C., Scapin, D.L.: Ergonomic criteria for the evaluation of human-computer interfaces. Journal 79
22. Jakob, N.: Usability Engineering. Journal, 358 (1993)
23. Norman, D.A.: Emotional Design: Why We Love (or Hate) Everyday Things. Journal (2005)
24. Jeongyun, H., Dong-Han, H., Sanghyun, P., Chiwon, S., Wan Chul, Y.: A framework for evaluating the usability of mobile phones based on multi-level, hierarchical model of usability factors. Interact. Comput. 21, 263–275 (2009)
25. Young Seok, L., Sang, W.H., Tonya, L.S.-J., Maury, A.N., Kei, T.: Systematic evaluation methodology for cell phone user interfaces. Interact. Comput. 18, 304–325 (2006)
26. Rodolfo, I., Cristian, R., Silvana, R., Cristhy, J., Virginica, R.: Usability Heuristics for Touchscreen-based Mobile Devices. Journal (2012)
27. Apted, T., Collins, A., Kay, J.: Heuristics to Support Design of New Software for Interaction at Tabletops. Journal (2009)
28. Sandrine, R.: An empirical study of speech and gesture interaction: toward the definition of ergonomic design guidelines. Journal (1998)
29. Sandrine, R.-R., NoëLle, C., Pierre, D.: Expression constraints in multimodal human-computer interaction. Journal (2000)
30. Alex, W.S., Harshada, P., Sarah, C.S., John, R.W.: Developing speech input for virtual reality applications: A reality based interaction approach. Int. J. Hum.-Comput. Stud. 69, 3–8 (2011)
31. Android Design Principles, http://developer.android.com/design/index.html (retrieved March 27, 2013)
32. iOS Human Interface Guidelines, http://developer.apple.com/library/ios/-documentation/UserExperience/Conceptual/MobileHIG/Introduction/Introduction.html (retrieved March 27, 2013)
33. Microsoft Surface User Experience Guidelines, http://www.microsoft.com/en-us/download/details.aspx?id=19410 (retrieved March 29, 2013)

Developing Playability Heuristics for Computer Games from Online Reviews

Miaoqi Zhu and Xiaowen Fang

School of Computing, DePaul University, Chicago, IL, U.S.
miaoqi.zhu@gmail.com,
xfang@cdm.depaul.edu

Abstract. This paper demonstrates a revised lexical approach for developing game playability heuristics by examining a large number of online game reviews. Game usability, which is better labeled as playability, has been receiving attention from researchers in the areas of HCI and Game Studies. Despite some early research efforts on this topic, most studies are generally qualitative in nature and don't cover a wide range of games. Inspired by the lexical approach used in personality psychology, we employed a revised method to investigate playability by analyzing players' languages. In our previous research, 6 factors were extracted about essential characteristic of game play experience [39]. This study aims to develop playability heuristics rules based on adjectives converging on factor perceived as playability, the top factor among the six.

Keywords: usability, playability heuristics, lexical approach.

1 Introduction

Although many studies have been conducted to evaluate productivity software in the area of Human-Computer Interaction (HCI), few of them have be dedicated to developing heuristic rules for hedonic systems such as computer games. In fact, some HCI professionals are still relying on the traditional usability evaluation/inspection techniques to detect potential usability issues of computer games.

Barr, Noble and Biddle ([3]) note that computer games are not made to support user-defined tasks and thereby differentiate themselves from productivity software. It is fair to say that some usability heuristics may not be applicable to computer games. For instance, user control and freedom in games may deviate from its original definition for desktop applications. We also argue that it is imperative to develop new heuristics for computer games because they are a different type of software system. The notion is that playability is a better measure, and it goes above and beyond traditional usability heuristics for computer games.

Previously there are a handful of attempts to define playability and playability heuristics. For instance, Malone ([20]) recommends three basic principles of designing an enjoyable interface for educational games: challenge, fantasy and

A. Marcus (Ed.): DUXU 2014, Part I, LNCS 8517, pp. 496–505, 2014.
© Springer International Publishing Switzerland 2014

curiosity. Federoff ([11]) proposes the first set of playability heuristics in the light of traditional usability heuristics ([27]). More recently, Pinelle, Wong and Stach ([31]) come up with a list of heuristics by analyzing 108 PC game reviews from GameSpot.com. This array of work presents different perspectives and approaches; however, they are typically derived from a small sample of games and do not necessarily reflect what game players truly think.

Motivated by the lexical hypotheses in the field of personality psychology, this paper presents a process of developing playability heuristics via a revised lexical analysis. The premise is that players need to use natural languages to describe play experience and characteristics of computer games. Over an extensive period of time, words are created to encode critical information pertaining to playability. As a result, any important playability issues must be reflected in players' languages.

Six major factors were extracted from 696,801 structured reviews covering thousands of games in a previous study [39]. Based on the same set of reviews and adjectives loading on the factor of playability, we adopt a grounded theory ([21]) approach to consolidate existing heuristics and discover unknown heuristics. In the following sections, we will discuss 1). Usability and computer game playability; 2). A revised lexical approach and prior analysis of adjectives; 3). A new method to explore playability heuristics.

2   Usability and Computer Game Playability

While usability looks familiar to most HCI scholars and practitioners, it may not be the single best measure for computer games considering the basic components of gameplay. We argue that playability is a more accurate term for game evaluation, and it is related to usability. In this section, we will compare them in depth and review existing playability heuristics.

2.1   Usability and Playability

Usability is defined as "the extent to which a product can be used by specified users to achieve specified goals with effectiveness, efficiency and satisfaction in a specified content of use" ([13]). There are a number of usability engineering methods, among which is heuristic evaluation developed by Nielsen ([26]). While usability concerns the pragmatic side of HCI, the term of User Experience (UX) was created to embrace its hedonic property ([9]). Effie et al. ([9]) claim that UX is more about the sensation, subjective feeling, emotional, and satisfaction aspect of user-system interactions.

Evaluation of game usability and/or UX features a new wave of thinking in the intersection of HCI and Game Studies. There has been a heated discussion to differentiate usability from playability. Malone ([20]) maintains that it is important to distinguish toys-systems from tools-systems. Games belong to the former category and typically do not require users to have an external goal. Pagulayan et al. ([30]) indicate that they allow players to seek novelty in the interactive experience. In contrast, the productivity applications are meant to be consistent. Pinelle, Wong and

Stach ([31]) view game usability as "the degree to which a player is able to learn, control, and understand a game," and that it is just a prerequisite to have an outstanding usability. For utility software, Sauro and Kindlund ([34]) conclude that its usability can be measured by effectiveness, efficiency, and satisfaction. However, Federoff ([11]) criticizes that satisfaction is more critical for computer games.

There currently exist many definitions for game playability. A commonly referenced one is "the degree to which a game is fun to play and is usable, with an emphasis on the interaction style and plot-quality of the game; the quality of gameplay" ([36]). Fabricatore, Nussbaum and Rosas ([10]) suggest that "playability is the instantiation of the general concept of usability determined by understanding and controlling gameplay." Sánchez et al. ([33]) view playability as the UX in videogames and define it as "a set of properties that describe the Player Experience using a specific game system whose main objective is to provide enjoyment and entertainment, by being credible and satisfying, when the play plays alone or in company." But Nacke et al. ([25]) separate the concept of playability from player experience, as they believe that the former comes from an evaluation process on game designs. Paavilainen, Korhonen and Saarenpää ([29]) consider playability as the combination of gameplay and user interface, which links to concepts of intuitiveness, unobtrusiveness, fun, and challenge.

Research activities are witnessed in the intersection of usability and playability. For instance, the playability model proposed by Järvinen, Heliö and Mäyrä ([14]) show that the functional dimension actually corresponds to efficiency in the standard definition of usability. Moreover, the structural dimension is tantamount to heuristic evaluation for games. Christensen, Jørgensen and Jørgensen ([6]) invent a hybrid method of usability and participatory design, which has assisted in detecting potential gameplay issues in a self-developed game called "Takkar". Caroux and Vibert ([4]) recommend game designers to review display design standards from human factors research, particularly the proximity-compatibility principle ([38]). In the meantime, traditional usability techniques are also applied in game user research. For example, the play-testing group, founded by Microsoft Game Studios, provides positive feedback regarding the application of software usability methods in computer games. Medlock et al. ([22]) justify the value of software usability principles for games, and Cornett ([7]) confirms it by carrying out usability test on three massively multiplayer online role-playing game (MMORPGs) and one single-player role-playing game (RPG).

2.2   Playability Heuristics

To introduce major playability heuristics, Malone ([20]) mentions three motivational factors for designing enjoyable interfaces: 1). challenge, 2). fantasy, and 3). curiosity. He designed a series of experiments by controlling each game element at one time. The subsequent analysis resulted in a practical design framework. Although the study was based on an educational game, it has a far-reaching significance for ensuing game studies.

Federoff ([11]) establishes the first set of playability heuristics for games of entertainment purposes. Her work is worth attention in that it was presented in comparison to traditional usability heuristics. Moreover, she conducted the study inside a game company, which makes the results more applicable to industrial practice. Nevertheless, no formal validation process is found in the end.

Desurvire, Caplan and Toth ([8]) compile a collection of heuristic rules from literature review and expert review. To validate their Heuristic Evaluation for Playability (HEP), they deploy a 2-hour playability evaluation session through 4 user studies. The outcome demonstrates the heuristics' effectiveness in identifying playability issues. Korhonen and Koivisto ([17], [18]) develop the first playability heuristics for mobile games. To address the concern on their evaluation model, Korhonen, Paavilainen and Saarenpää ([19]) claim it to be platform-independent hence the heuristics can be applied to examine other genres of games.

Pinelle, Wong and Stach ([31]) propose their heuristics principles through analyzing 108 PC game reviews from GameSpot.com. They categorized problems identified from the reviews, which they then translated into principles that described them at a higher level. Their study, however, focuses primarily on game interface at the expense of pinpointing issues relevant to other gameplay components. Further, the sampled games are not enough to cover all the classes. Given the trend of social networking games, Paavilainen ([28]) introduces an initial set of social game heuristics based on two existing design frameworks ([15], [37]). The heading-level heuristics contain 10 items (e.g., spontaneity, interruptability, narrativity), and they will become more concrete as the projects continue.

On the other hand, the game industries also find dedicated professionals sharing the same interest. A game design veteran - Rouse, outlines a list of design expectations from the perspective of players ([32]). Those expectations in fact can be translated into playability heuristics.

3   The Lexical Approach and Prior Analysis of Adjectives

According to the essential steps of the original lexical approach, we have implemented a revised method to inspect game-descriptive adjectives in the reviews contributed by various stakeholders (e.g. developer and player). The results suggest the success of our approach. It also produces a cluster of adjectives highly relevant to playability from which we will explore playability heuristics. This section will briefly discuss the core concept of the lexical approach and our analysis of game adjectives.

3.1   The Lexical Approach

The lexical approach is originally proposed to understand human personality. Since the characteristics of personality are not directly observable, there have been many ideas of developing personality taxonomies ([16]). However, a common weakness among them is the lack of an inclusive source that provides sufficient instances for each attribute. This problem was finally addressed when researchers resort to a readily accessible resource – natural languages such as English.

The lexical hypothesis states that when salient individual differences are socially relevant to life, these distinctive attributes will be encoded into a nature language. If more people agree to the same difference, it is more likely to be described by similar terms. To exercise the lexical approach, a researcher must first locate personality-descriptive adjectives in a dictionary ([1]). As an initial list is ready, it must be consolidated by removing rarely-used personality-descriptors. A final list is then sent to a large sample of subjects, and they will be asked to provide ratings on the extent to which each adjective describes their own personalities.

Based on the personal trait groups created by Allport and Odbert ([2]), Cattell ([5]) became the first researcher to obtain 12 personality factors via oblique factor analysis. However, when other scholars re-examined the correlation matrixes from Cattell's experiments, they found that only five personality factors stayed consistent ([35]). It is now the well respected Big-Five personality model ([35]).

3.2   Prior Analysis of Adjectives

A revised lexical approach was proposed and implemented in our prior study[39]. To summarize, seven stages were involved: 1). Collecting a large body of game reviews from mainstream game websites. We downloaded 30,252,536 review documents (e.g., user comments, expert reviews, etc.) from three sites (i.e., Gamespot.com, Gamestop.com, IGN.com); 2). Building an initial dictionary of game-descriptive terms. Approximately 11,000 unique adjectives were found by referencing the lexicon library of WordNet ([12], [23], [24]); 3). Extracting adjectives' ratings from players. Due to the size of the adjective list (n = 11,000), it would be difficult to conduct a large-scale survey study. An alternative and arguably better solution was then proposed and employed to convert structured reviews into a binary matrix. For each review document, "1" indicates the presence of an adjective in the document, and "0" implies its absence; 4). Running the first factor analysis. We carried out an exploratory factor analysis with varimax rotation, and this step discovered 70 factors; 5). Consolidating the list by grouping each adjective's synonyms and antonyms into one feature space if their correlations were also significant. A new rating table was constructed in the similar manner as the third step. However, instead of registering binary data, the absolute number of distinct adjectives was used as the value of each feature; 6). Running the second factor analysis. This round of analysis resulted in 6 distinct factors, which allows us to define the factors more precisely; 7). Exploring the traits of computer games. Two researchers independently labeled each factor by interpreting its adjectives in the context of gameplay.

These six traits are conceptualized as: playability, creativity, usability, action, sensation, and strategy. Playability, ranked as the top trait, seems to be the most important factor among all based on the variance it accounted for. We argue that the adjectives converging on this factor will likely reveal different aspects of playability. Therefore, playability heuristics can be established from them because they no doubt represent subjective perceptions of a large number of game players.

4   A New Method for Exploring Playability Heuristics

The general approach we take is to match playability related adjectives with any existent heuristics identified by prior research and any adjectives that are left alone become potential candidates for new heuristics. To obtain a list of existent playability heuristics, we first revisited the literatures of game designs and playability. The goal is to match the adjectives with potential design and/or heuristics principles. If an adjective is not clearly associate with a known heuristic or the context of its use is not clear, actual game reviews containing this adjective were examined to determine whether a new heuristic rule is warranted..

Similar to the grounded theory approach, for each group of terms, sufficient raw materials were examined until no additional new information was present. It was also observed that many of the heuristics may cross-reference adjectives of different groups. Below we are presenting a portion of the initial list.

Table 1. Selected playability heuristics and associated adjectives

Playability-related Adjectives	Playability Heuristics
Pretty, beautiful, nice, nasty, pleasant, respectable	• The game characters look adorable (e.g., beautiful, intelligent, interesting) to players; • Impressive setting designs can facilitate presence.
Hard, solid, challenging, strong, tough, serious, tricky, rough, soft, stale, severe, punishing, troublesome, grueling, easy, difficult, available, smooth, comfortable, user-friendly, abundant, simple, plain, complex, mere, bare	• The game should be easy to learn but hard to master; • The players should not be given severe punishment and/or penalty if failing difficult tasks; • The level of challenges is well-balanced; • The interface is user-friendly and easy to navigate to locate available features; • The Artificial Intelligence (AI) needs to assist players when they have difficulty dealing with tricky tasks; • Players should be able to overcome challenges eventually and feel a sense of accomplishment.

Table 1. (*continued*)

Sound, complete, intelligent, substantial, stable, sensible	<ul><li>Players are instructed to make intelligent decisions and carry out sensible actions;</li><li>The outcomes of players' actions must make sense to them;</li><li>Players understand the story line as a consistent and/or stable vision;</li><li>Non-player characters behave in a manner that is sensible in context of the story and setting.</li></ul>
Different, various, diverse, opposite, unusual, contrary, variant, polar, mean, normal, average, typical, natural	<ul><li>There should be various tasks for each stage of playing in order to create an enduring gameplay;</li><li>The controls are mapped in a natural way, and the game's default settings must follow typical ones from games of similar kind;</li><li>The game can be manipulated in a number of ways or explored through various modalities.</li></ul>
Boring, tedious, dull, tiresome	<ul><li>The tediousness during game-play can be solved by adding different tasks and adjusting the pacing of gameplay;</li><li>Customizations (e.g., control, sound, color) can help minimize possible tediousness.</li><li>Game mechanics are not mundane.</li></ul>
Repetitive, repetitious	<ul><li>The tasks in the games should not be perceived to repeat themselves;</li><li>When the same mistakes are made again, there should not assistance instead of the same penalties;</li><li>Repetitive activities can be reduced by simplifying controls.</li></ul>

5   Next Step

We are in the process of consolidating the list by removing repetitive and ambiguous rules. The next step is to substantiate playability heuristics drafted from above stage. Since the objective is to create a set of player-centered playability heuristics, finding empirical support for each rule is crucial. We are planning to adhere to three procedures for this task: 1). All the reviews will be retrieved and ordered according to the frequencies of involving adjectives (e.g. emotional) in the rule; 2). For each proposed heuristics, certain adjective patterns (e.g. emotional impact, emotionally connected) and pertinent subjects (e.g., character, story) will be gleaned from highly-ranked reviews; 3). Queries will then be constructed using the information obtained from previous step. 4). Essential statistics will be reported and compared such as how many times the targeted rules are mentioned by players or how many games contains this rule. Given the unprecedentedly large-volume reviews, only important playability issue can survive this step, as they are supposed to apply to a wide range of computer games and they should be mentioned by a considerably large number of players.

References

1. Ashton, M.C.: Individual Differences and Personality. Academic Press, San Diego (2007)
2. Allport, G.W., Odbert, H.S.: Trait-names: A psycho-lexical study. Psychological Monographs 47, 1 (1936)
3. Barr, P., Noble, J., Biddle, R.: Videogame values: Human–computer interaction and games. Interacting with Computers 19(2), 180–195 (2007)
4. Caroux, L., Le, B.L., Vibert, N.: Maximizing players' anticipation by applying the proximity-compatibility principle to the design of video games. Human Factors 53(2), 103–117 (2011)
5. Cattell, R.B.: Confirmation and clarification of primary personality factors. Psychometrika 12(3), 197–220 (1947)
6. Christensen, L.J., Jørgensen, T.T.Y., Jørgensen, A.H.: Developing a hybrid of MMORPG and LARP using usability methods: The case of Takkar. In: DIGRA Conference "Level Up", Utrecht (2003)
7. Cornett, S.: The usability of massively multiplayer online roleplaying games: Designing for new users. In: Proceedings of the SIGCHI Conference on Human Factors in Computing Systems, pp. 703–710. ACM Press, New York (2004)
8. Desurvire, H., Caplan, M., Toth, J.A.: Using heuristics to evaluate the playability of games. In: CHI 2004 Extended Abstracts on Human Factors in Computing Systems, pp. 1509–1512. ACM Press, New York (2004)
9. Law, E.L.-C., Roto, V., Hassenzahl, M., Vermeeren, A.P.O.S., Kort, J.: Understanding, scoping and defining user experience: a survey approach. In: Proceedings of the SIGCHI Conference on Human Factors in Computing Systems, CHI 2009, pp. 719–728. ACM Press, New York (2009)
10. Fabricatore, C., Nussbaum, M., Rosas, R.: Playability in Video Games: A Qualitative Design Model. Human-Computer Interaction 17(4), 311–368 (2002)
11. Federoff, M.: Heuristic and Usability Guidelines for the Creation and Evaluation of Fun Videogames. Unpublished Master Thesis, Department of Telecommunications, Indiana University (2002)
12. Fellbaum, C.: WordNet: An Electronic Lexical Database. MIT Press, Cambridge (1998)
13. International Organization for Standardization. ISO 9241-11: 1998: Ergonomic requirements for office work with visual display terminals (VDTs) - part 11: Guidance on usability. International Organization for Standardization, Geneva (1998)

14. Järvinen, A., Heliö, S., Mäyrä, F.: Communication and community in digital entertainment services. Prestudy Research Report. Tampere University Press, Tampere (2002)
15. Järvinen, A.: Game design for social networks: Interaction design for playful dispositions. In: Spencer, S.N. (ed.) Proceedings of the 2009 ACM SIGGRAPH Symposium on Video Games, pp. 95–102. ACM Press, New York (2009)
16. John, O.P., Angleitner, A., Ostendorf, F.: The lexical approach to personality: A historical review of trait taxonomic research. European Journal of Personality 2, 171–203 (1988)
17. Korhonen, H., Koivisto, E.M.: Playability heuristics for mobile Games. In: Proceedings of the 8th Conference on Human-Computer Interaction with Mobile Devices and Services, MobileHCI 2006, pp. 9–16. ACM Press, New York (2006)
18. Korhonen, H., Koivisto, E.M.: Playability heuristics for mobile multi-player games. In: Proceedings of the 2nd International Conference on Digital Interactive Media in Entertainment and Arts, pp. 28–35. ACM Press, New York (2007)
19. Korhonen, H., Paavilainen, J., Saarenpää, H.: Expert review method in game evaluations: Comparison of two playability heuristic sets. In: Proceedings of the 13th International MindTrek Conference: Everyday Life in the Ubiquitous Era, pp. 74–81. ACM Press, New York (2009)
20. Malone, T.W.: Heuristics for designing enjoyable user interfaces: Lessons from computer games. In: Proceedings of the 1982 Conference on Human Factors in Computing Systems, pp. 63–68. ACM Press, New York (1982)
21. Martin, P.Y., Turner, B.A.: Grounded theory and organizational research. The Journal of Applied Behavioral Science 22(2), 141–157 (1986)
22. Medlock, M.C., Wixon, D., Terrano, M., Romero, R., Fulton, B.: Using the RITE method to improve products: A definition and a case study. Usability Professionals Association (2002), http://www.microsoft.com/playtest/publications.htm
23. Miller, G.A.: WordNet: A lexical database for English. Communications of the ACM 38(11), 39–41 (1995)
24. Miller, G.A., Beckwith, R., Fellbaum, C., Gross, D., Miller, K.J.: Introduction to WordNet: An on-line lexical database'. Journal of Lexicography 3(4), 235–244 (1990)
25. Nacke, L.E., Drachen, A., Kuikkaniemi, K., Niesenhaus, J., Korhonen, H.J., Hoogen, V.D.W., Kort, Y.: Playability and player experience research. Paper presented at DiGRA 2009: Breaking new ground: Innovation in games, play, practice and theory, London (2009)
26. Nielsen, J.: Usability engineering. Academic Press, Boston (1993)
27. Nielsen, J., Molich, R.: Heuristic evaluation of user interfaces. In: Proceedings of the SIGCHI Conference on Human Factors in Computing Systems: Empowering People, pp. 249–256. ACM Press, New York (1990)
28. Paavilainen, J.: Critical review on video game evaluation heuristics: Social games perspective. In: Proceedings of the International Academic Conference on the Future of Game Design and Technology, pp. 56–65. ACM Press, New York (2010)
29. Paavilainen, J., Korhonen, H., Saarenpää, H.: Comparing two playability heuristic sets with expert review method: A case study of mobile game evaluation. In: Media in the Ubiquitous Era: Ambient, Social and Gaming Media, pp. 29–52. Information Science Reference, Hershey (2012)
30. Pagulayan, R.J., Steury, K., Fulton, B., Romero, R.L.: Designing for fun: User-testing case studies. In: Funology: From Usability to Enjoyment, pp. 137–150. Kluwer Academic Publishers, Dordrecht (2003)

31. Pinelle, D., Wong, N., Stach, T.: Heuristic evaluation for games: Usability principles for video game design. In: Proceeding of the 26th Annual SIGCHI Conference on Human Factors in Computing Systems, pp. 1453–1462. ACM Press, New York (2008)
32. Rouse III, R.: Game design: Theory and practice. Jones & Bartlett Learning, Boston (2010)
33. Sánchez, J.L.G., Simarro, F.M., Zea, N.P., Vela, F.L.G.: Playability as extension of quality in use in computer games. In: Proceedings of 2nd International Workshop on the Interplay Between Usability Evaluation and Software Development, I-USED, Uppsala (2009)
34. Sauro, J., Kindlund, E.: A method to standardize usability metrics into a single score. In: Proceedings of the SIGCHI Conference on Human Factors in Computing Systems, pp. 401–409. ACM Press, New York (2005)
35. Tupes, E.C., Christal, R.C.: Recurrent personality factors based on trait ratings. Journal of Personality 60, 225–251 (1992)
36. Usability-First,
   http://www.usabilityfirst.com/glossary/playability/
37. Ventrice, T.: Building the foundation of a social future,
   http://www.gamasutra.com/view/feature/4210/
   building_the_foundation_of_a_.php
38. Wickens, C.D., Carswell, C.M.: The proximity compatibility principle: Its psychological foundation and relevance to display design. Journal of the Human Factors and Ergonomics Society 37(3), 473–494 (1995)
39. Zhu, M., Fang, X., Chan, S., Brzezinski, J.: Building A Dictionary Of Game-Descriptive Words To Study Playability. In: CHI 2013 Extended Abstracts, Paris, France, April 27-May 2. ACM, New York (2013); ACM 978-1-4503-1952-2/13/04

Media and Design

Designing Real-Time: On How Events Affect Audiovisual Narrative

Marcus Bastos

PUC-SP, Brazil
info@contradiccoes.net

Abstract. *Eventuality: designing real-time events* presents projects developed by Marcus Bastos aiming to explore new formats of filming and editing, as a result of real-time technologies and their effects on audiovisual cultures. Design aspects will be highlighted, and contextualized by a broader discussion about concepts such as event, constructed situation, heterotopy, and others that describe momentarily occurences capable of shifting the functioning of an established system (be it a narrative, an algorithmic procedure, a form of ocuppying a stage or a specific region of a city).

Keywords: Event, constructed situation, hetorotopy, real-time, audiovisual, filming, editing.

1 Introduction

Contemporary society is increasingly defined by real-time events. Auto-publication systems and other platforms that allow instant commenting and sharing of content allow processes of communication in which collective updating, contextual framing and immediate reactions result in environments which are constantly evolving. Such environments behave according to custom settings, that make then specific to each and every user. User and location, among other variables, generate unique renderings of such systems. For that reason, they are not only accessed in real-time, but manifest that particular configuration only in that specific moment and context. This is applicable to every forms of networked mediations, though particularities of photos, sounds or videos means that specialized systems have proper characteristics according to their emphasis (be it hosting a collection of posts, sharing sets of images, or managing clips and playlists). Similarly to Heraclitus famous quote, it could be said that nobody access the same Facebook, Twitter, Youtube or Pininterest page twice.

The aim of this paper is to discuss how this real-time platforms are affecting audiovisual language, both in terms of filming and editing. Distribution could also be a topic, but it will not be highlithed at the moment, since the focus of this paper will be the design process of low-cost mobile units or editing interfaces, used mostly in live performances staged by means of improvising, or recreating dramaturgic situations. On the discussed projects, several aspects of real-time generations of images will be addressed, from generative procedures to modifications of given scripts or scores

A. Marcus (Ed.): DUXU 2014, Part I, LNCS 8517, pp. 509–518, 2014.

affected by live data or audience participation. Though technological aspects are crucial for this sort of experiment, they will not be taken as determinant. On a society overly defined by the devices and applications it uses, experimentation can be taken as a space to examine alternative perspectives, and sometimes they are also the result of performatic tactics of criticism, rather than technological deconstruction.

In terms of structure, the article will be divided in two distinct parts: a conceptual discussion of the concept of *event*, and others related with momentary occurrences; and a discussion of projects developed by the author exploring how new formats of filming and editing change audiovisual language. Although related, both parts are not an strict conversation. Some aspects of the conceptual discussion are broader, and address the cultural context in which the projects were created, rather than specific topics or issues developed. The projects are affected by the discussed context, but sometimes explore more specific questions, or isolated features of eventuality: *Visible Cities* uses existing webcam live feeds. *Tosco Street View* and related projects explore portable / moving filming units. *fluxes* deal with well-established vocabularies of generative visuals. *Streaming Concert* use voip to allow remote musicians to improvise onstage during a performed score.

1.1   Events

Events that occur in real time tend to be associated with immediacy. The word implies non-mediation, which might sound obvious but is worth mentioning, for the sake of the argument developed below. The difficulties of defining real-time will not be addressed on this article, since this would be material enough to generate a completely new one[1]. The existence of a shared, reasonably consensual, perception of a mutual and networked present that unfolds, as people interact with it, will be considered enough justification to discuss design possibilities to develop devices and interfaces that gather or edit data both on networks or wired cities. As Douglas Rushkoff puts it, in Present Shock, our "society has reoriented itself to the present moment. Everything is live, real time, and always-on. It's not a mere speeding up, however much our lifestyles and technologies have accelerated the rate at which we attemp to do things. It's more of a diminishment of anything that isn't happening right now — and the onslaught of everything that supposedly is"[1].

This perception happens nowadays as a result of an over-mediated environment, and despite the fact that ancient and newer forms of transmission equally mediate language in real-time. Nothing happens out of the bubble of present, so there is a

---

[1] Some of this problems were discussed in "Mundo em Tempo Real" (World in Real Time) and "iMaGeNSoNS: sincronias entre acontecimento e narrativa" (iMaGeSouNS: sincronicities between event and narrative", articles in which the author of this paper review ideas of theoriticians such as Bachelard, Bazin, Deleuze, and others, to discuss different concepts of time, showing how the continuous of past and present and its always updated relations result in the perception of passage of time, of an existing know and then, of a possible here and gone. Our relation with the context that surrounds us results of an interweaving of inputs and impulses that is already sophisticaded enough, without most recent technologies of mediation, in which the interval between action and response is closer to those of bodily interactions.

paradox not to be disconsidered when we put emphasis on the real-timeness of current media processes. A not so obvious example of real-time mediation is an instrument, that amplifies sound waves and transmits them in form of vibrations in the air. A more explicitly mediated one is the satellite, that codifies audiovisual signals and transmits them (again, in form of aerial waves!) to a TV set. On both situations, the moment in which the mediated element is generated (either the sound or the TV image) almost coincides with the moment in which it is perceived by its recipient (either the listener of the sound or the TV watcher). So, what are the differences on recent processes of mediation, that results in a valorization of real-time phenomena and instantaneity?

Contemporary technologies are more explicitly perceived as real-time mediations because they depend on user agency. Simultaneity seems to be more easily identified in processes that happens by means of shared actions, where the passive position is nonexistent. That happens because the idea of presence is culturally associated with body participation: one is present when its body testifies an occurrence or interferes on it. And bodily actions are usually understood as distinct from device based actions: the body is perceived as immediate, devices are perceived as mediators. This understanding of presence as a bodily positioning endures, despite experiences such as that of a phone call. Since the 19th century people interact from a distance. Yet, the several forms of telepresence known throughout history did not radically change the assumption of presence as a bodily feature, until very recently.

Mc Luhan states that "the age of anxiety and of electric media is also the age of the unconscious and of apathy /.../ With our central nervous system strategically numbed, the tasks of conscious awareness and order are transferred to the physical life of man, so that for the first time he has become aware of technology as an extension of his physical body. Apparently this could not have happened before the electric age gave us the means of instant, total field-awareness"[2]. It could be argued that this process was modified, as forms of agency appeared and shook people away of the passive role as consumers of language. Agency obliges people to leave their position of apathy. Touching a screen with a mouse (or directly, with the finger) blurs the distinction between mediator and mediated. Interfaced body and devices are allowed to perform joint actions, thus installing a shared present, a space of mutual existence. Of course, social and cultural processes are complex textures of numerous divergent, conflicting, discrepant elements. So, if recent political uprisings or people's habits of communication indicate a culture of action and participation, other aspects of current society points towards exclusion and lack of access. The reasonable conclusion would be that the present times are marked by tensions and conflicting models that dispute alternative futures, in a context of unclear outcomes.

The effect of augmented proximity produced by superimposing body, architecture and technology is enhanced by the experience of using interfaces that change, according to context and user profile. Environments that act in conformity with contextual parameters resemble organisms, in their capacity to adjust to situations. Technologies such as VOIP and social networks amplify the effect of a body that is, at the same time, remote and present. These mediated modes of presence reconfigure oral modes of communication, recursively mirroring through technological effects of sharing experiences in modes that were more akin to oral culture and its communal rituals of conversational exchanges. When touching a screen becomes as personal as talking with someone, people on the other side of the planet become more intimate than neighbors. With the aid of screens that transport (visual and sonore) fragments of a living room through high bandwidth connections, over there can become closer than right here.

Posting on interfaces in which people react and comment, seconds after content is available, produces an awareness of the passage of time, as if the present lasted more than the ephemerous moment one try to grasp, just to feel it vanished. On *Cristals of Memory*, Deleuze describes the bergsonian model of memory as a relationship of instants that shift away from the plane of experience, becoming virtual recollections of events[3]. Current networked technologies give materiality to this flux, in a distributed and cumulative format that display temporal succession in front of people's eyes. Social networks and intermittent webcam transmissions are equivalents of procedures tried in direct cinema or video art experiments, aiming to stress the passing of time (to quote the title of one of Bill Viola's well known pieces). The difference is that they are routinely, instead of exceptional. Dislocating to a different context Deleuze's affirmative, it would be possible to say that they present people to "something intolerable: their own routinicity"[3].

On that context, events are perceived as occurrences that shift away from routine, producing difference on seas of similarity. When Edgar Morin organized the *Communications* edition focused on the return of the event, he was probably searching ways of thinking about a world affected by the disruptive unfoldings of May 68, undeniably one of the most intense set of deviations and questionings of all sorts of routines in recent history[2]. According to Morin, in *Le Retour de L'événement*, the concept of event "a été chassé dans la mesure où il a été identifié a la singularité, la contingence, l'accident, l'irreductibilité, le vécu (nous interrogerons plus loins le sens de ce mot événement)"[4]. So an event can be associated with something that happened, unpredictably, on a certain moment, and is unlikely to repeat, at least on the exact configuration it once happened. Abraham Moles explains that events are "des types de variations perceptibles d'un environment qui n'ont pas été prévues par l'occupant du centre de cet environment"[5].

The polysemic and open definition proposed by Morin is, partially, resulting of the fact that his article presents a volume dedicated to multidisciplinary approaches to the concept of event, from sociological to historical, psychoanalitical and cybernetic. But the concept of event, in itself, deals with actions of certain openness and ungraspability (as stated by Moles, and also by Atlan, on the same publication). It would be incongruent to attribute predictable behaviors to an event, at least from the perspective of the action or object which is affected by its occurrence. Nevertheless, algorithmic description of such occurrences can be assumed as atributes of a given system. They are even necessary, in cases in which a system is modeled with parameters enough to trigger such unpredictable actions.

---

[2] May 68 was known, in France, as *l'évenement*, or the event.

The complexity of the situation that evolves towards certain event is a given, even if the event in itself turns out to be simple, punctual or subtle. This plasticity and openness makes the concept of event relevant to describe a lot of what happens on contemporary environments in which networks of different kinds interveawe and allow a multiplicity of connections (temporally and geographically synchronous and/or asynchronous). The velocity of communications through the internet and mobile networks foment a culture in which the majority of the world seems to be promptly available through the click of a mouse, or the swipe of a finger. On such context, remote actions seem to affect unrelated communities, collective arrangements seem to emerge without predictable patterns. The complexity of the system makes its occurrences ungraspable to its participants.

On this article, the concept of event will be mainly associated with an unusual, unexpected action or behavior, a happening that desestabilizes and redirects the functioning of a narrative. This particular understanding of the word is historically related to cybernetics, in which an event reorganizes the functioning of an algorithmic routine. In *Du bruit comme principe d'auto-organisation*, Henri Atlan states that "Un pas de plus dans cette direction était réalisé, lors de recherces formelles sur la logique de systémes auto-organisateurs, en attribuant aux organismes la propriété non seulement de résister au bruit de façon efficace, mais encore de l'utiliser jusqu'a transformer en facteur de organisation! /.../ Soit un système exposé a un certain nombre de réponses. Chaque sucession pertubation-résponse met le systemé dans un certain état. Parmi tous les états possibles, seuls certains sont acceptables du point de vue de la finalité (au moins aparante) du systemé, que peut être sa simple survie ou l'accomplissement d'une fonction"[6].

Designing narrative structures that are affected in real-time by events which will change it (a space modifying a stream of events) or that will build temporary spaces mixing worlds and narratives (a stream of events modifying a space) install transitory places. Such spaces mixes fiction and reality in complex ways. It is a game-like situation, in wich the city becomes scenario for movies that happen in real-time with participation of spectators, actors and devices, as they are simultaneously shaped by the real world features surrounding it. This space of interfacing of real and fictional, as well as collective and individual, suggests new narrative formats that can explore our contemporary will to constantly participate and react. Overlaying public and networked spaces as devices for narrative allow to design real-time events to propose unexpected formats, that confront an audience accostumed with social networking and immediate reactions.

1.2 Visible Cities: Designing a Multi-screen Space Fed by Webcams That Intermitently Films Public Areas

Created in 2009, with an award from Itaú Cultural Rumos Expanded Language program, Visible Cities is a web documentary and multi-screen installation. It was developed by the LAT-23 collective, which is composed of Denise Agassi, Marcus Bastos, Claudio Bueno and Nacho Durán. The online version generate automatic clips of 8 minutes, by randomly mixing pre-recorded and live footage from webcams organized in sets of pre-defined tags and listed on the project's database. The installation version fill a darkened room with 5 monitors that display the live cameras, organized according to a collection of tags periodically sorted. The premise is that intermittent images of a place result in a situation opposite to the one to be expected. The project proposes an exploration of the flipside of the event, by showing how cameras that continuously capture images of cities generate an excedent of repetitive and inocuos imagery. Also, the combination of images of similar situations in different places of the globe results in repetitions that reveal how cities share a lot of common architectural and situational structures.

As stated by Agassi, Bastos, Bueno and Durán, on the project presented to Itaú Cultural describing the conceptual proposal for the piece, "putting side by side different kinds of registers of the world, available online, highlights a universe of evident monotony". For that reason, *Visible Cities* "reveals a dialog with etnography, and its project of incorporating the dead times of recordings into documentary, as if by doing so it would be possible to neutralize the process of selecting a specific perspective, during the editing process. But there is also an evident provocation when it is clear that exhaustive and intermittent register reveals few about the captured world. Almost as if a totality of gazes suggested its flipside: an incapacity of seeing".

Fig. 1a. *Visible Cities* in the installation version exhibited at *Itaú Cultural*, in São Paulo: a real-time documentary using webcams feeds as ready-made footage, showing images of specific places around the globe, such as airports, parks, crossroads, harbours, etc. **Fig. 1b.** *Visible Cities* online interface: on the internet, the user can watch automatically generated 8 minutes clips, with images from pre-recorded and live webcams selected from the projects database.

Another aspect of Visible Cities is the automatic editing process, that create films that evolve in real-time from algorithmic decisions. Visible Cities aims to subvert the logic of filming and editing typical of cinema and video, with procedures of capturing online signal and tagging the resulting materials. The goal is to produce films in which live footage produce always unexpected results. It is impossible to anticipate what the online webcams embedded on the project's database will display. Also, by approximating then by a combination of tagging and spatial proximity, the piece stimulates arbitrary relationships between distant places. This kind of procedure relates to generative art, with the difference that the images are not generated, but edited through programming rules. Footage is already existing, but the spatial relations and order in which it will be displayed is generated every time the user clicks on the play button.

1.3   Tosco Street View: Designing Low-Tech Units for Filming Cities, as a Device for Real-Time Documentary

Created in 2011, with a commission from SESC, Tosco Street View is a portable filming unit that explores precariousness as a strategy to deviate from the ambition of exhaustive landscape reconstruction associated with technologies used to capture images from places, and recreate them three-dimensionally. Collecting data of all kinds to generate visualizations based on 3-D models shows that one aspect of contemporary society resembles the paradoxical dream of creating the most complete possible map of a place, described by Borges on his short story Exactitude of Science. A map that ironically, when finally resembles the territory it represents, is rendered useless. Referring to such a map is similar to wandering through the areas it represent, since its extension does not allow any sort of generalization of inference about what is mapped. Our times are experiencing an obsession with organization of large data sets that can be compared to this quixotesce procedure of excessive detailment. It seems to be a reaction to an uncontrollable overload of information, as well as a shift in capacity of representation, as a result of the appearance of devices that read pieces of information that are not perceptible by bodily instruments, as well as images of unprecedented resolution exhibited on screens of previously unimagined proportions. The outcomes, it seems, points towards ungraspabilities not so different from the fictional borgean exactitude.

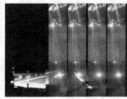

Fig. 2a. Preparing *Tosco Street View* to film in Piracicaba, during the SESC Circuit of Arts. This was the first version of the car, in which 3 cell phones and a tablet were used to capture images of cities throughout the state of São Paulo. **Fig. 2b. 2c.**The resulting material was used in *she, lonely, thinks of that*, a performance in which an actress would play the role of a woman who hits the road after being fired in a unexpected phone call, and revisits memories of her past through images and events occurring in the cities through which she passes.

The premise that structures Tosco Street View is that precarious and shattered images have their own share of informational insight, and that the ironic gesture of filming a city with a car that barely holds 4 low-res devices on its roof is, in itself, a statement that puts people to think about the times they live in. Unlike evangelists of resolution, a number of filmmakers and audiovisual artists have repeatedly defended precarious images as sources of their poetics. In she, lonely, thinks of that, the first piece created with images filmed with the Tosco Street View, this fragmentation is explored as a feature. The scenes of the car driving through cities were edited in stripes, both of the four cameras in simultaneous views, or one camera repeteaded 4 times, to strengthen similarities and discontinuities between the different perspectives of the shots.

She, lonely, thinks of that also research other aspects of eventuality, by means of an open narrative that adjusts to its context. The performance is created from a set of existing scenes, that are altered in two ways: it includes footage of the city where it will happen; the actress that plays the role of the main character interacts with the audience, and the generated situations dictates how the story will evolve. A live camera is used to include details of such interaction on the live mix, during the presentation. Also, elements of previous performances are included as new possibilities in future renderings of the project.

On its 2.0 version, the car uses streaming technologies and a feedback monitor to improve its presence on public space. Created to generate temporary TV stations aiming to provoke debates about local specific issues, the new version of the car benefits from low cost of portable tripods and existing apps to transmit video footage in real time, to upgrade into a more sophisticated unit, that allows scene selection and immediate transmition of the filmed materials. But this is not the most important unfolding of the project. Based on previous experience, this new version of Tosco Street View aim to foster more direct participation of audiences, as it films, and direct exchange of materials. The goal is to generate sound and video collections to produce real-time narratives about specific regions, mixing fictional and documentary elements.

Fig. 3a. 3-D project for the 2.0 version of *Tosco Street View*, including streaming technologies, a feedback monitor and an iPad that allow people to record testimonies to be mixed with the material captured by the roof cameras. **Fig. 3b.** *Perspectives* is a short film created with the *Tosco Street View* for the *Videoguerilha Festival;* subtitles highlight details of scenes, showing how the automatic mode of footage production, resulting from the fact that its driver does not have control of the filmed angles, can result in interesting surprises and flagrants of different aspects of urban life. **Fig. 3c.** *Remap* was also produced for the *Videoguerilha Festival*; data records of latitude, longitude and altitude of the cars trajectory while filming is used to automatically change hue, luminosity and saturation of the resulting scenes.

1.4   Fluxes: Designing Generative Ocupations of Space

Launched in 2010, with a commission from Paço das Artes, fluxes is an audiovisual piece that explores the contrast between geometric and non-geometric patterns, in live improvisations based on 4 different themes. It was created by Telemusik, a collective composed by Marcus Bastos, Karina Montenegro and Dudu Tsuda (and guest participation of Richard Ribeiro). Embedded in the generative / visual music tradition, the piece nevertheless seeked spatial forms of displaying materials as a form to broaden a usually temporal based format. Also, fluxes seeks a tension between analogical and digital effects of recurrency and repetition, and how they can evolve to distention and increasing variations.

Fig. 4a. With two screen in a 90 degree angle and two reversed projections from ceiling to floor, *fluxes* is performed in a space that involves the musicians, video artists, and even those in the audience who decided to step inside the projected area while the piece was performed: analog effects and real-time shape generators were used to produce an abstract environment ranging from geometry to complexity. **Fig 4b.** geometry/movement: screen capture of an improvisation with one of the visual patterns produced for *fluxes*.

Fluxes mixes aspects of staged performances traditions and installation, crossing pop culture with experimental languages. Real-time frictions of abstract visual and improvised sound occupy a space that was designed to dissolve the distance of italian stage formats. Here, there are no external inputs affecting the structure of the piece. The overall format is reasonably determined by a score and a set up. Events are rather the result of the musicians and video artist decisions, and how they react to each other, than a result of unpredictable parameters.

1.5   Streaming Concert: Designing Remote Ocupations of a Stage

Presented in 2011, as a hommage to John Cage's centenial, Streaming Concert proposes live improvistions of 3 pieces by Cage, with musicians distributed around the Globe. The technological project developed for the piece combines voip and syphon to embed remote calls from musicians that stream their images and sound, to be included on the live mix. Streaming Concert highlights the fragmented geographies existing as the result of real-time technologies of connection. Space gains a very different meaning, when people can telepresently performance. Distant interactions are not new, they happen since the 1970s, with well-know projects such as Hole in Space. On the current stage of such technologies, a further step is the possibility of lively manipulating this real-time inputs, transforming then in instantaneous footage for improvisation and mixing. It is a significant change, that shows how liveness, to use Paul Auslander's term, seem to have reached a very potent peek, in a society already fostered by processes in which instantaneity and mutual agency are crucial.

 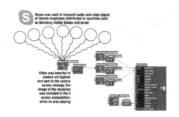

Fig. 5a. 3 screens were used to present live improvisation with images and footage related to Cage's imaginary (interviews, pictures, scores, etc). The central screen was used to insert live participations of remote musicians, that would send voip signal onstage according to a GMT based cue point. **Fig 5b.** Part of the Isadora project used to capture Skype audio and video and include it as a virtual webcam signal inside the composition used to perform *Streaming Concert.*

References

1. Rushkoff, D.: Present Shock — When Everything Happens Now. Penguin, New York (2013)
2. McLuhan, M.: Understanding Media. McGraw-Hill, London (1964)
3. Deleuze, G.: Cinema 2 - A imagem tempo. Brasiliense, São Paulo (2007)
4. Morin, E.: Le Retour de L'événement. Communications 18(18)
5. Moles, A.: Notes pour une typologies des événements. Communications 18(18)
6. Atlan, H.: Du bruit comme principe d'auto-organisation. Communications 18(18)

Post Media: Towards a User Interface Architecture

Jiří Bystřický[1] and Jan Brejcha[2]

[1] Catholic Theological Faculty, Charles University, Prague, Czech Republic
jiribystricky@seznam.cz
[2] Information Science and Librarianship, Charles University, Prague, Czech Republic
jan@brejcha.name

Abstract. The issue of the so-called "lived reality" of the contemporary world is largely dependent on the mediation process of "presence", especially on the technology of rapid data transport, covering a space of media reality such as an image of every day's living space. To explain the relationship between the reality of the mass media and conventional reality of everyday life it is needed to restore confidence to the present moment. The framework for understanding this relationship is through a certain revision of immediacy, *i.e.*, the way we report about the subject on a new spatial law in the media reality. Only then we get closer to the possibility of presenting the construction of a world in which man will be in control of forms in which the "presence" takes place.

Keywords: image, mediality, transparency, art, imaging, instrumentality.

1 Introduction

The issue of the so-called "lived reality" of the contemporary world is largely dependent on the mediation process of "presence", especially on the technology of rapid data transport, covering a space of media reality such as an image of every day's living space. To explain the relationship between the reality of the mass media and conventional reality of everyday life it is needed to restore confidence to the present moment. The framework for understanding this relationship is through a certain revision of immediacy, *i.e.*, the way we report about the subject on a new spatial law in the media reality. Only then we get closer to the possibility of presenting the construction of a world in which man will be in control of forms in which the "presence" takes place.

"... A combination of strategies: memorability being achieved by mixing effects of bizarre. So is developing the postmodern world of mestizos, where there is not searched for new, but for recombinations of the known. Ongoing bastardization of man, machine and sign. The new space law requires a new poetics of mixing." [9][page 53]

"The detachment of the subject from itself, its subservience to heteronomy, lies directly in the subject's essence." [6][page 217]

The provisional result of the use of modern computational systems in processes of transformation of contemporary society lies in a sudden and distinct change in

A. Marcus (Ed.): DUXU 2014, Part I, LNCS 8517, pp. 519–526, 2014.

perspective: changes in habitat on which a long-term pattern of traditional spatial and temporal law has been built. This law is gradually changing the technologically produced objects of "seeing": not only that they do not provide a sufficient difference between thinking and knowing, but they lead to "overlapping" the difference between the current display and its subsequent simulation, mainly by redirecting perspectives. In other words, rationality is too abstract and not very reflective, text and words become too differentiating, rather than unifying. In principle, the familiar "here" and "now" is replaced by "there" and "again". For more or less randomly appearing objects of the standard reality are overlapped by the production of mass media world and place before us their own finished images as previously identified objects, essentially as forwarded claims.

And from there it is just a short step to perceive visual electronic imaging complexes as a kind of facticity.

New spatial laws of imaging techniques combine the opinions that were previously necessary to process in the lived world, and only after share those opinions in an environment. On the contrary, understanding the coordinates of the objects in their processed world is almost impossible, and their acceptance does not require any active self-reference of the viewing subject, let alone a shared environment.

The game lies only in the pre-programmed calculations of the displayed points. Recent developments in IT quite subtly draw our attention to an effort to rearrange the model of cognition and knowledge that would be more appropriate and truer; it is, however, not the model of traditional realty, but of a "multiverse" reality. However, the far from ending desire for rewriting modernity is more or less the defining feature of the present time, say a special epoch, which fully utilizes practices that somehow in principle go beyond the boundaries of its own limitations.

Though we still linger in the wings of the world that we have created relatively hard and especially constructed socially, yet such a world is not quite a complete, concise and sufficiently domesticated area of our lives. We accept as a part of this world the apparatuses, techno-images, technologies or systems of mediation, whose influence is not only evident, but also changeable. With the gradual use of technology we use a different way of thinking, not so that we have changed the possibilities of our own dispositions, but we change fundamentally the strategies of their use. Some strategies are deliberate, some rather forced: anyway, the forms of our thinking take other appearances, as well as the ways in which the forms of thinking can be communicated. It seems that it is now the time to return to the unification and not to other forms of disintegration. For a start, we should recall what we find by using what we usually call "dispose of."

2   The Dispositive and Reflexive Mediality

"Society includes interaction. The difference between them is not a distinction between kinds of actions, societal versus interactional. Instead, it structures the undifferentiated domain of elemental operations, adding a capacity for abstraction that could not develop through interaction alone." [5][page 442]

"The autotransparency, to which the media lead us together with social sciences, is proving itself to be a mere revelation of plurality, and the mechanisms and the inner armature of our culture." [11]

If we look at current developments in philosophy of the media, one cannot but note that the almost uncritical reflection period is over, and it is necessary to make something like defragmentation of the empty contents and unintended consequences, which significantly reduced the capacity for critical reflection of complex called the media. In this paper we shall focus on two basic concepts, which challenge and certainly relativize the current extinct world of the media.

Briefly, we talk about the concept of the **dispositive**, from which it is essential to move towards **reflective mediality**, and to examine how it is possible to newly constitute the subject particularly in terms of a *pre-format of the very thought*. It is necessary to know with what "viscera", what "inner self", or technique of "laying", inserting, or founding the thinking in itself features. First we shall discuss this on a general level.

This is actually a more precise definition of the concept of difference, as it is understood and used not as an opening to a greater extent to the general, but on the contrary, i.e., as an internal and precise elaboration of internal links. The difference must allow an understanding of the difference between the term "medium" as an implicit difference between separate and autonomous in relation to the general, understood as a greater whole: allowing to develop individual differences and newer concepts of the concept of media, i.e. as a purely translational means. In this case, we it is some form of autoreference self-wrapped in a circle, from which it cannot set foot. The fundamental problem is the following:

There is a basic contradiction of things that cannot be compatible, especially without a negation in the simple unity of their media, i.e., where and in which way they appear, or become things. From the very contradictory principle of our world things cannot share the same medium, cannot satisfy the condition of agreement in the medium, because every form of 'thinghood' in Hegel's terms is disposed in an own medium for themselves: hence the contradiction between the concept of *medium* and *media* as a transferable format to approximately the same, which can then communicate, even as mass-media. From the perspective of the thing it is also clear that the thing is constituted by its own contradiction; the recognition lies precisely in the understanding and acceptance of their own negation, i.e., in the possibility of denial. The things can be themself only, when their own correlation with their differences is understood as an implicit unity, therefore, taken as a kind of game of opposites.

This is, however, exactly what the newer concept of media does not articulate, does not presuppose, and intentionally eliminate. "Yet; as thus opposed to one another they cannot be together in the simple unity of their medium, which is just as essential to them as negation; the differentiation of the properties, in so far as it is not an indifferent differentiation but is exclusive, each property negating the others, thus falls outside of this simple medium; and the medium, therefore; is not merely an Also, an indifferent unity, but a *One* as well, a unity which *excludes* an other. The One is the *moment of negation;* it is itself quite simply a relation of self to self and it

excludes an other; and it is that by which 'thinghood' is determined as a Thing."
[4][page 69][1]

It is now crucial to remind the wider socio-cultural and historic context:

"In light of this theological genealogy the Foucaldian apparatuses acquire an even more pregnant and decisive significance, since they intersect not only with the context of what the young Hegel called "positivity," but also with what the later Heidegger called Gestell (which is similar from an etymological point of view to dis-positio, dis-ponere, just as the German stellen corresponds to the Latin ponere). When Heidegger, in Die Technik und die Kehre (The Question Concerning Technology), writes that Ge-stell means in ordinary usage an apparatus (Gerät), but that he intends by this term "the gathering together of the (in)stallation [Stellen] that (in)stalls man, this is to say, challenges him to expose the real in the mode of ordering [Bestellen]," the proximity of this term to the theological dispositio, as well as to Foucault's apparatuses, is evident. What is common to all the terms is that they refer back to this oikonomia, that is, to a set of practices, bodies of knowledge, measures, and institutions that aim to manage, govern, control, and orient – in a way that purports to be useful – the behaviors, gestures, and thoughts of human beings." [2][page 12]

The dispositive is very closely related to what we know already from the time of Coser: namely the conflict theory, in response to Parsonian functionalism assuming a general consensus, both at the level of rationality and power and particularly its layout. According to Coser, is it on the contrary a conflict, a disagreement, which is latently present, and which introduces some dynamics into the social, and power relations, and accelerates the necessary solutions. Conflict, therefore, allows a better understanding of the concept of dispositive, because it is based on differential dynamic - static, followed by sensory and aesthetic configuration, followed by the ideal in the power tools of the subjectification processes. If we look at the general, common, thus to some positive elements of the different actors of the social relation, say the general consensus, we must also have in mind (Hegel), how one copes with the pressure that is created purely on her due to a indecision to unite the opposites. These opposites, however, cannot be otherwise than from the nature of its foundation different; it means that not united otherness, that is in a certain form kind of demonstrative, and according to Hegel, is the output of the impurity of the sense together with the sense's opposition to the purely abstract.

If this impurity of reason is to be somehow reconciled with positive elements, i.e. those that embody a particular richness of life, especially with the Platonic conception of the idea of goodness and beauty, it is essential that the latent disagreement is appropriately argued in favor of the general, whole, and not only in favor of idiosyncrasies, and separate parts. Here comes into play not only the concept of discussion, but also the notion of communication. For it is still true, that in any discussion in society, where there really is something we can discuss about, contains the structure of a latent conflict and misunderstanding, looking now away from the

---

[1] "... interlocutors do not make what they discuss in argument real. Existence is not concluded. The ontological argument is false. Nothing can be said about reality that does not presuppose it." (Lyotard, 1988: 32).

fact, that such a conflict can be deliberate and purposeful. In this respect, the assumptions themselves are in danger: the object and the subject of discussion is not something obvious, but rather a dispute, and must be established first.

"A dissensus is not a conflict of interests, opinions or values; it is a division inserted in ‚common sense': a dispute over what is given and about the frame within which we see something as given." [8][page 69]

The word is still somehow true, has always efficiency, and continues to serve its goal: i.e., understanding. The "word" in itself not only performs some work, expresses what it wants to say, and this is not just a work of the concept in the strict sense, but rather a very distinct but decisive "exclusivity of the word". In this sense we speak of exclusivity of the word as the process of spreading or expanding the territory of knowledge, the re-configuration of what can be said, and what is concealed by what is said. Nevertheless, or precisely because of it, it is an execution of the word as is the laying (Stellung), and the trajectory of the process of reconciliation of opposites, or the widespread irrationality of rationality (Weber).

"The words mean however what they [say], and the trajectory of the words actually indicates the processes that they can." [3][page 146][2]

Before we recall the concept of communication procedures, that does not solve the problem, but rather complicate it, let's add to the listed so far the aesthetic dimension of this concept. Aesthetics is more resistant to the referred simplification and elimination of subtle differences, because it takes into communication separate modes of expression. Aesthetics is actually a division of the sensory and the discourse about sense. The actual difference of *vision through vision* and *vision through thinking* is closely related. As Kant indicated, the singularity of aesthetic sharing and the requirement of universality, that is connected, leaves the *"governor mentality"* in quiet repose. In fact, the governor mentality corresponds to the concept of self-reference closure.

The singularity constantly undermines and contradicts this mentality, just by what Virilio has described as a clear disproportion: *given is just information, but not sensation*; this is apatheia. This inertia prevents political power to take any initiative in the process of subjectification, and gives rise to the initiative of phenomenon.

"Dissensus does not refer to a conflict of interests, opinions or values, but to the juxtaposition of two forms of the sensory implementation of collective intelligence. Politics frames a sensory world of its own, a world in which a generic intelligence is implemented." [8][page 80]

If the force field of power, especially political power, which is based on configuration of interests in decision-making processes, as the logic of redistribution of highly valued goods, preferences of parts to the whole, and their mutual re-configuration, then it is quite clear that aesthetics is not moving in this field, and has

---

[2] "... the aesthetic phrase is the phrase par excellance of the faculty of presentation, but that it has no concept for which to present its sensible or imaginative intuition, it cannot therefore determine a realm, but only a field. Moreover, that field is only determined to a second degree, reflectively, so to speak: not by the commensurability between the capacity for presenting and the capacity for conceptualizing. This commensurability is itself an Idea, its object is not directly presentable. " (Lyotard, 1988: 168).

more the character of the above-mentioned reference aesthetics. Recall the basic definition, as for the mentioned above the reference aesthetics has a basic internal link to the relationship of dispositive and reflexive mediality. For aesthetics is bringing together in one unit the above basic components, which stand at the very beginning of the whole chain: thus the *laying, articulation, singularity* and eventually the *techné of mediation* - **reflexive mediality,** which constitutes the **modes of thinking.** Then the true *reality of display* in the artwork can be seen first and foremost as an expression of a balanced relationship between the individual and the universal. Therefore, it is not so much that one or the other were given prominence in the expression of their own content, but rather to ensure that the display itself *expressed balance* of both principles. That applies to, e.g., seeing and the seen, thought and imaginary, or in other words, to see through vision and the vision through thinking. Mastering this technique is then thought to enter the difference territory itself, logics of strategies and models of thinking and versions of the general and the particular, to the world of singularities and contingency, with which the subject compensates as much as possible and able.

We refer to the definition of the concept of media in G.W.F. Hegel, who suggests, which assumptions we work with, when we understand the problem of mediation too immediately, or in some simple naming of things. And that is always associated with understanding the negative (non-simple unity) in connection with the unity of the general, which make it at all possible at the moment of disengagement from its opposite.

"Negation is inherent in a property as a *determinateness* which is immediately one with the immediacy of being, an immediacy which, through this unity with negation, is universality. As a One, however, the determinateness is set free from this unity with its opposite, and exists in and for itself." [4][page 69]

Reflexive mediality therefore responds to the dual interpretation of the concept of the media, to the difference in negativity, the difference of simple distinction and the difference of exclusivity, i.e., distinguish the distinction primarily in a way, that the negative, the negation of its own otherness loses the priority, and as crucial becomes the difference distinguishing the otherness in the whole of unity: in what things they have in common in terms of objectivity, yet so subtly different in their own specification. If this media cannot mediate, it becomes a mere operator of a false unification. Therefore, it is not the objective of media philosophy to search forms of the identifying unification, but on the contrary, to search for non-identifying unity, that lets the things talk in itself and for itself.

Basically, this means that medium must be self-differing; otherwise it is not a medium whatsoever, but merely a transporting means. This has, however, in relation to the aesthetic the following consequences.

As already mentioned above, the *aesthetic* is in its own territory if it is only a "guarantor" of a definite and universal validity of a clear relationship of beauty and truth, difference of vision and visibility, or of display and image, and thus more or less free of the illusion of redundant displays and unnecessary reliefs of the real: as the *dispositive* behind images notes *unification,* not dissent, conflict and the artificial expansion thereof. Inventing controversial versions of the world, including aesthetic versions, does not mean inventing languages capable to formulate problems, of which the existing languages can hardly speak; it is rather the ability to create communication strategies that do not allow penetration through lines of discourse, and that frequently use and misuse the discourse. And how aptly observes N. Luhmann, mediating in itself still does not constitute communication. For we must always remember the internal difference of the "Word" itself: there is a considerable difference between the word *communicated* (a mere articulation of content) and *shared* (implicit understanding). Remember the classical formulation of Wittgenstein:

"Most of the propositional and questions to be found in philosophical works and not false but nonsensical. Consenquetly we cannot give any answer to questions o this kind, but can only point outthat they are nonsensical. Most of the propositions ang question of philosophers arise from our failure the understand the logic of our languague. " 4.003 [12][page 19]

However, understanding the logic of our language, or rather the structure of its formation is one important condition, but there is another: What leads our understanding of the language, so that we know what the language actually says? That propositions and concepts correspond somehow to what they describe? They correspond, but with the exception of convention. Here still remains in the game the term of medium, the differentiating factor of mediation that leaves the contradiction in details of the thing and its reification in a mutual distance and distinctive self-articulation.

This is only possible in a society retaining the specific differences, something like a dialect of its own, and not the leveling of a media society, where media are understood as mass media interaction.

".. in the media society an ideal of emancipation is promoted, instead of emancipatory ideals built upon the entirely explainable self-confidence, on a perfect awareness of who knows how things are (whether it is Hegel's Absolute Spirit, or a person who is no longer in Marx's sense a slave of ideology). Such an ideal of emancipation is built upon an oscillation, a pluralism, and results in an erosion of that principle of reality.... Today's people can finally realize, that perfect freedom is not that of Spinoza, that the perfect freedom is not ... knowing the necessary structure of the real and the adaptation to the real." [11]

In principle, we can say that the central distinction is still the concept of Hegel: medium within the meaning of implied emancipation from false unification, neglect of conflict, which is own to each thing, and is forcing to self-developing differences. Conversely, the current understanding of the concept of media is actually rather the opposite: the unification at the cost of leveling, the suppression of internal differentiation, and at the same time the pressure on a general support of sharing of the more or less similar, if not the same in its mediation.

This is similar to the identity of expression and identity of character, specifically with their relations in the bilateral transcript, flipping one to the other, to which pointed already Wittgenstein:

"Identity of object I express by identity of sign, and not by using a sing of identity. Difference of object I express by difference of sign" 5.53 [12][page 52]

Self-confidence is the recognition of determination of diversity and mutual relatedness with different and also with the internally contradictory: the same principle of contradiction, that non-simple non-unity, with which each self-consciousness becomes a differentiating self-determination, and in this regard the **media** as a factor of a mutual motion to itself and to its own conflict, whether such a movement is correct, valid and participating in the general, is not a replaceable concept of media. And it cannot be valid. These are two different principles dealing with the real and the simulacrum of the real.

From this perspective, it is clear that it will be more or less necessary to return to the concept of a resolution that outlined G.W.F. Hegel: to understand the concept of **medium** in its differentiating essence, in its relative relatedness to the general as a whole of possible further relations. On the contrary, the concept of *media* as it is now widely accepted, will be left.

Obviously, the time is not far, when we shall start to talk about the era of **post-media**. And to ensure, that the era of explicit description of the media world of simulations looked like a period of compliance with the reality, which, however, by saying what it says, conceals what cannot be told. In terms of art we can add:

"... art requires philosophy, which interprets it in order to say what i tis unable to say, whereas art is only able to say it by not saying it. " [1][page 96]

The medium in its essence allows communicating even, what can be translated into other forms. And by doing this, it fulfills exactly its destination.

References

1. Adorno, T.W.: Aesthetic Theory. Continuum (2004)
2. Agamben, G.: Was ist ein Dispositiv? Diaphanes, Zürich (2008)
3. Foucault, M.: The Birth of Biopolitics: Lectures at the Collège de France, pp. 1978–1979. Palgrave (2008)
4. Hegel, G.W.F.: Phenomenology of Spirit. Oxford University Press (1977)
5. Luhmann, N.: Social systems. Stanford University Press (1995)
6. Lyotard.J-F.: Political Writings. Taylor & Francis (2002)
7. Lyotard, J.-F.: Le Différend. University of Minnesota Press (1988)
8. Ranciere, J.: Dissensus: On Politics and Aesthetics. Continuum International Publishing (2010)
9. Sloterdijk, P.: Tau von der Bermudas. Über einige Regime der Einbildungskraft. Suhrkamp Verlag (2001)
10. Sloterdijk, P.: Uber die Verbesserung der guten Nachricht: Nietzsches funftes "Evangelium". Suhrkamp Verlag (2001)
11. Vattimo, G.: The Transparent Society. Parallax (1992)
12. Wittgenstein, L.: Tractatus logico-philosoficus. Routledge, London (1974)

Interactive Film: The Computer as Medium

Roman Danylak

University of Technology, Sydney
roman@emotional-computing.com

Abstract. The focus of this paper is to attempt to define some key qualities of what will be described as interactive film. Interactive film is the description of user interface experience, where the screen surface is seen as a continuous piece of film altered by data interactions, which are but edits to the film observed on screen. As such computer screen representations as a user experience are seen as the convergence of the medium of film with computer databases. The paper also examines the history of two other media, namely the book and painting over the last five hundred years as examples to understand how media – its form – and its content – the message behave, leading to interactive film.

Keywords: Science-fiction and DUXU, Interface Design and Convergence.

1   The Nature of Media

McLuhan's famous dictum, the medium is the message [1]– guides this paper and its content. The statement, when paraphrased, may be understood as - it is the nature of a medium that decides what messages can be transmitted; this underlines the view that the form of the technology, its nature and characteristics, dictates the content. The focus here is to understand the computer as a medium- its form, supporting the greater ambition of defining its messages - its content.

A medium - that which is in between - refers to material and non-material process-es for transmitting messages [2] Media forms include text, film, television and radio. A medium, of which media is the plural, is defined as 'something in between'. A medium then, is that which carries a message between the maker / sender and the receiver of the information, enabling communication. The air that carries our verbal utterances is a medium; a clay tablet with impressions marking the number of head of cattle is a medium. Media are communication technologies with a long history and are used to create inventory and portability of information through the senses, primarily of what is seen and heard, but this now also includes touch. A medium, from which the plural media is derived, simply means that which is in between, or that which is in the middle of two communicating individuals. In this way, paper is a medium carry-ing the message of written words to from the writer to the reader. Computers have a multimedia dimension in that many media, often interlinked, are present in the one machine [3].

A. Marcus (Ed.): DUXU 2014, Part I, LNCS 8517, pp. 527–536, 2014.

2   The Message of the Printed Book: The Rise of the Individual

It is worthwhile examining the last great period of new media invention – what is now very old media - and its effects upon society as a result of the messages that these media conveyed – towards building a model of medium and it message in computing. In European history, it was the invention of the mechanical printing press by Gutenberg in 1450 [4] that caused a revolution in individual perception giving rise to what we now know as the *individual*. The book, previously a hand-made object and therefore rare, was restricted knowledge and poorly dissemination. With the *advent* of mechanical cast moveable type, books become more readily available and by 1623 the publication of Shakespeare's first folio copies occurred some of which still exist to this day [5]. This ready, privately available information gives rise to the individual because it is the individual who can think and interpret for themselves the message of the author now having access to an otherwise absent medium. This singles a departure from the rigid preceding hierarchical feudal order and as a set of values is known as *humanism* [6].

Similarly, Machievelli's work *The Prince* [7] which highlights the rise of the individual, a person capable of subterfuge and able to scale the previously unassailable walls of medieval order. The Machievellian individual has a strong and complex inner life, a psychological dimension that is self-willed and self-driven. This is the dark side of Renaissance man; this is the other side of humanism, where humanism as defined through Thomas More's *Utopia* [8] showed a regard and consideration for the plight of the individual with early projections of social planning. The emphasis is on the individual mind and what it can produce with the information of the new media, the book. The humanist, both good and bad, emphasises the creative ability of the individual, which is still a dominant from a western perspective, and manifests in inventions like the *personal computer* (PC).

Further, Shakespeare's plays hold within them the archetypes of this new-self willed, mobile reading and writing individual. A number of his tragic characters fail in part because of their inability to understand and operate the new media of the day: the book. Macbeth, who does both read and write in the play [9], fails to *interpret* the riddle of the witches showing himself to be a poor reader. It is a tragic irony that this man who can both read and write is hasty and unreflective when listening to the prophecy of the witches, believing in a single interpretation of their message - that he cannot fail in his endeavours - propelling him into a sequence of murders which do not secure him his desired crown. Hamlet, on the other hand thinks extensively about the philosophical outcomes of life, with stage directions showing him reading a book [10]. But his sophisticated thoughts of life and death as typified in his soliloquy 'To be or not to be....' [11] hinder him, as he fails then to secure a successful revenge of his father's murder; Hamlet is an over-reader, unable to balance thought and action, not understanding how the new media of his day should fit into his world and serve his political ambitions. Whilst in *Julius Caesar* [12] it is Mark Antony, an ancient orator, who holds and unopened scroll – very, very old media – on which Caesar's will is written. He holds this and speaks to the crowd, emphasising the murdered Cesar's generosity but uses the presence of the unread document dramatically to reinforce a promise and thus swings political favour in his direction finally cornering his Brutus and the fellow murderers. Shakespeare has shown his audiences how the new media of the day can be used successfully or unsuccessfully to support individual ambition.

3   Painting: A Medium with a Message That Reflects Upon the Medium

Closer to the age of computing in the mid twentieth century, painting has offered intelligent discourse on how we see and experience the world. Painting is an innovative medium, creating new ways of seeing where the old vision is replaced by the new. That old media are absorbed by new media as McLuhan has stated [13], is also true for the aesthetics of painting. What follows is a brief commentary of significant art over the last century with an initial reference to the Renaissance, commenting on the role that machines have in the production of art and in human perception potentially offering a model for interactive film and computing.

To then jump some four hundred years we see in the work of Picasso's and Braques Cubism [14] a world dramatically changed by the new machines of the early 20th Century. At this time, a time when industrialisation is in full swing with the motor car, electricity, flight and the growth of massive industrialised cities, human experience was forced into a speed and complexity of experience that was entirely novel. What Cubism offered was an instantaneous view of the complexity of human experience; life was now not a matter of a single beautiful aesthetic view to be painted, but rather a clash of different sometimes jarring and conflicting views into one. At the same time what Cubism was resonating with the new science of psychology, which both Freud and Jung were evolving at the time, the interiority of the individual. Cubism also resonated with new

Pablo Picasso - Weeping Woman 1937
© Succession Picasso/DACS 2007

Fig. 1. Picasso *Weeping woman,* 1937 (Google image http://images.google.com/images)

viewpoints in science, namely Einstein's theory of Relativity, supporting the notion that knowledge evolved from the single privileged observer was a limited view of how reality was constructed. Cubism in this way, was a medium with a new message and expressing the new complexity of the individual (see Figure 1).

Painting, a light based medium, is however subverted by photography [15]. The process of manual mimetic depiction is suddenly automated and a window on the life as reality is made. The new image making of photography made redundant the craft of drawing and realistic painting obsolete. Photography spread rapidly and became popular and was made available to a mass consumer public. The new here had also absorbed the old medium. The same with magnetically recorded sound by Edison; the translation of the word into text in one swoop is made redundant. When sound and light converge in the form of film [16], with the understanding that successive photographic frames delivers an illusion of movement, just as perspective delivered the illusion of space, then the process of mimesis, or reproducing reality as we see it, is complete. At this time also Duchamp, with the exhibition of the pissoir at a Paris exhibition in 1917 [17] and giving it the title *Fountain,* he was announcing the redundancy of the old media in art. The pissoir, an ironic and cheeky object to submit as an art object, is of course industrially made by machine after an original form has been made by a single craftsman. Duchamp was commenting wryly on the domination of the machine, that the artisan, the maker by hand was being made redundant by industrial processes.

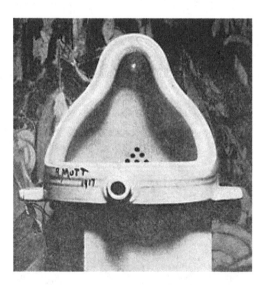

Fig. 2. Fountain 1917, Duchamp. Source: Wikipedia.

It was Warhol, in the 20th Century, however who suggested that not all was lost in the land of art as a result of machine made art. Instead of decrying the loss of painting, he invented a visual aesthetic in his work, the aesthetic of mass produced images. Warhol emphasised that *repetition* was an aesthetic principle, which indeed it is. In his work of Elvis Presley pulling a gun (see Figure 3), it is the multiple representations of the drama of pulling a gun – an extreme act – that highlights the fact that the message is change by the repetition, its impact lessened and modified by the machine reproduction. Whilst in his multiple works of Marilyn Munroe, the changes in chromatic key of the woman most popularly known in the mass media of the day as the most beautiful of all women, indicated that the new palette and brush of the artist was push button colour selection, replacing brush and canvas (see Figure 4).

Fig. 3. Presley Gun: Warhol. Source: Google images.

Fig. 4. Monroe: Warhol Source: Google images

Richter then follows Warhol, a popular contemporary artist of the late 20th and early 21st century. His approach was to develop an aesthetic of an image-producing machine that malfunctions, a machine that like Warhol's produces images but produces not as designed or ordered. The work might be the refuse of any common colour-copying machine in any office in the world. His work is on canvas and is hand made, creating an irony from the early departures of Duchamp (see Figure 4).

Fig. 5. Image Richter 'Abstraktes Bild (Source http://www.telegraph.co.uk/culture/art/art-news/)

In summary, in the artworks we see a strong and well-developed habit of artists using their medium in ways that often reviews and comments upon the limits and potentials of the medium. The artworks discussed show an understanding of how a medium may be superseded by a newer, more technically or intellectually evolved medium. Many of the artists discussed addressed the problem by repositioning or re-tasking the old media meaning that new perspectives on the new tools appeared. In short, they asked what the medium was in its new form and shaped messages to that medium accordingly.

4   The Qualities of Interactive Film

The approach here in examining medium and message is not so much philosophical as material: how does the medium perform and what can it say taking into account the impact of media and their messages as evidenced in past epochs? A single distinction is made here, in that the depiction of on-screen images by computer systems will be understood here as *interactive film*: film, because of the pervasive real and animated images; the motion; and interactive, because these images change with the addition of any data through exchange of information with data bases.

To look at any personal computer or smartphone it is in plain view that the computer is a machine that makes other machines [18]; it absorbs older forms of media be it text, images, sound and simulates their real functions virtually. The notion is quite useful and in part is responsible for the difficulty in being able to define its characteristics as a medium making messages because of the scale and complexity. The singular, object associated nature of media and media machines is historical and physical; printing presses, cameras, typewriters, microphones etc. and so on are knowable and have stand alone functions. The explosion of what are known as apps in mobile computing generating $200 billion of business in 2004 [19], is the result of this 'machine making other machines' capacity. Hence, rapid proliferation and a change of scale into million if not billion of interactions and more, is a central feature of the medium and its messages.

Interactive film, which is what we see as the computer screen surface, is then the result of convergence. The word *convergence* is often used inaccurately and creates more confusion than understanding. The word 'converge' suggests that things are becoming focused into a single almost absolute point. The real underlying principle of interactive film is a marriage between film and programmed interaction, the re-patterning of data. Hence this compounding of the two processes, one the simulation of a material process, the other electronic - brings about the invention of screen representations whilst also referring to a database. The *telegraph* is also a convergence; electrical conductivity was converged with the intellectual / physical process of speech. The notion that the current of a wire could be interrupted and that the interruption of the current could follow a code representing the sonic alphabet was a marriage, a convergence.

Essentially there are three main characteristics that support calling the medium of the computer, interactive film:

The first is the **presence of touch** as a predominant interaction mode [20]. If we take the example of the ever-popular smart phone and tablet interface now in extensive use, the management of the user applications is through a gentle left and right motion finger touch motion. Clearly this resembles film in its early manifestation travelling through an edit machine (see Figures 5 (a) (b)).

Fig. 6. (a) Manual film editing; Source Google images simulating film Human touch is an essential (b) Smartphone surface Source: Google images

The current success of smart phone technology is the result of adopting a film metaphor by designers. The design of the surface is useful from a user perspective in that the volume of information for the user is limited by the left and right movement. A constant difficulty for the designer is the appearance of overwhelming amounts of data representations; for the user, the visualisation of user functions must be coherent and not lead to cognitive overload. The adoption of the film as a material design metaphor has solved this pervasive and difficult problem with astounding commercial success resulting.

The **second is convergence of the data-base with the film surface**. The constant movement of the film surface to and from the database is a unique feature of interactive film. This is best understood from the perspective of *interaction*; we can say that each viewing of a screen presents us with a new frame. Film traditionally operates as a medium travelling in a single playback direction delivering the illusion of movement at 26 frames per second. The computer readily delivers the playback of digital film copying its analogue form. The other depictions of media forms are also film projections but they are often still frames. Rather than travelling along the axis of time, the graphic user interface (GUI) refreshes the image in the database, adding or subtracting data as directed. In this way the refreshes screen can be understood as a film edit, or a new frame in the original experience of the screen. A significant difference in the traditionally fixed film playback and interactive film is that fixed film is repeatable and passive. Interactive film may be repeatable in its original form and unaltered by interaction and commands sent to databases makes the relationships between the interactive entirely film unique [21] .

The **third is the nature of representations** classified as either realistic or animated, a distinction that is typical of film [22]. The photographic basis of film allows itself to make either real or animated depictions.

Fig. 7. (a) Real photographic images (b) Animated representations Source: Google images

The real, is that which has an apparent parallel from the image to world which we share and experience; animation is the capacity to draw or fabricate illustrations which have life-like qualities, often described as that traditionally has also relied on a photographic process. A look at any smart phone and the representations of its applications indicates a strong mix of both the real and animated. The distinction often goes undetected (see Figures 6 (a) (b)).

5   Conclusion

The focus of this paper has been to briefly survey select examples of older and contemporary media up to and including the computer at the moment its absorbs old media and to describe the characteristics of new media. One modern medium stands out in the process and that has been the medium of film, and as discussed, it is interactive film – the convergence of film with database interaction – that best describes the medium of emerging human computer interaction.

From the viewpoint of the emergence and socialisation of the book, we can see that a type of person, the individual, was not only the content – the message – of the medium, as featured in Shakespearean texts, but that the mechanical reproduction of the medium and invention of that time also encouraged individual interpretation to occur through increased access to information. Importantly, this is a manifestation of sound.

It is noteworthy that painting has been a medium that has a highly functional and practical beginning in terms of perspective drawing. It's evolution however has gone far beyond that, displaying a capacity to self reflect in ways that responded to other media technologies and to crises of redundancy in the art form, creating innovation within the medium. The capacity of painting to do so is very interesting and may explain its long-standing success to take a dominant role culturally for so many centuries. Importantly, this is a manifestation of light.

In the case of interactive film we are still only just beginning to understand the behaviour of the medium. The three qualities – transport, interaction, and the dual representation of the real and the animated – are highly significant factors in the current success of the computer. The summary here has been focused more on the medium rather than the message, a result of the still overwhelming development and invention of the technical aspects of computing. Importantly it is the recording of both sound and light that are at the foundation of film, absorbing both book and painting.

References

1. McLuhan, M., McLuhan, E.: Laws of Media; the New Science, p. 7. University of Toronto Press (1988)
2. Dictionary, Electronic Oxford American Dictionary Version 1.0.2, Software (2005)
3. Dijk, J.V.: Digital Media. In: Downing, J.D.H. (ed.) Sage Handbook of Media Studies, USA (2004)
4. McLuhan, M.: Understanding Media. McGraw Hill, Toronto (1964)
5. Shakespeare, W., Mouston, D.: First Folio 1623 Facsimilie, Applause, New York (1995)
6. Hayles, K.N.: How We Became Posthuman. University of Chicago Press (1999)
7. Machievelli, N.: The Prince and other writings. Canterbury Classics Baker and Taylor (2014)
8. More, T.: Utopia. Broadview Press (2010)
9. Shakespeare, W.: The Tragedy of Macbeth. Reimer, A.N. (ed.). University of Sydney (1980)
10. Shakespeare, W.: Hamlet, Reimer, A.N. (ed.). University of Sydney (1985)
11. Ibid. Act III sc. iii

12. Shakespeare. W., Julius Caesar. Spevack, J. (ed.) New Cambridge Shakespeare, Act 3 sc.i
13. McLuhan, M.: Understanding Media. McGraw Hill, Toronto (1964)
14. Hughes, R.: Shock of the New. Knopf, New York (1981)
15. Manovich, L.: The Language of New Media. MIT (2001)
16. Hughes, R.: Ibid
17. Hughes, R.: ibid
18. Crogan, P.: Games, simulations and serious fun: An interview with EspenArseth. Scan: J. Media Arts Culture 5, 1 (2008)
19. Varshney, U.: Mobile Commerce: a new frontier. Computer 33(10)
20. pp. 32–38, USA (October 2000)
21. Danylak, R., Edmonds, E.: Touch as the act of signification; naming as a key design concept for gesturally intuitive interactive space. In: Engage: Interaction, Art and Audience Experience, pp. 62–67. CCS Press, University of Technology, Sydney (2006)
22. Danylak, R., Edmonds, E.: The planning and experience of time and space in three gestural media: theatre, film and interactive film. Int. J. Arts and Technology 5(1), 1–16 (2012)
23. Kelty, C., Landecker, H.: 'A Theory of Animation: Cells, L-systems, and Film'
24. Grey Room, pp. 30–63 (Fall 2004)

Digital Self: Fiction and Non-fiction on the Internet

Ana Carol Pontes de França, Luciano Rogério de Lemos Meira,
and Marcelo Márcio Soares

Federal University of Pernambuco, Brazil
acpsicologa@gmail.com, luciano@meira.com, marcelo2@nlink.com

Abstract. By tradition, cognitive science uses the computer metaphor and psychological models that attempt to explain human complexity isolating the subject of sociocultural plot. Breaking with cartesian dualism, we invite the reader to consider the virtual-real continuous, in which the self is constituted as a discursive construction, social and narratively structured that emerges and develops in sequences of dialogical action established by partners located in time and space. Accordingly, we address aspects of communication and interaction on subjective relationships and intimacy we have with others while navigating on the internet. Paradoxically, in digital culture, fiction and non-fiction walk intertwined, supporting our practices with resources that allow us to compensate for the lack of a physical body. Basing on these assumptions, we investigated how the continuities and discontinuities occur in discursive ways in which people relate to themselves while transits on virtual and physical scenarios. For that, we turn to the ethnographic method. More specifically, we used: video version of the classic A Christmas Carol by Charles Dickens; interview protocol about personal continuity interrelated to the film, the self and Orkut, and clippings Orkut profiles of respondents. Three subjects participated in the study: one male and two females, aged between 20 and 30 years. Paying attention to the pragmatic aspect of the utterance or speech, we chose the enunciation because it reveals the voices of the "I" positions that connects the agent of speech to the audience in communicative practices of sustaining themselves. In the analysis, we grouped the responses according to the content that corresponded, in this case, to the "I" positions in the narrative act. Thus, we identify two levels of analysis: in the first one, the subject is engaged in a process of authorship, in the second one, the subject acts as if he/her were another. In such circumstances, the positions taken by the subject allow him/her to move through the imagination, as though in space, in accordance with changes in situation and time. By this study, we concluded that: 1) affinities, likes and interests are anchors that people use at virtual world to bring them what they know of the physical world, 2) the number of singularities (other "I" s) are interconnected to affinities, likes and interests, whose associations are located in the virtual environment on the links (symbolic places) between profiles and communities (writing, photos, images, audio, video), as well as between users and developers (aid terms , security center, etc.), 3) people do not connect to the internet just because they are geographically distant, but mainly because they seek answers, seek to establish that the communicative ties closer together; 4) while communicating, the user may oppose the idea that others have of him/her, if different from the others, although simultaneously is engaged in groups that make he/she similar to and different from each other as a communal.

A. Marcus (Ed.): DUXU 2014, Part I, LNCS 8517, pp. 537–547, 2014.

Keywords: Digital Culture, Semiotics, Human-Computer Interaction, Sense of Self.

1   Introduction

To authenticate our access online in an Orkut1 profile we have to registry our user "name" and password. Doing that, we announce our entry to the digital network. At that moment both, the system and other users in the network, are notified of our presence.

This presence makes it possible to consider a body - metaphorically - in motion. In such situations, message and body are intertwined, becoming an event in which the subject is presented as a sign. [1]

Using the language, a person "enter" his presence, occupying a particular place in a network of relationships. This body configuration, in turn, affects the other, producing emotions, sensations and ideas that diversify according to the context.

On Orkut, virtual profiles are highlighted. But similar to what happens in our everyday life, when we create a virtual profile, we are asked to answer 'who am I?', which is clearly not always such an easy task, although we often have to do so.

Fill the field 'who am I' in Orkut requires a lot of creativity, because every time the users do, personal characteristics emerge at the virtual environment, which although similar, are published in different ways, while occur changes in situation and time.

As in the diaries of yore, these users now have a symbolic "place" to record everything that seems meaningful to them in the moment [expectations, desires, aspirations, frustrations, riots, hopes, loves, dislikes, etc..]. However, unlike those, now a days we have many technological resources available that enable us to publish, re-edit and even delete content and people of our lives, including ourselves.

This ephemeral aspect of Orkut reveals our transience that is related to cultural aspects and to the historical moment in which we live. Always in search of ourselves, we establish discursive, intimate and public links, which allow us to contact the various characters (a social Other or other "I"s and their respective "me"s) [2] that co-inhabit our world - internal and external, physical and virtual - who actively collaborate with the composition of our own story life, helping us to ensure our own continuity in time.

This multitude of actors, metaphorically embodied to the environment [3], helps the user to communicate and interact and it's for that audience he addresses his message.

Therefore, for communication to occur, it is necessary that the interlocutor advertise himself, be acknowledged and update himself constantly and simultaneously. In this case, the Other, albeit imagined, occupies a crucial place in the process, because the design and communicative action depends of this Other to legitimize and complement itself. [4]

---

[1] `www.orkut.com`

Whereas dialogue as (an inside and outside) speech activity, is uninterrupted, we can note that the user of Orkut is involved in a network of social negotiations whose beginning is far prior to participation on digital network relationships.

Conceive language and communication in these terms implies consider the notion of genesis involved in the emergence and development of a sense of self, which is reached when the communication intertwines the context and socio-cultural practices.

So, before they meet and hold talks at Orkut, users gathered and reported to each other in different contexts, both physical and virtual: participating in work, education and leisure activities, writing a diary, reading a book, using search engines, forums and online discussion lists, etc..

In these interactions, these individuals seek answers, albeit unpredictables, regulated by a semiotic field of possibilities that shapes the historical and social context filled with multiple voices. [5, 6, 7]

For those particularly involved, the historical and situational aspect allows them to weave the dialogical wire that gives life to the narrative act, so that the process of constitution of a sense of self revels itself as a live, creative, dynamic and changeable process.

Dialoguing and interacting with others, the person appropriates the language and transforms it, leaving marks of style while transiting the different scenarios that make up the human experience. [1]

Thus, as occurs in presencial situations, the Orkut user, while composes a virtual profile, shows up as a subjectivity marked by revised and renegotiated positions through an irreversible time [6, 7], which gives a situational character to negotiations set out in language-game. [8]

Through these positionings, the subjects respond to each other composing discursive links between profiles and communities, which allows the subject to relate the voices of others that precede the anticipated responses of the audience (prospective dialogue with others).

Addressing a message to the addressee, even imagined, the user of Orkut is also marked by these others in their finishes: in the choice of verbs, pronouns, the use of deictic, abbreviations, intonations and textual organization, so these personal boundaries conferred by interlocutors in the narrative act when they respond to each other, characterizes collaborations in the environment, making specific relationships between network components.

Despite these characteristics, users guide their online actions from affinities, common tastes and interests which, in turn, approximates users of what they know about the physical world, which works as bridges between communities, profiles and developers (when reporting illegal actions on network security center, for example).

Thus, Orkut, an alternative cultural support, contributes to moments of personal and collective continuity and change, being related: 1) to creativity - when the user reinvents himself, resorting to the use of abbreviations, accents, emoticons, pictures, audio and video, and 2) to the opening for the new - as it enables the user to integrate the past into a future still under construction.

2   Method

In order to better understand how the 'I' construction on the Internet happens, we seek to rescue users opinions that allow them to support their own continuity inscribing themselves in existence despite the changes in time.

In such circumstances, it was possible to observe the connections on subjects' history, in which their own culture participates. That lead us to consider that culture exerts significant influence, modeling the minds of those who are under its influence [9], while simultaneously supports narrative constructions.

Such constructions, in turn, relate to broader aspects of social, political and ideological-cultural training as part of a process that depicts the macro-social structure on human interactions and about relationships they establish to each other, with the artifacts and with the environment.

In this sense, the narrative is taken from a comprehensive and interpretative framework of discourse in which the intersubjectivity and semiotic mediation are fundamentally integrated into the course of events.

To consider the narrative production in these terms represents an advance at the methodological approach, given that the narrative leaves the mere tool condition, composing the scenario in which the subjects mutually constitutes each other, as well as the researcher too, revealing to be epistemologically possible to the necessary balance between facts, concepts and theories in psychological science. [10]

2.1   Research Goals

Taking into account that literature and other media often discuss the existence of a Virtual 'I' totally divorced from face-to-face experience and from physical existence, we propose to investigate and understand how the 'I' construction on the Internet occurs.

As in old diaries, users usually write their own personal information on Orkut, highlighting situations and events while they compose the virtual profile itself.

However, unlike the old diaries, locked and hidden in secret or in difficult to access locations, on Orkut, users publically exposes themselves, so that all that a user posts can be read by numerous people connected to the network.

Given the current situation, we came across some questions that guided our actions as a researcher:

Given the changes experienced by us, how to explain the identity and the continuity sense in our everyday mutant experiences?

How the self takes shape on online and offline transit?

How utterance participates in this process?

In which aspects people re-present themselves on a virtual environment?

From these personal questions, we propose to investigate how the continuities and discontinuities occur in discursive ways in which people talk about themselves while they transit between physical and virtual scenarios, in order to understand how the subject in relation to another, ensures his/her own maintenance over time and space amidst a constant process of change.

For this, we focused on personal positionings taken by the participants in both personal interview and in Orkut profile, considering that the user is invited to refer him/herself and the others in a network of relationships online.

2.2 Participants – Field

Given that Orkut is predominantly used by young people, we chose to perform the study with students from Federal University of Pernambuco (UFPE), considering the possibility of access them in their educational institution.

Observing the ethical criteria needed to complete the study, we began the recruitment of participants, which occurred in a three weeks period, when they were contacted on their classrooms, located on UFPE's College.

On that occasion, they gave their name, phone, email and Orkut profile for contact. During the contact stage, once more we asked the students if they were interested in participating in the study. If we obtained an afirmative answer, we scheduled a day, time and place for an interview.

However, the participation in the interview and the consequent continuation of the study depended on the voluntary acceptance, obtained in the Term of Consent, signed and dated by volunteers moments before the interview.

The possibility to withdraw from the study at any time was offered to the participants, if they so desired.

2.3 Procedures

An interview was scheduled with each participant in order to understand how the self continuity occurs over time despite the changes in life story. That happened in a classroom located on the premises of the Post-Graduate Program in Cognitive Psychology at UFPE.

Initially, we invited participants to watch the movie A Christmas Carol (MGM, 77 minutes, color, 2004), and then respond to an interview, adapted from studies by Chandler et. al. [11]

By the interview, we seek to access the participant's opinions about the possible aspects of continuity and discontinuity in their own lives and about the lives of the film's protagonist (another social).

The opinions of the interviewees about the character's history, Ebenezer Scrooge, the protagonist of the film, are indispensable to the study because the way the informants "read" the story of this other, they take into account all those who consider significants on that occasion.

To do so, we based on the contributions of Chandler et al. [11], we took as reference the material used in the investigation of the self continuity by this author.

The procedures were intended to:

1) request to the participants to talk about their own experience of continuity along their own life story;

2) ask participants to describe, with as much detail as possible, both in the present time as five or ten years ago, as more meaningful in their life stories, emphasizing that

what they tell about their own history, in the past and present, are in fact different (changes in their own life);

3) ask respondents how they can reconcile their previously exposed conviction about their own continuity, if they clearly offer evidences about their own personal changes. [11]

In this phase, participants:

a) Watched the video version of the "classic" A Christmas Carol, by Charles Dickens;

b) Answered a semi-structured interview, about the events on the character's life story;

c) Were invited to explain the character's changes and continuities throughout history.

Then, participants were asked to:

d) Talk about the changes and continuities that occurred in their own lives [11]

e) Talk about the changes and continuities that occurred in their lives after publishing a profile on Orkut, placing it historically.

Thus, the interview about the participant's own self follows the interview about the character (social Other). The order of the story presentation, the media in which it was presented, as well as semi-structured interview that follows the presentation of these materials was based on procedures used by Chandler et al. [11].

The interviews were recorded on digital audio and video files for later transcription.

3   Data Analysis

In search of integrating the multiple relationships of parts to the whole, and in order to overcome the dichotomies frequently employed at the time – objective vs. subjective, individual vs. social, internal vs. external –, Vygotsky discusses the question of method, opposing the element analysis, proposing to seek an analysis by units and setting the unity as one instance of clipping that retains the properties of the whole that is intended investigate. [12]

Paying attention to the pragmatic aspect of the utterance or speech, we chose the enunciation because it manifests itself as the voice of an 'I' position that connects the audience to a communicative agent - in person or imaginatively incorporated - in self maintenance practices.

Accordingly, we focus on discursive links that intertwines the voices of others that are previous to the person to the answers that the person anticipates in function of a supposed audience, so that the person can secure his/her location in time and space that allows up his own existence.

Thus, the mutually constitutive relationship self-other, the utterance allows us to distinguish , moment by moment , various 'I' positions assumed by the person in the narrative act, that through a narrative space-time location, is rescued from the polysemic flow . [5, 6, 7, 11]

Based on these assumptions , we highlight the main features of utterances , which are essential to our analysis [1] :

• The utterances are addressed to an audience (social Other or other 'I 's and their 'me's);
• The contours of the utterances are delimited by alternating speech;
• The utterances are a unity of meaning;
• The meaning of the utterance establishes relationships between the different author's positionings;
• The utterances reveal judgments;
• Each utterance presents design and communicative action with characteristic ways of finishing;
• Being a "finished" form, anticipates the responses of the other, hoping that the other complements him/herself (incompleteness and inconclusiveness).

To this end , we became filiated to a notion of subjectivity that sets itself through different positionings taken along an irreversible time. In this sense, the dialogical wire that weaves a web of meanings and senses, links the voices that precede and follow the enunciation making possible to guarantee the sense of continuity in the midst of changes that occur in the situation and time.

These multiple author's addresses, the affective aspects involved in such diversity of positions as well as the creativity and innovation that emerge in the process are often neglected in traditional analyzes of the content and discourse .

Accordingly, we chose the qualitative approach of the phenomenon, based on Hermans [5] and Valsiner [6 , 7] , by possibility to rescue the personal attempts of continuity, albeit in a fictional way, facing the changes experienced by users in different scenarios that takes shape in the human experience of addressing the discourse to another.

The interest about developmental dynamics is related to the sense of continuity (identity) facing the changes that occur over time. That directed our efforts to accurately trace the phenomenon investigated, which allowed us to conduct our analysis on a micro-genetic level.

From our point of view, this level of analysis allows us to monitor, second by second, the interdependence of intersubjective phenomena, which in this study is linked to the 'I' positions in dialogue.

These different positions allow us, as researchers, to understand the ontogenesis on the constant flow of microgenetic episodes that also relates them to the environment.[7]

To do so, we consider that discursive practices integrate, compose, transform and transits through different scenarios that integrate the virtual and presencial human experience of addressing speech to another, which is comprised, in this study, by the three moments of the interview about the personal continuity of participants: about the film , about the self and about Orkut as well as by clippings of semiotic mediation on the internet.

Next, we highlight the type of analysis proposed by Hermans [5] and Valsiner [6, 7], from which we could analyze the whole by its component parts that, in turn, operate in dynamic, integrated and coherent way, organized to produce a wide variety of phenomena of higher order. That contributed even so we could identify the interrelationships between an 'I' narrator and an 'I' narrated.

3.1   Typology Analysis

According to Hermans [5], the sense of continuity in the dialogical self involves:

• The empirical components that belong to the person (whatever one might call 'mine'): the body, the mental states, people and things in the world, the environment and everything that is familiar and allows a physical and symbolic extension of the subject;
• Temporal relationships translated into spatial relationships, or in other words, the transition between the past and the present into the future (the plot);
• The external domain of the self (the socio-cultural 'body': the family, the nation and the other groups of belonging).

In this sense, we adopted the 'I' positions as a theoretical reference analysis [5, 6, 7], considering that the narrative identities - composed by different parties that establish dynamic relationships between them: goal, author, events, scenery, characters and plot - take place in the language and are modeled from the dialogic relationships established by the interlocutors.

According to Goffman [13], so we can interpret what is being narrated, we need to realize the connectives which function as clues that contextualize the speech. Taking these clues as a reference, we can frame the narrative action.

To Goffman [13] the interpretation of the animation in the narrative requires that our attention be focused on the characters and on the clues that reveal their evidences because the narrator not only informs the listener, but creates a drama that surrounds and affects the audience.

For this, we make use of strategies that connect the audience's attention, so that both we, the authors, as the others, are involved with the plot, as occurs, for example, when people use verbal and non-verbal resources, ranging from gestures and glances to the use of direct and indirect speech by the interlocutors.

Taking these considerations as a starting point, we grouped the responses of the participants according to their content, which in this case correspond the 'I' positions in the narrative act.

In other words, to highlight the pragmatic aspects of communication, we focus on the socio-cultural practices of self maintenance mediated by signs since they involve situated dialogical actions of addressing the discourse to another, to an audience, albeit fictitious.

In this sense, we complement our analysis by considering some socio-cultural criteria often used in the organization of socio-communicative events: what for, whom, to whom, how, where and when, commonly observed on self maintenance practices. Those are related to the pragmatic conditions speech [14] which, in turn, confer organization and coherence to the narrative act.

Such conditions allow the person weave the dialogical wires that give life to the narrative act, while simultaneously integrating the various time slices and whatever else might call 'mine' the own account.

The pragmatic conditions of the narrative act, therefore, characterize the discursive links indispensable to the self maintenance practices, allowing the person connect the voices of others that precedes him/herself with the responses that the person anticipates because of a supposed audience, to ensure their own continuity amid a constant process of change.

Thus, the typology adopted reveals how people make sense about their own and the others continuity, because when the person talks, updates him/herself, highlighting past references and a possible future that allow to identify the sense of personal continuity in face of changing. [11 , 15]

Therefore, the historicity that emerges and integrates the participants utterances revels the past and possible (opening to a canon's rupture and to the emergence of the new).

Thus, in the participants utterances, the earlier and later manifestations are understood as 'true' for historical reasons [11], circumstantially considered plausible by the interlocutors.

That is, over time, the subject learns talk about him/herself, in relationship with others, about others and about the things in the world [what for, whom, to whom, how, where and when], reasoned on cultural traditions. These traditions, then, offer the person a repertoire of possibilities and constraints that make the narration itself intelligible to other members of the culture.

However, despite utterances produced by participants - in a sense - be socially shared making them intelligible to others, we also can see the personal creativity weave the plot of personal senses and meanings, at different times and by different ways, about events taken as similar - for example, talking about the self in presencial and virtual situations - which reveals a flexible, diachronic and human time, in the narrative composition of the his/her own life story.

These utterances also show the appropriation of cultural traditions when the person appoints, describes and contrasts the different versions of reality, which is closely related to the bond of belonging that he/she establishes with social groups and cultural manifestations, or, as Bruner [9] suggests, with a "community tool kit."

Thus, the discursive links built between different time slices, are closely related to self maintenance social practices by the members of a given culture [11] which, in turn, also reveals the full complexity that involves the change in the continuity-change dialectic synthesis.

4   Results

Multiple positionings of the self, in the transit between physical and virtual scenarios, were identified from participants' utterances. In this perspective, the characters that emerge on the users' addressing speech reveal all plurality and polyphony of the narrative identity of respondents in which their opinions are implicated in the complex plot composition, which involves the multiple positionings that ensure the creation of a sense of personal continuity amidst change.

5   Discussion

From this study we concluded that we should not restrict the human being existence to a physical existence. Although necessary, it can only be understood from something that complements it (the presencial and the virtual, the objective and the subjective, the factual and the imagined, the internal and the external, etc.), and to that we can establish a relationship of interdependence.

In this sense, the greatest contribution of this study involves a change of perspective of the human being in his/her relationship to the virtual environment. Contrary to what many people think, the internet is not divorced from the physical world. In this sense, artifacts play a social role and cannot be understood detached from social activities (even imagined) as well as from the active participation of the context that emerges in these actions.

Consequently, we are much more than "a node on the network", we are people, and as such, our online actions have, in fact, impact on offline and physical situations: versions of dialogues we have with others on physical world can be extended to virtual environments and return to physical scenarios, characterizing a continuous and uninterrupted dialogical process.

References

1. Peres, F.: Diálogo e autoria:do desenvolvimento ao uso de sistemas de informação. Tese de Doutorado. UFPE, Psicologia Cognitiva, Recife (2007)
2. Bakhtin, M.: Problemas da póetica de Dostoievski, 3ª edn. Forense Universitária, Rio de Janeiro (2002b)
3. Lakoff, G., Johnson, M.: Metaphors we live by. University of Chicago, Chicago (1980)
4. Mead, J.: Mind, self and society from the standpoint of a social behaviorist. University of Chicago, Chicago (1934), http://spartan.ac.brocku.ca/~lward/Mead/pubs2/mindself (accessed in February 2007)
5. Hermans, H.: The dialogical self: toward a theory of personal and cultural positioning. Culture & Psychology 7(3), 243–281 (2001)
6. Valsiner, J.: Temporal integration of structures within the Dialogical Self. In: Keynote Lecture at the 3rd International Conference on Dialogical Self, Warsaw (August 28, 2004)
7. Valsiner, J.: Scaffolding within the structure of Dialogical Self: hierarquical dynamics of semiotic mediation. New Ideas in Psychology 23, 197–206 (2005)
8. Hacker, P.M.S.: Wittgenstein: sobre a natureza humana. UNESP, São Paulo (2000)
9. Bruner, J.: Atos de significação. Artes Médicas, Porto Alegre (1997)
10. Machado, A., Lourenço, O., Silva, F.: Facts, concepts and theories: the shape of psychology's epistemic triangle. Behavior and Philosophy 18, 1–40 (2000)

11. Chandler, M., et al.: Personal persistence, Identity Development, and Suicide: a Study of Native and Non-native North American Adolescents. Monographs of the Society for Research in Child Development (April 2003)
12. Góes, M.C.R.: A abordagem microgenética na matriz histórico-cultural: uma perspectiva para o estudo da constituição da subjetividade. Cadernos CEDES 20(50), 9–25 (2000)
13. Goffman, E.: Frame analysis: an essay on the organization of experience. Harper & Row, New York (1974)
14. Araújo, I.L.: Subjetividade e linguagem são mutuamente excludentes? Princípios, Natal 14(21), 83–103 (2007)
15. Chandler, M.: Surviving in time: the persistence of identity in this culture and that. Culture & Psychology 6(2), 209–231 (2000)

The Bridge – A Transmedia Dialogue between TV, Film and Gaming

Herlander Elias

University of Beira Interior (UBI), Department of Communication and Arts, Covilhã, Portugal
HerlanderElias248@gmail.com

Abstract. The goal is to discuss the transmedia (TM) relationship in the game-film and game-TV dialogue. First we will analyze previous game-film transitions and releases so that a background is set up and further examinations become sustained. Secondly, we are to find how exactly works transmedia gaming (TMG) as the main object of study, the video game *Quantum Break* (QB) sets a new trend, which leads us to take on digital media studies, communication sciences, as a framework, to better understand this new "dialogue".

Instead of going for narratology or ludology we see this transmedia event of QB as a change in digital media. We start with concepts such as narrative, fiction, virtuality, but as the new audience condition is shaped by a TM dialogue, storytelling is marketing-driven, thus turning the public into a searcher/connector. We will explain how changes are leading to a new scenario.

Keywords: bridge, narrative, digital media, Lost, transmedia, videogames, searchers, interactivity, TV series.

1 Introduction and Problem

Transmedia (TM) is the ability in media content design of having storytelling, interaction and viewing experience of a narrative unfolding on different media. Transmedia Gaming (TMG) (Evans, 2011, 94) means this strategy applied to videogames. Games, TV and films are separate from each other, but as a new game as *Quantum Break* (QB) is determined to clear these boundaries, we expect more from game and TV-film cross-overs. Here is a new dialogue, which in practice means that the public, sometimes as viewers, or players, will watch and play on screen displays. The core formula is that the game developer, Remedy, is making "Junction Moments" to bridge the gap between passive and interactive imagery. Also, it is supposed to be a TV series where the things we see are useful for the gameplay, and vice-versa.

In this work we do not focus on the approaches of narratology or ludology. Instead digital media is the core. We see QB as a digital media phenomenon, something new, asking for a new behavior and setting up new rules. The problem in this research is "how exactly is this formula new?", and the hypothesis are:

A. Marcus (Ed.): DUXU 2014, Part I, LNCS 8517, pp. 548–559, 2014.
© Springer International Publishing Switzerland 2014

1. "Is TMG applying the formula used on *Lost*?"
2. "How does the *Lost* formula work out once applied to other media?"[1]
3. Ultimately, "Where does QB innovates, in which features to be more specific?"

1.1   Discussion about the Related Work

Before we discuss how a game as QB sets a new trend we have to remind how a TV show as *Lost* (ABC, 2004-2010) managed to revolutionize media[2]. *Lost* narrowed the gap between viewers and users — the TV world and the computer world. Narrative was its major asset, which was non-linear and cross-media. It's like having TV before and after *Lost*. As the Web has become a key site for engagement, and narrative devices are built to attract people in TV webcasts, as time goes by, the boundaries between film, games, Web search, TM and TMG will be more and more blurred.

From domains such as science fiction comes the idea about how all things are coming around "Narrative". Writer William Gibson assures in the *Zero History* novel: "consumers don't buy as much products as they buy narratives" (2010, 21). And in the same trend, Lunenfeld affirms: "now that the narrative surrounds us, it has become the new ground" (2011, 58). Of course we know the longer people consume narrative parts, the deeper will be the connection with the fiction world. Assembling meaning equals connection to media worlds.

But when it comes to post-*Lost* TV, as Sasaki underlines

"*viewers had the option of following only the series on TV, ignoring any other unique content broadcasted by a different medium. At the same time someone who was not aware of the TV show could accidentally 'see'/access some of these extra content leading to the main plot, the 'big narrative scheme'*" (2012, 20).

This means narrative is no longer just content, since it is also part of the media design, in the sense that the message is medium-shaped. So, as far as narrative works, extends and splits in different media the audience is kept entertained and spends more money in all things interconnected with narrative. There is a big narrative being woven, as Sasakis points too.

2   About References and Issues

The big step forward with *Lost* is that the show was at the same level as digital media content. *Lost* appears in this discussion of TMG because it is the first originally designed TV series to integrate viewers, searchers and players.

As for the TM, and TMG, the videography we have tested for this research led us to this results, in terms of distinctive categories: we believe that until some recent TM

---

[1] As Sasaki asked too in 2012.
[2] Long before we could think of a game becoming interdependent with TV series, as QB promises to work with, *Lost* was the real first TM/TV show to provide content also in gaming, and setting up Web communities as well.

products, games, TV and films were spinning off their foundries what we may call "Fake TM", meaning that some things were taking place, except true "continuity". So the categories in which most media we have examined fit in are "Sequentials" and "Interactive", being TM a big amount too. However "Total TM" is only achieved in *Quantum Break*.

Sequentials are basically games and films establishing a "mention" between them, in the sense that one refers the other. There is no hybrid universe or direct dependency in narrative[3].

After some time, interactivity becomes a contaminant agent, spreading its logic everywhere. We see as the first attempt to bridge games and films with *The X-Files* (Hyperbole Studios, Fox Interactive, 1999), the game based on Full Motion Video and classified as an "Interactive Movie". Here the connection is obviously established with *The X-Files*: (Carter, C., 1993), the TV series.

More recently, games such as *James Bond 007: Blood Stone* (2010), make sense if we watch *007: Skyfall* (Mendes, S., 2012) and *007: Quantum of Solace* (Forster, M., 2008) movies. A less known relationship is the one between Ridley Scott's 1982 *Blade Runner* and the non-linear game (Westwood Studios, 1997) version. Here we literally play the movie. *Avatar* (Cameron, J., 2009), the movie, and the game *James Cameron's Avatar* are successful (2009) in just connecting. Again, connections, interactive ones, are conceived as part of the plan.

Even in *Golden Eye* (Campbell, M., 1995) Bond film, there was a success coming from the connection with *Goldeneye* (1997) game for Nintendo N64. In recent past, Christopher Nolan's *Inception* (2010) movie mentions a previous chapter, called *Inception Animation Prequel – The Cobol Job* (Kirby, I., 2010), which turns this animated short itself into TM. *Iron man* (Favreau, J., 2008) connects with Marvel movies and spins-off into games in consoles. Long before these strategies, games such as *Medal of Honor: Frontline* (2002) tried a straight connection with movies like *Saving Private Ryan* (Steven Spielberg, 1998). People want to play movies.

More examples stand in the history of video games, providing versions of homonymous movies, as *Predator* (McTiernan, J., 1987). The trend then allowed *The Running Man* (Glaser, P.M., 1987) to become *The Running Man* (1989), the game. For quite some time, interactivity was an add-on to passive imagery. *The Terminator* (Cameron, J., 1984) became eight years later *The Terminator* by Virgin Interactive. This narrative universe links up with *Terminator 2: Judgment Day* (Cameron, J., 1991); and still today, *Terminator Salvation* (McG, 2011) considers previous releases as puzzle pieces.

---

[3] For instance, *The Avengers* (Whedon, J., 2012) movie is connected with previous Marvel movies such as *Captain America: The First Avenger* (Johnston, J., 2012) and *Thor* (Branagah, K., Whedon, J., 2011). The same strategy is identified in *Lara Croft: Tomb Raider* (West, J., 2001), which stands side by side with *Tomb Raider* (1996), the game. Many are the examples, though we highlight here the link between the *Halo* game universe and the movie *Halo 4: Forward Unto Dawn* (2012). *The X-Files: Fight The Future* (Bowman, R., 1998) and *X-Files: I Want to Believe* (Carter, C., 2008) were the kind of movies that tried to link books and movies of *The X-Files'* universe.

A story with a need to connect with digital environment is for sure *Tron* (Lisberger, S., 1982). What is unfolding now is merely the "Real TM" mode of gaming. It began in TV series as *Lost* and *24* (Cochran, R., Surnow, J., Fox, 2001-10), which pioneered the gameplay of episode stories or subplots. Now, TV series like Marvel's Agents of S.H.I.E.L.D.[4] (Whedon, J., ABC, 2013) are establishing a cluster of sense with the narrative of *Thor: The Dark World* (Taylor, A., 2013) movie.

Other situations exist, like the video game *Tom Clancy's Ghost Recon: Future Soldier* (Ubisoft, 2012), which release online live-action movies as *Tom Clancy's Ghost Recon: Future Soldier - Ghost Recon Alpha Official Film* (Ubisoft, Little Minx Production, Mikros Image, May 5, 2012). Since search culture is a common ground for the audiences of these media, we see links coming from different media regarding the same storytelling universes.

Besides *24*, *Lost* remains the best in connecting with gaming. In fact, *Lost* deliberate releases the TMG *Lost: Via Domus* (2008). The reference for everyone in TMG was until today *The Matrix* (Wachowski, A. & Wachowski, L., 1999)[5]. Still now, the industry model of connecting at least two releases is working good. Since the launch of *Assassin's Creed* [AC] (Ubisoft, 2007), every game in the AC universe expands the memory of the thief and its universe[6]. A smart case of linking movies to new games in a successful manner lies in *AVP - Aliens vs Predator* (2010)[7].

Some references from the past and the present share similar positioning, as the purpose of some releases was since ever to turn watchable images in controllable images, and otherwise.

Other known releases such as *Mirror's Edge,* a PlayStation 3 game, became an iPhone release too (IronMonkey Studios, EA Mobile, 2010). Beyond that, a *Mirror's Edge Comic* (Wildstorm Productions, Smith, M.D., Pratchett, R., 2009-10) version came up afterwards. Similar launches came from Disney, by upgrading the *Tron* universe[8].

By repositioning our discussion here about the game and film dialogue, we may see in video TM approaches establishing a more direct link. The *Lost Experience* (2004) ARG is a TM maneuver too, like *Lost: Missing Pieces* (Mobisodes/Websodes)

---

[4] Especially episode 8 (directed by Frakes, J., 2013).

[5] The movie universe of Morpheus, Neo and Trinity, along with *The Matrix Reloaded* (Idem, L., 2003), *The Matrix Revolutions* (Idem, 2003) and *The Animatrix* (Chung, P., et al, 2003) builds up a narrative so big, that only players of *Enter The Matrix* (2003) and *The Matrix: Path of Neo* (2005) were really comprehending what the whole story was all about. Not to mention, *The Matrix Online* (2005).

[6] Players get to play different history moments in *Assassin's Creed II* (Ubisoft Montreal, 2009) or in *Assassin's Creed IV: Black Flag* (Ubisoft, 2013), but everything is related with webmovies [*Assassin's Creed: Lineage 1* (26 October, 2009) and *Lineage 2* (17 November, 2009)] and even books (*Assassin's Creed: Desmond* [comic] (Ubisoft, France-Belgium, 2009).

[7] In which players control play any of the primary characters of the famous movies of *Aliens* or *Predator*, and manage to see the story from three points of view.

[8] By *Tron Legacy Interactive Graphic Novel* (Disney Digital Books, ScrollMotion, Stefano, A., et al, 2011) and *Tron Legacy* (Disney Digital Books, 2011), the comic.

(Bender, J., 2007). The elements we identify are both passive and interactive footage[9]. While new narratives are stitched together now, in previous TMG what we had was more like a parallel narrative. It happens in *The Running Man* game version of the movie with the same name (1987). Even though we may witness cases of dialogue from games to film and otherwise, or from games to other media, we have say that *The Matrix* universe stands as pioneer in the TMG scene[10]. Before *The Matrix* the game-film dialogue is not marketing-driven from scratch. There are stories side-by-side, objects which have resemblance, there are similar universes, but no technological homogeneity nor narrative major design. It's a fragmented mediascape. This is why we call it "Fake TM", as every game becomes a comic or a movie, regardless of which medium meets release in the first place. Stories play out in a disconnected manner.

One thing is to have a big narrative to which we plug into, and interplay works; while another is to have one fiction world merely emerging in different mediums that are consumed differently. Total TMG solves this last part.

In 1991 Toffler notices a "multi-channel society" (372), and today, narratives would not be a consumer product if there would be no multi-channels to go back to, as he pointed out. For Jenkins in 2006, "convergence" or TM it is something "(...) integrating multiple texts to create a narrative so large that it cannot be contained within a single medium" (95). The reason why we make convergence work is because we own different platforms. We are not into one medium, we are purchasing ranges of products. As a consequence, audiences can move across media.

Simon Bond is one of the authors noticing TM and marketing strategies as an interesting phenomenon. He says if we "use this knowledge to hone how screen-specific messages can work in unison in a multiscreen environment for maximum effect. No marketer has done this yet, but one soon will. And others will follow" (2012, 34). It means that now we surely are in the "multi"media age. But it has been a potential for marketing since ever. "Integration" is what makes audiences connect with the media[11].

3   Introducing New Perspectives

The breaking point in TMG is what *Lost* had already in its TM form: it provided "new entry-points" (Sasaki, 2012, 2) for audiences. Following this, "a transmedia fictional world is one in which the viewers can lose themselves in a range of different contexts

---

[9] Some examples seem *retro* but trigger new TMG events, like the upcoming *Half-Life* movie, out of a partnership between J.J. Abrams' Bad Robot Productions and Gabe Newell's Valve Software, since the fan film *Half-Life: Raise The Bar* got online (Machinima Prime, 4 October, 2013). The idea came from fans, as it did in the *Metal Gear Solid: Philantropy Part 1* and 2 movies (Hive Division, Talamini, G., 2009), being the latter both inspired in the MGS game universe (Kojima, H., Konami).

[10] Even with *The Matrix* comic prequels available in www.whatisthematrix.com (Access in April, 1999).

[11] Researchers as Evans notice too how "Transmedia narratives such as *Lost* and *Heroes* (NBC, 2006–2010) offered greater integration" (2011, 179).

and in which (....) the relationship between text, viewer and technology come into play" (Evans, 2011, 39). So contexts, platforms and media types are something that matters. Storytelling as to work despite the differences of any element. In TMG the challenge is one level above, because TV, film and games are speaking different engagement codes with the audience.

Usually, games are more studied as sociological issues or according to interface and programming themes, while TV causes many media studies and audience research to appear under the guidelines of reception of contents. There is a lot of concern about how games are made, and also how TV is understood. For this study of ours, since the object of study is TMG, more specifically QB, the videogame made by Remedy aspiring boldly to bridge the gap between both TV and game world, we choose to face the issue as a matter of digital media study. By examining previous media releases in terms of games, TV series, and motion pictures, we are able to point out patterns and connections between fiction domains, platforms and the kind of audiences these elements outline.

Rather than choosing narratology or ludology, we choose to understand the relationships between elements in order to see how people consume this fiction worlds (such as *Lost* is a major example); and secondly we ask "how could a TMG game establish a new domain?"

New perspectives are to be considered here. We could say, as Paul Magill, that imposed cultural authority is replaced by an "offered cultural resource" (2003, 3). And this resources work with "images". The media are making images available and we are their "connectors". The problem is that these images are no longer just "graphic". We live in a "post-image" era. "There is 'no longer any distinction between text and image, (...) everything is now image'" (Bruce Mau in Lunenfeld, 2011, 55).

In this context, audiences are consuming images, narratives, something big, digitally plastic, crossing any platform. There is a transition from text to context. In Sasaki's regard, for example, TM narrative is all about "multilayered plots" (2012, 23), which triggers new things, such as the idea of a media-environment[12]. As a consequence of this surrounding, we tend to look for things, we become "searchers" (Lunenfeld, 2011, xv-xvi), a typical condition of the post-television age.

Maybe we should look at TMG and the non-linear narrative plots as a revolution in interfaces. Usually, a user interface is understood as pertaining to human-computer interaction (Shedroff, Noessel, 2013, 3). It is still "all parts of a thing that enable its use" (Idem, Ibidem). And when it comes to TMG, we are on the fringe of TV, books and film, gaming and cinema, and text and image. This is why we are all "interfacing" with contents, TV shows, websites, social media, and games with stories that never end. There is a new interface at question in TMG, especially in QB.

Dealing with TMG is about solving "technological discontinuity". And the new model is brought by *Lost*. *Lost* stands as a language format and a media system for

---

[12] Perhaps we are becoming "prisoners of the nexus" (Baudrillard, 2010, 37), as we are becoming more "viewsers" (Sasaki, 2012, 2). It is getting harder to distinguish the viewer condition from the user condition, as all things are image, displayed on screens, and digital platforms surround us.

TM, not just a TV series. We think TMGs and narratives share the same engagement type.

What is occurring is that on one side there is passive-unleashed imagery, whereas active-interactive imagery lies on the other. TMG is becoming a model to make TV-video-film concepts closer to gaming-VR experiences. It is as if wherever we go, there is the story, the experience. "Images become a meaningful text in their own right" (Freedman in Kackman et al, 2011, 207). For the casual consumer each story makes sense, while for the narrative devotee any part assembles something greater. This is why Lunenfeld's idea of the "searchers" makes sense. After all, a fragmented media landscape, the media types and the new audience behavior trigger "connecting" events. Having a versatile storytelling enhances flow, continuity and simultaneity in narrative consumption.

It is true that audiences can now move across media; from television displays to mobile media (Evans, 2011, 40). We see that new figures are popping out of the new framework. Searching is becoming a default setting in-between watch and play. These are emancipated audiences, used to turn on many media simultaneously. According to one recent Google report, "Search is the most common bridge between devices in this sequential [or simultaneous] usage" (2012, 3). In effect, a new culture is rising, which is search culture, "fundamentally, based on conversational interaction and social participation, and it is booming" (Spurgeon, 2008, 25). The reason why curious audiences engage with puzzles is that they know and want to play and watch. They don't mind at all to search[13].

4   Providing Concrete Results

Many game to film or TV dialogues are to be considered as "Fake TM". One may distinguish these items, which are "Sequentials" (40 objects), linked between each other superficially, from those being "Interactive" (53 objects), thus interconnecting up with fiction items and/or add up interaction agency. The single total TM, and TMG object, is QB[14]. Despite this, we had to examine 29 video games, 35 films, 5 TV series and 2 anime movies. The total amount of videography ascends to 87 objects, already integrating the 16 TM items exclusively analyzed for this article.

After crossing theory, concepts and the media objects we have set ourselves to review, we expect to understand how before QB separate media have prepared the conditions to make TMG a reality. Besides, we hope to understand the concerns in terms of narrative design and the digital media concepts to follow in the near future. By comparing previous game-film dialogues and transmedia products, and crossing it with the information provided by QB game developers, we conclude that TMG is a working model for storytelling, digital media and truly making cross-media

---

[13] They are finding meaning in connector interfaces. However with no digitization, searchable contents and TM strategies would fail.

[14] By the time this research was conducted the QB version of the TV series was yet unreleased, as well as the game; this narrowed the elements necessary to finish this work in a more accurate way.

something for the masses, though it may begin with niche markets, because gamers and viewers are purchasing memberships.

Until this point, we come across a question asked by Sasaki, one yet to be answered: "how exactly the TM elements of the *Lost* formula could be applied in other cases?" As for now, we know that the reason behind *Lost*'s success is that there was TV, Web and game audience engagement. Not only looking at games and TV, but to digital media in a more wider sense, we hope to find in Google Reports, game developer officials' and media researchers' statements as well, how storytelling in a fragmented media landscape, media types and trends in audience behavior are triggering "connector" events. "Big-narrative schemes" may work well, as "continuity" is "on" too.

In present day, these are emancipated audiences, and they are product range owners. They watch, search and play. According to one recent Google report, there is a new form of interaction, whether in its sequential or simultaneous usage (2012, 3).

In our perspective TM is relying on a new "audience agency" (Evans, 2011, 95). TV wants to engage us as games do. Spurgeon believes also "consumers of these systems are more actively configured as users" (2008, 6), and this is the background in which Google states we are "multi-screeners" (2012, 2). The problem is not about the new TM or TMG products' launch we witness here, but the previous TM events that anticipate QB transmedia dialogues. We label some of the events as "Fake TM" since most narratives were merely adapted, from TV or motion pictures to games, and vice-versa. No narrative world was firmly designed, just parts with pre-set links in the story.

When it comes to QB, it positions itself as true TMG. Not to mention that it sets up story worlds, characters, multi-stranded plots, and audience-user engagement. In fact, we may understand, TV programs are becoming an experience. And "narrative" is *that* product we are all buying in one way or another (Gibson), because it is designed to develop storytelling across multiple media in order to provide different 'entry points' in the story (Nicoletta Iacobacci [2008] apud Sasaki, 2012, 19-20). Due to this, perhaps we should talk about "story 2.0" (Gottschal, 2013, 2), as we are not only concerned with linear reading, watching or gameplay. It seems that at Remedy studios [QB game developer] the future of TMG will be about "connections"; this is why they speak of "Junction Moment[s]" (Sam Lake in Trussler, 2013, 1)[15]. The rules applied by QB seem innovative.

The benefits for TMG are more audience engagement, more Web traffic in search engines, more ads in TV series streaming sites, and people playing games with friends and sharing moments in social media. The entire brand narrative of TMG benefits this machination. As longs as people are looking for ways to get inside the story, this system works. On the audience side, the benefits are more engaging stories available. The problems are such as: narratives will be made of a text-image fusion, media

---

[15] Which "lead into the next episode of the show. Immediately the first scene of the show is affected by the choice you made. It's very much alternate content depending (…). The idea is that it will feel relevant to the plot of the show. You'll learn important things that you'll need for the game" (in Futter, 2013).

purchase will be exclusively digital and audience experience is entirely controlled in webcasts, game streams and social media[16].

In sum, a new media audience is outlined, being passive optionally whenever participation is on pause mode. Cloud computing improved story connection and enhanced gameplay videos shared on social media (like in Sony PS4). We have learned with Sasaki that whenever consumer and spectator are the core of a campaign; or whenever a consumer performs many roles (viewer, player, reader, Web surfer), a TMG campaign is more likely to work nicely, because the same person is targeted for that purpose (2012).

In this sense, the question here is "what is TMG exactly?". We could advance something as a "narrative system for bridging gaps in media types". It is interesting that Evans notices too that the creation of a 'platform', becomes central" (2011, 173). In a strategic point of view, TMG is designed to improve purchase and consumerism, customer control and audience involvement[17]. Again, we may call to the discussion the issue of "interfaces", because TMG is a new interface for viewing and playing. If "Sci-fi interfaces" help create a reality that is coherent, and makes sense for audiences, then "audiences are a class of users" (Shedroff, Noessel, 2013, 310). TMG is definitely a sci-fi interface. Film becomes somehow playable and games turn out to be viewed, rendering all of us into user-players.

The central issue is "audience agency" (Evans, 2011, 95), which is a part of TMG. Like gamers are loyal to games rather than to the hardware, so TV viewers rather follow shows, than programming. We see new demographics in our time, because social geography changed. Even human interaction with digital media is altered[18]. There is a new dialogue in town, and it is called transmedia.

References

1. Baudrillard, J.: The Agony of Power (2007). Trans. Ames. Hodges. Intervention Series (6) (2010)
2. Bond, S.: Meet The Screens. BBDO / Proximity Worldwide / Microsoft Advertising, New York, NY (2012), http://advertising.microsoft.com/meet-the-screens-research (access in May 2, 2013)

---

[16] There is also the danger of having audiences to pay for every single bit of the experience in the name of pursuing the next story chapters or in customization modules of characters, stories and items. Memberships are an industry "must" to spread even more.

[17] In Marsha Kinder's perspective, TM is more associated with the creation of "'supersystems', described as 'a network of intertextuality'" ([1991] in Evans, 2011, 19). TMG stands up in this logic. The greater the network of intertextuality, then the deeper the invoement.

[18] For Simon Bond: the multiplicity of screens surrounding us enhances our attention and improves engagement (2012, 34). However it is odd, the more different the screens, or media gear, we have, the more content is spread. Doubts grow, curiosity leads to searching in separate media. The new thing is that somehow contents are held hostage in a sort of "metaconvergence", to which we are heading to at high-speed, as noticed by Toffler (cit. in Ries; Ries, 2005, 58).

3. Evans, E.: Transmedia Television: Audiences, New Media And Daily Life. Comedia series. Morley, D. (ed.). Routledge, New York (2011)
4. Futter, M.: Remedy's Sam Lake Details Quantum Break's Transmedia Approach. In: Game Informer (November 22, 2013), http://www.gameinformer.com/b/news/archive/2013/11/22/remedy-s-sam-lake-details-quantum-break-s-transmedia-approach.aspx (access in December 18, 2013)
5. Gibson, W.: Zero History. G.P. Putnam's Sons, New York (2010)
6. GOOGLE. The New Multi-Screen World: Understanding Cross-Platform Consumer Behavior, US, Google Insights, Sterling Brands, Ipsos (August 2012), http://www.google.pt/think/research-studies/the-new-multi-screen-world-study.html (access in November 4, 2013)
7. Gottschall, J.: Story 2.0: The Surprising Thing About The Next Wave of Narrative. In: Fast Company, CoCreate.com (2012), http://www.fastcocreate.com/3020047/story-20-the-surprising-thing-about-the-next-wave-of-narrative (access in November 1, 2013)
8. Kackman, M., et al.: Flow TV: Television in The Age of Media Convergence. Routledge, New York (2011)
9. Lunenfeld, P.: The Secret War Between Downloading & Uploading - Tales of The Computer as Culture Machine. MIT Press, Cambridge (2011)
10. Magill, P.: The Crisis of Branding And The Theory Needed to Solve It. Symposium on The Coevolution of Technology-Business Innovations (September 24, 2003), http://www.almaden.ibm.com/coevolution/pdf/magill_paper.pdf (accessed in January, 2014)
11. Ries, A., Ries, L.: A Origem Das Marcas. Editorial Notícias, Lisbon (2005)
12. Sasaki, D.M.: Transmedia Storytelling And Lost: Path to Success. Master's Thesis in Digital Culture, University of Jyväskylä, Department of Art and Culture Studies (2012), https://jyx.jyu.fi/dspace/bitstream/handle/123456789/38244/URN:NBN:fi:jyu-201207192109.pdf?sequence=1 (access in December 1, 2013)
13. Toffler, A.: Os Novos Poderes, Lisbon, Portugal, Livros do Brasil (1991)
14. Trussler, J.: Quantum Break to Have a "Transmedia" Approach to Storytelling. Here's Your Remedy. In: Awesome Games (November 27, 2013), http://www.awesomegames.co.uk/quantum-break-to-have-a-transmedia-approach-to-storytelling (access in December 18, 2013)

VIDEOGRAPHY

Anime
Animatrix, The (Chung, P., et al, 2003)
Tron: Uprising (Lisberger, S., McBird, B., 2012-)

Films
007: Casino Royale (Campbell, M., 2006)
007: Skyfall (Mendes, S., 2012)
007: Quantum of Solace (Forster, M., 2008)
Avatar (Cameron, J., 2009)
Avengers, The (Whedon, J., 2012)

Blade Runner (Scott, R., 1982)
Captain America: The First Avenger (Johnston, J., 2012)
Golden Eye (Campbell, M., 1995)
Halo 4: Forward Unto Dawn (2012)
Inception (Nolan, C., 2010)
Iron man (Favreau, J., 2008)
Lara Croft: Tomb Raider (West, J., 2001)
Lord of The Rings (Jackson, P., 2001-2003)
Matrix, The (Wachowski, A. & Wachowski, L., 1999)
Matrix Reloaded, The (Wachowski, A. & Wachowski, L., 2003)
Matrix Revolutions, The (Wachowski, A. & Wachowski, L., 2003)
Predator (McTiernan, J., 1987)
Running Man, The (Glaser, P.M., 1987)
Saving Private Ryan (Steven Spielberg, 1998)
Terminator, The (Cameron, J., 1984)
Terminator 2: Judgment Day (Cameron, J., 1991)
Terminator 3: Rise of the Machines (Mostow, J., 2003).
Terminator Salvation (McG, 2011)
Thor (Branagah, K., Whedon, J., 2011)
Thor: The Dark World (Taylor, A., 2013)
Tron (Lisberger, S., 1982)
Tron Legacy (Kosinksy, J., 2010)
X-Files, The: Fight The Future (Bowman, R., 1998)
X-Files: I Want to Believe (Carter, C., 2008).

TV Shows
24 (Cochran, R., Surnow, J., Fox, 2001-10)
Agents of S.H.I.E.L.D. (Whedon, J., ABC, 2013), episode 8 (Frakes, J., 2013)
Lost (Abrams, J.J. et al., ABC, 2004–2010)
X-Files, The: [Série TV] (Carter, C., 1993)

Videogames
Assassin's Creed (Ubisoft Montreal, Ubisoft Entertainment, 2007, PS3)
Assassin's Creed IV: Black Flag (Ubisoft Montreal, Ubisoft Entertainment, 2013, PS3)
Assassin's Creed II (Ubisoft Montreal, Ubisoft Entertainment, 2009, PS3)
AVP - Aliens vs Predator (Rebellion, Sega of America, 2010, PS3)
Blade Runner (Westwood Studios, Westwood Studios, 1997, PC)
Enter The Matrix (Shiny Entertainment, Atari, Inc., 2003, Xbox)
Goldeneye (Rare, Nintendo America, 1997, N64)
Halo 2 (Bungie Studios/Microsoft, 2004, Xbox)
Half-Life (Valve, Sierra Online, 1998, PC)
Half-Life 2 (Valve, Sierra Entertainment, 2004, PC)
James Bond 007: Blood Stone (Kate Saxon, 2010, PS3)
James Cameron's Avatar [videogame] (2009)
Last of Us, The (Naughty Dog / SCEA, 2013, PS3).

Lost: Via Domus (Ubisoft Montreal, Ubisoft, 2008, Xbox 360)
Matrix Online, The (Monolith, Warner Bros, Sega of America, Inc., 2005, PC)
Matrix, The: Path of Neo (Shiny Entertainment, Atari, Inc, 2005, PS3)
Medal of Honor: Frontline (Dreamworks Interactive, EA Games, 2002, PS2)
Metal Gear Solid Digital Graphic Novel (Kojima Productions, Konami, 2006, PSP)
Metal Gear Solid II: Sons of Liberty (Kojima Productions, Konami, 2001, PS2)
Metal Gear Solid V: Ground Zeroes (Kojima Productions, Konami, 2014, PS4)
Mirror's Edge (DICE, Electronic Arts, 2008, PS3)
Red Dead Redemption (Rock Star Sand Diego, Rock Star Games, 2010, PS3)
Running Man, The (Emerald Software, Grandslam, 1989, CBM 64)
Terminator, The (Virgin Interactive, Virgin Interactive, 1993, Sega CD)
Tomb Raider (Core Design, Eidos Interactive, 1996, PS)
Tom Clancy's Ghost Recon: Future Soldier (Ubisoft Paris, Ubisoft, 2012, PS2)
Tron (Bally, Midway, 1982, Arcade)
Tron: Evolution (Propaganda, Disney Interactive, 2010, PS3)
X-Files, The (Hyperbole Studios, Fox Interactive, 1999, PC)

TRANSMEDIA
. Assassin's Creed: Desmond [comic] (Ubisoft, France-Belgium, 2009)
. Assassin's Creed: Lineage 2 [movie] (17 November, 2009). Available on
www.youtube.com/watch?v=fJXpcuAZb3Q (Access in 1 December, 2013).
. Assassin's Creed: Lineage 1 [movie] (26 October, 2009). Available on
http://www.youtube.com/watch?v=vcE8xJkK6t4 (Access in 1 December, 2013)
. Dead Space. Issue 1-6 (Electronic Arts, Johnston, A., Templesmith, B., 2008)
. Inception Animation Prequel – The Cobol Job (Kirby, I., 2010)
. Lost: Missing Pieces (Mobisodes/Websodes) (Bender, J., 2007)
. Half-Life: Raise The Bar [film] (Fan film, Machinima Prime, 4 October, 2013). Available on
www.youtube.com/watch?v=YiKcWZHeMG4 (Access in 1 December, 2013)
. Metal Gear Solid: Philantropy Part 2 [film] (Hive Division, Talamini, G., 2009). Available on
www.youtube.com/watch?v=tUctkLjstIw (access in 1 December, 2013)
. Metal Gear Solid: Philantropy Part 1 [film] (Hive Division, Talamini, G., 2009). Available on
www.mgs-philanthropy.net (access in 1 December, 2013)
. Mirror's Edge (IronMonkey Studios, EA Mobile, 2010, iPhone)
. Mirror's Edge Comic (Wildstorm Productions, Smith, M.D., Pratchett, R., 2009-10)
. Quantum Break [videogame] (Remedy Entertainment, Microsoft Studios, 2014, Xbox One)
. Tom Clancy's Ghost Recon: Future Soldier - Ghost Recon Alpha Official Film (Ubisoft, Little
Minx Production, Mikros Image, May 5, 2012). Available in
www.youtube.com/watch?v=le2AeTub3mo (Access in August, 2012)
. Tron Legacy Interactive Graphic Novel (Disney Digital Books, ScrollMotion, Stefano, A., et
al, 2011, Apple iPad)
. Tron Legacy [motion comic] (2011), Dir. Disney Digital Books, Apple iPad, US.

Fishtank Everywhere: Improving Viewing Experience over 3D Content

Lucas S. Figueiredo[1], Edvar Vilar Neto[1], Ermano Arruda[1],
João Marcelo Teixeira[1,2], and Veronica Teichrieb[1]

[1] Federal University of Pernambuco, Recife PE 50740-560, Brazil
{lsf,excvn,eaa3,jmxnt,vt}@cin.ufpe.br
cin.ufpe.br/voxarlabs
[2] Federal Rural University of Pernambuco, Recife PE 52171-900, Brazil
www.deinfo.ufrpe.br

Abstract. The goal of this work is to analyze the user experience of the motion parallax effect on common use displays, such as monitors, tvs and mobile devices. The analysis has been done individually for each device and comparing each other to understand the impact on the immersion of such media. Moreover, we focused on understanding the user impression on the change of an usual passive visualization paradigm to the interactive visualization possibility allied to the motion parallax effect.

Keywords: depth perception, cross platform experience, fishtank effect, interactive visualization.

1 Introduction

Since the early stages of Virtual Reality research the perception of depth is a highlighted issue. Among the explored depth cues there is the motion parallax as an option for interactive visualization. Motion parallax is the effect that allows the user to distinguish depth on the scene by moving his viewpoint (i.e. user eyes). The perception of the third dimension comes by the intrinsic comparison of which object in the scene is moving faster or slower in relation to the viewpoint displacement.

This type of depth perception is simulated on planar displays by a technique called Fishtank Virtual Reality, which uses the information of the user viewpoint (usually gathered by an additional sensor) to change the scene according to this movement. Considering the current availability of depth cameras and new face detection and tracking algorithms, the Fishtank technique gains space in the common use scenario. Moreover, as we show later, nowadays it is possible to enable the effect without requiring the use of glasses or any other additional attached sensors or displays. That said, it is possible to apply the Fishtank technique on nearly any 3D content on present devices.

The user experience of the Fishtank Virtual Reality technique working on different displays has been evaluated in this work. In our experiment, people used applications (e.g. 3D rendered games) coupled with the Fishtank Virtual

A. Marcus (Ed.): DUXU 2014, Part I, LNCS 8517, pp. 560–571, 2014.

Reality technique and without it. The effect experience was analyzed regarding its relevance and the user satisfaction and acceptance of the technique. For this, after the participants completed the proposed tasks, they participated on a semi-structured interview and answered a Likert-scale questionnaire, aimed to collect subjective impressions.

The paper is structured as follows. Section two exposes the chronology and the background concepts about the motion parallax illusion. Section three explains the proposed methodology and experiment. Section four shows the experiment results and analysis. Finally, section five presents the conclusion and future work.

2 The Fishtank Virtual Reality Technique

2.1 Chronology

This section provides information regarding the history and evolution of the Fishtank Virtual Reality technology, from the 1960's when it was only an utopic idea, to nowadays when it is possible to apply it also on telepresence scenarios with real content displayed. This list is not intended to cover all scientific works related to the technology; instead it points important marks along its history.

In the year of 1965, Ivan Sutherland, known by the research community as the "father of virtual reality", discussed about what the "ultimate display" should look like [14]. He stated that such utopic device should pose as a window to the virtual world, capable of simulating a complete immersive environment, seamlessly from reality itself. Beyond displaying 2D images, it should also provide tridimensional perception, different smells and tactile experiences. By conveying such information, it would be possible to exploit most human senses.

In 1992, Steuer contributed to the definition of the term Virtual Reality [13]. Up to this date, the concept was directly related to the hardware being used, instead of being based on sensations the users experienced. It then defines Virtual Reality in terms of telepresence, in a way that the physical person is transported to and feels like being in a different world (the virtual one). From this moment on, all the hardware used were simply considered instruments or means to implement telepresence. Later in 1992, the first system capable of changing the viewing perspective as the user changed his position was created [4]. Since the displays at that time were CRT and curved, a mathematical model was required to cope with such display shape. This work was named "High Resolution Virtual Reality", since it claimed to have a higher resolution than the head-mounted displays at that time, but it was later called "Fishtank Virtual Reality". In 1993, Ware et al. [15] compare the Fish Tank technique in two distinct scenarios: alone and combined with stereoscopy. This was the first work to relate the technology with other similar systems. Back in 1999, Brooks Jr. et al. discussed several issues regarding virtual reality, from its definition to its history, the technology it requires and devices typically used [2]. Finally, it lists the open problems and remembers us that we are still far from Sutherland's "ultimate display".

In 2006, Demiralp et al. compare the Fish Tank approach to a CAVE environment [5]. The important conclusion of this work was the suggestion that

Fish Tank systems are more effective than CAVEs. In 2008, Kooima generalized perspective transforms so that they could mathematically describe distorted frustums [10]. Such knowledge is necessary in order to correctly distort the viewing frustum to create a Fish Tank Virtual Reality system. In 2009, Maksakov developed an extension for the Fish Tank Virtual Reality technique that comprises much larger screens and cooperative work by using separate viewports [12]. This work solves a previous limitation of the technology because it was not designed for team cooperation. By using a device attached to each user's head, it was possible to modify the scene view accordingly. In 2010, Andersen et al. propose the combination of oblique perspective changes with stereoscopy [1]. They also propose a modified graphics pipeline in order to achieve applicable results, specifically targeting games.

In 2011, Francone et al. explore the application of head-coupled perspective in mobile devices by means of their camera and a face tracking algorithm [8]. It manages to track the user's face, estimate its position, and use it to change the perspective of the scene. This creates the impression of 3D perception in mobile devices and can be used to improve user experience. In 2012, Halamkar et al. redefine Virtual Reality as a computer-simulated environment [6]. They categorize different levels of Virtual Reality, some factors that one should consider when designing such environments, its origins, probable future and challenges that have still to be overcome in order to create ideal virtual environments. Later in 2012, instead of simulating the 3D environment on the TV screen, Heirichs et al. make use of a real scene captured by a robotic camera [7]. The camera position is controlled by tracking the user's head position in order to simulate the Fish Tank Virtual Reality effect, which is associated with the parallax effect to create a 3D perception illusion.

2.2   How It Works

The purpose of the Fishtank technique is to simulate a display behaving like a glass window to the 3D content. This simulation requires the knowledge of the user viewpoint in real time. The new pose of the scenes virtual camera is then calculated in order to render the 3D content considering the new viewpoint but without changing the original viewport (which represents the boundaries of the glass window metaphor). Figure 1 illustrates the concept.

Motion parallax can be experienced in a speeding car, as it can be perceived that trees located far away move slower than the ones closer to the car. The human brain uses this depth cue to define which objects are closer based on their angular relative motion to the observer. Its reasonable to say that during motion, our brain analyses the sequence of different images of an object, which were acquired from different points of view, and combines them together in order to estimate its depth. In contrast, the binocular depth cue of stereoscopy helps humans and other animals to estimate distances from objects without necessarily being in relative motion to them. The slightly two different images formed in each eye retina is sufficient to infer depth, and judge distances accurately. If theres no motion involved, motion parallax simply doesnt work, thus, making

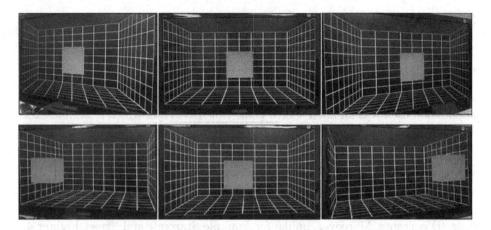

Fig. 1. Top: three different viewpoints of 3D content displayed on a monitor with regular visualization. Bottom: three similar viewpoints of the same 3D content displayed using the Fishtank approach, improving depth perception and immersion.

stereoscopy the main depth cue in such scenarios. A Fishtank Virtual Reality system uses motion parallax as its main depth cue to convey depth perception. Depending on the distance between the object and the observer, motion parallax can be even more important depth cue than stereoscopy itself [3].

To generate the motion parallax depth perception, the system must deform the viewing frustum and move the camera pose according to the users viewpoint position. Thus, a way of tracking the users head position is needed. Formerly, it was done by attaching extra tracking devices to the users head [15], [12], but this approach has inconveniences regarding user physical freedom. Hence, a good solution should not require extra devices attached to the users body. Nowadays, its possible to solve this problem by tracking the users head 3D position on images retrieved from a webcam or similar sensors. Even trackers which can only retrieve the 2D position of the users head, with the addition of an extra step can be used to estimate the 3D viewpoint of the user head based on the image bounding box.

By tracking the 3D position of the users head (x,y,z) a dynamic asymmetric frustum is defined as a function of the users head position. The frustum deforms according to the users current viewpoint, being responsible for half of the motion parallax effect. The other half of the effect is performed by displacing the virtual camera position (without rotating it) according to the users head new position. This displacement brings the virtual screen viewport (four points defining the virtual window) to the same position it was before the distortion of the frustum. As desired by the effect, only the virtual camera point of view changes according to the user head movement, maintaining the virtual screen on the same place. By using this mechanics, it is possible to apply the motion parallax nearly on any 3D rendered content and on any device with head or face tracking capabilities.

3   Cross-Platform Experiment

The main goal of the proposed experiment is to understand the impact of the motion parallax effect over different platform experiences. With that in mind, the setup simulated three different scenarios, namely a TV-like scenario, a Desktop scenario and a Mobile scenario, using the same application over each one. The application used was an open source game called GLTron, which is available for download and can be compiled for PC and Android devices.

3.1   Case Study Application

The choice of GLTron as the case study application aimed to promote a more engaging activity, exploring game mechanics as an enrichment of the experience over 3D contents. Moreover, unlike for example Starcraft and Street Fighter 4, GLTron is a game that needs to be rendered in 3D, because the interaction depends on that. This factor adds relevance to the depth perception and 3D environment exploration by the user. The simplicity of the GLTron interaction is also in favor of a more abrangent experiment, which requires minor user training and still can be challenging and engaging.

The game consists on controlling a futuristic motorcycle on a large and limited square area by turning it to the left or the right. During the movement each player motorcycle creates a wall following its path and this wall blocks the way of every player on the scene. The game was conducted with a single human player and other three artificial intelligence players. Figure 2 illustrates the GLTron game.

The game was compiled to run on each scenario, and then it was properly coupled with head/face tracking capabilities and the needed calculation of both frustum and virtual camera displacements. All three scenarios explored existent tracking technologies, which are widely available. The scenarios are shown in Figure 3 and detailed as follows.

3.2   Scenarios

The first scenario was intended to be a living room experience, in which the user has a 50 inch screen space (displayed by a projector), which was set about 3 meters away from him. In this case the user point of view was tracked using the Kinect device and the body tracking algorithm provided by the Microsoft Kinect Toolkit. Usually the algorithm tracks twenty body points but it was set to the seat-mode in order to be robust to both cases of the user standing and seated. The captured head 3D point was then used as input for the Fishtank effect. In this scenario the user was able to explore the effect seated or if wanted, he could walk in the room (within the Kinect field of view). To interact with the game a Xbox joystick was provided, so the experience aimed to be a game-like activity common in Xbox equipped living rooms.

The second scenario setup consisted of the user seated on a table with a laptop. The face tracking was performed using the laptop webcam images and a tracking algorithm called Face TLD (also known as Predator) [9]. Face TLD is able to

Fig. 2. GLTron game screenshots

detect the user face and track it over time, improving the tracking results as it learns the appearance of the user face. The algorithm, after some execution time, is able to track the user face even considering the head inclination over shoulders and the rotation to left and right. The result of the tracking is a bounding box containing the user face, which is further transformed in a 3D point using the camera horizontal field of view information and providing an average real size width (in meters) for the bounding box. In this case the user was free to decide if he wanted to interact with a joystick or using the laptop keyboard.

The last scenario aimed to reproduce the game experience on mobile devices. The used device was a tablet, and the face tracking was performed by a native Android function for face capturing. The tracking result is a 2D bounding box of the face, which is later converted to a 3D point in order to be used as input for the needed distortions.

3.3 Methodology

The experiment was conducted starting with a few questions about users profile and related to previous experience with games and gesture interaction. A minor test was also conducted to help them discover their dominant eye, this way this information could later be used to adjust the best 3D position as result of the tracking phase.

In sequence, the motion parallax effect was explained and a simple cubic room interactive example was shown to illustrate the functioning of the effect and help

Fig. 3. The three different scenarios tested. Top-left: Mobile. Top-right: Desktop. Bottom: TV-like.

users understand what happens when they move the head and why it happens. This step was necessary since some users may initially be confuse about the effect as a way to control the virtual camera rotation, besides, it is important to make users understand that the interaction of coming closer to the screen does not make the 3D objects to appear bigger. Essentially the opposite occurs, since the idea is that the virtual objects are linked to the real world, and their occupied screen space should decrease once the user comes closer, precisely to compensate that motion. The window metaphor was used to aid the explanation, helping users to understand that when they are closer to a window it is possible to see more of the other side in the same screen space.

After that, users experimented each described scenario with and without the motion parallax illusion. The goal was to play the game for a small amount of time (around five minutes) and try to win at least once on each condition (with and without the effect). This goal was set mainly to help the users engagement with the application, for example encouraging them to visually explore the game 3D world. The experience was observed and documented, and at the end of each scenario some questions were answered. The questions were the following: 1) The use of the effect provides a better visual exploration of the scene; 2) The effect extended immersion in the game scenario; 3) It was more fun playing with the effect. Each question was answered using a 1-5 Likert scale in which 1 means disagree completely, 3 means no impact and 5 means agree completely.

At last, a semi-structured interview was conducted to gather insight about the user overall experience. The guiding questions were: 1) Does the fishtank effect tend to improve user experience? Why? 2) Would you want to see this effect working on other 3D applications? Other games? 3) Were there any differences in experiencing the effect over the different scenarios/displays? What was the difference?

4   Results

A total of six users participated on the experiments, five male and one female, with their age varying from 19 to 29 years old, four having the right eye as dominant and two the left one, and all of them had previous experiences with 3D games and gesture interaction applications. Although the tests were performed with a small group of users, the provided insight was enough to understand main aspects of the interaction coupled with the motion parallax effect across the experimented platforms. Moreover, the users profile showed to be relevant to the experiment considering they already had experience or experienced all three proposed scenarios on common day interactions. This way they were able to correlate the test experience to real life and better answer questions like the one which asks about the use of Fishtank systems on existing applications (question 2 of the semi-structured interview).

The functioning of the effect was easily understood by the users as well. Additionally, on each platform, before playing the game using the effect the user experienced the effect on a static scene, to be familiar with the viewpoint changing inside the game and also to understand the impact his movements would have on the gameplay. Another important aspect of the used game (GLTron) is that during the experience the user is compelled to laterally observe the virtual scene in order to preview further collisions or other approaching players.

4.1   TV-Like Results

This setup drew amusement from most users at the first moment. They started to walk in the room and experience the effect. They had the option to stay seated, even though all of them (after a few seconds of being seated) decided to play the game standing and moving around to explore the virtual scene according to their gameplay needs. The influence on gameplay can be further analyzed and maybe used on the game design. For example, in this case, when using the effect a common move was reproduced by most users. They went in a straight line near and alongside one of the stage boundaries (from where no surprises could arise) and then moved to the other side of the screen to better visualize the other part of the scene from where other players could come and block the path.

As side-effect was perceived as the users intended to move the viewpoint by crouching in order to better see the horizon. Normally this viewpoint is not available, but since the users had the possibility to explore the visualization sometimes they sacrificed their comfort in order to better play the game. This lead to another thought of experience design in which the application should consider that sometimes the user may exploit the provided visualization freedom in a way that may not be wanted in first place (e.g.: the game is made to be played for hours, in a comfortably seated position).

When the users played the game without the effect they immediately felt the difference. A common behavior was to reproduce the interactive visualization movements but after a few tries they were disappointed but convinced that they would have to play without this possibility. One of the users at the first moment of experience without the effect said hey, its a lot different.

4.2 Desktop Results

In general, the playing experience using the effect on the laptop was not well accepted. The first perceived problem was the face tracking output jitter and drift. These are common tracking problems and have always been a challenge for all sort of algorithms. The jitter is result of the tracking imprecision and produces a shaking effect even if the tracked object remains still. The drift problem is a behaviour in which the tracking result is always delayed in relation to the real tracked object position. The Face TLD algorithm is a state of the art solution for tracking faces, still, its results present an amount of jitter and drift which turns the interactive visualization in a not reliable experience.

Another perceived point was that since the user is seated in front of the laptop in a more restricted body position the head movements are not effective as wanted. Even when the virtual camera accompanied the head correctly (regardless the jitter and drift problems) the viewpoint displacement was not enough to show the intended part of the scene, and the user could not move further due to the camera field of view limitation and also due to body position limitations (since the user was seated). Once this was perceived additional experiments were conducted using an increased movement effectiveness, i.e. the head movement was set to move more than the normal ratio, and this way the virtual camera moved the double of the normal movement to facilitate scene exploration. In this variation we perceived the effect could be effectively used to explore the virtual scene, which means a scale factor between the head movement and the virtual camera displacement may be useful. This additional test was conducted out of record and did not influence the responses showed in Figure 4.

4.3 Mobile Results

Regarding the face tracking, a similar issue to the laptop emerged in this case. The used algorithm was the face capturing available on the Android 4.3 version and returned the bounding box of the face, which later was converted to the face 3D point. The jitter and drift were also present and undermined the interaction. On the other hand, the horizontal field of view of the tablet front camera was wider than the laptop one and the movement restriction was not an issue since it was easier to move the head in relation to the device. So regardless the tracking precision and response time issues, the virtual scenario exploration was successful (without the need of any scale factor).

Another interesting behaviour was observed in which the users instead of moving the head to see from a different point of view, rotated the tablet to one side or to the other. Since the effect uses the relationship between the user face and the screen, the rotation interaction produced a similar result, showing the same desired virtual scene part on the screen. This type of interaction was more comfortable, requiring minor physical effort, thus it was reproduced along the experience time.

On the other hand, this rotation movement presents two issues. The first is that the relationship between the real world and the virtual world is changed once the user moves the mobile device. This does not occur in the other two scenarios since the display is fixed in the real world. By moving the tablet the virtual world moves accordingly, this way the impression is that the tablet is a window to the virtual world however this virtual world is coupled on the tablet and does not have a fixed relationship with the real environment.

The second issue related to the rotation interaction was present when the user choses to rotate and at the same time had to press the left or right in order to turn the motorcycle. Considering these two simultaneous movements, it was perceived that sometimes the user reaction was side-inverted in response to his needs.

Figure 4 presents the overall results of the objective questions about visual exploration, immersion and fun. As discussed before, the issues presented by the tracking algorithm impacted user experience on the Mobile (tablet) and Desktop (laptop) cases. On the other hand the living room (TV-like) experience was very well accepted.

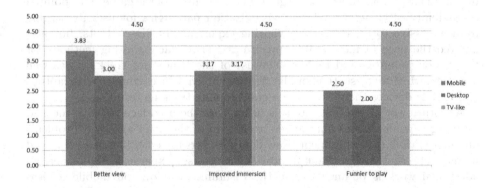

Fig. 4. Result comparison for the three tested scenarios. The values represent the mean scores given by all six tested subjects.

The semi-structured interview returned interesting additional feedback as well. Here follow some of the user responses on question 1 asking if the fishtank effect had improved the experience: "Yes, because you feel more immersed in the game. This game is improved with the effect" and "In an ideal scenario, I think it has the potential to improve the experience".

Question 2 asked the users if they would like to use the effect on other games or 3D applications: "It would be cool. Because it lets us look at the best objects", "Yes, I think it would be really cool if there was a more stable version" and "Yes, because with this effect it was possible to play in a fun way. Without it I would have found the game boring".

Finally, question 3 asked about the experience on the different scenarios: "Yes, the screen size influences. Using the tablet is worse because you keep your hands attached to the device and by moving the device I often moved the camera unintentionally", "Yes, the Kinect provided the best experience, because the sensitivity was higher. When comparing them, the Desktop version presented almost none viewpoint change" and "The tablet was the worst experience. It was the worst way of controlling the camera and holding the device, it was annoying and tiring".

5   Conclusion

We have applied and analyzed how the Fishtank Virtual Reality technique can be significant and useful for immersive interactions in different common displays, such as monitors, TVs and tablets. In our study, we could notice that users had no difficulties in comprehending the technique. However, while using it in the performed experiments, some issues arose mainly related to current face tracking solutions and scenario restrictions. The case study application was the GLTron game, and the effect showed to be more than a cosmetic improvement, being useful for the gameplay, providing additional visualization capabilities that improved user performance on the game and enjoyment of the game. This pointed a possibility of changing different visualization paradigms for users, emerging from a passive to an interactive viewing experience of 3D contents, but also pointed the need of more stable, precise and faster face tracking methods for the use on monitors and tablets. The use of the Kinect for tracking was well accepted, which suggests that similar depth-enabled devices coupled with laptops and mobile devices should provide a good enough tracking result.

As future works, the first intent is to improve the used face tracking method by using new algorithms and devices to get rid of the jitter and drift problems observed during the experiment. New depth sensors are emerging nowadays and it may represent a significant improvement on user experience. Moreover, an additional work is planned to use the Fishtank technique on mobile devices also including the devices additional sensors to correctly place the virtual world registered to the real environment. Moreover, this technique can be applied to Augmented Reality scenarios, making the tablet or smartphone look like a transparent glass (rather than a window metaphor presented on the Virtual Reality case). This way, the user should experience the augmentation more naturally.

References

1. Holst, J., Andersen, A.S., Vestergaard, S.E.: The implementation of fish tank virtual reality in games: Exploring the concepts of motion parallax simulation and stereoscopy (January 2014)
2. Brooks, F.P.: What's real about virtual reality? IEEE Comput. Graph. Appl. 19(6), 16–27 (1999)
3. Cutting, J.E., Vishton, P.M.: Perceiving layout and knowing distances: the integration, relative potency and contextual use of different information about depth. In: Epstein, W., Rogers, S. (eds.) Handbook of Perception and Cognition. Perception of Space and Motion, vol. 5, pp. 69–117 (1995)
4. Deering, M.: High resolution virtual reality. In: Proceedings of the 19th Annual Conference on Computer Graphics and Interactive Techniques, SIGGRAPH 1992, pp. 195–202. ACM, New York (1992)
5. Demiralp, A., Jackson, C.D., Karelitz, D.B., Zhang, S., Laidlaw, D.H.: Cave and fishtank virtual-reality displays: A qualitative and quantitative comparison. IEEE Trans. Vis. Comput. Graph. 12(3), 323–330 (2006)
6. Halarnkar, P., Shah, S., Shah, H., Shah, H., Shah, A.: A review on virtual reality. IJCSI International Journal of Computer Science Issues 9(6), 323–330 (2012)
7. Heinrichs, C., McPherson, A.: Recreating the parallax effect associated with fishtank vr in a real-time telepresence system using head-tracking and a robotic camera. In: ISMAR, pp. 283–284. IEEE Computer Society (2012)
8. Laurence, N., Francone, J.: Using the user's point of view for interaction on mobile devices. In: Conference Proceedings of IHM (October 2011)
9. Kalal, Z., Matas, J., Mikolajczyk, K.: P-n learning: Bootstrapping binary classifiers by structural constraints. In: 2010 IEEE Conference on Computer Vision and Pattern Recognition (CVPR), pp. 49–56 (June 2010)
10. Kooima, R.: Generalized perspective projection (January 2014)
11. Lee, J.C.: Hacking the nintendo wii remote. IEEE Pervasive Computing 7(3), 39–45 (2008)
12. Maksakov, E., Booth, K.S., Hawkey, K.: Whale tank virtual reality. In: Proceedings of Graphics Interface, GI 2010, pp. 185–192. Canadian Information Processing Society, Toronto (2010)
13. Steuer, J.: Defining Virtual Reality: Dimensions Determining Telepresence. In: Communication in the Age of Virtual Reality, pp. 33–56. L. Erlbaum Associates Inc., Hillsdale (1995)
14. Sutherland, I.E.: The ultimate display. In: Proceedings of the IFIP Congress, pp. 506–508 (1965)
15. Ware, C., Arthur, K., Booth, K.S.: Fish tank virtual reality. In: Proceedings of the INTERACT 1993 and CHI 1993 Conference on Human Factors in Computing Systems, pp. 37–42. ACM, New York (1993)

The Database on Near-Future Technologies for User Interface Design from SciFi Movies

Jun Iio[1], Shigeyoshi Iizuka[2], and Hideyuki Matsubara[3]

[1] Chuo University, 742-1 Higashinagano, Hachioji-shi, Tokyo, 192-0393, Japan
iiojun@tamacc.chuo-u.ac.jp
[2] Kanagawa University, 2946 Tsuchiya, Hiratsuka-shi, Kanagawa, 259-1293, Japan
shigeiizuka@gmail.com
[3] Canon Inc., 3-30-2 Shimomaruko, Oota-ku, Tokyo, 146-8501, Japan
hmatsubara574@gmail.com

Abstract. Science fiction (SciFi) feature films offer viewers a glimpse into the future, revealing unique interfaces, social systems, and complex human relations. In this paper, we report a trial conducted by the Science Fiction Special Interest Group (SIG-SciFi) to gain insight into probable human-centered design (HCD) trends and the database of scenes collected to be used as good references for futuristic design. Characteristic scenes from the movie *Minority Report*, *X-Men II*, and *The Island* were analyzed. Our argument and analysis began with a top-down arrangement of scenes in descending order of importance. Then, extracted characteristic scenes were classified hierarchically while considering the worldview of the movie. As a result, suggestions were obtained pertaining to the direction of HCD in the near future. The results of this analysis are arranged into the database which can be immediately applied as a design tool.

Keywords: human centered design (HCD), user experience (UX), science fiction (SciFi) movie, user interface, database.

1 Introduction

In recent years, the importance of human centered design (HCD) is growing not only for industrial products but also for providing services. Simultaneously, especially in the highly-networked information society, various services are implemented as information-technology (IT) system. That results in forcing many designers to create a new form of interface design.

For instance, consider the interface of smartphones. Although similar mobile terminals as personal digital assistants (PDA) have been proposed in the early days of digital era, could anyone imagine the interface currently provided for the modern smartphones, in a previous decade? Obviously, there is a limit of imagination if they try to create their new designs based on the idea of an extension of existing interface technologies.

So we have to discuss another way to create novel designs. As a solution for this question, our research group asked for some ideas from science fiction (SciFi)

A. Marcus (Ed.): DUXU 2014, Part I, LNCS 8517, pp. 572–579, 2014.
© Springer International Publishing Switzerland 2014

films. That is, we considered that the human-machine interactions represented in the SciFi films had a possibility to indicate a big suggestion to our user interface design in the near future.

In 2011, the special interest group named SIG-SciFi was organized in the Human- Centered Design Organization Japan (HCD-Net), in which members try to find some hints for their ideas in SciFi films. SIG-SciFi has maintained its activities until now, and we got several results useful for everyone involved in the HCD business activities. This paper reports our results and gives a proposal of a database system which can be a useful tool for designers.

2   Database and IP Problem

SciFi movies contain several remarkable scenes in terms of a showcase of futuristic user interfaces. A collection of such scenes could be of some help. However, it will be more effective if such scenes are provided in an organized way. To make it widely used, its sources should be comprehensive, that is, it is better that scenes are gathered from a number of SciFi movies (Figure 1).

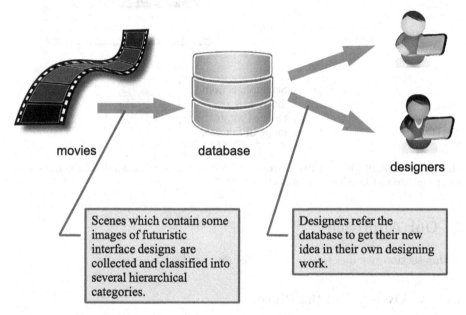

movies   database

designers

Scenes which contain some images of futuristic interface designs are collected and classified into several hierarchical categories.

Designers refer the database to get their new idea in their own designing work.

Fig. 1. The database record should have scene description, how to use them, class and category, and small clip from the original movie

In addition, it needs to be solved that the database does not violate intellectual properties (IP). For example, Shedroff and Noessel[1] published a book analyzing many scenes in SciFi movies, in which novel user interfaces were shown. In their book, many screenshots captured from the SciFi movies. To avoid violation of the IP rights of original movies, all of the pictures are small and stay in the confines of quotation (Figure 2).

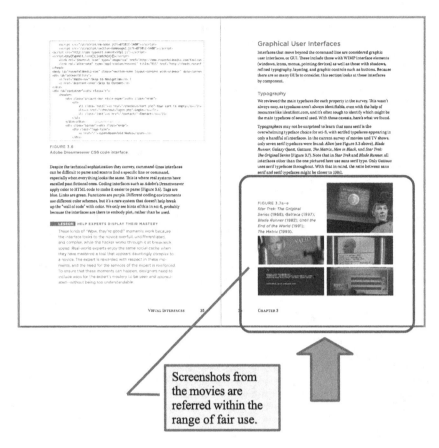

Fig. 2. Only small pictures taken from the SciFi movies are available in the book to avoid violation of intellectual properties

3 Our Approach

In this section, we describe overviews of our method and results.

3.1 An Overview of the Process

The members of SIG-SciFi carried out their tasks and discussions in the following procedure.

1. The target movie is decided by discussions and votes.
2. Each member watches the movie and extract the remarkable scenes.
3. In the regular meeting, the scenes are arranged, by taking what is good and by leaving what is bad (Figure 3).

Guessing an intention of the interface shown in each scene from the viewpoint of what makes it easier, each participant describes the concept into a yellow card.

Fig. 3. By estimating the intended purpose of the interface in each scene, each participant describes the concept on a yellow card

4. Based on the information of scenes arranged by previous process, a database model is created. It has a hierarchical structure and the scenes are categorized in a several groups by means of objectives of the interface design.

Our discussion has gotten started with *Minority Report* (2002). The movie has been studied so widely that it has been considered as a landmark of near-futuristic interface in the interface design community[2,3,4]. Nearly 30 specialists from institutions such as MIT scrutinized various interface-related technologies depicted in this movie. After the prototype of our scene database was finished, the target of our discussion was moved on to *X-Men II* (2003) and *The Island* (2005).

3.2   Results of Classification Analysis

Several examples of comments for the typical scenes in *Minority Report* are shown in Table 1[1].

Figure 4 shows an example of the database, in which scenes extracted from the movie are categorized into several groups and the groups are hierarchically arranged from large classes to small classes.

A scenario to utilize the database is as follows:

---

[1] Discussion was conducted in Japanese because all of the members are Japanese citizen. Therefore, the original examples are written in Japanese.

Table 1. Examples of scenes selected from *Minority Report*

Title	Description
Smart feedback	Heart warming message is provided when the system need to atract user's attention.
Simple and easy to understand	Simple function and operation fitting together with real world are easy to understand.
Visualization of operation	In the scene where data are copied into a memory device with translucent liquid-crystal-display, operating principle can be seen directly.
Humane interface	Light is turned on by calling "I'm home," which is a user interface operated by natural conversation.
Transportation device	Vehicle which can run horizontally and vertically has two entrance, a driver who entered from both of them can operate the vehicle. Not only automatic operation but also automatic operation are available.
Overlay display of information	A scene showing detectives analyze precognitive images delivered by *precogs* using gloves and gestures. Time scale is shown overlaying on the video image.
Natural operation (1)	Splitting, enhancing, and discarding. Gesture operation is suited for particular operations using big screen.
Natural operation (2)	Playing and editing video (images) on the over-head projector, with the gloves for gesture recognition.
Data visualization	Visualizing the data transfer. Information display on the memory card. Data can be handled as if they are some objects.
Scene recognition and verbal operation	Controlling devices by verbal commands.
Partly volumetric display	In the stereoscopic vision by projection, some target objects are extracted and displayed in the three-dimensions.
Visualization of images in brain	Playing the images in *precogs'* brain, extracted by the helmet-type devices.
⋮	⋮

1. A user consults the database with ambiguous awareness of his/her problems. The database offers large categories to fit the ambiguous problems.
2. After a large category is selected, smaller groups within the category are chosen in terms of its solutions represented most appropriately.
3. User could get an idea to solve the problem according to the case study shown in the scenes selected from the database.

The uniqueness of our database is that not only the literal information but also a fragment of movies specified by the data record are provided. Visual information has a strong power to explain so that it makes user imagine how the interfaces can be used.

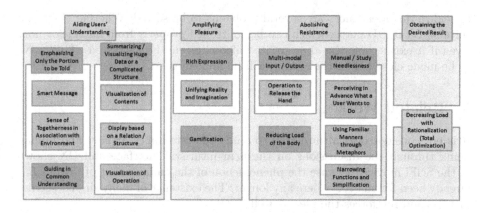

Fig. 4. Classification of user interfaces shown in *Minority Report*

4   Solution for the IP Problem

Previously mentioned, the database contains visual information and it is considered useful to explain how the futuristic interface is effective. However, the IP problems should be eliminated if the database is open to public. It needs to provide some techniques to avoid IP violation because the movies are protected by the copyright law.

Now we are planning to make the database which can provide fragments of movies without IP violation, by means of connecting the database and a DVD/BD player which can be controlled by the database (Figure 5). In order

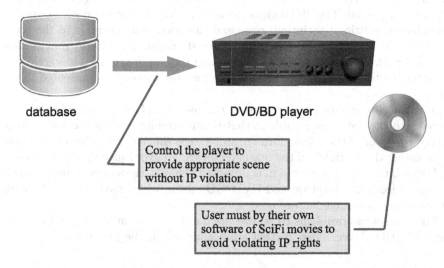

Fig. 5. A system being planned that contains the database and the DVD/BD player in order to avoid the IP problem

to realize this idea, there are several problems to be solved; Whether there is a suitable DVD/BD player which can be controlled properly from outside or not? Even if it exists, how the appropriate video clips can be extracted? They have to be made clear before the system will be implemented.

5   Related Work

It is not considered as absurd trial to study the relation of artifact and human being through the discussions on the near-futuristic interface and UX shown in the SciFi movies, because the phenomenon of the embodiment of fictions has already been found everywhere any longer. The existence of many similar studies justifies and reinforces the idea as well.

For instance, Schmitz, *et al.*[5] has reported a survey on the user interfaces drawn in SciFi movies. Fishwick[6] also pointed out that gaining ideas from SciFi was practically effective in his discussion on the modeling environment in the future.

In addition, Marcus comprehensively discussed on the relation between the computer human interaction (CHI) study and SciFi movies. In his paper[7], he describes that SciFi movies and CHI are tightly connected and that they have been developed complementally influencing each other. He also noted that not only CHI researchers learn from SciFi but also authors of SciFi should learn from CHI researchers in order to create smarter representations of the interaction.

6   Conclusions and Future Work

In this paper, activities and results of SIG-SciFi organized in HCD-Net Japan has been explained. The SIG members implemented the database whose records contains scene title, description, class and category, and timecode to the scene concerned in the movie. Scenes were collected famous three SciFi movies, *Minority Report*, *X-Men II*, and *The Island*, and they were arranged hierarchically according to the objective of the user interface fascinatingly represented in the movie.

A small clip of movies representing the user interface in details should be stored into the database record, so that it can visually explain the scenes intuitively. However, if the movie data are stored into the database directly, it would be violating the IP rights of the original movies. To avoid such violation, a novel and little bit tricky system design is proposed. That is, the source of movie clip is separated from the database and DVD/BD media, which have proper IP rights to the owner of the media, are used.

There are some problems to realize the database system in cooperation with the DVD/BD player. These further studies are left as the future work.

References

1. Shedroff, N., Noessel, C.: Make It So, Interaction Design Lessons from Science Fiction. Rosenfeld Media (2012)
2. Kammerer, D.: Video Surveillance in Hollywood Movies. In: Surveillance & Society, CCTV Special (eds. Norris, McCahill and Wood), vol. 2(2/3), pp. 464–473 (2004)
3. Sarkar, S.P., Adshead, M.D., MRCPsych, G.: MRCPsych: What Price Security? — A Review of Steven Spielberg's Minority Report. Journal of American Academy of Psychiatry Law 30, 568–570 (2002)
4. Kim, H., Kitahara, I., Sakamoto, R., Kogure, K.: An Immersive Free-View-point Video System Using Multiple Outer/Inner Cameras. In: Proceedings of the 3rd International Symposium on 3D Data Processing, Visualization and Transmission, pp. 782–789 (2006)
5. Schmitz, M., Endres, C., Butz, A.: A Survey of Human-Computer Interaction Design in Science Fiction Movies. In: Proceedings of the 2nd International Conference on INtelligent TEchnologies for Interactive enterTAINment, INTETAIN 2008, Article No. 7 (2008)
6. Fishwick, P.A.: Toward an Integrative Multimodeling Interface: A Human-Computer Interface Approach to Interrelating Model Structures. Simulation 80(9), 421–432 (2004)
7. Marcus, A.: CHI at the Movies and on TV. Fast Forward Column, Interactions 13(3), 54–55 (2006)
8. Marcus, A.: Sci-Fi and HCI: The Last Hundred Years of the Future. In: Tutorials on APCHI 2012 (2012)

User Interfaces That Appeared in SciFi Movies and Their Reality

Masaaki Kurosu

The Open University of Japan
masaakikurosu@spa.nifty.com

Abstract. In this paper, future image of the user interface (UI) that appeared in SciFi movies are critically reviewed, especially in terms of their reality. Some ideas of the UI in SciFi movies were actually manufactured as the product but most of them are not. Reasons for the validity in the real world are examined and it is proposed how we should deal with the ideas of the UI in SciFi movies. The concept of meaningfulness is examined as the criterion for validating ideas of the future UI.

Keywords: Science-fiction and DUXU, SCI-FI and DUXU: Film as the Future Information System.

1 Introduction

Early SciFi movies such as "Le Voyage dans la Lune" by Meliers, G. (1902) contained many futuristic but unrealistic ideas on artifacts including the rocket launched by a canon, the rocket with only the cabin inside it, the rocket without any shock absorber for landing, and so many other strange ideas.

Fig. 1. A scene from "Le Voyage dans la Lune" (1902) by Meliers, G.

A. Marcus (Ed.): DUXU 2014, Part I, LNCS 8517, pp. 580–588, 2014.
© Springer International Publishing Switzerland 2014

Fig. 2. A scene from "Le Voyage dans la Lune" (1902) by Meliers, G.

The concepts of the rocket using the liquid fuel and the space suit were proposed by Tsiolkovskiy, K.E. (1857-1935) almost at the same time with the movie by Meliers. Considering this temporal relationship, Meliers might have created the movie just for the entertainment and he might have no intention for using the scientific information for the purpose of improving the reality of the movie.

The year 1902 was 7 years after the invention of first cinematograph by brothers Lumiere. Movies at the end of 19th century and very early years in 20th century were mostly for recording objects and facts. Hence it is not a mystery why Meliers was motivated for the direction of entertainment and not for the scientific validity.

Fig. 3. A scene from "Metropolis" (1927) by Lang, F.

Later in 1927, Lang, F. directed "Metropolis" in which the famous robot and the laboratory to create it are shown. But the robot was described as something mysterious and no logical explanation was given to its creation. The laboratory also seemed to be "something" with many gadgets.

Even in 1950s, "The day the earth stood still" by Wise, R. described some magical and mysterious alien and its robot with no scientific validity.

Fig. 4. A scene from "The Day the Earth Stood Still" (1951) by Wise, R.

But "2001 a space odyssey" by Kubrick, S. (1968) described seemingly scientific spaceship and computer robot "HAL". But the lamps, buttons and levers on the operation console only seemed to be scientific and do not seem to be valid.

Fig. 5. A scene from "2001: A Space Odyssey" (1968) by Kubrick, S.

In this century, SciFi movies such as "Minority report" (2002) by Spielberg, S. described a detailed interactive operation of the system that might have been influenced by the development of non-verbal interface and other research trends in HCI. Although the interface of the system does not seem to be the one that could be realized by the current technology and the usability of the system seemed to be not good, the scientific description has advanced so much compared to previous SciFi movies.

Fig. 6. A Scene from "Minority Report" (2002) by Spielberg, S.

HCI researchers may be able to get some hints from these movies in terms of the future user interface. But the author thinks it is time now to consider about the triad relationships among SciFi movie directors, HCI engineers and usability professionals (or the quadruple relationship by adding industrial designers). SciFi movie directors describe the dreamlike interface while the usability professionals focus on the real usability and the feasibility in the real world. The HCI engineers stand in between these two. You can find many gadgets invented by such engineers at such HCI conferences as ACM SIGCHI where the purpose of the invention is not clear and it is ambiguous whether it is targeted to be used in the real world by real users for any practical goal achievement.

The future of SciFi movies makes us think the direction of HCI research if they are going in the right path. The author thinks it necessary to let the face of HCI researchers be directed toward the real life meaningfulness and the face of SciFi directors in the opposite direction, i.e. full of imagination that should be based on the current technology but should not be confined by the real future development of the current technology. SciFi is the fiction and should be full of dreams.

2   Realistic Prediction

There are some descriptions of the future UI that could successfully predict the future of products and systems. One example is the image of sweeping robots described in Luc Besson's "Fifth Element" (1997). When a glass fell on the floor and is broken, two types of round robot appeared and started sweeping the glass on the floor.

Fig. 7. A Scene from "Fifth Element" (1997) by Besson, L.

The image and the movement of the sweeping robot are quite similar to those of "Roomba" of which "Roomba 500 series" first appeared in the market in 2007. The difference of the robot sweeper in the movie and "Roomba" are 1). The robot sweeper detects the location of the clashed glass and goes directly to the target, and 2) "Roomba" does not include the broom-type and cannot collect large fragments of the glass. It is not clear if "Roomba" was developed by being inspired by the movie. But the movie made a correct prediction regarding the idea of automatic sweeping robot.

Fig. 8. A view of Roomba working on the floor

Another example is the gesture manipulation of visual images in "Minority Report". Although the necessity of the bodily manipulation is not clear in the movie and one can think of the mouse or hand operation on the wide screen as an alternative, the application of "Kinect" by Microsoft at the scene of surgery in the hospital is quite reasonable. During the operation, doctors have a need of viewing the relevant X-ray and other visual images when necessary. But, for the purpose of controlling the possible contamination, physical operations by using the pointing device is not desirable. In this situation, the gesture manipulation of visual image is quite meaningful.

Fig. 9. A scene from "Minority Report" (2002) by Spielberg, S.

Fig. 10. A scene of operation at the hospital using Kenect

In these two examples, it is not clear if SciFi movies gave the suggestion to the developer of the product and the system. But, at least, there is a close coincident between the SciFi movie and the real development of the product and the system.

3   Unrealistic Prediction

On the other hand, there are so many unrealistic predictive images on the future UI in SciFi movies. One example is the image of the future traffic system.

Fig. 11. A scene from "Metropolis" (1927) by Lang, F.

Fig. 12. A scene from the futuristic image of Tokyo (http://military38.Comarchives 28071211. html)

The image of future traffic system in Figure 11 and 12 includes highways running through buildings with almost no bridge girders. It is impossible from the viewpoint of structural mechanics and, furthermore, meaninglessly running high up.

Fig. 13. A scene from "Minority Report" (2002) by Spielberg, S.

Figure 13 is the famous scene of vertical moving traffics on the outer surface of the building in Minority Report. It is amazing but, at the same time, let us ask the question "why will traffics have to run on the outer surface of the building?".

These images are just for the entertainment and tickles our imagination. In other words, futuristic images in SciFi movies are in most cases just for fun and are not aiming at the prediction of the real future.

4   Meaningfulness

SciFi movies are full of new ideas that attracts people's attention. But in the real life, the novelty alone will not work if the new artifact has nothing meaningful that previous artifacts have not had. This is true not only to the SciFi movies but to all the products and systems in the market. Real products should have to be purchased and used and the situation is severer than just the movies. Customers and users may be attracted by the novelty, but, in the end, what matters is the meaningfulness. Artifacts with less meaningfulness will be wasted.

In this sense, what we find in SciFi movies will attract our attention but it is not because of its meaningfulness but of its novelty. Hence, there may be cases where SciFi movies will make a good prediction but it is just a rare thing and we can't expect SciFi movies as predicting our future life.

References

1. ASCII, Roomba 780 Review (2011)
2. http://www.youtube.com/watch?v=te1YgVqvaiA
3. Besson, L.: Fifth Element (1997)

4. Kubrick, S.: 2001: A Space Odyssey (1968)
5. Lang, F.: Metropolis (1927)
6. Meliers, G.: Le Voyage dans la Lune (1902)
7. Microsoft, OPECT Surgery Driven by KINECT Japanese Version (2013)
8. Spielberg, S.: Minority Report (2002)
9. Tsiolkovskiy, K.E. (based on Wikipedia)
10. Wise, R.: The Day the Earth Stood Still (1951)
11. Unknown (?) Tokyo in (2011),
    http://military38.comarchives28071211.html

Bridging the Gap

Methods and Teaching of F-A-S-T - Framing-Art-Science-Technology

Deborah Schmidt[2], Grit Koalick[2], Sebastian Gassel[3], Christian Sery[1],
Rainer Groh[2], and Markus Wacker[3]

[1] Academy of Fine Arts, Dresden, Germany
`sery@hfbk-dresden.de`
[2] Technische Universität, Dresden, Germany
`{deborah.schmidt,grit.koalick,rainer.groh}@tu-dresden.de`
[3] Hochschule für Technik und Wirtschaft, Dresden, Germany
`{gassel,wacker}@htw-dresden.de`

Abstract. *Bridging The Gap* discusses necessities and methods of a transdisciplinary approach at the intersection of art, science and technology, including human computer interaction (HCI) and its various subjects. Research work that combines artistic and scientific approaches benefits substantially from artistic perception and the sensibility to questions beyond their regular environment beyond the work's associated environment. The transfer of knowledge, methods and communication strategies foster a transdisciplinary debate, discussing impacts of existing and emerging technology driven phenomenons. The paper provides a depiction of methods and communication of each discipline to carve out the coherence of transdisciplinarity in praxis. F-A-S-T is introduced as a cooperative project of scientific and artistic institutions where a student's existing profession is amplified by complementary knowledge, methods and collaborative project oriented work. It explores new roles and formats within the interaction between art, science and technology. The aim of the paper is to encourage further research regarding transdisciplinarity and the establishment of corresponding educational programs.

Keywords: design philosophy and duxu, education.

1 Foreword

Funded by the European Social Fund (ESF), by the federal state of Saxony via the Sächsische Aufbaubank and the Saxony Ministry for Science and Art (SMWK), F-A-S-T is a pilot project developing and evaluating a new postgraduate program at the intersection of art, science and technology. Supervised by the project lead of Prof. Christian Sery (Professor for Interdisciplinary and Experimental Fine Art), Prof. Markus Wacker (Professor for Computer Graphics) and Prof. Rainer Groh (Professor for Media Design). The following paper is based on the collaborative work of the

A. Marcus (Ed.): DUXU 2014, Part I, LNCS 8517, pp. 589–600, 2014.

authors together with Jonas Loh[1], Claudia Schötz[1], Svenja Wichmann[1], Axel Berndt[2] and Erik Zimmermann[3].

2   Introduction

In the last decades, computer-based interfaces have changed from technoid machines In the last decades, computer-based interfaces have changed from concrete devices with limited operational functions to fully integrated sensoric components of the human living environment. Interlinked in data-driven networks these technologies increasingly propagate into every-day life. Their research is no longer limited to commercial and academic interests. A vast growing 'Do-It-Yourself' culture is creating unexpected experimental tools and innovative projects outside of industrial mass production, contributing to the research into existing and emerging technologies. According to Ramocki, such a unique process of creativity is synonymous to artistic practice [Ramocki]. He suggests that, for example, the discipline of interaction design can benefit from a methodical dialogue with the arts. Through technological empowerment an approximation of epistemological methods and materializations is able to bridge the disciplines, leading to new forms of research and artistic practice which often form a sketch of possible futures. Prejudices against highly specialized disciplines must be overcome to achieve this goal. Art and science both expand the field of knowledge, though addressing distinct aspects of research. Typically scientific research includes working with documentation material, the construction of hypotheses, and often evaluative, empirical and applied works. In the context of transdisciplinary work, artistic research may also use the same procedures, but is not necessarily committed to scientific research standards. According to Klein, "art is the act of playing with frames – or a framed aesthetic experience" [Klein, 2010]. Scientific research in this context should be able to review itself within multiple framings. Reflexivity of process is already a part of scientific research, but usually limited to the specific disciplinary background. Seen from this angle, debates on the principles of scientific research methods should gain depth.

The remainder of the paper is organized as follows. We will describe examples of existing transdisciplinary projects and show their different ambitions in reference to scientific and artistic research. We encourage reflection and subsequent enrichment of HCI with unusual perspectives from the margins of interpretation. Furthermore, we will characterize conceptions of art and science, focusing on their methodical approaches and communication strategies. We discuss integrated approaches to combine the disciplines on different levels of strategy. Regarding future research challenges, we state that transdisciplinary education is of mutual interest. Within this transdisciplinary framework, we introduce the concept of a postgraduate curriculum called F-A-S-T Framing-Art-Science-Technology that conveys methods, independent of discipline, to students. The curriculum is demarcated from the accepted idea of art as an illustration of science and science as an inspirational tool for art. It focuses on project-oriented collaborations in-between art, science and technology. The program has already been evaluated in test runs. Primary experiences in breaking up the rigidity of traditional interdisciplinary prejudices and then solidifying constructive collaborative transdisciplinary working-relationships and possible future institutions of interaction will be exemplified. Finally we set our work in relation to scientific demands. Our current efforts in enhanced communication tools as well as prospects arising out of the current test periods with students are described. We conclude by encouraging scientific and artistic educational institutes to create inter-institutional structures. This paper aims to brace awareness for the advantages of transdisciplinary work in art, science and technology.

3   Related Works

This chapter reviews different aspects of transdisciplinary work. First, an artwork reflecting a technology-based interaction process is introduced. Next, research projects combining artistic and scientific methods are shown. Finally, a brief view on the scientific publications about research at the intersections of art, science and technology is given.

Artists regularly cross paths with HCI while creating interactive installations or dealing with perceptive aspects of media-based works. Technologically based processes may be reversed in their purpose to exaggerate a new status of perspective within an artistic moment. A performative work by Cohen and van Balen called "75 Watt" stages an assembly-line machinery, which produces a 'futile' object [Cohen & van Balen]. Its only purpose is to demonstrate the motions the workers are bound to perform, when assembling the object. The work was based in China. It addressed inter alia the engineering term 'black box' as an "abstraction [that] allows for the design of ever more complex products in ever more complex processes, resulting in a belief that there is very little we can not engineer", but that also "creates multiple layers of disconnection [..] between the designer and maker, [..] between technology and people, [..] between head and pin" [Cohen & Van Balen].

While the use of computer based technology is evolving in the context of art, current research strategies of both scientists and artists often remain exclusive. The following projects are successful counter-examples, though motivated by different objectives.

The performance-installation „Brain Study" staged by Klein presented an assembly of simplified functional parts of the brain controlled by one actor respectively [Klein, 2004]. The brain activities were perceived through sonification of the actor's neuroscan. The actors were trained to intentionally create certain brainwaves as a response. The resulting sound composition of all brain parts showed patterns of cognition, retention and emotion while remaining an artistic musical piece. The group was later asked to present their findings on EEG sonification at medical conferences, because it could be processed faster by test persons than the conventional visualization of EEG. Klein also worked together with musicians and biologists in a research group at the Cluster of Excellence Languages of Emotion at Free University Berlin. In a project called "Do birds tango?" the group analyzed the relevance of rhythm in songbird communication by pairing newborn birds with trained musicians who adopted the role of the birds language teacher [Scharff & Klein, 2010]. In summary, it can be stated that artistic methods are used to elaborate on research issues that science cannot yet answer conventionally.

The Future Lab of the Ars Electronica based in Linz, Austria is a place where international artists and scientists collaborate on research and orders from economy. They can also take residence and work individually while still being an influence to the transdisciplinary assemblage of the Lab. Within the Lab, processes are envisioned "as sketches of possible future scenarios in art-based, experimental forms" [Ars Elektronica]. While being profitable through collaborations with industry partners and developing patentable technology, they contribute to scientific education through workshops and the Ars Electronica Center and are highly innovative in current research fields of aesthetics, design, computer based interaction, robotics and virtual environments.

The fact that artistic and scientific researchers should approach a subject from different perspectives is also thematized by Amowitz et al. who considered that new challenges in interactive scenarios may not be solvable by scientifically established paradigms [Arnowitz, et al.]. The authors broke interaction issues down to communication problems between the interface and the user. Their statement is that „if you identify an artist who has addressed a problem that you are confronted with, then that artist is presenting a proven method of communication" [Arnowitz, et al, p. 14). The relevance of collaborative and transdisciplinary research is slowly heading toward scientific debates, e.g. through the Digital Arts and Interaction Community that has been part of the CHI conference since 2012 [England, et al.].

4   Motivation

As already mentioned, not only open scientific questions may be superiorly accessible when addressing them from a contrary point of view. The role of people who get addressed by artists and the role someone plays as the user of a sensitive device can be comparatively discussed as a form of communication between a medium of presentation and its target. The increasing adoption of computer-based interaction environments into everyday life thrusts HCI issues further into disciplines like sociology, medicine, philosophy or architecture. Topics evolve with social and emotional stakes. The complexity of HCI processes increases rapidly, leading to less evaluative scenarios [Poppe & Rienks]. Therefore future challenges such as interactive devices in public spaces create a necessity to approach them from various perspectives and to think through the implications of possible scenarios. The outcome of a materialized thinking process is not intended to solve a problem per se but rather to identify a question that is then communicated in a provoking manner fostering a debate. Art as a medium of critical reflection has the ability to discuss technological phenomena, such as 'rapid prototyping' or the 'Big Data' hype, in an intriguing way that communicates possibilities, but also possible risks. We need speculative notions of future challenges to show their context on a scale science may yet not be able to estimate. Overlapping thought processes can lead to a profound gain of knowledge, which is why a combined scientific and artistic education could lead to new ways of research. Positive trends in open-source software and hardware and emerging Do-It-Yourself communities favor such concepts. We will later propose a structure of a program that could provide exactly such an education. Priorly we will present a more general point of view on comparative aspects of scientific and artistic research.

5   Section Thinking, Communication and (re-)Presentation

For a better understanding of the challenges of cooperative thinking and working across the disciplines, one needs to recall the given structure of science and art.

The disciplines of science and their frontiers reflect their historic development: Objects of research, theories, methods, and research purposes define the identities of single subjects and disciplines and their responsibility for certain problems. But they are no given theoretical frontiers or frontiers of objects. Therefore, the complexity of actual problems increasingly does not fit the framework of singular disciplines, e.g. environmental and political challenges or the crafting of a successful future. Mittelstrass speaks of an "asymmetry of problem development and scientific development" [Mittelstraß, p. 3].

Different forms of cooperation can compensate for this difference. That scientific questions are answered through cooperation of scientists with different professional background is usual. 'Interdisciplinarity' could be understood as an increased form of cooperation, in a concrete project with undetermined duration.'Transdisciplinarity' would then mean a permanent cooperation that transgresses the boundaries and changes the structure of scientific disciplines permanently [Mittelstraß, p. 3].

In our context the term 'transdisciplinarity' does not only include scientific, but also artistic disciplines. Therefore, not only the subdivision of science is debatable; it is also the separation of art and science as two antithetic categories of thinking and knowledge production itself that is no longer appropriate. Art and science have been progressively disjoined and understood as apparently independent sectors over the last 300 years. Such categorization reached its zenith in modern times with the "functional differentiation between diverse spheres of action" [Reckwitz, p. 32]. In contrast to the classic modern separation of the sciences and the arts, it is the common grounds of artistic and scientific research that have been highlighted by the current discourse. Accordingly, Bippus notes that a clear distinction of disciplines is only possible on the level of (re-)presentation, but not fundamental on the level of research processes [Bippus, p. 15].

To overcome thinking in disciplinary boundaries, communication and exchange of research results has to go beyond the experience of single subjects and the scope of individual projects. Publications are the distributional medium of scientific research. They are a representation of expert communication, characterized by textual and linguistic complexity, differentiation, and comprehensiveness. They (re-)present research processes and results with the help of conventionalized text forms and scientific images. Publishing transdisciplinary results is a tightrope walk between the different disciplines and their conceptual clarification and theoretical framing. Artistic research uses the scientific forms of (re-)presentations in an (for classical scientific research) unconventional manner and questions their mechanisms sceptically. According to Bippus, artistic research is a provocation, simply because it follows a different course and achieves its results differently [Bippus, p. 10].

Transdisciplinary communication is complex since it happens either between dialogue partners of different scientific disciplines or between scientists and nonscientists. Communication difficulties arise because the dialogue partners possess different states of knowledge and diverse methods of knowledge discovery, convey varying interests, morals, concepts and beliefs. The first goal is therefore to establish a common vocabulary as a basis for mutual understanding. The point is not only to inform one another about a certain research question, as seen and understood from different perspectives, but to gain a deeper common understanding as a basis for design- or decision-making processes by. Transdisciplinary thinking requires an education program that reflects, avoids and abolishes methodical prejudices.

6   Research Methods and Didactic Methods

Methods are the way of doing something. In the context of science, methods are investigation procedures targeted on research results. Scientific methods are planned, goal-oriented and systematic. Method books represent methods to ensure their transparency, each discipline defines certain methods for solving certain problems. In consequence scientific methods should be objective and repeatable.

Artistic research also uses various methods, but in contrast to scientific methods, these are not necessarily conventionalized, reproducible and linear (even though they can be). The method, and the question of the method, are inherent subject matters of the artistic process itself. Malterud compiles a list[1] of competences to describe art as a general phenomenon and states: "Methods are individual as well as field-based. Processes are run by single persons in their personal way, or in corporate settings like theater or concert rehearsals. For all contemporary practice, challenging methods and settings will be part of the work." [Malterud, p. 25]. The idea of the uniqueness of the artist is opposed to the idea of transparency and repeatability as known from science. To sum it with Frayling, scientists prefer "words rather than deeds", whereas artists, craftspeople and designers do "deeds not words" [Frayling, p. 1].

Creativity methods provide further methodical indications. They mediate between analytical and intuitive principles: Creativity methods are often experimental and unconventional processes to consequently and systematically induce innovations. With their help, basic creative mechanisms can be described that are known in science

---

[1] The list of competences includes technical skills and hands-on expierence, creativity, courage, curiosity, attention, reflection, concentration, patience, knowledge of and insight into the field, knowledge of and ability to make use of relevant theory, notions of context, and notions of quality criteria in the peer community. Abilities to set up methodical experiments relevant to the project are needed, as well as competences of organization: locating and staging, communicating with partners, assistants, sponsors, and producers. [Malterud, p. 24]

on the one hand and design and possibly in art on the other. Due to their historic genesis, creativity methods can be comprehended as techniques of cultural and knowledge engineering, as well as techniques of memory, invention, and design across the disciplines. [Marais, p. 230]. This leads us to the question of transdisciplinary methods.

As specified above, problems of transdisciplinary are complex and individually different. They should offer answers, which a single discipline cannot give. Since they go beyond the scope of a discipline, they require case-by-case methods. Mittelstraß states that transdisciplinarity defies theoretical forms (e.g., the methodical form). [Mittelstraß, p. 1]

Transdisciplinarity uses various methods of different disciplines. Therefore, the knowledge about individual methods, and also about field-based methods, is necessary. This approach is given either by transdisciplinary teams or by transdisciplinary method books as suggested by Bergmann et al. The authors gathered different transdisciplinary (scientific) projects and analyzed their methods. They organized them according to seven integration strategies to guarantee transparency and repeatability. [Bergmann, et al.]:

1. Integration through conceptual clarification and theoretical framing
2. Integration through research questions and hypothesis formulation
3. Screening, using refining, and further development effective integration scientific methods
4. Integrative assessment procedures
5. Integration through the development and application of models
6. Integration through the artifacts, services and products as boundary objects
7. Integrative procedures and instruments of research organization

A pursuing question is, to what extend the documentation and classification of transdisciplinary processes in a method book is a useful tool for the extremely diverse interface of art, science and technology.

Our methodical considerations are the basis of the teaching at F-A-S-T. Our main objective is to develop a transdisciplinary platform where art, science and technology meet. Therefore, we introduced project-based work as the central format of our course. Within this form of teaching, students are asked to identify questions on a given relevant topic and to concentrate on possible responses. Project-based work puts a stronger focus on unconventional thinking and the iterative process of e.g. making prototypes, rather than on final objects, products, or solutions.

Project-based work is common didactic method in the fields of Art, Design and Media Computer Science. It is focused on independence, iteration and diversity, rather than on classical forms of teacher-centered education. The lecturer has the role of an initiator who selects topics and regulates process. Ideally, the class is formed by students with diverse backgrounds and prior knowledge in their respective fields to enable an in-depth-discussion. This arrangement of specifically selected topics, the transdisciplinary composition of the group, the processual and project-oriented work and the subsequent critical discourse, distinguish F-A-S-T from other education programs.

7   F-A-S-T - An Educational Vision

Research-based knowledge production is a common practice in any discipline. Still, differences between the disciplines are often identified in the respective general approaches and the used methods. In order to bridge this gap between art, science and technology, transdisciplinary educational approaches are of mutual interest. This particularly includes the teaching of artistic and scientific methods, communication and presentation forms. With this vision in mind, the cross-university project F-A-S-T Framing-Art-Science-Technology aims to develop a postgraduate course at the intersections of art, science and technology. In the course of this cooperative project, test runs were conducted, approaches were evaluated and the development of a curriculum is currently in progress. The working groups primarily consisted of representatives from the fields of design interactions, fine arts, architecture and media computer science and design. The focus of the curriculum has been influenced by this fact, without being limited to it.

One of the first fundamental questions was related to the topics and competencies that must be imparted in order to permit transdisciplinary work and research. In order to get to the point of transdisciplinarity, the students need a common understanding of disciplinary methods and topics. Based on this knowledge, current topics and state-of-the-art technologies can be analysed transdisciplinary. Regarding the forms of teaching, it soon became apparent that the focus should lie on project-based learning in the combination of seminars, workshops, colloquia and presentations. With this combination the students will be provided with target skills, such as reflexivity, communication, documentation, prototyping and scenario development.

In the interest of analysing and evaluating the approaches and questions, three independent test runs of one to 6 months were conducted with different focuses and participants. The topics and conditions varied thematically from rather specific to more general topics. Due to the voluntary, non-committal participation - less regulations and guidelines were imposed than one would commonly define in a running program. Furthermore, an optimal representation of the target group, which should equally consist out of students of art, science and technology, was not possible. Nevertheless, these insights were very valuable for the construction of the curriculum, especially with regard to the conveyed contents, techniques and methods. Moreover, it has been shown that the contents cannot be provided by existing courses, leaving behind the necessary context and transdisciplinarity. It was possible to draw conclusions about the preferable forms of teaching, the liberality of tasks and qualifications of the teachers. Concerning this, a tandem supervision between one mentor specialized in the field of humanities and arts, and another teacher in charge of mentoring the practical project work, such as the design, has been proven to be beneficial. These act as mediators between the disciplines and encourage the reflection of the knowledge areas and project work within colloquia. In the case of more advanced technical topics, contacts within the institutions should exist in order to give an entry point into a particular field of art, science or technology providing in-depth knowledge.

Taking the results of the test runs in consideration, F-A-S-T is currently developing a curriculum. The students will participate in thematically alternating projects and - while working on practical experiments - transfer the theoretical knowledge, research approaches and methods into practice. With every project, the context and the general conditions will change, allowing to evolve the designated target skills. The necessary knowledge support is provided by two additional components of the curriculum - the theoretical and technological influence streams. The theoretical inflow comprises theories and methods of disciplinary topics in order to produce a transdisciplinary context. The modular technological inflow provides the students with a wide practical relevance by imparting newest technology and back-and-forth workflows from analog to digital. The educational offer is completed by a public lecture series with alternating specialized lecturers, presenting their discipline and transdisciplinary ways of working. This already established fluctuating lecture series permits an immediate response to trends and achievements in research areas.

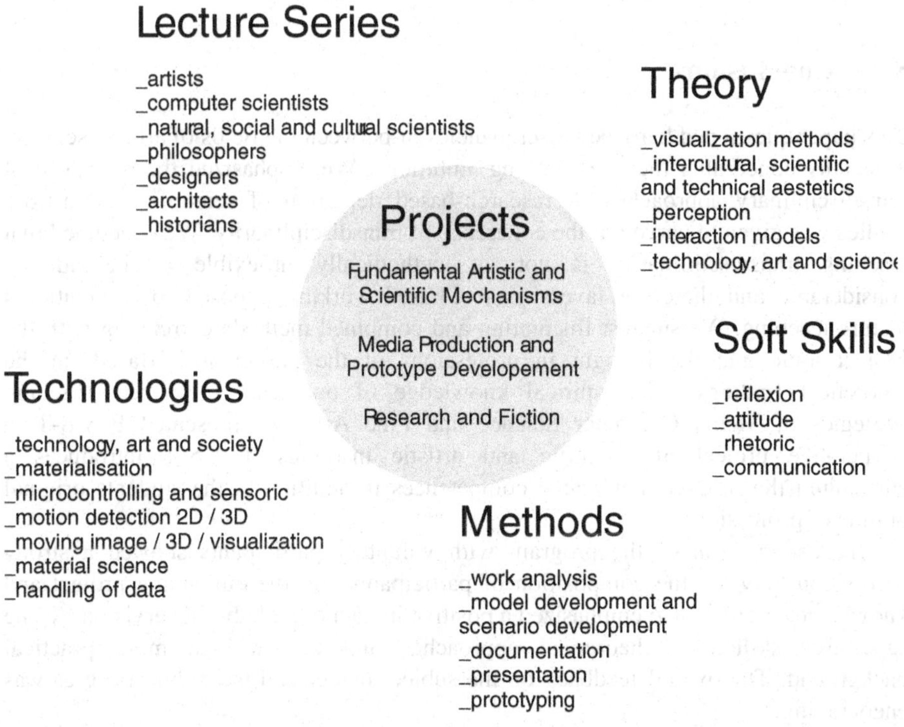

Lecture Series

_artists
_computer scientists
_natural, social and cultual scientists
_philosophers
_designers
_architects
_historians

Theory

_visualization methods
_intercultural, scientific
and technical aestetics
_perception
_interaction models
_technology, art and science

Projects

Fundamental Artistic and
Scientific Mechanisms

Media Production and
Prototype Developement

Research and Fiction

Technologies

_technology, art and society
_materialisation
_microcontrolling and sensoric
_motion detection 2D / 3D
_moving image / 3D / visualization
_material science
_handling of data

Soft Skills

_reflexion
_attitude
_rhetoric
_communication

Methods

_work analysis
_model development and
scenario development
_documentation
_presentation
_prototyping

Fig. 1. The project work in the center of the curriculum is supported theoretically and technically

Since transdisciplinarity can not be mapped onto a particular method and thus does not provide a clear result definition, graduates of the educational program will not learn a new pre-defined profession. It is rather the case that the own professional skills will strongly improve and, more importantly, a transdisciplinary competency profile will evolve (see). Due to this perspective change, the work in the respective discipline of the students will become many-faceted. In the field of HCI - as an example - the project work will strongly focus on the analysis, abstraction and materialization of processes, as well as on the conception of prototypes. From a theoretical perspective, the curriculum will be supported by knowledge from media theory, aesthetics perception theory, alternative design and presentation models. Courses on information visualization or the teaching of current interaction technologies serve as a practical inflow.

Running and evaluating the test runs and lecture series showed proof of an increasing acceptance regarding the program and revealed a profound interest in bridging the gaps in-between the topics, approaches and mindsets of art, science and technology. Furthermore, the inter-institutional base of F-A-S-T immensely increased the network of accessible experts and cooperation partners that students can refer to. As a perspective, the capacities of the City of Dresden - in terms of research, creativity and industry - could gain promising intersections.

8   Conclusions

This paper questioned hardened discrepancies in-between the fields of art and science, especially concerning their researching ambitions. We emphasized the relevance of transdisciplinary approaches. A research-based depiction of scientific and artistic studies was given to carve out the coherence of transdisciplinarity. We concluded that teaching transdisciplinarity is not as methodically inflexible as individually considerable and therefore favors project-based working opposed to conventional lecture teaching. We suggest fluctuating and combined methods correlating with the project topic and the brought in professions of the participants. Based on the theoretical findings and empirical knowledge of our team in current teaching strategies of Media Computer Science and Fine Arts, we presented F-A-S-T, a cooperative project of scientific and artistic institutes. F-A-S-T introduces a curriculum that imparts applicable competences in addition to the students original outline of profession.

The last test run of the program with voluntary participants showed a strong correlation between the composition of participants and the outcoming project and knowledge assets. It also emphasized a positive impact of a double supervision by one supervisor skilled in theoretical approaches and one with a more practical background. The overall feedback on the subject matter and the public lectures was encouraging.

These results are primarily empirical. The test runs only lasted maximally half a year and our experiences are hard to generalize. For that reason further scientific investigations regarding this topic should be made. There are art schools with diverse approaches to teach within transdisciplinary aspects like the design interactions program at Royal College of Art [Royal] or the master degree program "Art & Science" at the Angewandte Wien [Art & Science]. Further efforts to establish truly overarching education opportunities between art and science and associated institutions should be made.

9   Outlook

F-A-S-T is an ongoing project. The current test run with participants will be finalized and evaluated. Similar projects may help to establish an appreciation of transdisciplinarity between art, science and technology in education, research, economy and society. Currently we pursue an approach to create a decentral interactive visual term network. This could help to connect detached research or educational projects of different institutes and should also be discussed in the context of HCI. Nevertheless, a new research understanding as a base of teaching is needed to qualitatively discuss moral, ethical, political and aesthetic questions in a technology based context. Interinstitutional structures for transdisciplinary work environments should be established and socially adapted.

References

1. Ramocki, M.: DIY: The Militant Embrace of Technology. In: Adams, R., Gibson, S., Arizona, S.M. (eds.) Transdisciplinary Digital Art: Sound, Vision and the New Screen. CCIS, vol. 7, pp. 26–32. Springer, Heidelberg (2008)
2. Klein, J.: The Other Side of the Frame Artistic Experience as Felt Framing Fundamental principles of an artistic theory of relativity (2010)
3. Cohen, R., Van Balen, T.: 75 Watt,
   http://www.cohenvanbalen.com/work/75-watt
4. Klein, J.: Brain Study: Installation with interconnected brain players,
   http://aroseis.de/brst/ebrainstu.htm
5. Scharff, C., Klein, J.: Do birds tango? Biological origins of rhythm as a carrier of emotions, http://www.artistic-research.de/projects/
   current-projects/emolution/do-birds-tango?lang=en
6. Ars Elektronica: Future Lab, http://www.aec.at/futurelab/en/
7. Arnowitz, J.S., Priester, R., Willems, E., Faber, L.: Mahler, Mondriaan, and Bauhaus: using artistic ideas to improve application usability. In: 2nd Conference on Designing Interactive Systems: Processes, Practices, Methods, and Techniques, pp. 13–21. ACM Press, New York (1997)
8. England, D., Fantauzzacoffin, J., Latulipe, C., Edmonds, E., Sheridan, J.G., Pobiner, B.-K.N., Reeves, S., Tanaka, A.: Digital Arts and Interaction Community 2012: Building Bridges (2012), http://java.cms.livjm.ac.uk/homepage/staff/
   cmsdengl/arts2012.htm
9. Poppe, R., Rienks, R., van Dijk, B.: Evaluating the future of HCI: Challenges for the evaluation of emerging applications. In: Huang, T.S., Nijholt, A., Pantic, M., Pentland, A. (eds.) ICMI/IJCAI Workshops 2007. LNCS (LNAI), vol. 4451, pp. 234–250. Springer, Heidelberg (2007)

10. Mittelstraß, J.: Methodische Transdisziplinarität – Mit den Anmerkungen eines Naturwissenschaftlers –. Technologieabschätzung – Theorie und Praxis 14(2), 18–23 (2005)
11. Reckwitz, A.: Die Erfindung der Kreativität: Zum Prozess gesellschaftlicher Ästhetisierung. Suhrkamp, Berlin (2012)
12. Bippus, E.: Kunst des Forschens. Praxis eines ästhetischen Denkens. Diaphanes, Zürich (2009)
13. Malterud, N.: Can you make Art without Research? In: Caduff, C., Siegenthaler, F., Wälchli, T. (eds.) Art and Artistic Research, pp. 24–29. Scheidegger und Spiess, Zürch (2010)
14. Frayling, C.: Research in Art and Design. Royal College of Art Research Papers, 1 (1993/1994)
15. Marais, C.: Methodische Imagination. In: Tröndle, M., Warmers, J. (eds.) Kunstforschung als ästhetische Wissenschaft, pp. 203–242. Transcript Verlag, Bielefeld (2012)
16. Bergmann, M., Jahn, T., Knobloch, T., Krohn, W., Pohl, C., Schramm, E.: Methods for Transdisciplinary Research: A Primer for Practice. Campus Verlag, Frankfurt (2012)
17. Royal College of Art: Royal College of Art, http://www.rca.ac.uk/
18. Art & Science: "Art & Science" at the Angewandte Wien, http://www.dieangewandte.at/artscience/

Film – System – Communication

Katrin Vodrazkova

Charles University in Prague
Department of Information Science
Czech Republic
vodrazkova.katrin@gmail.com

Abstract. The paper shows the relation between two models of reality, possibilities of media thinking and combination of binary and complex systems – film as the social and mainly future information system, and fundamental way of operations and usability. We should draw a line between the two types of reality – the real reality and the film reality, and two levels of observing – *what* we are observing (primary reality, facts) and *how* we are observing (secondary reality, film imaginary double-reality, the reality of mass-media, observing of an observation). Film as the social and information system creates a special form of the construction of fictional reality.

The most important point for complex information systems is to understand one informative message. On the basis of understanding of information further communication can continue in each social system. Film communicates in its second reality through the mediation of Other-reference. So there is a difference between Self-reference and Other-reference in the information system. This difference produces new information and new relations, surprise and new cognition and knowledge. Other-reference is the clue for understanding of information and communication systems, relation between the system and its environment, sci-fi and film interface.

Keywords: difference, double-reality, complexity, film, future information system, future design, mediated reality, Other-reference, recursive structure, system communication, system reference, usability.

1 Film and System Communication

The paper shows the model of film as the future information system, the specific area of sci-fi space, and most importantly the difference between **two system references**: the **Self-reference and *Other-reference***, which is typical for system communication and which creates the difference between the **real reality and double-reality**, occuring primarily in the film, moving images, displaying technique and social system. The background for the research will be found in the Luhmann´s system theory, based on the conception of *complexity* of social systems.

Luhmann´s system theory is on the one hand a contribution to post-media and information studies, and on the other hand an application of a system which is active, ingenious, and influential, like a biological or lively organism. This is the way social

A. Marcus (Ed.): DUXU 2014, Part I, LNCS 8517, pp. 601–609, 2014.
© Springer International Publishing Switzerland 2014

systems show the paradoxes of mediated reality. In the case of an information system like film, we are speaking about the double-reality. The social complexity is the conception that mostly influences the behavior and system communication.

The sci-fi space and virtual user interface, the second reality of moving images, consists of symbolic communication, special system communication. In this environment there is the Other-reference above all, that influences the internal Self-reference which exists only in the system inside and has no ability to move from one point to another one.

Why is **film** defined **as the future information system**? What kind of information is it producing? And how the double, mediated, so the film reality, and science fiction user interface influence the processes of human thinking and user experience in the system communication? Why is the *Other-reference* as a special kind of system reference important for the system communication in the sci-fi space, virtual reality, and for the communication process of each user? On the scheme bellow we can see the design of the film system and sci-fi user interface that consist of two types of references and models of reality:

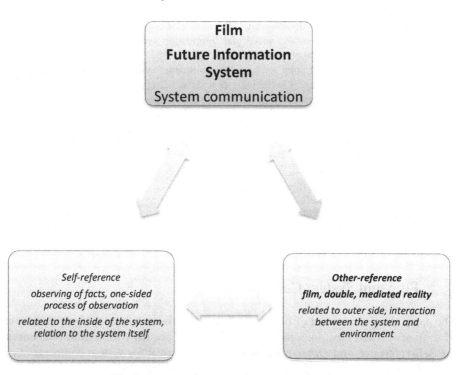

Fig. 1. System reference and two types of reality

The *Other-reference* **has ability to move from the outside to inside**, that means from the mediated reality of virtual environment back into the system, where only the Self-reference exists – on the inside. This is the important point and idea of the system communication theory and conception of the film as moving, imaging, information but also informative system and its information design.

The *Other-reference*, with its reflexive disposition, is the main concept of **forming of new forms** and of all elements in the sci-fi environment, which instigates the processes of creating new ideas or new conceptions and providing new information. The *Other-reference* is the link to answering the question of **how to understand the way from inside (system) to outside (environment)**, how to clarify this specific direction in relation to the users who are watching and observing something, and how to explain the processes in the information system which is still moving from one point to another points.

Film as the future information system and its double-reality based on the Other-reference are producing the system communication and special system interaction. The science fiction area is communicating with the users in all times and combinations – in the past, in the present and also in the future.

The Other-reference is able to provide the feedback for understanding each topic. Film is always providing new information and talks to the users and observers who are watching facts, but the film itself as a special information system is based on the second level of observation – double reality model: observation of the observers. And this is the way to influence the users seeing and thinking in the future, and how to understand new future trends of imaging techniques, which are working as designed, and second science fiction life. Within the concept of Other-reference the users could better understand the future design and usability of film, moving image, mediated reality.

The film as an information system is a kind of **recursive system** with specific **functions** on the one hand, and on the other hand it is able to create special **topics**, determinated not by the external values of knowledge, objectivity or social interest, but rather regulated by the internal binary code of *information – non-information* (related to the Niklas Luhmann´s system theory of social systems).

The system coding and recognizing of information and non-information is the background for the formation of **usability** and system communication in each information system related to the user experience and thinking, special knowledge and cognition.

On the grounds of the binary coding each social system is able to select new information which is informative, and communicates this information in accordance to its reflexive and recursive structure to all users who are part of the virtual environment and who are investigating how the cognitive processes and system communication in the particular social and information system work. They are asking for usability of the complex system, that means they are looking for the system reference, the *Other-reference*.

The complex social, information, and cognitive system is based on three basic layers. On the scheme below we can analyze the process of system communication and identify the relation between the two system references:

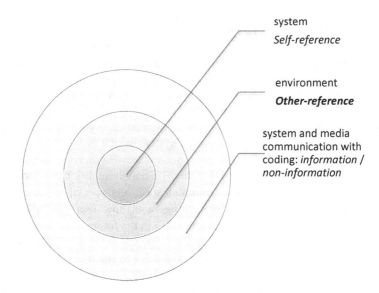

system
Self-reference

environment
Other-reference

system and media
communication with
coding: *information /
non-information*

Fig. 2. System communication

The system communication, existing in each social system, chiefly in film and its production of science fiction interaction and user experience, consists of **system operations** based on binary coding (yes – no) in the very complex system, and **system observation** (the system theory differentiates the system observation of facts or subjects – this is the real and primary reality – from the observation of how other observers are observing other observers in the social system – the case of the second, virtual, mediated reality, important and typical for film or system of massmedia).

The first line, observation of facts, is connected with the *Self-reference*. The other way around the second level of the system observation gives a definition that ***Other-reference*** is beeing produced the ´observation of observation´ within the mediated reality). Luhmann´s system theory focuses on the concept of self-description and self-reproduction of the technical code in each active system. This is the prerequisite for the functioning of all future information systems and the post-information society.

On the scheme bellow we can see the constituents that are designing and building the **construction of the system reality**, the model of reality of each social and information system, based on evolutionary theory. Niklas Luhmann described the model of social systems and system reality divided into three parts: **biological, social and psychologically systems**.

As a psychologically system we understand the person, man, human being, whereas the social system is the society, and it can also be culture, art, system of imaging methods or displaying techniques (based on double-reality model by producing of specific system construction, like film or sci-fi user interface, virtual reality), system of massmedia or for example law, management, theology and system of information design.

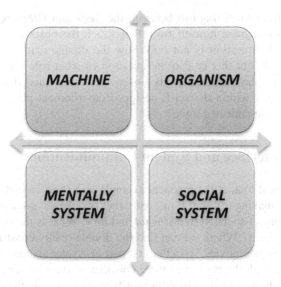

Fig. 3. System theory

The research question of the future information systems and future trends in new imaging methods is that nobody knows, how the specific quality - the system *Other-reference* - exactly works; how is it designed and implemented in each system environment, where the boundaries between the internal system and its external environment are, and what all is forming new information, new interactions, new concepts, new topics, new operations and new functions?

The motives, themes and topics are preconditions for the system communication and especially for the understanding of every informative information (that could be a new message, but also for example a new thought of something what somehow motivates all elements in the system or what is moving in the system environment). The system *Other-reference* is able to show how to better describe and fully understand not only the processing of creation of new information, but mainly the difference between the model of real reality (facts) and the mediated reality (film, usability of sci-fi implements).

The **complex social system like film**, second level of observation within its double-reality and representation of all three dimensions of time, offers more possibilities than the users could use in their daily life. The system complexity forms the selection of new information, new form and new concepts.

There is a distinction between two system references, auto-reference (Self-reference, displaying the primary reality of facts and internal side of each system) and system environment within the mediated reality. Only one type of information is acknowledged as informative, new information, in the current time. Here we are talking about the current possibility, in contrast to the virtual, second reality that recognizes the time dimensions (past, present, future). This is the model of two system references in the sci-fi system environment.

We always have to distinguish between the *Self-* and *Other-reference*. Also the observer has to recognize himself from that which the observer is observing in the relevant time. The question is not only how the double-reality and observation of second level work, but this is also the question of what role (better say how many roles the observer plays and shows, as a user, viewer, listener) does and should each user as an observer within the sci-fi designed environment play, how will the user understand the communicated topic?

2   Sci-fi Interface and System Communication

In this part we will look at the practical example as a short case study of the concept of *avatar* and making of the film, with the two basic questions regarding the Luhmann´s theory of social systems: *what* and *how*. What is the film reality? How is the sci-fi reality built? Where we can find the double-reality construction and system communication in the movies, so in the first part of Avatar and further episode? James Cameron started with the project of three episodes of the film **Avatar**. In the second episode he will show the model of future sci-fi interface within the construction of the system of sci-fi city and future environment. James Cameron will differentiate between the earth and hell´s gate. Initially would the earth have been shown in the film as an entrance sequences. As we can see on the picture bellow, the sci-fi town is displayed as a polluted urban city centre with the pump in the middle of this future town (Duncan, Fitzpatrick 2010: 80 – 81).

Fig. 4. Future digital city

The **future urban city**, environment of the humans, is described and will be analyzed as a contrast between the centre and home tree of Na´vi (original inhabitants of Pandora). Avatars lived in a harmony with the pure nature and original symbols like forest spirits, nature organism or other living creature. This is a very **special social system**, for example if the avatars wanted to move to another place and communicate with each other they use the special signals and connect their tail with the specific animal (for example for riding on avatar´s horses). So there is a difference between the nature system of living and the industry world where the newest technology is used. But what is the real and latest news? What kind of social system is the most efficient regarding the *sense-making* as Niklas Luhmann analyze in his theory of social systems and two different types of system reference? Where we can find the real reality in comparison to the double-reality model, in which social system? How we can recognize and get to know the future trends of thinking? Could we find the *Other-reference* there?

The new concept of James Cameron´s future urban city would like to image a digital city with the new model of seeing and thinking related to the trends of new displaying and digital techniques. This concept of **future digital city** shows the relation between the film reality and **digital media**. In the current information society we live in we call the media *post-media* because of the post-information model of our society. Therefore the Luhmann´s theory of the social systems constitutes the background for post-media-theory and post-information model of thinking about the media and society. The background we could find in the Luhmann´s social systems theory is forming and providing new forms, new conceptions, new ideas, new images, new systems and new imaging methods. The design for displaying of the future urban digital city found James Cameron in the model of Japanese industry area. That is a good example for analyzing the time, scope, speed and milieu, so the difference between the system itself and its system environment.

The *Other-reference* is a part of the double-reality model. Luhmann called this model within the second reality: **second-order cybernetics**. This is the direction of the Luhmann´s operative constructivism, described as *cybernetics of cybernetics*, so the second level of the observation. Regarding the example of the future digital city, we could see on the picture bellow, how this sci-fi model of the city is watching not only itself (*Self-reference*) but also all observers who are watching **facts** on the first level and other observers and observing systems on the second level **how** they are observing (*Other-reference*). Each observer could observe the facts that are produced by the future city as a whole **future information system**. This is a special construction of the operations with all specific functions and production of complex system communication, difference of the information and non-information.

There is also a difference between the observing and watching. The process of watching is connected in all cases with the medium of eye. Also in the first episode of Cameron´s *Avatar* we found the dynamic, active and moving **medium of eye**, the background and fundamental medium for understanding of the double-reality model of system communication and future information thinking, double-coding and computing. The pump in the second episode of Cameron´s Avatar has a function similar to the eye. It is located in the centre. It constitutes the centre. It forms the centre. It is the center as a complex system with its sci-fi and dynamic environment. The observation is a very complex system that could activate the operations and functions on the second level of seeing, thinking and cognitive process. The mode of second-order observation is based on the special design – **difference between the** *Self-reference* (the system) **and** *Other-reference* (and its system environment) in each system in our information society. This is the difference between what one knows from the specific social system and what one has really seen (the model of watching facts in comparison to observing: observation of other observers). The difference between the two types of system reference describes the model of real and system reality. The real reality is different.

But, what is most important – not only the binary coding of *yes-no* model of thinking, more likely the system complexity, the complex relations in each system. Therefore we could find in connection with the double-reality model many of the particular varied realities – more than one real reality and also many of the second realities (f.e. film reality or mass-media reality). Each separate reality has its own active living cycle. We can find many examples in digital or second live, film or music. For example if someone (man as the psychical system in the Luhmann´s system theory of all social systems in our post-information society and digital live of moving images) see some image within the motion and sound, and there are also other humans (psychical systems) at the same time in the particular space, everyone perceives some image with all the other elements on another way. Therefore each person rates his or her *reality* and its construction to *the reality*, his or her own reality. So many social systems, many double-reality models are producing **many separate realities**. Sometimes we could be confused, what reality we live in or we stay in at the moment, and how we can recognize individual forms of the model of complex system reality. Because each of the system has its observation mode, observing process with the specific irritation for forming of new information and new forms, and construction of the reality in comparison to the system environment with the functionality of the *Other-reference*.

3   Conclusion

Luhmann´s system theory is the background for understanding of **active systems** behaving like a lively organism, construction of a specific mediated double-reality and system communication. The system theory shows a timeless concept of media thinking, that could be used for all systems in the contemporary information society and also for virtual model of reality (film, moving image, motion capturing). On the scheme bellow we can see the fundamental components that could explain a very complex relation in each social and information system, in each science fiction environment, in each virtual user interface, and the conception of **complexity** *per se*.

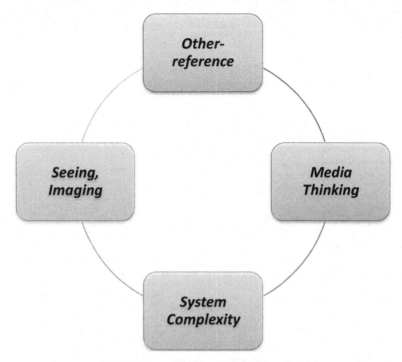

Fig. 5. Film as the Future Information System

This is the model of two types of system references, the difference between: *Self-* and *Other-reference*, based not only on binary coding, but first of all on the **system complexity** that is forming new complex relation, new ideas, new conceptions, new topics, new information. This is the way the internal system communicates with its external environment. And this is the implement for explaining and understanding all attractive themes and functions in each system, but also the way and questions of *how* to understand one informative message within the system communication.

References

1. Duncan, F.: The Making of Avatar. Harry N. Abrams, New York (2010) ISBN 9780810997066
2. Luhmann, N.: The Reality of Massmedia. Stanford University Press, Stanford (1996) ISBN 9780804740777
3. Luhmann, N.: Art as a Social System. Stanford University Press, Stanford (2000) ISBN 9780804739061
4. Deleuze, G.: Cinema 1: The Movement-Image. University of Minnesota Press, Minneapolis (1989) ISBN 9780816614004
5. Deleuze, G.: Cinema 2: The Time-Image. University of Minnesota Press, Minneapolis (1989) ISBN 9780816616770
6. Hofstadter, D.: Gödel, Escher, Bach: An Eternal Golden Braid. Basic Books, New York (1999) ISBN 9780465026562

Design and Creativity

User Experience Technique in Computer Digital Arts Production: Paper Prototyping Used as Material to Define Intentionality

Marília Lyra Bergamo[1,2]

[1] University of Brasília, Brasília, Brazil
[2] Federal University of Minas Gerais, Belo Horizonte, Brazil, supported by FAPEMIG
(Minas Gerais State Foundation for Research Support)
marilialb@eba.ufmg.br

Abstract. This papers aims to describe the historical introduction of paper prototyping techniques into interface development, what they basically consist of, and how such techniques can be applied on the development of Computer Digital Arts. With some examples applied on Digital Arts graduation courses at the Federal University of Minas Gerais in Brazil, this technique has proven to help the development of the artist's intentionality, rather than blocking creativity. It helped students to focus on important concepts that needed to be transmitted by interaction, while usability made the piece friendly where it needed to be friendly. Thus, young art students have been acting in a traditional way when experimenting with materials, not only physically and visually, but also with the interactive environment that should be considered as material in Computer Digital Arts.

Keywords: Mental Model Design, Usability Methods and Tools, Computer Digital Arts.

1 Introduction

The postmodern word interface is as common as its function. A few years ago, still between the 1970s and 80s, the discourse about the human-machine interface was fundamentally scientific, and technological domain of the exact sciences. Over the years, as ubiquitous computing became real, interface ceased to be a term associated only with the field of technology, and became a part of the discourse of the social sciences. It is only natural, since interface means mediation and, as such, communication. However, in this process, interface between man and machine has not lost its technological nature; it was born in the context of computer use, that is, a state machine. Thus, interface is historically the development of man's relationship with computational processing information.

For this reason, some interface development features are culturally intrinsic to every field that uses computation and human-machine interaction. This should also be true when Computer Digital Art is produced. But, because some discourses in Art are

A. Marcus (Ed.): DUXU 2014, Part I, LNCS 8517, pp. 613–621, 2014.

so eager to defend the importance of flaws in creative processes, the idea of using techniques that are related to usability found an inhospitable environment at traditional fine art schools. This is, sometimes, unfortunately a reality.

However, creative schools with focus on design usually do not have the same problem and user experience techniques such as paper prototyping with interfaces has gained importance with the introduction of new students. Due to their familiarity with industrial production and concept development, some kind of prototyping should naturally be used when developing interfaces. In specific, paper prototyping has become a very important tool, because it allows the development of the design concept with potential to usability tests. As a result, user experience techniques with paper prototyping are fully accepted in design, as well as in other creativity areas. Nevertheless, it still seems to be left out of most Computer Digital Arts methodology. Art practices are usually very experimental as regards the materials used, and the results achieved are somehow incorporated into the final piece. This is true when it comes to Computer Digital Arts,. However, it does not mean that intentionality related to functionality available on the piece does not need testing.

The Federal University of Minas Gerais presents a different reality. Some Digital Art students practice user experience techniques in the early years of their education. Paper prototyping, in special, has provided art students with the best practical approach to experimenting with interaction, the same way they already do when dealing with visual and physical materials. Such students are motivated to think of interaction both as sketching and as materialized practice. This paper will present the historical approach to those techniques on design literature, as well as paper prototypes produced by students.

2   Historical Introduction on the Relationship between Design, Art, and User Experience Techniques

The early years of the development of computer interfaces are marked by the adoption of interface as translation among media. Consequently, we watched the development of models that related men and machines focusing on textual cognitive models. According to Johnson [4] and Moggridge [7], with the development of the mouse device, direct manipulation in two-dimensional space created by computational procedures became possible. This was a very important step towards the development of interfaces. With direct manipulation came the metaphor for the transposition of the visual analog world to computer interaction. Interfaces then became graphic, and part of the cognitive visible world. This characteristic brought visual fields of knowledge and the development of interfaces closer together, since the same basic principles that govern visual arts have also been explored in human-machine interaction.

Among the various professionals who were involved in this area, graphic designers were by nature qualified professionals for this type of development. Graphic designers work with visual art principles in order to produce communication pieces, and therefore began to understand interface as a new working field, often in partnership with professional computer programming. According to Moggridge [7], the duo Tim Mott and Larry Tesler is a good example of these partnerships. Tim Mott was challenged by the idea of working out the new publishing system for Xerox Corporate, which he considered completely unusable for others than the people who built it. They worked together building the still used metaphor of an office desktop: all computer files were transformed into documents that could be carried and dropped onto a printer or into a trashcan.

The beginning of this century saw the emergence of some pieces of artwork created by computer processing that involved not only direct manipulation or input textual data [1]. Of course this did not occurred in isolation. As an example, the field of automation carried out studies that involved theoretical and practical concepts of two different disciplines: computing and electronics. The result of this combination may be seen in art works such as those of artist Daniel Rozin [3] and his mirrors. The image captured by the camera and processed by the computer is transformed into physical behaviors through electronics. His mirrors are physical representations of the pixel; these units behave as the smallest visible units of the piece, and translate the camera view into units that are both virtual and physical.

As a result of this, some contemporaneous interfaces are treated as tangible, and presuppose the existence of physical devices capable of communicating with the computer. Besides the interface sensible capacity (sensors and actuators), computational processing is now incorporating cognitive intelligence, making this medium increasingly complex. Interfaces are coupled with artificial intelligence and mechanisms of perception of human behavior. It can also recognize user actions and information processing input. Joining the recent technological developments in the area of mobile telephony, the coupling of gestures in two-dimensional interactive spaces, and motion capture techniques, the development of interfaces has become essentially multidisciplinary, a kind of space where several professionals work differently although with equivalent levels of importance. Among these, product designers found a fertile working ground, due to the fact that commercial product design now incorporates computational procedures. Daniel Rozin [3], for example, was trained as an industrial designer, and his work uses customized software.

3   User Experience Techniques Used in Computer Digital Art Development

The Federal University of Minas Gerais Animation and Digital Arts Graduation Program offers disciplines in both areas, but most of the students are more interested in animation. Young art students are very reluctant to study digital art. The origin of this reluctance towards the digital art field is coding and programming. Although being a part of the School of Fine Arts program, some of the initial disciplines concerning these topics are given at the College of Computer Science. Difficulty in learning coding is a reaction to the inability to understand the foundations of digital technology. Curiously art students are excellent at digital drawing, and very proactive to experiment with digital graphic tools. Nevertheless, as regards how and what these tools are built for, they have no interest.

Coding is a frustrating activity if done repeatedly due to lack of planning. Moreover, it may be even harder to recode when users do not know how to use the interface, and as a result of this, not only codes but the entire piece need to be rebuilt. This is an old lesson for the computer industry, for which specific commercial goals are essential. However, art students have no such goals to achieve, but simply intentions. While coding mistakes may be interesting to digital animation, this is not true when it comes to interaction. In Computer Digital Art, codes are finishing settings of a previous material, the interaction itself, and through user experience techniques art students can experiment with this interaction. Tools such as personas, use-case diagrams, scenarios and paper prototyping are introduced to design students in their first or second semester, but art students do not have access to this information on their course's curriculum. As result of this, teaching interface design to art students has been a laboratory of user design techniques.

The first technique introduced to art students is conceptual modelling. Rather than writing, art students are encouraged to draw, and are constantly motivated to specifically draw how the interaction piece would work. On this phase, it is important to think about the physical and graphic information, and draw sequences of how people would be interacting with it. Buxton's book, Sketching User Experience [2], is particularly applied to create conceptual models as it presents drawing as an essential tool to think about interaction. One interesting point is that when art students finish sketching conceptual models, they immediately want to start coding. After thinking about interaction through drawing, coding suddenly turns into something interesting.

Good exploratory sketches can help art students to discover their intentions, but not to understand their target audience. Thus it is important to motivate students to create personas, use-case diagrams, scenarios, flowcharts and navigation maps in order to understand how users would act through interactive digital art pieces. Although this is an important part of the process of mapping user experience, art students are unmotivated to do it. No important improvement in discovering the effectiveness of intention has been observed in art students while using those tools. Specially scenarios are less helpful to the process. On the other hand, when art students are asked to transpose interaction onto paper, and create art pieces that pretend to be working in computing environments, motivation can be again observed. Art students take time creating and recreating their interfaces with paper; it makes them think as product and graphic designers. They found it easier to make changes directly on paper prototype than rewriting something on the scenarios. This attitude is not equal to use-case diagrams and flowcharts, and art students found them very useful when preparing their prototypes.

Art students are asked to prepare paper prototypes to perform between two or three tasks that are fundamental to their intentions. Those prototypes are tested with volunteer users. That consequently leads to another two sections of paper prototyping redesign, in which art students have to go back to their activities of discovering what can be improved in order to better apprehend their intentions towards the audience. User tests show art students the wide range of reactions people may have while dealing with interfaces, and this is the specific material they need to experiment with before carrying out any coding or exhibition in Computer Digital Art.

4   Student's Work Examples

This section presents four selected works of art students that were produced according to the description in the last section. All of them had conceptual models, user experience documentation and paper prototypes, and were selected along the years of 2012 and 2013. These projects have gone through two or three different versions of paper prototyping since its conceptual modelling and documentation, and all usability problems and versions will be presented in result tables.

4.1   Share a Smile Application

This project was produced by student Débora Mini Almeida in 2012. The application basically consisted of sharing smiles around the world. The student has defined the piece intentions as something like: sharing smiles as a way to make people happier.

Fig. 1. Share a Smile Application Conceptual Model, drawing by Débora Mini Almeida, 2012. This image was modified. Textual note descriptions in Portuguese were eliminated in this paper presentation.

Table 1. Table of results from usability tests on paper prototyping, Share a Smile Application

Problem	Prototype Version	Priority	Solution found
Excess of information to sign in.	1	Medium	Sign in form with e-mail address and agreement only.
While reading email, application was interrupted, and users were unable to return the smile	2	High	The student wants to make people happy with smiles, but interrupting users did not work. A waiting icon was placed on the top the device.
Users were annoyed for not knowing where the smile came from	2	Medium	A flag was placed together with the smile picture
Users could not identify where the flag was from	3	Medium	Flags were replaced by names of countries

4.2   Artificial Stars Installation

Created by Isadora Morales in 2012, Artificial Stars Installation was inspired by a Chinese comic book called *Knite*. Set in a Chinese metropolis, the book presents a character who is part of a group frustrated by the impossibility of seeing stars in the night sky of the city. They then decide to create artificial stars. In the comic book these stars are cloth kites with small lamps. The conceptual model is an installation of gas balloons with wires and lights. Balloons could be controlled by a mobile device application, which enabled them to physically follow the user's geographic position value within a predetermined perimeter of the installation. The installation paper prototype was mainly focused on: 1. How users would react to the application; 2. How users would be coordinated by the application; and 3. How the application would let users know if they were followed by any balloon. For the user tests, a black gas balloon with Christmas lights tied to a string was used.

Table 2. Table of results from usability tests on paper prototyping, Artificial Stars Installation

Problem	Prototype Version	Priority	Solution found
Users were annoyed for having to sign in to be followed	1	High	No personal identification was needed to enter the software, only the geographic position and an ID should be generated, without the user's knowledge, to queue users.
Users could not identify which balloon was attached to them.	1	High	A feedback color tag was placed on each balloon.
Users did not manage to identify which color tag was attached and again did not identify which balloon was attached to them.	2	High	A map of all balloons was created as a feedback for users, and the one that followed the specific user was highlighted.

4.3   Interactive Mirrors Installation

Projected by Matheus Guedes de Paula in 2012, the interactive mirrors would be screens coupled with cameras simulating mirrors, to be placed in public bathrooms, and changing rooms at clothing shops. The screens would show a virtual person interacting with the audience, asking questions, playing games, and so on. His prototype was more a performance test, and an actor was hired to follow a specific script simulating the artificial intelligent software intended.

Fig. 2. Conceptual Model of Interactive Mirrors Installation. This image was modified. Textual note descriptions in Portuguese were eliminated in this paper presentation.

Table 3. Table of results from usability tests on paper prototyping, Interactive Mirrors Installation

Problem	Prototype Version	Priority	Solution found
Users kept looking at the actor on their backs	1	low	A real time projection was screened on a white paper attached to the mirror.
Users kept touching the real projection	1	Medium	Reactions to touch actions were inserted in the script, depending on where the touch happened.

4.4 Virtual Graffiti Installation

A project by Diego Falabella, Geisa Souza, Jessica Hissa, João Marcos, Lídia Soares, Saulo Ishutani and Teiciany Sena, 2013. Inspired by street art and its intense criticism against graffiti expression, the work intends to bring together the audience and reflections about the theme. The interface protopype is a spray can interface that helped the audience to produce virtual images in graffiti.

Fig. 3. Virtual Graffiti Installation. Paper prototyping installation in 2013, photographed by Marilia Bergamo

Table 4. Table of results from usability tests on paper prototyping, Virtual Graffiti Installation

Problem	Prototype Version	Priority	Solution found
Users had questions on how to save the screen	1	Medium	Change position of saving icon
Users do not understand how to scrabble, paint or interact with the screen.	1	High	The spray can interface was redesigned; some buttons were eliminated and placed on the screen, where users were more focused. A color panel was placed on the floor.
User cannot restart the installation after finishing drawing	2	High	A restart button was included on the spray can interface.
Color panel was stepped on	2	Medium	Colors are now chosen by being stepped on

5   Conclusions

The experience of teaching user-centered methodology with art students has led to three important conclusions about this process in this specific environment. First of all, this methodology has been applied to the earliest moment of the creation process. For this reason, it is important that some flexibility can be applied, especially, to the documentation. Documentation is important, but art students draw more out of pleasure, which means that some documentation can be conceived in sketching, and this sketching should be considered as an early stage of the user-centered process in art environments.

This conclusion leads to a second one, that some usability principles, such as feedback, restrictions and consistency should be incorporated into the minds of art students during the entire sketching process. In other words, because those creations are usually not very related to previously existing solutions, usability heuristic recommendations are, sometimes, of little use. As a result, if the principles are understood and accepted beforehand by those students, their drawings and sketches tend to be created incorporating usability right from the very start of the creation process.

At last, the third conclusion is about the prototyping methodology. Paper prototyping in digital art should be an amplified concept of low fidelity prototyping. Paper can be used, but all other kinds of cheap materials have been used, such as balloons and broomsticks. For this reason, any low fidelity, which won't cost the students too much money or time to develop, becomes material to experiment with interaction itself. Also this prototyping methodology in digital interaction art has demonstrated that the environment where the tests take place plays an important role in the process of acquiring user information. Sometimes performances are necessary, like in the Interactive Mirrors Installation, and at other times, the dark outdoor environment was fundamental, like in the Artificial Stars Project. This means, once again, another level of flexibility in the process of user testing. Classrooms, for example, do not suit as a good unbiased place for testing. On the contrary, the environment becomes part of the prototype itself.

In conclusion, with these prototypes and sketches, and more flexible methodology incorporated into usability principles, art students have demonstrated a better apprehension of user-centered concepts, and have observed the importance of such concepts for the audience, which consequently leads to acquiring clearer intentions.

References

1. Bolter, J.D., Gromala, D.: Windows and mirrors: interaction design, digital art, and the myth of transparency. MIT Press, Cambridge (2003)
2. Buxton, B.: Sketching User Experiences: Getting the Design Right and the Right Design. Morgan Kaufmann (2007)
3. Danil Rozin Interactive Art (2014), http://www.smoothware.com/danny/ (retrieved January 21, 2014)
4. Johnson, S.: Interface Culture: How New Technology Transforms the Way We Create and Communicate. Harper Collins Publishers Inc., New York (1997)
5. Jordan, P.W.: Designing pleasurable products: an introduction to the new human factors. Taylor & Francis, London (2000)
6. Laurel, B., Mountford, S.J.: The Art of human-computer interface design. Addison-Wesley, Reading (1990)
7. Moggridge, B.: Designing interactions. MIT Press, Cambridge (2007)
8. Norman, D.A.: The design of everyday things, 1st Doubleday/Currency edn. Doubleday, New York (1990)
9. Snyder, C.: Paper Prototyping: The Fast and Easy Way to Design and Refine User Interfaces. Elsevier, San Francisco (2003)

Cultural Creativity in Experience Design Model

Shu Hsuan Chang[1], Chi-Hsien Hsu[2], and Rung Tai Lin[3]

[1] Graduate School of Creative Industry Design, College of Design,
National Taiwan University of Arts, Taiwan,
Department of Commercial Design Vanung University
mikejsc@gmail.com
[2] Graduate School of Creative Industry Design, College of Design,
National Taiwan University of Arts, Taiwan
assah16@gmail.com
[3] College of Design, National Taiwan University of Arts, Taiwan
rtlin@mail.ntua.edu.tw

Abstract. Experience economy is on the upgrade in the world and experience has become a new type of marketing mode and brand value. Its connotation is to satisfy the mental and spiritual needs of consumer. Popular cultural concept of consumption in global village era emphasizes on local culture value of itself on the contrary. Therefore, the study believes it makes the consumer experience local culture through marketing design and identify the local culture via interaction further. In the marketing design taking local culture as experience can make the consumer understand the historic background, characteristics and cultural essence deeply. With additional story and entertainment design and construction, it is conductive to promote identification of consumer to local industries and increase consumption willingness. The study takes Majoee as case to study and analyze local culture. On the basis of experience literature overview, it takes conversion as experiential marketing design, proposes design conversion method and construction mode. The purposes of the study are as the following. First, it discusses experiential marketing design related literature theoretical basis. Second, it takes "Local Culture" as the theme of experiential marketing design mode. Third, case study takes Majoee as the theme of experiential marketing design mode. In the conclusion, it proposes to take "Cultural Creativity" as the theme of experiential marketing design strategy and feasibility. The importance of the study is to apply humanity and characteristics of local culture to convert into design transfer media through theoretical basis of semiotics. Then it merges cultural design as experiential marketing to promote local culture values and construct an experiential marketing design conversion mode to be taken as reference for cultural experiential marketing application.

Keywords: Local Culture, Experiential marketing, Majoee, Semiotics.

1 Introduction

Economic value has been into experience economy era in current stage. (Pine II & Gilmore, 1998) In the experience economy era, marketing strives to create valuable

A. Marcus (Ed.): DUXU 2014, Part I, LNCS 8517, pp. 622–630, 2014.

experience. (Schmitt, 1999) Experiential marketing indicates current completion methods are identical, and it is difficult to highlight differences on its performance, benefits, quality and services. Therefore, what the consumers want is to move their emotions and stimulate their spiritual needs. Schmitt proposes the concept of experiential marketing. Experiential marketing is to focus on the experience of consumer. It mainly relies on "experience media" to provide consumer with consumption experience situation and feel the value of "experience" products. While the current cultural creativity industry takes local culture to combine with creativity situation and commercial mechanism to promote and develop cultural creativity. Consumers can rely on experience mode to recognize multi-culture and increase industrial value. Therefore, it integrates cultural elements as experience design, provides development mode reference, and relies on Majoee case to discuss and understand creativity mode of experience design and intensify the connotation layer.

The study purposes are specifying as the following:

1. To discuss how to apply theme experience design on local culture.
2. To use the theories of experience and semiotics related scholars to construct basic development experience design.
3. To take culture as creativity design to experience the conversion mode of marketing.

2   Literature Review

The root of "experience" is to turn industry marketing thought to customization of service gradually, bring different feeding in the heart of consumers and create meaningful memory relying on personal involvement. As the different requirements of different layers of customers, industrial experience design also strives for different layers.

2.1   Experiential Marketing

Experiential Marketing theory scholar Schmitt (2000, Wang, Y. Liang ,X. Trans) believes that it makes the product or service create a kind of experience by providing sensing, appealing and creativity & situation related experiences. It is a kind of lifestyle marketing and social identity activities and makes efforts to provide s new experience for the consumers, and create different experiencing forms for the customers via 5 groups of strategy models, i.e. sense, feel, think, action and relationship and make the customers have a wonderful consumption experience. Pine II &Gilmore (1998) induces experience design to five method elements to describe the tendency of experiential marketing, i.e. the key point of market does not focus on marketing performance and effectiveness of products, but to shape the customer experience. The contents are described as the following (Table 1).

Table 1. Five Method Elements of Experience Design

Experience Design Element	Design Connotation	Execution Method
Set a theme for the experience	It is primary for to construct a good theme. Experience theme shall be clear, concise and attractive to let consumers feel the industry provided connotation clearly.	Take personal handling to deepen the sense of belonging and memories. Strengthen the experience of consumer to the space and event, and form interaction experience.
Shape impression and harmony with positive cues	Overall situations and personnel of consumption fields must be consistent with the theme. In this way, the consumers will have unforgettable memory.	Six pints to shape impression: 1. Time. 2. Space. 3. Technology. 4. Authenticity. 5. Qualia. 6. Specifications
Eliminate the negative factors	To shape perfect experience, it shall eliminate negative information which weakens the theme impression.	Eliminate all objects which may disperse the theme and concentrate on service essence and values.
Add souvenir	Design memory values. Souvenir is the memory for the field experience.	It shall provide souvenir sales, giving and independent making services.
Focus on five kinds of sensory stimulation	The more sense organs are involved in the experience, the more effective it will be to deepen the impression and difficult to be forgotten.	Use rich experiences to provide customers with entertainment, learning and relaxing requirements.
Provide experience for sales	When the industry provides experience for product sales, it is the start of industrial transformation.	Take appropriate costs to make consumers pay attention to the service quality and connotation.

Data Source: The data of the study is collected from Pine II and Gilmore (1998).

2.2   Semiotics Study

Currently, many studies have also applied semiotics in anthropology, sociology, history of ideas, cultural history, aesthetics, art and other fields, and become the interpretation language for connotation.   Saussure believes symbols generate meaning by the relationship between them, and the connotation of design can be applied on the basis of cultural symbols, which can show the connotation meaning and value of design. French semiotician Barthes (1972) explains the meaning of symbols and culture. He believes object is often away from the meaning of itself in human cultural life, while demonstrates the special cultural meaning termed as "denotative meaning ". Special meaning contained in the cultural society is involved in the cultural layer. Outreach righteousness based on the symbolic is expressed via the emotions of applicator, and it belongs to "connotative meaning". Hofstede (2005) points out Symbols, Heroes, Ritual & Norm and Value are the four key elements in our culture. Moreover, the four elements are all tangible symbols and existed in daily life of all nations' culture, which is deserved for all designers to take the tangible symbols as the ideation of   creativity. In the book Chinese Semiotics (Zhou,2000), it also proposes that it has constitutive property, causality, meaning and social domination association method behind the cultural phenomena due to cultural semiotics. (Li, 1993) It can provide us the root causes to understand the cultural creativity or cultural diffusion.   That is to say, using cultural conversion method can seek to get rich times and conduct data collection and analysis for symbols, ritual practices, relationships, character, values and other materials, and then covert into application elements.

2.3   Meaning of Semiotics

The study of semiotics linguists Saussure (1983) takes linguistics as the starting point. He believes symbol is composed of "Signifer" and "Signified". The Signifer is to transmit the physical entity of symbols, such as sound, shape and materials. It is perceived by our senses as "expression". The Signified is to transmit the concepts or ideas of symbols, i.e. the involved psychological concepts of symbol, which is a kind of "concept". Generally called symbols can be divided into verbal symbol and non-verbal symbol. Verbal symbol is the accumulated results of long-term "creativity" of human. It constructs historical events, social context, cultural scale, and even the inner world of subject and private space etc (Zhou,1993). Currently, exegetics or semantics summarizes the linguistic meanings and divides the meaning into "original meaning", "extended meaning" and "borrowed meaning". (Tan,1981) The connotation of "extended meaning" and "borrowed meaning" is echoed with the connotation of "Signifer" and "Signified" of Saussure.

3   Study Method and Process

Experiential marketing can be showed through the application of cultural element. Cultural symbol itself also has "indicative meaning" and "implied meaning". Therefore, the connotation of experience design conversion can rely on the application of semiotics to show the meaning the values. The symbol application of designer is to achieve the design purposes and communicate and transmit information with the participators. However, it is deserved to discuss and study for the whole thought process of designer on how to master the element and convert the element into symbols to transmit required information.

   The study purposes of the paper are just to convert the cultural element into experience design and cast into field situation design so as to achieve the aims of experiential marketing. The study has total 5 steps and "Experience Design Model" is summarized by integrating the above literatures. (Fig 1) First, it takes experience design element as the content setting. Second, it is the culture property selection, which is divided into substance, material, behavior, customs, ideology and intangible spirit. (Hsu, & Lin, 2011) Third, analyze characteristic culture and select figure, culture, geography, landscape, property (Hofstede, 2005) and four key elements of culture: symbols, model figures, ritual norms and values as experience element application. Fourth, it applies Signifer and Signified of semiotics to interpret conversion design on cultural, history, custom and other connotations. Fifth, it uses cultural symbols to covert the connotation meaning of experience design and merge the four aspects in experiential marketing theory (Pine & Gilmore, 1998), "Entertainment", "Education", "Esthetic" and "Escapist" in the field space design. An environmental situation which is conductive to create memory and concretization of experience connotation are sufficient to produce memory to the consumers. On the basis of it, it develops experience design model.

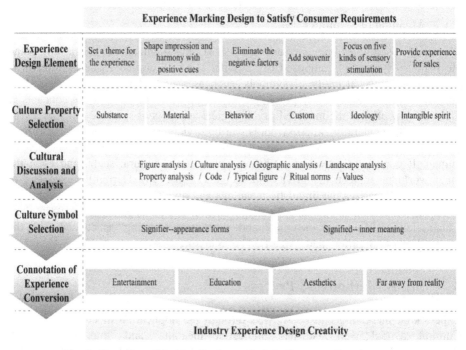

Fig. 1. .Experience Marking Design to Satisfy Consumer Requirements

4   Case Study of Cultural Creativity Conversion Experience

"Taiwan" has a kind of market competitive advantages with qualia and value identification. (World Chinese Entrepreneurs, 2010) and it is located in Dali, Yunnan, which has long cultural history and beautiful scenery. Hence, Majoee takes "land of idyllic beauty", "return to the original nature", "Far from the Hubbub" and

"Happy Life" as core ideas to be converted into design connotation. There are six scenarios coming from "Free" concept, including self-owned scenarios: Martial art, Secret manuscript, Disciple, Kung Fu, Discuss, and Practice.

4.1 Local Culture Conversion Experience Design

Set the Theme for the Experience-Form the Unique Sect. Majoee takes the "Exquisite Chess Board" plot in the Semi-gods and the Semi-devils of Jin Yong's novel as accommodation room No, and takes chess piece to select room. After selection, the young knight errant (service personal) will lead you to the room. The room is also furnished distinctively. The tea plantation is located at the high position of Mountain Cang, Dali, where can look into the Erhai Sea from a high place. It is suitable to be far from the hubbub and be as conversion development process.

Shape Impression and Harmony with Positive Cues-Secret Book Viewing. The knight errant will takes "Tea Cooking and Martial Discussion" storytelling plots at fixed time to provide "Pu'er Tea Valuable Book" for tea selection experience and provide customers with historical allusions to understand the Pu'er Tea, from Tea-Horse Road to the shape of Pu'er Tea, then to classification of Pu'er Tea and production year related knowledge, tea making and tea cooking technology, so that the visitors can have deep experience travel of Pu'er Tea.

Eliminate the Negative Factors-Disciple Selecting. Experiential marketing takes closing and personal sensing as the appeal to go into the tea plantation to pick tea leaves personally and experience the history the people's commune period. Then, the visitors will feel the temperature of tea plants and enjoy the fun of tea picking. Furthermore, it uses tea plant adoption to deepen the memory of local place. Majoee also takes tea plant adoption mode to maintain interaction relationship with visitors continuously, and send tea plant caring and growing photos the adoption visitors to cause the willingness of consumer to return for another visit.

Add Souvenir-Secret Gongfu Emerged. In the transition mode from tea plant to scenic tea plantation, visitors are asked to visit the making process of Pu'er Tea. With the fold song of Bai nationality, tea making process of Majoee is taken in show method. Tea fixing, rolling, drying, fermentation, steaming and pressing to tea cakes and final packaging process to finished products are shown in front of the visitors. The consumers will witness the whole making process and arouse the willingness to buy. Finally, it is taken as souvenirs with combination of memory to bring back home.

Focus on Five Kinds of Sensory Stimulation-Clam Kongfu Discussion. (Jianghu Feast) Yunnan is rich in traditional Chinese medicine and mushroom mountain products. The herbs and organic foods are taken as the calling to attract visiting tourists. In addition to enjoy local delicious food, it can also give consideration to healthy. However, it uses the martial plot in The Semi-gods and the Semi-devils as the name of each dish. When the young knight errant serve the dishes, they will tell the story of history and martial arts. The tourists also get impression memory and topicality on Dali style.

Provide Experience for Sales--Hidden Cultivation. After selecting room via turning the chess piece, tea storytelling, dish storytelling and tea picking experience, visitors go back to the room and have as rest. When in the room resting, in continues the experience of local culture. Continuing with the meaning of martial arts door selected in the "Exquisite Chess Board", the connotative story in the door number shall be merged into the indoor layout. Collaborated with the aroma loved and selected by the visitor, lit incense is disseminated and filled in the room slowly and visitors can soak for a bath to relax the body completely, which is like far from the hubbub and in the land of idyllic beauty.

In one word, 6 plots of experiential marketing conversion for Majoee converts the culture into the experience design process and the concept development of design application. It is collected as in Fig 2.

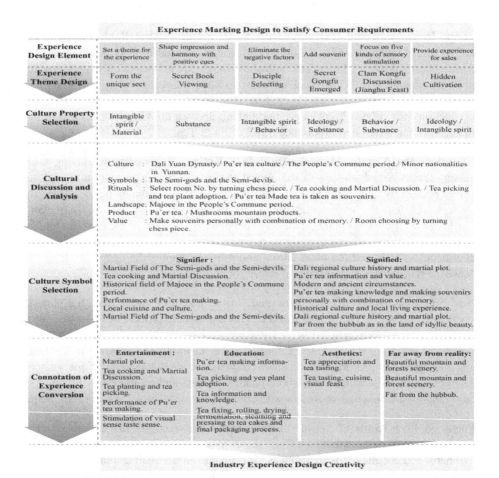

Fig. 2. Majoee Culture Conversion and Experience Design Process (collected by the author independently)

5   Conclusion and Suggestions

According to the semiotics literatures and experience theories, the study constructed experience design mode takes the Majoee case to analyze the contents and results and illustrate the marketing mode of converting culture into experience is applied in relationship construction of consumer. It enables to provide more persuasive proof and obtain deeper connation value. The contribution of the study is to make illustration in three dimensions. Cultural experience design can repackage the local culture and rethink the symbolic significance of cultural codes from it. It is conductive to enhance cultural awareness and cultural acceptance. Cultural creativity design industry transforms the culture and applies it in experiential marketing. It is conductive to improve brand differentiation of the industry in the market, and has identity and competitive power. For research purposes, with the local culture as the theme of the story, it collects and plans to provide a transformed thinking and reference.

It has changes in consumer patterns. At the beginning, consumers pursue a variety of different experience to obtain unforgettable experience and memories and get real spiritual needs satisfactory. Industrial creativity value lies in providing consumers with new value experience, and the culture is always the best source of creativity. Just through experience design, it can allow consumers to understand the background, features, uniqueness and culture of local industry, meet the demand and increase inner impressions of consumption and degree of recognition, which will all leave memories to achieve consumption and brand reputation. In this study, it takes Majoee case to interpret the marketing method of converting culture into experience in order to provide reference principle for conversion mode. Follow-up studies still need to think deeply on value-added constructive method of cultural creativity.

References

1. Barthes, R.: Mythologies. Marion Boyars, New York (1972)
2. Barthes, R.: Mythology (Hu, Q.Q., Hu, Q. L.Trans.). Guiguan Press, Taipei (1998) (Original work published 1972)
3. Chang, S.H., Hsu, C.H.: Cultural elements used in experiential marketing research. National Yunlin University of Technology (2001) (April 2013)
4. Hofstede, G.: Cultures and Organizations: Software of the Mind. McGraw-Hill, London (2005)
5. Hsu, C.H.: Case study of Taiwan aboriginal culture conversion using cultural product design. Institute of Industrial Design, Chang Gung University, Taipei (2004)
6. Hsu, C.H., Lin, R.T.: Cultural product design process. Journal of Design 16(4), 1–18 (2011)
7. Li, Y.Z.: Introduction to the theory of semiotics. Social Science Literature, Beijing (1993)
8. Pine II, B.J., Gilmore, J.H.: The Experience Economy: Work is Theatre & Every Business a Stage. Goods & services are no longer enough, USA (1999)
9. Pine II, B.J., Gilmore, J.H.: The Experience Economy (Jia, Y.L., Lu, W. Trans.). Cites Press, Taipei City (2003) (Original work published 1999)

10. Pine II, B.J., Gilmore, J.H.: Experience true (Qiu, R.M. Trans.). Tianxia Press, Taipei City (2008) (Original work published 1999)
11. Saussure, F.: Course in general linguistics. McGraw-Hill, New York (1966)
12. Schmitt, B.H.: Experience Marketing (Wang, Y. Liang, X. Trans.). Time Experss, Taipei City (2000) (Original work published 2000)
13. Trompenaars, F., Hampden-Turner, C.: Riding the Waves of Culture: Understanding Cultural Diversity in Business. Nicholas Brealey, London (1997)
14. Tan, Q.J.: Chinese of language study. Taiwan Business Press, Taipei (1981)
15. World Chinese Entrepreneurs. In: Wu, T.J. (ed.) Chinese "Fun Taiwan" phenomenon. World Chinese Entrepreneurs (8), pp. 32–33. World Chinese Entrepreneurs, Taipei City (2010)
16. Zhou, Q.H.: Semiotics of Chin. Yangzhi Press, Taipei (2000)
17. Zhou, H.S.: Meaning: Hermeneutics of inspiration. Taiwan Business Press, Taipei (1993)

Keeping Creative Writing on Track: Co-designing a Framework to Support Behavior Change

Paul Doney[1], Rebecca Evans[2], and Marc Fabri[1]

[1] Leeds Metropolitan University, United Kingdom
{p.doney,m.fabri}@leedsmet.ac.uk
[2] Minty Man Limited, United Kingdom
towritetrack@gmail.com

Abstract. The application of persuasive technology in web-based and mobile phone-based systems is well established, particularly in the health domain. However, a greater understanding of the effectiveness of the techniques deployed is needed to facilitate the successful transfer of research findings into practical applications. The context explored here is that of creative writing and the potential use of persuasive technology to foster and support a productive writing routine. Employing a user-centered design approach, we conducted surveys and a co-creation workshop with writers. Goal setting and regular writing, combined with self-monitoring, were key indicators of an effective writing practice. Group and mentor support were also highlighted. Based on our findings, we developed the architecture for a mobile personal writing coach. We evaluated the architecture against existing frameworks, finding good congruence. This supports our long-term goal of creating a universal framework, applicable to a wider range of behavior change interventions, domains and users. The design considerations reported in this paper go some way towards that goal.

Keywords: Behavior Change, Goal Setting, Design Thinking, User-Centered Design, Co-Design, Methodology.

1 Introduction

The application of persuasive technology to support positive behavior change has had significant success in the health domain with symptom trackers and management systems; in particular for physical and mental health, with specific examples for smoking cessation, weight loss and exercise [32][16]. Another arena has been reducing energy consumption [6]. These studies have resulted in a number of models for future systems to follow, whether that be from the perspective of underlying psychological theories, the use of persuasive interface design techniques [9] or architecture of functional components [23]. In parallel with this research effort, the availability of smart phones has facilitated a growth in productivity and tracking applications. These applications reflect many of the characteristics of those developed as part of research programs, although many have been developed within a commercial environment such as HealthMonth [12] and Runkeeper [29] and Lift [17].

A. Marcus (Ed.): DUXU 2014, Part I, LNCS 8517, pp. 631–642, 2014.

In this paper we report on the design of a framework for facilitating positive behavior change in creative writers, applying a user-centered approach. The research with users was undertaken to support the design phase of the proposed development of a mobile website, which will function as a personal writing coach. The goal of the website will be to assist aspiring and active writers to improve their writing practice and consequently meet their writing goals.

2   Background

The UK has an established and thriving creative writing sector, with 150 university level courses, and many thousands of short uncredited courses offered by organizations like Arvon [4] which has been running courses since 1968, The Guardian [11] and Faber [8] as well as short courses run in local libraries, colleges and by organizations like WEA [33]. Other tools to support aspiring and active writers include magazines like *Writing Magazine* [30], *Writers Digest* [7] and *Mslexia* [25]. Further to this, there are websites and apps offering advice, writing prompts, and allowing writers to post work and get feedback from writing communities; examples include National Novel Writing Month [26], Writers Café [3] and Wattpad [31].

Despite the creative writing sector offering such a variety of tools for supporting writing, our research identified a gap in the provision for supporting positive behaviors related to managing writing goals and promoting effective routines. Both of which could be offered through persuasive technology. This presented an opportunity for practical innovation and the proposal for application architecture to meet this gap. Given this, our work reported here is driven by the hypothesis that a route to writing success is based on developing a regular writing routine which is goal-based and measurable. Core to this is a focus on positive behavior change and fostering habits which can be tracked by the individual writer.

The suggestion that goal setting and habit change could be a more effective route to writing success than, for example, generating ideas, was tested with a large group of writers through a series of online questionnaires, a workshop using personas, and a small sample of paper-based writing trackers. This paper reports the results of this research and proposes a practical framework for behavior change and goal setting for creative writers. We then develop this framework into the application architecture of a mobile website-based personal writing coach called "Write-Track" [34].

3   Related Work

The desire to drive positive behavior change supported by technology is evident from meta studies examining web based systems [32] and mobile devices [27]. In persuasive technology research there has been a concerted attempt to apply established models of behavior change, including the Trans-Theoretical Model (TTM) [14], Theory of Planned Behavior (TPB) [1] and Social Cognitive Theory (SCT) [5] – either individually or in combination. TPB has been identified as a relatively successful online intervention model [32], but Michie et al [24] observed that even when interventions have been underpinned by established models, this is often done so minimally and without due consideration being given to all potential variables. From a system design perspective, this critique is understandable as the models in question are typically an attempt to illustrate interactions between various factors and therefore do not provide a clear framework for development. To test whether a system applies a model, an examination of the variables inherent within them can provide a framework.

Michie's Behavior Change Wheel [24] labels the three high level influences as Motivation, Capability and Opportunity. These closely mirror the work of Fogg [9], who similarly considered Motivation and Ability as key, but introduces the importance of Triggers. Triggers raise motivation or ability to the level where an individual is able to perform the target behavior; alternatively a trigger may simply act to nudge an individual who already has the ability and motivation but just needs a timely reminder [9]. SCT and TPB also present the path to behavior change as one that is dependent on a triad of influences, with SCT drawing attention to opportunity derived from the impact of environmental and personal factors [5] and TPB considering motivation in the guise of personal attitudes and perceived norms [1]. Both focus on self-efficacy as the key trigger for promoting a target behavior. In contrast, TTM is hierarchical and sequential, which offers designers a model that can more easily be transferred into a development framework or indeed an automated interaction. TTM identifies seven stages of change starting from a position of ignorance, through preparing for behavior change, through action and onto long term maintenance [14].

Whilst accepting the importance of behavioral models as an influence on system designers, some have sought to extend these to develop a framework that encompasses the experience of software systems design [13][28]. This move towards drawing lessons from different domains in pursuit of effective guidance for systems developers seems natural, with systems for behavior change being increasingly examined from an HCI perspective by commentators with a background in digital design.

Lockton et al [20] observed that design to influence behavior is not a domain specific pursuit and that attempts have been made in various domains such as architecture, medicine and web design to develop 'How-To' guides. Lockton offers the *Design with Intent Toolkit* to help direct designers of behavior change systems [19], presenting lessons learned from a multitude of domains. More recently Lockton et al [21] have begun to develop a set of behavioral heuristics as a means of defining further guidance. Anderson [2] offers a card-based 'Mental Notes' reference system for interfaces designers, drawing from psychology to capture insights into human behavior that can be applied to the design of websites or other software applications.

The adoption of web-based delivery to support behavior change has the advantage of being dynamic and unbiased, but all too often initiatives focus on the provision of information and underuse the technological potential [18]. The emergence of more interactive applications that include tracking, triggers, reminders and communication demonstrate that there is a clear shift towards exploiting technology more fully [15][27]. Extending this progression from theory to practical application, guidelines have been offered for design principles aimed at behavioral intentions [10], design patterns to influence user behavior [19] and persuasive information architecture [23].

4   Research and Investigation

Practical experience of working with writers indicated that there may be a gap in support available that is aimed at fostering an effective writing routine. It was therefore hypothesized that a route to writing success is based on developing a regular writing routine, which is goal-based and measurable. This hypothesis was tested with writers through a series of online questionnaires, a workshop and a small sample of paper-based personal diary studies.

4.1   Scoping Questionnaire

The aim of the questionnaire was to explore whether goal setting and a regularized writing routine offered an effective route to writing success, when compared to other techniques and approaches. Respondents were recruited by using the Twitter feed of co-author Rebecca Evans and the Arvon Foundation. Both these feeds are used to communicate with writers and in particular those that have attended an Arvon creative writing course. The use of Twitter potentially narrowed the target audience from all creative writers to those that are actively using technology. Using this approach, a convenience sample of 142 writers responded to the questionnaire which was delivered via Survey Monkey in two tranches between January and June 2013.

Results. 85% of respondents wanted to write more regularly and, of these, 90% wanted to write every day. Main obstacles to this were failure to develop good writing practice (61%) and difficulty finishing a project (57%). Key reasons were lack of time (56%) and lack of discipline (50%). In contrast, 76% of respondents found that ideas came to them easily, and 71% replied they found it easy to find inspiration. Main sources for inspiration were deadlines (75%), encouragement (61%) and competitions (35%); with on-going motivation being derived from writing groups (53%) potential success in competitions (51%) and going on a writer retreat (45%). Writers measure the success of achieving goals by completing a full project (50.7%), subjective evaluation (45.8%) and getting published (45.1%). Only 4.2% of respondents said they do not measure success in any way. Of the 97 participants who responded to whether they would be interested in using technology to improve their writing practice, 64% said they'd like to, 22% said no and 14% said they don't know.

4.2   Workshop

To seek further insights into potential responses to the problem domain, whether that be technological or otherwise, a structured workshop was devised. The aim of the workshop was to gain a deeper understanding of the strategies and methods employed by writers when confronted with particular challenges. In advance of the workshop 11 personas were developed, capturing the lives and characteristics of writers that were not meeting their goals. Each persona consisted of a detailed one-page description. Below are brief summaries of three of the personas:

- **Molly is maddened by motherhood** - Molly has two children under five, a part time job, and spends her spare time running a busy household. She has always written and is part way through a novel - she feels a loss of identity by not being able to realize her creativity.
- **Dan's difficult second novel** - Dan has a two book deal with a publisher. It took him ten years to write the first book, now he needs to deliver the second in 18 months. He's scared he can't write this book and is worried he is a one hit wonder.
- **Master of Arts Madeline** - Madeline has completed her MA in creative writing – she's got talent, great ideas, a short story collection and a first draft of a novel. She thrived in the college environment - now she needs to develop the practice on her own and is struggling without external deadlines.

In the first half of the workshop, participants formed groups of 2-4 and drew on their own experience to empathize with the aspirations and challenges that each persona presented. Then they identified a range of potential interventions to address the frustrations of their persona. These were narrowed down to the two favored interventions for each participant group. Participants were then introduced to the Fogg Behavior Grid [9] prior to being asked to examine the interventions they had identified and collectively place the identified interventions into the most appropriate grid cells. Each group was then provided with an information card about the grid cells relevant to their interventions and asked to re-examine their chosen interventions and develop suitable behavior change strategies, considering triggers, motivation and ability.

The workshop format was trialed with a small group of postgraduate students from a Creative Technology course. No changes were made following the trial. The actual workshop took place during May 2013 with 24 active writers as participants, forming 8 groups. Each group considered a different persona.

Results. Groups generally identified with their personas well and had no problems generating ideas for interventions. For example, the suggestions for 'Madeline' were:

- Get together with the course colleagues
- Enter competitions to provide deadlines
- Look for enthusiasm and encouragement, be around nice people (e.g. at festivals)
- Read out work at live shows where audience members perform at the microphone
- Set realistic goals
- Do small pieces of work at a time

The two favored interventions developed from above suggestions and then placed onto the Behavior Grid were to a) join a support group (Blue Dot – do a familiar behavior one time), and b) seek feedback from a mentor (Green Span – do behavior for a period of time). Overall, interventions proposed by the groups could be split into four broad categories:

1. Lifestyle changes to overcome difficult hurdles (6)
2. Goal setting as a focus for motivation and/or provision of a trigger to action (4)
3. Feedback in the form of social interaction or from experts as mentoring (4)
4. Improved time management to release time for writing (2)

Once all groups narrowed their suggestions down to the two favored interventions each, using the Fogg Behavior Grid as a reference point, feedback (13 occurrences) and goal setting (5) emerged as key interventions. Suggestions for lifestyle changes, although popular during the initial brainstorm, played only a minor role in the end.

4.3   Personal Diary Study

At the same time, we ran a personal diary study with 15 writers during one week in May 2013. The purpose of the study was to explore qualitatively what types of goals writers set and how they monitored their progress against them. We chose a personal diary method because this generally yields high accuracy when compared other methods, such as questionnaires or retrospective interviews. The diary study was presented as a paper-based writing tracker. Participants were asked to record, over five consecutive days, any goals they had set themselves and their progress against them. Volunteer participants were recruited from attendees at a writing retreat and were a mix of ages and genders. At the beginning of the week they were asked if they had set any goals for their writing, and what these were. Each day the writers were asked 3 questions: 1) Did you write today? 2) How did it go? 3) How did you feel about your writing today? At the end of the week they were asked if they had met their goals, whether and how they usually measured goals, if it is useful to do so, whether they found it useful to keep track of their writing and how they felt about it.

Results. Allowing writers to articulate their goals without a prompt generated a range of different goals. Some were very specific and number based, therefore easy to measure: *15,000 – 20,000 words per week; 3,000 – 5,000 words a day; 2-4 chapters of a book.* Others said they planned on completing comedy sketches or the first draft of a novel or new draft of a manuscript. Though these are not defined numerically they are still closed goals with specific end points.

Some writers focused on planning their work, rather than writing a certain amount, for example outlining a novel, plotting a novel and writing the first few chapters. Others looked at editing a radio play or a short story, or reviewing and restructuring a draft of a novel. These types of goals may be complex to measure, but there is still a specific end point so writers can say whether they achieved it or not.

Writers were asked about the usefulness of setting goals and many found it a positive experience: *"It has become like a diary record and allowed me to reflect on how my writing picked up pace."* Another said: *"[Goals] help me focus. I feel better about myself when I meet them at the end of each day and I am motivated to set more."*

There was an opportunity for writers to comment on the act of tracking itself. Again the role of motivation was mentioned: *"Keeping track was an additional motivation."* This was especially the case when writers looked back over the week. *"It's interesting to see the cumulative effect through a week of responses to writing. It only takes minutes and once it is established as a habit I imagine it could become a valuable tool for supporting work."* Another found that poor past performance actually made them write more: *"It showed me that I am goal driven because [when] I felt that I am failing to reach my target I worked and forced myself more."*

The structure of the tracker worked for writers, *"I found the 3 part structure very simple and it made me see what I'd actually done."* With some saying they would like to continue with the practice: *"I'll be incorporating this in my daily practice from now on."* Another saying: *"I wish I'd done it years ago!"* Finally one writer suggested how the tracker could be extended: *"I could imagine having tracker support groups getting together to share findings – more about the reflection on the process than the amount of words completed or hours spent writing."*

4.4   Final Questionnaire

A final questionnaire was devised, with a particular focus on exploring writing goals and habits. Twitter was again utilized to generate a convenience sample and the questionnaire was delivered using Survey Monkey, with 183 writers taking the survey during September 2013.

Results. Key findings were that 54% of writers set themselves goals, with only 16% being clear that they did not motivate themselves at least partially through goal setting. Of those that set goals 28% actively tracked progress, with 45% undertaking at least some limited monitoring. When asked to identify goals, the most popular were:

- Measurable closed goals such as time spent, number of pages written (per week, month), or number of words per day, week, fortnight or month (examples given included 500, 800, 1,000, 1,500, 4,500, and 5,000)
- Goals based around sections of writing or parts of a project, such as completing a chapter, scene, outline, article, poem, collection, novel (per day/week/month etc)
- Some writers set annual goals or aspirations such as submitting to agents, sharing with friends or peers
- Others saw the goal as an achievement of a routine, or meeting a deadline for a competition or from other external sources like publishers or agents

When selecting goals from a pre-defined list, the completion of part (56%) or a full (53%) project were the most popular; with both external deadlines (52%), words written (45%) and internal (45%) deadlines featuring strongly. The potential to share goals was questioned and an equal (32%) percentage of respondents were inclined towards sharing as those that felt their goals should be kept private. However, a greater proportion of those that were undecided were inclined (20%) towards sharing than those that were dis-inclined (13%). Only 3% said they had no goals.

4.5   Discussion

Writing regularly emerged as a key ingredient of having a good writing practice. The main barrier to this, interestingly, is not lack of ideas or inspiration, but lack of time and discipline. Questionnaire results clearly pointed towards goal setting and tracking of progress as a highly effective way of developing good writing practice. Interestingly, the tracker study revealed that the simple act of setting a goal can, for some, be enough to spur on writing – even without much tracking and follow-up. And the easier it is to set goals and track progress, the more likely it will become a habit.

Further, a focus on emotions as a key part of the goal setting emerged – it may not be just about the actual achievement but how people felt. It appears that setting writing goals increases feelings of well-being associated with achievement. There are many ways of measuring success in writing: from outlining a writing plan or completing a draft, over writing a set number of words per day to completing a project and getting published. What all these have in common is that they are easily measurable and characterized by set end points. The 2nd questionnaire identified the importance of having easily trackable milestones and deadlines and ticked off when completed.

Both the workshop and the diary study provided evidence that peer support, peer feedback and joint activities can be strong motivators to increasing writing and forming new positive habits. The first questionnaire also pointed towards contact with other writers, in a regular group or during a residential, as a strong motivator for writing. The opportunity for reflection – on both writing process and progress – within a group emerged as a potential catalyst for fostering motivation and forming habits.

5   Proposed Application Architecture

Drawing on insights gained from our research, we developed a proposal for the application architecture of the personal writing coach. It was clear from engagement with writers that managing goals and gaining feedback were central elements. Our architecture aims to deliver the elements through four inter-connected components:

Goal Setting. Enables users to make personal commitments and help them develop regular habits. Users have the option to define goals for specific projects or for their writing in general. Goals can be open ended or closed, with defined deadlines such as submitting to a competition. Goals may be user-defined or selected from suggested popular goals. Reminders are sent to assist users track progress.

Tracking and Analysis. Tracking could be as simple as allowing users to log that they have written that day or monitor against their goals by ticking them off, for example writing for a certain time or completing a defined number of words. Over a period of usage it will help users recognize what stops them writing and helps them to develop good writing practice and the conditions that support it. The application aggregates collected data and feedback on how the community of users is performing.

Groups. By making a goal public, the user joins a group of people with the same goal and has some awareness of what other group members are doing. Groups provide a means for users to share their experience with others and gain feedback (either automated or personalized). Having public goals is seen to be a crucial component for success in helping writers to progress. Groups are set up around pre-set goals, for example: write five days a week; write 500 words a day; write for a competition.

Resources. A wealth of support material is already available to writers, and this section does not duplicate but instead manage and signpost users to reliable sources, thereby fulfilling a mentoring role (albeit in a passive way). Resources are searchable, give access to support materials and provide links to further information. This section will grow through the use of a moderated forum, providing opportunities for peer support and feedback. It will feature a facility allowing writers to create their own personalized scrapbook of resources containing notes, photos, links etc.

5.1   The Architecture in Context

To evaluate the proposed architecture we examined it with reference to the Fogg Behavior Model [9] and the information architecture design suggested by Marcus et al for the series of Machine designs [22][23]. We chose Fogg because the model it is perhaps the most discussed and referenced model in the Persuasive Technology domain. We chose Marcus' Machine because it too was developed using a user-centred approach albeit in a completely different domain, so any parallels would arguably point towards domain-transferable concepts and architecture components.

Fogg Behavior Model (FBM). Fogg [9] suggests that motivation and ability must combine at a level such that an effective trigger will prompt action in support of a target behavior. Notably, Fogg suggests that boosting motivation and ability should be considered secondary in any intervention, with the design of timely triggers being critical if the intervention is to be effective. In examining the Writing Coach proposal against FBM, a precise mapping was not expected as the design was developed pragmatically in a commercially oriented environment, rather than a research-driven one. However, tables 1 and 2 illustrate that the proposed architecture has high congruence:

Table 1. Fogg Behavior Model Mapping (high level)

FBM Factor	Mapping to Personal Writing Coach
Ability	Users self-defined as writers or aspiring writers,
	Resources to boost knowledge, Advice from peers and/or experts
Motivation	Goal tracking and Encouragement from peers/ experts
Trigger	Tracking data, Reminders, Peer comparisons

The FBM offers further granularity to the three main factors, and by mapping these to our Personal Writing Coach architecture, a more complete picture emerges.

Table 2. Fogg Behavior Model Mapping (detailed level)

Factor	Factor Component	Mapping to Personal Writing Coach
Ability	Time	Lack of time was found to be the main barrier to writing
	Money	No significant mapping
	Physical Effort	No significant mapping
	Brain Cycles	Provision of resources
	Social deviance	No significant mapping
	Non-routine	Ideas of others through direct contact or resources
Motivation	Pleasure/Pain	Meeting targets/ achieving goals
	Hope/Fear	Setting goals
	Acceptance/Rejection	Receiving positive feedback
Triggers	Spark	Writing prompts
	Facilitator	Mentor support
	Signal	Reminders, results of comparative analysis

By mapping the application at this finer level of granularity some gaps can be seen. It could be argued that the application holistically supports a planned approach to writing and therefore aids time and lifestyle management, but there are no explicit aspects of the application that address the broader aspects of an individual's personal situation. Two of the elements of Ability, namely *physical effort* and *social deviance*, did not find a map in the context of creative writing. There is however a strong mapping against all aspects of motivation, particularly in support of pleasure, hope and acceptance. There are no elements in the application that explicitly focus on pain, fear, or rejection; although the peer support mechanisms could result in feedback that focuses on the predicted impact of not achieving set goals. The reminders and tracking analysis provide reliable signal triggers and the communication with other users could result in the provision of facilitator triggers, but this is considered to be too unreliable to provide a significant mapping. Fogg [9] notes that spark triggers could be considered annoying, so the absence of a strong mapping here is considered appropriate.

Aaron Marcus and Associate's (AM+A) Machine Architecture. AM +A's proposal for a Health Machine [22] provides an in-depth design overview including a proposed generic information architecture for the health domain. This builds on an earlier proposal for a Green Machine [23] aimed at facilitating environmentally sustainable behavior. Whilst both these initiatives vary from the context of creative writing, the architecture itself lends itself to adaptation to other domains. AM+A's architecture offers 5 high level components, as illustrated in Table 3. A further 6th level was omitted as it was considered too context-specific.

In contrast to the expectations with regard a mapping to the FBM, it was expected that the information architecture proposed for the personal writing coach would have strong links with that proposed by AM+A, primarily as both have been developed against a background which includes the presence of many similar applications. The notable exception is AM+A's proposal for a *My Challenges* component. AM+A propose that users should be provided games and a reward-based system as part of their application. This gamification can be found in many on-line environments, but nothing emerged during the design stage of the personal writing coach to suggest that gamification techniques would be well received. Notably, compared to FBM the writing coach architecture omits any aspects that target motivation through the negative emotions of pain, fear and rejection. Somewhat related to this, AM+A propose that predicted outcomes based on current practice should be included as part of My Future, potentially illustrating an unwelcome, and painful, future.

Table 3. Machine Architecture Mapping

Machine Component	Mapping to Personal Writing Coach
My Condition – tracks exercise, weight, food, etc.	Tracking and comparative analysis
My Future – goal setting & visualization of goals	Goal Setting and dreams
My Tips – recommendations & user guidance	Resources and personal scrapbook
My Challenges – game-based activities to educate	No significant mapping
My Friends – social support & communication	Group membership and communication

6   Conclusions

The hypothesis that a route to writing success is based on developing a regular writing routine which is goal-based and measurable, was tested through the application of a user-centered co-design process. The hypothesis was supported by the combined results from the questionnaires and workshops that were delivered. The design process was also used to devise a framework for a mobile website to support positive behavior change, through the application of persuasive technology. Website development is currently underway [34] and the next stage of our work will be test and evaluation.

The framework that emerged was evaluated by completing a mapping exercise, comparing it with models by Fogg [9] and Marcus [22]. Overall the mapping provided good model congruence. While there was some variance in frameworks, these were minor, indicating that models developed primarily in a health context are transferrable to novel domains. This supports our long-term goal of creating a universal framework, applicable to a wide range of behavior change interventions and domains.

References

1. Ajzen, I.: The Theory of Planned Behavior. In: Lange, P.A.M., Kruglanski, A.W. (eds.) Handbook of Theories of Social Psychology. SAGE Publications, London (2012)
2. Anderson, S.P.: Seductive Interaction Design. Berkley, New Riders (2011)
3. Anthemion Writer's Cafe, http://www.writerscafe.co.uk
4. Arvon Foundation, http://www.arvonfoundation.org
5. Bandura, A.: Social Cognitive Theory. In: Lange, P.A.M., Kruglanski, A.W. (eds.) Handbook of Theories of Social Psychology. SAGE Publications, London (2012)
6. Cowley, B., Moutinho, J.L., Bateman, C., Oliveira, A.: Learning principles and interaction design for 'Green My Place'. Entertainment Computing 2, 103–113 (2011)

7. Writer's Digest, http://www.writersdigest.com
8. Faber Academy, http://www.faberacademy.co.uk
9. Fogg, B.J.: A behavior model for persuasive design. In: Proceedings of the 4th International Conference on Persuasive Technology. ACM, Claremont (2009)
10. Gotsis, M., Wang, H., Spruijt-Metz, D., Jordan-Marsh, M., Valente, T.W.: Wellness partners. JMIR Research Protocols 2, e10 (2013)
11. GuardianWriting, http://theguardian.com/guardian-masterclasses/creative-writing-courses
12. Health Month, http://healthmonth.com
13. Hilgart, M.M., Ritterband, L.M., Thorndike, F.P., Kinzie, M.B.: Using Instructional Design Process to Improve Design and Development of Internet Interventions. J of Medical Internet Research 14, 98–115 (2012)
14. Kennett, D.J., Worth, N.C., Forbes, C.A.: The contributions of Rosenbaum's model of self-control and the transtheoretical model to the understanding of exercise behavior. Psychology of Sport & Exercise 10, 602–608 (2009)
15. Lau, P.W.C., Lau, E.Y., Wong, D.P., Ransdell, L.: A Systematic Review of Information and Communication Technology-Based Interventions for Promoting Physical Activity Behavior Change in Children and Adolescents. J. of Med. Int. Res. 13 (2011)
16. Lehto, T., Oinas-Kukkonen, H.: Persuasive Features in Web-Based Alcohol and Smoking Interventions: A Systematic Review of the Literature. J Med. Int. Res. 13(19) (2011)
17. Lift, https://lift.do
18. Litvin, E.B., Abrantes, A.M., Brown, R.A.: Computer and mobile technology-based interventions for substance use disorders. Addictive Behaviors 38, 1747–1756 (2012)
19. Lockton, D., Harrison, D., Stanton, N.A.: The Design with Intent Toolkit (2012) ISBN 978-0-9565421-0-6
20. Lockton, D., Harrison, D., Stanton, N.A.: The Design with Intent Method: A design tool for influencing user behavior. Applied Ergonomics 41, 382–392 (2010)
21. Lockton, D., Harrison, D.J., Cain, R., Stanton, N.A., Jennings, P.: Exploring Problem-framing through Behavioral Heuristics. IJ. of Design 7(1), 37–53 (2013)
22. Marcus, A.: The Health Machine: Mobile UX Design That Combines Information Design with Persuasion Design. In: Marcus, A. (ed.) HCII 2011 and DUXU 2011, Part II. LNCS, vol. 6770, pp. 598–607. Springer, Heidelberg (2011)
23. Marcus, A., Jean, J.: Going Green at Home. Information Design J. 17, 235–245 (2009)
24. Michie, S., Van Stralen, M.M., West, R.: The behavior change wheel: A new method for characterising and designing behavior change interventions. Impl. Science 6 (2011)
25. Mslexia, https://www.mslexia.co.uk
26. National Novel Writing Month, http://nanowrimo.org
27. Pagoto, S., Schneider, K., Jojic, M., Debiasse, M., Mann, D.: Evidence-Based Strategies in Weight-Loss Mobile Apps. American J. of Preventive Medicine 45, 576–582 (2013)
28. Ritterband, L.M., Thorndike, F.P., Cox, D.J., Kovatchev, B.P., Gonder-Frederick, L.A.: A Behavior Change Model for Internet Interventions. Ann. of Beh. Med. 38, 18–27 (2009)
29. RunKeeper, http://runkeeper.com
30. Warners Writers Online, https://www.writers-online.co.uk/Writing-Magazine
31. Wattpad, http://www.wattpad.com
32. Webb, T.L., Joseph, J., Yardley, L., Michie, S.: Using the Internet to Promote Health Behavior Change. J. of Medical Internet Research 12 (2010)
33. Workers Education Association, http://www.wea.org.uk
34. Write-Track, http://www.write-track.co.uk

Challenges in Designing New Interfaces
for Musical Expression

Rodrigo Medeiros[1], Filipe Calegario[1], Giordano Cabral[2], and Geber Ramalho[1]

[1] Centro de Informática, Universidade Federal de Pernambuco, Av. Prof. Luis Freire, s/n,
Cidade Universitária. Recife – PE, CEP: 50740-540, Brasil
[2] Departamento de Estatística e Informática, Universidade Federal Rural de Pernambuco,
Rua Dom Manuel de Medeiros, s/n. Dois Irmãos. Recife – PE, CEP: 52171-900, Brasil
prof@rodrigomedeiros.com.br, {fcac,glr}@cin.ufpe.br,
giordanorec@gmail.com

Abstract. The new interfaces are changing the way we interact with computers. In the musical context, those new technologies open a wide range of possibilities in the creation of New Interfaces for Musical Expression (NIME). Despite 10 years of research in NIME, it is hard to find artifacts that have been widely or convincingly adopted by musicians. In this paper, we discuss some NIME design challenges, highlighting particularities related to the digital and musical nature of these artifacts, such as virtuosity, cultural elements, context of use, creation catalysis, success criteria, adoption strategy, etc. With these challenges, we aim to call attention for the intersection of music, computing and design, which can be an interesting area for people working on product design and interaction design.

Keywords: design challenges, digital musical instrument, new interfaces for musical expression, user experience, interaction design.

1 Introduction

The whole way we interact with machines is changing, since gestures, movements and direct graphic manipulation are co-existing with keys, buttons and pointers [1, 2]. In the musical context, these new interface technologies open a wide range of possibilities in the creation of Digital Musical Instruments (DMI) or New Interfaces for Musical Expression (NIME), artifacts that connect inputs (interface controllers) and outputs (sound synthesis modules) according to a mapping strategy [3].

Despite 10 years of research in NIME, reported in conferences (such as New Music for Music Expression, and International Computer Music Conference) and journals (such as Organised Sound, Journal of New Music Research and Computer Music Journal), it is hard to find artifacts that have been widely or convincingly adopted by musicians. In fact, there are very few NIME virtuosi or professional musicians who adopted them as their main musical instrument. Few exceptions of commercial success are the artifacts related to electronic music, DJ interfaces and controllers.

A. Marcus (Ed.): DUXU 2014, Part I, LNCS 8517, pp. 643–652, 2014.
© Springer International Publishing Switzerland 2014

We believe there are some design challenges that may help to explain the state of the art in NIME research and practice, which are not well described, analyzed together or explicitly discussed in the literature. Topics such as usability, efficiency or fun are not obvious when applied to new musical instruments design, indeed.

This paper aims to discuss some challenges related to the design and the development of NIME, which presents a series of particularities due to their digital and musical nature. In fact, some issues are specially hard, such as how to deal with virtuosity, how to include cultural elements surrounding the artifact, how to consider the musician context in his/her experience in using the artifact, how to catalyze the creation of new artifacts, how to define what is a successful design, how to promote adequately the adhesion of adopters, etc.

We hope that, enumerating these interesting challenges, this paper will instigate people working in product design and interaction design, particularly in user-centered design and user experience (UX), to pay more attention this intersection of music, computing and design. We believe that HCI studies can provide important principles, methods and techniques for NIME development. In turn, we will try to show that HCI domain can take advantage from NIME design challenges, beyond the music domain [4].

In order to make its scope clearer, we would like to stress that this paper discusses musical instruments as artifacts to be used by professional musicians in all their potential. We are not interested in discussing the design of musical toys, artifacts created to make the experience of playing music easier for a non-professional public [5]. Even though musical toys may be important in some contexts, such as for musical initiation, promotion and education, they do not present the same design challenges.

The next section presents the definition and some examples of NIME. The following sections present some challenges on how to design NIME, divided into two parts: Section 3, the challenges of being digital, and Section 4, the challenges of being musical.

2   DMI and NIME

A digital musical instrument "consists of a control surface or gestural controller, which drives the musical parameter of a sound synthesizer in real time" [3]. It can be separated in three parts: (a) the input or gestural control; (b) the output or sound synthesis; and (c) the mapping strategies between input and output. In literature, some authors make distinctions between DMI and NIME definitions. However, it is not a consensus. In this paper, this distinction is not relevant for our main discussion and we assume that both definitions are synonymous.

These new musical interfaces can be classified by the resemblance to existing acoustic instruments: augmented musical instruments, instrument-like gestural controllers, instrument-inspired gestural controllers, alternate gestural controllers [3]. It is a diverse universe of artifacts with different natures. The following examples show the range of this variety: the hyperinstruments [6], AKAI EWI [7], Yamaha

WX5, Hands [3], Radio Baton [8], Reactable [9], Laser Harp, illusio [10], Tenorion [11], Novation Launchpad, Monome, Faderfox, and QuNeo [12].

As the physical constraints of acoustic instrument do not exist in NIME, the design of these new interfaces are more flexible concerning the coupling between input gesture and generated sound. Therefore, new ways of producing live music arise and go beyond the traditional concept of musical instrument which focused on controlling how notes are played [12]. NIME extends note control to process control, e.g. with simple gestures, the musician can trigger not only set of notes, but pre-recorded samples, loops, sound effects, etc. Consequently, the performer engages in different activities when playing those new interfaces: create, when interacting with notes and the sound synthesis parameters and control, when triggering processes as samples, loops [12].

3   Challenges of Being Digital

In this section, we enumerate some problems faced when designing digital musical instruments, compared to when designing acoustic instruments [13]. Identifying these problems is important to better understand the challenges discussed in Section 4.

3.1   The Mapping Problem

Contrary to acoustic instruments, which impose physical constraints to their design and fabrication regarding the connection of the input (possible gestures) to the output (sound generation), the design of NIME has more freedom. Due to the separation between gesture input and sound output, the mapping strategies are the essence of digital musical instruments [14]. Different mapping strategies for the same set of inputs and outputs affect how the performer reacts musically and psychologically to the instrument [15]. Those strategies are virtually countless [14]. Paradoxically, this advantage is a problem, since there is no established method or tool to guide the NIME designer to define how interfaces gestures should be adequately mapped into sound variables [16].

3.2   Audience Understanding and Engagement

Strongly related to the mapping problem is how does the audience understand the performance? Since the gestures and the produced sound have not necessarily a direct connection, the audience may not understand what is happening, and consequently, does not feel engaged during the appreciation [5]. If the audience is expecting something related to a musical instrument, they can get frustrated by the lack "observable primary causation" [12]. In the literature, this is called transparency, which can be defined as "the psychophysiological distance, in the player and the audience minds, between the input and output of a device mapping" [17]. In short, the creation of meaningful and perceivable connections between human action and sound is not only an issue for the musicians, but also for the audience [18]. There are some possible solutions for this problem, such as the use of well-designed visual feedback; visual cues as instrument's appearance, visualization of interaction and visualization of sound output; interaction metaphors [5]. However, this problem remains opened.

3.3   Sensor Limitations

All design projects have to deal with technical limitations and musical instruments is not an exception. Specifically, it's needed to take into account sensors and actuators limitations. The limitations comprise three subtypes: real time (latency and jitter), precision (the AD conversion requires the quantization of continuous quantities. Thus, the granularity and the way information is represented may be a problem), and information richness (some important data may be ignored by sensors).

3.4   Embodied Relationship and Haptic Feedback

In acoustic instruments, the excitation of notes and the sound generation are intrinsically linked. With the dissociation of these two components, the musician can explore limitless possibilities. However, he/she loses a strong relation with the concrete body of the instrument, what Payne describes as an embodied relationship [12]. For instance, "A pianist can see and locate a specific key before playing it, can use the resistance of the key-action mechanism to help know how hard to press the key, and can use the feeling of adjacent keys to keep track of hand position" [19]. NIME design must face how to provide haptic feedback to the performer.

4   Challenges of Being Musical

In this section, we enumerate some challenges involved in designing digital artifacts that we be used to create and play music.

4.1   Expressivity and Virtuosity

Probably the most important artistic property of a musical instrument (digital or not) is to enable the player to be expressive, i.e. to "effectively convey meaning or feeling" [20]. Traditionally, music expressiveness is coded by musicians through a subtle control over some sonic attributes of individual notes and musical phrases, such as timing, volume, timbre, accents, and articulation [19]. Artistic expressivity is also required for instruments oriented to process control rather than notes, which is the case of DJs performances using a turn-table, for instance.

As a consequence, an obvious challenge in designing a musical instrument is to enable sophisticated, fine-grained and subtle control of input gestures with their correspondence in sound output [21]. Indeed, it is not enough to build an instrument that plays notes. It should enable to play notes with a particular timbre, intonation, intensity, etc. This requirement make all the problems discussed in the previous section harder [19]. The sensors must deal with a large amount of subtle gestures, the sound synthesis must include the control of various sonic parameters, and the I/O mapping must deal with one-to-many, many-to-one, and many-to-many mappings and combinations of parameters.

These are other challenges in designing NIME as a result of the expressiveness need. In fact, musical expression requires not only an excellent control interface, but also virtuosic mastery of the instrument by the human player. Virtuosity is that "great technical skill" [20] that enables the player to master so well the subtle controls of the instrument that he/she can perform other cognitive activities as the music interpretation [22]. The lack of virtuosity may inhibit music expression, since a virtuoso does not only successfully realize a highly difficult task, but he/she does it expressively [23].

Mastering musical instruments demands years (some authors claim 10 years [24]) of studying and practicing. In other words, professional musicians are ready to spend hours in a daily-basis trying to master an interface that was created more to be expressive than to be easily usable [25]. Some instruments might even "hurt" new users (e.g., fingers of a beginner guitar player, or the lips for a trumpet player), but they still go on.

In terms of designing new instruments, a consequence of this concerns the evaluation of the artifact, which is an essential activity in the development process [26, 27]. If the artifact is supposed to be used by a virtuoso, how to know that an identified execution problem is a design error or a natural barrier that would be overcame by training? How the musician evolution could be taken into account in the evaluation protocol of the artifact? The concept of usability or UX in the context of NIME may be far trickier than we are used to discuss in most of HCI studies.

Another consequence of the "virtuosity factor" concerns user adoption. How to convince and favor people to engage in experimentation a new artifact that will demand huge amount of hours of dedication? Is there any kind of reward strategy that could be useful for motivating adopters? This problem is even harder in designing NIME, because contrary to conventional acoustic instruments, there is no virtuoso demonstrating how far one can go with a given instrument, which establishes somehow a standard.

Moreover, there is almost no musical repertoire created to draw the attention of potential adopters or to contribute to the technical advances of the instrument [25]. Learning a conventional instrument is helped by a body of technical knowledge, created over dozens of years (or centuries) and transmitted by teachers, books, concerning how to efficiently practice the instrument. How to be sure that the adopters are practicing is the most effective and efficient way, given that the instrument is entirely new? How to create a new instrument, its musical repertoire and its studying method in the same time stamp?

4.2   Context of Use and Stakeholders

Another important challenge is that the designer must be aware of the context in which the instrument will be played, since it may influence the musician satisfaction, and, consequently, the instrument adoption and refinement [12, 28].

There are different contexts of use. For instance, a performer can play solo or in a group. Also, he/she can improvise, play a predefined score or accompany others. There are equally different mindsets depending on the activity the musician is doing: studying, rehearsing, or facing an audience. Each context may demand different properties from the instrument. For example, playing with others may demand a minimum level of volume for the instrument to be listened; the requirement of playing an established repertoire may lead to a tonal instrument; etc.

The design process is harder when one needs to deal with multiple contexts that may substantially influence the musician experience of use. How to conceive an instrument which simultaneously serves to different purposes such as make solos, to accompany, to be played collaboratively, to compose, to perform before an audience? How to identify the needs of each context and how to take into account the different contexts characteristics in the design process?

Another important challenge related to context of use is the stakeholders' point of view. According to Payne, "any implementation of a new musical interface must therefore consider the ecology of this environment" [12]. There are different perspectives and stakeholders, such as the audience, the performer, the composer, the designer and the manufacturer [18, 28], involved in NIME design and use.

As discussed in the section 3.2, meaningful connections between musician actions and the generate sound should be provided to the audience. The emotional exchange and communication between the performer and the audience is an important factor in the performer satisfaction. Thus, if the audience did not like the performance because NIME was not understandable or exciting, this will influence the instrument adoption by the musician. How to incorporate coherently in the design process the stakeholders' perspectives? In particular, given that user experience is normally studied between the user and the artifact, how to go from the user-artifact binomial to an user-artifact-audience tripod?

4.3   Evolution and Success Criteria

One of the components of a design process is to be able to evaluate if the designed artifact is successful or not [29, 30]. This raises two questions: What defines success of NIME? How to incorporate success measures in the NIME design process?

The discussion of criteria success for NIME is not mature enough. This is probably due to the fact that lots of NIME are created to be used by the very creator [31]. Contrary to HCI community, where it is clear that artifacts or experiences must be designed to be used by someone else [2, 26, 29], the observation of some basic design principles is not always done by NIME practitioners or researchers.

We can group the success criteria discussed in the literature into two categories. The first one concerns the intrinsic measurement of quality, i.e. how the artifact fulfilled some requirements related to ergonomics, sound quality, visual feedback, fine-grained gesture control, embodied relationship, ease of use, efficiency, learning curve, etc. [31]. However, which are the most important criteria? How does the context or stakeholder perspective influence the criteria choice? Is it enough to fulfill these requirements to guarantee NIME adoption?

The second category includes various criteria (adhesion, impact, lifetime, commercial success, etc.), all of them requiring long time to be measured. This represents already a challenge, since we need the criteria during the development phase. However, even on the long-term, these criteria may be not objective enough.

One can say that an instrument has a high adhesion when it is adopted by a wide audience, when it is popular or it had a commercial success (number of units sold, sales volume or growth). The problem with this notion is that some are vocationally 'generic' and others highly specialized [32]. A specialized instrument may do not sell a lot, but be a success to a particular musician community.

The impact of an instrument is understood as how it has helped to create new music genres, new playing styles outstanding artworks [23]. The problem is that this takes a lot of time, cannot be planned in advance and depends on lots of variables, including cultural ones.

Persistence or lifetime is indicated as the most trustable measure of musical instruments success, Paine [33], for instance, says that "if we agree that acoustic instruments are 'successful' interfaces for music making, an assumption supported by the period of time they have persisted and the ubiquitous nature of traditional interfaces (...)".

In fact, the evolution of acoustic instruments is based on trial-and-error process that can take centuries [34]. Therefore, the results about the design process can only be evaluated after very long periods of time. For a demanding and growing area, a relevant challenge is how this process can be accelerated. How can we decrease a 100-years process into a, for example, 2-years one? Can an iterative process with short iterations and with an intense relation with artists and early adopters (user-centered design [26]) be a productive approach to achieve shorter instrument design processes?

4.4   Beyond the Artifact

Another basic challenge is that music is enveloped in a culture, sometimes bringing semantics or symbolism. For example, it is common to find musical instruments deeply related to their original region, nation, or people, as well as to particular attitudes. In other words, the musical instrument is more than just the artifact. It invokes the cultural elements that surround it. Thus, it is important to understand not only the conjuncture in which the instrument is inserted, but the strategies of adhesion.

For example, the adhesion of an instrument may be deeply related to a musical repertoire produced with it. "Some started playing after having been inspired by some music and, in particular, the sound of the instrument" [35]. There is a virtuous cycle related to the repertoire, the demonstrations and the instrument. Demonstrations need a repertoire, a set of compositions that can be played with the instrument. These compositions can even transmute into a new style. With demonstrations, potential musicians can understand what can be done with the instrument and engage in learning it.

For instance, let's take a look at the electric guitar and the Rock n'Roll. It's easy to imagine what can be done with an electric guitar by listening to some rock songs and watching some performances of rock musicians. This can attract new players and those new players, as they play the instrument, can go further in generating new repertoire and playing techniques.

The actual problem is that these strategies are frequently off the hands of the designer. What can a designer do if the success of a NIME highly depends on factors related to more than just the artifact? It won't be better if designers practice in planning marketing strategies? Even if this is often a responsibility of other professional, there are marketing strategies specific for musical instruments and designers could take advantage of it. In summary, it is important to know all the possible adhesion strategies, since it may provide shortcuts to a more successful instrument.

Shouldn't designers be closer to the final artists? For example, inviting composers to test the instrument may be good to generate a repertoire for it. Working together with an artist in a piece may also be very important, because "without a piece, it's difficult to gain acceptance" [5].

5   Conclusions

In this paper, we enumerate a series of design challenges for NIME that have not yet been systematically organized or deeply addressed in the literature. With the growth of the demand and the possibilities of building new interfaces for music expression, we believe that having those challenges more clearly stated, we can go a step towards better artifacts and more engaging user experience.

We believe that HCI expertise can improve NIME development. In turn, HCI can also take advantage from NIME area. The challenges presented here are a fertile research field and can provide fruitful insights for product and interaction design outside the musical domain: artifacts that requires a long time to acquire skill, that deals with different contexts of use, whose stakeholders play an important role, and whose use is deeply influenced surrounding culture, community, marketing, repertoire, etc.

As future work, we consider to deepen the relation between HCI and NIME by systematically discussing the crossover between HCI tools, techniques and processes with the NIME design challenges presented in this paper.

Acknowledgements. This research is partially funded by CAPES and CNPq.

References

1. Saffer, D.: Designing Gestural Interfaces. O'Reilly Media, Inc. (2008)
2. Moggridge, B., Smith, G.C.: Designing interactions. The MIT Press (2007)
3. Miranda, E.R., Wanderley, M.M.: New Digital Musical Instruments: Control and Interaction Beyond the Keyboard. A-R Editions, Middleton (2006)

4. Wallis, I., Ingalls, T., Campana, E., Vuong, C.: Amateur Musicians, Long-Term Engagement, and HCI. In: Holland, S., Wilkie, K., Mulholland, P., Seago, A. (eds.) Music and Human-Computer Interaction, pp. 49–56. Springer (2013)
5. Lyons, M., Fels, S.: Creating new interfaces for musical expression. In: SIGGRAPH Asia 2013 Courses on - SA 2013, pp. 1–164. ACM Press, New York (2013)
6. Machover, T.: Hyperinstruments: A composer's approach to the evolution of intelligent musical instruments. Organ. Sound., 67–76 (1991)
7. Vashlishan, M.J.: The Akai Electric Wind Instrument (EWI4000s): A Technical and Expressive Method (2011)
8. Mathews, M.: Radio Baton (2005), http://www.csounds.com/mathews/
9. Jordà, S., Geiger, G., Alonso, M., Kaltenbrunner, M.: The reacTable: exploring the synergy between live music performance and tabletop tangible interfaces. In: Proceedings of the 1st International Conference on Tangible and Embedded Interaction (2007)
10. Barbosa, J., Calegario, F., Teichrieb, V.: Illusio: A Drawing-Based Digital Music Instrument. In: Proceedings of the International Conference on New Interfaces for Musical Expression (2013)
11. Nishibori, Y., Iwai, T.: Tenori-on. In: Proceedings of the International Conference on New Interfaces for Musical Expression, pp. 172–175. IRCAM—Centre Pompidou (2006)
12. Paine, G.: New Musical Instrument Design Considerations. IEEE MultiMedia, 76–84 (2013)
13. Magnusson, T., Mendieta, E.: The acoustic, the digital and the body: A survey on musical instruments. In: Proc. Int. Conf. New Interfaces Music. Expr., pp. 94–99 (2007)
14. Rovan, J.B., Wanderley, M.M., Dubnov, S., Depalle, P.: Instrumental gestural mapping strategies as expressivity determinants in computer music performance. In: Proceedings of Kansei-The Technology of Emotion Workshop, pp. 3–4. Citeseer (1997)
15. Hunt, A., Wanderley, M.M., Paradis, M.: The Importance of Parameter Mapping in Electronic Instrument Design. J. New Music Res. 32, 429–440 (2003)
16. Calegario, F., Barbosa, J., Ramalho, G., Cabral, G., Finch, G.: Sketchument: Empowering users to build DMIs through prototyping. Organised Sound 18, 314–327 (2013)
17. Murray-Browne, T., Mainstone, D., Bryan-Kinns, N., Plumbley, M.D.: The medium is the message: Composing instruments and performing mappings. In: Proceedings of the International Conference on New Interfaces for Musical Expression, pp. 56–59 (2011)
18. O'Modhrain, S.: A framework for the evaluation of digital musical instruments. Comput. Music J. 35, 28–42 (2011)
19. Dobrian, C., Koppelman, D.: The E in NIME: Musical Expression with New Computer Interfaces. In: Proceedings of the International Conference on New Interfaces for Musical Expression, pp. 277–282 (2006)
20. Merriam-Webster: Merriam-Webster's collegiate dictionary. Merriam-Webster (2004)
21. Jordà, S.: Digital Instruments and Players: Part II – Diversity, Freedom and Control. In: Proceedings of the 2004 International Computer Music Conference (2004)
22. Hunt, A., Wanderley, M.M., Kirk, R.: Towards a Model for Instrumental Mapping in Expert Musical Interaction. In: Proceedings of the 2000 International Computer Music Conference, pp. 209–212 (2000)
23. Gurevich, M., Stapleton, P., Bennett, P.: Designing for style in new musical interactions. In: Proceedings of the International Conference on New Interfaces for Musical Expression, pp. 213–217 (2009)
24. Wanderley, M.M., Orio, N.: Evaluation of Input Devices for Musical Expression: Borrowing Tools from HCI. Comput. Music J. 26, 62–76 (2002)

25. Oore, S.: Learning advanced skills on new instruments. In: Proceedings of the International Conference on New Interfaces for Musical Expression, pp. 60–64
26. Preece, J., Rogers, Y., Sharp, H.: Interaction Design: Beyond Human-Computer Interaction. Wiley (2002)
27. Laurel, B.: Design research: Methods and perspectives. The MIT Press (2003)
28. Kvifte, T., Jensenius, A.: Towards a coherent terminology and model of instrument description and design. In: Proceedings of the International Conference on New Interfaces for Musical Expression, pp. 220–225 (2006)
29. Buxton, B.: Sketching User Experiences: Getting the Design Right and the Right Design. Morgan Kaufmann (2010)
30. Lowgren, J., Stolterman, E.: Thoughtful interaction design: A design perspective on information technology. The MIT Press (2004)
31. Jordà, S.: Digital Lutherie (2005),
    `http://dialnet.unirioja.es/servlet/tesis?codigo=19509`
32. Jordà, S.: Digital instruments and players: part I—efficiency and apprenticeship. In: Proc. Int. Conf. New Interfaces Music Expr., pp. 59–63 (2004)
33. Paine, G.: Towards Unified Design Guidelines for New Interfaces for Musical Expression. Organised Sound 14, 142 (2009)
34. Sachs, C.: The History of Musical Instruments. W. W. Norton & Company, Inc. (1940)
35. Green, L.: How Popular Musicians Learn: A Way Ahead for Music Education. Ashgate Publishing (2002)

Collaboration Space for Creative Knowledge Work – Analysis of Industrial Pilots

Mika P. Nieminen, Mikael Runonen, Mari Tyllinen, and Marko Nieminen

Aalto University School of Science
Department of Computer Science and Engineering
P.O. Box 15400, FI-00076 Aalto, Finland
{firstname.lastname}@aalto.fi

Abstract. In this paper we describe our experiences piloting a collaboration space DiWa that supports creative group-based knowledge work. The developed prototypes of the system were piloted at three industry and public sector partners in Finland conducting product development and city zoning and at one research institute involved in service design in Beijing, China. The system design was based on extensive literature review, observations and interviews at the partners. The results presented in this paper are derived from four one month long pilots using the DiWa prototype that were studied using observations, interviews and questionnaires. Main results are the observed differences in the use of collaborative spaces and work practices between the Finnish users and their Chinese counterparts. The paper concludes with eight recommendations for the design of collaboration spaces.

Keywords: Collocated collaboration, interactive spaces, supporting knowledge work, cultural differences.

1 Introduction

This paper describes our experiences and results from a set of month-long industrial pilots using the developed DiWa collaboration space. DiWa space incorporates parallel use of large displays to enable fluent information sharing during collocated collaborative tasks. Earlier systems with similar technology of features, lately also known as blended spaces [1], include dedicated ubiquitous group work facilities with large visual displays [2], combining digital and analog tools to support meetings [3] and use of large multi-display arrays and multi-user interactions [4].

In the DiWa space separate computers are connected to each other using a shared document repository, implemented using a network attached server, and a specially developed communication protocol based on pragmatic multicast [5]. Some of the computers are desktops with large touchscreen displays located permanently in the DiWa space (shown in figure 1) and some are laptops carried into the facility by users. They all can be connected to each other to form a single collaboration system by installing a small control application (depicted in figure 2) that resides on the top of each screen providing necessary means to control and share files to other desktops.

A. Marcus (Ed.): DUXU 2014, Part I, LNCS 8517, pp. 653–662, 2014.
© Springer International Publishing Switzerland 2014

Fig. 1. DiWa collaboration space used for a product review

The DiWa space also includes advanced memory support functionalities (described in detail in [6] and [7]) that allow the collaborators to mark important events. Event marking automatically saves the contents of the attached displays and a voice recording surrounding the event. A visualized timeline of all project activities, including marked events, accessed files and the times of collaboration sessions enables users to easily return to them.

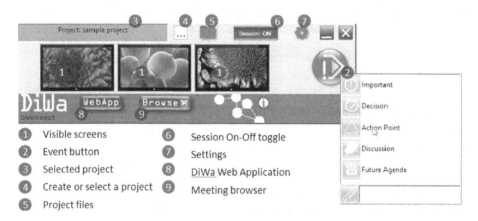

Fig. 2. The user interface of the DiWa Control Service with open event menu

1.1   User-Centered Design Process for a Group Work Space

The applied User-Centered Design (UCD) process consisted of a systematic literature review, observations at actual context of use, interviews with relevant stakeholders, iterative development of a collaboration space prototype and piloting it at the premises of our industry and public sector partners.

Literature review. A systematic literature review of 49 search terms to five sources delivered 13.6 million hits. 907 articles were individually browsed of which 168 summaries were written. Based on the summaries the collected articles were grouped into eight categories: Group Work, Work Practices, Space Design, System Design, Interaction, Requirements, System Possibilities and Video [8].

Requirements Elicitation. During a field study we observed 12 collaborative situations and interviewed 22 participants. In combination with the literature review this produced 82 individual requirements for an interactive collaborative space. Main findings include collaboration, support of conventional work practices, parallel and uninterrupted use and physical properties of a collaboration space. [8]

Action Research and Prototypes. The development of the DiWa prototype was scheduled to three six months periods. In the beginning the prototype development was solely guided by the original system requirements, even though our partners were invited to review the first concept demonstrators in fully facilitated group sessions. In the second phase the initial prototype version was tested internally. The usage was mainly by university students and researcher on an invitation only basis. In the final phase included the full scale pilots at our partners described in the next section.

The development was based on participatory action research approach [9] were iterative prototyping always introduces a new intervention that tries seamlessly to build on top of the previous encounters. This was particularly evident during the consecutive pilots, where every pilot case received an updated version of the prototype with increased maturity, as also shown by the SUS study in the results section.

2   Industrial Pilots

In the pilots the collaboration space was taken to the field and used for real work activities at the participating companies and organizations. A similar collaboration system was also built at a research institute in China to learn about potential cultural differences in the use, utility and acceptance of our solution. The pilot locations in chronological order were:

1. Kemppi, a manufacturer of arc welding equipment. Pilot site was situated in Lahti, Finland.
2. Konecranes, a manufacturer of industrial lifting equipment. Pilot site was situated in Hyvinkää, Finland.
3. City of Vantaa: City planning and zoning. Pilot site was situated in Vantaa, Finland.
4. Beijing Research Center of Urban Systems Engineering. Research institute specializing in elderly care service design. Pilot site was situated in Beijing, China.

All pilots shared a common blueprint. For each site, the system was assembled in an appointed space. Once the system was up and running, an introductory session was given to all future users of the DiWa Space. This session was meant to both inform the users about the pilot procedure and to motivate them to use the system by communicating its potential benefits. After the introduction, the system was available for use in the partner organization for 4-6 weeks.

One condition was set for all new users of the DiWa Space. Before starting to use the facility, the users were asked to fill out a pre-use questionnaire. This questionnaire included both closed-ended and open-ended questions regarding their experiences in group work and dedicated group work spaces, expectations towards using DiWa and practices of taking and making use of notes.

For the first two pilot sites a researcher observed one team on each of their visits to the DiWa space, while other teams used the facility by themselves after the initial visit. The researcher took the role of a passive observer but switched to active participation when the users required technical assistance or had questions on how to use the system or how to proceed.

Post-use questionnaires and user interviews were conducted at the end of each pilot. A post-use questionnaire was used to validate and compare findings from the pre-use questionnaires and gather additional data about the usage. Enclosed in the questionnaire was also positive/negative System Usability Scale (SUS) [9]. The interviews were semi-structured and considered themes such as experiences of working in the DiWa space in general, usability issues and differences between the DiWa space and other group work facilities that the users were familiar with. The interviews were carried out with great care not to introduce any concepts that were not expressed by the interviewees first. Afterwards the interviews were transcribed as whole. The order between post-use questionnaires and interviews was chosen on the basis of not causing a bias to questionnaire answers by interviewing first.

The same procedure was repeated in the Chinese pilot. However, because none of the researchers were fluent in Mandarin Chinese, some compromises had to be made. Since the pre-use questionnaire was rather straightforward and simple, it could be translated to Chinese by our local partner. The semi-structured interview question framework and post-use questionnaire were more complex and more sensitive to exact tone and necessitated be first written in English by the researchers and then translated to Chinese by a professional translation agency. The interviews were recorded and then transcribed. This operation was reversed for the results, i.e. the interview transcripts and questionnaire results were translated to English also using a translation agency. In order to obtain comparable data, two persons from the Chinese partner were coached to carry out the interviews in Chinese in a similar manner to those conducted in Finland.

3   Analysis

All 17 interview transcripts and open-ended answers from questionnaires were coded according to a predefined scheme by two researchers using ATLAS.ti. The following a priori codes were used:

- **Memory Support.** All statements discussing the memory support functionality of the interactive space or related aspects.

- **Reasons for Returning.** Statements and reasoning that discussed incidents where users returned to their notes or other materials from a previous meeting.
- **Expectations.** Statements answering questions such as "What users expect the system to be?", "What kind of functionalities it will contain?" and "What kind of changes there will be in their everyday work?". Also expectations towards change in attitudes were included.
- **Realization.** As a reflection of expectations, Realization served as a vehicle for how users experienced the usage of the system in contrast to their expectations. This code did not contain only system-specific observations but also changes in facilities.
- **Opinions and Attitudes towards Group Work.** Opinions and attitudes set the level of how interested users are about group work in general. These codes acted as a filter through which other codes were viewed.
- **Current Situation.** An assessment of work conditions in general. These conditions included current facilities, current practices and current tools.
- **Taking Notes.** Whenever users specified that they took notes of some kind or discussed anything related to such activity.
- **Work Practices.** A collection of newly gained means and practices after using the system and getting familiar with it.
- **Problems.** These could include difficulties with facilities, equipment failures, workflow problems, or alike.
- **System Evaluation.** Similar to Realization with a small difference. Whereas Realization captures experiences vis-à-vis expectations, System evaluation is for statements that contain assessments about system's usability and functionality.
- **General Observations.** A repository of statements that did not fit into any other codes but still carried interesting information.

Most of the codes contained several sub-codes and supplementary grounded sub-codes were added when necessary. Furthermore, passages were coded as negative, neutral or positive according to the tone in which the interviewee presented her notions. This categorizing was only done when the researcher could deduce the tone from the context with certainty.

Once coding was finished, all the codes were revisited by two researchers. The analysis was continued using hybrid card sorting [10], where some of the categories were decided in advance. The first four categories were imported from the original user requirements: user-centric approach, work practices, space design and adaptability. During the sorting new categories emerged: change management, considering the collaboration space as a tool, integration to existing systems and the feasibility of the designed solution. In order to make the categories raised by the qualitative analysis more beneficial, approachable and practical for our project partners, it was considered appropriate to formulate the results as recommendations.

4   Results

In the following subsections we outline the results from our studies and draw comparisons between the Finnish pilots and their Chinese counterpart.

4.1   SUS Study

A SUS study was carried out as part of the post-use questionnaires. The results are shown in table 1. The SUS score for the first Finnish pilot was 54.7 which according to Bangor et al. [11] falls barely into the category of "marginal" or "ok" in adjective ratings. For a system that would be used daily as a tool for a group of designers, such value would be less than desirable. However, we argue that for a prototype system with numerous known technical flaws and missing features, this is acceptable.

As Finnish pilots progressed, the system was developed further and many of the programming errors were fixed. This is reflected with an ascending score between pilots (54.7 | 65.5 | 73.8). For the third pilot the score over 70 can be considered as "acceptable" [11]. However, as the sample size is small whereas the standard deviation is very large, this value should be treated with some reservation.

Even though the system version used in the Chinese pilot was developed the furthest, the SUS score given to it was the lowest. This lower score was possibly caused by misplaced expectations towards the system and some critical errors in the system. Due to the language barrier, the researchers were not able to sufficiently communicate that some functionalities were deliberately left outside the piloted system. The most sought after features not found in the DiWa space were cloning the desktop of a personal laptop to the shared screens and ability to participate to a collaboration session from a remote location. These expectations persisted throughout the pilot. One catastrophic programmatic error in the DiWa system was that documents with Chinese character encoding were not supported. This meant that the Chinese users could not use their files "as is", but they had to rename them when used in the DiWa space.

Table 1. SUS scores for all pilots

Pilot site	N	Score	STDEV	MEDIAN
Finland #1	9	54.7	8.0	
Finland #2	5	65.5	6.0	
Finland #3	2	73.8	33.6	
Finland all	16	60.5	13.1	57.5
China	8	51.6	14.5	
Total	24	57.5	13.1	58.8

4.2   Taking Personal Notes

Reasons for personal note taking and the amount of notes taken were rather similar both in Finland and in China. However, there are clear differences in the note-taking tools and in the ways of taking notes. Finnish users are generally more traditional, sticking to pen and paper or computers when writing or drawing their notes, while in China also smart phones and digital camera are used often. The use of audio recordings was also significantly more common in China.

Based on the answers, it can be said that in China DiWa had less impact on the practices of taking personal notes than in Finland. In Finland taking personal notes was diminished during the pilots, whereas in China the use of pen and paper increased and the use of smart phones decreased.

The DiWa functionality for marking important events was not commonly used during the pilots. This was observed the same both in Finland and China. The participants in Finland shared several views on the reasons for not using the functionality. The voice recording functionality was seen producing too much information, and there were concerns that event marking would have a negatively effect on the discussions and decision-making. On several occasions the users could see the need for such functionality afterwards, but the novelty of this new practice made it difficult to remember to use it. In China, a clear difference was seen in the attitudes towards recording meetings. Participants hoped to receive full recordings of the meetings and several requests for video recordings were stated.

There were some differences between China and Finland in the ways of returning to previous meetings. Photographs, audio and video recordings were used more in China compared to Finland where these tactics were not generally used. However, the things that participants identified as important about the meetings held in the DiWa space were similar: common memorandums and other collaborative documents were regarded the most important. Chinese respondents wanted to have a full record of everything that happened in a meeting, while the Finnish respondents frowned upon this idea.

4.3   Group Work Practices

The pre-use questionnaire included questions about how beneficial group work is seen and if respondents preferred "working alone" to "working in groups" of different sizes and modes. Somewhat surprisingly, there was no significant difference in answers between Finnish and Chinese respondents relating to group work practices. Finnish and Chinese users alike deemed both informal and formal group work beneficial. However, it is noteworthy that no one regarded working in groups larger than 6 persons the most effective.

When the users were asked to compare the DiWa space to other group work spaces or meeting rooms, there was again no real difference between the Finnish and Chinese responses. According to the aggregate results out of 24 responses on a 5-point scale with a neutral value in the middle, 18 rated the DiWa Space to be more suitable for their activities than other options. 17 regarded it as more pleasant and 14 appreciated the décor more when compared to previously used group work facilities. Ease of use was considered worse by 13, which can be contributed to the technical difficulties encountered with the prototype system. 10 users valued the understandability of functionalities lesser.

5   Recommendations for Designing Collaboration Spaces

Combining the potential benefits of new technology with the best work practices requires adopting multiple perspectives to design and can be quite challenging. Based on our study, we describe here eight recommendations for designing collaboration spaces. These recommendations are specifically targeted for the organizational decision-makers responsible for procurement or development of collaboration systems or facilities for collaboration.

Design for the Users. Designing collaboration spaces requires deep understanding of the workers' existing best practices. These practices can be slightly different for all employees, even within the same unit or department. The collaboration space should not be an arbitrarily placed generic meeting room based on an organizational chart but instead it must be tailored to fit the users, their needs and practices. Its design must be based on the needs of the employees and not separately planned and procured by corporate IT, facilities management or outlined based on the product offerings of technology vendors.

Embrace the Change. New tools, systems and work facilities inevitably change work practices. This change is often slower than expected and sometimes the promoted change never takes place. Careful planning, truthful marketing and well-timed information sharing enables successful change management. Communication of the proposed changes to the existing, even preferred, practices is most efficiently carried out by a well-known and trusted colleague that can act as a product champion.

Allow Well-Proven Work Practices. One should never deny the traditional and well-proven work practices, even when actively developing and adopting new ones. Especially tasks that rely on fine motor skills (sketching or drawing by hand) or include learning by doing (developing product ideas using post-it notes) are more natural and effective than using available digital solutions.

Invest in the Space. Where the collaboration space is situated affects its usage dramatically. If the space is readily available it will be used, but any additional steps, like cumbersome reservation systems, lessen the usage. The overall pleasantness of the space is increased by attractive décor, good ergonomics and well-functioning ventilation. These aspects become more important if the working sessions tend to last longer. The size of the space needs to comply with its intended use. All our observed cases suggest that bigger is better.

Preserve Adaptability. The collaboration space must be able to transform to meet the needs of different kinds of practices and group sizes. More flexibility is gained with adjustable furniture and by providing variety of both analog and digital tools to cater the preferred working habits of differing users.

Mind the Tools. A collaboration space and its supporting ICT systems should be seen as tools for a specific task. It is essential that the space does not obstruct the execution of work tasks it is supposed to support. Interruptions in the usage, software bugs and encountered usability problems have a negative impact on work performance and satisfaction. They can irrevocably damage the users' trust towards the system and destroy their continuing motivation to use it.

Anticipate Integration to Other Systems. Any new collaboration system must integrate seamlessly to the organization's existing ICT infrastructure. The parties responsible for IT policies, privacy and data security should be engaged already in the planning phases to the development of a new collaboration space. Their role will become even more important during the adoption of the new system and they are eventually responsible for providing necessary training and support.

Consider the Feasibility. Simply adding a few large displays does not deliver answers on how to use them effectively and how to share information fluently. However, collaboration systems and facilities supporting multiple displays and multiple simultaneous users can easily become exceedingly complex. The currently available operating systems do not readily support multiple concurrent users, so it is necessary to make compromises. The complexity of the desired collaboration facility directly translates to a need for more tailoring and easily leads to higher equipment and development cost.

Acknowledgements. This research has been made possible by the funding from Tekes – the Finnish Funding Agency for Technology and Innovation, and the participated companies Kemppi, Konecranes, Suomen Yliopistokiinteistöt and the City of Vantaa. In addition we would like to thank our friends and partners at the Beijing Research Center of Urban Systems Engineering.

References

1. Benyon, D., Mival, O.: Blended Spaces for Collaborative Creativity. In: Designing Collaborative Interactive Spaces: An AVI 2012 Workshop, Anacapri, Italy (2012)
2. Borchers, J., Ringel, M., Tyler, J., Fox, A.: Stanford interactive workspaces: a framework for physical and graphical user interface prototyping. Wirel. Commun. IEEE 9, 64–69 (2002)
3. Haller, M., Leitner, J., Seifried, T., Wallace, J.R., Scott, S.D., Richter, C., Brandl, P., Gokcezade, A., Hunter, S.: The NiCE Discussion Room: Integrating Paper and Digital Media to Support Co-Located Group Meetings. In: Proceedings of the 28th International Conference on Human Factors in Computing Systems, pp. 609–618. ACM, Atlanta (2010)
4. Jagodic, R., Renambot, L., Johnson, A., Leigh, J., Deshpande, S.: Enabling multi-user interaction in large high-resolution distributed environments. Future Gener. Comput. Syst. 27, 914–923 (2011)
5. Gemmell, J., Montgomery, T., Speakman, T., Crowcroft, J.: The PGM reliable multicast protocol. IEEE Netw. 17, 16–22 (2003)
6. Tyllinen, M., Nieminen, M.: Supporting Group and Personal Memory in an Interactive Space for Collaborative Work. In: Yamamoto, S. (ed.) HIMI/HCII 2013, Part III. LNCS, vol. 8018, pp. 381–390. Springer, Heidelberg (2013)

7. Tyllinen, M., Nieminen, M.P.: Memory Support Functionality in a Collaborative Space - Experiences from the Industry. Presented at the 11th International Conference on the Design of Cooperative Systems, Nice, France (May 27, 2014)

8. Nieminen, M.P., Tyllinen, M., Runonen, M.: Digital War Room for Design - Requirements for Collocated Group Work Spaces. In: Yamamoto, S. (ed.) HIMI/HCII 2013, Part III. LNCS, vol. 8018, pp. 352–361. Springer, Heidelberg (2013)

9. Brooke, J.: SUS-A quick and dirty usability scale. Usability Eval. Ind. 189, 194 (1996)

10. Hudson, W.: Card Sorting. In: Soegaard, M., Dam, R.F. (eds.) Encyclopedia of Human-Computer Interaction. The Interaction Design Foundation, Aarhus, Denmark (2012)

11. Bangor, A., Kortum, P.T., Miller, J.T.: An empirical evaluation of the system usability scale. Intl J. Human–Computer Interact 24, 574–594 (2008)

Ornamental Images and Their Digital Occurrences

Michael Renner

Visual Communication Institute, The Basel School of Design, HGK FHNW,
University of Applied Sciences and Arts Northwestern Switzerland,
Academy of Art and Design
michael.renner@fhnw.ch

Abstract. In the first part of this paper, the historical debate about ornamental images is summarized and interpreted. This leads to the understanding that ornamental images can be seen as a recurring phenomenon, welcomed or abolished, but always present in different occurrences throughout cultural history. In the second part, three different periods of digital technology are distinguished and ornamental images of those eras are analyzed. Based on these studies a conclusion is inferred isolating specific aspects, positioning the chosen digital examples as a continuation of a historic sequence of ornamental images.

Keywords: Digital Aesthetic, Iconic Research, Ornament, Complexity, Generative Design, Visual Communication, Practice Led Iconic Research.

1 The Historical Discourse on Ornamental Images

Ornamental objects of craft and architecture are sources of our early cultural history. They date back long before there is proof of a written discourse concerning their role and meaning. If we look at ceramic artifacts from the Pottery Neolithic (6000 – 1500 BC), the period when the ceramic technology was discovered in Mesopotamia, Asia and Europe by early societies after farming and cultivating crops had begun, we find many examples of pottery showing ornamental décor. We can only guess why the ornaments at the time have been added to the body of the pots and why the purely functional purpose of a vessel was considered to be not enough. Besides the material affirmation of the ornament, an early critical reflection upon the meaning of ornaments can be found in Aristotle's rhetoric [1]:

"Your language will be appropriate if it expresses emotion and character, and if it corresponds to its subject. 'Correspondence to subject' means that we must neither speak casually about weighty matters, nor solemnly about trivial ones; nor must we add ornamental epithets to commonplace nouns, or the effect will be comic, as in the works of Cleophon, who can use phrases as absurd as 'O queenly fig-tree'."

The ornamental is described here as an inappropriate form of speech which does not correspond to the subject and is an exalted addition to the essence of narration. This leads to an ironic and absurd expression. In the writings on poetics, Aristotle grants the ornamental a certain position among other elements of language [2]. He defines good

A. Marcus (Ed.): DUXU 2014, Part I, LNCS 8517, pp. 663–674, 2014.

style in poetry as being clear without being mediocre. According to Aristotle, it is necessary to use unusual words to raise above the pure functionality of language.

"A certain infusion, therefore, of these elements is necessary to style; for the strange (or rare) word, the metaphorical, the ornamental, and the other kinds above mentioned, will raise it above the commonplace and mean, while the use of proper words will make it perspicuous."

Without giving a definition, the description of good style asserts a clear status to the ornament by contributing to overcome the mean. In contradiction to the above quoted part of the rhetoric, the ornament does not have to be an unnecessary addition. It becomes an element with an ambiguous status denoted with positive characteristics contributing to good style, or with a negative idea as an unnecessary addition to the essential element of language.

If we leave the early rhetoric and poetic discourse behind and turn to the philosophical debate of aesthetics, Kant's Critique of Judgement (1790) [3] is considered one of the most influential statements about the inquiry into the beautiful. He defines the aesthetic experience as a feeling of disinterested pleasure (§26). He explains that all objects of nature can not be measured mathematically but only aesthetically and therefore we can not formulate a definite concept of what is beautiful in nature. A beautiful object has to be experienced and the senses make the evaluation. Furthermore, the aesthetic measurement is relative and is always an evaluation between objects while the mathematical measurement is absolute. Regarding ornaments we can find in Kant's Critique of Judgment a similar ambiguity as described above. He elaborates on the status of ornaments as follows (§14):

"Even what we call ornaments [parerga], i.e. those things which do not belong to the complete representation of the object internally as elements but only externally as complements, and which augment the satisfaction of taste, do so only by their form; as for example [the frames of pictures, or] the draperies of statues or the colonnades of palaces. But if the ornament does not itself consist in beautiful form, and if it is used as a golden frame is used, merely to recommend the painting by its charm, it is then called finery and injures genuine beauty."

With this description we get closer to a definition of the ornament. It is not something necessary for the representation of an object. It does not make an object more or less recognizable in the sense of an abstracted description and it is not part of a memorized schematic generalization in order to recognize something. But the ornament contributes purely by the harmonic relationship of its form, without a mimetic function, to the satisfaction of taste as an individual experience related to a common understanding of the beautiful. In the description, a paradoxical evaluation becomes apparent again. If the ornaments are isolated from the essence of the content they have a negative effect and become empty forms inhibiting the aesthetic experience.

Considering this two-folded idea of the ornament, the elaboration on painting is even more surprising. In paragraph 51 of the Critique of Judgement Kant discusses the division of the beautiful into subsections. The division can be made into artificial aesthetic ideas and natural aesthetic ideas. He considers the division into two categories, the art of expression of thought and the art of intuition, but he refused this possibility as too abstract. He preferred to divide the beautiful into three areas; the art of speech (rhetoric and poetry), the art of form and the art of playful sensations (color and music). The formative art consists of the plastic art and painting. Painting is defined as an aesthetic experience resulting from a mimetic function or the arrangements of natural or artificial objects in a repetitive manner such as in landscape gardening. Painting proper is creating an illusion in the beholder through its mimetic function stimulating imagination, whereas the arrangement of decorative elements are fostering imagination purely by the relationship of their forms. But the ornamental painting and painting proper follow the same goal to foster imagination as a free process of thought in the beholder. According to Kant, the judgment of taste depends in all the arts on the effect of form in regard to imagination. In this definition, the ornament is assigned an independent role and leaves behind its irrelevance as an addition to an essential experience.

Other aspects of the ornamental were developed by Karl Philipp Moritz (1756 – 1793), just shortly after the Critique of Judgment had been published. Moritz was appointed in 1789 as a professor for antiquity at the Royal Academy of Fine Arts in Berlin, where he lectured students who studied fine and applied arts. In his publication "Pre-Terminology for a Theory of Ornament" [4], Moritz does not complete a reformulation of the ornament. Even though we have to consider his publication as a preliminary stage for a fully developed theory prevented by his death in 1793, we find a range of terms presenting the ornament under a new point of view. Already in the introduction, the analogy of perceiving nature such as leaves of a tree and looking at decorations (Zierrath) is described as equal in evoking mental processes (p. 4). Furthermore, to decorate is described as a uniquely human drive as important as the drive to do science or art (p. 5). In the discussion of the bodily occurrences of humans and animals, the terminology *Uniformity* and *Variety* provide a starting point to understand the ornamental repetition in nature and art as a result of a common principle of creation which leads to harmonious occurrences (p. 11). The ornament can be understood therefore in a psychological reading as a longing to understand the principles guiding the process of creation. In this context, terms such as *Imitative Instinct* and *Addiction to Innovation* used by Moritz, refer to the creative context and can be read as two methods to come up with unseen images (p. 56). Even though the idea is not elaborated on in great detail, Moritz addresses the question of when form is merely a variation of some known and existing image, and when does a form overcome being a mere alteration within a given principle?

We have turned now already to the processes of image creation and left behind the ornament debate which is led purely by the effect of the image on the beholder. Gottfried Semper (1803 – 1879), architect and art critic, has emphasized the influence of the technique and material quality on the crafts. In his elaboration on the cultural development he declares weaving as the starting point from which all handcraft, art and architecture originated. He considers weaving of fences and textiles for clothing to be closely related to the first occurrences of the ornament. The orthogonal structure of warp and thread are according to Semper responsible for the discovery of an ornamental décor as a result of simple alterations in the weaving process [5]. The recognition of the effect caused by rhythmic abstract compositions in textiles are declared by Semper furthermore, to be the springboard of art in general (p. 113). While Semper intends to prove the influence of weaving technique and materiality on other crafts, art and architecture, Alois Riegl (1858 – 1905) refuses the exclusive focus on these two components. In his "Historical Grammar of the Visual Arts" he defines the origin of Art in the human drive to imitate nature. Symmetry and rhythm are, according to Riegl, not merely an effect of the "Medium" (materiality and technique) but existed already before weaving was invented as a basic human drive to imitate nature. As inference of this idea, Riegl attempts to connect historical and cultural contexts through the occurrence of comparable ornamental motifs [6] [7].

The re-occurring focus on ornament throughout the centuries, selectively summarized above, is proof of the intriguing power of this iconic phenomenon. At first glance it seems that the modern movement of the 20th Century has banned the ornamental for reasons expressed in Adolf Loos' polemic essay "Ornament and Crime" [8]. A closer look at facades realized by modern architects (Mies van der Rohe, Marcel Breuer, le Corbusier) [9] or paintings by modern artists (Piet Mondrian, Wassily Kandinsky, Jackson Pollock) [10], show a new ornamental aspect which is caused by repetitive visual elements and their various alterations. In reference to George Kubler and his description of cultural development as a sequence of occurrences originating from a common problem [11], we can describe the ornamental image as a linked sequence of solutions to the question of how imagination and aesthetic experience can be stimulated (Kant) or how a principle of creation can be visualized (Moritz). The following analysis of digital images with an ornamental structure is based on the issues of analog images described above.

2   Ornamental Images in the Digital Age

If we turn now to the analysis of digital ornaments we can refer again to Gottfried Sempers idea of defining a work of art or craft as the result of its function, the characteristics of the material chosen for the object, and the tools involved in the process of design. Even without the support of these three points as exclusive influences on art and design, we find an analogy in the famous formula "The medium is the message" by Marshall McLuhan pointing at the dependence of form on the medium [12]. Functionality of the message can only be achieved within the medium (materiality, tools). The following analysis of digital ornament examples is conducted with the aim to describe the shift of the phenomenon within the constraints of digital technology.

2.1   Ornamental Images in the Pioneering Phase of the Computer Era

During 1965, three exhibitions of computer-generated images were shown [13]. Georg Nees presented his work at the Technical University Stuttgart in February. The work of Michael Knoll, generated since 1961 at the Bell Laboratories in Murray Hill New Jersey, was exhibited in April at the Howard Wise Gallery, New York. Frieder Nake had a show with his images in November at the Gallery Wendelin Niedlich in Stuttgart. The results of these early experiments are proof of inquiries exploring the possibilities of image generation through computer code. Looking at these images, it is evident that the computer artists were interested to explore whether the programmed image is able to imitate the individual stroke of an artist. In Frieder Nake's work "13/9/65 Nr. 2" (also known as Hommage to Paul Klee, 1965, plotter drawing, ink on paper) or Michael Noll's "Four computer-generated random patterns" (based on the composition criteria of Mondrian's "Composition with Lines", 1965), the orthogonal structure of the images is dominant. Both image series imitate a repetitive flow of gestures by the randomized variation of a basic description of a specific form. In this alteration of a principle, the images become ornamental in the sense that they show unity and variety based on a common underlying principle. The beholder perceives a variety of similar forms related to each other but they can neither be recognized as mimetic representation of an object, nor as signs pointing to something. We can describe the mentioned images as second generation artwork merely created to find the limits of the technical capabilities of the computer with the literal meaning of Max Bense terminology "artificial art" [14].

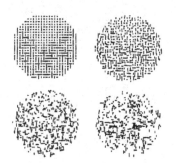
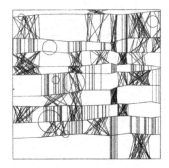

Fig. 1. Left: Michael Noll: Four computer-generated random patterns based on the composition criteria of Mondrian's "Composition with Lines", 1965. Right: Frieder Nake: 13/9/65 Nr. 2, Hommage to Paul Klee, 1965. Digital Art Museum, DAM, (www.dam.org).

In contrast to the work of art generated with traditional means, the computer generated ornamental image lets us access the underlying principle in the form of programming code and unveils to a certain degree the mystery of a creative process. Guided by the fascination of mastering a principle of creation in nature through a mathematical description, a second category of images can be distinguished. The image "Gravel-Texture" (Schottertextur) by Georg Nees from 1968 shows a sequence of twelve squares from a geometric, horizontal alignment at the top to a scattered arrangement of the squares at the bottom of the composition. We can imagine a sequence of square objects exposed to external powers gradually disintegrating the orderly arrangement. Even though we can not say what the squares depict, we can follow the imitation of a process we are familiar with from the experience with physical objects. The title of the project confirms and supports the reading of the image. Georg Nees' image series "Octagons" (8-ecke) also represents a variety of similar possibilities to connect eight points through lines. With the systematic arrangement, the beholder is overseeing a field of options and can compare the variations, perceiving similarity and difference.

Both images "Gravel-Texture" and "Octagons" explore randomly generated values in order to imitate natural variety. The lack of curves is obvious in these early images realized by computer code. They can be declared as ornamental with a number of arguments: (1) The most obvious argument is based on the observation that the compositions consist of elements used in a repetitive way varying in position or form. (2) Both images provide an aesthetic experience through the ambiguity of their meaning. A direct mimesis and denotation of the forms are missing. (3) The images are ornamental because they present a principle of generating variety by following a natural process. (4) The mathematical description of the principle becomes accessible and repeatable in these generative processes. The creation of images becomes a repeatable process such as an experiment in the sciences.

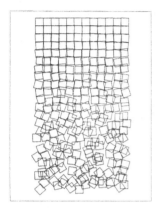

Fig. 2. Left: Georg Nees: Gravel-Texture (Schottertextur), 1969. Digital Art Museum, DAM, (www.dam.org). Right: Georg Nees: Octagons (8-ecke), 1964. compart, center of excellence computer art, (http://dada.compart-bremen.de).

The Fractal images emerging in the beginning of the 1980's can be seen as a further development to imitate and recreate an underlying principle of nature with a mathematical code. Benoît Mandelbrot discovered the equation named after him in 1979 and his visualizations of the mathematical discovery allowed a popular understanding of self-similarity as a principle in nature [15]. The visualizations mark a peak of the confrontation between the natural and the artificial. Their broad reception in science and art is an indicator of the basic longing for the understanding of the powers behind nature and other complex systems found in risk management or economy. The self-similarity of these images at different levels of zoom, makes them a unique type of ornamental self-reference, and complements the idea of randomly generated variety of the earlier computer graphics.

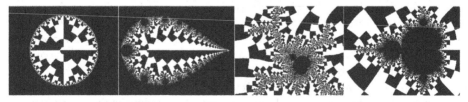

Fig. 3. Heinz-Otto Peitgen, Peter H. Richter: Binary decomposition, 1986. The Beauty of Fractals. Images of Complex Dynamic Systems, p. 74, Berlin 1986.

2.2   Ornamental Images in the Early Stage of the Personal Computer

In the exhibition of Georg Nees' work at the ZKM in Karlsruhe 2006, there was a small woven carpet exhibited consisting of black and white stripes. Nees had woven the carpet on a children's loom altering black and white according to the toss of a dice. It was his interest in randomly generated images that lead him to the loom [16]. In reference to Gottfried Sempers idea of situating weaving and its orthogonal structure as the beginning of the ornament, we can also consider the computer-generated images in the phase of the emerging personal computer technology in the mid 1980's under the aspect of the ornamental. The aesthetic of the early drawing software is strongly influenced by the orthogonal structure of the pixel-raster. In contrast to the programmed images which were executed with an automated drawing table (Zuse Z64 Graphomat) moving a pen over paper, the technology as an affordable output device, connected to the personal computer, was the dot matrix printer. As the name of the printer conveys, any image executed with this technology follows a matrix based on pixels. Experimental investigations were made by designers and artists to explore the new possibilities of the digital tools. The wrapping paper designed by Mara Jerman in 1985 at the Basel School of Design is a typical example that integrates the dot matrix aesthetic with a project [17]. In opposition to the work achieved by programming code, the aesthetic of the software tools does not address the concept of presenting a field of options by varying the execution of one algorithm. The images are rather examples of collage in which textures of different density, gestural strokes drawn with the mouse, and typographic elements are composed through the possibilities of the copy and paste functions provided by the software. Since the pixel was at that time a one bit (binary digit) entity, textures were employed to achieve a gray scale effect. The MacPaint interface from 1984 shows the matrix was not only used to fake grayscale but also to offer a palette of textures and patterns. Once they were filled into a shape, the designer could alter them according to his/her imagination. These possibilities, provided by the software, allowed a free combination of existing and self generated ornamental textures and patterns. They have fostered the use of ornamental elements along with the promotion of a combinatory process provided by the copy and paste function [18].

Fig. 4. Mara Jerman: Wrapping paper for citrus fruits designed with MacPaint, 1986. Swiss Typographic Magazine 4, p. 3 – 18, Zürich 1986.

Fig. 5. Susan Kare: Drawing in MacPaint for the release 1.0 of the MacPaint software, 1984. Wikipedia, (http://en.wikipedia.org/wiki/File:MacpaintWP.png).

The addition of low cost scanners to the personal computer made it possible to scan photographic images as bit map images, imitating gray values with a larger or lower density of a randomized pixel texture. Depending on the setting of the resolution, more or less abstraction was achieved. In the following test sequence of transferring a continuous tone image into a bit map, we can perceive a diminishing role of the mimetic and an increase of the self-referential function of the squares with decreasing resolution. In this technical process of abstraction, the ornamental is a principle applied to the conversion of gray values without paying attention to the mimetic aspect of the represented object.

Fig. 6. Amir Berbic: Systematic reduction of the bit map resolution applied to a portrait photograph, Summer Workshop 2009. Archive of the Basel School of Design HGK FHNW.

2.3   Ornamental Images in the Beginning of the 21st Century

The further development of standard software and authoring tools enable designers today to choose and to combine the processes of digital image generation described above. The resolution of the image description, as well as the input and output devices are no longer prescribing an orthogonal structure onto design solutions. Generative processes defining procedures of image generation and standardized software tools can be combined more of less ad libitum. If we see the ornamental image not purely as a result of materiality, tools and techniques, but also as a means to accommodate a specific need of the beholder, we can ask again what kind of digital images with an ornamental effect have been created with the actual technology. Three examples are discussed in the following section which stand for a continuation of the historic sequence of iconic phenomenon of ornament.

The thesis project of Simon Koschmieder conducted at the Basel School of Design (HGK FHNW) in 2004, explored the possibilities of an interactive installation in public space. The installation was designed to engage people in the play of image generation. The interaction with the image generating hardware and software was based on the interpretation of sound level, movement, and color. Live video footage was captured, interpreted, and altered through processing code [19] and the resulting images were projected onto a large wall of the space. The alterations of the video image can be grouped in three categories. (1) The captured image is interpreted according to a set of rules applied to a grid. In the specific case each square was filled with a color sample of the underlying life image. Furthermore, the squares were divided diagonally and the darker the section of the life image, the larger the area of the gray overwriting of the actual color became (Fig. 7. left). (2) A sequence of live images was displayed and continuously updated. Through the small interval of the frames captured and the gradually changing orientation of the frames, the projection was read as an assembly of transforming elements (Fig. 7. middle). (3) The third interpretation of the life captured video image was transformed in a way that the mimetic function of the image was completely lost. The interpretation of video data resulted in a repetitive composition of similar but never equal elements (Fig. 7. right). Something all of the discussed images have in common, is that the ornamental effect is achieved by a repetition which is addressing the flexibility of a formal principal (not proncipal). It is not the square pixel, nor the imitation of a natural variety, but an abstract play of similar forms and their relationship presented through dynamic transitions which is characteristic for these images.

Fig. 7. Simon Koschmieder: E-Walls, Thesis 2004. Archive of the Basel School of Design HGK FHNW.

Another example is the image series "Path" by Casey Reas. He describes the images as a movement of a synthetic neural process [20]. They are characterized by repetitive lines which are similar to hand drawn marks in their variation and unity. In their organic flow, they remind one of colored ink dissolving in water. As the title confirms the images are meant to imitate an originally natural process of neurons. We can explain the image series "Path" with the aim of ornamental images to address a principle of nature showing variation and unity. As described above, this aspect was the first time addressed by Carl Philipp Moritz and is also apparent already in the early stage of programmed images. It is the fascination of artificial nature which is further developed in the images of Casey Reas through the mastering of curves and the resulting organic shapes achieved in his and Ben Fry's programming platform "Processing" [19]. Furthermore, the specification of "Path" as a movement of a synthetic neural process is pointing to another characteristic of digital ornaments. A synthetic neural process is most likely described by an immense amount of data indicating which neuron is activated at what time. The design of images based on data has become increasingly available through the possibilities of data storage and processing.

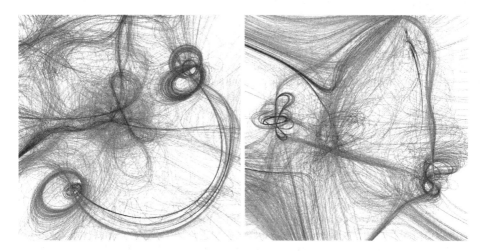

Fig. 8. Casey Reas: Path, 2001, (http://reas.com/)

The project "Big Atlas of LA Pools" conducted 2013 by Benedikt Groß and Joseph K. Lee [21] has isolated 43,000 swimming pools of the Los Angeles area from digital maps publicly available. They have used online services such as "clipping farm" or "amazon mechanical turk" to isolate, locate, verify and assemble pools to a thematic atlas of Los Angeles. This procedure generates images that pretend to visualize information. The amount of data – in this specific case the shapes of the pools – appears as a repetitive accumulation of similar shapes causing an ornamental effect. Only with a closer analysis can we perceive that there are not many small pools, midsize pools seem to be more rounded and large size pools are often organic. But the reading of the midsize pools might just be an effect of the accumulation of lines and is not clearly inferable from the image. We may understand this kind of information visualization as a "data ornament". It is characterized by an overwhelming accumulation of similar entities creating a loss of significance of an individual measurement in the visualization.

The design decisions do not follow the aim of reduction or explanation of a complex situation, but rather follow the aim to create an aesthetic experience or even achieve the experience of the sublime in the beholder [22].

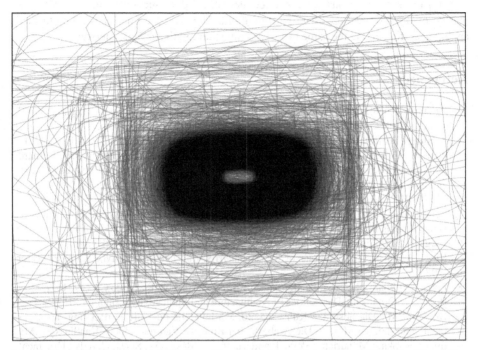

Fig. 9. Benedikt Groß, Joseph K. Lee: The Big Atlas of LA Pools, 2013, (http://benedikt-gross.de/log/2013/06/the-big-atlas-of-la-pools/)

3   Conclusion

In the first part of this paper the theoretical discourse about the ornament has been summarized briefly. The ambiguity of the ornament as a negative and unnecessary addition or a core element of an aesthetic experience has been addressed. Furthermore, the ornament has been identified as an image category representing a principle of creation in nature as well as in art and design.

Referring back to the continuation of the historical sequence of the ornament, we can identify the following points as achievements of the digital image generation processes: In the early era of programmed images, the confrontation of the natural, which is visible in the output, and the artificial, which is recognizable in the mathematical description in a form of the computer code, has found a new form which can be interpreted as a continuation of representing unity and variety (Karl Philipp Moritz). In the early phase of the personal computer textures with orthogonal structures can be seen as another revival of textile design principles. But they overcome these constraints through the technical possibilities of combination and figuration leading to collage-like compositions. In the 21st Century, the ornamental image is no longer bound to repetition of a static form.

Variety is achieved by generative procedures calculating the individual instance of an element from a set of live data coming from a flow of images or a dynamic data stream captured in a digital network.

With these observations we can infer the fruitful continuation of the historical sequence of ornamental images in the digital era. The digital occurrences relate to their analog ancestors and at the same time overcome them with aesthetic innovation.

References

1. Aristotle: Rhetoric, translated by W. Rhys Roberts, Mineola NY, book III, paragraph 7, p. 129 (350 B.C.) (2004)
2. Aristotle: Poetics, translated by S. H. Butcher, Mineola NY, Part XXII (350 B.C.) (1997)
3. Kant, I.: Critique of Judgement, translated with Introduction and Notes by J.H. Bernard, 2nd revised edn., London (1914), http://oll.libertyfund.org/title/1217 (January 19th, 2014)
4. Moritz, K.P.: Vorbegriffe zu einer Theorie der Ornamente, Berlin (1793)
5. Semper, G.: Style in the technical and tectonic arts, or practical aethetics, translated by Harry Francis Mallgrave and Michael Robinson, Los Angeles (1879, 2004)
6. Riegl, A.: Problems of Style, translated by Jacqueline E. Jung, New York (2004)
7. Riegl, A.: Historical Grammar of the Visual Arts, translated by Evelyne Kain, Princeton (1993)
8. Loos, A.: Ornament and Crime, translated by Michael Mitchell, Riverside CA (1904, 1998)
9. Picon, A.: Ornament: The Politics of Architecture and Subjectivity, London (2013)
10. Brüdelin, M.: Die abstrakte Kunst des 20. Jahrhunderts oder die Fortsetzung des Ornaments mit anderen Mitteln. Die Arabeske bei Runge – Van de Velde – Kandinsky – Matisse – Kupka – Mondrian – Pollock und Taaffe. In: Beyer, V., Spies, C. (eds.) Ornament. Motiv – Modus – Bild, München, pp. 349–374 (2012)
11. Kubler, G.: The Shape of Time. Remarks on the History of Things, New Haven/London (1962)
12. McLuhan, M.: Understanding Media: The Extension of Men, Cambridge (1994)
13. DAM, Digital Art Museum (February 1, 2014), http://dam.org/artists/phase-one/frieder-nake
14. Bense, M.: Aesthetica. Einführung in die neue Aesthetik, 2nd edn., Baden-Baden, p. 337 (1982)
15. Mandelbrot, M.: The Fractal Geometry of Nature, New York (1982)
16. Video-documentation of the exhibition "Georg Nees – The Great Temptation) at the ZKM Karlsruhe (2006), http://www.youtube.com/watch?v=CRVCX2A_YUA (February 1, 2014)
17. Jerman, M.: Wege zur Typographie. Swiss Typographic Magazine 4, 3–18 (1986)
18. For another typical example see: April Greiman, Design Quaterly 133, Does It Make Sense? Walker Art Center, Minneapolis (1989)
19. Processing web site, http://www.processing.org (February 1, 2014)
20. Reas, C.: http://reas.com/path_p/ (February 1, 2014)
21. Groß, B.: http://benedikt-gross.de/log/2013/06/the-big-atlas-of-la-pools/ (February 1, 2014)
22. Kant, I.: Critique of Judgement, translated with Introduction and Notes by J.H. Bernard, 2nd revised edn., § 25, London (1914), http://oll.libertyfund.org/title/1217 (January 19, 2014)

Affording Creativity and New Media Possibilities

Zoie So

Department of Visual Studies, Lingnan University
8 Castle Peak Road, Tuen Mun
Hong Kong SAR
zoieso@ln.edu.hk

Abstract. Developers compete to design the computational commodity with the most user-friendly interface. While this allows massification, it also defines boundaries. In operating these devices, users are afforded little creative freedom. We do well to question a technology that is not conducive to freedom. By no means should our interactions with computers force us into robotic submission. Following commands unreflectingly only serves to dull the mind. On the other hand, designing programs that allow users to decide over operational parameters serves to point the direction to human technological freedom. They share a common approach to the object, which should adjust to the body as the body does to it, in a reciprocal alliance that responds to particular situations. In addition, DIY and studio art practices afford the necessary skills and mindsets for sensible HCI and yield us the power to optimize our chances of designing a world defined by openness.

Keywords: Affordance, Creativity, Skill Development, Coupling, Embodiment, Disembodiment, DIY, Frugal Innovation, Studio Art, Modular Design, Openness.

1   Introduction

The addition of some specimen of computational technology to every aspect of human life has spawned in us an augmented sense of technophobia. Immersed in a lake of digital technology, our inner fear drifts to its reflection at the surface. The fear is caused in part by users' passive compliance with electric power machines and their mysterious intelligence. Apocalyptic dreams of robotic dominance or the end of electric power are popular themes for sci-fi plots[1]. Humans paralyze and gradually dehumanize, corrupted by convenience, efficiency, and computational accuracy. Homo-sapiens evolves into a sheepish homo-babulus, as digital intelligence gains omniscience and rises to omnipotence. Though these musings seem exaggerated and unrealistic, it is in fact not difficult to discern the tendencies in our everyday

---

[1] A list of some technophobic novels as example is: Frankenstein (1818) by Mary Shelley, The Island of Dr. Moreau (1896) by H.G. Wells, Cell (2006) by Stephen King. In addition, Sci-Fi movies such as Metropolis (1927), 2001 Space Odyssey (1968), The Terminator (1984), Wall-E (2008), and Avatar (2009) can dramatically display such fear.

A. Marcus (Ed.): DUXU 2014, Part I, LNCS 8517, pp. 675–685, 2014.
© Springer International Publishing Switzerland 2014

applications of computational technology that resonate with such a dreadful reality. Fascinated by the ever new capacities of cutting-edge, state-of-the-art computation, it would nonetheless be sapient to consider their influence over users -a.k.a. human beings. In this paper I aim to illustrate that while most existing Human-Computer Interaction (HCI) design models still feed technological dependence, there is however innumerable means of developing technology in ways that inspire creativity and are conducive to the users' innate bent for innovation. I declare our mission to identify this potential and to support thereby the realization of our will for a sensible HCI: our gift to future generations.

2   Computation's Complexity and Simplicity

To begin our journey in identifying a sensible HCI model, let us trace back a bit the history of computer development. Computational technology has grown continuously in sophistication and complexity ever since the appearance of the first models of binary computers during the 1950s.[2] Direct operation of giant electro-mechanical systems was succeeded by the invention of programs using symbolic coding, which subsequently gave way to the application of metaphoric couplings where text and graphics express computational commands to users. The changes taking place through different generations of computer design capture various dimensions of HCI[3]. More recent advances have aimed at making digital technology increasingly accessible to the public and thereby have significantly contributed to the popularity of all-in-one personal computing and the creation of a ubiquitous digitalized environment. Contributing to defining modern life, desktop computers, personal digital assistants (PDA), smart phones, ticket booths and central air conditioning systems are, by all means, like the air: everywhere and all around us. In spite of their actual mechanical complexity, user-"friendly" designs aim at erasing all operational complication. They seek to make it "effortless", like the inborn act of breathing, and to transform – surreptitiously– our operation of them into an unconscious behavior.

Abstraction and interfacial *coupling* [4] achieve simplification, which in turn contributes to user accessibility. Coupling is a way of establishing relations between functional entities, such that a chain of associations is formed linking otherwise disparate actions. The chain links body movement, mechanical design, electronic operation, symbolic manipulation and visual metaphors. The skill required by the user to fulfill computation is thereby diminished. Users can operate the system at skin level from the tip of the iceberg. The desktop model, which induces paralysis by restricting our physical body to one place –and seems to aim at some kind of physical absenting, suppression, vanishing, destruction–, conditions gestures and action to

---

[2]   Bruce Wands, "A Timeline of Digital Art and Technology", *Art of the Digital Age*, 210-211, Thames & Hudson, New York, 2006.

[3]   Paul Dourish, "A History of Interaction.", In *Where the Action is: The Foundations of Embodied Interaction*, 1-11, The MIT Press, Cambridge, Massachusetts, London, England, 2001.

[4]   Dourish, "Foundations.", *Where the Action is, 138-154.*

repetition ad absurdum, and with the internet has enabled us to connect to the outside world through couplings. This situation can potentially send the user into a second-order world of representations and couplings, giving rise to the problem of virtual and disembodied cyberspace.

Often technology is a black box to users, who no longer understand the inner workings. These powerful black boxes have gradually become the backbone of convenient city life. They rapidly penetrate our being to reshape habits and semiotics. Meanwhile, we remain outside of them. It is not inherently wrong to apply simplified designs in certain practical contexts, but the inertia of operating at the surface as a rule discourages the moment-to-moment, situation-specific refinements of users and limits their creative performance potential. Consumerism further fuels the mindless drive towards technology. User-friendly products are designed for replacement and not repair. The sealed computation black boxes conceal conspiracies of designed and programmed obsolescence that fuel economic interests. Critics believe consumers are wickedly kept from this information to favor the corporations. However difficult it is to measure the current extent of such immoral activity, its role in depleting Earth's resources requires more attention. Taking preventive measures to discourage and penalize such wasteful behavior would be most fitting.

3   Affordance and Affording Creativity

Paul Dourish is a scholar of embodied interaction and ubiquitous computing. We turn our attention to his clarification of the term affordance. In addition, his adoption of Heidegger's phenomenological approach to meaning in everyday life can further illustrate the degree to which HCI design induces disembodiment, frustration, and alienation within real life settings.

According to Dourish, the psychologist J.J. Gibson defines affordance as a "property of an environment"[5], approached ecologically by a subject via visual perception. Subjects observe their environment and generate an understanding of the possible actions afforded by this environment in relation to their body. A jar in high position affords only some tall people to reach, the gap between the sofa and the floor affords only some small hands/ kids' hands to have the freedom of movement in that space, or the access to reach their lost toys there. Following Gibson's analysis, Donald Norman further explores this concept in this book *The Design of Everyday Things* (1988). Norman highlights the relation of form and function in the design of everyday objects and of human-computer interfaces.[6] Affordance can be designed by thoughtful consideration and arrangement. Action and participation are partially determined by the potential embedded in an object by design. A cup handle affords an easy hand grasp. The shape and size of the handle is designed in proportion to the shape and size of the human hand. Therefore the shape of a hand affords the handle a range of possible shapes.

---

[5]   Dourish, "Being-in-the-World.", *Where the Action is,* 117.
[6]   Paul Dourish, "Being-in-the-World.", In *Where the Action is,* 118-119.

I would soon argue here that instead of simply affording expected actions, a sensible HCI model must afford creativity and skill development. The notion of situated actions, expounded by British anthropologist Lucy Suchman, provides a firm axis from which to propound my argument. The framework emphasizes the importance of the specific normal context of situations. Computational designs are often built on the basis of the "antecedent conditions and the consequences of human actions"[7]. They work within a closed system of finite operational possibility, affording decision-making users a series of choices. By contrast, real life situations, under the continuous influence of complex social and environmental factors, involve a human communication and interaction impossible to pre-formulate. They are conversations that, to achieve an overall coherence of the person and the unit of computation require moment-to-moment adjustments and ongoing revision. Suchman's view is that sensible computational designs should serve as resources for situated actions without restricting their own local and circumstantial practical possibilities. At present, most computational units have preset limitations. It is important that users gain awareness of the limitations and find ways to compensate for them.

So what can users do after gaining this awareness of the computational limitation? Let us take a look at how it is exactly that people engage with their tools and computational devices through the lens of Heidegger's phenomenological concept of meanings in everyday life. Being-in-the-world (Dasein) is one of Heidegger's key concepts. We engage with the world by encountering meanings driven by practical affairs. The distinction between ready-to-hand (zuhanden) and present-at-hand (vorhanden) gives a more concrete description of the encounters. Dourish further applies Heidegger's conception literally to our use of tools, namely to computer interfaces.[8] A mouse works as an extension of its user's hand. Unreflective of the mouse's existence, the mouse is ready-to-hand to the user. Were the mouse to reach the edge of the table and the user to notice, the mouse would, if only fleetingly, appear to the user as present-at-hand. Dourish believes tools can function well only when they exist as ready-to-hand.[9] This, I believe, is an oversimplified interpretation of the user/tool relation in the context of real situations. The relation is actually very unstable, and a shift between ready-to-hand and present-at-hand is continuously taking place. The user's world is highly complex. Often tools conceptually fuse, often they are conceptually severed, being in some way ready and present almost at once. More in tune with Suchman's notion of situated actions, we can investigate the way users engage with tools on a moment-to-moment basis, and leave aside the simplistic notion that tools become invisible when people are efficient.

The development and resultant ripeness of the technique with which a tool is used is dependent on repetition and refined through accumulated experience. The technique of writing with a pencil, for instance, is never ultimately stabilized and undergoes

---

[7]   Lucy Suchman, *Human-Machine Reconfigurations: Plans and Situated Actions*, 31,
       Cambridge University Press, West Nyack, New York, USA, 2006.
[8]   Paul Dourish, "Being-in-the-World.", In *Where the Action is*, 106-110.
[9]   Ibid.

ceaseless modification: there is improvement on the path to mastery, adjustment is a function of how frequently we write, different contexts demand different speeds, the surface of inscription plays a role, language has an influence over technique, recipient and destination impact effects, injury conditions.

In short, every encounter with a tool -itself a complex entity- involves a stabilizing and a destabilizing of skills, and every application of skill is influenced by a previous level of skill, by accumulated experience, and by the aim of the application. My experience of writing with a sharp pencil will influence the way I write with a blunt pencil. I may gradually apply less force on the pencil as it blunts to maintain an even line thickness. Moreover, the location of the writing in relation to our body changes throughout the writing action. In writing on a page from left to right and from top to bottom with a sharp pencil that blunts one stroke at a time, our technique is a function of our accumulating experience within a situation of absolute change that demands dynamic adjustment. Paradoxically, a static technique would only produce inconsistency. We destabilize the technique and reestablish it with subtle movements. An unrealistic linearity is implied by designs based on false notions of stability in a world of predictable imperatives. The strict model of solid design is bound to break by sheer pressure -for change is unrelenting.

The notion that a setting's affordance is not preset but changes over time as a function of experience (i.e. the user's encounters with objects within a context) is related to the aforementioned observation that using tools is a dynamic learning process requiring constant skill adjustment and development. A master ceaselessly returns to the novice stage. With an awareness of the nature and limitations of computation design, and through gradual acquisition of the skill of in situ embodiment, we prepare the ground for creative solutions to flourish. Prompted by Norman's idea of designing a cup handle's affordance, I hereby propose we endeavor consciously to afford this awareness of the nature and limitation of computation the power to afford us, artists and engineers the ability to design HCI platforms that afford creativity through the development of skills. The choices we make concerning technology and education are changing our future. Are we sufficiently aware that these factors interbreed and sensitive to the concomitant realities? Should we be content simply to transit mechanically from transient awareness to ready-to-hand invisibility?

4   DIY and Studio Creativity

Meanwhile, the practice of Do-It Yourself (DIY) and studio art can shed some light on how to incite the creativity of participants and how to promote innovative solutions and original interactions. The phrase "Do-It-Yourself", which already appears in a 1912 US advertisement, became common during the 50s.[10] DIY referred at first to home improvement, decoration and maintenance work performed by householders

---

[10] Matt Watson and Elizabeth Shove, "Products, Competence and Meaning in the Practices of DIY", Paper, European Sociological Association Torun 2005, Poland, 2005.

who refrained from employing professionals. It has now been extended to other DIY activities like furniture production, clothes making and computer assembly. Matt Watson and Elizabeth Shove emphasize DIY's emergent character, and not budget concern, as a key motivation to people's involvement in production that can easily be out-sourced.[11] In vein with Suchman's notion of situated action, Watson affirms that needs change in the context of local everyday practice, and therefore plans must be contingent and temporary.

He mentioned that in the process of completing a planned DIY project often reveals new needs, adjustment and jobs that needed to done before the planned tasks. The unpredictability of DIY practice further develops DIYers' competence and confidence, thus allows new possible DIY projects to evolve in the future.[12] Enhanced by knowledge obtained from school, friends and family, and read about in DIY manuals and internet forums, such competence remains virtual until DIYers actively synthesize and harness their existing knowledge, experience and skills through practice and through engagement with tools, materials and the specific conditions of their DIY tasks.

"[DIY] is the work, of coordination of tools, materials, competence, confidence, body and the fabric of the home that places DIY at such a complex location in relation to the conventional boundaries of social scientific analysis, the boundaries between leisure and work, consumption and production, and ultimately between human and nonhuman." (Watson and Shove 2005)

Alongside this, the frugal DIY approach to technology in Cuba portrays another inspiring reality. *Technological Disobedience*[13] is a term coined by Cuban Artist/Designer Ernesto Oroza in his study of the lifestyle of frugal innovation in Cuba in response to severe isolation and scarcity of resources since the 1960s,[14] when a vast number of American investors, professionals and technicians left Cuba. 'Disobedience' refers to a violation of a product's unity, a disregard for its aesthetic integrity, a lack of concern for safety and legal regulations and a willingness to take risks, and a breakthrough from the typical product-consumer model of other developed countries, overturning a closed system to break open and unleash unexpected unrealized solutions. Invention, reinvention, improvisation and repair are demonstrated by ordinary Cuban citizens, who display awesome skill in applying with novelty various materials and parts of complex machines. Their understanding of how things work coupled with an ability to extract an unlimited potential from limited resources is truly impressive. I was in Cuba for two weeks in 2008 and witnessed a makeshift fair with old amusement park rides in Pinar del Río. The machines looked exotic, most of them tattered and repaired, looking almost like oversized tin toys lit by

---

[11] Ibid.

[12] Ibid.

[13] "Ernesto Oroza, Technological-disobedience", Last modified January 28, 2014, http://www.ernestooroza.com/category/technological-disobedience-project/

[14] "Cuba's DIY Inventions from 30 years of Isolation", MotherboardTV, Last modified June 20, 2013, http://wn.com/exact/MotherboardTV

tungsten light bulbs. Traces of repair were unabashedly exposed, a silver fork used to control a swinging ship, a few strong men using muscle power to start and to brake the ship, wires tied with knots from the rotational train to the central pole… All these surreal facts were fusing live with real Cuban music, and a cheerful and optimistic atmosphere ruled. [Fig.1] Like the artist that I am, I set out to capture my observations in video and began to design a way to display the video in a form that could evoke similar technological relations. I thought of constructing a six-channel video installation without the luxury of eight separate projectors. I appropriated several magnetic door stoppers to function as 360° pivots and attached a tiny mirror to each one. [Fig.2] Each magnetic joint could be manipulated with precision to control the direction of reflection of the video projected onto its respective mirror, and simple hand adjustments could be made to adapt the installation to the height, width and depth of different rooms. It was first installed in a projection room close to my studio. I was aware of my limited budget and knew that fine video screens were beyond my grasp. While I puzzled over a solution, the A2 sketching papers on my studio desk caught my attention. The newspaper-like texture of the sketching papers matched surprisingly well my impression of Cuban style. For the presentation, I invited visitors to use these papers to capture the video projections reflected by the six tiny mirrors mounted on the magnetic pivots. The images had a sharp focus only if they were caught "in mid-air" by the papers, and looked blurred when they hit the walls. My guests walked around the room, viewing my video document of Cuban amusement machines as phantoms appearing on paper. [Fig.3] The work was named *Warm Technology*, to glorify a Cuban creativity that demonstrates a special reciprocal relationship between the people and their technological devices and system. Faced with an imperative for on-site adjustment, functional appropriations provide the needed flexibility and openness for a successful engagement with an otherwise deficient technology.

Fig. 1. Video Screenshots of *Warm Technology*, captured in Pinar del Río, Cuba, 2008

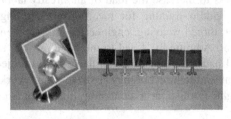

Fig. 2. Magnetic door stoppers with mirrors

Fig. 3. Video Installation, *Warm Technology*

I have found the influence and merits of studio art practice central to the discussion of affordance of creativity to reflect a similar spirit. At the interface of meditative thinking and material engagement, of concept and bodily involvement, where stress is laid on the power of imagination and on promoting the development of new forms of expression, the exercise of problem finding and solving, of restricted and situational improvisation, finds a liberated space to manifest.

Reflecting in this light, I have set out in my own art practice as research vehicle to explore how computational interfaces and digital image displays afford creativity through a choice in setting.[15] In several of my studio works I rethink and rework my own media. Aware of the idiosyncrasy of living in a computer age, and not wanting merely to display my seal with digital projectors on monitors, I built an image machine for visitors to actually enter and modulate, gaining thereby the peculiar ability to influence an iridescent image at hand on display. Named LSD (Liquid Soap Display) as a deviation from a sophisticated market product –the LCD monitor– it challenges the passive viewing practice pervading the industry of digital imagery by giving rise to an interactive dialogue between visitors and the image generated in situ in real time, made possible by the soap solution and the huge lens membrane generated. Moreover, I bring notice to the way viewers participate in the process of image perception at the physical, biological, and cognitive levels. In a different work called Wood Digit, I make a reference to early forms of the computer, like the Jacquard Loom, and to modern software packages so popular among new media artists. I designed a programming platform for generating sequences of patterns using thousands of interwoven nylon threads mounted on a wooden structure that allows control over the length of the threads, the programmed parameter of my artistic display. The weaving process was extremely tedious and technically challenging. I was constantly reminded of the gap between theory and practice, and found myself struggling between digital logic and physical properties. Problems arose at almost every step in the process to increase the load of an already labor-intensive project. It served as a complete studio training for me, in wood cutting, programmed laser cutting on plastic sheet, thread weaving, engineering, and mathematical calculation of programmed movement. Admittedly, I had to integrate most of the multi-disciplinary skills and knowledge I had learnt thus far. All these studio projects have allowed me and my visitors to think through technology. I strive in my work to afford creativity, in action and in thought. Furnishing a technology that affords creativity is a way of

---

[15] "Zoie So- Art Laboratory", Last modified in 2013, www.zoieart.com

contributing to the design of humanity's humanity. The creative practice of DIY and studio art does more than merely provide a possible model for an HCI model that affords creativity. The enormous experience and acquired skills undertaken in both DIY and studio art practice equips a person with the competence and confidence needed to interact with computational technology in a way that furnishes creative solutions to unspecified local site-specific conditions.

5   Modular Possibilities

Preoccupied with openness and improvisation, Dourish urges designers to focus on providing means for exploiting appropriation and articulation of resources, that they may be incorporated into the practice specific to each situation, allowing users to reach and act upon the technology, and more importantly making possible the extraction, examination, manipulation and rearrangement of units. He asserts that coupling management and meaning construction should be relayed by designers to the users. Yet this kind of unmitigated transparency exposing users to a hard-core numerical programming language is impracticable and perhaps even impractical.[16] The Cuban frugal approach, though fascinating, may not suit citizens of developed countries with sufficient resources and unwilling to risk safety and to challenge law. Dourish's alternative is to design a "macro" programming and thereby to increase the ability of users to define couplings and to participate in the design process.[17] Along these lines, modular design provides flexibility between specificity and exchangeability. Acting upon electric sockets, which are a global variable, universal adaptors and transformers function as constants executing local and global coordination.

Modular Design is widely implemented in architecture and interior design, a common example being the mobile furniture units of office spaces. Workstations built from modules can respond to functional variations and can be both re-assembled and expanded upon to adapt to an ever-changing workforce. The units of modular design are not limited to a uniform shape. Bicycles and computers, for instance, take parts responding to functional variation and upgrading. Modular design commonly makes use of connectors with highly compatible standard links to mediate modules, a feature that makes recombination feasible, simple and economical. USB (universal serial bus) protocols, which allow interconnection of various computer and electronic devices, support both data and power transfer. The personal computer serves as a hub to link keyboard, mouse, external hard drive, printer, scanner, digital camera, bluetooth adapter, and can power or charge these devices simultaneously.

The model of modular design depicts an open system that in principle allows for unlimited incorporation of new modules, providing devices with the flexibility to adjust to situational demands. The USB device can double as a cooling fan, a hand

---

[16] Malcolm McCullough, "Technology: Situated Types", *Digital Ground: Architecture, Pervasive Computing, and Environmental Knowing*, 117-119, The MIT Press, Cambridge, Massachusetts, London, England, 2004.

[17] Ibid.

warmer, an LED desk light, a keyboard mini dust-vacuum, a self-inflating pillow mounted on a laptop, all of it made possible by the open nature of the USB. This also contributes to reducing technological waste. Most current computational models follow the sealed blackbox design, purporting user-friendliness while perpetuating the wasteful practice of acquiring devices that cannot be repaired once damaged, or incur unreasonable repair costs, rendering useless a device with most of its parts intact. The absurd reality is that a new device is usually cheaper than repair of a broken one.

Concerned about the unnecessary waste generated in the smart phone market, a team of three members: Dave Hakkens, Gawin Dappe and Tomas Halberstad started a design group under the name of Phonebloks in 2013 that today boasts 979,260 supporters.[18] The group is devoted to realizing a modular design for the smart phone, which they promote with the slogan "a phone worth keeping"[19]. Their modular design for smart phone has detachable blocks connected to a common base that holds everything together. Modular blocks are self-contained, and each works as a separate Wi-Fi, Bluetooth, battery, operation speed, data storage, antenna or audio unit. Users can customize, upgrade and repair each phone block independently. Ideally, with different companies contributing to the development of these functional blocks, users could enjoy great liberty in choosing and composing blocks, and could go as far as to design their own. Technological functions are broken down into units and can be recognized and studied separately, allowing users themselves to determine the coupling of visual metaphors and the assignment of semantic values, as the device's mode of operation is itself revealed through operation. This kind of open modular system serves genuinely as a root for creative potential and provides ample resources for high exchangeability in multiple and varied cases.

6   Conclusion

The metaphor put forth by American scholar Malcolm McCullough further enriches our musings over designs of computer interaction: Classical musical instruments facilitate personal growth and increase creativity through skill practice, and this creativity flourishes when bodily engagement is tightly channeled through the physicality and nature of the instruments.[20] The experience is a tangible one of sense making. Musicians are encouraged to mediate with and to understand their instruments, and not to look at them merely as responsive devices, as means to solving problems promptly or performing a specific task.

Our ever-changing world demands embodied responses to various moment-to-moment conditions that require a semiotic understanding. Computer design is to consider local and global compatibility and the adjustments specific to their respective nature. The flexibility and openness of models such as modular design afford customization, sensitive appropriation and improvisation. In DIY and studio art practice artists generate the know-how needed to accomplish tasks, as they engender

---

[18] "Phonebloks", Accessed February 10, 2014, https://phonebloks.com/en
[19] Ibid.
[20] McCullough, "Technology: Embedded Gear", *Digital Ground*, 85.

awareness of materiality through first-hand involvement and deep reflection upon the relation of consumer and product.

A sensible HCI model would afford users the power to engage with computers in a flow of creativity that exploits experience and acquired skills. In furthering competence and confidence through active engagement with computational devices and the environment, creative solutions and original situations emerge in the process. Sensible HCI designs require a degree of understanding that discourages oversimplification and ultimately resists the inertia of ignorance. Human interactions with computers are to advance a platform wherefrom to generate sense and meaning. Through embodiment, skill development and reflection on the nature of the relation, this platform is to be a stepping stone for human creativity. To afford creativity is not to enforce patterns. Rather, it is a freedom-favoring way to design how we want to be, for ourselves and the generations to come: open.

References

1. Wands, B.: A Timeline of Digital Art and Technology. Art of the Digital Age, pp. 210–211. Thames & Hudson, New York (2006)
2. Dourish, P.: Where the Action is: The Foundations of Embodied Interaction. The MIT Press, Cambridge (2001)
3. Suchman, L.A.: Human-Machine Reconfigurations: Plans and Situated Actions. Cambridge University Press, West Nyack (2006)
4. Watson, M., Elizabeth, S.: Products, Competence and Meaning in the Practices of DIY, Paper, European Sociological Association Torun 2005, Poland (2005)
5. Ernesto Oroza-Technological Disobedience, http://www.ernestooroza.com/category/technological-disobedience-project/
6. Cuba's DIY Inventions from 30 years of Isolation, http://wn.com/exact/MotherboardTV
7. Zoie So- Art Laboratory, http://www.zoieart.com
8. McCullough, M.: Digital Ground: Architecture, Pervasive Computing, and Environmental Knowing. The MIT Press, Cambridge (2004)
9. Phonebloks, https://phonebloks.com/en

basil.js – Bridging Mouse and Code Based Design Strategies

Ludwig Zeller[1], Benedikt Groß[2], and Ted Davis[1]

[1] Academy of Art and Design Basel HGK FHNW,
Visual Communication Institute / The Basel School of Design,
Vogelsangstr. 15, 4058 Basel / Switzerland
{ludwig.zeller,theodore.davis}@fhnw.ch
[2] Benedikt Groß, Werastr. 134,
70190 Stuttgart
bg@benedikt-gross.de

Abstract. In this paper we present our JavaScript library basil.js that makes scripting and automation in Adobe InDesign accessible to designers with little previous knowledge in programming. We outline how we derived our API design from the Processing project and applied it to Adobe InDesign. We explain the benefits of combining code and mouse based design strategies within one software package and show how creative users can benefit from the possibility to extend their existing software tools. Lastly the current state of our project is reported and application examples in the form of student projects are given.

Keywords: Generative design, computational aesthetics, tool development, tool modification, educational programming language, Adobe InDesign, Processing, JavaScript.

1 Introduction and Motivation

Digital approaches for print publishing became the common practice in the 1990's. Today, Adobe InDesign is the de facto standard and both a respected and reliable tool for the creativity of layout designers. Thus, it is the primary software package that is used by students and staff in education and third-party commissions.

The Basel School of Design has a long tradition in the education of young designers and a high expertise in visual communication through editorial, book and information design. It is one of our main goals to expand the methodologies of design and to educate students in developing a set of individual, unique styles and aesthetics. One possibility to achieve this is bringing the students in contact with programming and the development of generative and/or interactive digital systems.

We see generative design as an interesting possibility for our students in order to create a unique visual language and handwriting. In particular we are interested in the creation of digital, visual tools as an individual means of expression. The complex behavior of a self-executing formal system such as a programming language can offer both control and surprise. Often the production of partly unexpected output yields an interesting source of inspiration.

A. Marcus (Ed.): DUXU 2014, Part I, LNCS 8517, pp. 686–696, 2014.

2   Tools for Designers

2.1   Generating Design through Code

The introduction of digital desktop publishing to the mass market in the 1990's brought the step from designing something by hand to using screens and mouse driven interfaces in order to do the same thing. Working with the computer obviously made the design experience less tangible, but on the other hand it also promised a vast set of new possibilities like the use of digital fonts, "copy-and-paste" and the "undo" function.

Generative design is the use of formal rules in the shape of algorithms in order to produce a design output. For instance Processing [1] is one of the most commonly used software platforms for this purpose and has become increasingly popular over the past decade. After moving from hand to mouse we have moved from creating with the mouse to creating through code. Or to be more precise the idea of procedural design is being revisited. Before the WYSIWYG paradigm had been established by the computing industry in order to make computers more accessible to a wider audience, the expression through code already had been a very common way to produce visual output. Designers and artists such as Manfred Mohr, Georg Nees and Frieder Nake have been active in the pre-GUI era of visual computing [2]. Nonetheless, their work was already circulating around the core concepts that we link with generative design nowadays.

Already these protagonists faced the situation that generative design is at the border between two different worlds. Common assumptions for this clash of roles put the idea that "artists and designers can't program" against the idea that "a programmer can't design". Therefore, educating designers in this field is an interdisciplinary endeavor. While computational design and art was already known in the 1960's as mentioned above, the idea that artists and designers would program these formal rules themselves was not necessarily commonplace back then. Frieder Nake describes in his article "Teamwork zwischen Künstler und Computer" a cooperating system consisting of an artist, a human programmer, a computer and a visual output machine such as a printer or monitor [3]. This exemplifies a major difference of today's generative design practice where it became normal that the artist and programmer are the same, broadly educated person. An explanation for this could be the availability of easy to use programming environments, our current zeitgeist that is influenced by the tight integration of computers in daily life and an according curriculum in art and design education.

But it has to be emphasized that basil.js and its integration in education is not aimed at making a programmer or even software engineer out of a designer, but to allow for visual experiments and results with greater ease and fewer requirements of their technological knowledge. Additionally we find that creating generative design within an existing WYSIWYG software package such as Adobe InDesign offers a useful bridge between generating through code and adjusting by mouse.

2.2   Modifiable Meta Tools vs. Closed Design Platforms

In general, tools are enabling and limiting at the same time. In the words of Marshall McLuhan: „First we shape our tools, thereafter they shape us." [3] We think and perceive the world and its possibilities through the functional facilities we possess and know. Or to put it in the words of Ludwig Wittgenstein and his thoughts on the borders of "Welterkenntnis": "the limits of language mean the limits of my world". [4]

Many software packages have a closed, specialized nature. They offer a valuable set of pre-defined, common solutions for specific problems. They are relatively easy to learn and use, but their extension is difficult. A programming language on the other hand is a kind of meta tool that allows for questioning the set of available methods and for extending it by creating new tools.

In fig. 1 a number of common software tools and languages are put into a relation of required learning time to the amount of aesthetical quality that is pre-defined by their use. Packages such as the Adobe Creative Suite are relatively easy to learn for beginners offering a great starting point into the world of digital content creation and manipulation but are meant to be used as deployed.

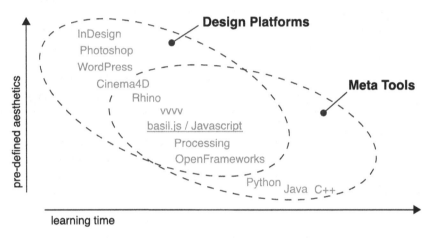

Fig. 1. Mapping common design/programming tools regarding their pre-defined aesthetics and required learning time [Adapted from 5]

On the other far end of the scale you find lower-level programming languages such as Java and C++. These require a far greater amount of time to learn, but on the other hand offer a tremendous amount of possibilities, since eventually e.g. C++ is the foundational layer of software packages such as InDesign. Unfortunately due to the extreme requirements to the user's experience in software design, bringing designers in direct touch with these languages is usually an inappropriate strategy. It would mean a too demanding involvement of them into an area that does not belong to their aesthetical interest. Nonetheless, this might be a meaningful option for some extreme scenarios.

Looking into the middle range of the graph we find software dialects such as Processing, which bundles a subset of the existing possibilities of Java into an easier to learn approach for graphics programming. Complex software packages such as Maxon Cinema 4D that feature built-in scripting facilities are usually relatively easy to learn and allow for the adaptation of the package's tools in order to realize complex and unique projects. JavaScript is regularly used as the language of choice for built-in scripting, since its powerful interpreter engines are available to software developers to integrate into their software.

We found that both specialized and adaptable approaches have benefits and downsides. In the case of using code as a medium for visual expression the benefits are the ability to build your own tools, to foster the precision of your digital computing, to gain control over your digital production techniques and ideally to discover previously unseen aesthetics.

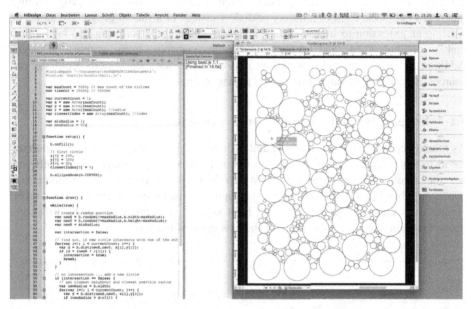

Fig. 2. basil.js code in the Adobe ExtendScript Editor (left) populated a page with circles in Adobe InDesign (right)

But we aren't advocating that code is the best way to design. Instead we want to highlight that there are disadvantages as well, such as the designer not receiving an immediate visual feedback, the manual fine-tuning of generated output is hard or even impossible, it is building upon a very different skill set than design itself and is therefore unintuitive to learn for designers. Therefore, offering a design environment that enables both the possibility for manual mouse based and algorithmic code based design tools is helpful. With Adobe InDesign containing a JavaScript programming interface it becomes a mix between a closed design platform and a modifiable meta tool.

3   Introducing basil.js

The aim of the developer team was to incorporate these scripting facilities in our teaching curriculum. We invited Benedikt Groß to offer an InDesign scripting workshop to our students in Spring 2012. We found out that the Java API of the co-existing software package "InDesign Server", which has been the starting point for the

JavaScript API, is aimed at professional software engineers. This can be derived from its very high-end pricing, the database-driven pipelines it is intended to be connected with and the formal style of coding it requires. Therefore this programming interface is unfortunately especially hard to be learnt and used by designers, who usually do not have much or any experience in programming. This seems like a contradiction since the GUI version of Adobe InDesign is obviously aimed at graphic designers.

basil.js in order to make the InDesign JavaScript API more approachable for designers and artists. This can be seen in the tradition of educational programming languages but in the form of a library or dialect instead of a full language. We aimed at creating an extension to InDesign that brings automation and scripting into layout and makes computational and generative design possible from within InDesign. Additionally, it also includes workflow improvements for data imports from various sources, indexing and complex document management.

3.1   Bridging WYSIWYG and Generative Design

As mentioned above bridging mouse and code based design paradigms was important for us in this project. Fig. 2 explains a common basil.js usage scenario: on the left you see the Adobe ExtendScript Editor, which is used for developing, running and debugging basil.js scripts. While we recommend using this default editor, other coding tools can also be used. On the right side of the screen an Adobe InDesign project is open that shows the result of the execution of the script.

Fig. 3. Manually drawn vector lines have been used as an input for a basil.js script that transforms these according to algorithmic rules

The program filled the page with non-intersecting circles at different sizes. Different to Processing, these circles are then available as live entities within Adobe InDesign and therefore can be altered and deleted through the mouse just like manually produced graphical elements. Fig. 3 shows another example in which manually designed vector paths are being used as an input to the basil.js script on the left. In this case the original vector lines that made up simple typographic characters are being replaced with modulated sine waves that follow the exact path of the original manual input and can be configured in more detail by setting variables in the script.

3.2   Designing an Accessible API

Since the original Adobe InDesign JavaScript API was so hard to use for students we wanted to design basil.js to be significantly easier for integration into our curriculum. Processing has been an important and efficient part of our curriculum already for a number of years and therefore was suitable as a role model for starting basil.js. Since we already teach Processing for a couple of years and made good experiences with this, we took that platform as an inspiration. This brought us to the following question: What made Processing so widely adopted and is it possible to translate this to Adobe InDesign?

```
var doc = app.activeDocument;
var layer = doc.layers.add("layer with a line");
var color = doc.colors.add({model: ColorModel.process,
space: ColorSpace.CMYK, colorValue: [20,100,50,0]});
var lines = doc.graphicLines;
var newLine = lines.add( layer );
newLine.strokeWeight = 1;
newLine.strokeColor = color;
newLine.paths.item(0).entirePath = [[0,0], [300,400]];
```

Code snippet 1: Adding a line with a new color to a new layer without basil.js

```
b.layer("layer with a line");
b.stroke(20,100,50);
b.line(0,0,300,400);
```

Code snippet 2: Same task executed with basil.js

Without conducting an in-depth case study we concluded that the open-source spirit, the well integrated user community, the availability of online learning material and galleries, the integration in academic curricula world wide and its easy to grasp structure made Processing successful. We decided to transfer this "spirit of Processing" to Adobe InDesign by offering a similar programming API and online community. The initial goal to be 100% compatible to Processing codes could not be achieved, but suitable programs can be converted in a short amount of time.

We analyzed the existing functionalities of the Processing and InDesign API and selected a subset that would be especially useful in a common print design scenario. The according InDesign core functions were redesigned in its usability from the viewpoint of a visual designer and have been code-wrapped into basil.js. Processing uses very short and clear names, avoids the Java typical camel case naming and provides overloaded method signatures for getters and setters depending on the argument count. Additionally, the Processing toolkit loads most of its functionality into one very big class. From a software engineering point of view this could be seen as a clearly bad practice, but this avoids the need to understand more sophisticated concepts of organizing codes in classes, packages and software design patterns. Again, we took this as a guideline for our own development.

For many casual scripting tasks we managed to highly reduce the code complexity compared to native InDesign code and therefore improved the experience for the scripting designer. For instance in order to draw a line with a new color on a newly created layer we managed to replace the relatively complex code in snippet 1 with the shorter basil.js version in snippet 2. Please note that this comparison leaves out all the error detection and convenience that basil.js is offering on top of that basic functionality.

The most obvious difference in the two coding approaches can be seen in the demanded sequence of function calls. In the Processing style you are first setting default colors for fillings and strokes, default stroke weights, etc. before you actually apply a stroke to the canvas. This sequence stays in the metaphor of actually using a pencil: once you've taken it at hand its visual characteristics are applied to all the following strokes you are going to bring to the paper. The InDesign API on the other hand demands you to configure the appearance of each single stroke after it has been placed to the canvas. A very modular approach from a professional programmer's perspective, but completely counter-intuitive to graphic designers. This kind of gap between InDesign's API and a designer's understanding of the production of visual output can be seen throughout large parts of the API. In the above example this can also be observed in the overly explicit configuration of new colors and the actual creation of the line: First an "empty" and therefore invisible stroke object is added to the document and only after that the visual features such as colors and even the actual geometric appearance (start and end point) are defined. Without deeper knowledge we assume that the Processing team faced similar awkwardness when they wrapped the desired visual functionalities of the Java Advanced Window Toolkit (AWT) into their dialect.

We managed to keep the naming conventions of Processing for many functions such as color(), line(), rect(), etc. in order to make the transition from Processing to basil.js easy. In cases where no direct Processing equivalent was available we tried to invent new functions with a similar coding style in mind. Unfortunately, we had to bind basil.js to a global object "b" in order to avoid namespace collisions with third-party JavaScript libraries that would occur in a global scope. This is a limitation of JavaScript compared to the well-organized Java language.

4   Project Discussion

Since education is the primary goal in this project, we started to integrate basil.js in the seminars at our institute as a test-run since Winter 2012. The public release took place in February 2013. Since then a number of projects have been created, of which three three examples will be presented briefly.

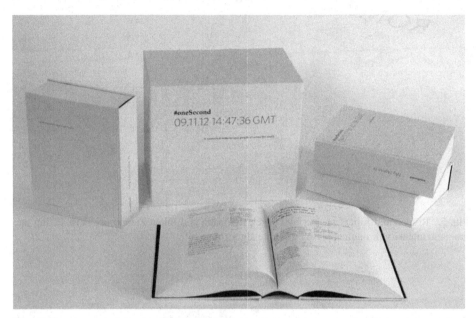

Fig. 4. #oneSecond project by Philipp Adrian. Archiving the data generated in one second on Twitter as a four volume print publication.

In fig. 4 we see Philipp Adrian's project *#oneSecond* that has been advised by Prof. Marion Fink. A one second time span on Twitter has been recorded with the help of a commercial marketing analysis service. The collected data was then transformed and decorated with additionally aggregated information about the involved users and their location, preferences, languages, etc. In total over 4000 tweets were archived in this manner, which lead to a four-volume book publication. While not directly being a generative design project *#oneSecond* gives a good example of how basil.js and InDesign can be used for customized data flows and template based print presentation.

The project *"Romeo and Juliet"* by Patrick Baumann and Inken Zierenberg shown in fig. 5 takes Shakespeare's entire play transcription and presents it in small point size on five posters. basil.js was then used to draw lines between all occurrences of the words "Romeo" and "Juliet". Together the poster series indirectly produces a visual representation of the narrative dramaturgy of the story by showing increasing and decreasing densities of line connections. In this example it was helpful to use InDesign's typesetting engine that works together seamlessly with basil.js in order to find the positions of individual words in flowing text.

Fig. 5. "Romeo and Juliet" project by Patrick Baumann and Inken Zierenberg. Visualizing the dramatic intensity through applying a simple algorithmic rule.

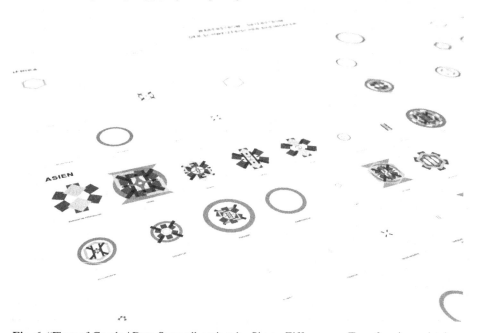

Fig. 6. "Flow of Goods / Data Stream" project by Simon Ziffermeyer. Transforming a database from the Swiss border police to an encoded visual system.

Finally, fig. 6 shows the project *"Flow of Goods / Data Stream"* by Simon Ziffermeyer. This project consists of several data visualizations of the import and export numbers at the Basel Rhine harbor in the form of posters and a book publication. Simon received these numbers separated according to the different types of goods as well as destination and origin countries as Excel tables and loaded the information with basil.js. These numbers were then being mapped to a visual system of overlaid pictograms that make up visual collages in order to give a quickly graspable representation of several numeric values at a glance. This project shows how basil.js is used in a more traditional generative design scenario and benefits from the fact that manually prepared vector shapes can be easily used and duplicated through code.

5   Conclusion

In this paper we positioned today's generative design approach as a revisiting of early concepts of computational design after the introduction of WYSIWYG platforms in the 1990ies. We described the possibilities of adaptable design tools in the creation process and discussed the integrated combination of mouse and code based design paradigms.

In this picture we introduced basil.js as a contribution to our research and education agenda at the Visual Communication Institute in Basel. It has been explained how we improved the accessibility to Adobe InDesign's scripting facilities for non-experts through partly redesigning its programming API. We exemplified the aesthetical explorations that are made possible through bringing automation and scripting into the WYSIWYG design and layout process such as processing and transforming large amounts of external data and to generate designs that would be too time demanding to achieve without code. The aesthetical and practical benefits of the tight iteration between feeding mouse-based designed assets into the generation and transformation through formal rules and vice versa have been shown. Eventually we outlined meaningful areas of specialization for our project that can be seen as an extension for existing poster and book projects in Adobe InDesign, the intense work on typography and its manual corrections as well as the usage in generative book projects.

An open-source project like basil.js is successful if it is used in the outside world and joined by other developers. We already have received submissions both in the form of design projects and pull requests on Github. Additionally, it will be important to see which kind of aesthetical use and innovation this project will see in its near future.

Acknowledgements. Many thanks to Stefan Landsbek for contributing the initial JavaScript architecture, Prof. Michael Renner for making the support through the Visual Communication institute possible, Philipp Adrian for contributing the backend system of the basiljs.ch website, the be:screen GmbH that provided valuable technical assistance, Ken Frederick for contributing a user interface package and other additions as well as our students for giving us error reports and brilliant inspiration in our beta stage.

Special thanks go to Ben Fry and Casey Reas for starting Processing, the processing.js team for providing an open-source Processing port to JavaScript [7] that we partly ported to basil.js and Jürg Lehni for his Scriptographer [8] project that gave us a starting point of inspiration for scripting within the Adobe Creative Suite.

References

1. Fry, B., Reas, C.: Processing. Software platform and website,
   http://www.processing.org
2. Büscher, B., Hoffmann, C., von Herrmann, H.-C.: Ästhetik als Programm, Max Bense / Daten und Streuungen. Diaphenes, Zürich (2004)
3. Nake, F.: Teamwork zwischen Künstler und Computer. FORMAT Nr 11, 38–39 (1967)
4. McLuhan, M.: Understanding Media. Extensions of Man. McGraw-Hill, New York (1964)
5. Wittgenstein, L.: Tractatus Logico-Philosophicus (1921)
6. Groß, B.: Tools and Authorship in Computational Design. MA Dissertation, Royal College of Art, London (2012)
7. Processing.js, an open-source port of Processing to JavaScript,
   http://processingjs.org/
8. Lehni, J.: Scriptographer. Scripting environment for Adobe Illustrator,
   http://scriptographer.org/

Author Index

Abbas, Aneela   III-391
Abbas, Mazhar   III-245
Abdullah, Manal   III-255
Abu Hassan, Roaa   III-273
Abulkhair, Maysoon   III-273
Acartürk, Cengiz   II-373
Aderhold, Andreas   II-3
Adıyaman, Öner   IV-164
Ahmad, Maqbool   II-346, IV-446
Ahmad, Usman   III-442, III-574
Akbar, Salman   III-442
Alaçam, Özge   II-373
Alangari, Nora   IV-105
Alawi, Aisha   III-347
Al-Behairi, Salha   III-347
Aldayel, Haifa   IV-105
Aldaz, Gabriel   III-3
Alessio, Pedro   II-550
Alfayez, Aljohara   IV-105
Alharbi, Rawan   IV-105
Alhudhud, Ghada   IV-105
Ali, Wasif   II-346, III-391
Aljehani, Roaa   III-273
Aljindan, Rania   IV-105
Al-Khalifa, Hend S.   I-415, II-15
Almeida, Ana   IV-3
Almutairi, Badr   II-28
Al-Muzaini, Mashael   III-347
Al-Negheimish, Hadeel   IV-105
Alomar, Dania   IV-105
Alomari, Ebtesam Ahmad   II-38
Al-Qahtani, Nada   III-347
Alrajhi, Wafa   IV-105
Al-Razgan, Muna S.   I-415
Al-Rubaian, Arwa   IV-105
Al-Sabban, Lana   III-56
Al-Salhie, Layla   II-383
Al-Shahrani, Mona D.   I-415
Alshathri, Ashwag   IV-105
Alssum, Lama   IV-105
Altaboli, Ahamed   IV-199
Alvarez, Jaime   III-281
Alves, Márcia Maria   II-732
Alwaalan, Sara   IV-105

Al-Wabil, Areej   II-383, IV-105
Al-Zuhair, Mona   II-383
Amaral, Fernando Gonçalves   I-273
Ancient, Claire   IV-113
Andrade, Rafael de Castro   III-184
Araújo, Cristiano C.   II-313
Arfaa, Jessica   II-50
Arrieta, Abel   III-643
Arruda, Ermano   I-560
Arshad, Sidra   III-391
Aşçı, Sinan   II-173
Asghar, Usman   III-574
Ashraf, Imran   IV-446
Asif Butt, Tayyab   III-423, III-442, III-574
Asimakopoulos, Stavros   IV-358
Atnafu, Solomon   III-482
Auinger, Andreas   I-402
Aziz, Azizan   III-605, III-616

Babadr, Mona   III-273
Bach, Ursula   II-636
Backhaus, Nils   III-400
Badewi, Amgad Ali   III-495, IV-392
Bakker, René   IV-403
Banerjee, Banny   III-520
Bansemir, Bastian   I-3
Baranauskas, M. Cecília C.   IV-208, IV-273
Barattin, Daniela   I-185
Barros, Gil   II-509
Barros, Helda Oliveira   II-501
Barros, Marina L.N.   I-437
Barros, Rafaela Q.   IV-124
Barroso, João   III-452
Bastos, Marcus   I-509
Batchelor, John   III-719
Battaiola, André Luiz   II-732
Baumlin, Kevin   III-125
Beato, Rosemary   III-125
Befort, Marcel   II-463
Bengler, Klaus   I-329
Bergamo, Marília Lyra   I-613
Berger, Arne   I-25

Bertholdo, Ana Paula O.   I-33
Beul-Leusmann, Shirley   I-217
Bilgin, Gökhan   II-234
Billestrup, Jane   II-71
Bischof, Andreas   I-115
Bockermann, Christian   II-393
Böhm, Victoria   I-14
Bolchini, Davide   III-217
Brandenburg, Stefan   III-400
Brandse, Michael   II-669
Brangier, Eric   I-425
Braseth, Alf Ove   III-326
Braz, Alan   IV-381
Brejcha, Jan   I-45, I-519
Breyer, Felipe   II-184, II-647
Briggs, Pam   I-229
Bristol, Kelly   IV-319
Brizolara, Paulo Leonardo Souza   II-521
Brod Júnior, Marcos   III-207
Brown, Vanessa   I-86
Buchdid, Samuel B.   IV-208
Burchell, Kevin   III-594
Bystřický, Jiří   I-519

Cabral, Giordano   I-643
Cabreira, Arthur   II-279
Cagiltay, Kursat   III-155
Cakir, Hasan   III-155
Calegario, Filipe   I-643
Camba, Jorge   II-405
Campos, Fábio F.C.   I-437, I-484, II-81
Candello, Heloisa   IV-381
Cao, Yin   II-586
Carmo, Ubiratan   II-647
Casalegno, Federico   IV-71
Castadelli, Gilson Ap.   II-193
Catalá, Andreu   IV-220
Chammas, Adriana   II-213
Chang, Chun-Chieh   II-417
Chang, Huang-Ming   IV-220
Chang, Shu Hsuan   I-622
Chapman, Lorraine   IV-12
Chen, Kun   II-586
Chen, Szu Han   II-562
Chen, Szu-Miao   III-265
Chen, Wei   IV-220
Chien, Sheng-Fen   III-265
Choi, Heejin   II-678
Choi, Jin-Ghoo   II-346, IV-446

Choi, Joohee   II-678
Chung, Wynnie (Wing Yi)   IV-285
Chunpir, Hashim Iqbal   III-495, IV-392
Cicek, Filiz   III-155
Clarke, Auren   III-542
Çömlekçi, Fatih   II-62
Contero, Manuel   II-405
Cook, Allison   III-562
Correia, Walter F.M.   I-437, II-81
Corsini, Massimiliano   II-3
Coventry, Lynne   I-229
Craven, Michael P.   III-15
Cronje, Willie   III-530

Dagge, Ricardo   III-653
Dalianis, Athanasios   II-481
da Luz, Alan Richard   II-688
Damena, Michael   II-334
Danylak, Roman   I-55, I-527
Dar, Hafsa Shareef   III-462
Darvishy, Alireza   IV-133
da Silva, José Carlos Plácido   IV-90
da Silva, Tiago Silva   I-33
Davis, James   III-338
Davis, Ted   I-686, II-425
De Amicis, Raffaele   II-223
de Carvalho Correia, Ana Carla   II-521
de Castro, Jacqueline Aparecida G.F.   II-203
de Castro Lozano, Carlos   IV-141
de França, Ana Carol Pontes   I-537
De La Torre, Fernando   III-103
de Lemos Meira, Luciano Rogério   I-537
de Miranda, Leonardo Cunha   I-74, II-521
Deng, Yi-Shin   III-265
De Paula, Rogério Abreu   IV-381
Desmarais, Michel C.   I-425
Desouzart, Gustavo   III-662
De Troyer, Olga   II-158
Dias, Cristiani de Oliveira   IV-141
Díaz, Marta   IV-220
Di Staso, Umberto   II-223
Doney, Paul   I-631
Dörflinger, Michael   I-402
Duarte, Emília   II-541, II-742, III-369
Duffy, Vincent G.   III-507
Dumpert, Jennifer   III-583
Dyson, Mary C.   III-164

Eibl, Maximilian   I-25
Ejaz, Hassan   III-423, III-442, III-574
Elias, Herlander   I-548
Emiliano, Rodrigo   III-452
Eschrich, Brian   II-533
Esin Orhun, Simge   IV-185
Esteves, Felipe   III-643
Estupiñán, Sergio   II-541
Evans, Rebecca   I-631

Fabri, Marc   I-631
Fadel, Luciane Maria   II-92
Faheem, Muhammad   IV-446
Falcone, Daniela   II-647
Fang, Xiaowen   I-496
Farnsworth, Carol   IV-232
Faroughi, Arash   I-64
Feijó, Valéria Casaroto   II-323
Feldhaus, Lea H.   I-173
Fernandes, Fabiane Rodriguez   II-104
Fernandes, Maria Goretti   IV-124
Fernandes Cavalcante, Victor   IV-381
Ferreira, Carlos   II-541
Figueiredo, Lucas S.   I-560, II-550
Filgueiras Vilar, Ernesto   III-653,
   III-662
Filippi, Stefano   I-185
Fischer, Holger   I-206
Flanagan, Patricia J.   III-675
Flora, June A.   III-520
Ford, Rebecca   III-530, III-542
Frangoudes, Fotos   II-699
Frankjaer, T. Raune   II-435, IV-253
Frazão, Luís   III-452
Freitas, Daniel   II-550
Freitas, Sydney   II-615
Fuks, Hugo   III-643
Furugori, Satoru   III-281

Gandhi, Rajeev   III-103
Garcia, Regina A.   II-15
Gassel, Sebastian   I-589
Gatsou, Chrysoula   IV-244
Geabel, Abeer   III-273
Gehring, Bettina   IV-412
Gençer, Merve   II-234
Genes, Nicholas   III-125
George-Palilonis, Jennifer   III-217
Geraci, Renae   I-86
Ghinea, Gheorghita   III-482

Gilgen, Daniel   II-435, IV-253
Göktürk, Mehmet   IV-23
Gomes, Luiz Vidal   III-207
Gomes Sakamoto, Sarah   I-74
Gomez, Rafael   IV-261
Gonçalves, Rafael   I-352
González de Cossío, María   III-411
Good, Alice   III-25, IV-113
Goode, Walkyria   I-86
Gotsis, Marientina   II-699
Govind Joshi, Suhas   III-141
Graf, Holger   II-3
Granollers, Toni   I-340, I-475
Green, Steve   I-393
Greiner-Petter, Moritz   I-96
Gris, Iván   II-720
Grønli, Tor-Morten   III-482
Groh, Rainer   I-3, I-130, I-589, II-488,
   II-533
Groß, Benedikt   I-686
Güney, Serhat   II-62
Guo, Sisi   II-586
Guo, Yonghui   IV-49
Gutiérrez Posada, Julián Esteban
   IV-273

Habel, Christopher   II-373
Hakeem, Shahd   III-56
Hakkarainen, Kai   I-142, II-246, II-289,
   II-301
Ham, Jaap   IV-328
Hamachi, Rieko   IV-32
Hamad, Safwat   II-148
Hammerschmidt, Christopher   III-34
Han, Ting   IV-469
Hanibuchi, Shumpei   IV-297
Hannich, Frank   IV-412
Hannß, Franziska   I-3
Harries, Tim   III-594
Harrison, Anna   IV-261
Hassan Al-Sayed, Alaa   III-56
Hastreiter, Isabella   I-104
Haubert, Lisa L.   II-699
Hayashi, Elaine C.S.   IV-273
Haydell, Tyler   III-3
He, Ning   II-446
He, Shan   IV-71
Heibach, Christiane   III-687
Heidt, Michael   I-25, I-115

Heimgärtner, Rüdiger   I-123, I-445,
    IV-39
Heiskala, Mikko   I-261, II-246, II-301
Held, Theo   II-754, IV-232
Hellweg, Daniel   II-711
Hernández Rubio, Erika   II-269
Hertlein, Franziska   I-371
Hesse, Jan   II-533
Hessey, Sue   II-562
Hinderks, Andreas   I-383
Hirai, Nobuhide   I-240, IV-458
Hoffmann, Max   II-636
Hollerit, Bernd   I-445
Holtzblatt, Karen   IV-232
Hsu, Chi-Hsien   I-622
Hsu, Wei-Lin   III-173
Huang, Ting-Yi Chou   III-173
Hung, Yah-Ling   III-44
Hussain, Mubbashar   III-391
Hussein, Idyawati   II-116
Hwang, T.K. Philip   II-417
Hwang, Ula   III-125

Ibrahim, Lamiaa Fattouh   III-56
Ibrahim Mohammed Ahmed, Asmaa
    III-56
Iftikhar, Shahzaib   III-423, III-574
Iio, Jun   I-572
Iizuka, Shigeyoshi   I-572
Illyas, Abbas   III-423, III-574
Imai, Michita   II-606
Inami, Masahiko   II-606
Inoue, Hiroaki   I-240, IV-458
Ip, Emily   IV-285
Iqbal, Muddesar   II-346, III-391, IV-446
Irshad, Azeem   IV-446
Ito, Kyoko   IV-297
Iuliucci, Nicholas   II-127

Jain, Samay   III-103
Jakobs, Eva-Maria   I-217
Jastaniah, Khlood   III-273
Jennings, Elizabeth M.   III-164
Jerzak, Natalia   I-453
Jeschke, Sabina   II-636
Jeske, Debora   I-229
Jeurens, Jasper   IV-403
Johnson, Michael   II-405
Jordan-Marsh, Maryalice   II-699

Joyce, Ger   I-465
Joyce, Mary   I-250
Ju, Wendy   II-598
Jun, Bong Gwan   II-763
Jung, Yvonne   II-3

Kamiya, Kei   III-281
Kammer, Dietrich   II-533
Kampf, Constance   III-554
Kang, Kyeong   I-55
Kannry, Joseph   III-125
Kaplan Akilli, Goknur   III-155
Karapantelakis, Athanasios   IV-49
Karasu, Necdet   III-155
Karlin, Beth   III-562
Kasugai, Kai   III-628
Kato, Satoshi   I-240, IV-458
Keck, Mandy   I-130
Kelner, Judith   II-184, II-647
Khalifa, Amal   II-148
Khan, Muhammad Sikandar Lal   II-574
Khashman, Nouf   II-139
Khokhar, Muhammad Faraz   III-423,
    III-442, III-574
Kikuchi, Senichiro   I-240, IV-458
Kim, Hyun Jung   II-763
Kim, Jea In   II-763
Kim, Min Soon   III-125
Kirakowski, Jurek   I-250
Kito, Akira   III-281
Knoll, Christian   III-293
Koalick, Grit   I-589
Kojo, Inka   I-261
Kon, Fabio   I-33
Koryzis, Dimitris   II-481
Kozak, Karol   II-533
Kramer, Joseph   IV-152
Krause, Sascha   I-104
Kremer, Simon   I-163, IV-308, IV-370
Krempels, Karl-Heinz   I-217
Kuijper, Arjan   II-3
Kulpa, Cínthia Costa   I-273
Kumar, Janaki   IV-61
Kurdi, Heba A.   II-148
Kurosu, Masaaki   I-580
Kuru, Armagan   III-63
Kuru, Hakan   III-63

Laamanen, Tarja-Kaarina   I-142
Lai, Fung Ha Sandy   III-305

Lai, Jennie   IV-319
Lamontagne, Valérie   I-153
Landa Ávila, Irma Cecilia   I-285
Landim Goya, Julia Yuri   II-203
Lang, Alexandra R.   III-15
Lapczyna, Esther   I-130
Lasternas, Bertrand   III-605, III-616
Lee, Jaeki   II-678
Lee, Lin-Chien James   I-296
Lee, Sunmin   IV-285
Lei, Tian   II-586
Leifer, Larry   III-3
Lemos, Rafaela   I-318
Li, Haibo   II-574
Li, Shupin   II-289
Li, Xun Rong   II-794
Lilley, Mariana   I-465
Lima, Ricardo Cunha   II-463, III-184
Limeira, Carlos Dias   IV-339
Lin, Ming-Huang   I-296
Lin, Rung Tai   I-622
Lin, Tingyi S.   II-455
Lindemann, Udo   I-163, IV-308, IV-370
Link, Michael W.   IV-319
Little, Caroline   I-86
Liu, Dongyuan   II-586
Liu, Gang   IV-469
Liu, Xu   II-586
Liu, Yu-Chieh   III-530
Lochner, Berit   I-3
Loftness, Vivian   III-605, III-616
Lopes, Cristiano   II-279
Lu, Ke   II-446
Ludwig, Thomas   III-495, IV-392
Lympouridis, Vangelis   II-699

Macedo, Vanessa   I-308, I-318
Magliocchetti, Daniele   II-223
Mahmood, Zainab   III-432
Mahmud, Murni   II-116
Makino, Yasutoshi   II-606
Mankodiya, Kunal   III-103
Marcio Silva, Caio   I-308, I-318
Marcus, Aaron   II-258, III-583
Mareis, Claudia   I-96
Martin, Jennifer L.   III-15
Martins, Edgard Thomas   III-317
Martins, Isnard Thomas   III-317
Martins, Laura Bezerra   III-72
Martins, Marcos André Franco   III-195

Masip, Llúcia   I-475
Maslo, Semir   I-64
Matos, Rui   III-662
Matsubara, Hideyuki   I-572
Matsuoka, Yoshiyuki   III-281
McCulloch, Malcolm   III-530
McDonald, Susan   IV-81
Medeiros, Ligia   III-207
Medeiros, Rodrigo   I-643
Mehak, Shakra   III-442
Melo, Claudia de O.   I-33
Melo, Filipe   III-662
Ménard, Elaine   II-139
Meneses Viveros, Amilcar   II-269
Menezes, Bianca H.X.M.   II-313
Menezes, Thiago   II-550
Michailidou, Ioanna   I-163, IV-308, IV-370
Midden, Cees   IV-328
Miesler, Linda   IV-412
Milde, Jan-Thorsten   II-358
Mitchell, Diane   III-338
Miwakeichi, Fumikazu   I-240, IV-458
Mo, Yunjeong   III-605
Mobeen, Sara   III-442
Monat, André S.   II-463, III-184
Monowar, Muhammad Mostafa   II-38
Mont'Alvão, Cláudia Renata   II-213, III-83, IV-173
Morgan, Corey   IV-81
Mukherjee, Ananya   IV-71
Mulling, Tobias   II-279
Mushtaha, Abdalghani   II-158
Mushtaq, Adeel   III-442, III-574
Mustafa, Faizan ul   III-442, III-574
Muukkonen, Hanni   II-246, II-289
Muzaffer, Umar   III-423, III-574

Nakamura, Ricardo   II-773
Nara, Hiroyuki   I-240, IV-458
Nascimento, Renato   IV-339
Neidlinger, Kristin   II-598
Neves, Maria   II-81
Nieminen, Marko   I-653
Nieminen, Mika P.   I-653
Nishida, Shogo   IV-297
Nishimura, Hidekazu   III-281
Nixon, Ken   III-530
Noda, Hisashi   IV-32
Nomiso, Lúcia Satiko   IV-423

Noriega, Paulo   II-541, II-742, III-369,
    IV-3
Noronha, Sunil   IV-152
Novick, David   II-720
Nunes Marciano, Juvane   II-521

Ogata, Masa   II-606
Okimoto, Maria Lúcia L.R.   I-318, I-329
Olaverri-Monreal, Cristina   I-329
Oliva, Marta   I-475
Onal, Emrah   IV-81
Onal, Olga   IV-81
Orehovački, Tihomir   I-340
Orlandini, Guilherme   II-193
Osman Md Tap, Abu   II-116
Öztürk, Özgürol   IV-164

Pai, Shantanu   IV-232
Palomäki, Eero   II-246, II-301
Park, Soomi   III-731
Paschoarelli, Luis Carlos   II-104, IV-90,
    IV-423
Passerino, Liliana Maria   IV-141
Patsoule, Evelyn   IV-434
Paula, Danielly F.O. de   II-313
Paulillo, Christopher   III-338
Paulin, Rafael Eduardo   II-732
Pelczarski, Michal   III-699
Penn, Joe   III-530
Penzenstadler, Birgit   III-562
Pereira, António   III-452
Pereira, Pedro   II-742
Pereira, Roberto   IV-208
Petkov, Bojana   III-326
Pinheiro, Mariana   II-550
Pinho, André Luís Santos de   IV-339
Plácido da Silva, João Carlos Riccó
    IV-90
Plewes, Scott   IV-12
Pohl, Hans-Martin   II-358
Portugal, Cristina   III-230
Poulos, Irina C.   II-699
Prado León, Lilia Roselia   I-285
Presumido Braccialli, Lígia Maria
    II-193

Quaresma, Manuela   I-352, II-213,
    IV-173
Quarles, Diane   III-338

Rafi, Zeeshan   II-346
Ramalho, Geber   I-643
Rasool, Saqib   II-346, III-391
Rauterberg, Matthias   IV-220
Rebelo, Francisco   I-453, II-541, II-742,
    III-369, IV-3
Reis, Bernardo   II-647
Renner, Michael   I-663
Renzi, Adriano Bernardo   II-615
Requejo, Phil   II-699
Rettie, Ruth   III-594
Ribas Gomez, Luiz Salomão   II-323
Richert, Anja   II-636
Rigas, Dimitrios   II-28
Říha, Daniel   II-661
Rino, Marcelo V.   II-203
Rivera, Laura   III-125
Rivero, Antônio   II-184
Rızvanoğlu, Kerem   II-173, IV-164
Rodriguez, Ania   II-127
Rolim Filho, Epitácio Leite   II-501
Rosenthal, Paul   I-115
Rügenhagen, Eva   II-754
Ruggiero, Wilson   IV-71
Runonen, Mikael   I-653
Ryan, Neal   III-103

Sadek, Suzan   III-56
Salcines, Enrique García   IV-141
Salo, Kari   II-334
Sambhanthan, Arunasalam   III-25
Samsel, Christian   I-217
Santaella, Baltazar   II-720
Santa Rosa, José Guilherme   IV-339
Sato, Koichiro   III-281
Sauer, Stefan   I-206
Savage-Knepshield, Pamela   III-338
Schall, Andrew   I-86, I-363, IV-347
Schiphorst, Thecla   IV-285
Schmeil, Andreas   III-91
Schmidt, Deborah   I-589
Schmuntzsch, Ulrike   I-173
Schneidermeier, Tim   I-104, I-371
Schranz, Christine   II-624
Schrepp, Martin   I-383
Schulze, Inken   III-293
Schuster, Katharina   II-636
Schwalm, Maximilian   III-628
Scupelli, Peter   III-605, III-616
Seitamaa-Hakkarainen, Pirita   I-142

Sery, Christian   I-589
Shafiq, Muhammad   II-346, III-391, IV-446
Shahzadi, Syeda Sana   III-432
Shakya, Udeep   II-334
Shalash, Wafaa M.   III-347
Sharahili, Bayan   III-347
Sharma, Vinod   III-103
Sheikh, Farzan Javed   III-462
Sheikh, Javed Anjum   III-462
Shi, Chung-Kon   II-763
Shimizu, Shunji   I-240, IV-458
Shin, Jeongbeom   II-763
Beul-Leusmann, Shirley   III-628
Silva, Fernando   III-452
Silveira, Aline   II-647
Silveira, Milene Selbach   I-33
Simon, Andreas   III-687
Şişaneci, İbrahim   IV-23
So, Woonsub   II-678
So, Zoie   I-675
Soares, Marcelo Márcio   I-437, I-537, II-501, III-317, IV-124
Solanki, Alkesh   I-123, I-445
Soriano, Jared   III-125
Souto, Virginia Tiradentes   II-472
Spiliotopoulos, Dimitris   II-481
Spillers, Frank   IV-358
Spinillo, Carla Galvão   III-34, III-115, III-184
Stage, Jan   II-71
Stamato, Cláudia   IV-173
Steinert, Martin   III-3
Stickel, Christian   II-358
Stones, Catherine   III-44
Suggs, Suzanne   III-91
Sugiura, Yuta   II-606
Sumavsky, Ondrej   III-542
Szafer, Dafna   III-3

Takei, Kuniharu   III-710
Tao, Yonglei   I-197
Tariq, Sahar   III-432
Teichrieb, Veronica   I-560, II-550
Teixeira, João Marcelo   I-560, II-550
Thalen, Jos   III-357
Thomas, Jeffrey   III-338
Thomaschewski, Jörg   I-383
Thorsnes, Paul   III-542
Thum, Frederick   III-125

Tomimatsu, Kiyoshi   II-669
Ton, Thanh G.N.   III-103
Torpus, Jan-Lewe   III-687
Trapp, Anna   III-400
Tribe, James   III-719
Trocka-Leszczynska, Elzbieta   III-470
Tsukida, Ichiro   IV-32
Tsuruga, Takeshi   I-240
Turpin, David   II-699
Tyllinen, Mari   I-653

Ünlüer Çimen, Ayça   IV-185
ur Réhman, Shafiq   II-574

van der Voort, Mascha   III-357
van der Waarde, Karel   III-132
van Moorsel, Aad   I-229
van Schaik, Paul   I-393
van Turnhout, Koen   IV-403
Vartiainen, Matti   II-246, II-289, II-301
Vasconcelos, Luis A.   II-184, II-647
Vasconcelos de Melo, Hugo Fernando   III-72
Vázquez Ceballos, Dario Emmanuel   II-269
Vega, Katia   III-643
Verghese, Shiny   I-393
Viana, Bruno Santos   II-773
Vicario, Juan   II-720
Vilar, Elisângela   III-369
Vilar, Ernesto   III-369
Vilar Neto, Edvar   I-484, I-560, II-81, II-550
Vilimek, Roman   III-293
Virtanen, Juho-Pekka   I-261
Vodrazkova, Katrin   I-601
von Saucken, Constantin   I-163, IV-308, IV-370
Voyvodaoğlu, Tansel   II-234

Wacker, Markus   I-589
Wang, Yuanqiong (Kathy)   II-50
Wanner, Danilo   II-782
Watanabe, Eiju   I-240, IV-458
Wetzlinger, Werner   I-402
White, Catherine   II-562
Whittow, Will   III-719
Wiederhold, Maximilian   I-217
Wigham, Laurie   III-583
Wilberforce, Nana   III-605, III-616

Wilkosinska, Katarzyna   II-3
Winfield, Catherine   IV-71
Winkler, Clemens   III-731
Wojdziak, Jan   I-3, II-488
Woldmariam, Mesfin F.   III-482
Wolff, Christian   I-14, I-104, I-371
Woll, Anita   III-141
Wu, Cheng-Tse   III-378
Wu, Guan Shang   II-794
Wu, Qiong   II-794
Wu, Yu-Ting   III-378
Wüthrich, Adrian   IV-412

Ximenes da Silva, Sérgio   I-437
Xiong, Luyao   II-586

Yang, Chao-Yang   III-173, III-378
Yantaç, Asım Evren   IV-185

Yaqub, Nadeem   III-391
Yigitbas, Enes   I-206
You, Hsiao-Chen   III-265
You, JongJun   II-678
Yun, Ray   III-605, III-616

Zan, Özgür   II-234
Zeller, Ludwig   I-686
Zhang, Ada   III-103
Zhang, Chenlu   III-605
Zhang, Lulu   II-446
Zhang, Qi   II-586
Zhang, Yinting   IV-469
Zhao, Chuncheng   IV-469
Zhao, Jie   III-605
Zhu, Miaoqi   I-496
Ziefle, Martina   I-217, III-628